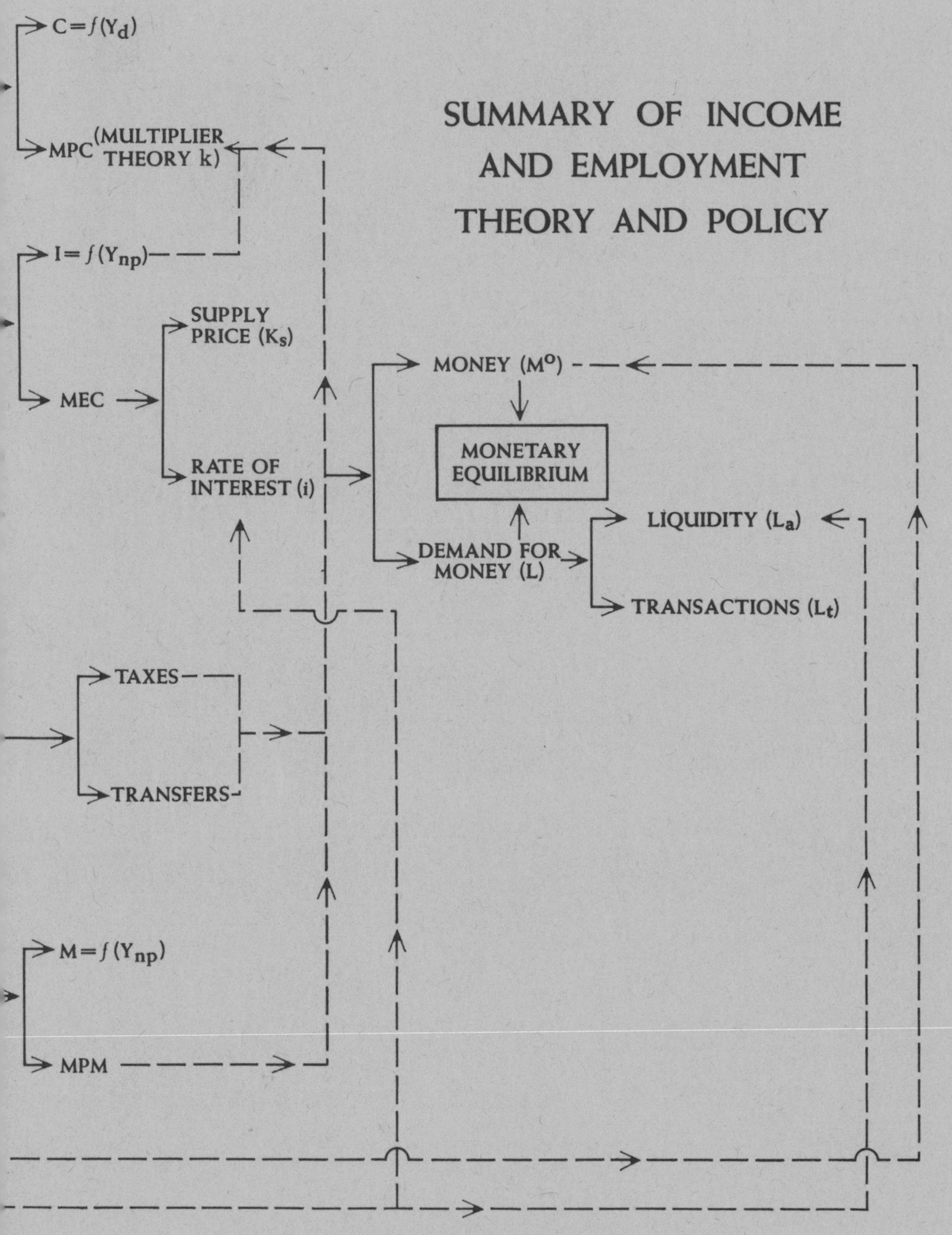
SUMMARY OF INCOME AND EMPLOYMENT THEORY AND POLICY
C=f(Yd)
MPC (MULTIPLIER THEORY k)
I=f(Ynp)
SUPPLY PRICE (Ks)
MEC
RATE OF INTEREST (i)
MONEY (Mo)
MONETARY EQUILIBRIUM
LIQUIDITY (La)
DEMAND FOR MONEY (L)
TRANSACTIONS (Lt)
TAXES
TRANSFERS
M=f(Ynp)
MPM

Income, Employment, and Economic Growth

FOURTH EDITION

Supplementary to this text
Macroeconomics: Problems, Concepts, and Self-Tests
Fourth Edition, by Harold R. Williams

WALLACE C. PETERSON

UNIVERSITY OF NEBRASKA

Income, Employment, and Economic Growth

FOURTH EDITION

W · W · NORTON & COMPANY · INC · NEW YORK

Published simultaneously in Canada
by George J. McLeod Limited, Toronto.
Printed in the United States of America.

Library of Congress Cataloging in Publication Data
Peterson, Wallace C.
Income, employment, and economic growth.
Fourth Edition
Includes bibliographical references and index.
1. National income—United States. 2. Labor supply—United States. 3. United States—Economic policy—1961– 5. United States—Economic policy—1971– I. Title.
HC110.I5P43 1978 339.373 78–2795
ISBN 0 393 09069 8

1 2 3 4 5 6 7 8 9 0

To Eunice, Cary, Shelley,
and the memory of my brother Harold

Contents

Part II The Basic Theory of Income and Employment

Part III Money, Interest, and Income

Part IV Inflation, Growth, and the Business Cycle

Part V Aggregate Income Distribution

Preface

Recent shocks to the economy at home and abroad have put many fundamental tenets of macroeconomics to severe new tests. At no time in the post-World War II period has the challenge been greater to develop and refine our understanding of the forces which drive the aggregate economy. I have tried to capture this spirit in the present edition. The entire text has undergone a critical and painstaking revision, intended not only to update the policy discussions but to tighten and sharpen the exposition of key ideas, principles, and concepts.

My primary aim, as in earlier editions, is to set forth a clear, accurate, and complete explanation of contemporary macroeconomics. A textbook should equip students to understand and apply economic principles with a minimum of outside help, thus freeing the instructor to explore in the classroom special facets of the analysis and current policy issues. The emphasis throughout is upon economics and understanding economics, not quantitative manipulation. As before, mathematics is used sparingly, although where appropriate there are mathematical appendixes for those students interested in the derivation of key propositions.

Two broad aspects of this revision merit special comment. First, there is more stress than ever on making certain that the text reflects the real, serious problems of our era, both in the theoretical and policy discussions. Every effort has been made to introduce the student early to policy issues as they arise in connection with the discussion of theory and to tie both theory and policy into what is actually happening in the world today. Second, the text strives to analyze fairly the currents and controversies which now swirl through macroeconomics. There is much less agreement now than there was some years ago on the body of theoretical ideas which makes up contemporary macroeconomics. The three main idea streams now moving through the profession involve the standard neoclassical interpretation of Keynes, the monetarist challenge to much of Keynesian economics, and a growing chorus of criticism within the ranks of macroeconomic theorists directed toward the neoclassical synthesis.

What changes and innovations have been introduced to accomplish the overriding objective of keeping the exposition current with developments both in and outside the discipline? Most important are two entirely new chapters.

• Chapter 13 ("Stabilization Policy: Overview and Appraisal") seeks to do several things. It begins with a general discussion of the nature of monetary and fiscal policy, including comment on the new congressional budget act and how it works. From this point the chapter moves into an analysis of how *in theory* such policies can be applied. Special attention is given to the "crowding out" thesis. The latter part of the chapter includes a detailed discussion of the application of both monetary and fiscal policy in the post–World War II era. It also attempts to show what these policies can and cannot achieve given the present limits of macroeconomic theory.

• Chapter 16 ("Business Cycles and Forecasting") deals with a phenomenon which once again has taken a central place in economic discussions, even though many economists in the 1960s believed the cycle had been tamed and all but eliminated from our national economic life. The nature, measurement, and causes of the cycle are analyzed. The chapter includes a section on economic forecasting which describes the major forecasting techniques and evaluates their effectiveness.

A number of chapters, while not altogether new, have been extensively reorganized and rewritten. In the first part of Chapter 7 ("Investment Spending and Investment Finance") the theory is developed within the traditional Keynesian framework, an approach which ties investment spending strongly to expectations and uncertainty with respect to the future. Two basic approaches to investment spending are presented. The first develops an investment demand schedule based upon the Keynesian concept of the marginal efficiency of capital. The second deals with investment spending within the context of a demand for capital schedule, an approach based upon the present value (discount) formula and the concept of a demand price for new capital. This permits a better and more direct comparison with the supply price for new capital, an approach which draws upon the supply and demand concepts students usually master in the principles course.

An entirely new—and major—section has been added on the financing of investment. The intent of this new section is to show how borrowing affects the asset-liability structure of the firm, and how uncertainties in this realm may spill over and influence investment spending. The analysis goes well beyond the typical approach which treats the financial side of investment spending mostly by recognition that the rate of interest is a measure of the cost of financing. The student is also introduced to the concept of borrower's risk and lender's risk, two ideas important in *The General Theory*, but which have not been incorporated into most intermediate macroeconomic texts.

This chapter has been strengthened by enlarging the section on the interaction between the multiplier and the accelerator, including adding a demonstration of how self-generating cycles may ensue from this interaction. There is also a new section which summarizes the state of empirical findings on relationship between investment spending, the rate of interest, and the level of income.

Key modifications and additions have been made in Chapter 8 ("Public Expenditures, Taxes, and Finance"). A new section, pitting theory against actual practice, analyzes developments from the 1964 tax cut to the most recent policy decisions by the Carter administration. Material on built-in stabilizers has been expanded, including data on their effectiveness in the 1969–70 and 1974–75 recessions. Perhaps most important is the attention now given to the financing of government deficits.

In Chapter 9 ("International Transactions and Aggregate Demand"), the discussion of the general nature of the balance of payments has been shifted from an Appendix to the beginning of the chapter, a change urged by a number of readers. The chapter contains new material on flexible versus fixed exchange rates, material which assays the impact of different exchange systems on the international economic position of an economy and how the latter affects both income and employment. Chapter 10 ("Money and Interest") now includes an enlarged discussion of the nature of money, including explanation of the different measures of money used by the Federal Reserve System, and an analysis of the process of money creation which does not duplicate the usual T account approach found in most beginning texts, but does develop some general principles of money creation which will be of value to the student. There is also new material on both empirical findings and theoretical analyses relating to the demand for money and the rate of interest.

Although structure of Chapter 11 ("The Modern Quantity Theory") is essentially unchanged, the basic explanation of how the modern quantity theory works now traces out in detail the transmission mechanisms of the monetarist model and compares it to its Keynesian equivalent. Further, attention is given to the major empirical findings which have resulted from the monetarist challenge to mainstream Keynesianism, including the Friedman-Meiselman study, the work of the St. Louis Federal Reserve Bank, and the principle critiques of their efforts.

Chapter 12 ("General Equilibrium and the Neoclassical Synthesis") now consists of three major parts. It opens with an analysis of macroeconomic general equilibrium using the standard IS-LM approach developed by J. M. Hicks. This is followed by a new section entitled "The Neoclassical Synthesis" which develops fully what has become in the post–World War II era the standard interpretation of Keynes, with labor-market equations and the price level introduced into the Keynesian IS-LM model. The chapter ends with a review of the growing body of theoretical criticism directed toward the neoclassical model, a movement which includes such economists as Joan Robinson, Sidney Weintraub, Axel Leijonhufvud, Robert Clower, Hyman Minsky, Paul Davidson, and others.

Chapter 14 ("The Economics of Inflation") has been thoroughly redone. A new section on what is wrong with inflation has been added, an important change because in the past most macroeconomics texts have slighted the social consequences of inflation. Second, cost-push as a source of inflation now receives far greater emphasis, since the market power lodged in large corporations and trade unions has become a major causal factor in the economy's endemic inflation. Third, there is a new section on the Keynesian theory of the price level. This section draws heavily on aspects of Keynes often neglected by macrotheorists; in particular, his belief that inflation was closely linked to movements in money wages and productivity. The chapter concludes with an expanded treatment of the Phillips Curve and the accelerationist theory, as well as a detailed analysis and critique of incomes policies tried out in the 1960s and 1970s.

There are a number of other important though less extensive changes. In Chapter 4 ("Employment, Unemployment, and the Classical View") the discussion of the meaning of full employment has greater depth; special attention is given to the employment problems of minorities, teenagers, and women. This chapter also has an expanded discussion of the concept of equilibrium as an analytical tool, including comment upon its uses and limitations. In Chapter 5 ("Principles of Aggregate Supply and Demand") the discussion of Keynes's concept of an aggregate supply schedule is expanded and a new section on statics and dynamics has been added.

As with earlier editions, Professor Harold R. Williams of Kent State University has developed a workbook especially designed for this text. Many instructors will find this workbook a valuable adjunct which enables students to review and undertake applications of the theoretical material found in the text.

As is true for most writing, an author can never fully acknowledge the many persons to whom he is indebted. But there are always some people to whom a special thanks is due. This text is no exception. I especially appreciate the detailed and thoughtful reviews of the third edition given me by Professors Roger N. Waud of the University of North Carolina and Ziad Keilany of the University of Tennessee at Chattanooga. Both these critiques were extremely helpful in undertaking this revision. Professor John J. Spitzer of the State University of New York at Brockport also gave me some excellent critical comments on parts of the third edition and helpful suggestions for the organization of ideas in this revision. Professor Hyman Minsky of Washington University offered good advice at various times as this revision was under way. A number of my colleagues here at the University of Nebraska-Lincoln have given me the benefit of their comments and suggestions, for which I am grateful. They include Professors Edward

Day, Wayne Dobson, Harish Gupta, Ernst Kuhn, Thomas Iwand, and Campbell McConnell.

A special word of thanks is due Donald S. Lamm, Mary Cunnane, and Ruth Ridler for their skill and efficiency in editing the manuscript. I, of course, accept full responsibility for all errors.

Finally, I want to express deep appreciation to my wife, Eunice, for the strong support she has always given me, not just in this current revision, but in prior revisions and the first writing of the text.

Acknowledgment: For kind permission to quote from *The General Theory of Employment, Interest, and Money*, I wish to thank Harcourt, Brace & World, Inc., Macmillan & Co. Ltd., and the Trustees of the Estate of the late Lord Keynes.

Wallace C. Peterson

Income, Employment, and Economic Growth

FOURTH EDITION

1

The Nature and Scope of Economic Analysis

When Jimmy Carter became president in January 1977 he confronted an economy being whipsawed between too much inflation and too much unemployment. Like Gerald Ford, his predecessor in the Oval Office, President Carter, through his economic advisers, could draw on a vast and evolving body of economic knowledge to grapple with the complex problems of an ailing economy. Other post-World War II presidents—Johnson, Kennedy, Eisenhower, and Truman—faced similar circumstances, as will presidents in the future. Economics will not give us pat answers to tough, complex problems. But, like all science, its knowledge is both evolutionary and cumulative. Thus, the economic tools available to a president today to combat difficult and intractable economic issues are better, more comprehensive, and more usable than those at the disposal of Franklin D. Roosevelt, who on entering the White House in 1933 confronted an economy in almost total collapse.

To a large degree, the present state of our understanding and knowledge about the overall management of the economic system is a result of a "revolution" in economic thinking set in motion in the mid-1930s by a distinguished British economist, John Maynard Keynes. In 1936 Keynes published *The General Theory of Employment, Interest and Money*[1], a

1. John Maynard Keynes, *The General Theory of Employment, Interest and Money* (New York: Harcourt, Brace & World, First Harbinger ed., 1964).

work destined to change for all time the manner in which people thought about the working of the economic system in advanced Western countries. The impact of Keynes on theory has been so great that few would disagree with John Kenneth Galbraith of Harvard University, in calling *The General Theory* "the most influential book on economic and social policy in this century. . . . By common, if not yet quite universal agreement, the Keynesian revolution was one of the great modern accomplishments of social design."[2] As another observer has said, "finance ministers around the world approach the problems of economic management through an analytical framework which, perhaps for want of a better word, commentators rightly call Keynesian."[3]

What kind of a book is *The General Theory*? Basically, Keynes set out to write a book that would explain the forces which shape and determine the level and rate of growth of national production and employment, a subject not well understood either by economists or the layman prior to the catastrophic depression of the 1930s. In this he succeeded exceedingly well; *The General Theory* laid the basic foundation for what has become a highly developed body of economic theory and policy directed toward the most pressing problems of the economy as a whole—output, employment and unemployment, economic growth, and inflation.

Although Keynes is unquestionably the prime architect of how most economists think about the problems described above, his basic interpretation of how the economy works has not gone unchallenged. In recent years Professor Milton Friedman, a University of Chicago economist and Nobel laureate., has emerged as a leading theoretician in this area. In a broad sense Professor Friedman operates—as do nearly all modern economists—in a Keynesian framework, but he stresses a different set of explanatory variables than do economists who adhere more directly to the ideas found in *The General Theory*. In a monumental work published in 1964, *A Monetary History of the United States*,[4] Professor Friedman, in collaboration with Anna Jacobson Schwartz, developed his basic thesis, that the money supply is the most important single, strategic variable in determining the economy's short-run performance. Most economists do not accept wholly either the Keynesian or monetarist approach in its pure form, although much of the work at the "frontiers" of economic theory involves the testing and refining of these theories.

In essence, the foregoing three paragraphs are what this text is all about. Its intent is to help the student understand the entire framework of modern economic analysis regarding the performance of the economy as a

2. John Kenneth Galbraith, "Came the Revolution," *New York Times Book Review Section*, May 16, 1965.

3. D. E. Moggridge, *Keynes* (London: The Macmillan Press, Ltd., 1967), p. 9.

4. Milton Friedman and Anna Jacobson Schwartz, *A Monetary History of the United States* (Princeton: Princeton University Press, 1964).

whole, including discussion of the contributions that many other economists have made to this branch of economic knowledge since publication of seminal works by Keynes and Friedman. We confront a bewildering variety of difficult problems at the national level, including the especially knotty one of how modern societies can obtain reasonably full employment without inflation. There are no magic or costless answers for this and other related problems of the whole economy. But no worthy answers will be forthcoming without continuing efforts to probe into and understand the forces that determine the economy's over-all performance.

There is an excellent statement in *The General Theory*, which, if kept in mind, will help the reader attain a healthy sense of perspective about the usefulness of economic theory in providing specific answers to practical problems. After a rather lengthy technical discussion on the inflation problem, Keynes shifted to a more philosophical vein,

> The object of our analysis is, not to provide a machine, or method of blind manipulation, which will furnish an infallible answer, but to provide ourselves with an organised and orderly method of thinking out particular problems; and, after we have reached a provisional conclusion by isolating the complicating factors one by one, we then have to go back on ourselves and allow, as well as we can, for the probable interaction of the factors amongst themselves. This is the nature of economic thinking."[5]

"To provide ourselves with an organised and orderly method of thinking out particular problems . . ." It would be difficult to come up with a more succinct statement of the nature and value of economic analysis—or economic theory. Every reader should engrave this in the forefront of his or her memory!

The branch of economics that is the subject of this book is termed macroeconomics; it centers on the analysis and performance of the economy as a whole. *Macro* is a Greek work meaning "large" or "big." Hence macroeconomics is concerned with those economic problems that are large in the sense that they embrace the entire economy: the determinants of the total output of goods and services; the factors that influence the levels of employment and unemployment and the economy's rate of economic growth; and movements in the general level of prices.

The branch of economics concerned with the behavior of the individual entities of the economy, such as the business firm and the consumer household, is microeconomics. *Micro*, too, is a Greek word, meaning "small." In contrast to macroeconomic analysis which concerns itself with over-all levels of production and employment, microeconomics focuses on equally valid and important questions relating to the composition of the national ouput, the allocation of economic resources among alternative uses, and the distribution of products and income among the members of

5. Keynes, p. 297.

the society. Economists often refer to the macro branch of economics as income and employment theory, and the micro branch as value and distribution theory.

Although macro- and microeconomics are distinct branches of economic analysis, usually studied separately, this should not lead one to the false conclusion that they are wholly unrelated. On the contrary, a close connection necessarily exists between them, for the behavior of the large aggregates studied in macroeconomics traces back ultimately to the behavior of the individual business firms and households in the economy. For example, total consumer spending in the economy will obviously depend to a large degree upon how individual consumers behave in various situations. In a broad sense, macroeconomic behavior involves the aggregation of individual economic behavior. A word of caution is in order here, though, for one must not fall into the trap of the *fallacy of composition*—that is, assuming what is true for a part is necessarily true for the whole. Thus, while macroeconomics involves aggregation, it does not follow that the behavior of the aggregates is always the same as their individual components. This is why it is necessary to study aggregate economic behavior as a separate area.

Before proceeding with our discussion of the nature of economic analysis, it is useful to consider carefully the fundamental conditions which give rise to the science of economics. These underlying conditions are extremely important for they serve not only as a basis for a broad, formal definition of our subject matter, but also offer useful insight into the manner in which the process of defining a subject-matter area exerts a powerful influence upon its scope and content.

Economics is rooted in an age-old human problem, often described as the wants-means dilemma. The *wants* of human beings are virtually unlimited in scope; the *means* available for the satisfaction of these wants are scarce. This is an idea worth some hard thought. It is not our basic biological wants—our needs for food, shelter, and clothing—that are unlimited. It is our social or cultural wants that fit this category—that is, those wants which arise out of the society or culture in which we live. These wants, accentuated in the modern world by television and advertising, are explosively "open-ended." Everywhere people find themselves overwhelmed by rising aspirations for an ever-changing, ever-improving material standard of life. It is out of this situation that the economic problem arises, for the scarce resources of a society must be allocated among competing wants in a way that permits the maximum satisfaction of those wants. In this sense, economics is the study of scarcity and choice, for if means were not believed to be scarce in relation to wants, the economic problem would not exist. Thus, a formal definition of our subject matter might read: *Economics is the organized study of the processes by which scarce resources are allocated among alternative and competing wants with the objective of obtaining a maximum satisfaction of these wants.*

This formal definition of economics is called traditional because the scarcity theme is nearly always present when the subject matter of economics is defined. It is important that we examine this definition carefully to be aware of some of the assumptions and implications imbedded in it.

Implications of the Traditional Definition of Economics

The traditional definition of economics connotes efficiency; accordingly, economists have made the notion of efficiency the focal point of much of their study. To the economist, efficiency has two major facets. First, there is the problem of efficiency in the allocation of resources among competing wants. In this context, the notion of efficiency implies that the producing and consuming units of the economy should be so organized that the community gets the maximum of the things it wants in the amounts wanted; microeconomic analysis focuses on this problem. Second, and on a different plane, there is the problem of efficiency in the utilization of resources in the economy; resources must be utilized to the fullest extent possible within the existing framework of custom, law, and other institutional practices. Idle resources are evidence per se of inefficiency as long as any wants remain unsatisfied. It is from this idea that we derive our concern with the *level* of employment of economic resources, a macroeconomic problem.

Economics thus acccepts the concept of efficiency as a part of the social ethic; it is assumed to be a desirable goal. This demonstrates that economics rests upon assumptions which are, in the final analysis, value judgments, for although few people would question the idea that efficiency is a good thing, it is nonetheless an assumption that can be neither proved nor disproved.

A second element in the traditional definition of economics concerns the matter of human wants. Most modern textbooks in economics assert, either explicitly or implicitly, that the material, or economic, wants of human beings are unbounded. Some recognition may be accorded to the idea that wants, in a fundamental sense, are culturally determined, but beyond this, it is generally presumed that they are subject to increase without limit. Usually the matter is dropped at this point. The practical effect is to exclude virtually any analysis of the relative merit of different wants from the formal body of economic analysis. Wants are presumed to be given data, and the major task of the economist is to gauge the efficiency with which scarce means are applied to the satisfaction of these wants. Since, as a practical matter, it is impossible to separate wants from what people regard as good, this is, perhaps, tantamount to saying that the economist as an economist has no concern with either the immediate or ultimate values of society.[6] Placing wants outside the domain of the economist may lead to a divorce between economic analysis and economic policy, which may or may not be desirable. We will have more to say about this later in the chapter.

A third implication of the traditional definition of economics is the idea that economic activity is primarily directed toward consumption; consumption of goods and services is the means by which the wants of human beings are satisfied. In this view, goods and services are desired because they possess *ultility*, that is, they have the capacity to satisfy wants, whereas work, or the process of producing goods and services, represents *disutility* and is by implication distasteful. This idea is derived from a concept of human nature which sees man as a kind of passive creature whose major need is to satisfy the urge to consume—the economic man who appeared so frequently in the early literature of economics. At best, though, this is a partial view of human nature, which ignores, among other things, the creative activity that many argue is vital to a purposeful life. This oversimplified view of human nature has caused economists to devote their energies to analysis of the behavior of man as a consumer, to the comparative neglect of man as a producer. Productive activities are viewed as only an adjunct to man's assumed primary goal of maximizing satisfactions. It is not our purpose at this point to discuss the merit or lack of merit in this aspect of economic analysis and its underlying psychology of human behavior, but simply to cite another instance of the influence exercised by an assumption implicit in the traditional definition of economics.

Our discussion so far should warn the reader that assumptions with value implications may be present in such a prosaic matter as the definition of an area of study. And if this is true for a definition, it may also be true for the body of analysis built upon that definition. The significance of this for the study of economics is that a complete separation of analysis and policy (that is, values) may not be possible; more on this point later.

6. It is not difficult to see why economists have traditionally shied away from consideration of the relative merits of the different wants of people in society. Wants are satisfied through the consumption of goods and services and this process is, in the last analysis, a highly subjective matter. Since economics has not yet developed satisfactory techniques for making interpersonal comparisons, there seems to be no way in which the economist can objectively determine that certain wants ought to be satisfied in preference to others. For an attack upon this traditional viewpoint see J. K. Galbraith, *The Affluent Society* (Boston: Houghton Mifflin, 1958), esp. chaps. 10, 17, and 22. See also Myron E. Sharpe, *John Kenneth Galbraith and the Lower Economics* (White Plains, N.Y.: International Arts and Sciences Press, 1973), esp. pp. 23–32.

Moreover, in economics, as in any discipline, the student should always seek out and make explicit the assumptions upon which any analysis is based. This is particularly necessary in economics because often extremely elaborate analyses are erected upon the foundation of a few, relatively simple assumptions. Failure to be aware of the existence of such underlying assumptions and their implications and limitations will lead to confusion in thought and action.

Science and Economics

We identified economics as a study of the processes by which goods and services are produced, exchanged, and consumed. The data of the economist are variables such as price, production, consumption, wages, interest rates, and taxes, but these economic quantities are not primarily significant in themselves. Their significance arises from the fact that they represent the factual evidence of the economic behavior of human beings, which is the economist's real concern. Human behavior in the economic realm manifests itself through measurable quantities like those enumerated above.

This being the case, it follows that economics is a social science. E. R. A. Seligman divides sciences into two categories: the natural sciences, which are concerned with the universe, and the mental, or cultural, sciences, which are concerned with what takes place in man himself—in the realm of his mental life. The latter can be further divided into those dealing with man as a separate individual and those treating man as a member of a group. Thus,

> the phenomena . . . related to group activities are commonly called social phenomena, and the sciences which classify and interpret such activities are the social sciences. The social sciences may thus be defined as those mental or cultural sciences which deal with the activities of the individual as a member of a group.[7]

Economics, then, is a social science because it aims at an understanding of the economic aspects of organized or group behavior by human beings.

Having classified economics as a social science, we must take up two additional questions concerning the character of the discipline. The first relates to the nature of science itself, and the second to the authenticity of the claim that economics is truly a scientific discipline. Without answers to these questions it is practically impossible to comprehend either economics as a body of knowledge or what the economist seeks to accomplish.

7. E. R. A. Seligman, *Encyclopaedia of the Social Sciences*, vol. 1 (New York: Macmillan, 1930), p. 3.

The Nature of Science

There is no exact, absolute, or final definition for the word *science*. In its most general sense, science has to do with the process of knowing; the Latin root *scire* of our modern English word *science* means "to know." But "to know" implies understanding, which means "to be able to explain." This definition of science, while technically correct, does not go far enough, for we need to know in a more specific way how science seeks to achieve understanding. What do we mean, in other words, by "understanding" and by "being able to explain"?

Classification · Understanding involves, first, the classification of things, or phenomena, and second, the discovery or observation of uniformities among the phenomena so classified. Classification, which is the oldest form of scientific activity, attempts to bring order to the universe external to man by seeking out similarities between things and placing them in groups, each group being designated by a name or symbol which is representative of all things brought into it. Classification is a necessary first step toward understaning; it provides the basis for the creative act of finding relationships between phenomena, which lies at the heart of all scientific activity. Professor Jacob Bronowski describes this creative act as being the discovery of hidden likenesses in facts or experiences which are separate. In such facts or experiences the scientist "finds a likeness whch had not been seen before; and he creates a unity by showing the likeness."[8]

Generalization · The creative act of discovery means the establishment of meaningful generalizations (that is, general statements) pertaining to relationships between phenomena. Such generalizations are meaningful in the sense that they attempt to explain phenomena in the world by linking them together in a cause and effect relationship. The construction of such generalizations, or laws, is the true essence of scientific activity.

Scientific laws are formulated as "if . . . , then . . ." propositions, which is to say that they assert some event or thing will happen if certain conditions are present or satisfied. Formulation of scientific statements as "if . . . , then . . ." propositions implies cause and effect relationships. Scientific generalizations, in other words, explain by virtue of the fact that they describe a causal relationship between phenomena. A note of caution is in order here: Causation should not be confused with correlation, although this happens at times. Correlation is a statistical concept which involves a relationship between two variables such that the value of one is *uniquely* related to the value of the other. It is well known, for example, that a correlation exists between the price of a good and the quantity sold (the

8. J. Bronowski, *Science and Human Values* (New York: Julian Messner, 1956), p. 35.

economic "law" of demand). Correlation, however, does not reveal anything about the reasons (that is, the causes) for a relationship. Causation is nearly always complex and difficult to ascertain. Even though an observable relationship may exist between phenomena, the causal significance of such a relationship is not always readily apparent. In the last analysis, attributing a particular cause to a particular effect requires the exercise of the most careful kind of judgment For example, in the matter of the relationship between price of a good and quantity sold, causation tends to run from price to sales. How do we know? Only careful study of the actual behavior of buyers in real markets indicates that buyers generally respond to price and not the other way around.

To say that scientific laws are essentially "if . . . , then . . ." propositions means that all such laws consist of two parts. The if part implies that all scientific laws rest upon certain assumptions concerning the data under investigation. The particular function of the assumption is to describe the condition, or circumstances, under which the generalization possesses validity. For example, it is a well-accepted principle of physics that all bodies fall at a constant rate of acceleration: approximately thirty-two feet per second. But this is true only if the body is falling freely in a vacuum. In this instance the assumption serves to specify the conditions under which the physical law of falling bodies is valid. The conditioning role of the underlying assumptions of a scientific proposition can be illustrated by an example drawn from the economic field. The reader may recall from his earlier study that in equilibrium the business firm will produce at the output level at which marginal cost is equal to marginal revenue. But this general statement as to the behavior of the business firm is true if it can be assumed (1) that the firm is seeking to maximize its profit and (2) that the firm possesses full knowledge of the relevant cost and revenue schedules. Only if these conditions are present does the generalization hold.

The second part of any scientific law consists of the conclusion derived by the process of logic from the basic assumption or postulates. Thus, a scientific law starts with one or more assumptions about the data under investigation and proceeds to derive the logical consequences of these assumptions. Mathematics often enters the picture at this point, since all sciences use mathematics to some degree in the process of drawing conclusions from a set of assumptions. The use of mathematics, though, should not obscure the fact that the essential activity at this stage of the scientific process involves logic. The behavior of the business firm described above is a case point. If the assumed conditions—desire to maximize profit, and knowledge of the relevant cost and revenue curves—are present, logic leads us inevitably to the conclusion that the firm will operate at the level at which marginal costs and marginal revenues are equalized. This is so because the firm can always increase its total profit by expanding output as long as marginal revenue is greater than marginal cost, or by contracting output when marginal cost is greater than marginal revenue. The logical consequence of our assumptions is that the firm will seek to operate at a particular level of output. Taken together, the assumptions and the conclusion derived from them constitute the essence of a scientific law or principle.

Validity · How do we determine whether or not a particular scientific law is valid? Validity depends upon the correct use of logic in deriving conclusions from a given set of assumptions. If the rules of logic are not applied correctly, a generalization will not have validity, irrespective of the merit of its underlying assumptions. More important, a generalization must succeed in explaining that which it sets out to explain. Its conclusions must be compatible with the observed behavior of the data under investigation. Empirical observation is, in other words, the final test of the validity, or truth, of any scientific generalization. This means that a scientific principle should predict what will happen under a stipulated set of circumstances, but it does not mean that such a principle must be an exact and detailed mirror of the real world. Experience can never conclusively prove a generalization to be absolutely right, for there will always remain the possibility that a different generalization might better explain the situation under investigation. What empirical observation does show is that the conclusions reached in a scientific principle are (or are not) in accordance with the facts of reality.

Realism in the Assumptions · Does the validity of the principle require that its assumptions be realistic? This, unfortunately, is a question that cannot be given a categorical yes or no answer. In one sense, the answer is no, for, as we have already seen, the formal validity of the principle is a matter solely of its logical derivation from the underlying assumptions, irrespective of the degree of realism present in the latter. Moreover, the question of exactly what constitutes realism is not easily resolved. To illustrate, let us recall once again the physical principle that governs the acceleration of falling bodies. Strictly speaking, the underlying assumption of the principle can hardly be termed realistic, as we rarely find a vacuum existing in the real world. But we know that conditions approximating this assumption do exist often enough in the real world; therefore the principle does serve to explain the behavior of the falling bodies. What we seek is reasonable accuracy in both assumptions and generalizations.

Much the same may be said concerning the assumption frequently employed in economic analysis which asserts that the business firm seeks to maximize its profit. In a literal sense, this assumption is not realistic, for many other considerations besides profit motivate the behavior of the business firm. Nevertheless, generalizations erected on this assumption may be valid because they provide us with an explanation of the behavior of the firm in a particular situation that can be confirmed by an appeal to empirical fact.

If by realism in our assumptions we mean something that represents an exact duplication of an extremely complex real world, the validity of a principle cannot be judged in this way simply because such realism cannot possibly be attained. But if by realism we mean some kind of approximation to the real world that serves usefully as a basis for constructing generalizations that can be tested empirically, our assumptions ought to be realistic. This assertion is consistent with our earlier statement that the formal validity of the principle depends strictly upon the correct use of logic in deriving conclusions from a set of assumptions, for unless the latter are in some way rooted in reality, the principle concerned will be without relevance, and thus the question of validity will be meaningless.

The Value of Science · In the foregoing section we said that science is an activity that seeks to discover meaningful relationships in the complex world of reality that lies about us. It is now proper to raise the question of the value of such activity. What, in other words, is the utility of science? To some, given the fact that our age has witnessed a seemingly unending series of scientific accomplishments of obvious usefulness, this question may seem quite unnecessary. Yet, the question is important; unless we understand clearly why we value scientific activity, we will not fully comprehend the essential nature of science. The vague, and perhaps intuitive, feeling of the average citizen that scientific activity is in some sense desirable is not sufficient for our purposes.

Let us state, first of all, that the creative process of scientific generalization is useful simply because it enables human beings to understand why things happen as they do. Man has an overwhelming sense of curiosity concerning himself, his world, and the universe; the word *why* is perhaps the most important word in the human vocabulary. Scientific generalization is a means—on a high intellectual level, to be sure—whereby human beings satisfy the deeply rooted urge to know the why of things.

There is, moreover, another and related sense in which scientific knowledge is essential to mankind. To say that human beings want to know the why of things is tantamount to saying they want to make sense out of the external world. In seeking to do this, man is confronted at every turn with an overwhelming and enormously complex array of facts. To make sense of the external world requires a broad frame of reference that gives order and meaning to the vast array of facts. This is exactly the task of scientific generalization—or theorizing; generalizations provide the necessary frame of reference through which the facts of reality are related to one another and, thus, rendered intelligible. The practical and absolute necessity of generalization, or theory, as a basis for intelligent comprehension of the complex world of reality cannot be overestimated. The so-called practical man who wants facts and scorns theory is really not practical at all, as facts in themselves are quite meaningless. The practical man differs from the theorist in that he engages in implicit, haphazard and often semiconscious theorizing as a means of organizing facts. The vagueness of the theorizing of the practical man often protects fallacies in his theories from discovery and, as a consequence, errant nonsense is put forth as truth. No one really escapes the burden of theorizing. There are only better or worse theories, simple or more complex theories, implicit or explicit theories.

A second basic reason for the utility of scientific principles is simply that they enable us to predict what will happen or take place under certain circumstances. To be able to anticipate the outcome of a particular situation or action is obviously a matter of some value. Although the terms *prediction* and *forecasting* are often used interchangeably, it is useful in economics to draw a distinction between them. As used in this text, prediction has a narrower connotation than forecasting. It means the determination of the outcome of events within a specific "if . . . , then . . ." frame of reference. It is a term, in other words, which applies to a specific generalization.

Consider, for example, the economic law of demand: In general, people purchase more of a commodity at a lower price and less at a higher price. Thus, if price changes we can predict that sales will go either up or down, depending upon the direction of the change in price. The predictive value of scientific generalizations in economics is frequently limited to providing information on the direction that events may move as a result of some specific change.

Forecasting on the other hand, means estimating precise future values for specific economic quantities on the basis of known values for other economic quantities. This requires knowledge of the exact form of the relationship between the phenomena being observed. During the last several decades *econometrics* emerged as an important branch of economics concerned with the development of mathematical models as forecasting devices for future changes in the economy. The meaning of both *econometrics* and the term *model* as applied to economics is discussed more fully in a subsequent section of this chapter. At this point it will suffice to say that successful economic forecasting requires an economic model plus an accurate information system, which is to say we must have reliable data about what has happened in the economy in the past.

In the daily routine of living we constantly encounter situations involving prediction and forecasting, in the sense of anticipating behavior of people or events on the basis of knowledge currently available. These range from the daily forecast of the weather to the expectation of a businessman that by means of a sale he can increase the volume of goods sold. Whether or not such situations are described as a prediction or a forecast is less important than understanding that all such anticipations of behavior rest upon generalizations. Once again, though, we must proceed cautiously, because the predictive value of the scientific law always pertains to a *general* class or group of things but not to any *specific* or individual entity within the class or group. For example, the law of demand asserts that, other things being equal, people will purchase more of a given commodity at a lower price than at a higher price. But this law, or generalization, does not tell us whether any particular individual will respond at all times in this way to a change in the price of a commodity; it only tells us that this kind of behavior can be expected of people under certain stipulated conditions. The reader is urged to remember that the predictive value of a generalization will be limited by the character of its underlying assumptions. The "if" portion of the principle necessarily defines one set of conditions under which accurate prediction is possible. In the law of demand the assertion that more units of the commodity will be sold at a lower than a higher price follows only *if* all other things are equal and *if* consumers are rational in the sense that they seek to maximize the satisfaction derived from the expenditure of their incomes.

Finally, we can say that scientific generalizations possess great utility because they enable human beings to exercise control over their social and physical environment. Prediction implies control, for without a knowledge of what will happen under a particular set of circumstances there is no way either to bring about or to prevent the occurrence of a specific event. The use of the word *control* in this context must be carefully understood. In popular usage the word frequently connotes restraint—particularly physical restraint; here, however, control is meant in a broader sense—the use of the knowledge gained from generalization to accomplish human purposes. Scientists and engineers, for example, have made use of our knowledge concerning the behavior of gases under various conditions to develop the internal combustion engine and, from it, the automobile. This area of control is, in other words, roughly the area of applied science and technology wherein use is made of scientific generalizations to achieve a vast variety of practical objectives. In economics such practical objectives include reducing unemployment, controlling inflation increasing economic growth—to name but a few. Recent national administrations—Kennedy-Johnson, Ford, and Carter—have at times used tax cuts to attain one or more of these and other objectives. The possibility of using tax adjustments as a policy (i.e., control) instrument stems from the validity of scientific generalizations about economic behavior.

The spectacular achievements of applied science are visible to everyone, and include such diverse accomplishments as the most recently developed antibiotic drugs and the exploration of space by manned and unmanned vehicles. This is the aspect of science most familiar to all of us and which most often captures the public imagination. Yet behind the exciting spectacle of scientific achievement in the modern age lies the much less dramatic task of developing generalizations, without which none of the miracles of modern science would be possible. The matter of attempting to discover or develop new generalizations that describe and explain relationships between phenomena in the real world is sometimes characterized as pure science, because the persons engaged in this type of activity may not have any immediate concern with any possible practical application of the knowledge they discover. At best though, there is no sharp dividing line between science that is pure and science that is applied; both are an essential part of an activity that seeks to enlarge man's ability to understand and control his environment.

The Scientific Character of Economics

What is the basis for the claim that economics is a scientific discipline? The primary objective of economic study is development of generalizations—or principles—that explain relationships between economic phenomena. Like all scientific generalizations, economic principles are basically "if . . . , then . . ." statements to which a casual significance is imparted. Thus, if our contention is correct that the key characteristic of scientific activity is the discovery of generalizations that explain the why of things, economics is clearly entitled to scientific standing.

Earlier, we pointed out that economics is a social science because it deals with human behavior. Since economics concerns itself with human behavior, some may wonder if it is really possible to have a science of economics. Is it not true that human behavior is, more often than not, wholly capricious? Many persons would argue that man is a free agent and thus uniquely different from all other natural objects, living or inanimate. Under such circumstances, how can useful predictions be made about such an uncertain thing as human behavior?

At first it might seem that the obvious answer is that one cannot make such predictions, but a little reflection should convince us that such an answer is too glib and superficial. It is possible to generalize about human behavior because when human beings live together in organized society they behave most of the time in orderly—and predictable—ways. If they did not, chaos would result and civilized living as we know it would be impossible. The reader might reflect for a moment on the extent to which the successful completion of his daily activities depends upon the assumption that the scores of people he has contact with each day will behave in a predictable fashion. A simple example is the use of red, green, and yellow lights to control the flow of automobile traffic.

The behavior patterns characteristic of civilized societies manifest themselves in a multitude of ways, ranging from simple customs, or folkways, such as the wearing of particular types of clothing, to highly complex organizational arrangements for achieving the political, economic, or religious ends of a society. Whether the behavior patterns of a society are simple or complex, it is the business of the economist, as well as other social scientists, to develop and improve generalizations that seek to describe and explain these patterns of behavior.

A useful notion which pervades most economic analysis is that of *maximizing* behavior. Essentially, it means that human beings will act in such way as to maximize what they perceive as their economic well-being. Thus, the businessman tries to maximize profits, the worker his or her wages, and the consumer the satisfaction to be obtained from the consumption of goods and services. Adam Smith, the founder of modern economic analysis, commented on this propensity a long while ago. "Every individual," he said, "is continually exerting himself to find out the most advantageous employment for whatever capital he can employ. It is his own advantage, indeed, and not to that of society which he has in view."[9] Smith's language is a bit quaint, coming as it does from the eighteenth century, but the meaning is unmistakable. If the word resources (including labor power) is substituted for Smith's "capital" in the foregoing sentence, we have a clear statement of the maximizing idea. A *caveat* is in order, however. The maximizing notion is one of those assumptions found so frequently in economics that have a useful role to play, but which are not literally true (recall our discussion of realism earlier in this chapter).

Before leaving this question, it is necessary to say something about the problems posed for economics as a science by the assumption that man is a free agent. We shall not seek to resolve the philosophical problem of whether or not men possess free will. We need to recognize as a practical matter that man is a thinking being and that this has some vital consequences for economic study. Because man has the power of thought, and because, too, he can learn from experience, he is able to bring about change in society, or, put differently, to establish new behavior patterns. Therefore, a given set of conditions may not produce the same response at one time and place as they do at another time and place.

The foregoing makes prediction in economics and the other social sciences inherently more risky than it is in the natural or physical sciences, but it precludes neither the fact that there are uniformities in human behavior nor the possibility that such uniformities can be discovered. Economics must develop generalizations concerning economic behavior and make use of the predictive character of all such generalizations. The student of economics should remember that man, because he possesses

9. Adam Smith, *The Wealth of Nations* (New York: Random House, 1937), p. 421.

the power to think, can if he so chooses, take cognizance of the predictive element embodied in a generalization and by so doing modify the outcome. This fact does not change the basic character of economics as a scientific discipline, but it does mean that economics is much less exact than such sciences as physics or chemistry.

Some Characteristics of Economic Generalizations

One aspect of economics that causes concern to students is the abstract character of economic generalizations or economic theory. Abstraction is often considered unrealistic; hence economic theory seems to have little or no practical value. But this attitude stems from a failure to understand fully and clearly why an economic generalization, principle, or theory must necessarily be abstract.

Abstraction

The object of all scientific inquiry is to understand, not simply to reproduce or reconstruct reality. The world of reality is a complex of forces so vast that no one could possibly comprehend all their interrelationships. If progress is to be made toward the understanding of reality, it is essential to simplify the complexities of the real world. We can do this by directing our investigation toward the forces, or factors, believed to be of strategic importance for an understanding of how things do work in the real world. This is nothing less than the process of abstraction. Thus, economic generalizations and theories are not detailed, photographically faithful reproductions of a portion of the real world, but are, rather, simplified portraits whose purpose is to make the real world intelligible.

It is important to understand that abstraction is a characteristic of theory in any discipline, including the biological and physical sciences. The major difference between the social sciences and the natural sciences is not in the degree of abstraction, but in the fact that the social sciences are generally unable to resort to a laboratory to determine the validity of their principles. We shall return to a discussion of this point shortly.

The Concept of a Functional Relationship

Another important characteristic of economic generalizations concerns the form in which these generalizations or principles are often presented. Since the economic aspects of human behavior usually are manifested in the form of economic quantities, such as prices, outputs, incomes, and wage rates, economic principles frequently can be stated in mathematical form. The most common practice in this respect is to express the principles of economics in the form of a *functional relationship* between economic variables.

The concept of a functional relationship between variables is essential to an understanding of the nature of economic analysis. In fact, this is perhaps the most important concept the reader can grasp. If one fully and clearly understands the nature of the functional idea, the way to a thorough comprehension of economic analysis is open. A *functional relationship exists between two variables when they are related in such a way that the value of one depends uniquely upon the value of the other.* Such a relationship can be expressed in equation form as follows:

$$y = f(x) \tag{1–1}$$

An equation of this form reads "y is a function of x." It means, simply, that the variable represented by the letter y is related in a systematic and dependable way to the value of the variable represented by the letter x.

The concept of a functional relationship enables us to express symbolically (that is, in mathematical form) the essence of a particular economic principle or generalization. For example, the economic law of demand can be expressed in equation form as

$$Q_d = f(P) \tag{1–2}$$

which means that the quantity demanded for a particular commodity is a function of its price. By itself the above equation does not tell us anything more than that quantity and price are linked together in a systematic and dependable relationship. Knowledge of the exact nature of the relationship between these two variables requires more information than can be obtained from the equation alone, a point to which we shall return subsequently.

Although the functional concept is an important tool for economic analysis, there are limitations inherent in the concept that must be appreciated if it is to be used effectively. In the first place, the fact that two variables are related to one another in a functional sense does not mean that the one is the *cause* of the other. Cause is not easily determined. To determine cause requires keen judgment and a broad knowledge of the situation under study. The law of demand provides an excellent example of the need for the careful exercise of judgment. The mathematical expression of this law simply tells us that the variables, quantity demanded and price, are functionally related. For a clearer understanding of the nature of this relationship we must be aware of the behavior of buyers in a market situation. More precisely, we must know whether the quantity demanded varies as the price varies, or conversely, whether price varies as quantity demanded varies. If we can answer this, we will be in a position to say something about the causal relationship that may exist between these variables. Since we are discussing the behavior of buyers in a market situation and not the behavior of suppliers of the commodity in question, the more reasonable conclusion would be that buyers will vary their purchases in accordance with changes in price. But this is to say that in the equation, quantity demanded (Q_d) is the dependent variable, and price (P) is the independent variable, for quantity demanded varies (inversely) with price and not the other way around. If we say this, does it not also mean that we have identified price as the immediate—although not necessarily sole—*cause* of the quantity demanded by buyers? In any common-sense meaning of the word *cause* the answer to this question would obviously be yes.

A second important aspect of the functional concept is that a particular variable may be a function of a number of other variables. For example, to say that the quantity demanded of a commodity is a function of its price does not mean that the quantity demanded cannot at the same time be a function of variables besides price. In the case of the law of demand, many things besides price affect a buyer's decision as to the amounts of any specific good he will purchase at any particular time. Thus, we might say that the quantity demanded of a good is a function not only of price, but of the buyer's income, the price of other goods, the buyer's expectations as to future prices, and perhaps a host of other factors.

The fact that an important economic magnitude may be functionally linked to a number of variables presents a difficult problem for economic analysis, particularly when some of the variables cannot be quantified. The usual way in which economists solve this problem is by resort to the device of *ceteris paribus*, "other things are equal." This procedure involves analysis of the relationship between two or more variables on the basis of the assumption that all other variables that might influence the outcome of the situation remain constant. This is a kind of intellectual equivalent to the laboratory procedure that is commonly followed by the physical or biological scientist. The investigator seeks to analyze in isolation the relationship between the variables or factors believed to have the most strategic significance in determining the value of the phenomena under investigation. An extremely clear exposition of the nature of *ceteris paribus* is found in the following statement by Alfred Marshall:

> It is sometimes said that the laws of economics are "hypothetical." Of course, like every other science, it undertakes to study the effects which will be produced by certain causes, not absolutely, but subject to the condition that *other things are equal*, and that the causes are able to work out their effects undisturbed. Almost every scientific doctrine, when carefully and formally stated, will be found to contain some proviso to the effect that other things are equal: the action of the causes in question is supposed to be isolated; certain effects are attributed to them, but only on the hypothesis that no cause is permitted to enter except those distinctly allowed for.[10]

10. Alfred Marshall, *Principles of Economics* (8th ed. London: Macmillan, 1925), p. 36.

Model Building in Economics

The notions just discussed—abstraction and the idea of a functional relationship—are often brought together in a formal fashion in economic models. A model frequently is a physical representation, often in miniature, of something that exists or can be observed. Anyone who has visited a planetarium has seen a model of the solar system. Almost everyone is familiar with model airplanes and model cars. Less familiar, perhaps, is the idea of a nonphysical representation, or model, of something as large, complex, and intangible as the economic system. Yet, this is quite possible, and, increasingly, models of varying degrees of complexity are being used to represent many facets of the economy, including the entire national economy.

What is an economic model? Obviously, and as the term suggests, it is a representation of all or part of the economy. Specifically, an economic model usually involves representation in mathematical form of the way in which the various parts of the economy are interrelated. The mathematical form for a model may be either geometric or algebraic. The kind of diagram found in any elementary text which shows how an equilibrium price is established by the intersection of supply and demand schedules is an example of a simple economic model presented in geometric form. In this case, the model is that of the market process. The same process can be presented in algebraic form, as is done on page 20.

An economic model is expected to show the relationships that exist between measurable economic magnitudes. These are called *variables* because they are capable of changing. Any magnitude which is assumed to remain constant is termed a *parameter*. Such models should have the ability to predict the change in a particular economic variable as a result of change in one or more other economic variables.

Technically, the mathematical equations which show the relationships believed to exist between the economic variables constitute the *structure* of the model. Specific numerical values for any of the constants (or parameters) which appear in the equations are estimated from actual, historical data. For example, econometric models which depict the whole economy usually show that consumption spending is a fixed proportion of income. The coefficient (parameter) which shows this proportion is estimated from the ratio between consumption and income in the past.[11]

In macroeconomics, econometric models have grown rapidly in number and complexity in recent years. Some of the econometric models now in use are of such complexity that they may include three hundred or more equations. What is important to understand, though, is that the role of

11. This does not mean that consumption spending cannot be related to other variables besides income. The relationship that may exist between consumption and any other variables would have to be estimated separately, again using actual, historical data.

equations in an econometric model is to specify in algebraic terms the relationships that make up the model. In the United States, econometric models of the American economy have been developed by such diverse groups as the Federal Reserve Board, the President's Council of Economic Advisers, the Office of Business Economics of the U.S. Department of Commerce, the Brookings Institution (a private research organization in Washington, D.C.), and academic economists at many of our major public and private universities.

Irrespective of their complexity, all econometric models have certain features in common. First, and no matter how many equations they embrace, they are still abstractions—simplifications of the real world. Putting more equations into a model does not change this basic fact. Second, the variables in an econometric model are characterized as either *exogenous* or *endogenous*. An exogenous variable is one whose value is determined by relationships which lie outside the model, whereas an endogenous variable is one whose value is determined by the relationships that lie within the model. Finally, an econometric model may be *closed* or *open*. It is closed in a mathematical sense if the number of equations and the number of variables are equal, but it is open whenever the number of equations is less than the number of variables. When the number of equations and the number of endogenous variables are equal, the model can be solved mathematically by the method of simultaneous equations. For models with a large number of equations, the use of a computer is an obvious necessity.

The elements of an economic model can be illustrated simply by the use of the well-known proposition from elementary economics that the price of any good or service is determined by the interaction between demand and supply schedules. Such a model of market price determination can be formulated in terms of the following equations:

$$Q_d = f(P) \tag{1–3}$$

$$Q_s = f(P) \tag{1–4}$$

$$Q_d = Q_s \tag{1–5}$$

The first two equations specify the relationships involved in the model, namely that quantity demanded is a function of price and quantity supplied is a function of price. The third equation specifies that in equilibrium the market will be cleared, which is to say that there is some price at which quantity demanded and quantity supplied are equal. Since there are three equations and three unknown endogenous variables—Q_d, Q_s, and P—the model is complete and capable of solution.

The use of models in economic analysis—especially mathematical models—is fraught with several dangers. Since the relationships specified in the model depend upon what was happened in the past, a model may suggest a continuity in economic events that does not really exist. Statistical trends are necessary and useful for understanding the past and forecasting ahead, but we should not lose sight of the fact that they are in a sense artificial. History is not a smooth trend line; it is a series of discontinuous and unique events. Second, a model may give a misleading impression of greater constancy in economic relationships than experience justifies. Economic generalizations—principles or theories—do show us what will happen under specific circumstances, but we must not forget that in the real world economic circumstances are never exactly the same as the economy moves forward through time. Finally, models may become "frozen" as reality moves on and the model remains unchanged. For an economic model to be useful, it must reflect the reality of the economic structure.

Let us add a further word of caution with respect to the use of the functional concept and models in economic analysis. Reducing economic generalizations to the form of a functional relationship between quantitative magnitudes suggests more precision in our knowledge of economic behavior than is really the case. Mathematics is a precise discipline, and its use in conjunction with economic analysis may be misleading. We have already observed that the generalizations of economics and the social sciences are usually less exact than those of the physical or biological sciences. This, of course, does not prevent us from using mathematics in economic analysis, but it does require that we guard ourselves against the temptation to view the principles of economics as a set of exact relationships akin to the laws of physics or chemistry. We should also be on guard against another danger, which is the temptation to view the medium—mathematics—in which the economy's structure often is explained as the reality. Models are sometimes elegant in their construction and design, but we should not try to force reality into the confines of a model simply to preserve that elegance.

The Methods of Economic Analysis

Economics, as we have seen, is an area of knowledge that can be fitted into our broad definition of science as an activity that explains relationships between phenomena by the process of generalization. Equally important for comprehension of the scientific character of economics is an understanding of the methods employed in economic analysis—that is, its methodology.

Methodology refers to the techniques and procedures used by the economist to acquire knowledge and understanding of economic processes. More specifically, it concerns the techniques employed in the construction and verification of economic principles. Unless these techniques are sound, economic generalizations will have little value. In passing, it must be emphasized that there is no single and best methodology suitable for all areas of science. The appropriate technique will depend largely upon the kind of data under investigation; some methods of investigation are wholly applicable in some areas and not at all applicable in others.

The Deductive Method

The most characteristic method of economic analysis has been one usually described as *deductive*, or *hypothetical*. In essence, deduction involves the establishment of certain basic premises or assumptions concerning the strategic determinants of economic behavior and then, by reason or logic, inferring their consequences. John Stuart Mill called it the *a priori* method, by which he meant "reasoning from an assumed hypothesis."[12]

The deductive method as applied to economics consists of three major steps. The first is to postulate assumptions about the determinants of economic behavior in a particular situation. The nature of these assumptions deserves careful attention. Critics of the deductive method argue that the assumptions underlying the laws of economics are imaginary and unrealistic; consequently, any deductive system erected upon such assumptions is without significance. But in a purely formal sense, as already noted, the imaginary or nonimaginary character of the underlying assumptions does not matter; in the abstract the validity of a principle depends solely upon the correct use of logic in deriving the consequences of a given set of assumptions.

However, it is not accurate to say the basic assumptions of economics have no empirical—that is, factual—basis. Professor Lionel Robbins, an eminent British economist, asserts that the underlying postulates of economics are "all assumptions involving in some way simple and indisputable facts of experience relating to the way in which the scarcity of goods, which is the subject matter of our science, actually shows itself in the world of reality."[13] In other words, the assumptions of deductive economics consist of shrewd and imaginative observations about human behavior. To illustrate, we spoke earler of the assumption that the business firm seeks to maximize profit, and, as a consequence, does or does not do certain things. With respect to any particular business firm the empirical content of this assumption may be relatively low, for the factors that actually motivate a specific firm in a specific real world situation are many

12. John Stuart Mill, *Essays on Some Unsettled Questions of Political Economy* (London: Longmans, Green, 1877), p. 143.

13. Lionel Robbins, *An Essay on the Nature and Significance of Economic Science* (London: Macmillan, 1949), p. 78.

and complex. Yet as an insight into the forces that determine the behavior of business firms in general, the assumption of profit maximization is meaningful because it is a realistic description of a major, strategic determinant of economic behavior in a market economy. This is so even though an assumption of this kind can never be fully tested by experience. Ludwig von Mises has said that the "end of science is to know reality" and that "in introducing assumptions into its reasoning, it satisfies itself that the treatment of the assumptions conceived can render useful service for the comprehension of reality."[14] Consequently, an assumption like that of profit maximization, even though it may not be wholly accurate in an empirical sense, can be a tool of great power and usefulness for the comprehension of reality.

The second step consists of determining the consequences that will ensue from the performance of the assumed determinants of economic behavior. This is the purely deductive part of the process, because the essence of deduction, as John Stuart Mill said, consists of reasoning from given premises to their necessary conclusion. Success in this stage of the process depends primarily upon the correct use of logic, although in contemporary economics formal logic is supplemented in many instances by mathematics, a form of logic.

The last step in the deductive method is verification, which consists, in essence, of testing the conclusions reached by the process of logical inference against observed reality. The problem of verification is especially knotty in the social sciences because, as pointed out earlier, usually it is not possible to conduct controlled experiments to determine the validity of a generalization. The merit of the controlled experiment is that by rigidly regulating the conditions under which a particular event takes place, the investigator can isolate the effects of a change in any one of the factors that enter into the situation under study. Verification of a particular hypothesis is achieved through the repetition of the experiment until sufficient experience is accumulated to either sustain or disprove the hypothesis.

In all the sciences that concern themselves with the group behavior of human beings, the strict application of the controlled experiment as a means of verifying hypotheses is usually impossible. This is because the social scientist normally can not bring a part of society into the laboratory and re-create experience over and over again under strictly identical conditions. In the social sciences, consequently, evidence for the validity of a generalization depends most of the time as Mill said, on "the limited number of experiments which take place (if we may so speak) of their own accord, without any preparation or management of ours; in circum-

14. Ludwig von Mises, *Human Action* (New Haven: Yale University Press, 1949), p. 858.

stances, moreover, of great complexity and never perfectly known to us."[15] Mill's "limited number of experiments" are to be found in recorded facts of human experience, statistical and historical, and it becomes the task of the economist or social scientist to search patiently through the complex fabric of events of the real social world for necessary evidence to verify his generalizations. This task is not as hopeless as it may first appear, for, as Professor Milton Friedman has pointed out, experience does provide us with an abundance of evidence, although the interpretation of this evidence is at once more difficult and less dramatic than that arrived at by the controlled experiment.[16] In spite of the difficulties that economics may present with respect to verification, the final and necessary test of the validity of any economic generalization is observed reality.

The Inductive Method

In contrast to the analytical, or deductive, technique of analysis, there exists an alternative method that is described as empirical, or inductive. The process of induction involves the establishment of generalizations or principles on the basis of a number of specific instances or facts. It is said to be empirical because adherents of this method of analysis assert that generalization or the formulation of principles can come only after there has been an extensive complication of the raw data of experience. The latter may consist of historical data of an essentially qualitative character, or statistical data. The historical method and statistical method are sometimes cited as specific modes of investigation which fit into the broader framework of induction. The major differences between deduction and induction from the point of view of logic are well stated in the following quotation:

> By *deduction* in logic is meant reasoning or inference from the general to the particular, or from the universal to the individual. Still more specifically deductive inference signifies reasoning from given premises to their necessary conclusion. *Induction* is the process of reasoning from a part to the whole, from particulars to generals, or from the individual to the universal.[17]

15. Mill, p. 147. Experimentation is not wholly impossible in economics, however. During the first half of the 1970s the federal government sponsored a series of experiments to determine the effect of a guaranteed income (a "negative income tax") on work incentives and the reduction of poverty. Early findings indicated no significant reduction in the number of family heads holding jobs or seeking work because of an income guarantee. This was not a controlled, laboratory experiment in the strict sense of the term, but controls were in effect during the experiment. They were designed to isolate as nearly as possible the effects of an income guarantee on work incentives.

16. Milton Friedman, *Essays in Positive Economics* (Chicago: University of Chicago Press, 1953), p. 10.

17. Wilson Gee, *Social Science Research Methods* (New York: Appleton-Century-Crofts, 1950), p. 206.

Some economists have argued that the inductive method is the only truly scientific method of analysis and that if economics wants to achieve and retain standing as a scientific discipline it must become more and more inductive in its analytical techniques. This point of view is summed up in the following statement by Colin Clark:

> Not one in a hundred (of the academic economists)—at least of all those who are most anxious to proclaim the scientific nature of Economics—seems to understand what constitutes the scientific approach, namely, the careful systematization of all observed facts, the framing of hypotheses from these facts, prediction of fresh conclusions on the basis of these hypotheses, and the testing of these conclusions against further observed facts.[18]

Professor Clark's statement is representative of what some economists today probably regard as an extreme position with respect to the proper techniques for the acquisition of economic knowledge of a scientific character. Many economists argue that deduction and induction are complementary rather than alternative or opposing techniques of investigation. There can be no such thing as pure induction or empirical research without some preconceptions of what is important and the way in which things are related—in short, without some hypothesis to guide the investigation. This is exactly what the deductive process provides, and, without it, empirical research would degenerate into an incomprehensible accumulation of facts. On the other hand, pure deduction is equally an impossibility if economic analysis is to be something more than an exercise in abstract logic. Deduction without a factual content—that is, without induction—is just as empty and meaningless as induction or empirical research without some preconceptions—that is, without deduction.

The foregoing remarks on the deductive and inductive methods of analysis and their applicability to the science of economics suggest an important conclusion: There is no unique or single method of investigation or analysis that can appropriately be labeled the scientific method and which is the only proper or permissible technique to be used for the discovery and elaboration of scientific generalizations. Professor Max Black of Cornell University has defined the scientific method as "those procedures which, as a matter of historical fact, have proved most fruitful in the acquisition of systematic and comprehensive knowledge."[19] Such a broad definition is undoubtedly as good as any that can be devised, for even a cursory examination of the history of science will show that the development of scientific generalizations nearly always involves an amalgam of observation, experiment, speculation, and reasoning.

18. Colin Clark, *The Conditions of Economic Progress* (London: Macmillan, 1940), pp. vii–viii.

19. Max Black, "The Definition of the Scientific Method," in Robert C. Stauffer, ed., *Science and Civilization* (Madison: University of Wisconsin Press, 1949), p. 81.

Economic Analysis and Economic Policy

Any discussion of the nature of economics would be quite inadequate without consideration of the policy aspects of economics. The word *policy* refers to some course of action that is designed to realize or bring about some specific objective or end. Policy is concerned with what we want and how we get it. Economic policy thus has to do with the means that individuals, groups, or a whole society may utilize to achieve ends or objectives that are primarily of an economic nature. A distinguished economist and first chairman of the President's Council of Economic Advisers, Edwin G. Nourse, once defined economic policy as

> a sophisticated—that is, an intellectual rather than emotional—way of defining ends to be sought and adopting promising means of pursuing those ends. Perceiving business life as a complex social process about which, in spite of its vagaries, we have some hard-won understanding, policymaking expresses a faith that we can have some measure of control over the outcome.[20]

Since economic policy is concerned with the ends or objectives of society, it involves *value judgments*; it is concerned with questions of what ought to be. It is important that the significance of value judgments be recognized, for individuals and groups usually have deeply held convictions about the economy and how things ought to be, and such convictions profoundly affect their behavior. Value judgments concerning the proper ends of economic activity are important, too, because they are the source of much that is controversial in economics. Disagreement in economics stems not so much from disagreement over the economic objectives being sought, but over the appropriate means for the realization of these ends.

With this understanding of the nature of economic policy and its significance as a source of controversy in economics, we are prepared to discuss the relation of economic analysis to economic policy. Once again a word of warning is in order, for economists are not in agreement among themselves as to the manner in which these two facets of economics are related to one another. This being the case, we shall begin by describing briefly the major positions that economists hold in respect to the relationship between economic analysis and economic policy.

At one extreme of the spectrum of possible attitudes is the positivist view that economic analysis and economic policy are two separate aspects of economics which simply cannot be mixed. This particular point of view asserts that economics is a positive science, which means it is an activity that concerns itself only with the discovery of generalizations of the kind

20. Edwin G. Nourse, *Economics in the Public Service* (New York: Harcourt, Brace, 1953), p. 6.

we described earlier; it is completely divorced from any consideration of values. John Neville Keynes in his classic work, *The Scope and Method of Political Economy*, defined a positive science as "a body of systematized knowledge concerning what is," and contrasted it with a normative, or regulative, science, which he defined as "a body of systematized knowledge discussing the criteria of what ought to be, and concerned therefore with the ideal as distinguished from the actual."[21] Professor Friedman asserts that "positive economics is in principle independent of any particular ethical position or normative judgments."[22] In sum, the positivist view holds that the economist must, if he is to retain his claim to scientific objectivity, confine his activities to the discovery of significant relationships among economic phenomena and remain scrupulously neutral toward ends or goals of society.

It is doubtful that most economists today accept without reservation the positivist view of the nature and scope of economics. For one thing it is argued that values cannot be separated from analysis because economics is a social science and the social sciences possess significance only to the extent that they contribute to the solution of real social problems. If this is a valid contention, it means that economists and other social scientists can hardly avoid becoming involved in some fashion with the ends or goals of the society of which they are a part. The reader will recognize, of course, that this particular attitude is itself a value judgment, but it is one, nevertheless, that many competent economists share. For example, Professor John H. Williams, a former president of the American Economic Association, states, "Economic theorizing seems to me pointless unless it is aimed at what to do. All the great theorists, I think, have had policy as their central interest, even if their policy were merely laissez faire."[23]

The viewpoint of an economist like Williams does not necessarily refute the positivist position that economic analysis can be neutral in the sense of being completely detached from value judgments, but it suggests that such an economics, if it really could exist, might be a barren discipline.

The phrase "if it really could exist" brings us to the second major reason why some economists assert that economic analysis cannot truly be free of value judgments. The more fundamental objection to the positivist viewpoint is that values are inevitably a part of the analytical techniques employed by the economist. Value judgments are, so to speak, built into economic analysis to such an extent that it is vain to expect that economics can be a science completely detached from all value considerations. Several reasons may be suggested as to why this is so.

21. John Neville Keynes, *The Scope and Method of Political Economy* (London: Macmillan, 1891), p. 34. J. N. Keynes was the father of John Maynard Keynes.

22. Friedman, *Essays in Positive Economics*, p. 4.

23. John H. Williams, "An Economist's Confessions," *American Economic Review*, March 1952, p. 10.

The first concerns the definition of a scientific discipline. Definitions are necessary in any science, for without them there would be no way of knowing where one field of inquiry begins and another leaves off. This is true even though definitions must often be quite arbitrary. The determination of content and scope for any area of intellectual inquiry is basically a matter of determining what is important and what is not important, which in turn implies that no scientific discipline can even be defined without the exercise of value judgments.

Closely related to definition is the terminology used in economics. Gunnar Myrdal, a distinguished Swedish economist and Nobel laureate, says

> . . . nearly all the general terms current in political economy, and the social sciences generally, have two meanings: one in the sphere of "what is," and another in the sphere of "what ought to be." The word "principle," for instance, means, on the one hand, "theory," or "basis of a theory," or "working hypothesis within a theory." But the word "principle" may also mean an "aim of conscious striving" or a "chief means of attaining a postulated end" or a "general rule of action". . . . From a scientific point of view nearly all our terms are for this reason "value-laden."[24]

A second argument concerns the selection of areas to be investigated within the confines specified by the definition of the subject. This, too, involves value judgments, for whenever a selection is made it implies that some things are more important than others. In economics, the choice of the areas for study and analysis is largely influenced by the problems that are of concern to a society at any particular historical epoch. If economic analysis is largely a by-product of the economic problems that beset human societies from time to time, it is difficult to perceive how such analysis can be wholly divorced from values. Since the problems of a society in some sense reflect the values and value conflicts of that society, it logically follows that these will be reflected, too, in the areas selected for investigation and analysis by the economist.

Finally, it can be argued that most, if not all, economic generalizations or principles necessarily contain within themselves specific implications in the matter of economic policy. If economic analysis has its origins in economic problems, then it would seem reasonable—and logical—that such analysis should point the way to a solution of these problems. But if this is the case, then it can hardly be said that the analysis is neutral with respect to values. One or two simple examples will suffice to illustrate this point. Economics has developed an elaborate body of principles that explains how prices are determined and resources allocated through the mechanism of the market. This elegant structure of principles is some-

24. Gunnar Myrdal, *The Political Element in the Development of Economic Theory* (New York: Simon and Schuster, 1954), p. 19.

thing more than a scientific explanation of the mechanism of the market, for it implies, among other things, that certain types of market arrangements lead to a more favorable—or better—allocation of resources than others. Another case in point is the theory of comparative advantage, which provides a scientific explanation of the basis for trade between nations. It does this, but it also implies that a policy of free trade is desirable if a nation seeks to maximize the material well-being of its citizens. The latter goal, the reader will recall, appears to be one of the value premises implicit in the traditional definition of economics.

The question that we have raised concerning the relationship between economic analysis and economic policy is an especially difficult one for which no final or definitive answer really exists. This is an issue that we should not take lightly, especially in view of the traumatic experiences we have lived through in the last few years. We are a democratic society, but the tragedy of the Vietnam war and Watergate should have taught us that even a democratic government can threaten and mislead its citizens. This has a bearing on policy simply because policy action usually requires some kind of intervention by the government into the economy. In this century the professed aim of public intervention has been to improve the welfare of citizens, but it does not follow that the consequences of government behavior are always benign. Government action is needed in the economic management of our society, but we also need to be alert to the dangers that an excess of government can pose for the rights and well-being of citizens. The viewpoint favored in this text is that economics cannot be a pure science, detached from the great issues of public policy of our day. This in itself is a value judgment. But it arises out of the conviction that economics is worthwhile and a discipline deserving of public support *only* to the extent that it can contribute something of genuine value toward the solution of real and pressing human problems.

I
The National Income

2

Fundamentals of National Income Accounting

The behavior of our economy is not one of steady growth toward higher and higher levels of material production; rather, it typically moves forward in a series of sharp upward thrusts, frequently followed by contractions in economic activity. The economy's performance has a distinctive fluctuating character, as witnessed by the output path shown in Figure 2–1. How does the economist measure the forces behind the erratic and somewhat cyclical path that the economy follows over time? This chapter and the next are addressed to that question.

First, it is necessary to understand clearly the meaning and use made of the word *income* when reference is made not to the income of the individual citizen or business firm, but to the income of the whole economy. Specifically, we seek in this chapter to define and analyze the nature of national income and related aggregates that have to do with the over-all performance of the economic system. In Chapter 3 we shall describe in detail some important measures that economists and statisticians have developed for recording the economy's performance.

The Nature and Uses of National Income Accounting

The techniques of national income accounting developed in the United States and other nations during the last half-century are not fundamentally different from the accounting systems developed for and utilized by

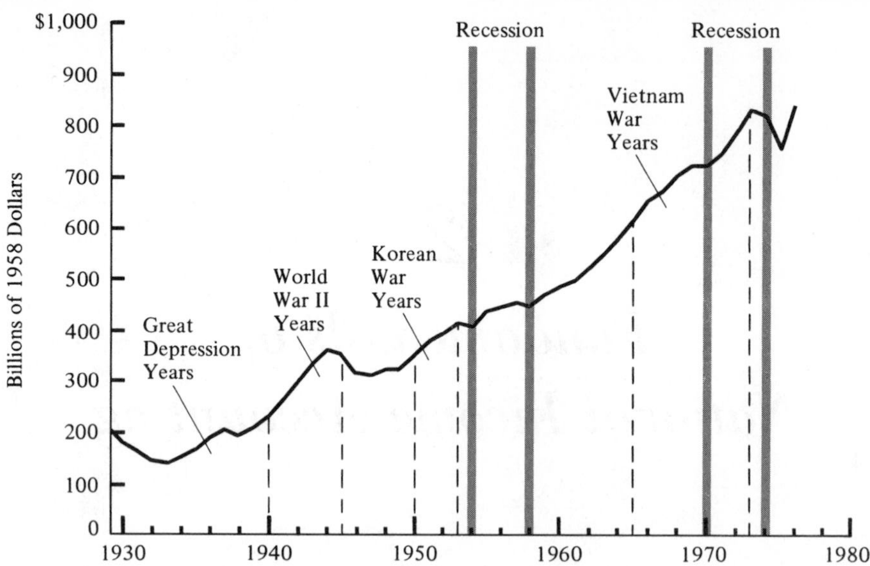

Source: Historical Statistics of the United States; Economic Report of the President, 1975

FIGURE 2–1. Growth of U.S. National Output
(GNP in billions of constant dollars)

business firms. All accounting systems have as their common purpose the measurement and communication of accurate, numerical information concerning the economic and financial activities during a specified period of time of some entity (such as the household, the business firm, or the nation).

Many readers are familiar with the typical accounts employed by the business firm, like the balance sheet and the profit and loss statement. These accounts provide a numerical record of the activities of the business firm. To conduct the affairs of his firm successfully, the businessman must have at his disposal accurate and current information concerning sales receipts, expenditures, and the profit of his firm. From information provided by the firm's accounting system, the businessman judges the state of economic health of his enterprise. The businessman could not possibly make intelligent policy decisions respecting future operations of the enterprise without adequate information concerning what has taken place in the firm in the recent past.

National income accounting is designed to do for the economy as a whole what more traditional forms of accounting do for the business firm. That is to say, the basic objective of a system of national income accounting is to provide a systematic and factual record of the performance of the economy during a specified period of time.[1]

1. In the United States, national income accounting got a major start in 1920, when the National Bureau of Economics Research, a private research organization, began

Responsibility for compilation of the statistical data that go into the accounts of the system rests with the Bureau of Economic Analysis of the United States Department of Commerce. The statistics of national income are published at periodic intervals in the *Survey of Current Business,* a monthly publication of the Department of Commerce. The Commerce Department has published two important supplements to the *Survey of Current Business* (in 1951 and again in 1954) entitled *National Income,* which describe in detail not only the concepts employed in the United States' system of national income and social accounting, but also the sources and methods utilized in the compilation of the statistics of income for the whole nation.

The most important use of national income accounting[2] is in the formulation of economic policy, primarily by governments, but also by business firms and labor organizations. Since the great Stock Market crash of 1929 there has been a vast expansion in the role played by government (federal, state, and local) in the economy; between 1929 and 1976 for example, the purchase of goods and services by all levels of government rose form 8 percent of national output to 21.6 percent.[3] As a consequence, public policies relating to taxes and expenditures have become one of the most strategically important determinants of the over-all performance of the economic system. Given the growing complexity of the modern economy, detailed statistical information on the performance of the economy as provided by systems of national income accounting is indispensable in developing intelligent and workable public policies. One of the most important applications of national income accounting is to trace fluctuations and growth in total activity, as in Figure 2–1. Aggregate data of this nature provide us with useful information about the use and availability of resources in the economy. When national income data are broken down into different sectors and industries, we are able to gain important insights into the structure and anatomy of the economic system. Such

---

extensive work on the measurement of national income. After the onset of the Great Depression and as a result of a 1932 Senate resolution, the U.S. Department of Commerce began to compile national income statistics for the American economy. Professor Simon Kuznets, the fourth economist awarded a Nobel Prize in this field, directed the early work of the National Bureau on national income measurement and worked closely with the Department of Commerce in preparing its first estimates. These latter were published in 1934 as a report, *National Income 1929–32.* For a more detailed review of the history of national income accounting, see John W. Kendrick, *Economic Accounts and Their Uses* (New York: McGraw-Hill, 1972), chap. 2.

2. National income accounting is a broad and descriptive term covering a wide variety of economic accounts that apply to the economic system. The best known of these include national income and product accounts (the subject of this and the following chapter), flow of funds accounts, input-output analysis, balance of international payments accounts, and statements of national wealth. For a detailed discussion of various forms of national income accounting see Kendrick.

3. U.S. Department of Commerce, *Survey of Current Business,* April, 1977.

information is invaluable in analyzing the effect of specific policies on prices, production, and employment in different parts of the economy. Further, interrelationships between different parts of the economy are clarified. Business firms, too, make use of national income data, especially as a background for important business decisions pertaining to production, purchasing, borrowing, and capital spending.

The usefulness of national income data reaches beyond the domestic economy. Important comparisons between nations can be made on the basis of their respective national income accountings systems, especially because the terminology and conceptual framework for such systems are becoming increasingly standardized. National income accounting as developed in this and the following chapter is the most widely used frame of reference for making forecasts and projections of economic activity.

Income and Wealth

Having sketched out the nature of national income accounting, we shall analyze, first, the concept of income and, second, the meaning of income in reference to the whole society. A similar discussion on wealth will follow; then we shall discuss the relationship between income and wealth.

The Concept of Income

As a concept there are a number of different ways in which income can be defined, but the one thing common to all definitions is the idea that income is a *flow* phenomenon. By a *flow* is meant something that is *measured over time.* For the individual the income flow is usually thought of in terms of money received between two points of time, although one might just as readily—and correctly—conceive of it as a flow of satisfactions during a period of time. The business firm, too, usually thinks of income as money received over time. But no matter how we choose to define income from the point of view of the individual or the firm, the crucial element in our definition is that of flow.

This last statement brings us to the question of what we mean when we talk in terms of the income of the whole society—what, in short, is the meaning of *national income*? We emphasized that the basic purpose of national income accounting is to provide a factual record of the performance of the economy. Since economic activity aims at satisfaction of human wants, and since want satisfaction results from consumption of goods and services, the performance of the economy must be measured in terms of the amount of productive activity taking place in a period of time. Productive activity, however, culminates in the output of valuable goods and services; thus income from the standpoint of the whole society is a *flow of output over a period of time*. Let us inject a word of caution: The income of the whole society, even though normally measured in money terms, in not the same as the aggregate of all money incomes received by persons in the economy. Flows of money income do not always represent or correspond to output flows, and increases in money flows do not always mean that there has been an increase in output flows. We shall develop the reasons for this in greater detail subsequently.

If the basic definition of income in a social sense is that of a flow of output, this presents a difficult problem in measurement. Output consists of a vast and heterogeneous quantity of goods and services that cannot be added together unless they can be reduced to a common unit of measurement. As a practical matter, the only way in which we can add together all the different kinds of goods and services produced by the economy during a period of time is by reducing them to their money value. Money value is the common denominator which enables us to sum up and reduce to a single figure the complex aggregation of goods and services contained in the economy's flow of output during some definite period.

It is possible to reduce the economy's flow of output to its monetary valuation because in a market economy practically all productive activity will be reflected in money transactions. Most activities that are productive —which lead to the creation of goods and services—are carried on through the mechanism of the market and will thus carry a price tag. If a way can be found to summarize all the monetary transactions that reflect productive activity, it becomes possible to measure in money terms the total income, or flow of output, of the society.

While, in principle, the summing of money transactions describes the technique by which the output of the whole society is measured, several qualifications to the above statement should be noted. For one thing, all monetary transactions do not necessarily reflect current productive activity; this is the case with sales of secondhand goods or the purchase and sale of various financial instruments, such as stocks and bonds. Second, some productive activity does not pass through the mechanism of the market and thus is not reflected in a monetary transaction. The labor of the homemaker is a case in point. Finally, money itself is not a stable unit of measure since the value of money fluctuates as the general level of prices changes. These important qualifications to the general principle that the productive activity of the economy is reflected in monetary transactions will be examined in detail in a later section of this chapter.

The Circular Flow of Income and Product

Income, as we have seen, is a flow phenomenon. But it is important to note the *circular* character of this flow. This basic concept is illustrated in

Figure 2–2. Output originates in the producing units of the economy—including the government as a producing entity—and moves from them to the economy's households, which are not only the ultimate users of the economy's output, but also the owners and suppliers of the economic resources that enter into the creation of output. The existence of a flow of output means there must be a corresponding flow of inputs, for the essence of the productive process is the transformation of the services rendered by the economic resources of land, labor, and capital into economically useful goods and services. Thus, as shown in Figure 2–2, the underlying real economic process consists of a continuous, circular process whereby inputs of resources are transformed by the economy's production units into goods and services. The thoughtful reader will recognize that this is a simplified view of the matter because it lumps all goods and services together and assumes that all of the output is directed toward the households of the economy. This is not actually the case because some of the output consists of capital or investment goods, for which firms rather than households are the ultimate users. Moreover, households do not spend all of their income, as some is saved and some is taxed. These facts, though, should not cloud our understanding of the basically circular character of the economic process.

The input and output flows that constitute the essence of the economic process are matched by two flows of money—one of income and one of expenditure. According to Figure 2–2, which outlines the productive process in a market economy wherein resources are privately owned and most production decisions are privately made, resource owners exchange the service of their resources for money incomes, while the pro-

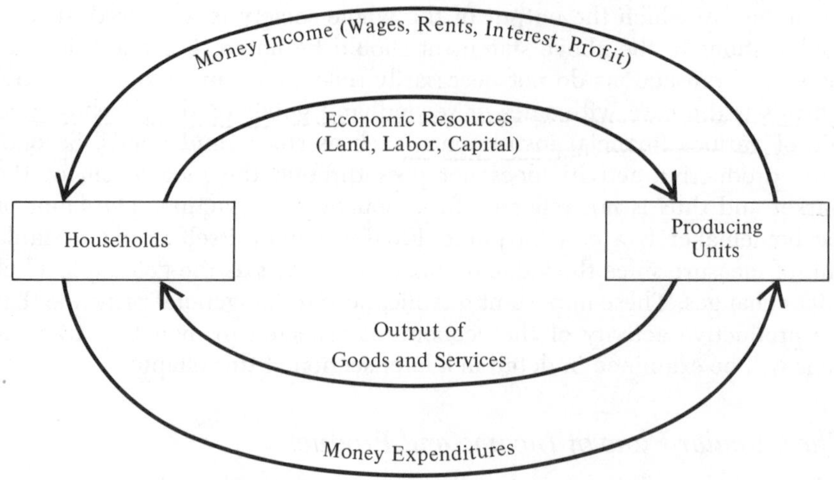

FIGURE 2–2. The Circular Flow of Economic Activity

ducing entities of the economy exchange their output of goods and services for the flow of expenditures originating in the households of the economy. The flow of income and expenditure matching the real flows of the economy is seen to be circular in the same sense that the underlying flows of product and services of economic resources are circular.

The circular flow diagram, even though oversimplified, illustrates a number of important propositions relating to the economic process and the flow of income. First, the diagram shows that income (or output) creation involves an interaction between the two basic kinds of markets that exist in the economy. Exchanging the services of economic resources for money incomes, depicted in the top half of the diagram, reflects transactions taking place in the resource (factor) market, while the expenditure of money income for the economy's output, depicted in the lower half of the diagram, represents the total of transactions taking place in the economy's market for goods and services. Second, the circular flow diagram aids in understanding why the flow of income, the flow of output, and the flow of expenditures for output are necessarily equal, *once they have taken place*. The reason for this equality is that all of these flows are different measures of the same thing—the volume of productive activity in the economy. Since the circular flow analysis reveals that the total flow of current income is always equal to the value of current output, this means that the productive process will always generate sufficient total money income to purchase the current output of the economy. This does not mean, however, that all the income so generated will be spent by those who first receive it, as some may be saved and some may be taxed. There may be spending by business that offsets saving and by government that offsets taxes, but this does not necessarily have to happen.

The Concept of Wealth

Wealth and income are concepts so closely related that it is easy to confuse them and not see that they are distinctly different entities. As a starting point, let us define *wealth* as all material things which possess economic value. Wealth, in other words, consists of goods that can command other goods and services in exchange. Several aspects of this definition should be noted. First, our definition limits wealth to tangible or material things, which is to say that intangibles (for example, services) are excluded. Second, wealth is a *stock* phenomenon in contrast to income, a *flow* phenomenon. Wealth is a concept that relates to the total material things existing at a moment of time. Contrast this with the income concept which has to do with the flow of output or money over a period of time.

The basic difference between wealth and income is reflected in the way in which the two are measured: Income can be measured only by reference to some distinct period of time such as the day, the week, the month, or the year, whereas wealth can be measured only by reference to a specific moment of time, such as the final day of the week, the month, or the year. This difference can be illustrated with reference to the balance sheet and the profit and loss statements of the business firm. The balance sheet is analogous to the wealth concept; it reveals the position of the firm in terms of its assets and liabilities at a given moment of time, usually the close of business on the last day of the year. The profit and loss statement, on the other hand, is analogous to the income concept; it depicts the receipts and expenditures flowing into and out of the firm during a specific period of time, usually one year.

Finally, it is important to note that wealth, because it involves stock of goods, is exhaustible, while income, because it is a flow, is capable of being continuously renewed. Wealth, in other words, can be wholly used up. The corollary to this is that the renewal of wealth used up in production must come out of what is produced. It is also true, of course, that within a specific period most income is normally used up, but the income flow will be renewed in the next period as long as the economic resources that are the basic source of income are not destroyed.

The distinction between a stock and a flow extends beyond income and wealth to other economic variables. The labor force, for example, is a stock variable, but the loss of jobs is a flow, since it makes sense to measure the latter with reference to a specific time period, a week, a month, or a year. Much of the time there is a stock counterpart to a given flow—as in the relationship between wealth and income—but not always. Wages, for example, are a flow variable, since they represent the amount of money a worker receives over a period of time. But there is no such thing as a "stock of wages," the size of which is affected by the flow variable. No hard and fast rule exists to tell whether a stock component exists for any particular flow—only common sense and a careful examination of the flow variable in question can determine this.

Resources—land, labor, and capital—can be destroyed, worn out, or otherwise depleted, but this would simply have the effect of stopping the income flow until new resources are generated.

Problems in the Measurement of Wealth

In any discussion of wealth, particularly in reference to the economy as a whole, distinction must be made between *wealth* and *claims to wealth*. Wealth consists of material things of economic value, while claims to wealth are, in effect, evidences of ownership, such shares of stock or deeds or claims that do not necessarily involve ownership, such as bonds, paper money, and other debt instruments. From the viewpoint of the individual, the distinction between wealth and claims to wealth is not critical; the individual, in reckoning his personal wealth position, usually counts both the material items of wealth in his possession, such as a house or land, as well as intangible claims in the form of bonds, shares of stock, and money in the bank. This is a logical position as far as the individual is concerned because for any single individual both the material wealth and claims to wealth that he owns possess exchange value, and can, if necessary, be converted into purchasing power. There exist in the economy many different markets for the purpose and sale of claims to wealth. Organized security markets such as the New York Stock Exchange are a good example of the latter.

For the economy as a whole, however, the distinction between wealth and claims to wealth is vitally important. When we are trying to measure or get an inventory of the material wealth of the society, it would be illogical to add up all goods and all claims to goods as well. This would give us a total in which everything has been counted twice. In the economy as a whole the value of all material things would just equal the sum total of all claims possessing exchange value because every material item of wealth must be owned by an individual, a group of individuals, some type of business entity such as the corporation, or by some kind of governmental unit.

In taking inventory of the wealth of a community or the nation, there is an immensely difficult and complex problem of valuation. Wealth can be measured only if valued in some such common denominator as money. Normally items of wealth are valued in money terms as a result of their purchase and sale in a market, but for many items of wealth that ought to be included in a national inventory this method of valuation is simply not possible. What, for instance, is the value of a great public library or hospital? A national park or forest? Or an ancient building of great historical significance? For items of wealth such as these and, perhaps, for resources which are bought and sold only infrequently, there can only be an arbitrary judgment as to their real value.

Our discussion of the nature of wealth would not be complete without comment on the basic categories of material wealth existing in any society. The most fundamental classification distinguishes between natural resources and resources that are man-made. In the first category we find all natural wealth, which is to say land and the values inherent in land—fertility, mineral deposits, and climatic characteristics. These things are basically gifts of nature, even though their economic value over time may be modified by man's actions. Within the category of man-made resources it is necessary to distinguish between wealth possessed by consumers or households, which is often thought of as nonproductive, and wealth possessed by firms, which is regarded as productive (because its services are employed in the production of future output.) It is not literally true, of course, that items of personal wealth—for example, automobiles, refrigerators, washing machines, and other household appliances—are nonproductive, since they render services to their owners. Granted this, it is still desirable to distinguish items of consumer wealth from the society's stock of productive instruments in the form of buildings and various types of capital equipment. In determining the productive potential of any society, it is wealth in the form of productive instruments that is of critical importance. Wealth in the form of capital goods represents a dynamic and procreative element in modern society because the real function of such goods is to produce other goods and services.

How much tangible wealth is there in the United States? John W. Kendrick, estimates that at the end of 1975 the nation's net *real* wealth (corrected for changes in the value of the dollar) totaled $5,684 billions—a staggering sum that amounts to an average of $13,212 for every man, woman, and child residing in the United States. For the nation as a whole, 36.5 percent of tangible wealth consists of equipment, 44.9 percent structures, 10.1 percent land, and 8.5 percent inventories (stocks of goods on hand). Professor Kendrick also discovered that since the nation was founded in 1776, *real* wealth per person grew seventeenfold, a figure which means that on the average it more than doubled every fifty years.[4]

The Concept of Human Wealth

In recent years some economists have applied the wealth concept to the investment by human beings in skills and knowledge. The skills, education, and knowledge that human beings acquire is in a broad sense a form of capital that contributes in a significant way to the process of production. Professor Theodore W. Schultz, one of the early advocates of the idea that economic analysis should take into account human as well as material capital, points out that not only does wealth in the form of human skill and knowledge require investment for its creation, but this form of wealth has grown in Western societies at a much faster rate than other, nonhuman types of capital. Further, Professor Schultz says, the growth of human capital may be the most distinctive feature of the modern economy, contributing more to the growth of output over the long run than conventional forms of wealth.[5]

Measurement of the economic value of human capital presents formidable statistical difficulties, although roughly speaking, the net worth of an individual's human capital depends on the income he or she can expect to earn over his or her working life. Chapter 7, "Investment Spending and Investment Finance," gets into the problem of how the current economic

4. John W. Kendrick, "Measuring America's Wealth," *Morgan Guaranty Survey*, May 1976, pp. 6, 10.

5. Theodore W. Schultz, "Investment in Human Capital," *American Economic Review*, March 1961.

value of any item of wealth (or capital) which produces an income is determined. Aside from statistical difficulties in measuring human capital, there is a reluctance—and perhaps even a repugnance—among economists and others to suggest even remotely that human beings might be looked upon as capital goods. As Professor Schultz points out, to regard human beings as capital that can be augmented by investment runs counter to deeply held values, primarily because of the long struggle of Western man to rid society of any form of slavery or indentured service.[6] Nevertheless, economists have continued to refine the concept of human capital and to measure its value. In the 1960s the concept provided a rationale for more spending on education, since it was widely held that investment in human capital would contribute as much or more to the growth of the economy than other sources of wealth. Second, it appeared that spending for education might work to lessen inequality in income distribution. This seemed logical because studies showed a high correlation between income earned and educational levels attained. Raising the educational level of persons at the lower end of the income scale would thus tend to lessen inequalities.

Since the 1960s hope for the latter outcome has diminished. This is due in part to the fact that income distribution did not change significantly over the decade, in spite of substantial increases in high school graduation rates and in the ratio of college graduates to nongraduates.[7] Also, more recent studies challenge the basic assumption of an important correlation between educational attainment and income. This is the theme of the now famous Coleman report on education and school and an equally prestigious study by Christopher Jencks on inequality.[8] These studies have not gone unchallenged, and, further, they should not obscure the fact that low income groups and minorities often do not have a fair opportunity to make the kind of long and costly personal investment that is needed if they are to improve their skills and knowledge.

Interactions of Income and Wealth

We have outlined some of the basic differences between income and wealth; it is important also to have a clear understanding of the way in which they are linked together.

Our fundamental definition of income from the point of view of the

6. Ibid.

7. Alice M. Rivlin, "Income Distribution— Can Economists Help?" *American Economic Review*, May 1970, p. 10.

8. James S. Coleman, *Equality of Educational Opportunity* (Washington, D.C.: Department of Health, Education, and Welfare, 1966) and Christopher Jencks et al., *Inequality: A Reassessment of the Effect of Family and Schooling in America* (New York: Basic Books, Inc., 1972).

whole society is that of a flow of goods and services. Given this definition, a key question is: What use or disposition is made of the economy's income? The simplest answer is that whatever the economy produces in any particular period of time must either be consumed or not consumed. To consume output means, of course, to use up goods and services in the satisfaction of human wants. If a good or service can satisfy a human want it is said to have utility. Consumption, therefore, involves the using up of utilities as wants are satisfied. Production, on the other hand, involves the creation of utilities so that wants can be satisfied.

But what happens to the output that is not consumed during the income period in which it is produced? This output becomes an addition to the existing stock of wealth of the economy. Here we have the essential relationship between income and wealth; whenever current income exceeds current consumption the stock of wealth automatically is increased, and whenever current consumption is in excess of current income the stock of wealth will automatically be reduced. The relationship between the flow of income and consumption and the stock of wealth may be likened to a reservoir of water, in which the water level (that is, the stock of water) depends upon the rate at which water flows into the reservoir as compared to the rate at which water flows out of the reservoir. If the rate of inflow is greater than the rate of outflow the water level within the reservoir will rise, while if the rate of outflow is greater than the rate of inflow the water level will drop.

If some part of the current output of an economy is not consumed during the period in which it is produced *saving* has taken place. Two things about saving should be noted. First, saving, like income, is a flow phenomenon. The assets (real and monetary) of both a nation and an individual may increase because of saving. Second, saving is a negative act, since basically it represents the *nonconsumption* of current output.

There is, however, another facet to the nonconsumption of current output. The addition to the economy's existing stock of wealth that is the inevitable consequence of the act of saving is also defined as *investment*. In a fundamental sense, investment means a net addition to the stock of wealth of the economy. As we probe further into national income measurement and analysis we shall see that it is necessary for practical reasons to modify this definition, but this does not change the important underlying idea that the act of investment always involves something *real*, in the sense that it has to do with changes in the economy's stock of wealth. Another word of caution is in order here: This overly simple definition will have to be modified when we consider the difference between net and gross additions to the economy's stock of wealth.

The relationship between output and wealth should be viewed in another way. Not only is it true that the stock of wealth is augmented when the economy does not consume all of current output, but it is also true that output is a flow that has its origins in the size, quality, and use made of the economy's stock of both material and human wealth. The act of investment (discussed below) is essential if a society is to maintain intact—or increase—its stock of wealth. Unless the society makes provision for investment, the income flow will be imperiled.

Whenever we discuss or measure saving and investment in an *ex post*,[9] or after-the-fact sense, they are necessarily equal. This follows from the way in which we have defined these phenomena: If some part of the economy's current output is not consumed we say that saving has taken place, but by the same token we say that this represents investment because an act of nonconsumption will add to the economy's stock of wealth. The notion that investment and saving are identical when defined in this manner is highly important in economic analysis and one that will be encountered frequently in subsequent chapters.

Basic Components of National Income

Our discussion of the relationship of income and wealth provides the foundation for understanding the major categories of output and expenditure actually employed in national income measurement and analysis. Before we examine the major measures of national income and product currently constructed by the Department of Commerce, it is essential to have a clear understanding of the kinds of output that enter into these aggregates. The broad concepts discussed in the previous section must be translated into specific categories that are capable of measurement and practical use in a national income accounting system.

Consumption Goods and Services (C)

In most societies the largest proportion of current output will consist of consumer goods and services. These may be defined as goods and services designed to satisfy human wants. The usual method for measurement of the economy's output of consumer goods and services is through adding up the expenditures made by all households and private nonprofit institutions. Beyond this it is customary in national income accounting to break this category down into three subcategories: expenditures for consumer durables (automobiles, household appliances, household furnishings, etc.), nondurables (mostly food and clothing), and services. (In all subsequent

9. Economists use the term *ex post* to refer to values (spending, saving, etc.) that are measured by looking back after an event has happened. *Ex ante* is used to refer to values that involve looking forward to what is intended or planned to happen. For a further discussion of the concepts see p. 54.

discussion and analysis we shall designate this particular component of the national discussion output by the capital letter *C*).

The durable goods component of consumption expenditures presents us with a problem of measurement. A durable good (like an automobile) is essentially a consumer capital good. Typically such goods have a life span of a number of years, and their real economic value lies in the fact that they render a service to the consumer during this life span. In the case of an automobile, the service is that of transportation; in the case of a refrigerator, that of food storage and refrigeration. Since the basic purpose of national income accounting is to measure the amount of productive activity taking place in the economy during a specific period, the logical procedure would be to count the services rendered to the consumer during each income period by a durable good, such as an automobile, as a part of the income (or output) of that income period. This logical procedure has not been followed, however, because of the impossibility of measuring statistically the rate at which the economy's enormous stock of consumer durable goods delivers services to consumers. As a result, national income accountants and statisticians resort to the convenient fiction that all consumer goods, including consumer durables, are consumed during the income period in which they are purchased. The only important exception to this procedure is consumer housing, for purchases of new houses are treated as investment rather than consumption expenditures. This point will be discussed in the following section.

Investment Goods (I)

In a broad sense the investment goods category of the national output should consist of all additions to the economy's stock of wealth; this was the basic meaning we gave to the term *investment* in our previous discussion. From the standpoint of national income accounting, however, it has been necessary to modify this fundamental approach, primarily because it is impractical and statistically impossible to include all additions to the economy's stock of wealth in the investment goods category. (The capital letter I will be used in this and later chapters to designate the investment component of output.)

The usual practice in national income accounting is to measure the economy's output of investment goods by the expenditures made during the income period by the end-users (generally business firms) for goods of this type. The Department of Commerce classifies the following as domestic investment expenditure:

1. All purchases by business firms of new construction and durable equipment
2. All purchases of new houses, that is, all residential construction
3. All changes in inventories held by business firms

The rationale for this particular structure of classification warrants explanation. The first category, producer's plant and equipment, obviously consists of additions to the economy's stock of productive instruments. It is less clear, though, why purchases of new houses should be considered as investment goods. Actually the decision to include residential construction in the investment goods category is arbitrary, because one could argue with justifiable logic that the purchase of a durable item like a house, which renders a service to its owner over its lifetime, is basically no different from the purchase of other durable consumer goods such as automobiles, stoves, and refrigerators. The logic of such a position would be almost irrefutable if all newly constructed houses were sold to consumers or households. On the other hand, it would be equally logical to treat houses as a productive *capital* instrument if all houses were sold to business firms and then rented to the consumer, for in this case the house would clearly be a means for the provision of a service for which the consumer would pay. Actually this is what is assumed in national income accounting and measurement, even though a very large portion of the nation's houses are occupied by their owners. The basic reason for this procedure is that the much longer life of houses as compared to other consumer durables would make the fiction of the consumption of durables in the income period in which they are produced and sold quite absurd if applied to housing. The purchase of new houses, therefore, is treated as an investment expenditure in the income period in which the purchase is made, and a rent is imputed to the owner of the house in the case of owner-occupied housing during subsequent income periods. This imputed rent presumably represents the value of the service provided by the house to its owner over its useful life and thus becomes a part of the economy's output of consumption goods and services.

The inclusion of all changes in the volume of inventories held by business firms in the investment goods category is in accord with our earlier discussion of the fundamental nature of the investment process. Consumer goods, including those in process, and quantities of raw materials produced but not sold or used up during an income period necessarily represent an addition to the economy's stock of wealth. Such goods and raw materials represent a net increase in the inventories—or stocks of goods on hand—of the business firms of the economy. Thus changes in inventories properly belong in the investment goods category of the national output.

At this point the reader may wonder what happens if the stock of all types of goods held by business firms is drawn down during an income period. If this takes place there has been *disinvestment* insofar as inventories are concerned. Whenever the net change in inventories is negative, sales are being made from stocks rather than current output. This implies that expenditures reflect not only current output but output from some previous period. Thus if we hope to measure current output by expenditures, it is necessary to deduct expenditures that represent the using up of past output. Broadly, the process of disinvestment means that the economy has consumed more than it has produced during an income period; consequently there will be a reduction in the economy's existing stock of wealth. From an *ex post* viewpoint, disinvestment is conceptually identical with *dissaving*, as the latter takes place whenever current consumption exceeds current output.

Gross and Net Investment · In a discussion of the investment goods category of the economy's output it is important to distinguish between investment that is gross and investment that is net. Once the reader understands the difference between gross and net investment there will be no difficulty in understanding the difference between gross and net output, a distinction that is useful in economic analysis. Basically, gross investment refers to the output of all goods in the investment goods category during an income period. This total is gross because it includes capital goods for replacement and for additions to the economy's stock of physical wealth. It is logical that some part of the economy's current total output of investment goods should constitute replacement for the portion of the economy's existing stock of productive wealth used up in the course of producing the current output. The productive process requires use of capital instruments in conjunction with other resources in order to secure an output, and whenever capital equipment is used it will experience wear and tear. Thus, in any income period some part of the total stock of capital equipment or productive wealth will ultimately be exhausted and have to be replaced. The share of the total investment goods output that serves to replace worn-out capital instruments is termed *replacement investment*. There are serious statistical problems with respect to measurement of this magnitude, but we shall defer any discussion of these to a later point.

If we subtract from the total output of investment goods in any income period the amount representing replacement investment, we are left with a total *net investment*. This total is net because, if our figure for replacement purposes is accurate, the difference between this figure and the total must represent the amount by which the economy's stock of productive wealth has increased during the current income period. Thus, net investment refers to the process by which a society increases its stock of productive capital instruments. If, during an income period, net investment is positive, the economy will have experienced an absolute increase in its physical stock of productive wealth, which will mean that its ability to produce goods and services will have been enlarged. On the other hand, if net investment is negative, there has been a reduction in the economy's total stock of productive wealth, a development that normally implies an impairment of productive capacity.

Government Purchases of Goods and Services (G)

Up to this point we have discussed two major categories of output: consumption goods and services, and investment goods. In general, it is the practice in national income accounting to measure the amount of output in each of these categories by the expenditures made during the income period by the end-users of each kind of output, namely households and other nonprofit institutions (if consumption goods and services are involved), and business firms (if investment goods are involved). This is possible because the bulk of the goods and services that fit into these categories are produced and sold on a private basis through the mechanism of the market; consequently, expenditure totals are a good indicator of output.

The above classification, however, is incomplete, as it leaves out a third important category—the output of the public (or government sector) of the economy. Use of the word *output* in connection with the activities of government may at first glance strike some readers as strange, yet this is a perfectly appropriate and proper use of the term. The public sector of an economy produces a vast array of economically valuable goods and services, ranging from material things like highways, parks, dams, and schools to intangibles like police and fire protection, the services of judicial systems, and the activities of regulatory bodies, such as the Federal Trade Commission. Output originating in the public sector differs from output originating in the private sector primarily because it has a collective character. Public sector goods and services also differ from privately produced goods and services because the decision to produce the former is a political one—made through government—whereas the latter is private, that is, made by individual producers in response to the quest for profit.

In general, the output of the public sector consists of goods and services that normally would not be produced by private firms, or if they were produced, would not be produced in sufficient quantities. Such goods and services are collective in the sense that they are indivisible, which is to say that their benefits accrue to society as a whole. The individual, to be sure, benefits from their production, but only by virtue of the fact that he is a member of the society in which such goods are being produced. The nation's judicial system is a case in point, for certainly all members of a nation receive some benefit, intangible though it may be, from the existence of a system of courts, yet there is no practical way to measure the amount of this benefit that accrues to each citizen. And if the benefit cannot be measured individually, then it is impractical to attempt to produce the good or service privately.

The basic distinction between collective and private goods and services can be seen through application of the *exclusion principle.* If there is no practical way to exclude a person from obtaining the benefits of a good or service—as in the instance of flood control—the good or service is clearly collective in nature. On the other hand, if persons not willing to pay directly for the benefit are excluded from the use of the good or service, it is clearly of a private and individual character. The reader should note carefully that this latter point does not mean that such a good or service could not be produced and sold on an individual basis by a government unit. Packages, for example, are delivered by the government (the Postal Service) and by a private, profit-making firm (United Parcel Service).

Of course, not all the goods and services produced by the public sector are clearly of a collective and indivisible character. Education, for example, can be—and is—produced and sold on an individual basis. In spite of this, the greater portion of education is produced collectively. If our system of public education were entrusted to private enterprise for production at a profit, there would not be an adequate supply of educational services. The well-being of the whole society would be endangered. The same is true with respect to other goods and services produced by the public sector, such as highways, parks and recreational areas, dams, and many different types of services. The private production and sale of such goods and services is clearly not impossible, but in most instances the private plus the social benefit would be small as compared to the benefit that results when such goods are produced on a collective basis.

In addition to their social character, goods and services produced in the public sector differ from privately produced goods and services in another important way. In the private sector of the economy output is normally disposed of by sale to the end-user of the output, but in the public sector the usual procedure is to distribute this output without charge to the society as a whole. Governments, in other words, do not normally sell on an individual basis the collective goods and services which it is their responsibility to provide. This means that we cannot measure the value of the output of the public sector in the same way that we measure the value of the private sector, namely by the total of expenditures made by those who purchase the different categories of output. Since the output of the government sector is distributed free to all or most members of the community, the only practical measure of the value of this output is in terms of what it costs to supply it to the community at large. In order for the public sector to carry out its function of providing the economy with an array of collective goods and services, it must obtain economic resources; generally, it does this either directly through the hire of labor, or indirectly through purchase of part of the output of the private sector. Therefore, the public sector's purchases of goods and services constitute the input of resources necessary to the output of collective goods and services. In national income accounting government purchases of goods and services are used as a measure of the portion of the total output that originates in the public sector. (It is the usual practice to designate this category of output by the capital letter G.)

Transfer Expenditures (TR) and Taxes (TX)

It is necessary to distinguish another and important type of government expenditure that does not enter into the computation of output totals. These expenditures, which occur at all levels of government, are called *transfer payments*, primarily because they involve transfers of income by the government from group to group rather than the acquisition of resources necessary to the production of governmental output. Transfer expenditures, in other words, provide income (real or monetary) to the recipients of such expenditures, but the governmental unit does not receive either goods or services in return. Old-age pensions, unemployment compensation, aid to dependent children, and various forms of aid to war veterans are common forms of transfer payments. Insofar as the national economy is concerned, interest on the public debt, as well as subsidies to business firms, are considered to be transfers. Transfer expenditures may be viewed in another way, too, for they are, in a sense, negative taxes. Just as the recipient of a transfer payment does not directly provide the governmental unit making the payment with an equivalent value of either goods or services in exchange, neither does the government, in collecting taxes, provide each citizen individually with an immediate and equivalent value of goods or services in exchange. Transfer expenditures, in other words, are a one-way flow of income from the government to the individual or business firm; taxes, on the other hand, are a one-way flow of income from the individual or the business firm to the government. It is in this sense that we can also speak of taxes as being negative transfers. (In subsequent discussion in this text we shall designate transfer expenditures by the symbol *TR* and taxes by the symbol *TX*.)

Net Exports (I_f)

The category of national income known as net exports is equal to the difference between a nation's exports of goods and services and its imports of goods and services. If there are no *transfers* of income to or from foreign residents, net exports may also be identified as *net foreign investment*, designated as I_f. This latter definition is subject to a number of qualifications (see Chapter 3), but for the moment it will serve as a working definition of foreign investment. A nation's exports represent expenditures for its output that originate outside the nation's borders, while a nation's imports represent spending by its residents for output that originates in foreign countries. If a nation's exports of goods and services exceed its imports of goods and services, net foreign investment is positive. On the other hand, if imports of goods and services are in excess of exports of goods and services, net foreign investment is negative. Positive net foreign investment increases the claims of the residents of a country against residents of other countries; negative net foreign investment does the reverse.

Since we seek in our discussion to link the various categories of the national output to expenditures made by end-users for each of these categories, it is important to understand the sense in which net exports constitute an expenditure category. If exports of goods and services exceed imports, the difference should be counted as an addition to the other categories of expenditure, the total of which is a measure of the national output. On the other hand, if imports of goods and services exceed exports, the difference should be subtracted from the sum of the other categories of expenditure. Expenditures by the nation and its residents for imported goods and services are normally included in the other categories of expenditure, since there is no practical way to distinguish the exact portion of expenditures for imports in each category. Consequently, total expenditures by residents for imported goods and services should be deducted in order to avoid counting them as output. This will be done automatically by making the net foreign investment category negative whenever imports of goods and services exceed exports of goods and services.

Net foreign investment is similar in its economic effects to expenditure for investment goods. Expenditure leading to production of capital goods has the effect of creating money income within the economy equal to the amount of the expenditure. But there is not created in the same income period an offsetting volume of consumer goods and services, owing to the durable character of capital goods which produce value equal to their cost in the form of consumer goods only over their entire life—which usually encompasses several income periods. An excess of exports over imports (positive net foreign investment) will have the same economic effect, because the production of goods and services for export creates money income in the national economy, but no offsetting volume of goods and services for domestic purchase is available. If imports fall short of exports, an excess of money income over the total of goods and services available for purchase during the income period exists. This excess is equal to the difference between exports and imports. On the other hand, an excess of imports over exports means that the physical volume of goods and services available for purchase by the nation and its residents is in excess of the amount of money income created by the process of producing the national output. Expenditures on imported goods and services, it may be noted, are similar in their economic effects to saving, because use of any part of current income to finance the purchase of imported goods means that a part of current income is not being spent on domestically produced output. This is the same thing that takes place when some part of current income is saved. Thus, in an economic and conceptual sense, imports of goods and services are a counterpart of saving, whereas exports of goods and services are a counterpart of domestic investment.

Fundamental Identities among National Income Components

The manner in which the various component parts of the national output fit together can be expressed symbolically and summarized in a series of *identity equations.* An identity equation defines one variable in terms of other variables; it is an equation asserting an equality which is true by definition. Such equations are normally derived by taking a total (or aggregate) and expressing it as the sum of its parts. Identity equations are to be contrasted with *behavior equations,* which express a relationship between variables. Behavior equations are not necessarily true in the same sense as identity equations. They are a mathematical statement of a hypothesis concerning economic behavior and, consequently, the relationships involved in such equations are causal in nature. If we say, for example, that total consumption expenditures equal expenditures for consumer durables plus expenditures for consumer nondurables plus expenditures for consumer services, we would have an identity equation, because these three forms of consumer expenditure represent the component parts of the total consumer purchases of goods and services. If we let C stands for total consumption, C_d spending for consumer durables, C_n spending for nondurables, and C_s spending for services, the identity equation reads as follows:

$$C \equiv C_d + C_n + C_s$$

In such an equation the right and left sides are equal by definition—they cannot be unequal. The equation is always true for all values of C_d, C_n, and C_s.

On the other hand, if we assert that total consumption expenditures are a function of (that is, depend upon) current income, this would be a behavior equation, for it expresses a hypothesis about economic behavior. Such a hypothesis might be expressed in equation form as follows (see Chapter 6 for more detailed analysis):

$$C = a + bY$$

This is a behavior equation which says that total consumption spending is determined by the particular values assigned to *a, b,* and *Y. In this equation a* and *b* are parameters, that is, economic magnitudes whose values are fixed. There is only one unique value for C, depending on the values assigned the parameters and Y (the symbol used for income).

For our series of identity equations that describe how the component parts of the national output fit together, we will use the following symbols:

Y = the national output and income
I = investment expenditures (output of investment goods)
I_f = net foreign investment (net exports)
C = consumption expenditures (output of consumer goods and services)
S = saving

G = **government expenditures for goods and services** (output of community or collective goods)
X = **export expenditures** (domestic output that is exported)
M = **import expenditures** (foreign output that is imported)
TR = **transfer expenditures**
TX = **taxes**

Let us start with an imaginary but highly simplified economic system which has no government and no economic ties with any other nation. In this hypothetical system the origin and disposition of income can be expressed symbolically as follows:[10]

$$Y \equiv C + I \tag{2–1}$$

$$Y \equiv C + S \tag{2–2}$$

Equation (2–1) states that output (and income) has its origin in expenditures for consumption goods and services and investment goods. To put it in a different way, we can say that output consists of consumption goods and services, and investment goods. Equation (2–2), which relates to the disposition of current income, expresses the idea that income created in the productive process must be either consumed or not consumed (that is saved). The C in Equation (2–2) also represents expenditures for consumption goods and services.

From these equations we can derive a third equation showing the identity between saving and investment. Since income and consumption are common terms in both of the above equations, it follows that investment and saving must be equal to one another. Thus

$$I \equiv S \tag{2–3}$$

This particular identity states in symbolic terms an idea already discussed, namely that saving and investment are identical whenever we are discussing these magnitudes in an *ex post* sense. The above identities are *ex post* equations because they are descriptive of that which exists or is actual; they do not in any way describe economic behavior in an intended, planned, or *ex ante* sense. This point about the *ex post* identity of saving and investment is stressed because lack of understanding of the exact sense in which saving and investment are always equal has been a cause of serious confusion in economic thinking in the past. The reader should recognize that these two magnitudes must be identical in an *ex post* sense because of the way in which they are defined, but this does not mean that the amounts saved and the amounts invested in the economy in any specific income period always coincide with the amounts that firms or

10. Since these are identity equations we shall use the identity sign $\equiv$ instead of the equality sign $=$.

persons *intended* to save and invest. The latter is an entirely different matter, which we will analyze thoroughly at a later point in the text.

We can proceed closer to reality in the development of our identity equations by dropping the assumption of an economy without a government. We will retain for the moment, however, the assumption that our economy has no relationships with other economies; in other words, it is a closed economy. Let us assume, too, that the only function of our government is to provide for collective goods and services; it does not engage in transfer expenditures. On the basis of this set of assumptions we would have the following identities:

$$Y \equiv C + I + G \qquad (2\text{–}4)$$

$$Y \equiv C + S + TX \qquad (2\text{–}5)$$

$$S + TX \equiv I + G \qquad (2\text{–}6)$$

$$S \equiv I + (G - TX) \qquad (2\text{–}7)$$

Equation (2–4) means that output consists of consumption goods and services, investment goods, and collective goods, or that output has its origin in expenditures by consumers or households, by business firms, and by governmental units. Equation (2–5) relates to the disposition of income, and shows that with the introduction of government a third alternative is now available for the disposition of current income, namely taxes. The economic effect of taxes is similar to saving because taxes also represent a nonexpenditure of current income for consumption goods and services.

Equation (2–6) is a modification of the saving-investment identity. It is made necessary by the introduction of government expenditures and taxes. Saving plus taxes, both of which are leakages from the current income stream, are equal to investment plus government expenditures for goods and services. Investment and government expenditures are offsets to leakages in the form of saving and taxes. Equation (2–7) is a further modification of the above identity, for if taxes are transferred to the right-hand side of the equation, it means that saving is equal to investment *plus* the government deficit or *minus* the government surplus.

The terms *deficit* and *surplus* as used here do not in any way refer to the budgetary situation of the federal government. Rather, these terms refer to the current income and product transactions of all governmental units in the economy. For example, if the current expenditures of the public sector for goods and services are in excess of total taxes collected then the public sector has incurred a deficit on its income and product transactions. Insofar as the public sector is concerned, dissaving has taken place because governmental units have spent more than their income, the latter being derived from taxation. If G − TX is placed on the right-hand side of Equation (2–7), it must be positive, because the total saving of the economy must cover investment expenditure plus the amount of the deficit of the public sector.

On the other hand, if the tax collections of the public sector are in excess of the current expenditures of governmental units, then there is a surplus in the income and product transactions of the public sector. This would be a form of governmental saving, for expenditures are less than current receipts. Again if G − TX is placed on the right-hand side of the same equation, it should be negative, as the total saving, S, of the economy is now less than investment expenditure and must be augmented by governmental saving.

We are now able to drop the last of the simplifying assumptions with which we started our discussion, namely the assumptions of a closed economy and of no transfer expenditures. When we drop these assumptions, our structure of identity equations becomes realistic, describing accurately how the component parts of the national output fit together. Consequently, we now have the following series of identity equations.

$$Y \equiv C + I + G + X - M \tag{2–8}$$

$$I_f \equiv X - M \tag{2–9}$$

$$Y \equiv C + I + G + I_f \tag{2–10}$$

$$Y \equiv C + S + TX - TR \tag{2–11}$$

$$S + TX - TR \equiv I + G + I_f \tag{2–12}$$

$$S \equiv I + G + I_f - (TX - TR) \tag{2–13}$$

Equation (2–8) is essentially the same as Equation (2–4), except that we have now added expenditures for exports and subtracted expenditures for imports. Since the difference between exports and imports is equal to net foreign investment, as in Equation (2–9), the basic identity equation describing the origin of output and income takes the form shown in Equation (2–10).[11] The existence of transfer expenditures means that we must modify the equation describing the disposition of income to take such transfers into account. This is done in Equation (2–11), in which transfer expenditures are subtracted from taxes. Since transfers are, in effect, negative taxes, they offset taxes as a leakage from the current income stream. Moreover, once we have introduced transfers into the system, they must be deducted from the components on the right-hand side of the disposition of income equation, or else they would be counted twice. This is the case because transfer expenditures are income to the recipients of such expenditures, and as such can be a source of consumption expenditures, saving, or tax payments just as much as income derived from the process of production. Thus, transfer expenditures will be

11. This assumes no transfers to or from the rest of the world.

reflected in consumption, saving, and taxes, in Equation (2–11), showing the disposition of current income.

Finally, the basic saving-investment identity is modified to take into account net foreign investment, which offsets not only saving and taxes in the same manner as investment and government expenditures, but also the effect of transfer expenditures, on the deficit or surplus of the public sector with respect to income and product transactions. Thus, saving plus *net* taxes (TX − TR) is equal to investment plus net foreign investment and government expenditures for goods and services in Equation (2–12). If net taxes are shifted to the right-hand side of this equation, the basic identity equation relating saving and investment takes the form shown in Equation (2–13).

Current Data and Identity Equations in an Open Economy

The identity equations that pertain to an open economy with transfers may be verified by fitting to them actual data from the national income and product accounts for the United States for 1976. The data have been rounded to the nearest whole number; therefore the details may not add to the totals. First, we have the equation for the origin of gross national product:

$$Y \equiv C + I + G + X - M \tag{2–14}$$

$$\$1{,}707 \equiv \$1{,}094 + \$243 + \$361 + \$163 - \$155 \tag{2–15}$$

These data are in billions of dollars in 1972 prices and are obtained from the *Survey of Current Business*. Note that in 1976 the United States had a surplus in its foreign trade, X − M.

The equation for the disposition of the GNP may be written:

$$Y \equiv C + S + T_n \tag{2–16}$$

In the above equation T_n is equal to *net* taxes and is the difference between total taxes, TX, and transfers, TR. When the data for 1976 are fitted to this identity showing the disposition of the gross national product, we have:

$$\$1{,}707 \equiv \$1.094 + \$287 + 327 \tag{2–17}$$

The basic saving-investment (Equation 2–13) identity now becomes:

$$S \equiv I + I_f + G - T_n \tag{2–18}$$

In the above equation I_f is equal to the difference between exports X and imports M.

With 1976 data fitted to the equation, we now have:

$$\$287 \equiv \$243 - \$8 + \$361 - 327 \tag{2–19}$$

This equation shows that in 1975 there was a deficit on the income and product transactions of the public sector, which is an offset to saving.

3

Measurement of National Income and Product

In the last chapter we analyzed the fundamental concepts which underlie most systems of national income accounting. We turn now to discussion of the techniques of national income and product measurement. While the techniques described in this chapter are those developed and employed in the United States, they are similar to the techniques utilized by other nations. In general, systems for national income and product measurement differ more in detail than in substance.

Our analysis of national income accounting in the United States begins with discussion of the national income aggregates that are the best-known of all measures of national income, and which, further, are in wide use as indicators of the economy's performance. Specifically, the five aggregate measures we will discuss are: (1) gross national product, (2) net national product, (3) national income, (4) personal income, and (5) disposal income. The first three of these are measures of both product and money income flows, while the latter two are measures of money income flows only.

Gross National Product

Gross national product, also called gross national income or gross national expenditure, is the best-known and most widely used of the various statistical measures developed to gauge the economy's performance. It is defined as *the current market value of all final goods and services produced by the economy during an income period.* The normal income period for most national income accounting systems, including that of the United States, is the calendar year. As an expenditure total, gross national product (or GNP as it is usually called) represents the total purchases of goods and services by consumers and governments, gross private domestic investment, and net foreign investment. As an income total, GNP shows both the total income created as a result of current productive activity and the allocation of this income. The output total included in the GNP figure is described as gross because it does not take into account capital goods that have been consumed or worn out during the process of production. It is termed national because it refers to the productive activities of the nationals of a particular nation, including the contribution to current output of property resources owned by these nationals. Table 3–1 shows GNP data for the United States for the period 1929–76.[1]

Final and Intermediate Goods and Services

In defining GNP, we stated that it is a measure of the economy's output of final goods and services during an income period. In national income accounting, it is necessary to distinguish between *final goods and services*, which are the end products of the economy, and *intermediate goods and services*, which normally are thought of as goods and services purchased for resale. We must make this distinction to avoid double-counting. Intermediate goods and services enter into the production of final goods and services. Therefore, if we added up expenditures for final goods and services as well as expenditures for intermediate goods and services, we would count the same goods and services twice. This would give us an exaggerated total for GNP. For example, the production of bread involves several stages and several transactions. Wheat is produced by the farmer and sold to the miller, who in turn processes the wheat and produces flour, which is sold to the baker, who uses it to produce bread. In this simple example wheat and flour are intermediate products, whose value will be reflected in the value of the final product, bread. This being the case, it would be an error to add separately the value of the wheat produced by the farmer, the value of the flour produced by the miller, and the value of the bread produced by the baker.

There is no exact rule by which we can clearly determine whether a good or a service is an intermediate or final product. In our example, flour is an intermediate product because it is sold to the baker for further processing. But if flour were sold directly to a homemaker it would be classified as a final product, since the homemaker is the ultimate user of the

1. As an identity equation *GNP* or Y equals $C + I + G + X - M$.

TABLE 3–1. Gross National Product or Expenditure, Selected Years, 1929–76 (in billions of current dollars)

Year	Gross National Product	Personal Consumption Expenditure	Gross Private Domestic Investment	Government Purchases of Goods and Services	New Exports of Goods and Services
1929	$ 103.1	$ 77.2	$ 16.2	$ 8.5	$ 1.1
1931	75.8	60.5	5.6	9.2	0.5
1933	55.6	45.8	1.4	8.0	0.4
1935	72.2	55.7	6.4	10.0	0.1
1937	90.4	66.5	11.8	11.9	0.3
1939	90.5	66.8	9.3	13.3	1.1
1941	124.5	80.6	17.9	24.8	1.3
1943	191.6	99.3	5.7	88.6	−2.0
1945	211.9	119.7	10.6	82.3	−0.6
1947	232.8	161.7	34.0	25.5	11.6
1949	258.0	178.1	35.3	38.4	6.2
1951	330.2	207.1	59.2	60.1	3.8
1953	366.1	299.7	53.3	82.5	0.6
1955	399.3	253.7	68.4	75.0	2.2
1957	442.8	280.4	69.2	87.1	6.1
1959	486.5	310.8	77.6	97.6	0.6
1961	523.3	335.0	74.3	108.2	5.8
1963	594.7	374.6	90.2	123.7	6.3
1965	688.1	430.2	112.0	138.4	7.6
1967	796.3	490.3	120.8	180.2	4.9
1969	935.5	579.7	146.2	207.9	1.8
1971	1,063.4	668.2	160.0	233.7	1.6
1972	1,171.1	733.0	188.3	253.1	−3.3
1973	1,306.3	805.5	220.5	269.9	7.4
1974	1,413.2	887.5	215.0	303.3	7.5
1975	1,516.3	973.2	183.7	339.0	20.5
1976	1,706.5	1,094.0	243.3	361.4	7.8

SOURCE: U.S. Department of Commerce, *Historical Statistics of the United States* 1975, data for 1929–45; *Economic Report of the President*, 1977; and *Survey of Current Business*, July, 1977, data for years subsequent to 1945.

product (as contrasted to the baker, who clearly is not the ultimate user). In order to distinguish between intermediate and final products in national income measurement, the Department of Commerce has adopted the working definition that a final product is one that is not resold, while an intermediate product is one that is purchased with the normal intention that it be resold.[2] Thus, in the example cited, wheat sold to the

2. U.S. Department of Commerce, *National Income*, 1954, p. 30. This document states the official position of the U.S. government on concepts and methods used in national income accounting in the United States.

miller and flour sold to the baker constitute intermediate products, because in both instances the products will be resold, although in altered form. Bread purchased by the homemaker normally will not be resold and therefore can be considered a final product.

Monetary Transactions and Productive Activity

Since GNP is a measure of productive activity, the basic technique for its measurement is through the summation of all monetary transactions that reflect productive activity. There is a problem here, for as pointed out in Chapter 2 some monetary transactions do not represent current productive activity, while certain types of productive activity, on the other hand, will not show up in any monetary transaction. The most common monetary transactions that are not measures of current output are: (1) those involving the purchase and sale of used or secondhand goods, because such goods constitute part of the output of a previous income period (2) those involving purchase and sale of various financial instruments, such as bonds and equities; and (3) transfer payments, both public and private. All of these transactions should be excluded from any monetary measure of current productive activity.

For productive activity not reflected in a monetary transaction, the homemaker's activities can again serve as an example. If she bakes her own bread, no monetary transaction reflecting the sale of a final product is involved, although there will be such a transaction if she buys her bread in the bakery or grocery shop. Yet in both instances productive activity has taken place. The same sort of thing takes place if a householder chooses to paint his own house rather than hire a professional painter to do the job. When the householder paints his house, productive activity occurs that is not reflected in the current GNP. But if he hires a painter, the resulting productive activity involves a monetary transaction and hence appears in the current output figures.

Ideally, GNP should be a measure of all current productive activity in the economy, irrespective of whether the activity is reflected in a market transaction. But as a practical matter it is quite impossible to measure with any degree of statistical accuracy the total value of all the "do-it-yourself" type of productive activity and other nonmarket transactions that occur in the economy. The U.S. Department of Commerce limits its data to economic production. The basic criterion used for classifying an activity as economic production is whether it is reflected in the sales and purchase transactions of the market economy. The only exception to this is that the Department of Commerce makes estimates of certain income and product flows that are not reflected in transactions in the market. The most important of these *imputations* (estimates of nonmarket production) are wages and salaries paid in kind rather than money, fuel and food produced and consumed on the farm, and the rental value of owner-occupied homes.[3] Aside from these imputations, the Department of Commerce does not attempt to measure and record productive activity that is of a nonmarket character. The decision as to what nonmarket production ought to be included in national income and product measures is necessarily an arbitrary one. There is no logical reason, for example, to include the rental value of owner-occupied homes and to exclude the value of the labor of the homemaker.

An Alternative Technique for Measuring Gross National Product

An alternative approach to the measurement of GNP is through a summation of charges against the output total or, in other words, through the allocation of the gross income created in the process of producing the economy's current output of final goods and services. (Allocations and charges are different names for what is basically the same technique of measurement.)

Table 3–2 summarizes the two techniques by which GNP can be measured. The right-hand side of the table shows the *expenditure* or *flow-of-product* approach to the measurement of gross output. It is a summation of expenditures for the four major categories of goods and services produced by the economy during the income period. The left-hand side of the table represents the *charges* or *allocations* approach to the measurement of output. It summarizes the total of charges levied against the income total, or shows the allocation of the total income.

Contemporary national income accounting practice recognizes two major types of charges against the value of GNP. The first of these is factor costs, or *income charges,* which consists of income received by the owners of economic resources in the form of wages, salaries, and other kinds of employee compensation; rents; interest payments; and profits. The other is *nonincome charges* and consists of capital consumption allowances and indirect business taxes.

Factor Costs · Basically, factor costs consist of necessary payments that have to be made in either money or kind in order to secure the services of the factors of production. The utilization of the services of these factors makes possible the production of goods and services. Items (1) through (7) in Table 3–2 are the factor costs for the gross national product of the American economy in 1976. Each of these is explained as follows:

Compensation of employees consists primarily of all wages and salaries and income and kind paid in return for the services of labor and, in addition, certain supplements to wages and salaries. These latter are contributions made by employers under the social security system (contributions

3. Ibid.

TABLE 3–2. Sources and Allocations of the Gross National Product, 1976 (in billions of current dollars)

Allocations of Gross National Product		*Origins of Gross National Product*	
1. Compensation of employees	$1,036.3	1. Personal consumption expenditures	$1,094.0
2. Proprietors' income	88.0	2. Gross private domestic investment	243.3
3. Corporate profits tax liability	64.7	3. Government purchases of goods and services	361.4
4. Dividends	35.8	4. Net exports of goods and services	7.8
5. Undistributed profits*	27.6		
6. Rental income of persons	23.3		
7. Net interest	88.4		
National income	**$1,364.1**		
8. Indirect business taxes	150.1		
9. Business transfer payments	8.1		
10. *Less:* Subsidies less current surplus of government enterprises	0.8		
11. Statistical discrepancy	5.5		
Net National Product	**$1,527.4**		
12. Capital consumption allowances	179.0		
Gross National Product	**$1,706.5**	**Gross National Product**	**$1,706.5**

*Includes Inventory Valuation and Capital Consumption Adjustment
SOURCE: U.S. Department of Commerce, *Survey of Current Business*, July, 1977. *Note:* Details may not add to total because of rounding.

by employees are included in the figure for wages and salaries), employer contributions to private pension plans, and various minor forms of labor income, such as compensation for injuries and pay for individuals in the military reserve.

Proprietors' income is a measure of the monetary earnings and income in kind accuring to all unincorporated business enterprises in the economy. This item is primarily a measure of the profits of sole proprietorships, partnerships, and producer cooperatives.

Corporate profits tax liability consists of the total of federal and state taxes levied against the earnings of all corporations in the economy.

Dividends represents the amount of corporation profits paid out to shareholders during the current income period.

Undistributed profits constitute the part of corporate profits neither paid out to the shareholders as dividends nor collected as taxes by federal and state governments. The sum of this item and the previous two items gives total corporate profits in the income period.

Rental income of persons equals the money income received by persons from the rental of real property, such as buildings and land.

Net interest is a measure of income in the form of interest payments received by individuals in the economy, with the exception of interest payments by government (federal, state, and local), and by consumers. The Department of Commerce states that interest on the public debt and interest paid by consumers are not a part of current production; hence they should not be treated as a factor cost.

It may be noted that the sum of items (1) through (7) in Table 3–2 is labeled national income. This is so because, fundamentally the term *national income* refers to the factor costs of the goods and services produced by the economy. We shall discuss this particular measure in more detail shortly.

Nonincome Charges · *Indirect business taxes* constitute the first type of nonincome charge against GNP The major types of taxes included in this category of nonincome charges are sales taxes, excises and real property taxes paid by business firms[4] These taxes are called indirect because it is assumed they are treated by business firms as a part of the cost of doing business; thus they will be included in the sale price of final goods and services produced. If such taxes are shifted forward, as the Department of Commerce believes, they will be reflected in the expenditure totals for the various component parts of GNP and, consequently, they must appear, too, on the allocations side of current GNP. But the total of indrect taxes cannot appear as a factor cost because they accrue to the government, and it is not the present practice in United States national income accounting procedures to treat government as a factor of production.

Capital consumption allowances, the other nonincome charge against GNP, ideally should measure the physical wearing-out of capital equipment during the year. Capital goods are a part of the economy's stock of productive resources and their use in the productive process will inevitably entail a gradual wearing-out of such assets. The amount by which the economy's stock of real capital has been used up (or consumed) during the current income period is what we try to measure through capital consumption allowances.

It is the practice of the Department of Commerce to measure capital consumption allowances by the sum of depreciation charges by private business firms against their current incomes, plus accidental damage to fixed capital occurring during the income period. The basic difficulty with this procedure is that charges by the business firm for depreciation do not accurately reflect the physical wearing-out of capital goods, for the purpose of depreciation charges from an accounting viewpoint is to allow the individual producer to maintain intact the money value of his equipment. For the most part, allowances made by the business firm for depreciation are based on various arbitrary formulas that have little relationship to

4. Ibid., p. 33.

either the actual physical life of the asset or its use in any particular year. In spite of these deficiencies, the Department of Commerce continues to use business charges for depreciation as the best available measure at the present time of the economy's consumption of real capital during the income period.

Two Minor Charges · Before we discuss the other four national income aggregates that, along with GNP, make up the five-family series of national income and product measures, two additional, though minor, charges against the output totals must be explained. These appear in Table 3–2 as the items "Business transfer payments," and "Subsidies less current surplus of government enterprises." Business transfer payments are transfers from business to persons; they embody charges against the output total for which no return in the form of factor income is received. Most consist of corporate gifts to nonprofit institutions and consumer bad debts. "Subsidies less current surplus of government enterprises" is really a combined entry. In moving from national income to GNP in Table 3–2, it is necessary to deduct subsidies from the national income total. They are factor costs on the assumption that they constitute a form of payment necessary to secure the services of particular factors, although they are not reflected in the market price of final goods and services. The current surplus—or profit—of government enterprise is not, on the other hand, a factor cost, because government is not regarded as a factor of production; yet the value of goods and services produced by government enterprise and sold through normal market channels will be reflected in the value of final product totals. Electric power produced and sold by a municipal power and light plant is an example of this type of entry. It is the current practice of the Department of Commerce to combine these two relatively minor charges against the output totals into a single item on the allocations side of GNP.

Other Measures of Product and Income

We have devoted a relatively large amount of space to discussion of GNP not only because it is the most widely used national income aggregate, but also because it is the best point of departure for consideration and understanding of the other aggregates that make up the Department of Commerce's five-family series of national income and product measures.

Net National Product

Net national product is defined by the Department of Commerce as the market value of the *net* output of final goods and services produced by the economy during the relevant income period.[5] In a theoretical sense it is a measure of the nation's output after allowance has been made for the consumption of capital in the current process of production. NNP is derived by subtracting capital consumption allowances from GNP. If business reserves for depreciation and the other items that enter into capital consumption allowances accurately reflected the real depreciation of the nation's stock of physical capital, net national product would accurately measure the amount of output that the nation could use for consumption, for the public sector, or for adding to the existing stock of capital without any impairment of productive capacity because of a failure to provide for the replacement of consumed items of real capital. Unfortunately, though, existing measurement techniques do not permit an accurate measurement of real capital consumption, so the net national product figure is not widely used.

National Income

We have already defined national income as the sum of the factor costs incurred during production of the economy's current output. More specifically, the Department of Commerce defines national income as the aggregate earnings of labor and property which arise from the production of goods and services by the nation's economy.[6] This measure is also described as the *net national product at factor cost* because it is a measure of the factor costs of the net output total. The national income is a concept of fundamental importance; it represents for the economy as a whole the amount of income earned by the owners of economic resources (land, labor, and capital) in return for supplying the services of these resources to the productive units of the economy. As such, it is the major source of money income or spending power for the purchase of the bulk of the national output. The national income figure can be derived either by summing up the total of factor costs incurred in producing the current output, or by deducting indirect business taxes and the other minor charges from the net national product total. It should be noted that the national income is both a measure of product (in the sense that it represents the factor cost of the current output) and a measure of money income earned by the factors of production.

Personal Income

Although the national income aggregate is a measure of income earned by the owners of economic resources through participation in the produc-

5. Ibid., p. 56.
6. Ibid.

tive process, it does not measure money income actually received by persons and households during the current income period. The reason is that some parts of earned (or factor) income are not actually received as money income by persons or households, while some households and persons receive money income that is not earned through supplying the services of economic resources to the productive process. The latter consists of transfer payments and interest income from consumers and government. Although the Department of Commerce defines personal income as the current income "received" by persons from all sources,[7] this is not strictly correct. The Department of Commerce normally measures personal income on a before-tax basis, but since some income taxes are withheld from wage and salary income, such income is not actually received. The intent, though, is to show the money income that persons are entitled to from all sources.

The usual procedure for obtaining the personal income measure is to deduct from national income the major categories of earned (or factor) income that are not actually received as money income by persons or households, and then add to this figure the total of transfer incomes received from both government and business. The major deductions are: (1) contributions to social insurance, (2) corporate profits tax liability, and (3) undistributed corporate profit. The chief forms of government transfer payments which must be added in are: (1) interest on the public debt, (2) pensions paid to retired persons, (3) unemployment compensation, (4) various forms of relief payments, and (5) benefits extended to war veterans.

Disposable Income

The final, widely used measure of income is that of disposable income, which the Department of Commerce defines simply as the income remaining to individuals after deduction of all taxes levied against their income and their property by all governmental entities in the economy.[8] It is obtained by deducting such taxes from the personal income total, and it represents a measure of the after-tax purchasing power at the disposal of persons or households.

Table 3–3 shows the relationships between the above five measures for selected years since 1929. This table should be studied carefully, for one can readily trace from the data some of the vicissitudes of the American economy over nearly 50 years. These range from the collapse of the depression years, and vast surge of growth during World War II, to the long postwar expansion.

7. Ibid.
8. Ibid.

Price Indexes and Comparisons over Time

The practice of the Department of Commerce is to report the money value of national income and product statistics in terms of the prices prevailing during the reporting period. Thus, GNP data for 1976 are reported in prices of 1976. If we are only interested in the statistics of income or output for a particular year, this does not create a special problem; but if we want to make comparisons between a number of years, then it is necessary to correct for changes in the general level of prices. This must be done because changes in the monetary value of product totals may result from either a change in the physical quantity of production or a change in the prices at which physical output is valued. The latter type of change is a distortion insofar as comparisons over time are concerned. If such comparisons are to be used meaningfully, it is desirable that we compare *real* changes rather than changes in value due to changes in price. Thus, the effect of price-level changes must be eliminated if income and product data for different years are to reflect real changes.

The procedure for eliminating the effect of price-level changes from income and product data is to divide the data valued in current prices by an appropriate price index This has the effect of converting the data to a constant-price basis, thus making possible comparisons of real changes over time. While the problem of constructing an appropriate index of prices is complex, the basic principles involved are relatively simple. For our purposes it is only necessary to have an understanding of the underlying rationale of the process of converting data valued in current prices into data valued in constant prices.

An index of prices is a device for comparing the amount by which one or more prices have changed over a specific period of time. Some specific year is selected as the *base year* (specific point of reference). Prices in all other years are measured as a percentage of the price in the base year. For example, if the price of wheat in 1972—our assumed base year—was $2.00 per bushel, and we found that in 1976 the price of wheat had risen to $3.50 per bushel, it would be correct to say that the price index for wheat in 1976 is 175 percent of the price in the base year, 1972. Thus, the price index for wheat in 1976 is 175 since the price index in the base year must be 100, that is, 100 percent. The problem is infinitely more complex when a larger number of prices is involved although again the technique for the construction of the price index is basically the same. If an index of the general level of prices is to be constructed, it is necessary to *weight* the various individual prices that enter into the general price level in accordance with their relative importance. Unless this is done, the resulting price index will not accurately reflect relative or percentage changes in the general level of all prices. For the construction of such a complex index as that of the general price level the two most important problems

TABLE 3–3. National Income and Product Measures: Selected Years, 1929–76 (billions of current dollars)

	1929	*1933*	*1939*	*1941*	*1945*	*1948*	*1952*	*1956*	*1960*	*1964*	*1968*	*1972*	*1976*
Gross National Product	**103.1**	**55.6**	**90.5**	**124.5**	**212.0**	**259.1**	**347.2**	**420.7**	**506.0**	**632.4**	**864.2**	**1,171.1**	**1,706.5**
Less: Capital consumption allowances	7.9	7.0	7.3	8.2	11.3	20.3	29.6	38.9	47.7	56.1	74.5	105.4	179.0
Equals: **Net National Product**	**95.2**	**48.6**	**83.3**	**116.3**	**200.7**	**238.8**	**317.6**	**381.8**	**458.3**	**576.3**	**789.7**	**1,065.8**	**1,527.4**
Less: Indirect business taxes*	7.4	8.3	10.7	12.1	19.2	19.8	31.8	34.9	46.3	58.2	78.6	113.9	163.3
Equals: **National Income**	**86.8**	**40.3**	**72.6**	**104.2**	**181.5**	**219.0**	**285.8**	**346.9**	**412.0**	**518.1**	**711.1**	**951.9**	**1,364.1**
Less: Social security taxes	0.2	0.3	2.1	2.8	6.2	5.4	9.0	12.9	21.1	27.9	47.1	73.6	123.8
Corporate income taxes	1.4	0.5	1.4	7.6	10.7	12.4	19.4	22.0	22.7	28.3	39.9	41.5	64.7
Undistributed corporate profits†	3.3	–3.7	1.1	3.2	3.8	9.7	7.5	9.8	11.0	20.2	20.8	26.0	27.6
Plus: Transfer payments	1.5	2.1	3.0	3.1	6.1	11.3	13.1	18.7	29.0	36.7	59.5	104.1	192.8
Interest paid by government and consumers	2.5	1.6	1.9	2.2	4.2	5.6	7.3	10.1	13.5	19.1	26.1	27.6	**41.9**
Equals: **Personal Income**	**85.9**	**47.0**	**72.8**	**96.0**	**171.1**	**208.5**	**270.4**	**330.9**	**399.7**	**497.5**	**688.9**	**942.5**	**1,382.7**
Less: Personal tax payments	2.6	1.5	2.4	3.3	20.7	21.0	34.0	39.7	50.4	59.4	97.9	141.2	196.9
Equals: **Disposable Income**	**83.3**	**45.5**	**70.3**	**92.7**	**150.2**	**187.4**	**236.4**	**291.3**	**349.4**	**438.1**	**591.0**	**801.3**	**1,185.8**

**Includes:* Business Transfer Payments, Subsidies Less Current Surplus of Government Enterprises, and Statistical Discrepancy.
†Includes: Inventory Valuation Adjustment, and other minor adjustments.
SOURCES: U.S. Department of Commerce, *Historical Statistics of the United States*, data for 1945 and prior years; *Economic Report of the President*, 1977, and *Survey of Current Business*, July, 1977, for subsequent years. Details may not add to totals because of rounding.

are, first, selection of the individual items (and their prices) that are to be included in the index and, second, assignment of the proper weights to each of the individual items that make up the index. Once these steps have been taken the remaining problem is simply that of selecting the proper mathematical technique for computation of the actual index.

The underlying reason for dividing data valued in current prices by a price index in order to get data valued in constant prices can be explained by means of an example. Let us assume that we want to convert GNP data for 1976 to 1972 prices so we can compare the actual physical change in GNP between these two dates.[9] Since, by definition, GNP is a measure of the monetary value of the current output,

$$GNP_{1976} = O_{1976} \times P_{1976} \tag{3–1}$$

This equation means that the value of current 1976 output is equal to the actual output (O) times the prices (P) at which the output is sold in that year. From our prior discussion of price indexes, it also follows that the index of prices for 1976, using 1972 as the base year, is equal to the ratio of 1976 prices to 1972 prices. Thus

$$\text{Price index for 1976} = \frac{P_{1976}}{P_{1972}} \tag{3–2}$$

If we divide the GNP data for 1976 by the above price index, the result will be a measure of the physical output of 1976 valued in the prices of 1972. The following equations show algebraically why this is true.

$$\frac{GNP_{1976}}{\dfrac{P_{1976}}{P_{1972}}} = \frac{P_{1976} \times O_{1976}}{\dfrac{P_{1972}}{P_{1976}}} \tag{3–3}$$

From Equation (3–3) it follows that

$$\frac{GPN_{1976}}{\dfrac{P_{1976}}{P_{1972}}} = (P_{1976} \times O_{1976}) \times \frac{P_{1972}}{P_{1976}} \tag{3–4}$$

9. The Department of Commerce uses 1972 as its base year for constructing GNP price *deflators*, i.e., indexes used to convert GNP data to constant dollars.

In Equation (3–4) the two expressions for 1976 prices, P_{1976} on the righthand side cancel out, and thus we have

$$\frac{GPN_{1976}}{\dfrac{P_{1976}}{P_{1972}}} = O_{1976} \times P_{1972} \tag{3–5}$$

By dividing GNP measured in current (1976) prices by the current (1976) price index, the GNP data are converted to a figure which values the current output in prices for a selected base year. Table 3–4 shows the

United States GNP in both current and constant dollars (or prices) for selected years since 1929. The table also includes in Column (3) the price indexes used to deflate the current dollar amounts.

Major Price Indexes

Three major prices indices are widely used in the United States. They are the consumer price index (CPI), the wholesale price index (WPI), and the GNP deflator. The consumer price index measures the changes in the prices of goods and services purchased by urban wage-earners and clerical workers, including both families and single persons. In the press it is often called a "cost of living index," although this is not strictly correct since it does not measure retail prices paid by all consumers. The index includes prices for aproximately 400 commodities and services. Along with the wholesale price index, it is compiled and published monthly by the Bureau of Labor Statistics of the U.S. Department of Labor.

The wholesale price index is the most comprehensive measure available for the general price level of commodities. It records month-to-month changes in the prices of all commodities sold in all the primary commod-

TABLE 3–4. Gross National Product in Current and Constant Dollars; Selected Years, 1946–1976 (in billions of dollars)

(1) Year	*(2)* GNP in Current Dollars	*(3)* Price Index 1972 = 100	*(4) = (2) ÷ (3)* GNP in Constant Dollars
1948	259.1	53.1	487.7
1950	286.2	53.6	533.5.
1952	330.2	58.0	548.5
1954	366.3	59.7	613.7
1956	420.7	62.9	668.8
1958	448.9	66.1	679.5
1960	506.0	68.7	736.8
1962	563.8	70.1	799.1
1964	635.7	72.7	874.4
1966	753.0	76.8	981.0
1968	868.5	82.3	1.051.8
1970	982.4	91.4	1,075.3
1972	1,171.1	100.0	1.171.1
1974	1,412.9	116.0	1,217.8
1976	1,706.5	133.9	1,274.7

SOURCE: *Economic Report of the President*, 1977, and *Survey of Current Business*, July, 1977

ity markets in the country, some 2,700 products, ranging from raw materials to finished goods ready for the retailer. The wholesale price index is available from 1890, the consumer price index only from 1913.

The index that provides the most comprehensive coverage for prices of all goods and services in the economy is the GNP deflator, an index constructed by the Department of Commerce. It is derived differently than the other indexes, in that it is found by dividing the actual GNP (GNP in current dollars) by the real GNP (GNP in constant dollars). The Department of Commerce constructs the constant dollar GNP series breaking the GNP down into the smallest parts or groupings for which appropriate price indexes (either at the wholesale or retail level) are available. Once this is done, the current dollar value for each component part of the GNP is deflated in accordance with the procedure described earlier. This will yield a figure for each part in deflated—or base-year—prices. Then all the categories can be added together to get the final (and correct) GNP total in constant (or base-year) prices. For many years the Department of Commerce used 1958 as its base year for the constant dollar GNP series, but in 1976 a switch was made to a new base year, 1972.

Limitations Inherent in Aggregate Measures of Income and Product

In spite of the fact that GNP and other aggregates discussed are in extensive use as measures of the material performance of the economy, they are subject to a number of limitations, particularly with respect to economic welfare (material performance and welfare are not always identical). The most important of these limitations can be briefly summarized.

Economic Versus Social Values · National income and product figures measure the economic rather than the social value of current productive activity. These data are largely limited to a measurement of economic value in terms of the market prices that different types of goods and services may command. But the market price of a good or a service may not accurately reflect the value to the society of the good or service in a more fundamental, philosophical sense. A society, for example, might spend identical sums on education and tobacco, and yet one would hesitate to assert that the social, as distinct from the economic, value of these two types of expenditures is the same. Professor Robert Lekachman puts it, ". . . the national income expert totals not only the value of oil pumped up from the Santa Barbara channel [from oil spills] or the Gulf coast but also the expenses of cleaning up beaches and salvaging fishing grounds in the wake of oil-well blowouts. . . . By current criteria, gross national product rises when auto sales increase, regardless of what may be happening to the quality of the enjoyments these arrogant chariots generate or the variety of adverse side effects for which they are responsible."[10] The basic problem here is that the social value of the national output is necessarily a subjective matter, dependent upon individual judgments concerning what ought to be. It follows that there are no simple, direct, or objective criteria for measurement of the social value of the national output. It is desirable, nevertheless, that the reader be aware of the distinction between economic and social value, and realize that the former is not always representative of the latter.

Economic Versus Social Costs · Much of what was said in the foregoing paragraph concerning economic and social values applies equally to economic and social costs. There is no necessary identity between the economic costs of producing the current national output and the social costs of the output. Economic costs include items such as factor costs, capital consumption allowances, and indirect business taxes—elements identified earlier as charges against GNP, and for which a monetary valuation is available. Social costs, on the other hand, relate to subjective and intangible phenomena such as the general deterioration of the physical and social environment as a result of current productive activity. For example, the beauty of the countryside may be irreparably marred, as has often happened in mining and industrial areas; rivers and the atmosphere may be contaminated through the disposal of industrial wastes; and disease and crime-infested slums may result as a by-product of industrial growth and urbanization. These costs are not measured directly by gross national product figures. Nevertheless, social costs are as much a part of the real cost of the national output as the more readily measurable economic costs, but because of their subjective nature there are no obviously certain criteria for judging their magnitude. Their existence, though, should be recognized by the serious student of economics.[11] Later in this chapter we shall discuss a pioneer effort to incorporate some social costs into the conventional measure of GNP.

There are, however, indirect ways in which social costs will be reflected in gross national product and other output measures. First, the money spent for workers and other resources needed to repair environmental damage from the past will be reflected in the output figures for the period in which such expenditures are made. Unhappily, as Professor Lekachman suggests, existing techniques for national income accounting and

10. Robert Lekachman, *National Income and Public Welfare* (New York: Random House, 1972), p. 7.

11. A leading proponent of this viewpoint is the British economist, E. J. Mishan. See his *The Cost of Economic Growth* (New York: Praeger, 1967). See also Robert Lekachman, *National Income and the Public Welfare Ibid.* chaps, 5, 6, and 7.

measurement cannot—or do not—distinguish between expenditures of this type and other expenditures which reflect newly created goods and services. Second, the expenditures that must be made to prevent further environmental deterioration or pollution also enter into gross national product accounting, although these expenditures do not directly increase either the quantity of goods and services we consume or our stock of capital instruments. Expenditures of this nature will probably grow rather than decrease in the future. One recent estimate put a $271 billion price-tag on pollution-control costs over the decade ending in 1985.[12] Finally—and even more subtly—the social cost of environmental deterioration may show up in the higher wage levels necessary to attract workers to such areas, and congestion and associated higher taxes in areas to which people flee to escape depressing surroundings.

The Value of Leisure · In any analysis of the economic welfare or well-being of a nation the amount of leisure time at the people's disposal should rank high in importance; yet the national income and product statistics do not measure directly the value of leisure to society. Over the last half-century the length of the average work week has fallen from sixty to seventy hours to about forty hours, a development that represents a drastic improvement in welfare. What this means, in part, is that people have been willing to "exchange" relatively fewer goods and services for more leisure. One needs to be careful on this point, however, for no simple "trade-off" is involved. The reason, of course, is that the productivity of the work force—what an average worker can produce in a unit of time—has also gone up, so it is possible to work less, and yet enjoy the same or even a larger bundle of goods and services as compared to an earlier time. It is in this sense that GNP figures do not—they cannot—measure directly the value of leisure to a society. Nonetheless, not many would question the proposition that a society which is able to produce a larger volume of material goods and services with an equal or even smaller expenditure of human effort is in a real sense better off.

Qualitative Changes in the National Output · In the discussion of price indices we pointed out the necessity for eliminating the distortion produced by changes in the prices of goods and services entering into the national income product statistics if comparisons were to be made of the national output at different points in time. Unfortunately, it is not possible to make the same adjustments for changes in the quality of goods and services. It is possible, for example, that the economy might spend (in terms of constant dollars) about the same amount today as it did ten years ago for television sets, but today's set is in a qualitative sense a vastly different product from one produced ten years ago. In some

12. *U.S. News and World Report*, February 7, 1977, p. 43.

instances, qualitative changes may be so great that for all practical purposes no basis exists for comparing the value of a product now being produced with the value of the same or similar product in an earlier period. In the present stage of development of national income accounting no satisfactory technique exists for taking into account qualitative changes in the income and product totals.

The Composition of Output · The various aggregates that we have been discussing are limited as measures of economic welfare because they do not tell us very much about the composition of the national output, except in the broad terms of consumption, investment, and government expenditure. The welfare implications of an increase in the national output (in constant dollars) cannot be assessed without some knowledge of the composition of that output. For example, real GNP in the United States rose sharply during the Vietnam conflict, yet it would be ridiculous to say that the whole of this increase represented an increase in our well-being. Moreover, over long periods of time the composition of the national output may change drastically. Today, transportation by air is commonplace; sixty to seventy years ago, this kind of service did not exist. Thus, to evaluate fully the welfare implications of an increase in a society's real national product, it is necessary to know the composition of the product total and changes that may have taken place in this composition over relatively long periods of time.[13]

The Distribution of the National Output · While national income and product data serve as highly useful measures of the economy's over-all productive performance, they do not tell us how the output total is distributed among the members of society. It may be noted that the data indicate how the national income is distributed with respect to various forms of income—that is, wages, rents, profits, and so on—but not how it is distributed to persons. It is impossible, though, to ignore the distribution of output (and income) in any analysis of the welfare implications of a given level of economic activity. There are no wholly objective or purely scientific criteria for proper distribution of output and income in a society. One reason is that economists have, for reasons that probably don't make a lot of sense to the lay person, largely taken themselves out of the "theoretical-philosophical question of how income ought to be distributed."[14] Nevertheless, those economists who feel that greater equality in the distribution of the national income is to be preferred to less equality tend to argue along these lines: that society's welfare will be increased if, for example, a thousand dollars is taken from a rich man and

13. Lekachman, chap. 3.

14. Alice M. Rivlin, "Income Distribution—Can Economists Help?," *The American Economic Review*, May 1975, p. 5.

given to a poor sharecropper with four or five children. The difficulty in this is that there are no objective criteria to tell us how far to push such a proposition.[15] In any event, some knowledge of the actual distribution of income in society, and some concept of how income ought to be distributed is necessary for an evaluation of the economy's performance in terms of economic welfare.[16]

Income and Output Per Capita · Finally, it is necessary to take into account changes in population as well as changes in real output totals if meaningful comparisons of economic welfare are to be made over time. A rise in real income will not bring an improvement in the material level of well-being if population grows at a faster rate than the output total. For many purposes it is desirable that the aggregate data of national output and income be reduced to a per capita basis before comparisons are made. Figure 3–1 shows in index number form the growth of real GNP and real GNP per capita since 1954. Note the slower growth of GNP per capita because of population growth.

The shortcomings described are not the only limitations involved in the use of national income statistics. The careful reader, who understands that such limitations exist, will exercise caution in drawing welfare conclusions from the performance data recorded in national income and product statistics. National income data are of great value for the measurement of the economy's performance, but they must be interpreted correctly.

The Search for Improved Measures of Product and Welfare

The limitations of currently used measures of national income and product have not gone unnoticed by national income theoreticians and statisticians. In recent years two approaches to the problem have emerged toward establishing better and more refined measures of output and well-being. One aim is to have statistics on economic output reflect social benefits, social costs, and leisure; a second aim is more far-reaching: to measure the social health of the nation in the same way that national income accounts have measured its economic health. Both of these are worthy of our attention.

Recently two Yale University economists developed an experimental *measure of economic welfare*—termed MEW—which is designed to con-

15. Ibid., p. 6.
16. Lekachman, chap. 4.

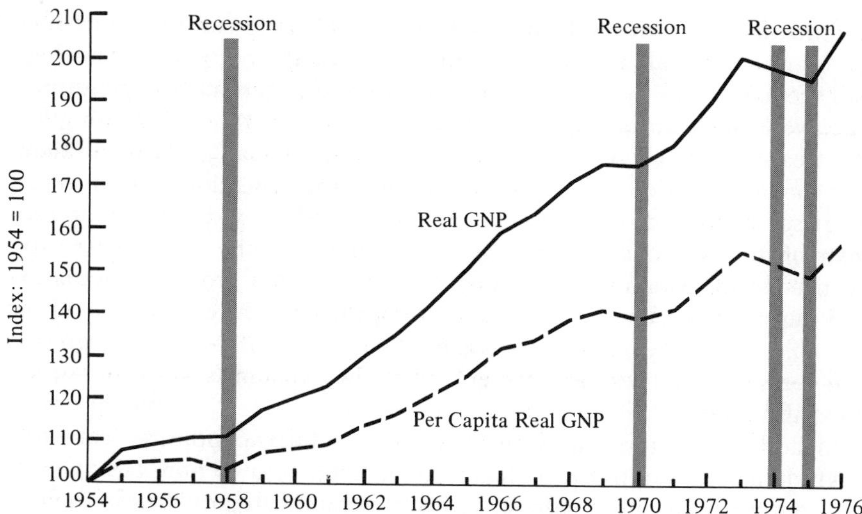

Source: Economic Report of the President, 1977

FIGURE 3–1. Real GNP and Real GNP Per Capita: 1954–76 (*1954 = 100*)

vert the conventional GNP figure into one that measures economic welfare.[17] As they point out, the major shortcoming of GNP is that it is an index of production, not consumption. Since presumably the main purpose of economic activity is consumption, any measure of economic welfare ought to be oriented toward consumption more than production. Their experimental MEW represents essentially a rearrangement of conventional national income data to reflect this point of view.

The necessary adjustments to GNP data fall into three basic categories:[18] (1) reclassifying GNP expenditure totals so as to get more accurate measures of consumption, investment, and intermediate products; (2) making estimates—*imputations*—for the value of the services of consumer and public capital, for leisure, and for household work; and (3) adding a correction that reflects some of the disamenities—i.e., social costs—of urbanization.

In reclassifying GNP final expenditures as normally reported in the U.S. national income accounts, Professors Tobin and Nordhaus adjusted capital expenditure figures in two ways. First, they enlarged the capital consumption category to include estimates of capital consumption for three

17. James Tobin and William Nordhaus, "Is Growth Obsolete?" in *Economic Growth* (New York: National Bureau of Economic Research, 1972). Professor Nordhaus was appointed to President Carter's Council of Economic Advisers in January, 1977.

18. Ibid., p. 5.

additional types of capital: the stock of privately held consumer durables, government capital, and human capital (see Chapter 2, p. 42). This logically follows from their reclassification of some government expenditures as capital expenditures (housing, education, transportation, for example), the treatment of all outlays for consumer durables as gross investment, and the classification of private expenditures for educational and medical purposes as investment in human capital. Second, they developed an estimate of the additional investment in all forms of public and private capital needed to sustain per capita consumption with a growing population and improving technology. This they term the growth requirement (Line 7, Table 3–5). The underlying assumption is that, if population growth and technical progress are present, then the economy's stock of capital must also grow.

In addition to the adjustments in the capital expenditures category, GNP data were adjusted to change some expenditures now classified as final output to an intermediate, or instrumental, category. These include such public expenditures as police services, sanitation, road maintenance, and national defense, the rationale being that most government expenditures—other than those of a capital goods nature—are necessary overhead costs in a modern nation.[19] Private expenditures reclassified as intermediate included a portion of personal transportation expenditures and all personal business expenses.

As pointed out earlier, national income procedures now in use include an imputation for rent on owner-occupied homes as a part of consumption and income. But no allowance is made for the value of leisure. This tends to understate economic welfare. Consequently, Professors Tobin and Nordhaus introduce into the calculation of MEW estimates of the value of leisure and nonmarket productive activities (housework and other home-produced services). These, of course, have a positive value.

The two final adjustments made by Tobin and Nordhaus to transform GNP into MEW involve estimates of some of the social costs, or disamenities, associated with urbanization, and of the value of services provided by government and private capital held by consumers. The main disamenities included in their calculations are pollution, litter, congestion, noise, insecurity, and buildings and advertisements offensive to taste that are characteristic of urban life. These they attempt to measure by calculation of a disamenity premium, which is based upon estimates of the additional income required to induce people to live in densely populated cities rather than in smaller communities and rural areas.[20]

What does all this add up to? The results for selected years are presented in Table 3–5, which shows the transition of GNP data in 1958

19. Ibid., p. 7.
20. Ibid., p. 49.

TABLE 3–5. Gross National Product and MEW, Various Years, 1929–65 (billions of dollars, 1958 prices)

	1929	*1935*	*1945*	*1947*	*1954*	*1958*	*1965*
1. Gross national product	203.6	169.5	355.2	309.9	407.0	447.3	617.8
2. Capital consumption, NIPA*	−20.0	−20.0	−21.9	−18.3	−32.5	−38.9	−54.7
3. Net national product, NIPA	183.6	149.5	333.3	291.6	374.5	408.4	563.1
4. Final output reclassified as intermediate expenditure							
a. Government	−6.7	−7.4	−146.3	−20.8	−57.8	−56.4	−63.2
b. Private	−10.3	−9.2	−9.2	−10.9	−16.4	−19.9	−30.9
5. Imputations for items not included in GNP (NIPA)							
a. Leisure	339.5	401.3	450.7	466.9	523.2	554.9	626.9
b. Nonmarket activity	85.7	109.2	152.4	159.6	211.5	239.7	295.4
c. Disamenities	−12.5	−14.1	−18.1	−19.1	−24.3	−27.6	−34.6
d. Services of public and private capital	29.7	24.2	31.0	36.7	48.9	54.8	78.9
6. Additional capital consumption	−19.3	−33.4	−11.7	−50.8	−35.2	−27.3	−92.7
7. Growth requirement	−46.1	−46.7	−65.8	+5.4	−63.1	−78.9	−101.8
8. Sustainable MEW	543.6	573.4	716.3	858.6	961.3	1,047.7	1,241.1
9. Sustainable MEW per capita							
Dollars	4,462	4,504	5,098	5,934	5,898	5,991	6,378
1929 = 100	100.0	100.9	114.3	133.0	132.2	134.3	142.9
10. Per capita NNP							
Dollars	1,945	1,205	2,401	2,038	2,305	2,335	2,897
1929 = 100	100.0	78.0	155.4	131.9	149.2	151.1	187.5

*NIPA-National Income and Product Accounts, or conventional Department of Commerce measures of Income and Product.
SOURCE: William Nordhaus and James Tobin, "Is Growth Obsolete?"

prices to sustainable MEW for the same years. The table also contains data showing the per capita values for NNP and sustainable MEW, including an index using 1929 as the base year. Two important findings emerge from these data. First, the estimates of measurable economic welfare (MEW) are much larger than both GNP and NNP, which means, of course, that our conventional measures of output seriously understate economic welfare. The main reason for this is the failure of conventional national income accounting to take into account the value of leisure and the worth of nonmarket activities, especially the services provided by the homemaker. Second, the data show that MEW, though larger in an absolute sense than GNP and NNP, has been growing at a slower rate.

Although the MEW concept still awaits refinement, it is at least a promising start. Not nearly so much progress has been made in efforts to construct a comprehensive system of social accounts that would measure the nation's social health in the same way that economic accounts measure the nation's material health. Some impetus in this direction was given by the release in 1969 of a report from the Department of Health, Education and Welfare urging the development of a set of social indicators and an annual *Social Report* on the model of the annual *Economic Report* of the President's Council of Economic Advisers.[21] Legislation was introduced into the Congress establishing a Council of Social Advisers and requiring the publication of an annual *Social Report*, to be transmitted by the president to the Congress. But there has been little support in recent years for such legislation.

What would a social report and social accounting attempt to do? Specifically, it would measure, via a set of social indicators, social progress or retrogression. According to HEW's *Toward a Social Report*, this would require the development of quantitative measures of the factors that help (or hinder) the individual citizen to live a full and healthy life within a decent social and physical environment. Among such factors listed in the HEW report are health and illness, the extent of social mobility, the quality of the physical environment, the extent and incidence of poverty, conditions of public order and safety, the availability of educational and cultural opportunities, and the existence and extent of alienation in society.

Obviously, formidable difficulties confront any effort to construct a set of social accounts comparable to the economic accounts now in use. Not only are many of the social factors inherently subjective in nature, but they do not lend themselves readily to quantification in index form. But the task is not impossible. In areas like health, education, and crime, for example, statistical data are being compiled and used in a manner that reflects improvement or retrogression. Slow but persistent progress can be expected in the development of statistical indicators in such areas. What is not likely, though, is the development of a single, unified statistic comparable to GNP that would be a barometer of the nation's social health. As the HEW report says, "It would be utopian even to strive for a Gross Social Product, or National Socioeconomic Welfare, figure which aggregated all relevant social and economic variables. There are no objective weights, equivalent to prices, that we can use to compare the importance of an improvement in health with an increase in social mobility. . . . Thus the goal of a grand and cosmic measure of all forms or aspects of welfare must be dismissed as impractical, for the present at any rate."[22]

21. U.S. Department of Health, Education and Welfare, *Toward a Social Report* (Washington, D.C.: U.S. Government Printing Office, 1969). For more details on the history and background of social reporting, see Daniel Bell, "The Idea of a Social Report," *Public Interest*, Spring 1969.

22. *Toward a Social Report*, p. 99.

II
The Basic Theory of Income and Employment

4

Employment, Unemployment, and the Classical View

We now begin formal study of the forces that determine national output, income, employment, and the price level in the modern economy. It is the objective of *macroeconomic* analysis to understand these forces. To place our study in historical perspective, we will examine the explanation given to the problem of the determinants of income, employment, and prices by the system of economic analysis known as classical economics. First, though, we shall consider what economists mean by the concept of employment and unemployment and demonstrate how employment is related to the output level.

The Meaning of Employment and Unemployment

The words *employment* and *unemployment* need to be examined carefully. The idea that full employment is a proper and desirable objective of public policy gained widespread acceptance in the United States and most of the nations of Western Europe during and immediately following World War II. In the United States, the Employment Act of 1946 gave legislative sanction to the view that the federal government has a direct responsibility for the level of employment and income prevailing in the economy. The act specifically stated:

> The Congress hereby declares that it is the continuing policy and responsibility of the Federal Government to use all practicable means consistent with its needs and obligations and other essential considerations of national policy, with the assistance and cooperation of industry, agriculture, labor, and State and local governments, to coordinate and utilize all its plans, functions, and resources for the purpose of creating and maintaining, in a manner calculated to foster and promote free competitive enterprise and the general welfare, conditions under which there will be afforded useful employment opportunities, including self employment, for those able, willing, and seeking work, and to promote maximum employment, production, and purchasing power.[1]

The qualifying phrases found in the Employment Act suggest, on the one hand, that full employment is not a social goal to be achieved at all costs and, on the other, that the federal government has other obligations ranking in importance with that of full employment. Increasingly, economists believe that stability of the general price level is a goal equal in importance to full employment. They believe this because they fear that continuous upward pressure on the price level not only dissipates the gains resulting from full employment, but jeopardizes the economy's ability to maintain conditions of full employment for any significant period of time. The tribulations of the federal government during the 1970s as it has sought—largely unsuccessfully—to develop policies to keep prices under control have dramatized inflation as a major macroeconomic problem.

Although the Employment Act makes maximum or full employment an objective of public policy it does not define exactly what constitutes a fully employed labor force. Yet without some conception of what is meant by full employment, administration of the act in any practical sense is impossible. The simplest definition of full employment is a situation in the economy characterized by an absence of *involuntary unemployment*. The latter exists when members of the labor force are willing to work at prevailing wages in their trade or occupation but are unable to obtain employment. If we let N' be representative of the labor force and N stand for the actual level of employment, then full employment exists in the society as $N' - N$ approaches zero.

The reader should note that we used the phrase *approaches zero* rather than *equals zero*. The reason for this is that absolute full employment of the labor force, which would prevail if $N' - N$ were equal to zero, is a condition that is seldom, if ever, attained in practice. In almost any society there is likely to be a varying amount of *frictional unemployment*, which results whenever persons in the labor force are temporarily out of work because of imperfections in the labor market. At any given time some workers will be in the process of changing jobs or occupations;

1. Employment Act of 1946.

others will be experiencing temporary layoffs caused by the seasonal nature of their employment, by shortage of materials in some industries, or by shifts in demand that reduce the need for some types of workers and increase the need for others. Many other similar factors cause some proportion of the labor force to be out of work for short periods of time.

Quite early in the history of the implementation of the Employment Act a 4 percent unemployment rate emerged as a rough measure of full employment in the American economy. Full employment not only means that frictional unemployment is at a minimum, but that the economy can attain such a level without the risk of serious inflation. The use of the adjective "rough" is deliberate, for between 1946 and 1961 the President's Council of Economic Advisers strongly resisted using any explicit figure to measure full employment. In January 1955, for example, Council member Arthur F. Burns told the Joint Economic Committee of the Congress that ". . . although 4 percent of the labor force is widely regarded as an approximate measure of the average amount of frictional and seasonal unemployment, the Council has not favored this or any other rigid figure to serve as a trigger to govermental action or as a measure of good performance.[2]

It was not until the Kennedy administration that an explicit figure for full employment was agreed upon. In the January 1962 *Economic Report of the President* the Council explicitly set a 4 percent unemployment rate as an interim goal, the expectation being that ultimately an even lower target figure could be established:

> In the existing economic circumstances an unemployment rate of about 4 percent is a reasonable and prudent *full employment target for stabilization policy* [emphasis added]. If we move firmly to reduce the impact of structural unemployment, we will be able to move the unemployment target steadily from 4 percent to successively lower levels.[3]

Under the Johnson administration 4 percent continued to be accepted as an appropriate target, and no attempt was ever made to lower the figure. For a while the Vietnam war made the question academic, since unemployment dipped below 4 percent for the four years 1966 through 1969.

During the Nixon and Ford administrations references to a specific target for unemployment practically vanished from the reports of the President's economic advisers. As inflation picked up steam in the 1970s, some economists began to abandon the idea that 4 percent represented even a satisfactory interim goal. In its 1972 report, the Council argued that 5 percent rather than 4 percent unemployment would be a more suit-

2. *Economic Report of the President: **Hearings***, 84th Congress, 1st Session (Washington, D.C.: U.S. Government Printing Office, 1955) p. 45.

3. *Economic Report of the President* (Washington, D.C.: U.S. Government Printing Office, 1962), p. 46.

able benchmark[4] mainly due to the fact that women and teen-agers constitute a growing portion of the labor force. In 1948, for example, less than 35 percent of the teen-age and female population was in the labor force; it is now around 50 percent.[5] Since both teen-agers and women have higher unemployment rates on the average than men (See Figure 4–1), this tends to pull the overall unemployment rate up. In the final report for the Ford administration, Alan Greenspan, chairman of the Council, reported that the outgoing Council believed the appropriate full employment rate for joblessness was 4.9 percent, but warned that inflationary pressure might set in even at an unemployment rate of 5.5 percent.[6] When the Ford administration left office, unemployment was running close to 8 percent.

As President (and, before that, as a candidate) Jimmy Carter stated that his primary goal was to bring the overall rate down to 4.5 percent as rapidly as possible. Organized labor, however, is pushing for legislation which would mandate government action to bring the unemployment rate for workers over twenty down to 3 percent within four years. Legislation to this effect was introduced in Congress in 1976 (the Humphrey-Hawkins Full Employment and Balanced Growth Act), but the bill remained bottled up in both 1976 and 1977. Late in 1977 President Carter endorsed a revised version of the Humphrey-Hawkins bill, one which called for reducing the unemployment rate for all workers over 16 to 4 percent in five years, but which did not provide any specific means whereby the government could attain this goal. The revised bill also called for "reasonable price stability," and stated that the goal of price stability should have equal weight with the goal of full employment. In its push for a mandated full employment job bill, the AFL-CIO is now calling the week ushered in by Labor Day "Full Employment" Week.

If a 4 to 5 percent unemployment rate is accepted as a working measure of full employment for the American economy under current conditions, employment appears to have been high much of the time since the end of World War II. Figure 4–1 traces unemployment in the American economy through a major part of this era. For the whole period—1948 through 1976—unemployment averaged 5 percent of the civilian labor force, although in just over one-half of those years (15) it rose above 5 percent. If we look at the data more closely, the record is uneven, for it was only during the years affected by the Korean war (1951–53) and the Vietnam war (1966–69) that average unemployment got below the Ken-

4. Ibid, 1972, pp. 108 ff.

5. Federal Reserve Bank of St. Louis, *Review*, September 1976, p. 7. In the same interval the number of men in the labor force declined from nearly 90 percent of the eligible population to less than 80 percent.

6. *Economic Report of the President* (Washington, D.C.: U.S. Government Printing Office, 1977), p. 56.

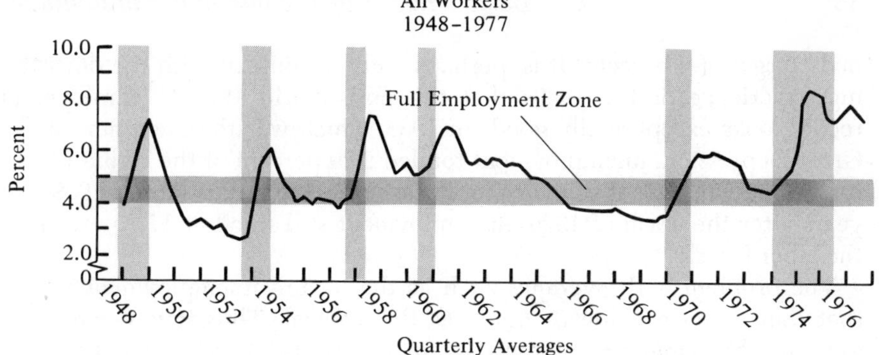

Note: Shaded Areas Indicate Recession Periods

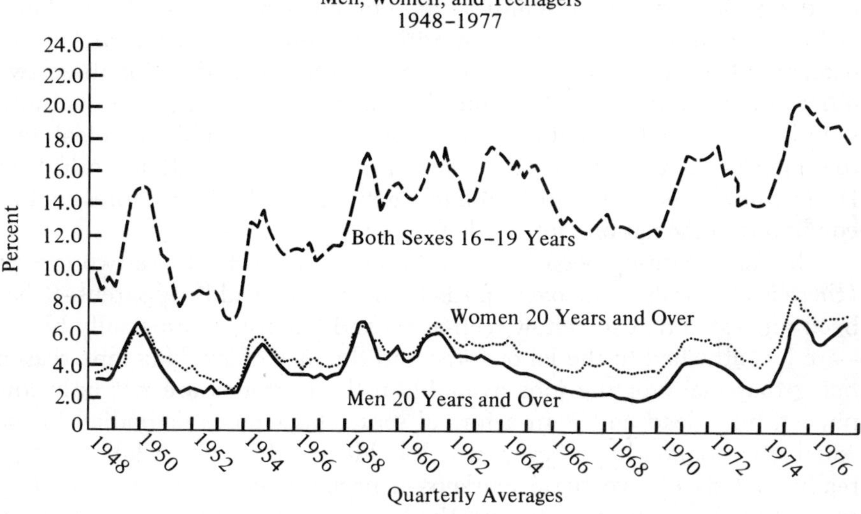

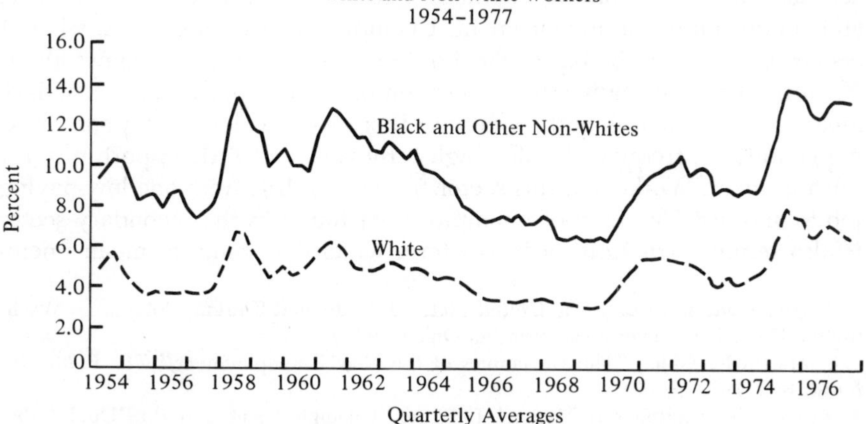

Source: U. S. Department of Labor.

FIGURE 4–1. Unemployment Rates
All Workers 1948-1977

nedy target of 4 percent. It is, perhaps, only in contrast with the devastating experience of the 1930s that the post–World War II employment record looks exceptionally good. In 1933, which was the low point of the Great Depression, unemployment totaled 24.9 percent of the civilian labor force—one worker out of every four was jobless. Even as late as 1939, ten years after the crash of 1929, unemployment still stood at 17.2 percent of the labor force.[7]

The problem with averages such as the overall unemployment rate is that they often exclude as much as they reveal. Thus it is essential to examine the remainder of the data in Figure 4–1 to see what has happened to particular groups in this period. What the two lower graphs in the figure show is that some segments of our society have never experienced anything that remotely resembles "full employment," by whatever standard it is measured. Blacks and minorities as well as teen-agers are in this category. The overall situation for women is not as bad as for these two other groups, but most of the time they have found it tougher to get jobs than have adult white males. What these statistics reveal is the bleak fact that most of the time during the years of high prosperity after World War II nonwhite minorities and teen-agers actually confronted depressionlike conditions in the nation's job markets.

Why this condition persists in good times and bad for these two groups (there is obviously some overlap) is by no means readily apparent. It has been suggested that somehow teen-agers and minorities—especially blacks—are less attached to the labor force and the idea of working, one reason being that many of the jobs available to both groups are not only low paying, but "dead end."[8] In a formal sense this view is embodied in the "dual labor market hypothesis," which holds that the nation's labor market really consists of two basic markets—a *primary* sector and a *secondary* sector.[9] In the primary sector are the better-paying, preferred jobs, characterized by good working conditions, reasonable employment stability, and opportunities for advancement. Unemployment in this sector, when it occurs, is best described as cyclical or "Keynesian," in that it comes about when the economy falls into a recession or depression. In the secondary sector, the situation is quite different; there we find low pay, poor working conditions, frequent layoffs, high turnovers, and little opportunity for advancement. Workers in this sector frequently drift from one low-paying job to another. The kind of unemployment found in the secondary sector is also termed *structural*, a broad term which has come to mean unem-

7. *Historical Statistics of the United States*, Bicentennial Edition, Volume 1 (Washington, D.C.: U.S. Government Printing Office, 1975), p. 135.

8. Martin Feldstein, "The Economics of the New Unemployment," *The Public Interest*, Fall, 1973, p. 14.

9. Peter B. Doeringer & Michael J. Piore, "Unemployment and the 'Dual Labor Market' ", *The Public Interest*, Winter 1975, p. 70.

ployment which is not frictional and which persists even when times are good.[10] Economists are by no means in agreement on the extent of such unemployment—obviously not all minority and teen-age unemployment is of this nature—but there is a developing consensus that such unemployment is much more difficult to cure than the "Keynesian" variety. The fact that there have been such high rates of joblessness for minorities and teen-agers in good times and bad ever since World War II attests to this.

Employment and Output

In the foregoing paragraphs we stressed that full employment for the nation's labor force has become a public policy objective of major significance for contemporary American society. It is equally important to point out that there exists a close link between the employment level and the output level. In other words, we can expect the amount of employment to vary more or less directly with the volume of production. Since the latter constitutes the real income of society, it follows that the employment level serves as an indicator of the economy's over-all performance. Conversely, the output level is a good indicator of the prevailing employment situation in the economy. This, of course, applies to the over-all average, not the specific employment situation for any particular segment of the labor force at any given time. Figure 4–2 shows how the unemployment rate fluctuates with the economy's output (GNP in constant prices), falling during periods of prosperity (a rising GNP) and rising during periods of recession (a declining GNP). As Figure 4–1 reveals, unemployment rates for particular groups are much higher on the average than the rate for all workers, but even these higher rates fluctuate pretty much in harmony with output changes.

The link between real income and the employment level is important for economic analysis because it embraces a number of simple, but fundamental, economic relationships. Basic to an understanding of the determinants of the level of production and employment is the concept of the economy's productive capacity, also termed potential GNP. At any time, there exists for the economy as a whole a given productive capacity, that is, a potential for the production of goods and services. Even in the short run the economy's productive capacity is not an exact or unvarying magnitude, for in practically all economies there is some flexibility in the maximum output that can be obtained over short periods of time. Nevertheless, all economies have some upper limit to the amount of goods and services that can be produced, and this upper limit will necessarily consti-

10. See *Economic Report of the President* (Washington, D.C.: U.S. Government Printing Office, 1975), p. 98 ff.

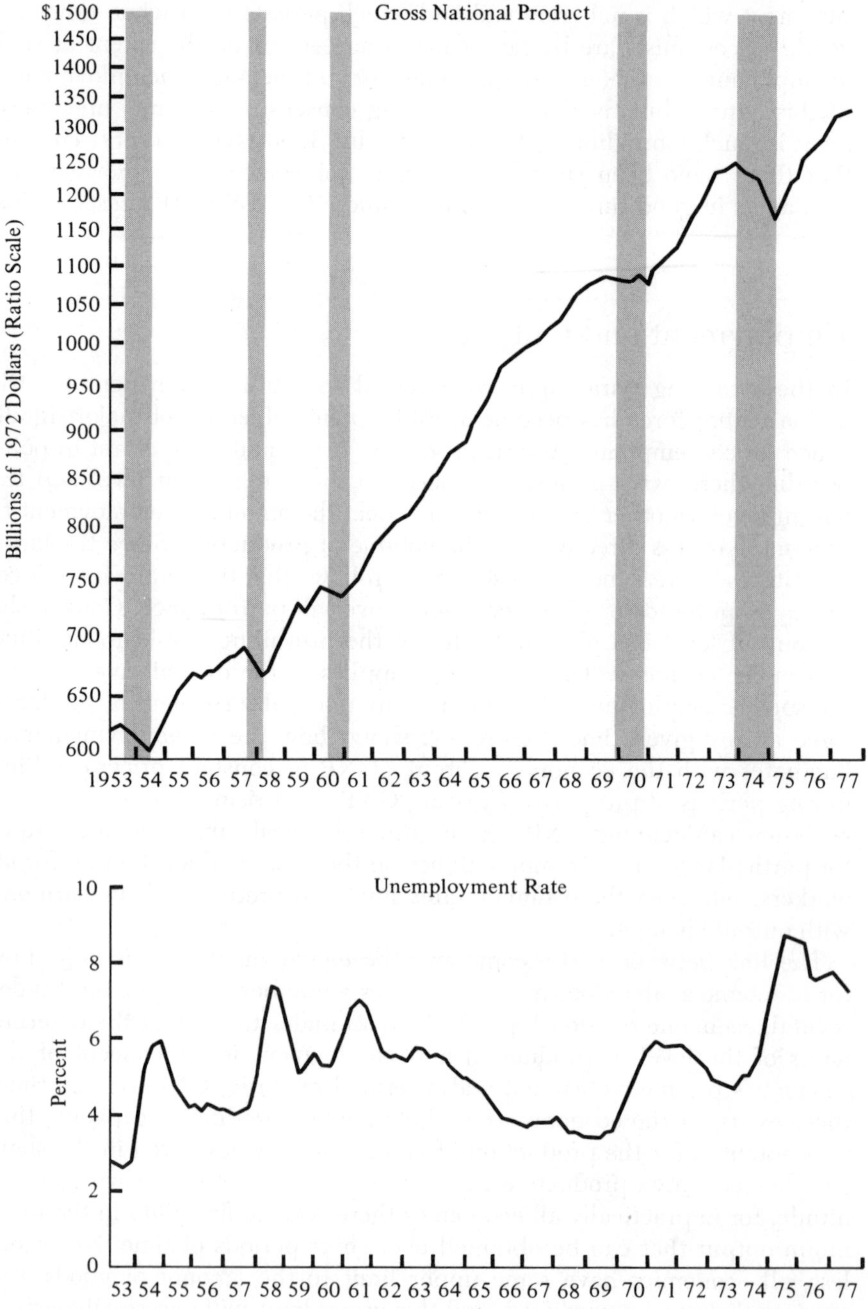

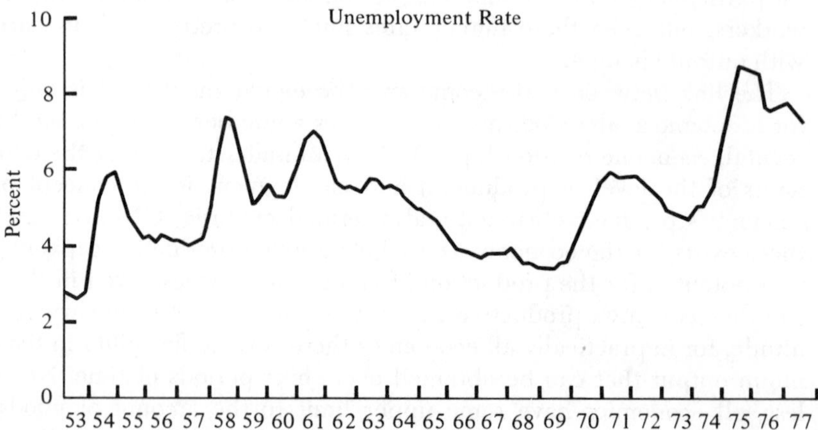

FIGURE 4–2. Actual Gross National Product and Unemployment Rate: 1953-1977

tute an economy's short run maximum capacity to produce. Over time, of course, this may change, as the process of economic growth brings about expansion in the economy's productive capacity. A *dynamic economy* is characterized by a continuously expanding capacity for production.

What determines the productive capacity of the economy? This is one of the most complex of all economic problems, yet the basic factors in the process can be readily identified. In the simplest sense, productive capacity depends upon, first, the quantity and quality of resources available to the economy; and second, the skill and efficiency with which these resources are brought together for the purpose of production. The latter concerns technology, for in its broadest meaning technology refers to the over-all level of effectiveness attained by an economy in combining resources together in the productive process.

The statements in the foregoing paragraph can be summarized symbolically by the following equation:

$$Q = f(N', H', R', K'; T) \tag{4–1}$$

In this and the following equations the symbols used have the following meanings:

Q = The economy's productive capacity (*potential GNP*).
N′ = The economy's labor force.
H′ = The standard hours of work per year.
R′ = The economy's stock of known and economically useful natural resources.
K′ = The economy's stock of capital or man-made instruments of production.
T = The level of technology prevailing in the economy.

The meaning of equation 4–1 is that the economy's productive capacity is a function of (the symbol f in the equation) the basic determinants listed above: the quantity of labor, the standard hours of work, natural resources, capital, and the level of technology. Note that the equation does not in any way specify the exact proportions in which the determinants of capacity are brought together, but merely states that productive capacity depends on these things. Because technology is not a stock, as are labor, capital, and natural resources, it is separated from the other variables by a semicolon. Technically, it is a *parameter,* whose value determines the output potential associated with specific quantities of the other three determinants.

The productive capacity of the economy can be defined, too, in terms of the fully employed labor force, N', and the average productivity of labor, P_r. The productivity of labor, or average output per man-hour (or some other time unit such as man-year), does not refer to the degree of skill possessed by labor in general, but rather to the efficiency with which labor power is employed in the productive process. Since the latter depends upon the quantity and quality of capital equipment and natural resources used in conjunction with labor, the following is a correct statement of the relevant relationships:

$$P_r = f(R', K'; T) \tag{4-2}$$

The equation states that the productivity of labor is a function of the quantity of natural resources and capital equipment, given the level of technology. This being the case, it follows that the economy's productive capacity is equal to the fully employed labor force, N', times the normal hours of work per year, H', times the average productivity of labor, P_r. When so stated P_r represents the normal *output per man-hour.* Thus, we have the equation

$$Q = (N' \times H \times P_r) \tag{4-3}$$

If we let P' represent the normal *output per man-year,* the equation would simply be

$$Q = (N' \times P'). \tag{4-4}$$

Just as the economy's productive capacity depends upon the quantity and quality of available resources, the actual level of output is determined by the extent to which these resources are being used. Output results from the utilization of productive capacity. In economics the physical relationship that exists between the input of resources and the output of goods and services in any given period of time is termed the *production function.* Stated in other terms, the production function embodies a functional relationship between the quantity of input and the quantity of output. In the short run it may take the following form:

$$Y = f(N, H, R', K'; T) \tag{4-5}$$

This equation means that—*given the stock* of natural resources and capital, as well as the level of technology—output is determined by the labor input (N) and the hours actually worked (H). It is also true that output can be defined as the product of the actual labor employed and the average productivity of labor. In such a formulation N may represent either actually employed labor or actual man-hours of work, depending upon whether we use output per man-hour or output per man-year. For example, if P' represents output per man-year, then N would stand for the actual number of people at work.

$$Y = N \times P' \tag{4-6}$$

The concept of the production function is depicted graphically in Figure 4–3, which shows output on the vertical axis and labor input (people at work) on the horizontal axis. The output curve will eventually level off because of diminishing productivity. On the curve labeled Y_a, an increase in the income level from Y_1 to Y_2 results when employment increases from N_1 to N_2. The same increase in income may be obtained with no change in employment if the entire production function shifts upward to the level depicted by the curve Y_b. This would result from a change in the stock of capital and natural resources, a change in technology, or a combination of the two.

The foregoing discussion provides a basis for an understanding of the close relationship over short periods of time during which it is assumed that the quantity of capital, natural resources, and the level of technology remain relatively fixed. By implication, then, productive capacity is also relatively fixed.

There is no way to define precisely the length of real time involved in the short run, although a satisfactory working definition is that it is long enough to permit some cyclical fluctuations in income and employment, but not sufficiently long to show a definite trend. The significant factor for our analysis is that the short run is not a long enough period of time to permit any really significant changes in the economy's productive capacity. Consequently, we may assume that the underlying determinants of capacity in Equation (4–1) have relatively fixed magnitudes, although the extent to which they are actually utilized in production is variable. This is particularly true with respect to the labor force, because the level of employment, N, can quite obviously depart rather widely at times from

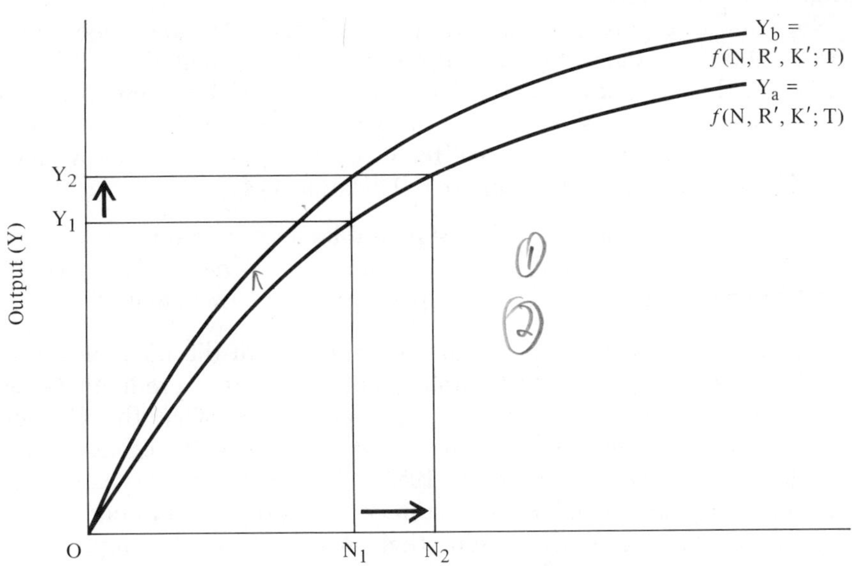

FIGURE 4–3. The Production Function

the size of the labor force, N'. For the economy as a whole the output level, Y, in the short run will tend to vary directly with the employment level N. Thus a good workable hypothesis is as follows:

$$Y = f(N) \quad (4\text{–}7)$$

In this formulation the level of employment, N, has meaning not only in relation to the over-all supply of labor, N', but also as a barometer of the extent to which the economy's productive capacity is actually being utilized. In the analysis to follow we will make frequent use of this simple but important notion that over relatively short periods of time employment and real income move together.

Productive Capacity and the Output Gap

For many years now, federal policy-makers have computed the economy's productive capacity, which they term potential GNP, and compared it with actual output, the purpose being to get a clear picture of how well the economy is performing in relation to its potential. In those years in which actual output falls short of capacity, the shortfall has been labeled the GNP gap. Figure 4–4 traces the relationship between potential and actual GNP since 1953.

Note that in Figure 4–4 there are two potential GNP lines, one designated "Old Potential GNP" and the other "New Potential GNP." The reason for the two lines is that in 1977 the Council of Economic Advisers recalculated potential GNP for all the years shown in the chart.[11] The basic formula used by the Council for measuring potential GNP is given by the following equation (compare to Equation 4–3):

$$\text{Potential GNP} = \begin{pmatrix}\text{Fully-}\\ \text{employed}\\ \text{labor force}\end{pmatrix} \times \begin{pmatrix}\text{Standard hours}\\ \text{of work}\\ \text{per year}\end{pmatrix} \times \begin{pmatrix}\text{Average}\\ \text{output per}\\ \text{man hour}\end{pmatrix} \quad (4\text{–}8)$$

From this equation it can be readily seen how both the unemployment rate believed to represent full employment and worker productivity, as well as working hours, influences potential output. What the Council actually did was to make the judgment that in mid-1955 the economy was actually operating at full capacity, 1955 being a benchmark year. From that time on potential GNP was estimated to grow at differing annual rates, depending upon the assumptions made about the appropriate unemployment rate for a fully employed labor force, as well as annual

11. *Economic Report of the President* (Washington, D.C.: U.S. Government Printing Office, 1977), pp. 52–56.

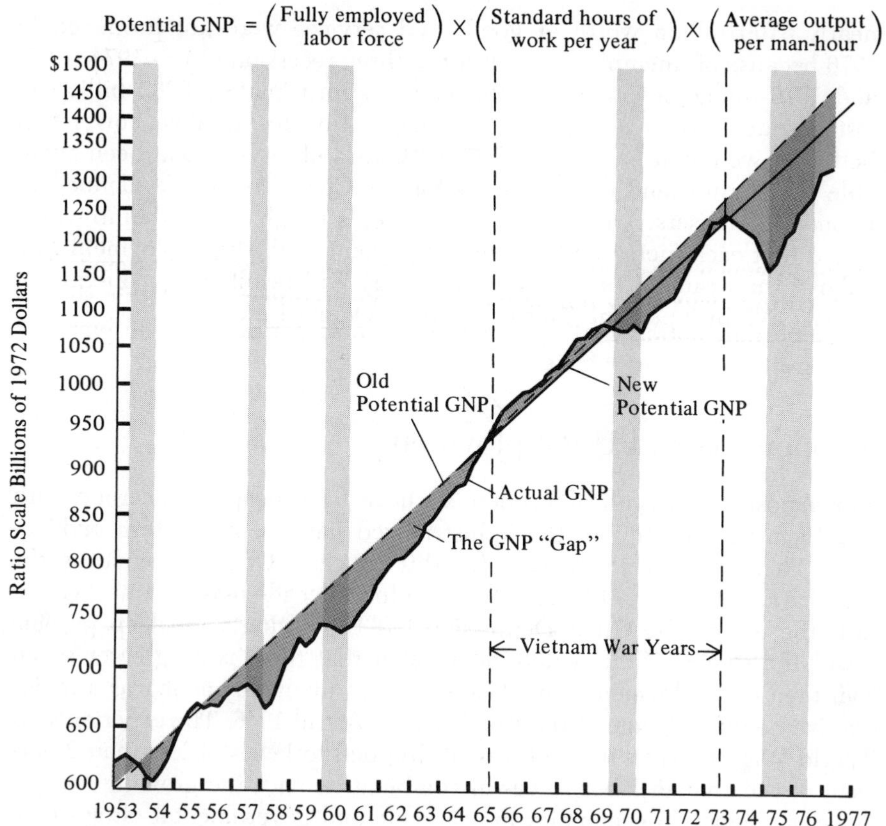

FIGURE 4–4. Actual and Potential Gross National Product 1953–1977

rates of change in productivity and working hours.[12] The main reasons for the reduction by the Council in 1977 of the potential GNP figure from earlier estimates were: first, that the full-employment benchmark was changed from 4.0 to 4.9 percent;[13] second, that there was a slowdown after 1966 in the annual average rate of increase in productivity. As a result of these new calculations, potential GNP in 1976 was $58 billion (in 1972 prices) lower than earlier estimates.

One use of the foregoing type of analysis is to dramatize the social costs of unemployment—that is, the output lost to the nation because a substantial part of its labor force is idle. Using the Council's revised figures,

12. This method of estimating potential GNP is not without criticism. For a critical review of the methods used by the Council of Economic Advisers and development of an alternative method see Edward F. Denison, "Has the Potential Output of the U.S. Economy been misstated?" *Monthly Labor Review*, December 1974, pp. 34–42.

13. The change was made gradually in that the Council in its calculations adjusted the full-employment rate upwards from 4.0 percent in 1955 to 4.9 percent in 1976.

nearly $100 billion worth of goods and services were not produced in 1976 because of unemployment. For the three recession years—1974, 1975, and 1976—unemployment cost the nation approximately $282 billion in lost output. It does not take much imagination to visualize how much better off we might have been if these goods and services had been available for our use and enjoyment. A former Chairman of the Council of Economic Advisers, Arthur Okun, developed a rough rule of thumb which stated that each increase of a percentage point in the unemployment rate (above the assumed full-employment rate) will result in a reduction of actual GNP by 3 percent. This is known as Okun's Law.

Economists and Unemployment

For almost half a century, economists have been deeply concerned with employment problems in the industrialized nations of Western civilization. There are several reasons for this concern. One, of course, is the traumatic experience of the 1930s, when for a decade mass unemployment was the norm. The Great Depression left the nation with deep psychic scars, the source of the widely held belief that there is no greater social evil than unemployment. The desire to erase unemployment was a major motive behind passage of the Employment Act in 1946. The experience of World War II—when unemployment dropped to levels of less than 2 percent of the civilian labor force—in combination with the growing acceptance of Keynesian economics in academic and governmental circles convinced many people that the nation did not have to accept unemployment as a norm. Unemployment is also an affront to the notion of efficiency that is deeply ingrained in most economists' thinking. Unemployment means a waste of resources, a condition that should not be tolerated if the economy is to succeed in providing a maximum of goods and services for the satisfaction of human wants.

This preoccupation with unemployment, however, has not always been at the forefront of the economist's concerns. It was not the case prior to 1929, when the views of the *classical* economists dominated the discipline. As the following section explains, their concerns were quite different, and unemployment was not seen as a major problem. Why, then, should we be concerned with their thinking? One reason is that by understanding classical analysis we sharpen our historical perspective, which enables us to appreciate more fully the cumulative nature of scientific knowledge. What we know today has developed from what was known in the past. Discussion of classical thought also provides some useful insights into ideas discussed in Chapter 1, especially those pertaining to economic "model" building and the predictive character of economic theorizing.

This will serve the reader in good stead in the chapters to come. Finally, knowing how the classical economists perceived the world enhances both understanding and appreciation for the major issues of economic policy that the United States and other advanced market economies have wrestled with since the Great Depression spurred a revolution in economic thought.

The Nature of Classical Economics

Classical economics is the system of economic analysis developed in England in the late eighteenth and early nineteenth centuries, which stood largely intact until the 1930s as the main body of economic principles accepted by economists. In his famous treatise, *The General Theory of Employment, Interest and Money,* John Maynard Keynes employed the term to characterize the followers of the early nineteenth-century British economist David Ricardo, and included John Stuart Mill, Alfred Marshall, and A. C. Pigou. These British economists were deemed by Keynes to be most representative of the classical system of economic analysis.[14]

The chief objective of classical analysis was to explain the working of a capitalistic economic system founded upon the institution of private property. Essentially this involved construction of a set of principles that would explain how a market structure of competitive prices functioned to determine what goods and services were to be produced, how resources were to be allocated for the production of goods and services, and how the final output was distributed to the owners of economic resources. In this scheme the motivating force was the self-interest of entrepreneurs, resource owners, and consumers seeking, respectively, to maximize profits, income, and satisfactions. Implicit within the theoretical structure of the classical economists is a set of propositions that purport to explain how the employment level is determined; it is this facet of classical thinking that will occupy our attention throughout the remainder of this chapter.

As a body of economic principles, classical economics rested upon two major assumptions. The first was that the economic order is dominated by the kind of rigorous competition which denies any control over prices to either the sellers of goods and services, or the sellers of the services of economic resources. This is what modern textbooks usually describe as pure competition. The social function of competition is to play a regula-

14. John Maynard Keynes, *The General Theory of Employment, Interest and Money* (New York: Harcourt, Brace & World, First Harbinger ed., 1964), p. 3. (Keynes's use of the word *classical* is not strictly correct, for actually the phrase *the classical economists* was originally used by Karl Marx and referred to Ricardo and his predecessors, including Adam Smith.)

tory role and insure that the free play of self-interest in the commodity and resource markets will lead to results that are desirable for the whole economy. Adam Smith, the father of modern economic analysis, was the first economist to develop the concept of a self-adjusting market economy. In the *Wealth of Nations* he made his famous statement to the effect that every producer, in seeking to promote his own gain, is led by "an invisible hand to promote an end that was no part of his intention."[15] This end is, of course, the general well-being, or the public interest.

The second underlying assumption of the classical economists was that man is a rational being. Rationality to the classical economists meant essentially the "pleasure-pain" calculus. Man, in other words, was a creature who sought to avoid pain and achieve pleasure. In all his activities, including those pertaining to economics, he would rationally attempt to order his affairs so as to maximize pleasure and minimize pain. The balancing of pleasure against pain—or gain against cost—is, according to the classical view, the strategic, motivating force in the economic system. As a consumer, man attempted to maximize the satisfaction derived from the expenditure of income; whereas as a resource owner or entrepreneur, he sought to maximize the return obtained from the sale of the goods and resources at his disposition. On the basis of this sweeping assumption concerning human nature, the classical economists constructed through deductive logic an elegant and complex structure of economic analysis, much of which remains valid and in use.

The Three Building Blocks of the Classical Theory of Employment

The phrase *the classical theory of employment* is to some extent a misnomer because none of the writings of the leading classical economists contains an explicit account of what were thought to be the chief determinants of the level of income and employment. Nevertheless, there exists in the literature of classical economics basic ideas relating to employment, which, when brought together, constitute a logical and coherent explanation of how the employment level is determined. Awareness of the existence of these ideas has largely come about since the publication of Keynes's *General Theory*. Since Keynes asserted that a major objective of his own treatise was to refute the classical theory, it was inevitable that the publication of *The General Theory* would stimulate thought and discussion among professional economists concerning the nature of the class-

15. Adam Smith, *An Inquiry into the Nature and Causes of the Wealth of Nations*, (New York: Modern Library, Cannan ed., 1937), p. 423.

ical system. As a result we now have a reasonably clear conception of classical employment theory.

In essence, the classical theory of employment consists of three propositions. The first of these is a theory of the demand for and the supply of labor, which was derived from the economics of the individual firm and generalized to apply to the economy as a whole. The second pertains to the level of effective demand for the economy as a whole. The third involves a theory of the general level of prices. Our discussion of classical employment theory will consist of a detailed analysis of each of these three building blocks of the classical system. First, though, we need to look at some underlying assumptions.

Some Microeconomic Foundations for Classical Analysis

To understand how the classical economists developed an explanation of the over-all employment level using schedules for the *aggregate* demand for and supply of labor, we must examine some basic propositions drawn from traditional economic analysis pertaining to the business firm and its behavior. There are two such key propositions: the concept of the production function (including the notion of diminishing productivity) and the principle of profit maximization.

Let us begin with the production function, a concept introduced earlier in our discussion of potential GNP. If we assume—as classical analysis does—that the quantity and quality of capital and natural resouces as well as the level of technology are fixed,[16] then the output of the individual firm will depend upon the quantity of labor it employs. At this point the profit maximization principle enters the picture. Classical economics assumes that the entrepreneur always attempts to maximize his profits; consequently, he will be guided by the profit-maximization principle in the use of labor just as he is in determining the appropriate level of output for his firm's operations. Essential to the most profitable use of labor is the principle of diminishing returns (or productivity).

According to the principle of diminishing productivity, the additional product resulting from the employment by the firm of additional units of labor will become smaller and smaller as the total labor used increases. In more technical language this principle means that in response to increased employment the *marginal physical product* of additional units of labor will decline. What interests the firm is the yield which results from the employment of additional amounts of labor. This depends not only upon the additional output it gets from additional labor—that is, the marginal physical product—but also on the price at which the additional

16. This is a standard assumption made in microeconomic analysis for the short run; that is, a period in which plant size is fixed and output varies only within the confines of the existing plant size.

↑ N, $\xrightarrow{\text{eventually}}$ ↓ MPP

units of output are sold. For the sake of simplicity, let us assume the firm operates in a purely competitive market. Insofar as the firm is concerned, this means that all output can be sold at a constant price. Because of diminishing marginal productivity, though, the *value* of the firm's marginal physical product will inevitably decline as more labor is employed.

Profit maximization requires that the firm adjust its level of operations to the point at which the value of additional output is just equal to the cost of that output. When this principle is applied to employment, it means that the firm should adjust its employment to that point at which the cost for the last units of labor hired is just equal to the value of the marginal physical product of that labor. If this is done the firm will be in a position of equilibrium in respect to its employment of labor. The cost to the firm of the additional (or marginal) amounts of employment depends upon the number of additional workers hired and the prevailing money wage. Thus, the firm's equilibrium position with respect to the employment it is willing to offer in a purely competitive situation is one in which the marginal physical product of the last workers hired multiplied by the price at which the product sells is equal to the number of workers in the last group hired multiplied by the money wage at which they are hired.

The Real Wage and the Employment Level

At this point it is essential to introduce the concept of the *real wage.* The *real wage* is the purchasing power of a given money wage, which depends upon the relationship between the money wage and the general price level. Symbolically, the real wage, W, can be defined as the money wage, w, divided by the general price level, p.

$$W = \frac{w}{p} \tag{4-9}$$

The real wage will fall if the general price level rises while money wages remain constant, because in such a situation the purchasing power of any given money wage would decline. The reverse will be true if the money wage increases while the general price level remains constant.

Let us now return to our discussion of the firm and examine how its equilibrium position will be affected by a change in *either* the general price level or in money wage rates. If we assume that our firm has an equilibrium position, then a fall in the money rate will upset this equilibrium by reducing the cost to the firm of the marginal physical product of the last group of workers hired, assuming no change in the product price. If this happens, the firm can employ additional labor. In fact, the profit-maximization principle requires that it do just that, but as additional workers are employed their marginal physical product will decline. Eventually, the firm will reach a new equilibrium position at which once again the value to the firm of the marginal physical product of the last group of workers hired will be just equal to their cost to the firm. *But it will be an equilibrium at a higher level of employment.* What is the significance of the foregoing? It is tantamount to saying that the employment level is an inverse function of the real wage, for if the money wage declines while the general price level remains unchanged, real wages will have declined. The same result will be obtained if the general price level rose while the money wage remained fixed. This would disturb the firm's equilibrium by increasing the value of the marginal physical product of the last group of workers hired and thus necessitate the same sort of upward adjustment in the employment level.

In classical thinking, therefore, the demand for labor is a function of the *real wage*, a proposition expressed as follows in equation form:

$$N = f(W) \tag{4–10}$$

The Aggregate Demand Schedule for Labor

The equilibrium we have just described pertains to the employment decision of the individual firm, but the same reasoning may be applied to the economy as a whole. For short periods of time, for the economy as a whole, as well as for the individual firm, labor is the variable input. Thus, employment for the whole economy can be increased up to the point at which the marginal product of the last increment of employed workers is just equal to the real wage. For the economy as a whole this is a condition of employment equilibrium. If ΔY stands for the change in real output and ΔN for the change in employment level, than $\Delta Y/\Delta N$ is the marginal product of labor for the whole economy. The equilibrium condition, that is, the employment level at which the marginal product equals the real wage, is thus

$$\frac{\Delta Y}{\Delta N} = \frac{w}{p} \tag{4–11}$$

By clearing fractions we arrive at the necessary condition for profit maximization:

$$\Delta Yp = \Delta Nw \tag{4–12}$$

In this equation the monetary value of the last increment of output equals the monetary cost producing this last increment of output.

The importance of the above is that the aggregate demand curve for labor is conceptually identical with the individual firm's demand schedule for labor. The aggregate demand schedule slopes downward to the right and, other things being equal, the volume of employment for the whole economy must vary inversely with the level of real wages. Figure 4–5 shows this relationship. Here in essence is the classical concept of the economy's total demand for labor. We may note in passing that Keynes in *The General Theory* accepted the view that demand for labor is inversely related to the real wage. He did not accept classical thinking with respect to the total (aggregate) supply of labor, however, a topic to which we now turn.

The Aggregate Supply Schedule for Labor

Classical ideas concerning the supply of labor may be expressed algebraically in the equation:

$$N' = f(W) \tag{4–13}$$

In this equation N' represents the number of workers in the labor force actively seeking employment. Supply, however, may be interpreted to mean not only the number of workers but the hours of labor supplied by both old and new workers. The equation simply states however interpreted that the supply of labor is a positive function of the real wage;

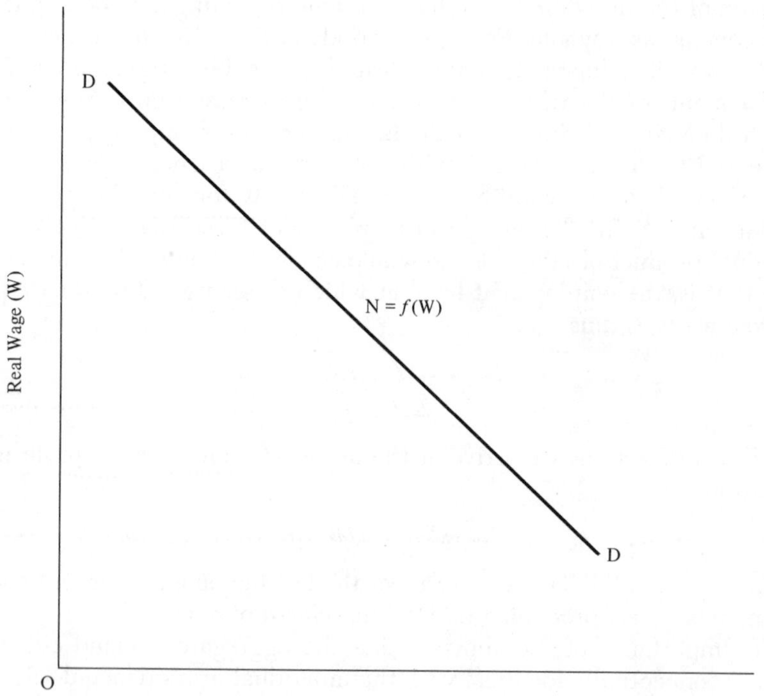

FIGURE 4–5. The Classical Demand Schedule for Labor

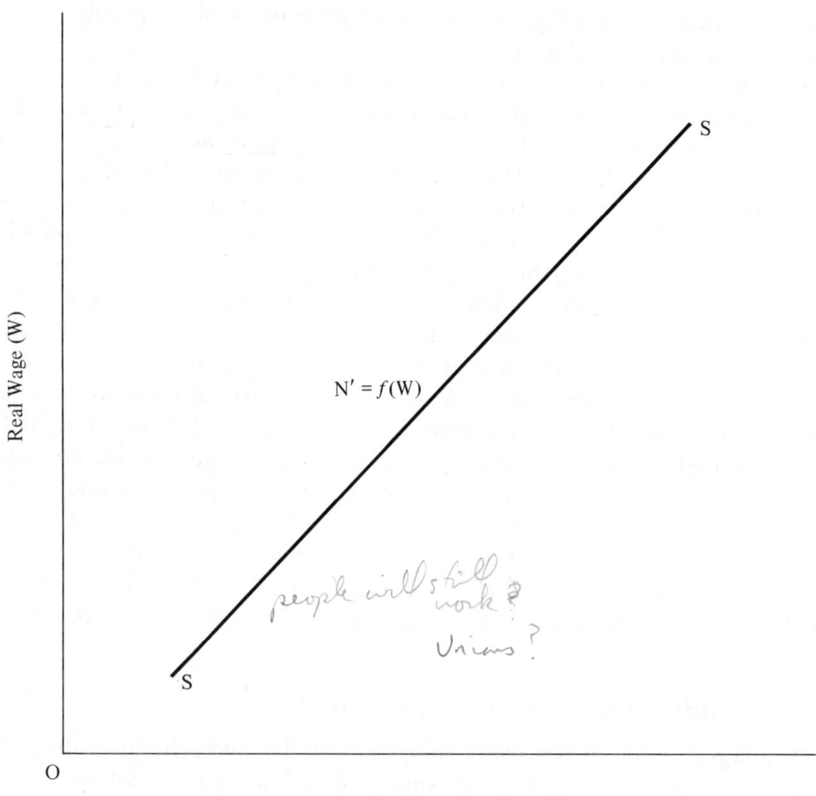

FIGURE 4–6. The Classical Supply Schedule of Labor

hence, the supply curve of labor in the classical system has a positive slope. This is shown in Figure 4–6.

The view that the number of workers seeking employment is a function of the real wage rests partly on the classical assumption that the worker, in offering his services in the labor market, seeks to maximize his income in the same way that the entrepreneur seeks to maximize his profit. Keynes, in speaking of this postulate of the classical analysis, said it means that the utility of the wage associated with a given volume of employment will be just equal to the disutility of that amount of employment.[17] Stated differently, the real wage represents that which is necessary to overcome the irksomeness (or disutility) of work and thus induce people to become employed. What this means is that there must be a "tradeoff" between work and leisure, a balancing of the gain to be gotten from consuming the goods and services which the money wage will buy (the real wage) and value of leisure to the individual. Since lei-

17. John Maynard Keynes, *The General Theory*, p. 5.

sure has value, a rational person will give some or all of it up only if he or she is rewarded for so doing.

The functional relationship between the supply of labor and the real wage is also based upon the classical assumption that workers and other resource owners do not suffer from the *money illusion.* The term *money illusion* was coined by the American economist Irving Fisher and refers to "a failure to perceive that the dollar or any other unit of money expands and shrinks in value."[18] In other words, the monetary unit is believed to be stable in value, and thus a rise in money income is considered, *ipso facto,* a rise in real income. Under these circumstances—that is, an economy suffering from the money illusion—the supply of labor could just as easily be a function of the money wage as the real wage. But this is not the classical view of the matter. Money, to the classical economist, is fundamentally a medium of exchange, a means to an end; they thought the use of money should not obscure the fact that basically the economic process is concerned with an exchange of goods for goods. Money is significant only because it is more convenient to have a generally accepted medium of exchange than it is to resort to barter. The implication of such a view is that resource owners, including workers, will value the services of their resources in terms of the real returns they can command.

The Equilibrium Level of Employment

The significance in the classical system of the two schedules discussed —the demand for labor and the supply of labor—is that, when brought together, they uniquely determine both the employment level and the real wage. Moreover, the classical demand and supply schedules for labor necessarily intersect at the level of full employment. The process by which employment and real wage are mutually determined in the classical analysis is depicted in Figure 4–7.

In the figure, DD represents the demand schedule for labor, while SS is the supply schedule for labor. Given these two schedules, competition in the market among employers for workers and among workers for employment will drive the real wage and the employment level to the values represented at the point of intersection of the two schedules. As long as the two schedules do not shift, no other level of either employment or real wages can prevail. If, momentarily, real wages were at the level represented by W_1, the number of workers actually seeking employment would be equal to the distance ON'_1. But at the W_1 level of real wages the amount of labor demanded would be equal only to the distance ON_1 The distance $N_1N'_1$, consequently, represents the surplus of workers seeking employment at the momentarily prevailing level of real wages.

18. Irving Fisher, *The Money Illusion* (New York: Adelphi, 1928), p. 4.

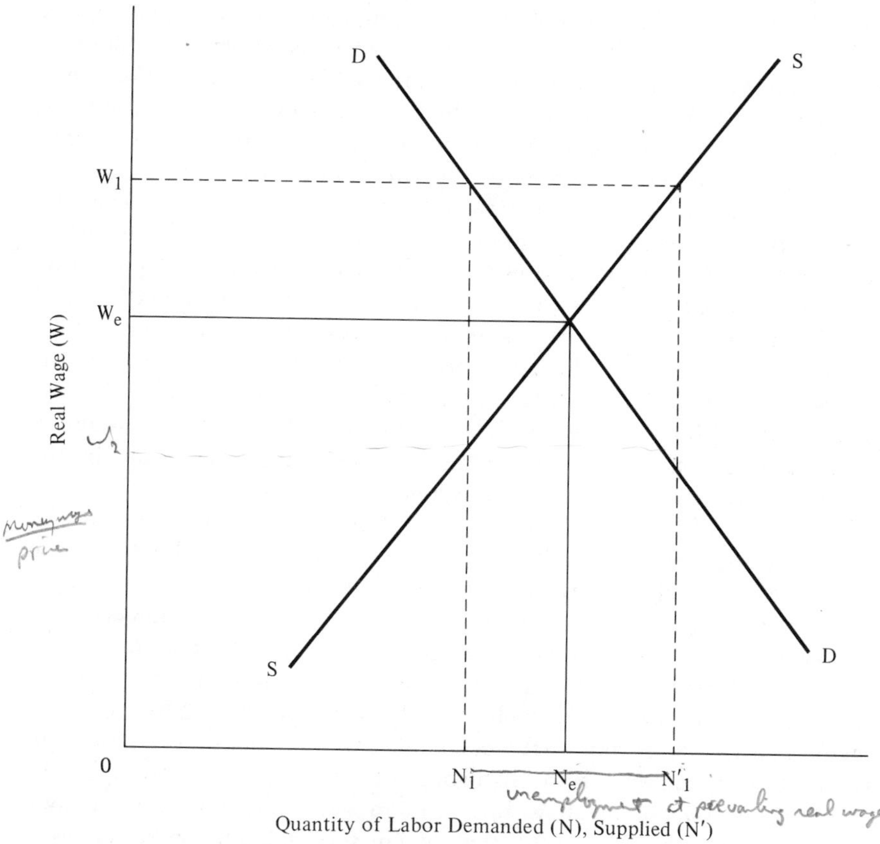

FIGURE 4–7. The Equilibrium Level of Employment

Competition for employment among these workers would lead some of them to offer their services to prospective employers at reduced money wages. As this happens, the real wage will decline, assuming other things remain constant, and employment will increase. Equilibrium in the labor market will prevail at the level of real wages W_e and the level of employment N_e. This is the essence of the classical explanation of how the economy's level of employment is determiend. The criticisms set forth by Keynes against this portion of classical employment theory will be examined at a later point in this chapter.

A Digression: The Concept of Equilibrium

The paragraph above illustrates one of the oldest and most important ideas used in economic analysis—the concept of an equilibrium. It is an idea borrowed from the physical sciences, where it describes a situation in which there is a balance between opposing forces. When this happens, the system of which the opposing forces are a part achieves a state in which any action taking place will repeat itself continuously. For example, the motion of the earth around the sun or the moon around the earth represents systems in a state of balance, so that the earth stays in its orbit around the sun and the moon in its orbit around the earth.

Equilibrium in a market situation treats economic phenomena as analogous to physical forces; they interact with one another, tending toward a state of balance. It is not a situation without motion, for an equilibirum price means that the inflow into the market (quantity supplied) is just equal to the outflow (quantity demanded). As long as there is no change in the balance between these two forces, price will not change. In the example above, the inflow is the supply of labor services and the outflow is the demand for the services of labor. Economists call such a situation *static equilibrium*, one in which there is no change over time in the underlying balance of forces in the system.

Equilibrium is a useful device in analyzing the many different types of situations encountered in the real-world economy. But it should not be confused with reality. It is rare—if ever—that we find a situation in the real world in which the economic forces are so precisely balanced that observed variables such as price, wages, income, production, and others remain fixed in their magnitude for a long period of time. Rather, equilibrium is an intellectual tool which can help us to understand how changes take place whenever any of the economic forces responsible for the outcome of economic events are disturbed. For example, we draw upon the equilibrium concept to show how and in what direction a price may change because the demand for the good or service being priced has been changed. The reader will be saved much misunderstading if he or she remembers that fundamentally equilibrium is a helpful concept but it is not reality.

Full Employment in the Classical Analysis

The equilibrium employment level determined by the intersection of the classical demand and supply schedues for labor has to be one of full employment. If any unemployment (aside from frictional unemployment) exists after equilibrium is obtained, it must be voluntary unemployment. This is true for essentially two reasons. First, the classical postulates imply that if nonfrictional unemployment persists after the equilibrium situation, it must be because some workers are demanding wages too high in relation to the marginal productivity of labor. If these workers are unemployed because of their refusal to accept lower money wages, their unemployment must be regarded as voluntary. If they would accept a reduction in money wages, the real wage would decline, other things being equal, and more employment would be forthcoming.

The second reason why the employment level is one of full employment is simply thaat the traditional theory maintains that *money* wage bargains between workers and entrepreneurs determine the *real* wage; consequently, the workers in general are in a position to determine their real wage (through money wage bargains), and, therefore, the level of employment. If this is true, it necessarily follows that any unemployment that actually exists at a given level of real wages has to be voluntary unemployment.

These classical conclusions, according to Keynes, are intended to apply to the whole body of labor in the economy, not just to the amount of labor utilized by a firm or by an industry. They are based, moreover, on the belief that a reduction in the general level of money wages in the economy will, in the short run, be accompanied by a similar, though not necessarily proportionate, reduction in real wages.

The Theory of Aggregate Demand

We observed that classical economic analysis purports to show how the volume of employment is determined in the economy, and why there cannot be any involuntary unemployment in the system resulting from a deficiency of the demand for labor. The level of employment determined in this matter is significant, too, because it also determines the level of production in the economy. Real income, according to our earlier discussion of the classical production function, is dependent on the level of employment; consequently, once we have determined the employment level, we have simultaneously determined output in the economy.

But these facts raise another question pertaining to the possibility of involuntary unemployment for the economy. For the economy as a whole, output is the same thing as real income, but real income is necessarily the basis of any economy's demand. The monetary value of current output is the same thing as the economy's gross money income. This means as Keynes phrased it, that "the income derived in the aggregate by all the elements in the community concerned in a productive activity necessarily has a value exactly equal to the *value* of the output."[19] This being the case, it raises the interesting possibility that there might be involuntary unemployment in the economy because of a deficiency of total or aggregate demand. If income (money or real) is, in fact. the basis for demand, is it not possible that the economy as a whole may fail to generate sufficient demand to consume all the goods and services produced in a particular income period? If this happened, there could be involuntary unemployment not because of any error in the classical analysis of the nature of the demand for and supply of labor, but because the economy as a whole failed to spend income at a rate sufficient to justify production at the level

19. Keynes, p. 20.

associated with a given volume of employment. In short, unemployment might result from overproduction.

Say's Law of Markets

The possibility of this kind of involuntary unemployment is denied by classical economic theory. It is denied because of the general acceptance by classical economists of a curious doctrine known as Say's Law of Markets. Jean Baptiste Say was a French economist of the early nineteenth century who disseminated and popularized the ideas of Adam Smith in France and elsewhere on the European contiment. His Law of Markets, which Galbraith described as having had the status of an article of faith with classical economists for over a hundred years,[20] is the formal expression of the idea that widespread and involuntary unemployment because of general overproduction is impossible. To put the matter slightly differently, there cannot be any involuntary unemployment because of a deficiency of total demand.

The simplest possible statement of this doctrine is that supply creates its own demand. The meaning of this statement, as pointed out by Keynes in his *The General Theory*, is that in some sense the whole of the costs of production must necessarily be spent in the aggregate, directly or indirectly, on purchasing the product. Every producer who brings goods to the market (that is, creates supply) does so in order to exchange them for other goods (that is, creates demand). Classical economics assumed that the end purpose of all economic activity is consumption, but consumption depends upon income, which in turn is derived from production. In consequence of this, every act of production must necessarily represent the demand for something.

The conclusion that follows from the assertion that all supply is potentially the demand for something is that there cannot be any general overproduction or deficiency of total demand for the economy as a whole. True, there may be some misdirection of production and consequently an oversupply of some commodities, but the pricing mechanism will correct this and cause some entrepreneurs to shift their output to other and more profitable lines. But such oversupply cannot be the case for the whole economy because the act of production always creates sufficient value or purchasing power to take off the market all goods and services produced. If there cannot be deficiency of total demand in the economy, it also follows that any involuntary unemployment because of the phenomenon of overproduction is impossible.

The most explicit statement in English of Say's Law of Markets is to be found in John Stuart Mill's *Principles of Political Economy*, a famed trea-

20. John Kenneth Galbraith, *American Capitalism: The Concept of Countervailing Power* (Boston: Houghton Mifflin, 1952), p. 22.

tise that represents one of the best and most comprehensive statements of the classical viewpoint. In a chapter devoted to a discussion of the impossibility of overproduction, Mill poses the following question and then proceeds to answer it with an express statement of the principle embodied in Say's Law.

> Is it . . . possible that there should be a deficiency of demand for all commodities, for want of means of payment? Those who think so cannot have considered what it is which constitutes the means of payment for commodities. *It is simply commodities.* Each person's means of paying for the productions of other people consists of those which he himself possesses. All sellers are inevitably and *ex vi termini* buyers. Could we suddenly double the productive powers of the country we should double the supply of commodities in every market, but we should by the same stroke double the purchasing power. Every one would bring a double demand as well as supply: everybody would be able to buy twice as much because everybody would have twice as much to offer in exchange. It is a sheer absurdity that all things should fall in value and that all producers should, in consequence, be insufficiently remunerated.[21]

As stated by Mill, Say's Law is expressed in barter terms. But the classical economists believed that the principle was equally valid if money were introduced into the analysis. In a monetary economy Say's Law is interpreted to mean that money income will automatically and continuously be spent at the same rate at which it is being generated through the act of production. If this is true, then money makes no difference and supply will continue to create demand.

Say's Law and the Classical Theory of Interest

One possible trouble spot in this otherwise harmonious picture is saving. Saving, as defined earlier, is the nonexpenditure of current income for currently produced goods and services. Thus, if some persons or groups in the economy save a portion of their money income there may be a deficiency of aggregate demand equal to the amounts being saved. This possibility, too, was denied by the classical economists, because, in their view, saving is nothing more than another form of spending. Specifically, it represents spending for capital goods. All saving, in other words, is automatically transformed into investment spending. Thus the act of saving cannot give rise to a deficiency of total demand or an interruption in the flow of income and expenditure. This belief of the classical economists is illustrated in the following statement by Alfred Marshall:

21. John Stuart Mill, *Principles of Political Economy* (London: Longmans, Green, 1936), book II, chap. XIV, sec. 1, p. 551. (*Ex vi termini* in Mill's quotation means: "By the meaning of the word.")

> The whole of a man's income is expended in the purchase of services and commodities. It is indeed commonly said that a man spends some portion of his income and saves another. But it is a familiar economic axiom that a man purchases labour and commodities with that portion of his income which he saves just as much as he does with that he is said to spend. He is said to spend when he seeks to obtain present enjoyment from the services and commodities which he purchases. He is said to save when he causes the labour and the commodities which he purchases to be devoted to the production of wealth from which he expects to derive the means of enjoyment in the future.[22]

The mechanism in classical thought that transforms saving (nonspending) into investment (spending for capital goods) is the rate of interest. The classical theory of interest is a necessary part of the classical theory of employment because it is the means whereby Say's Law remains valid in a monetary economy. Interest in the classical system brings the demand for investment into equlibrium with the willingness to save. Since investment represents the demand for investible resources, and saving represents their supply interest is the price at which the two are equated.

Figure 4–8 presents geometrically the essence of classical thinking with respect to the rate of interest. In the figure, DD is the demand for investible resources, while SS is saving, or the supply of investible resources. Since saving is nonconsumption, the act of saving releases resources from the production of consumer goods and services. The demand for these resources is similar to the demand for any economic resource, which is to say that it depends basically upon the productivity of the resource. Thus, the DD schedule in Figure 4–8 has its origins in the productivity of capital.

The latter is one of the key ideas in the entire fabric of classical economic thinking. Capital is not important simply as a form of spending which must, in a money-using economy, offset saving if Say's Law is to hold. It is also important because it is the chief means by which the economy progresses, the instrument for insuring economic growth and the enhancement of the material standard of life. Capital is wanted because it is productive, which is to say that the investment of resources in equipment and structures will yield an enlarged flow of output in the future. These aspects of the classical view of capital and its importance are analyzed in Chapter 15 which focuses on the principles of economic growth.

According to Figure 4–8 if individuals, households, and business firms attempt to save more out of current income than business firms want to spend for new capital equipment at the prevailing market rate of interest, forces will be set in motion that will reduce saving and increase investment until they are brought into equality with one another. For example, if the market rate of interest is at i_1 in the figure, this means that saving

22. Alfred Marshall, *The Pure Theory of Domestic Values* (London: London School of Economics and Political Science, 1949), p. 34.

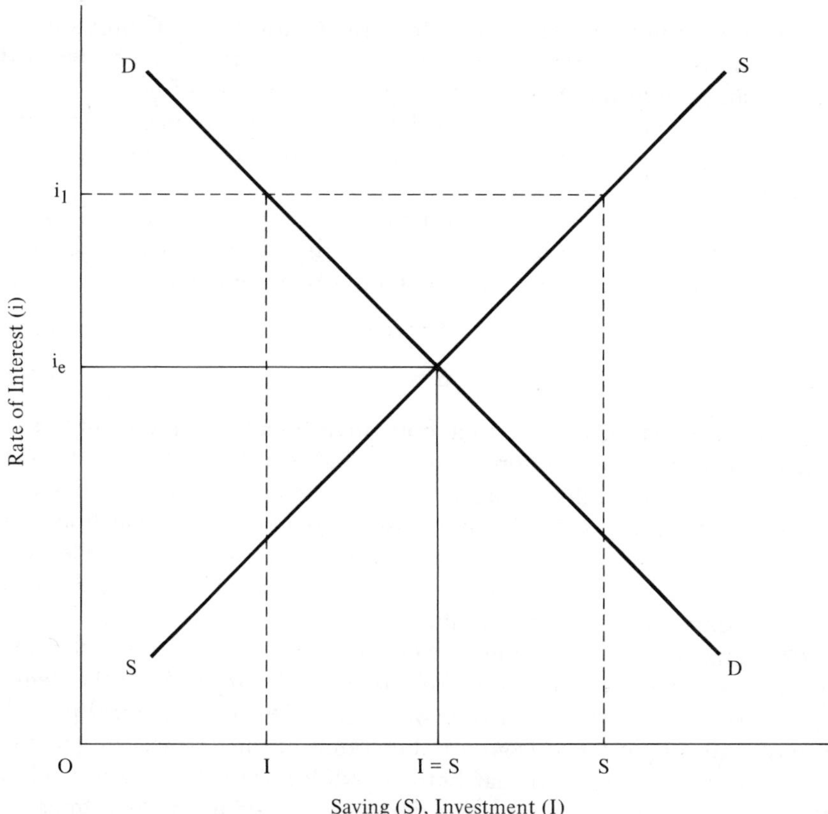

FIGURE 4–8. The Classical Theory of Interest

groups in the economy are attempting to save more than is wanted for the purchase of new capital equipment. But this disequilibrium will cause the rate of interest to fall, and as it falls the incentive to save will be lessened, while the incentive to invest (i.e., to purchase capital goods) will increase. Market adjustment will continue until the market rate of interest has reached the level at which the demand for and the supply of savings are equated. In Figure 4–8 this condition prevails at the indicated interest rate of i_e. As Keynes stated, the rate of interest in classical theory is the nexus that unites decisions to abstain from present consumption—that is, saving—with decisions to provide for future consumption—that is, investment. As long as this is the case, Say's Law remains intact.

This underscores another important classical idea, one which we shall explore further in Chapter 7 on investment spending and investment finance. Keynes saw interest as a nexus which united decisions to save and decisions to invest, but classical economists viewed it as the price which allocates output between present and future consumption. Marshall for example, described the act of saving as a decision to postpone consumption to the future, and the act of investment as a way of providing for future consumption. Hence, interest plays an allocative role between the present and the future. Since it also represents the cost of getting "investible resources," interest becomes a determinant of the amount of investment taking place. This is another idea which will be explored fully in Chapter 7.

To summarize, the following equations capture the essence of classical thinking about the rate of interest. All of the ideas discussed above are subsumed in the following investment and saving functions:

$$I = f(i) \tag{4–14}$$

$$S = f(i) \tag{4–15}$$

The above equations assert that both investment, I, and saving, S, are functions of the rate of interest. Since I and S in the equations (and the schedules of Figure 4–8)) are *ex ante* concepts, equilibrium exists only when I and S are equal. This prevails at the point of intersection of the investment and saving schedules shown in Figure 4–8. If $S > I$, the rate of interest will fall, and if $I > S$, the rate of interest will rise. Algebraically, the necessary condition for equilibrium is that $I - S = 0$.

One final point concerning the classical theory of interest should be mentioned. This has to do with the *interest elasticity* of both the demand scheduled for the supply schedule of savings. This is a technical point but one of some significance from a policy point of view, since, in general, it is the classical contention that both schedules are highly interest elastic. What this means is that both the demand for saving for investment and the supply of savings are sensitive to small changes in the market rate of interest. As a consequence, only minor changes are needed in the market rate of interest to bring about equilibrium between investment and savings. Through changes in the money supply and the rate of interest, monetary policy can bring about new levels of investment expenditure and thereby regulate the income and employment level. For most of the classical economists, however, questions of this sort were academic, because the whole structure of classical employment theory was designed to show that full employment is the normal state of affairs in the economy. Nevertheless, the reader should recognize that the classical assumptions concerning the interest elasticity of savings and investment schedules do carry with them certain specific policy implications.

The Theory of the Price Level

The final building block in the classical structure is the theory of how the general level of prices in the economy is determined. This theory also explains the role that money occupies in the classical scheme. Classical thinking about the price level is contained in what is known as the *quan-*

tity theory of money. In actuality there is no single quantity theory of money with which all the classical economists were in agreement. But the various versions of the quantity theory all focus attention on the relationship between the quantity of money in circulation and the general level of prices.

A good starting point for discussion of the quantity theory of money is the *equation of exchange*, which may be expressed algebraically in the following form:

$$M^o v = p \cdot Y \qquad (4\text{–}16)$$

In the equation M^o is the money supply; v the income velocity of circulation (that is, the number of times each unit of money turns over in income and product transactions during a given time period); p the general price level; and Y real income. Expressed in this form, the equation of exchange is simply a truism, for it must follow that the quantity of money multiplied by the number of times each unit of money is used in a period equals the goods and services produced during the period times the average price level for the goods and services. Each side of the equation represents a different way of describing the same thing. A truism, it should be emphasized, does not explain; it is not a "theory." But, as the following comments indicate, it may provide a convenient starting point for development of a theory.

To do this it is necessary to make assumptions about some of the variables contained in the truistic equation of exchange. This is what the classical economist did. In so doing they developed a theory, the *quantity theory of money*. This theory describes some basic causal relationships with respect to the role of money in the economy. For instance, the classical economists assumed that the velocity of circulation v was relatively stable. The velocity of circulation was believed to be deeply rooted in the habit patterns of the community and hence slow to change. Since full employment was the presumed outcome in the classical scheme, output also had to be a constant. Thus the only magnitudes that varied in the short run were the money supply, M^o, and the general price level, p.

To understand fully the classical relationship between the money supply and the general price level, it is first necessary to recall the classical attitude toward money. To the classical economists money was simply a medium of exchange. Its only important function was to facilitate the real process of exchange, which was one of exchanging goods for goods. As a consequence, the classical economists saw no reason why people would want to hold money as such. If an individual came into possession of additional amounts of money this simply meant that he had additional purchasing power at his disposal and, given the medium-of-exchange function of money, he would choose to spend it. In the classical view, therefore, more money in circulation in the economy could only mean more spending.

Let us see what this means in view of the above-mentioned classical assumptions concerning the stability of both N and Y. What will happen, in other words, if there is an increase in the supply of money in the economy? An increase in the money supply means more spending; if output cannot change because the economy is always at full employment, and if the velocity of circulation remains stable, then the only thing that can change is the general price level. In effect, then, the classical quantity theory of money asserts that the general price level, p, is a function of the supply of money M^o.

$$p = f(M^o) \tag{4–17}$$

It should be noted that this general statement does not tell us exactly how p varies with changes in M^o. A rigid version of the quantity theory holds that prices always vary in exact proportion to changes in the money supply, a view that also implies that v and Y do not vary at all in 4–17. Less rigid versions maintain that the price level tends to vary directly with changes in the money supply, although not necessarily in the same proportion. The latter is the more meaningful interpretation.

The classical theory of the price level can be depicted geometrically, as is done in Figure 4–9. Real income is shown on the vertical axis, while the general price level is charted on the horizontal axis. The $M^o v$ curve provides the necessary link between real income (output) and the price level. In mathematical terms this curve is known as a *rectangular hyperbola,* which is one in which the product of coordinate values on the two axes is a constant. This means that with fixed values for the money supply and the velocity of circulation, real income can rise only if the price level falls and the price level can rise only if real income declines. As long as the money supply and velocity are fixed, real income and the general price level must move inversely to one another.

The way in which an increase in the money supply will affect the general price level can be shown in the figure. Assume that Y_1 is the full employment level of output and that $M_1^o v$ represents the initial supply of money in the economy. Velocity is also a constant and given by v. Under these circumstances the general price level will be p_1. What will happen if the curve representing a constant volume of expenditure shifts upward to $M_2^o v$? Since we have assumed that the economy is already at the full employment level, real income Y cannot change. The only thing that can change is the general price level; it will rise to the level indicated by p_2 in the figure.

A Diagrammatic Summary

We have discussed the major propositions that make up the classical theory of employment. It is appropriate at this point to draw these propositions together and briefly summarize the essential features of the classi-

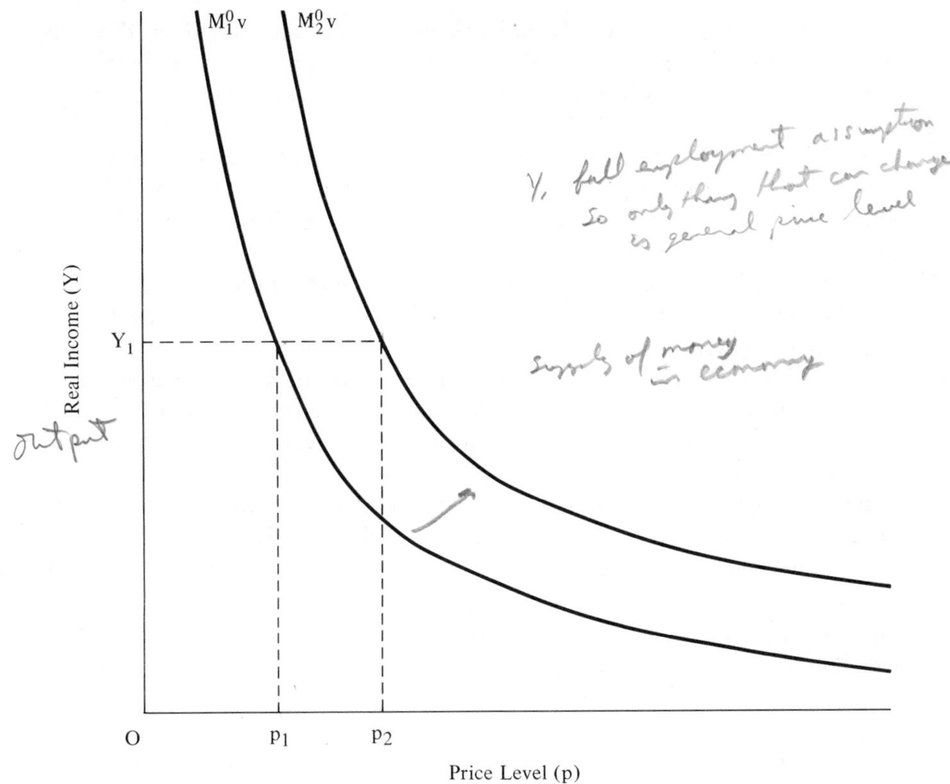

FIGURE 4–9. The Classical Quantity Theory of Money

cal theory. Figure 4–10 portrays geometrically the key elements in the classical theory of employment. We may summarize these as follows:

1. Part A in the diagram has two parts. The upper diagram depicts once again the classical production function. Its purpose is to show that with a *given* technology and a *fixed* quantity of resources other than labor, output depends uniquely upon the level of employment. To explain what determines the employment level, we must turn to the bottom portion of Part A, where, once again, are the classical demand and supply curves for labor. Interaction between demand and supply as shown here determines both the level of employment and the real wage. The classical equilibrium shown in Part A is a unique one involving output, employment, and the real wage.

2. Turn now to Part B. In the lower portion of Part B we introduce a new curve, one labeled w/p. This shows the price level (on the horizontal axis). The slope of the line (w/p) measures the real wage as determined by the demand for and supply of labor given in the lower portion of Part A. The upper portion of Part B shows how the monetary value of the real output level—determined from the production function in Part A—de-

pends upon the money supply and velocity. If the latter is given, then the money supply becomes the prime determinant of the price level and hence the monetary value of any real output level. By changing any of the variables in the classical system or shifting a relevant function, it is possible to trace through the impact of any such change upon output, real wages, employment, the price level, or money wages. To gain familiarity with the workings of the classical "model," the reader should work out such changes on his or her own.

3. Finally, Part C shows how Say's Law fits into the analysis by assuring the necessary equality between savings and investment so that there is no interruption in spending flows because of any deficiency in total demand. Note that in the classical model the rate of interest cannot have any impact upon the output level; its role is to determine the division of output between investment and consumption, as well as to insure that all savings flow into investment spending.

Before we turn to a discussion of the broad policy implications of the classical analysis, two things need to be said about the model we have been discussing. In the first place, the system is so constructed that it tends automatically toward a level of full employment. The demand for and the supply of labor curves have the role of determining the actual employment level, but they are so conceived that this employment level is

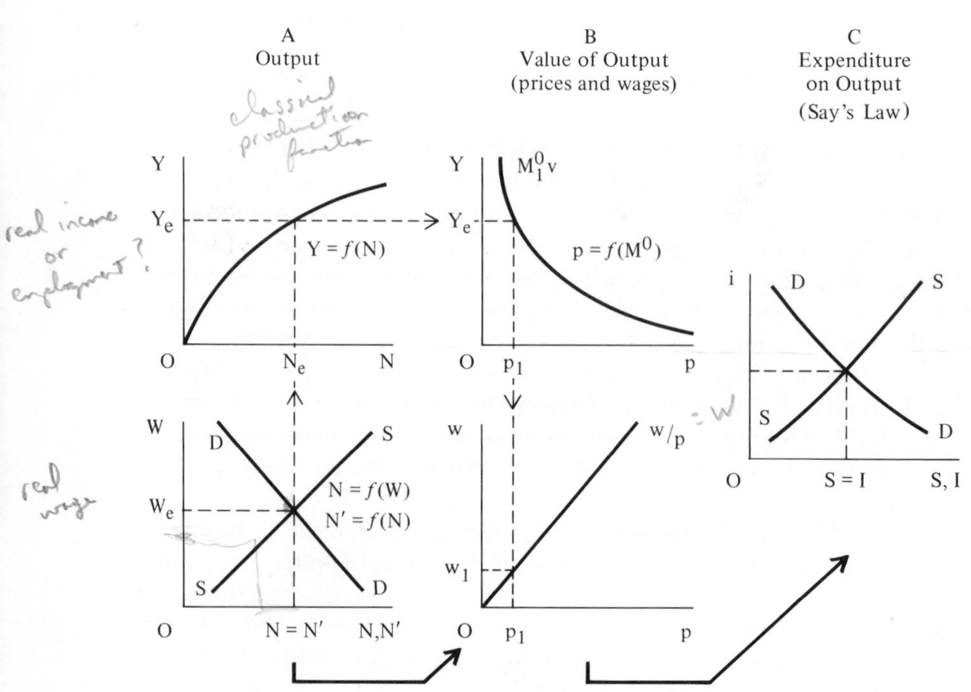

by definition one of full employment. Moreover, Say's Law of Markets, in conjunction with the classical theory of interest, makes certain that there is no possibility of involuntary unemployment in the system because of any deficiency of aggregate demand. Second, if there is within the system any temporary deviation away from the full employment equilibrium, the appropriate remedy is clearly indicated. This is a reduction in the real wage, which can be brought about either by an increase in the money supply, with its consequent effects on the general price level, or by a cut in money wages.

Policy Implications of the Classical Theory

The classical ideas just discussed consist of a structure of abstract ideas and relationships that purport to explain how the economy works in the determination of the income and employment level. These ideas form a body of economic theory. But like most other sets of theoretical ideas in economics, this particular set contains within itself significant implications for public policy.

The classical theory of employment implies a *laissez faire*, "hands-off" (or noninterference) policy that minimizes the extent to which government intervenes in the operation of the economy. In a broad sense there are two major reasons why government might intervene in the economy.[23] The first is that imperfections in the market economy may lead to an undue concentration of economic power in private hands. The second is that the private or market sector of the economy may not function sufficiently well to provide jobs for all members of the labor force actively seeking employment.

Actually both of the above possibilities are denied by the classical system. As we saw earlier, classical economists assumed that competition is a normal characteristic of the economy. The kind of competition they envisaged as being dominant in the economy was the *atomistic* variety, in which the number of firms in every industry is so great in relation to the demand for the output of the industry that no single firm can exercise any control over the price at which its product is sold. If no firm is in a position to exercise any control whatsoever over price, no firm (or person) can possess any real economic power over other firms (or persons). All firms and persons are at the mercy of the impersonal market forces of supply and demand. If this is a correct evaluation of the situation in the economy, then there is no basis for intervention by the state for the sake

23. This is aside from the fact that there are certain activities necessary to the functioning of a complex society that can only be done by the state; for example, maintenance of law and order and provision for national defense.

of redressing any abuse of private economic power. The latter does not exist in the classical scheme.

The second reason for state intervention is the continued existence of a significant amount of *involuntary* unemployment. As we have seen, classical employment theory leads to the conclusion that involuntary unemployment on a large scale for anything more than brief periods is an impossibility. If the economy has an inherent and automatic tendency toward equilibrium at full employment, then there is no real need for public intervention on the ground that employment is inadequate. Under such circumstances *laissez faire* is the appropriate policy.

Competition plays a vital role in this respect because its presence within the economic system insures the flexibility of wages and prices, including the rate of interest. The system will move toward an equilibrium at full employment only if wages respond instantly to the least discrepancy between the demand for and supply of labor in the market. The same holds true for the rate of interest, for, unless interest responds to any discrepancy between the demand for and supply of saving, the system will not attain the equality between saving and investment necessary to insure the working of Say's Law in a monetary economy. Price and wage flexibility stems from competition, and the more highly competitive the system, the more responsive wages and prices will be to market forces.

The Collapse of Classical Employment Theory

The classical theory of employment is no longer widely accepted, either by the general public or by academic and business economists. Few people today really believe that there is any automatic tendency for the economic system to reach equilibrium at the level of full employment. In addition, there are few economists who still support the classical analysis as a good theoretical explanation of how the employment level is actually determined.

The collapse of the classical theory of employment ushered in a new phase of economic thought, for this theory had enjoyed the support of practically all economists of any importance for nearly a century. This collapse can be attributed to two major factors: the experience of the Great Depression, and the appearance of an alternative—and more feasible—explanation of how the employment level is determined.

Until the 1930s, as Galbraith has pointed out, the American economy had never experienced a deep and prolonged depression.[24] In the past

24. Galbraith, p. 67.

there had been periods of unemployment and falling prices, but these were rarely of long duration, and were generally followed by a prompt recovery of the economic system to high employment levels. Until the 1930s, in other words, the experience of the American economy tended to confirm the classical theory and its conclusion that full employment was a normal condition. The fluctuations in income and employment which did take place could be explained as resulting from frictions and imperfections in the market, or else as the consequence of war and its aftermath.

All of this changed with the depression that began with the cataclysmic collapse of stock market values in the autumn of 1929 and continued until the wartime mobilization of the 1940s once again brought full employment to the American economy. For ten long years, serious and prolonged unemployment was the normal condition of the economy. Under these circumstances not even the staunchest defender of the classical analysis could seriously maintain that there existed within the economy forces that would automatically generate continuous full employment. The Great Depression was a social catastrophe without previous parallel in American economic life; classical employment theory simply proved to be incapable of coping with such a phenomenon. We pointed out earlier that experience is the ultimate test of the validity of any theory, and on this basis the classical analysis was found wanting.

The second reason for the collapse of the classical employment theory was the appearance of an alternative theory during the decade of the 1930s. While it is true that the facts of experience in the 1930s were clearly not in accord with the classical analysis, it is equally true that facts alone will not destroy a theory. As James B. Conant, former president of Harvard University, has said, "It takes a new conceptual scheme to cause the abandonment of an old one."[25] This took place in 1936 when Keynes published his *The General Theory*, the intellectual foundation of all modern employment theory.

Keynes's purpose in *The General Theory* was twofold. In the first place, he sought to demonstrate the basic failings of the classical theory of employment not so much by appealing to the facts of experience, but rather by demonstrating that the theory itself was internally inconsistent and logically untenable at a number of points. Second, Keynes sought to construct an alternative theory, or explanation, of how the employment level is determined in a complex industrial society. He called his treatise *The General Theory of Employment, Interest and Money* because he believed that the techniques and analytical tools characteristic of classical thinking were applicable only in the special case of full employment, while his own analysis was applicable at all levels of employment.

25. James G. Conant, *On Understanding Science* (New Haven: Yale University Press, 1947), p. 89.

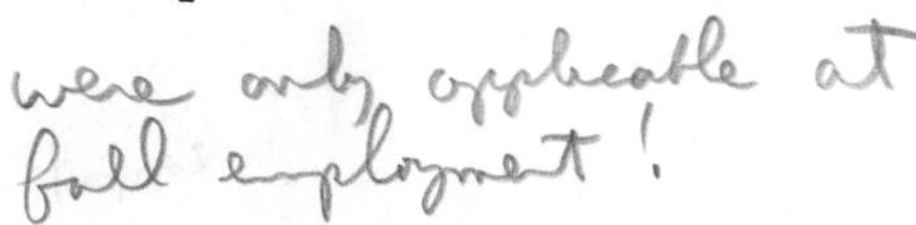
were only applicable at
full employment!

Keynes's theory of employment determination is basically the concern of the remaining chapters in Part II, but we may at this point allude briefly to his major criticisms of the classical theory, even though each of these will be examined later in more detail.

Keynes's criticism of the classical analysis is directed, first, at the classical view that the employment level and the real wage were determined by the intersection of the demand and supply schedules for labor; and second, at the idea that saving is, after all, nothing more than spending for capital goods. He refutes, in other words, the validity of Say's Law of Markets for a monetary economy.

In attacking the classical doctrine that the supply of and demand for labor determine both the real wage and the employment level, Keynes makes two points. He denies, in the first instance, that the supply of labor is a function of the real wage by pointing out that the workers do not normally withdraw from the labor market if there has been a fall in real wages as a result of a rise in prices with money wages unchanged.

> A fall in real wages due to a rise in prices with money wages unaltered, does not, as a rule, cause the supply of labor on offer at the current wage to fall below the amount actually employed prior to the rise of prices. To suppose that it does is to suppose that all those who are now unemployed though willing to work at the current wage will withdraw the offer of their labour in the event of a small rise in the cost of living.[26]

Keynes's second point concerns the relationship between money wages and prices. He refutes the notion that workers are in a position to determine the real wage and with it the volume of employment by the money-wage bargains they make with the employers. Workers cannot do this, he asserts, because money wages cannot move independently of the general level of prices. To prove his point Keynes utilizes analytical concepts developed by the classical economists in the area of price theory. Under conditions of pure competition and with a given demand schedule, prices will be governed by marginal costs expressed in money. This follows from the profit maximization principle which asserts that the firm will adjust output to the level at which marginal cost and marginal revenue are equal. Money wages will necessarily make up the major part of marginal costs. Consequently, any change in money-wage rates would cause prices to change in about the same proportion. If this analysis is correct, it means that changes in the money wage will not necessarily bring about any change in the real wage and with it a change in the employment level. Keynes thought that the classical economists were so preoccupied with the idea that prices depend on the quantity of money that they failed to see the implications inherent in their own analysis of the behavior of the business firm.

26. Keynes, p. 12.

The second major argument of Keynes strikes at the heart of Say's Law. In a monetary economy Say's Law reduces itself to the proposition that money income will auomatically be sent at the same rate at which it is being created by the process of production. Keynes contends in *The General Theory* that the classical economists reached this erroneous conclusion because they confused the proposition that all income must be spent at the same rate at which it is created with another proposition which is quite true, namely that the "income derived in the aggregate by all the elements in the community concerned in a productive activity necessarily has a value exactly equal to the *value* of that output."[27] In other words, there is a basic truth in Say's Law in the sense that output or productive activity is the source of income for the whole community, but it does not logically follow that income will necessarily be spent at a rate which will clear the market of all that is produced. Much of *The General Theory*, in fact, is devoted to showing why decisions to produce, i.e., to create income, will not necessarily always coincide with decisions to spend that income.

The classical theory of interest is a necessary part of Say's Law in a monetary economy, for the rate of interest joins the decision to save with the decision to invest. But this, too, is challenged by Keynes, who takes the commonsense view that decisions to save and decisions to invest are two different kinds of decisions that cannot be automatically linked together in any simple way. More importantly, he attempts to show through the development of an alternative theory that the rate of interest is not necessarily a nexus that unites the decision to save and the decision to invest. Once this link is severed between saving and investment, Say's Law breaks down and the way is open for the existence of involuntary unemployment due to a deficiency of total or aggregate demand.

Before concluding our summary of the Keynesian criticism of classical employment theory, one final point needs to be underscored. Although Keynes was a vigorous critic of the classical theory of employment, the reader should not conclude that Keynes rejected the whole of the classical tradition and body of economic analysis. Keynes explicitly accepted the validity of classical analysis in the area of price and distribution theory, as the following quote from *The General Theory* well illustrates:

> If we suppose the volume of output to be given, i.e., to be determined by forces outside the classical scheme of thought, then there is no objection to be raised against the classical analysis of the manner in which private self-interest will determine what in particular is produced, in what proportion the factors of production will be combined to produce it, and how the value of the final product will be distributed between them.[28]

27. Ibid., p. 20.
28. Ibid., p. 378.

In one other respect, Keynes was very much in harmony with the classical tradition, even though he rejected the employment theory of the classical economists. As we saw in our earlier discussion, the deductive approach was the typical methodology of classical analysis. In this sense Keynes remains close to the classical tradition because the methodology of *The General Theory* is basically deductive. This will become increasingly apparent in subsequent chapters.

5

Principles of Aggregate Supply and Demand

In this chapter we turn to a discussion of the principles which underlie modern employment theory, largely developed from the thought and writing of John Maynard Keynes. Specifically, the task of this chapter is to outline the essential characteristics of the modern theory, leaving to the chapters that follow a more detailed analysis of the component parts of the theoretical structure.

The Essence of the Income-Employment Problem

A logical point of departure for our study of income and employment determination is the concept of capacity. It will be recalled from the discussion in the previous chapter that capacity is defined as the economy's potential for the production of goods and services. If we begin with this concept, certain consequences logically follow. First, output will depend upon the extent to which this capacity is being utilized. This will be true up to the limits of capacity. Second, output will depend upon the level of employment as long as all resources other than labor are fixed. This brings us to the key question of modern employment theory: *What is it that determines the extent to which the economy's productive capacity is being utilized?*

In a sense the answer to this question is deceptively simple, for it is the *expectation* of the businessman that he will be able to sell what he produces which leads him to make use of the productive capacity at his disposal. The presumption here is that the output will be sold at prices that cover costs of production. Stated in more formal terms, productive capacity will be brought into use (or production will take place) whenever there exists the expectation that demand for the output will be sufficient to clear the market of what is being produced. Note carefully two points. First, this statement describes the conditions under which productive capacity will be utilized in a market economy, that is to say, an economy in which the basic decisions about what is to be produced and in what quantities are made by private individuals rather than public authorities. Second, the key word in the statement is *expectation*, which is a way of stressing the fact that production in a market economy is carried on, for the most part, in anticipation of demand.

If it is true that the expectation of demand is the essential condition required to bring productive capacity into use, it follows that *the theory of income determination in the modern economy is basically a theory of aggregate demand.* In other words, if we are to understand how the level of output and employment is actually determined, it is necessary that we understand how demand for the output of the whole economy is determined. In sum, aggregate demand is the crucial determinant of the level of income and employment during short periods when productive capacity is assumed to be relatively fixed. This is the central theme of *The General Theory.*

In the long run the income-employment problem is more complex. Over the long run productive capacity is subject to change. Thus, a long-run theory of income and employment determination must explain, first, changes in the economy's productive capacity over time; and, second, how aggregate demand adjusts over time to such changes. This is the essence of post-Keynesian growth theory which will be one of our concerns in Part IV.

The Aggregate Supply Schedule

The idea that there exists for the economy a given productive capacity which will be utilized in greater or lesser degree according to the aggregate of expectations held by entrepreneurs is represented in the aggregate supply schedule or function. As a concept, the aggregate supply schedule for the whole economy is very much like the supply schedule for any individual commodity. A typical supply curve for a commodity has a positive slope—that is, it slopes upward to the right—and shows the prices at which various amounts of the commodity will be forthcoming. It is an *ex ante* concept in the sense that it depicts the intended response of the suppliers of the commodity to varying circumstances. The schedule is, in effect, a series of *supply prices* for varying amounts of the commodity. The supply price for any particular quantity of a commodity is that price which will just induce the producer or supplier to continue to offer that quantity of the commodity on the market; thus the *supply schedule* shows the amounts of the commodity that will be forthcoming at any and all possible prices. The aggregate supply schedule represents not the response of a single producer supplying the market with a particular commodity, but the summation, in effect, of the responses of all producers supplying the whole of the output of the economy. It seeks to show, in other words, the conditions under which varying amounts of total output will be supplied or produced. It is in this sense that the aggregate supply schedule is conceptually similar to the ordinary supply schedule for a single commodity.

The Keynesian Aggregate Supply Function

In *The General Theory* Keynes defined the aggregate supply price of the output of a given amount of employment as "the expectation of proceeds which will just make it worth the while of the entrepreneur to give that employment."[1] What Keynes had in mind was a schedule which would show for any and all possible levels of employment the volume of receipts from the sale of output that would justify the varying quantities of employment. The receipts would have to be sufficient to cover all costs incurred by the entrepreneur plus a profit. Keynes believed that the entrepreneur would be seeking at all times to maximize his profit. The receipts —or expected proceeds—must cover costs plus profits for the economy's total employment in the same way that price must cover costs and a unit profit for the supply of a particular good or service. Such a schedule shows the amount of employment that entrepreneurs in the aggregate can be expected to offer on the basis of any and all possible volumes of proceeds from the sale of the output resulting from the different amounts of employment. In *The General Theory* Keynes linked employment, rather than output or real income, to expected proceeds because at the time he was writing (1936) statistical techniques for the accurate measurement of important aggregates such as GNP were not highly developed. He thought that employment constituted the best single measure of total or aggregate economic activity.

A highly simplified version of the Keynesian aggregate supply function is illustrated by the hypothetical data in Table 5–1, which relate employ-

1. John Maynard Keynes, *The General Theory of Employment, Interest and Money* (New York: Harcourt, Brace & World, First Harbinger ed., 1964), p. 24.

ment and expected proceeds. For the sake of simplicity we assume that labor is the only resource, and thus the only costs of production to be covered in the aggregate by the sales proceeds are labor costs. It is further assumed in Table 5–1 that the normal work week is forty hours, and that workers are employed for fifty-two weeks each year. In the table there are two schedules: Schedule *A* and Schedule *B*. Schedule *A* is based upon the assumption that the money wages of workers remain constant at $4.75 per hour, regardless of the actual level of employment or demand for labor. Schedule *B* is based upon the assumption that the money wage will rise as more employment is offered. This implies that, as the demand for labor increases, its price, i.e., the money wage, will rise. Note, too, that money wages rise in Schedule *B* at an accelerating rate as the employment level increases.

Let us examine each of these schedules in a little more detail. Schedule *A* shows what the minimum expected sales proceeds must be for entrepreneurs to offer employment to specified numbers of workers. For example, if employers in the aggregate are to offer employment to 88 million workers, the expected proceeds from the sale of the output produced by these 88 million workers must at a minimum equal $869 billion. Why is this? The $869 billion represents the total money costs of this amount of product which must be covered by sales proceeds if entrepreneurs in the aggregate are to continue to offer this amount of employment. Thus, the $869 billion is the aggregate supply price of this amount of employment. In Schedule *B* the aggregate supply price for each level of employment subsequent to 82 million is higher because of the assumption that the

TABLE 5–1. The Aggregate Supply Function

	Schedule A		Schedule B	
Employment (N) (in millions of workers)	*Money Wages (per hour)*	*Aggregate Supply Price (Z) (in billions of dollars)*	*Money Wages (per hour)*	*Aggregate Supply Price (Z′) (in billions of dollars)*
82	$4.75	$810	$4.75	$810
84	4.75	824	4.80	839
86	4.75	850	4.92	881
88	4.75	869	4.99	911
90	4.75	889	5.11	954
92	4.75	896	5.26	1005
94	4.75	928	5.44	1066

Note: 40-hour work-week and 52-week work-year assumed. Data rounded to nearest whole number.

money wage will rise from $4.75 per hour to $5.44 per hour as the total volume of employment climbs from 82 to 94 million workers.

Figure 5–1 illustrates graphically the Keynesian aggregate supply function.[2] In the figure, employment is plotted on the horizontal axis, and expected sales proceeds on the vertical axis. If we then plot the data of Table 5–1 we get the two curves shown in the figure. The one labeled *A* is the aggregate supply schedule based upon a fixed money wage of $4.75 per hour, whereas the schedule labeled *B* reflects the fact that the money wage may rise as the level of employment rises. The more rapidly the money wage rises with actual changes in the level of employment, the less responsive is the employment level to any given change in expected proceeds. Technically, this means that, as the elasticity of the employment level decreases, the money wage becomes more sensitive to any increase in the demand for labor. The aggregate supply schedule will become perfectly inelastic with respect to expected proceeds at the level of employment which represents full employment of the existing labor force. If, for

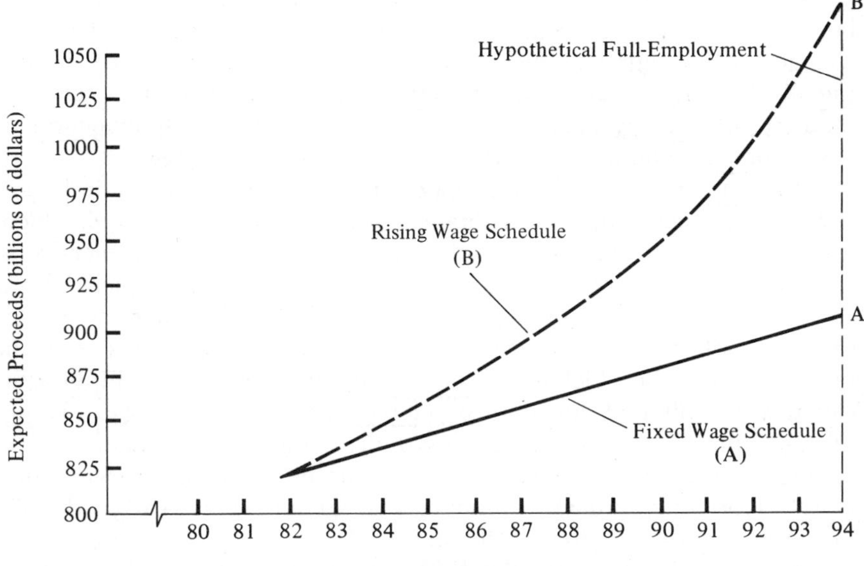

FIGURE 5–1. The Keynesian Aggregate Supply Function: Employment and Proceeds

2. The student should not confuse the above curves with the production function, which normally shows the relationship between employment and output. The supply schedule as depicted could be made more "realistic" by the addition of a "mark-up" factor to total labor costs which would represent the entrepreneur's profit. This does not change the basic principle involved, however. The aggregate supply "price" still must cover all the necessary costs associated with a given amount of employment.

example, the employment level of 94 million workers is the upper limit to the labor supply in our hypothetical economy, then the two curves, A and B, will terminate at this point. Since no more workers are available once employment has reached the 94-million level, actual employment cannot exceed this amount, irrespective of what happens to expected proceeds. This is shown in Figure 5–1 by the dotted line extending vertically upward at the 94-million mark on the horizontal axis.

Alternative Concepts of Aggregate Supply

The Keynesian aggregate supply function just examined linked employment to expected proceeds primarily because Keynes thought employment to be the most satisfactory measure of changes in the current output of the economy. Since publication of *The General Theory*, various alternative measures for determining total output have been developed. The extensive and rapid development of national income accounting has provided the economist with excellent techniques by means of which the heterogeneous complex of goods and services produced by the economy can be reduced to a single aggregate. Procedures for measurement of real changes in this aggregate over time are similarly well developed. Consequently, the aggregate supply function can be formulated in terms of total output (or real income) rather than the level of employment; this has become the standard practice in modern employment theory.

Such a formulation of the aggregate supply schedule is shown in Figure 5–2. The aggregate supply schedule is represented by the line *OZ*, which, it should be noted, bisects the origin at an angle of 45°. (Generally in modern income theory the aggregate supply function is depicted by a 45° line.) To understand the significance of the 45° line, the reader should recall that the aggregate supply schedule consists of a series of points, each one of which represents the supply price for the output associated with different amounts of employment. The aggregate supply schedule must show the conditions under which entrepreneurs in the aggregate will produce a particular volume of goods and services and more important, continue to produce that volume. This is what the 45° line in the Figure 5–2 attempts to do.

Real income is measured on both the vertical and horizontal axes of the figure, but the sense in which we are measuring real income differs for each of the two axes. The horizontal axis measures the money value in constant prices of the economy's current output of goods and services; but this also is equivalent to the total cost—including a normal profit—incurred by entrepreneurs in the aggregate in producing any given output. Statistically and in the aggregate, the value of any given quantity of physical output must be equal to the costs of producing that output. Thus, we can interpret the horizontal axis of the figure as a measure of current

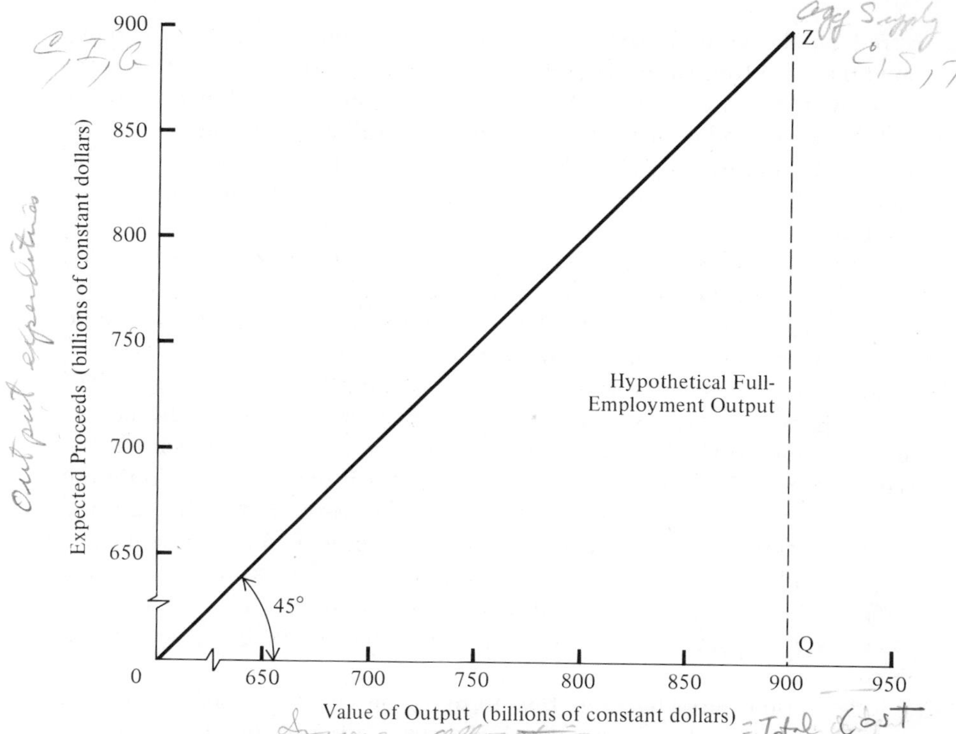

FIGURE 5–2. The Aggregate Supply Schedule: Expected Proceeds and Value of Output in Constant Prices

output seen from the viewpoint of the costs that entrepreneurs incur when they decide to produce a particular volume of goods and services. Specifically, the costs involved are listed earlier (Chapter 2) in the discussion of the allocations side of the gross national product: wages, rents, interest, profits, capital consumption allowances, and indirect business taxes.

Since the aggregate supply schedule, or function, must show the conditions under which any particular level of production will continue, it follows that entrepreneurs in the aggregate must receive a return flow of expenditures equal to the costs they incur if they produce any given aggregate of goods and services. Since Figure 5–2 measures real income (output valued in constant prices) on both the horizontal and vertical axes, the only possible line that will conform to the conditions described above is the 45° line that bisects the point of origin. In other words, if the vertical axis is viewed as measuring the flow of expenditures or expected proceeds in constant prices, then the 45° line must of necessity be the aggregate supply schedule, for each point on such a schedule represents the amounts that entrepreneurs must receive back as receipts (as measured on the vertical axis) if they are to continue to produce varying amounts of output (as measured on the horizontal axis).

As was the case with the Keynesian aggregate supply function, there will be some level of output which represents full employment for the 45° aggregate supply schedule. This may be represented by a point upon the horizontal axis, for once the economy has achieved full-employment (capacity production) no further increases in output are possible. In Figure 5–2 this point is represented by the vertical line ZQ. It is possible, though not customary, in modern income analysis, to combine the Keynesian aggregate supply schedule with the 45° aggregate supply schedule by measuring employment as well as output or real income on the horizontal axis. This can be done because each possible level of output will correlate with a specific amount of employment. Because of the law of diminishing returns, however, employment will not necessarily vary in the same proportion as output, a fact which makes it difficult to compute the exact amount of employment which might be associated with each and every possible level of real output (see footnote 2). As a consequence, most modern income theorists have been content to measure real income only on the horizontal axis and simply assume—correctly—that employment will vary more or less directly with changes in the level of real income.

One serious drawback to this formulation of the aggregate supply schedule is that the general level of prices "disappears." It disappears because of the use of deflated values for both output and expected proceeds. When Keynes wrote *The General Theory* this was not a serious problem because there was little concern in the depths of the depression of the 1930s about prices rising too rapidly when output expanded. In more recent years, however, this has not been the situation. We have frequently had rising prices (inflation) both when output is falling and when it is expanding.

Prices can be brought back into the aggregate supply schedule if we change the vertical axis in our diagram from a measure of output in constant prices to a measure of output in *current* prices. This is done in Figure 5–3. In the figure, we still measure real income on the horizontal axis. But the vertical axis now measures the current market value of output, which is its value in present prices. The aggregate supply function now takes on the shape of the curve $Z'Z'$. This curve shows that the general level of prices will rise with successive rises in real income.[3] As a consequence, the flow of expected proceeds that entrepreneurs must receive to induce them to continue to produce at varying levels must increase proportionally more than the increase in output. The closer the

3. This increase in the price level may be accounted for by an increase in unit costs of production as output expands because of diminishing returns, as well as an in-increase in wage rates and other money costs that ensue when production increases.

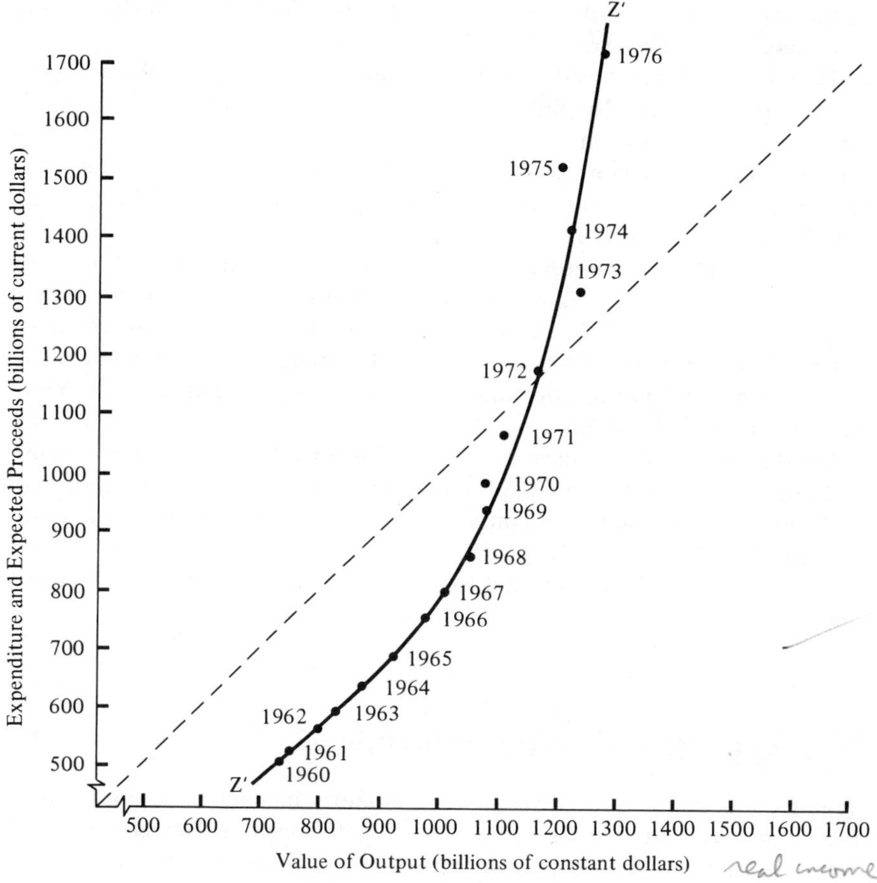

FIGURE 5–3. The Aggregate Supply Schedule: Expected Proceeds in Current Prices and Value of Output in Constant Prices

economy gets to full-employment and full-capacity output, the sharper will be the increase in the general price level; hence the steeper the rise in the aggregate supply curve *Z'Z'*. When the full-employment output level is attained, the curve becomes completely inelastic. Output will no longer respond to changes in the flow of expenditures. All that can happen from this point is a further upward shift in the general level of prices. The curve *Z'Z'* in Figure 5–3 was constructed from actual GNP data for the period 1960 through 1976. Values of GNP in both constant (1972) and current prices for each year are given by the dots next to each year shown. It may be observed that the fit of the *Z'Z'* curve, while not perfect, clearly reflects the concepts just discussed. The curve also shows the increasing vulnerability of the economy to inflation in recent years, especially since the mid-1960s. This is reflected in the increasing steepness of the curve from about 1965 onwards.

Thus far we have considered three different formulations of the aggregate supply function. No single one can be regarded as best, as each formulation has its uses in connection with different aspects of modern income and employment analysis. Nevertheless, the concept that is most widely employed in contemporary income analysis is the 45° aggregate supply schedule, and it is the one that we shall generally use in ensuing discussions. The 45° aggregate supply schedule permits us to formulate the entire analysis in real, i.e., constant-price terms, a useful procedure from the standpoint of the employment level. Modern employment theory asserts that employment can be expected to change primarily when there is a change in output, not necessarily where there is a change in the monetary value of that output.

We do not intend to ignore changes in the price level, an important subject dealt with in detail in Chapter 14. But in order to develop a thorough and sound understanding of contemporary employment theory, it is sensible to proceed in careful, building-block fashion, putting together first the basic structure of the theory and then adding the necessary complications one by one.

The Aggregate Demand Schedule

The second major analytical tool in modern income and employment theory is aggregate demand. Just as aggregate supply is conceived of as a schedule showing the expected proceeds necessary to induce a given quantity of employment or amount of output in the economy, aggregate demand is also conceived of as a schedule showing the amounts the major spending units in the economy are prepared to spend at each and every possible level of real income. It is a schedule that links real income and spending decisions for the economy as a whole. The idea that the aggregate demand schedule involves a relationship between decisions to purchase the different categories of output and the level of output itself is a gross oversimplification of a concept that is quite complex. But such a definition of the aggregate demand schedule is, nevertheless, a good point of departure for our analysis.

Figure 5–4 depicts the relationship described above. The line *DD* is the aggregate demand schedule. As in Figure 5–2, the vertical axis measures income as a flow of expenditure, while the horizontal axis depicts income as a flow of output. Thus, the curve *DD* can be said to represent the spending decisions associated with any and all possible levels of output, or real income.

Since the aggregate demand schedule seeks to show how much the

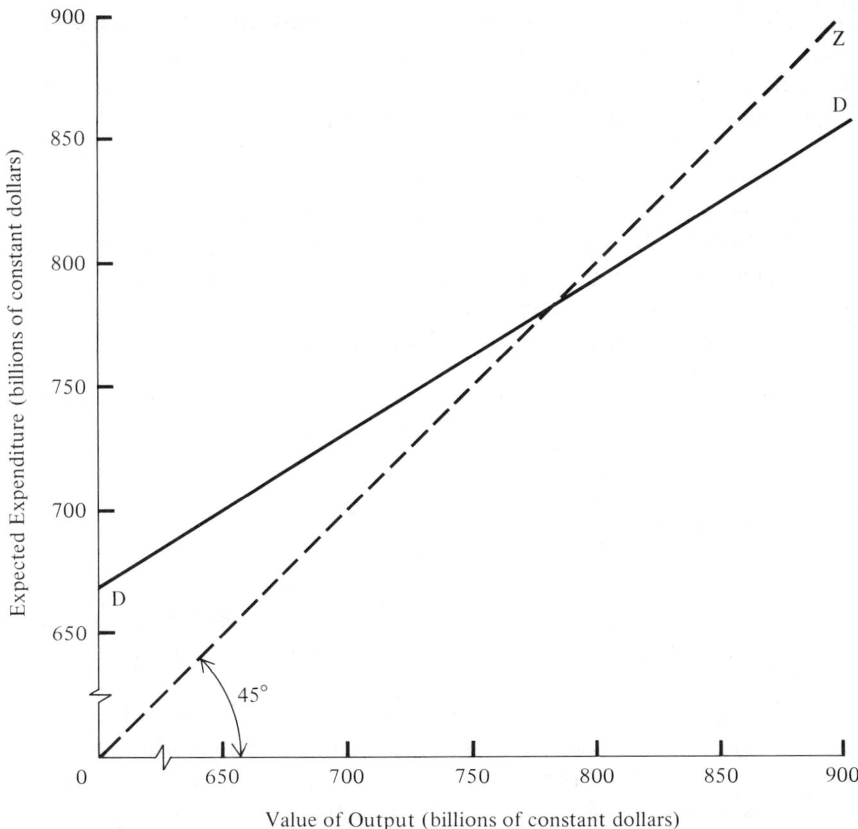

FIGURE 5–4. The Aggregate Demand Schedule

economy is disposed to spend for the various categories of output at different levels of real income, it is therefore an *ex ante* phenomenon. The aggregate demand schedule does not represent any particular level of statistical demand, but rather the demand that will prevail if certain conditions are satisfied. The notion of an aggregate demand schedule is important for our analysis because it underscores the fact that those who make the decisions to spend are not necessarily the same individuals or groups who make the decisions for production and employment. This will become fully apparent when we examine the process by which the income and the employment level is actually determined.

The Origin of Spending Decisions

Where do the spending decisions of the economy originate? Or, stated in different terms, who or what are the spending units in the economy? This is a question that concerns the component parts of the aggregate demand schedule, and a complete answer depends upon the discussion to follow in the next several chapters. But a brief answer can be given here that will serve to outline the basic problem involved in the analysis of demand for the output of the whole economy.

If we ignore for the moment any economic ties the economy may have with other nations, decisions to purchase a portion of the current output of the economy must originate in one of three major economic sectors: (1) the household, or consumer sector, which is the purchaser of consumer goods and services; (2) the business, or firm, sector, which is the purchaser of capital, or investment, goods; and, (3) the public, or government sector which is the point of origin for decisions relating to the economy's output of government, or collective, goods and services. In a symbolic sense, then, the schedule of aggregate demand will be equal to the sum of consumption, C, investment, I, and government expenditure, G, for goods and services. In other words,

$$DD = C + I + G \tag{5-1}$$

Since the aggregate demand schedule represents the spending intentions of the major spending units in the economy, a corollary question concerns the source of spending power at the disposal of these major spending units. In a monetary economy spending power requires access to a quantity of money, and thus the question pertains to the source of supply of money for the economy's spending units. Fundamentally, there are three possible sources of spending power for an individual spending unit in the economy. First, a spending unit may finance its current expenditures by drawing upon assets accumulated during past income periods. These may be in the form of holdings of money or in the form of other assets which can be converted to money. A household, for example, might finance some of its current expenditures by drawing down a savings account, or perhaps by the sale of some of its holdings of stocks or bonds. Second, current expenditures may be financed out of current income. For the household, or consumer, sector of the economy and for the bulk of government purchases of goods and services this is the typical pattern. Most of us as individuals have to depend upon our current money income to finance the major portion of our current expenditures.

In the past the more usual practice in the business sector of the economy was to finance capital expenditures by borrowing, rather than out of current and internal resources. Increasingly, however business firms are resorting to internal financing for major items of capital expenditure; moreover, the firm can, like the consumer, draw upon assets accumulated in past income periods to finance current outlays. But borrowing remains important as the third and final source of spending power for current expenditures. Consumers frequently resort to loans for financing large items of expenditures, such as houses, automobiles, and other durable goods, while it is quite commonplace for governmental units in the economy to borrow to meet a portion of ther current expenditures. National governments, we may note in passing, possess the unique distinction of having the power to create money.

These remarks about the source of the money that provides the basis for spending power in a monetary economy apply to the whole economy much in the same way as they apply to individual spending units within the economy. For the aggregate of all spending units, in other words, spending, or purchasing, power can be derived from current income, borrowing, or by drawing down previously accumulated cash balances. If all spending units resort to the latter two sources for some portion of their purchasing power, new or additional quantities of funds are injected into the economic system. How this comes about will be examined in greater detail later.

These various sources of purchasing power rule out the possibility of any simple and direct relationship between the spending decisions embodied in the aggregate demand schedule and the income level. One major component of aggregate demand, consumption, can be related functionally to the real income level, but this is not necessarily the case with the other two components. To repeat, the kind of schedule shown in Figure 5–4 is a simplification. Such a schedule, though, is an extremely valuable analytical tool, for what counts from the standpoint of the income and employment level is the willingness of the entrepreneur in the economy to make use of the economy's productive capacity. And this is directly tied to his expectations concerning demand, which, in turn, depend upon the decisions made by the major spending entities in the economy.

The Equilibrium Level of Income and Employment

The schedules of aggregate supply and aggregate demand take us directly to the heart of modern income and employment theory. The basic—and in many respects simple—idea that Keynes put forth in *The General Theory* is that the aggregate supply and demand schedules of the economy between them determine the level of income and employment. According to Keynes, "the volume of employment is given by the point of intersection between the aggregate demand function and the aggregate supply function. . . . This is the substance of the General Theory of Employment."[4]

The way in which aggregate supply and aggregate demand, considered together, determine the income and employment level is shown in Figure

4. Keynes, p. 25.

5–5. As in Figure 5–2 and 5–4 real income is shown on both the vertical and horizontal axes. Again the 45° line *OZ* is the aggregate supply function, while the schedule *DD* represents the aggregate demand function. Given these two schedules, the volume of income and employment will inevitably adjust to the level found at the point of intersection of these two schedules. This is represented by the income level Y_e, which is both the equilibrium income level and the equilibrium employment level.

The reason why income and employment must of necessity adjust to the level represented by Y_e and why this particular level represents income and employment equilibrium can best be understood if we analyze what will happen assuming for the moment that some other income level exists in the economy. The actual income level, as we have seen, can always be depicted by some point on the 45° aggregate supply schedule, as well as by points on the horizontal or vertical axes. (Since our analysis is framed in real terms, prices remain constant.)

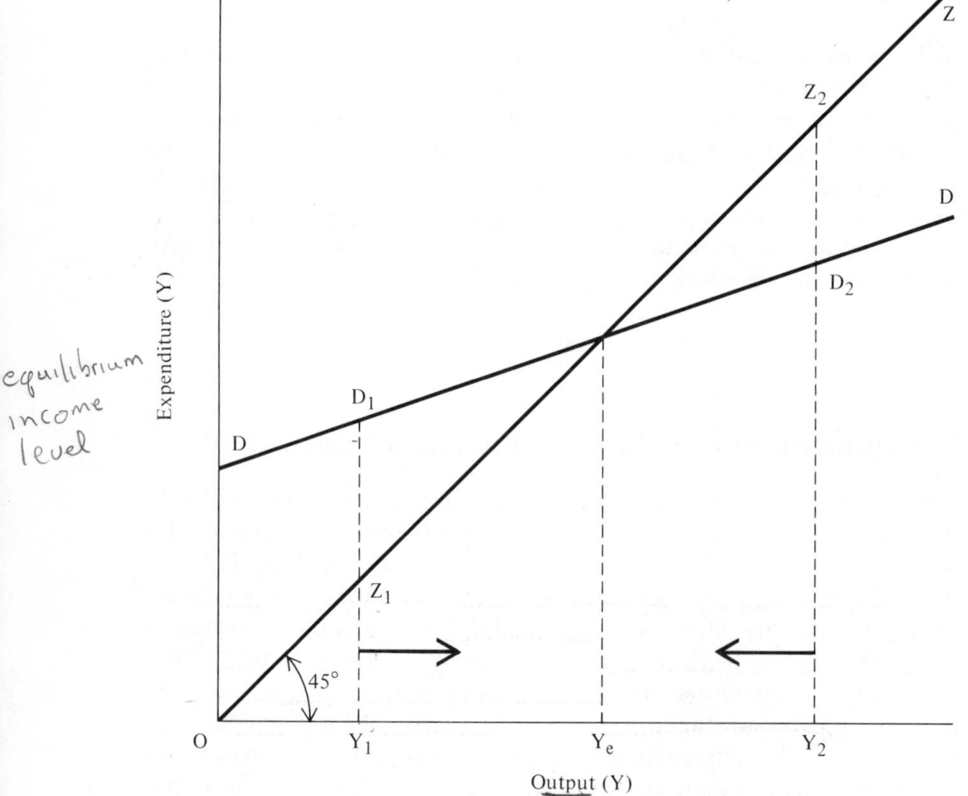

FIGURE 5–5. Aggregate Supply, Aggregate Demand, and the Equilibrium Level of Income

To illustrate, business firms (in the aggregate) anticipate or expect sales equal to Y_1Z_1; therefore, they will produce that amount of goods and services, paying out in the process income to owners of economic resources equal to OY_1. This, of course, equals Y_1Z_1, which is the same as the amount of income earned during the current period. To put it another way, Y_1Z_1 is the amount of income generated by the process of production.

What is the situation with respect to aggregate demand? The current income level, Y_1, is not an equilibrium income level, because at this particular level aggregate demand, *DD* exceeds aggregate supply, *OZ*. At the point Y_1 the *DD* schedule lies above the *OZ* schedule. Specifically, this means that at the income level Y_1, the spending intentions of all spending units in the economy are such that these add up to an amount equal to the distance, Y_1D_1, which is in excess of the current output or income level Y_1Z_1. In short, the demand for current output exceeds the supply of output. This is an unstable, or *disequilibrium*, condition that cannot be sustained; instead it will drive the economy toward higher levels of income and employment.

Let us look more closely at what is taking place in the current income period. In the first place, additional purchasing power over and above the amounts generated by current income is being injected into the economy's income stream. Diagrammatically, this is represented by the distance Z_1D_1, since the excess of aggregate demand over aggregate supply is a measure of the amount of purchasing power required beyond that being generated by the process of production. For our immediate purposes the exact source of this purchasing power does not matter; what does matter is that new spending power is being injected into the income system. If the distance Z_1D_1 is a measure of the excess of current spending intentions over current (actual) output, how will the spending plans of the economy's spending units be satisfied? Since our analysis is in real terms, we have precluded any increase in the general level of prices as a result of the excess of aggregate demand. But if we rule out price changes, and if current supply falls short of demand, there remains only one other alternative: The excess of aggregate demand must be satisfied by sales out of existing stocks (*inventories*) of goods. The distance Z_1D_1 represents not only the excess of aggregate demand over aggregate supply in the current income period, but also the amount by which current inventories of goods must be drawn down to satisfy this demand. From the standpoint of the whole economy, the distance represents *unintended (unplanned) disinvestment* in stocks. Such disinvestment is unintended because it results solely from the failure of production or output plans to coincide with spending plans in the current income period.

How does the situation that we have been describing appear from the point of view of the business firms of the economy? Typically, in this situation business firms will find their sales running ahead of current production, and they will revise their production plans upward for the next income period in the belief that the existing demand is a reliable indicator of demand in subsequent income periods. If most firms in the economy act accordingly, then output employment will rise throughout the whole economy. This process of adjustment will necessarily continue until a situation is achieved in which output and spending decisions coincide. In Figure 5–5 this is the situation depicted by the intersection of the aggregate supply and aggregate demand schedules.

The foregoing analysis serves not only to show the essentials of the process by which income and employment adjust toward equilibrium values, but also should underscore the fact that disequilibrium—which always implies change—occurs whenever expected, or *ex ante*, values diverge from actual, or *ex post*, values. In the analysis we have been pursuing, the expected aggregate demand of entrepreneurs would be at the level Y_1Z_1, which originally led them to produce output at the rate Y_1. But actual, or *ex post*, aggregate demand turned out to be at the level Y_1D_1. Changes in the income and employment levels in subsequent income periods stem from this initial divergence between expected and actual values. There is no inherent reason why expected and actual values should always coincide. Modern income and employment theory stresses that spending and output decisions are made by different groups or persons, so there is no reason to expect the two values to be always equal. The reader should note this carefully, for it is basic to the explanation of the *why* of changes in income and employment levels in the modern economy.

To round out our present discussion of the equilibrium income level, let us postulate a situation just the opposite of the one we have considered. Let us assume that in the current income period the supply of output is in excess of the demand for that output. In Figure 5–5 this is depicted at the income level Y_2, as measured on the horizontal axis. At this income level the aggregate supply schedule, OZ, lies above the aggregate demand schedule, DD. Output in the current income period equals Y_2Z_2, but spending decisions or current demand for that output only add up to the distance D_2Z_2, with the consequence that, for the income period in question, there is *unintended (unplanned) investment* in stocks or inventories. More money income or purchasing power is being generated by current output than is being spent on that output; once more, a disequilibrium situation exists.

The typical business firm sees this as an unhappy situation in which sales fall short of current production and the firm suffers losses. Unless an immediate change to a better sales position is anticipated, the firm will have no choice but to revise downward its production plans for subsequent income periods. As most firms in the economy do this, output and employment levels for the whole economy will decline. Such a downward adjustment of income and employment must continue until a point is reached at which the supply of output is no longer in excess of current demand for the output. This, again, is the situation shown in Figure 5–5 by the intersection of the aggregate supply and aggregate demand schedules.

A Numerical Example

The process of adjustment of income and employment to an equilibrium level can be illustrated by means of a simple arithmetical example that employs a set of hypothetical data pertaining to employment, aggregate demand, and aggregate supply. Table 5–2 provides these data. In Column (1) are shown the varying amounts of employment associated with different levels of aggregate output (or national income) for our imaginary economy. The various possible levels of national output are given in Column (2), which is the aggregate supply schedule. For each of these various output levels, producers will incur costs exactly equal to the value of the output produced. Column (3) is the aggregate demand schedule and shows the amounts that spending units are prepared to spend at each possible income or output level shown in Column (2). Column (4) tells us which direction income and employment can be expected to change in response to the various levels of aggregate supply and aggregate demand. Column (5) shows the unplanned inventory changes that result when *DD* and *OZ* are unequal.

In Table 5–2 there is only one possible income level at which total

TABLE 5–2. The Equilibrium of Income and Employment

(1) Employment (N) (in millions of workers)	*(2)* Aggregate Supply or National Income (OZ) (in billions of dollars)	*(3)* Aggregate Demand (DD) (in billions of dollars)	*(4)* Direction of Change in Income and Employment	*(5)* Unplanned Inventory Change
72	$660	$700	Rise	$ – 40
74	690	720	Rise	– 30
76	720	740	Rise	– 20
78	750	760	Rise	– 10
80	**780**	**780**	**Equilibrium**	–
82	810	790	Fall	+ 20
84	840	800	Fall	+ 40

spending in the economy is just equal to the value of current output. This condition occurs at an output level of $780 billion and an employment level of 80 million. At all other possible values for income and output disequilibrium is present. Suppose, for example, that current output is equal to $690 billion. At this level the aggregate demand schedule, Column (3), shows that spending units in the aggregate intend to spend at a rate of $920 billion. Total spending, in other words, will run ahead of total output by an amount equal to $30 billion. Under these circumstances, and in view of our explicit assumption that prices remain constant, there can be only one possible outcome—employment and production must rise. In these circumstances, the $30 billion of excess demand represents the amount by which stocks of goods will be drawn down during the income period so that the spending intentions of the spending units can be satisfied.

Just the reverse will hold true if output in any income period rises above the equilibrium level of $780 billion. If production proceeds, say, at an annual rate of $840 billion, producers are doomed to disappointment because at this particular income level the total of spending decisions in the economy amount to only $800 billion. Producers will find that inventories of unsold goods are accumulating at an unwanted rate of $40 billion per year. The reader should note carefully that the economy has not failed through its current productive activity to generate enough purchasing power to clear the market of all goods and services produced, but rather it has failed to spend this purchasing power at the same rate at which it is being created. This is the point at which Say's Law goes awry, because it assumes that income will always be spent at the same rate at which it is created. In this connection Keynes asserted that

> the conclusion that the *costs* of output are always covered in the aggregate by the sale-proceeds resulting from demand, has great plausibility, because it is difficult to distinguish it from another, similar-looking proposition which is indubitable, namely that the income derived in the aggregate by all the elements in the community concerned in a productive activity necessarily has a value exactly equal to the *value* of the output.[5]

Characteristics of the Income Equilibrium

The analysis so far attempts to explain how, in a most fundamental sense, aggregate demand and aggregate supply are the key determinants of income and employment levels. This is the crux of modern employment theory, for if the schedules of aggregate supply and aggregate demand are known, it is possible to determine both the income and employment level for the economy.

But—and this is a point of critical importance—the equilibrium level of

5. Ibid., p. 20.

income and employment brought about by the interaction of aggregate demand and aggregate supply will not automatically be one of *full employment.* Since decisions to produce and decisions to spend are made independently, it is largely a matter of chance whether or not they happen to coincide at a level of output that represents full employment of the economy's labor force. The economic forces embodied in the analytical concepts of aggregate supply and aggregate demand must of necessity drive the economy toward an equilibrium position, but there is nothing special in these forces that will in any way make full employment the normal state of affairs for the economy.

In fact, the basic lesson of modern income and employment analysis, in contrast to the classical theory, is that any level of employment may be normal in the sense that it may be sustained over a considerable period of time. For example, during the whole decade of the 1930s large-scale unemployment was the normal situation in the American economy. If there is a deficiency of aggregate demand, the economy will experience a *deflationary gap* and may reach equilibrium at less than full employment. On the other hand, if aggregate demand persistently runs ahead of aggregate supply, there will be an *inflationary gap*. The latter situation will be characterized by strong upward pressure on the price level and the per cent of the labor force unemployed will fall below the level normally thought of as full (Chapter 4). The essential point to remember is that in the short run the economy can achieve equilibrium of income and employment at levels that represent full employment, less than full employment, or even "overly" full employment. This last is made possible through inventory adjustments, that is, drawing down of inventories. No one level is in any sense inherently more normal than any other level. The economy does not—as the classical economists believed—automatically move through market processes toward such an equilibrium. It all depends upon the relationship existing at any given time interval between aggregate supply and aggregate demand.

But one should not assume that the use of the equilibrium concept as a technique for analyzing change means that the economy necessarily settles down into a steady situation with respect to income and employment. The main thrust of Keynes's great work is instability—not just the failure of the economy to attain full employment much of the time, but the inherently unstable nature of a market economy. The basic reason is that the economic forces which lie behind aggregate demand—especially investment spending—are highly unstable, a subject which we shall develop in greater depth subsequently. Thus, the economy may be tending toward an equilibrium as depicted in Figure 5–5 and Table 5–2, but before it reaches a stable situation, the aggregate demand schedule may change. How this type of change affects the system is discussed in the next section.

Changes in Income and Employment

Besides explaining how the level of employment is determined, the foregoing analytical framework serves to illuminate clearly the how and the why of change within the economic system. The vital principle running through our analysis is that change is the inevitable outcome of a situation in which expected and actual events do not agree, which is to say, change will occur whenever *ex ante* and *ex post* values do not coincide. Insofar as income and employment are concerned, this means that these magnitudes will be changing whenever aggregate supply and aggregate demand are not equal.

It is necessary to note, however, that within this rather broad analytical framework two distinct kinds of change can be envisaged. In the first instance, change may come about because, with given schedules of aggregate supply and aggregate demand, actual output or income fails to correspond to the demand for that output. This is the kind of situation depicted in Figure 5–5. The resultant change is the adjustment of the income and employment level toward equilibrium values that are based upon a given position for the schedules of aggregate supply and aggregate demand. Changes of this type originate with the producing units of the economy because they come about as a result of the failure of entrepreneurs to judge accurately the level of demand for the output of the whole economy.

Change is also involved in the movement of the economic system from one equilibrium level to another. In the short run such change results from a shift in the position of the aggregate demand schedule that occurs when the spending units of the economy are predisposed to spend more (or less) on current output at any and all levels of income. This shift in the position of the aggregate demand schedule will disturb a previously existing equilibrium between spending and output decisions, and thereby set in motion all of the forces involved in the adjustment of the economy toward equilibrium values for income and employment.

The latter type of change is illustrated in Figure 5–6. Schedule *DD* represents the original position of aggregate demand; output will adjust to the level Y_e, which is the intersection of the aggregate supply schedule, *OZ*, and the aggregate demand schedule, *DD*. If, however, aggregate demand shifts to the level represented by schedule *D′D′*, then the existing equilibrium income level, Y_e, is disturbed. The immediate consequence of this shift is to create a new situation in which aggregate demand at Y_e exceeds aggregate supply or output. This will set in motion forces making for change; income and employment will rise until a new equilibrium obtains at the level Y'_e. The important thing to note is that the original impetus for this type of change came from the spending rather than the producing units in the economy. One consequence of this

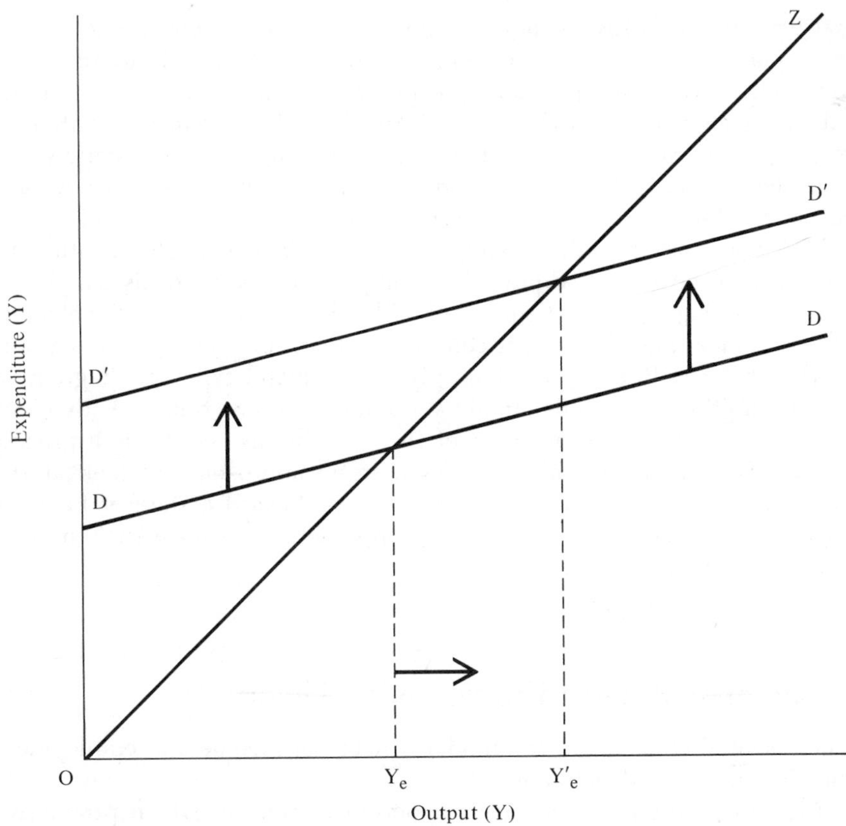

FIGURE 5–6. Aggregate Supply, Aggregate Demand, and Shifts in the Equilibrium Level of Income

type of change is that the increase in output may be greater than the shift in the aggregate demand schedule. Thus, there may be a *multiplier effect* associated with such shifts, a topic to be discussed in the following chapter.

Statics and Dynamics

The previous paragraph concerns a particular type of economic change, namely the shift from one equilibrium position to another. Technically, this is described as an exercise in *comparative statics*. In economic analysis the term *statics* applies to a situation in which the motion of the system is toward an equilibrium position, as in the examples discussed earlier of the movement toward an income equilibrium. Such a situation is deemed static because all of the underlying determinants of the schedules involved—the aggregate demand and supply schedules in the material we have been discussing—are "givens" (or parameters). The motion takes place in response to the economic forces embodied in these schedules—schedules whose positions are presumed known. When one of the schedules changes, as is shown in Figure 5–6, the system will shift to a new equilibrium position, but it still represents an essentially static situation because no further change can take place until there is a new disturbance. Hence the term *comparative* statics.

Dynamics, on the other hand, is a term which connotes continuous change and movement. Equilibrium diagrams of the kind discussed earlier in this chapter are not suitable for the discussion of constant change. One reason is that if change is continuous, then time must become a part of the analysis. But the usual supply and demand types of diagram so widely used in economic analysis do not embody time.[6] A dynamic approach will view the behavior of the economy as essentially a process taking place through time, whereas a static approach will look at the economy's behavior as a system which tends toward a state of balance. Neither approach is the only correct approach; both have their uses in helping us to real world economy.

Summary: Modern Employment Theory

The essential elements of the modern theory of income and employment may be summarized as follows:

1. In the short run, defined as a period of time in which productive capacity is fixed, the employment level will vary directly with the extent to which productive capacity is being utilized.

2. In the private sector of the economy the extent to which productive capacity is actually utilized depends upon the entrepreneur's expectation that his sales proceeds will be sufficient to cover the costs incurred in the production of any given volume of output. The aggregate supply schedule represents the formal, analytical expression of this idea, for it is a schedule showing the expected proceeds necessary to induce entrepreneurs in the aggregate to offer on a continuing basis a given amount of employment or produce a given output of goods and services.

3. The aggregate demand schedule associates spending decisions with differing levels of real income. It shows, in other words, the amounts that will be spent for output at each and every possible income level.

4. Given the aggregate supply and aggregate demand schedule for the economy, the equilibrium level of income and employment will be deter-

6. This comment applies to both supply and demand diagrams used to explain individual price behavior (microeconomic analysis) and aggregate supply and demand diagrams of the type discussed in this chapter (macroeconomic analysis).

mined by the intersection of these two schedules. There is nothing inherent in these forces of aggregate supply and aggregate demand to assure that this equilibrium will be one of full employment.

5. Change in the economy's level of income and employment results from the failure of the output and spending plans embodied in the schedules of aggregate supply and demand to coincide. In the short run such changes may take the form of a movement toward an equilibrium position, given an initial imbalance between output and spending, or a movement from one equilibrium position to another. This latter type of change is contingent upon a shift in the schedule of aggregate demand.

A Concluding Comment

The "model" of output and employment determination developed in this chapter and summarized above is sometimes described as an "income-expenditure" model, the reason being the emphasis it places upon the level of aggregate demand as a key to the output and employment level. It is probably the most straightforward interpretation of Keynes's *The General Theory*, a fact which makes it the ideal point of departure for serious study of all the many factors which enter into such a complex problem as the determination of output and employment in the modern economy. It is, of course, not the whole of contemporary macroeconomic analysis—only a starting point. The rationale for beginning with a simple model and proceeding from it to situations of greater complexity was well-stated by Keynes.

> The method of our analysis is, not to provide a machine, or method of blind manipulation, which will furnish an infallible answer, but to provide ourselves with an *organised and orderly method of thinking out particular problems* [italics added]; and, after we have reached a provisional conclusion by isolating the complicating factors one by one, we shall have to go back on ourselves and allow, as well as we can, for the probable interactions of the factors among themselves. *This is the nature of economic thinking* [italics added].[7]

This brief passage will serve as a useful direction-finder as we make our way through the complexities of modern economics.

7. Keynes, p. 297.

6

Consumption, Saving, and the Multiplier

In the preceding chapter, the point was made that in the short run aggregate demand is the key determinant of the level of income and employment. The reason is that aggregate demand determines the extent to which the economy's productive capacity will be utilized. The aggregate demand schedule is a summation of decisions to use the economy's output. But since the output of the economy consists of several different categories of goods and services, the demand for the output of the whole economy is a demand for the various categories of goods and services that enter into the national output. Structurally, aggregate demand (in a closed economy) consists of the sum of expenditures for consumer goods and services, C, investment, or capital goods, I, and government, or collective goods and services, G. In an open economy it is necessary to take into account net foreign investment, I_f

Given the underlying assumption that output and employment in the short run depend primarily upon the level of aggregate demand our basic task is to understand the forces that enter into the determination of the demand for the output of the whole economy. Since we have already identified the component parts of the economy's structure of total demand, the logical procedure is to understand the determinants of each of these component parts, following this with an analysis of how these parts are linked together to form a schedule of demand for the economy's whole output.

The Determinants of Consumption Expenditure

Keynes's basic hypothesis with respect to the volume of consumption expenditure in the economy is that *income is the prime determinant of consumption expenditure.* This is the case for the individual and for the economy as a whole. Keynes stated "aggregate income . . . is, as a rule, the principal variable upon which the consumption constituent of the aggregate demand function will depend."[1] To say that income is the prime determinant of consumption expenditure is not to say that there may not be other determinants. For the moment, however, we shall put aside any other possible determinants and concentrate on the variable of income.

Before we turn to a detailed analysis of the income-consumption relationship, it is desirable to consider which particular measure of income is appropriate for the analysis. Should we regard consumption as a function of GNP, national income, personal income, or some other income measure? Since we are concerned primarily with consumer behavior, it would seem logical that the income concept most appropriate to our analysis is one that most nearly approximates the idea of take-home pay. If there is validity to the hypothesis that income is a prime determinant of consumption expenditure, income in this context must mean the income which is wholly at the disposal of the consumer for consumption expenditure. Within the framework of national income aggregates, the particular measure that meets this requirement is *disposable income,* which, the reader will recall, is defined as the income remaining to individuals after deduction of all personal taxes. It is the closest approximation to take-home pay at the national level. Accordingly, contemporary income and employment theory has generally formulated the consumption function in terms of the relationship between disposable income and consumption expenditure. Consumption is thus held to be a function of disposable income.

If we assume that all saving other than capital consumption allowances originates in the household sector, disposable income will be equal to the net national product minus taxes and plus transfer payments. In equation form we have:

$$Y_d = Y_{np} - TX + TR \qquad (6\text{–}1)$$

In the discussion which follows in this and ensuing chapters *net national product* (Y_{np}) will be used as our basic income measure rather than gross national product, primarily because use of the latter in the algebraic models requires making the extreme assumption that saving even in the form of capital consumption allowances originates in the household

1. John Maynard Keynes, *The General Theory of Employment, Interest and Money* (New York, Harcourt, Brace & World, First Harbinger ed., 1964), p. 96.

sector. Use of net national product does not in any way change the basic analysis or principles.

In *The General Theory* Keynes suggested two basic ideas concerning the relationship between consumption and income. These ideas are the underpinning of the modern theory of consumption and saving. First, Keynes asserted that consumption expenditure is related to income in a systematic and dependable way. Symbolically, we have the equation

$$C = f(Y_d) \tag{6–2}$$

Keynes defined the functional relationship between a given level of income and the consumption expenditure out of the level of income as *the propensity to consume*.[2] It may be noted, parenthetically, that the functional relationship posited by Keynes is one that concerns real consumption and real income.

The second key idea is known as Keynes's fundamental psychological law.

> The fundamental psychological law, upon which we are entitled to depend with great confidence both *a priori* from our knowledge of human nature and from the detailed facts of experience, is that men are disposed, as a rule and on the average, to increase their consumption as their income increases, but not by as much as the increase in their income.[3]

Basically what Keynes meant is that when an individual's income increases he will spend more for consumption because of the increase, but he will not spend the whole of the increase. Some portion of the increase, in other words, will be saved. Keynes believed that this was especially true in the short run, for our consumption standards tend to become habitual, and are not quickly adjusted either upward or downward. If income rises, spending, and our standard of consumption, may not immediately adjust upward to a new and higher level. The reverse, it may be noted, will be the case when income falls.

The Consumption Function

In modern income and employment theory these two Keynesian ideas with respect to income and consumption are brought together in the concept of the *consumption function*, which may be defined as a *schedule showing the amounts that will be spent for consumer goods and services at different income levels*. The nature of the consumption function is shown in Figure 6–1. Aggregate real income is measured on the horizontal axis and real consumption expenditure on the vertical axis. The curve $C = f(Y_d)$ represents the consumption function; this curve shows the

2. Ibid., p. 90.
3. Ibid., p. 96.

amount of consumption expenditure forthcoming at any and all income levels.

The notion of the consumption function as a schedule follows logically from Keynes's definition of the *propensity to consume* as the functional relationship between income and consumption. This functional relationship can be represented by a schedule which shows the range of values over which the dependent variable (consumption) moves as a result of changes in the independent variable (income).

It should be noted that, *as a concept*, the consumption function is quite similar to the ordinary demand curve. The latter is the graphic representation of a schedule showing the amounts of a commodity or service that buyers are willing to purchase at any and all possible prices within a specified period of time. The ordinary demand schedule embodies the idea that quantity demanded is a function of price. Thus, it is correct to state the law of demand in the form of an equation, such as $q = f(p)$, in

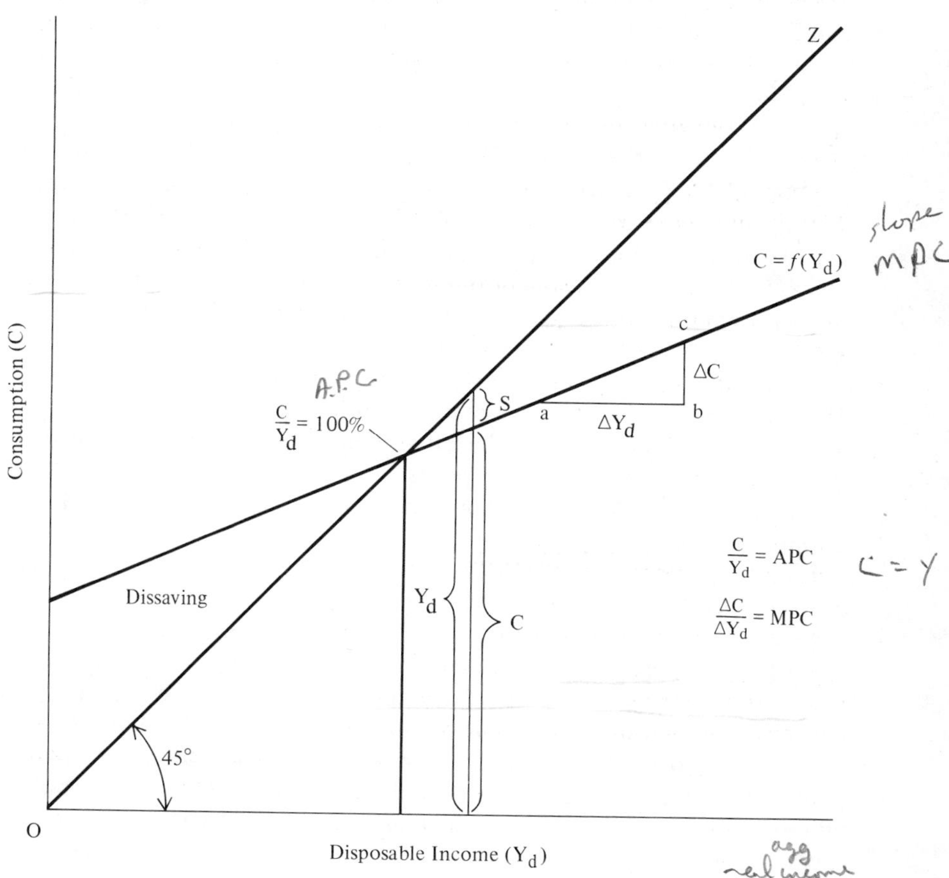

FIGURE 6–1. The Consumption Function

which q represents quantity demanded and p represents the price of a good or service. So it is with the consumption function, except that the two variables are disposable income (the independent variable) and consumption expenditures (the dependent variable).

The income-consumption schedule, like all similar schedules in economic analysis, is an *ex ante* phenomenon. The schedule shows intended values, that is, the levels to which consumers plan to adjust their consumption expenditures on the assumption that any particular income level is achieved and maintained for a reasonable period of time. The consumption function is presumed to define the normal relationship of consumption to income.

Technical Attributes of the Consumption Function

Although Keynes used the term *propensity to consume* to refer to the schedule relating consumption and income, modern employment theory usually uses the term *consumption function* to describe the schedule relationship between income and consumption. This will be the usage in this text. The *average propensity to consume* is the ratio of consumption to income, C/Y_d, at a specific level of income. It is the proportion of a given income that is spent for consumption purposes. This is the first significant attribute of the function. The average propensity to consume may vary as the income level varies. In Figure 6–1, for example, the average propensity to consume is 100 percent at the point at which the consumption function $C = f(Y_d)$ crosses the aggregate supply function, OZ. At this point, consumption is exactly equal to income. To the left of this point, the average propensity to consume will be more than 100 percent because at every possible income level intended consumption is greater than income. Thus the ratio C/Y_d will be greater than 100 percent. To the right of the point of intersection, on the other hand, the average propensity to consume will be less than 100 percent, because at every income level above that at which consumption and income are equal, intended consumption is less than income.

The second important attribute of the consumption function is the *marginal propensity to consume*. This concept is the formal expression of Keynes's fundamental psychological law, which, the reader will recall, states that men are disposed to increase or decrease their consumption by less as their income increases or decreases. We may define the marginal propensity to consume as the ratio of a change in consumption, ΔC, to a change in income, ΔY_d. With an increase in income, the marginal propensity to consume gives in percent the amount by which consumption will increase. If income declines the marginal propensity to consume measures—again in percent—the amount by which consumption expenditure will decline. If we assume, for example, that the marginal propensity to consume of the economy is 0.75 (i.e., 75 percent), consumption expenditure will increase by \$0.75 with every increase of \$1.00 in the income level and fall by the same amount with every \$1.00 decline in the income level.

In Figure 6–1 the marginal propensity to consume is measured by the slope of the consumption function, because, in mathematical terms, the slope of a line is determined by the ratio of the vertical distance to the horizontal distance (when movement takes place horizontally). Since consumpton, C, is measured on the vertical axis and income, Y_d, on the horizontal axis, the marginal propensity to consume must necessarily be the same thing as the slope of the curve. In Figure 6–1 the marginal propensity to consume can be depicted by reference to the triangle *abc*. The vertical side of the triangle is the change in consumption expenditure ΔC, while the horizontal side is equal to the change in income, ΔY_d. The reader should note carefully that as long as the consumption function is assumed to be linear—that is, drawn as a straight line—the marginal propensity to consume will have a constant value. The basic reason for this is that all triangles formed by ΔY_d and ΔC will be similar (in a geometric sense) to the triangle *abc*, and consequently the ratio of their vertical sides to their horizontal sides will always be the same. The marginal propensity to consume and its constant value is to be contrasted to the changing value of the average propensity to consume.[4]

In an analytical sense the role of Keynes's fundamental psychological law is to establish limiting values for the slope of the consumption function. In *The General Theory* Keynes held that normally the marginal propensity to consume is positive, but its value is less than unity. This means that the slope of the consumption function will normally be less than 1. Since we are not told anything further about either its shape or slope, there is nothing in the Keynesian law that precludes us from drawing a consumption function whose slope is such that the average and marginal propensities to consume are equal. Keynes's basic—and only—stipulation was that, as income increases, consumption will increase, but not by so much as the increase in income, and when income falls, consumption will fall, but again not by so much as the decrease in income. Keynes did not specify that consumption had to change either in proportion to or less than in proportion to the change in income. As a matter of fact, a change in consumption expenditure that is proportional to the change in income is just as compatible with the fundamental law as is a change in consumption expenditure that is less than proportional to the change in income.

The marginal propensity to consume relates to consumption expenditure that is *induced* by a change in income. Such a change can be viewed geometrically as a movement along a known consumption function, and

4. The above remarks do not necessarily imply that the income-consumption relationship must be linear. The consumption function may have a shape such that both marginal and average propensities to consume decline as the income level rises. For reasons of simplicity in analysis, however, most economists operate on the assumption that the consumption function is linear.

should not be confused with the change that may come about as a result of a shift in the consumption function itself. Keynes assumed that normally the consumption function is stable, so that most changes in consumption are induced by income changes. This means that fluctuations in the income and employment level are not likely to have their origins in the consumption component of the aggregate demand schedule.[5] Whether or not this particular conclusion is warranted remains to be seen; for the moment, though, our chief concern is with the marginal propensity to consume as a phenomenon having to do with induced changes in consumption expenditure. The analytical significance of the idea of induced consumption expenditures is that we find in such phenomena the basis of the theory of the multiplier, an aspect of modern income and employment theory that we shall develop in full detail later in this chapter.

Our discussion of the consumption function would not be complete without the algebraic expression of this relationship. If we assume the function is linear, as we did in Figure 6–1, the consumption function can be stated as

$$C = C_0 + aY_d \tag{6–3}$$

In the above expression, C is the level of consumption; C_0 is the amount of consumption when income is zero; a is the marginal propensity to consume. Geometrically, C_0 is the point at which the consumption function cuts the vertical axis, and a is the slope of the consumption function. The value of C_0 at zero income is wholly hypothetical, as there is no known instance of zero income for an entire society for any significant period of time. Students of algebra will recognize this equation for the consumption function as the formula for a graph of a straight line of the type depicted in Figure 6–1. A consumption function which has the characteristics of Equation 6–1 is usually described as a *cyclical* function, the reason being the pattern of actual data for the short-term fits such a schedule (See Figure 6–3).

The Saving Function

The counterpart to the consumption function is the *saving function*, which we may define as a *schedule showing the amounts that income recipients intend to save at different levels of income.* Saving is the nonconsumption of current income; because we are not at the moment con-

5. This comment needs to be qualified. Contemporary policy-makers clearly understand that one way to influence consumption spending (and with it the overall level of economic activity) is by changing taxes. A tax reduction, for example, will increase disposable income (Equation 6–1), which should lead to higher consumption spending. The Kennedy-Johnson administration did this in 1964, as did the Ford administration in 1975 and the Carter administration in 1977. The mechanics of tax changes and the income and employment effects are analyzed fully in Chapter 8.

cerned with any disposition of income other than consumption or saving, it logically follows that saving, too, is a function of income. In algebraic terms

$$S = f(Y_d) \tag{6–4}$$

Since we are assuming for the moment that consumption and saving are the only alternative uses of income, the saving schedule can be derived directly from the consumption function. At each income level intended saving will equal the difference between the aggregate supply function and the consumption function, and these are the amounts that should be plotted to derive a schedule as shown in Figure 6–2.

Since the saving function is conceptually similar to the consumption function, it is characterized by similar technical attributes. Thus the *average propensity to save* may be defined as the ratio of saving to income, S/Y_d, at a given level of income. It is the proportion of any given income that is saved. Like the propensity to consume, the ratio of saving to income may vary as the income level changes. At the intersection of the saving function and the horizontal axis (point *s* in Figure 6–2), the volume of saving is zero; hence the average propensity to save is zero. To the left of this point, the saving function drops below the horizontal axis, which means that saving is negative, or that dissaving is taking place. If this is the case, the saving-income ratio, S/Y_d, will be negative, which is as it should be, since the consumption-income ratio, C/Y_d, is greater than 1 under these circumstances. As long as we assume that consumption and saving are the only alternative uses of income, C/Y_d and S/Y_d must add up to unity. To the right of point *s*, the average propensity to save is not only greater than zero, but increases in value as the income level rises. The proportion of income saved increases as the income level increases.

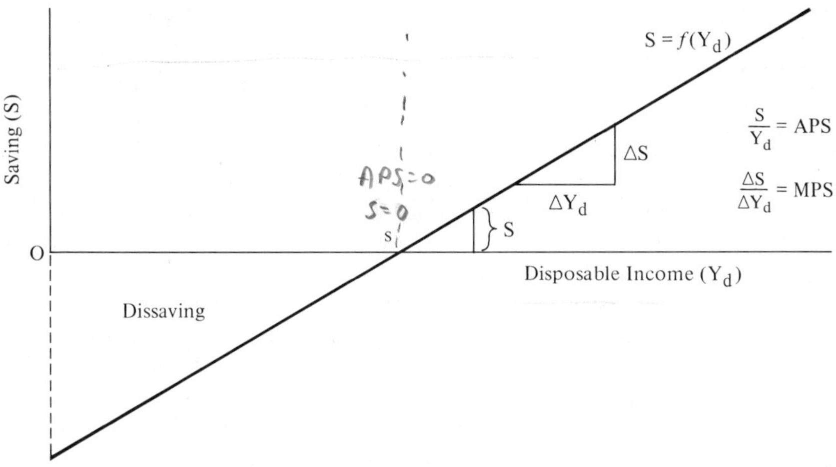

FIGURE 6–2. The Saving Function

The counterpart of the marginal propensity to consume is the marginal propensity to save. It is defined as the ratio of a change in saving, ΔS, to a change in income, ΔY_d. Analogous to the representation of the consumption function, the marginal propensity to save is depicted graphically by the slope of the saving schedule. If this schedule is assumed to be linear, the marginal propensity to save will have a constant value. Numerically, the marginal propensity to save is equal to 1 minus the marginal propensity to consume. This is true only so long as we adhere to our assumption that all income must be either consumed or saved. A marginal propensity to consume of 0.75 would mean a value of 0.25 for the marginal propensity to save, for if $0.75 is spent for consumption purposes out of an additional $1.00 of income, the balance of $0.25 is by definition saving. The ratio $\Delta S/\Delta Y_d$ must equal 0.25.

Empirical Verification

Up to this point in our analysis we have advanced two general propositions. The first of these is that consumption (and saving) is primarily a function of income, and the second is that the functional relationship between consumption (and saving) tends (in the short run) to assume the shape and character depicted by the schedules shown in Figures 6–1 and 6–2. But how well do these propositions accord with the facts of experience? In other words, do the statistical data pertaining to income and consumption expenditures tend to confirm the existence of the kind of behavior pattern embodied in the notion of the consumption function? Table 6–1 contains data on disposable income and personal consumption expenditures for the American economy for the period 1929–76. The table also shows the percentage of disposable income spent for consumption goods and services in each of these years. The data are computed in 1972 prices; thus we are dealing with real income and real consumption expenditures. A careful inspection of the data reveals a rather general tendency of consumption expenditure to conform to the pattern suggested by the Keynesian hypothesis. For example, from 1929 to 1933 disposable income declined, but the average propensity to consume rose. This is the type of behavior pattern for consumption expenditure suggested by the consumption function in Figure 6–1. From 1933 to 1937, a period in which disposable income was rising, the average propensity to consume underwent a decline. The same is true for the period 1938 through 1941. Between 1941 and 1945 the figures lose much of their value, since these were war years, and consumption expenditures as a percent of disposable income fell sharply because of wartime rationing, cutbacks in the production of consumer durables, pressures on the consumer to save and purchase war bonds, and general shortages of consumer goods and services. For the postwar period, beginning in 1946, disposable income has

TABLE 6–1. Disposable Income and Personal Consumption Expenditure: 1929–1976 (in billions of 1972 dollars)

	(1) Year	(2) Disposable Income	(3) Personal Consumption Expenditure	(4) = (3) ÷ (2) Propensity to Consume (in percent)	
	1929	$229.8	$215.6	93.8	
	1930	210.6	200.0	94.9	
	1931	201.7	192.1	95.2	
	1932	174.3	174.1	99.9	
	1933	169.7	170.7	100.6	
	1934	179.7	177.2	98.6	
	1935	196.6	188.1	95.7	
	1936	220.7	206.8	93.7	
	1937	227.8	214.3	94.1	
	1938	212.8	209.2	98.3	
	1939	230.1	220.3	95.7	
	1940	244.3	230.4	94.3	
WW II Years	1941	278.1	244.1	87.8	War Years
WW II Years	1942	317.3	241.7	76.2	War Years
WW II Years	1943	332.2	248.7	74.8	War Years
WW II Years	1944	343.9	255.7	74.4	War Years
WW II Years	1945	338.6	271.4	80.2	War Years
	1946	332.4	301.4	90.6	
	1947	318.8	306.2	96.0	
	1948	335.5	312.8	93.2	
	1949	336.1	320.0	95.2	
	1950	361.9	338.1	93.4	
	1951	371.6	342.3	92.1	
	1952	382.1	350.9	91.8	
	1953	397.5	364.2	91.6	
	1954	402.1	370.9	92.2	
	1955	425.9	395.1	92.8	
	1956	444.9	406.3	91.3	
	1957	453.9	414.7	91.4	
	1958	459.0	419.0	91.3	
	1959	477.4	441.5	92.5	
	1960	487.3	453.0	92.9	
	1961	500.6	462.2	92.3	
	1962	521.6	482.9	92.6	
	1963	539.2	501.4	92.9	
	1964	577.3	528.7	91.6	
	1965	612.4	558.1	91.1	
	1966	643.6	586.1	91.1	
	1967	669.8	603.2	90.1	
	1968	695.2	633.4	91.1	

TABLE 6–1. (*continued*)

(1) Year	(2) Disposable Income	(3) Personal Consumption Expenditure	(4) = (3) ÷ (2) Propensity to Consume (in percent)
1969	712.3	655.4	92.0
1970	741.6	668.9	90.2
1971	769.0	691.9	89.9
1972	801.3	733.0	91.5
1973	854.7	767.7	89.8
1974	840.8	759.1	90.3
1975	855.5	770.3	90.0
1976	890.7p	812.9	91.3

p = preliminary
SOURCE: U.S. Department of Commerce, *Survey of Current Business*, Oct., 1976; *Economic Report of the President*, 1977.

risen in relatively steady fashion. Consumption expenditure too has increased, but the average propensity to consume has shown, particularly in recent years, a greater tendency toward a constant value than was true of the prewar years. Note that in 1970 and 1971 the propensity to consume fell slightly, a consequence some economists believe of the temporary surtax on the personal income tax in effect at that time. Nevertheless, the postwar data appear to be roughly in line with the consumption function hypothesis.

A better view of the extent to which actual data conform to the Keynesian hypothesis can be obtained if we plot the data of Table 6–1 on a graph. This is done in Figure 6–3, wherein disposable income is measured on the horizontal axis and personal consumption expenditures on the vertical axis. When all the points representing consumption expenditure associated with disposable income for specific years are plotted, we have what statisticians term a *scatter diagram*. Such a diagram is highly useful for it helps us to determine whether or not values for two variables are related. As Professor R. G. D. Allen points out, if two variables are independent, then the value of one of the variables will be associated equally with large and small values for the other variable. In such a case the points will spread over the scatter diagram as if they were thrown there at random. On the other hand, if the value of one of the variables is uniquely determined by the value of the other variable, the points will lie on a line or curve that represents the *perfect* relationship between variables.[6] Such a line or curve is said to describe a perfect relationship in the sense that this would be the way in which the two variables are

6. R. G. D. Allen, *Statistics for Economists* (London: Hutchinson House, 1953), p. 120.

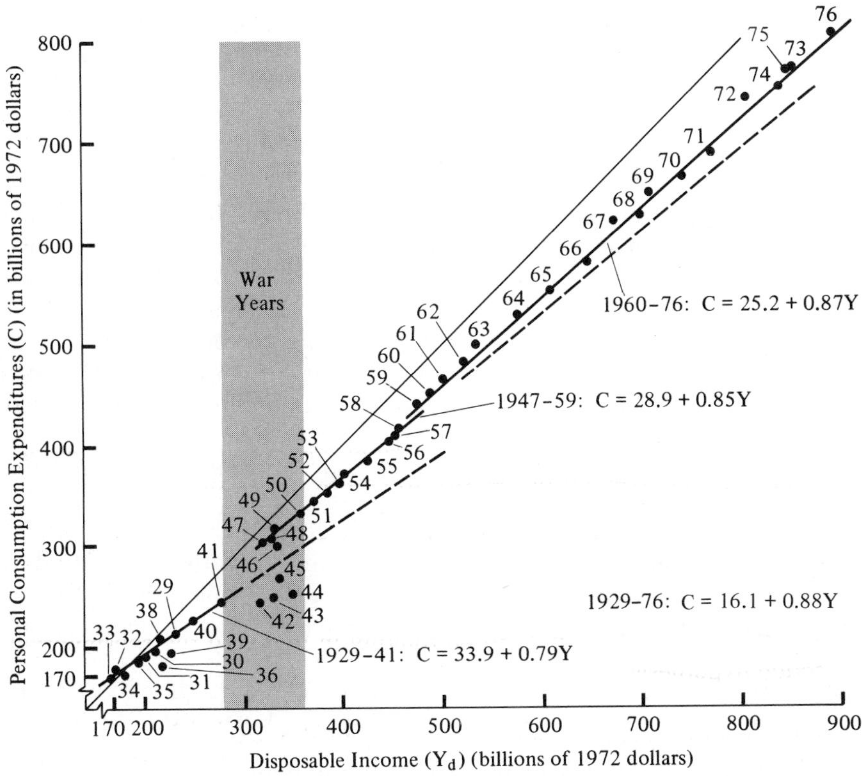

FIGURE 6–3. Consumption Expenditure and Disposable Income, 1929–72

related if the value of one of the variables was determined solely by the value of the other variable. This, of course, is rarely the case with any two variables in the real world.

The plotted data in Figure 6–3 fall into three distinct periods: 1929–41, 1947–59, and 1960–76. World War II was an abnormal period, as consumption expenditures as a percent of disposable income dropped well below prewar averages, the prime reason being the lack of consumer durables during the war. Thus, it is appropriate to look at the pre- and postwar periods separately. Keynes argued that the stability of the consumption function depended upon the existence of normal conditions, by which he meant the absence of wars, revolutions, or any form of social upheaval that might seriously distort the income-consumption relationship.

If we fit curves to the plotted data of Figure 6–3 we obtain three distinct schedules, one appropriate to each of the above-mentioned periods. Inspection of these curves shows, first, that the fit is not perfect, as all the points do not lie on the curves but, second, that there is a tendency for the actual data to be in accord with the consumption function hypothesis.[7] The general shape and slope of the curves is similar to the hypothetical consumption function of Figure 6–1. The fact that the fit of the curves is not perfect suggests that other factors besides income play a role in the determination of the level of consumption expenditure in the economy. Actually, there is nothing surprising in this, for neither Keynes nor any other modern economic theorist seriously maintains that income is the sole determinant of consumption expenditure. When we posit the notion of a functional relationship between income and consumption we are saying in effect that of the many factors that probably influence the level of consumption expenditure, income is of the most strategic significance. Later on we shall analyze some of the other factors.

Before we conclude our discussion of the empirical validity of the consumption function hypothesis, let us consider an additional fact revealed by the plotted data in Figure 6–3. It is apparent that these three curves differ from each other in both level and slope. In order to compare the three curves, we have extended the straight-line curve which best fits the appropriate data beyond the period to which the data applies (dotted lines in Figure 6–3). Note that the extension lies below the curve fitted to the next set of data. What is the significance of this? One possible answer is that the empirical data suggest the consumption function tends to shift upwards over time. The 1960–76 curve, for example, lies above the 1947–59 schedule, while the latter lies above the 1929–41 curve. There are good, logical reasons why this may happen, but we shall defer any further consideration of this point until later in this chapter when we discuss recent theoretical efforts to deal with the apparent phenomenon of the shifting consumption function.

The Process of Income Determination

Now that we have defined the consumption function, it is appropriate that we examine its usefulness as an analytical tool. In Chapter 5 we constructed a basic analytical framework designed to show how, in the short

7. In Figure 6–3 the schedules are fitted to the plotted data by simply drawing them in such a manner that they pass as closely as possible to all the dots. There are, of course, more exact and specialized statistical techniques for fitting a curve to data, but the approximation method employed here is adequate for our purposes. The lines which relate consumption to disposable income are called *regression lines*. Expressed as an equation, they take the form $C = C_o + aY_d$ (Equation 6–3). The empirical consumption functions for the three periods calculated from the data in Table 6–3 are shown in the figure.

run, the level of income and employment depends primarily on the aggregate demand function. It is desirable that we re-examine this framework with the objective of showing how the consumption function fits into the structure of the aggregate demand.

We shall assume a hypothetical economy in which there are only two categories of output or expenditure, consumption and investment. Table 6–2 contains data pertaining to this hypothetical economy. Column (1) in this table lists possible income levels for the economy (from 0 to $850 billion), while Column (2) represents the economy's consumption function, in that it reveals the intended consumption associated with these income levels.[8] The consumption function in this model is $C = 100 + .75Y_d$. This consumption function is also shown graphically in Figure 6–4. The 45° aggregate supply function (OZ in the figure) shows that the analysis is in real terms because output in constant prices is measured on both the horizontal and the vertical axes.

We shall assume that investment expenditure is autonomous with respect to the income level, that is, that the amount of investment expenditure is independently given—not determined by any of the other variables that enter into our hypothetical economic system. We are not implying that economic analysis has nothing to say about the determinants of investment spending. Rather, for the sake of convenience and analytical

TABLE 6–2. The Process of Income Determination
(in billions of constant dollars)

(1) Income Y_{np}	(2) *Planned Consumption* C	(3) *Planned Saving* S	(4) *Planned Investment* I	(5) *Aggregate Demand* $C+I$	(6) *Unplanned Inventory Change*
0	100.0	– 100.0	75	175.0	– 175.0
350	362.5	– 12.5	75	437.5	– 87.5
400	400.0	—	75	475.0	– 75.0
450	437.5	12.5	75	512.5	– 62.5
500	475.0	25.0	75	550.0	– 50.0
550	512.5	37.5	75	587.5	– 37.5
600	550.0	50.0	75	625.0	– 25.0
650	587.5	62.5	75	662.5	– 12.5
700	**625.0**	**75.0**	**75**	**700.0**	—
750	662.5	87.5	75	737.5	12.5
800	700.0	100.0	75	775.0	25.0
850	737.5	112.5	75	812.5	37.5

8. Since the hypothetical economy has only the two categories of output, consumption and investment, there are neither taxes nor transfer expenditures. Consequently, net national product and disposable income are identical. Thus: $(Y_{np} = Y_d)$. The consumption function is constructed such that the marginal propensity to consume has a value of 0.75.

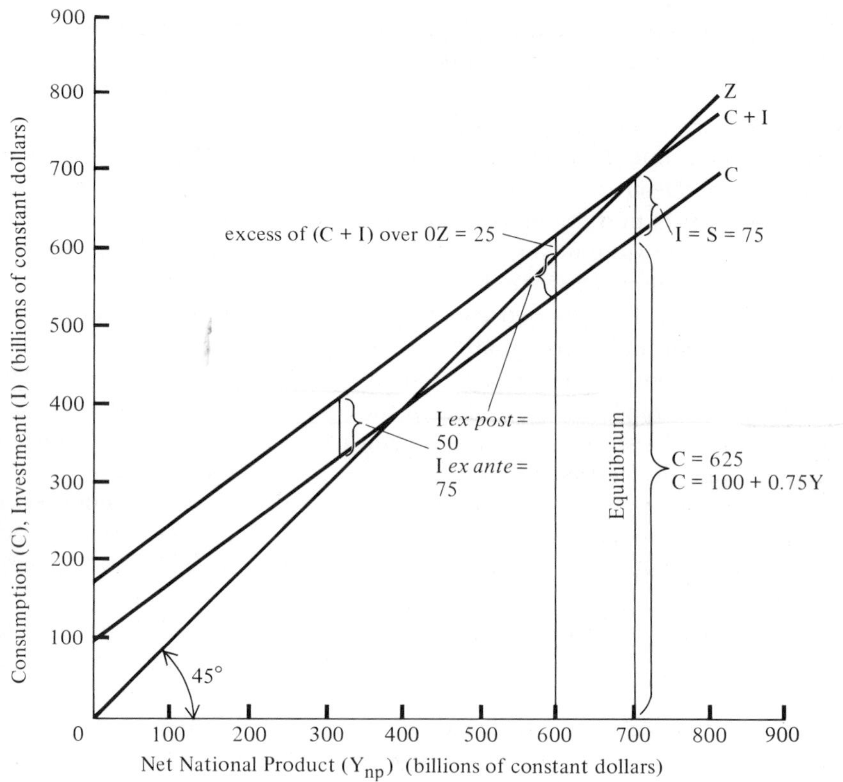

FIGURE 6–4. The Process of Income Determination

simplicity, we assume its value as given in the same sense that the schedule for the consumption function is given. Furthermore, we assume that the amount of investment expenditure will not change as the income level changes. Column (4) of Table 6–2 is this autonomous investment schedule. The term *schedule* is used deliberately here because the values shown are *ex ante*.

Since the schedule of aggregate demand consists of the sum of *ex ante* consumption and *ex ante* investment expenditure, we can construct this schedule for our hypothetical economy by adding an amount equal to autonomous investment to the consumption function. In Table 6–2 the results of this procedure are shown in Column (5). In Figure 6–4 we derive the aggregate demand function diagrammatically by drawing $C + I$ parallel to the consumption function and at a distance equal to the assumed value for autonomous investment expenditure. Thus aggregate demand is equal to the consumption function plus autonomous investment. We can express this idea algebraically in the form of an equation.

$$DD = (C_o + aY_d) + I \quad (6\text{–}5)$$

Given the fact that we have established an aggregate demand schedule, $C + I$, for this hypothetical economy, the process by which an equilibrium income level is attained is as described in Chapter 5. The equilibrium income (and employment) level is to be found at the point of intersection of the aggregate demand and aggregate supply schedules. On the basis of the data contained in Table 6–2 the income equilibrium is \$700 billion.[9] It is at this income level that the aggregate demand schedule of Figure 6–4 intersects the aggregate supply schedule. If actual income is below the \$700-billion level in any income period, a disequilibrium situation in which aggregate demand is in excess of aggregate supply will result. This will set in motion forces that tend to drive the income level higher. As long as aggregate demand is in excess of aggregate supply, income and employment will continue to rise toward the equilibrium position. Conversely, an income level above \$700 billion cannot be sustained because aggregate supply then runs ahead of aggregate demand, a condition that will lead to unwanted inventory accumulation and eventual cutbacks in output. A downward adjustment in income and employment levels would continue until output is once again in balance with total demand. Equilibrium is a situation in which producing and spending intentions coincide and, given the assumed schedules of consumption and investment for this hypothetical economy, the only income level at which such coincidence is possible is \$700 billion.

The Identity of Saving and Investment

In the discussion of the relationship between income and wealth in Chapter 2, the statement was made that saving and investment are necessarily identical when conceived of in an *ex post* sense. This *ex post* equality (or accounting identity of saving and investment as it is sometimes called) logically follows from the way in which we defined saving and investment. The basic identity equations for a simple economy in which consumption and investment are the only categories of output permit us to demonstrate that saving and investment must be equal. This equality holds good all the time.

There is, however, a condition in which saving and investment are not necessarily always equal. This is when saving and investment are conceived of in an *ex ante* sense, which means planned saving and investment. The claim that in one sense saving and investment are always equal, and that in another sense they are not necessarily equal, may at first glance seem to be logically impossible. For a number of years after the publication of Keynes's *The General Theory* lively controversy raged

9. See the Appendix to this chapter for construction of a simple algebraic model of income determination and its use to obtain the \$700 billion equilibrium figure.

among professional economists over the exact meaning of these concepts and the sense in which they were equal or not equal. Actually, however, it is not difficult to reconcile the seemingly contradictory claims.

Let us assume that the economy in Table 6–2 and Figure 6–4 has not yet attained an equilibrium income level. Income in the current period, let us say, is at the level of $600 billion. We know that this particular level cannot be maintained, but for the moment that is not of primary concern to us. We want to understand what is taking place during the current income period, irrespective of how income may change in subsequent periods. The consumption will be $550 billion. This is planned consumption expenditure, since the consumption function is an *ex ante* phenomenon. If planned consumption is $550 billion, then it follows logically that *ex ante* saving must equal $50 billion, because the saving function is the counterpart of the consumption function and is derived (in this hypothetical economy) by subtracting the consumption function from the aggregate supply schedule. But since the actual income level must always lie on the aggregate supply schedule, this is tantamount to saying the *ex ante* saving is equal to the distance between actual income and *ex ante* consumption.

But what of investment? Column (4) of Table 6–2 has already been described as the autonomous investment schedule. This means that the unchanging level of *ex ante,* or planned investment expenditure is $75 billion. But if investment *ex ante* is equal to $75 billion, while saving *ex ante* is equal to $50 billion, we have a situation in which these two entities are not equal. The failure of *ex ante* saving and investment to be in balance is a prime indicator of the existence of a disequilibrium condition with respect to the income and employment level; the income equilibrium must be defined in terms of equality between *ex ante* saving and *ex ante* investment.

There is nothing mysterious about the notion that saving and investment *ex ante* are not always equal, because there is no inherent reason why the intentions or plans of savers in the economy should always coincide with the intentions or plans of those undertaking investment expenditure. They may coincide, of course, although it is more likely that they will not.

Returning now to the idea that saving and investment *ex post* must always be equal, let us see how this concept of the identity between saving and investment can be explained through reference to the data of Table 6–2. By definition, saving is the nonconsumption of current income, so in this hypothetical economy saving *ex post* (or actual) must also be equal to $50 billion at the income level of $600 billion. Investment has been defined as the net addition to the economy's stock of wealth that results when the whole of current income (i.e., output) is not consumed. Thus actual investment in an income period is the difference between income and consumption. In the income period which we have under consideration, actual, or *ex post*, investment equals current income ($600 billion) minus current consumption ($550 billion), or $50 billion. This is the same as *ex post* saving during the income period.

At this point the reader may wonder how to reconcile *ex post* investment of $50 billion with *ex ante* investment of $75 billion. Since our analysis is constructed to rule out any change in the general level of prices, if planned investment runs ahead of actual investment, the difference between planned (*ex ante*) and actual (*ex post*) investment represents the portion of total demand that is satisfied through sales from *existing* stocks of goods. In Figure 6–4 it can be seen that at the $600-billion level of income this difference of $25 billion between investment *ex ante* and investment *ex post* is the identical amount by which the aggregate demand schedule exceeds the aggregate supply schedule. This $25 billion represents the amount of inventory *disinvestment* that has taken place in the income period because aggregate demand is in excess of aggregate supply. This inventory disinvestment is unplanned and comes about primarily because producers (in the aggregate) have underestimated the level of aggregate demand. It is *unplanned* investment or investment in stocks that is the balancing item between planned and actual investment.[10] Column (6) in Table 6–2 shows this magnitude for all income levels.

From the foregoing discussion we emerge with the important conclusion that equilibrium requires that saving and investment *ex ante* be equal. Equilibrium also means that *ex ante* and *ex post* values coincide. Disequilibrium exists if saving and investment are not equal in an *ex ante* sense, and whenever this is the case, forces are set in motion that make for a change either upward or downward in the income and employment level.

The Theory of the Multiplier

In Chapter 5 we pointed out that changes in the income and employment level can be of two distinct types. In the one instance, we have the kind of change just discussed that involves adjustment toward a specific equilibrium level, given known positions for the schedules that enter into the structure of aggregate demand. There is also the kind of change that takes place when an existing equilibrium situation is disturbed as a result

10. It is possible that there can be unplanned saving as well as unplanned investment. Unplanned saving may come about if consumption expenditure lags behind changes in income. In our analysis however, we are assuming that consumption expenditure adjusts immediately to any change in income. This is not necessarily the case in reality.

of a shift in the position of the aggregate demand schedule. A change of this type can be brought about by a shift in any of the schedules that constitute the aggregate demand schedule. This includes the consumption function, although most economists believe it to be highly stable under normal conditions. The implications of shifts in the aggregate demand schedule lead us into consideration of one of the most significant facets of modern income and employment theory, the *multiplier process*.

Let us assume, using data for the consumption function from Table 6–2 and Figure 6–4, that the autonomous investment schedule shifts upward by $25 billion. This means simply that at all the relevant income levels businessmen are prepared to spend for investment goods at an annual rate of $100 billion rather than $75 billion. Table 6–3 contains data for this new situation. Inspection of this table reveals that the effect of this increase in autonomous investment expenditure has been to shift the aggregate demand schedule upward by a like amount, namely, $25 billion. These new data for our hypothetical economy are plotted in Figure 6–5.

What has been the consequence for the income equilibrium of this upward shift in the schedule of autonomous investment expenditure and the upward shift in the aggregate demand schedule? If we look at the numerical data of Table 6–3 and the graphic presentation of these data in Figure 6–5, we are struck by the fact that the equilibrium income level has risen not by $25 billion, but by $100 billion. Here is a clear illustration of the multiplier process: An autonomous change in one of the variables that enters into the structure of aggregate demand has brought about a change in the income level several times greater than the amount of the initiating change. Technically, the multiplier can be defined as the *coefficient* which relates an increment of expenditure to an increment of income.[11] Keynes discussed the multiplier process entirely in terms of an *investment multiplier*, which he designated by the symbol k. The investment multiplier "tells us that, when there is an increment of aggregate investment, income will increase by an amount which is k times the increment of investment."[12] In algebraic form this idea is expressed as

$$\Delta Y_{np} = k\Delta I \qquad (6\text{–}6)$$

11. Basically the multiplier process is concerned with real changes. We are assuming that any change in expenditure for either consumption or investment goods leads to a corresponding increase in the output of these goods. This does not mean that a multiplier effect in purely monetary terms cannot take place in the economy. If, for example, there would be an increase in expenditure when the economy is at a level of full employment, the multiplier would still come into play, but the ensuing income changes would be wholly the result of changes in the general level of prices.

12. Keynes, p. 115. The net national product, Y_{np}, equals disposable income, Y_d, for in the simple system under discussion, which has neither taxes nor transfers the two measures of income are identical.

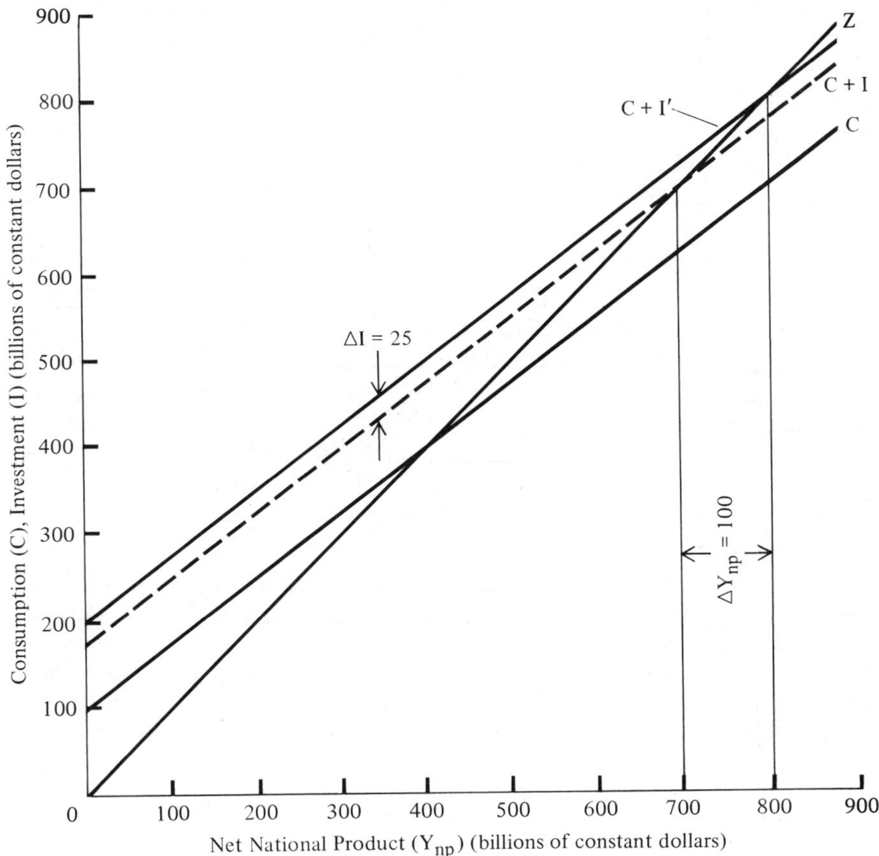

FIGURE 6–5. Multiplier Effect of a Shift in the Investment Function

From this equation it follows that we can define the multiplier as a ratio of a change in income ΔY_{np} to a change in investment, ΔI. Thus

$$k = \frac{\Delta Y_{np}}{\Delta I} \tag{6–7}$$

Although Keynes analyzed the multiplier process almost entirely in terms of the relationship between changes in investment and changes in income, the reader should not be misled into thinking that the multiplier effect is limited to changes in investment expenditure. Actually it is a coefficient that links any autonomous shift in aggregate demand to the consequent change in income. This point is emphasized because it is usually most convenient to introduce and discuss the theory of the multiplier through analysis of changes in the investment component of the aggregate demand structure.

What lies behind the fundamental idea of the multiplier that any change in the expenditure rate for any of the component parts of the aggregate demand schedule will have magnified effects upon the overall income level? To answer this, let us go back and trace what happens in the economy when, as is assumed in Table 6–3, there is an increase in the rate of investment expenditure equal to $25 billion. For the moment we need not be concerned with the means by which this extra $25 billion of investment expenditure is financed; all that interests us is that businessmen have increased their spending for investment goods by $25 billion.

When this happens, the first discernible result is that the producers or suppliers of investment or capital goods will find their incomes have risen by $25 billion, because increased spending for investment goods will lead to an increase in their production and, as more output is generated, incomes will rise. Thus, the primary effect of the increased spending for investment goods will be to create an equal amount of new income (in the form of wages, rents, interest, and profits) which will accrue to resource owners in the capital goods producing sector of the economy. What will happen after this? For the answer to this question we return to Keynes's assertion that whenever income increases there will be a strong tendency for the beneficiaries of such increases to step up their expenditures for consumption goods and services. In the case of our hypothetical economy, the beneficiaries of the initial increase in spending are those engaged in the production of investment goods. Since the members of this group have experienced a rise in their incomes, it is to be expected that

TABLE 6–3. Increased Investment and the Income Equilibrium (in billions of contant dollars)

(1) Income Y_{np}	(2) Planned Consumption C	(3) Planned Saving S	(4) Planned Investment I	(5) Aggregate Demand C + I	(6) Unplanned Inventory Change
0	100.0	– 100.0	100	200.0	– 200.0
350	362.5	– 12.5	100	462.5	– 112.5
400	400.0	—	100	500.0	– 100.0
450	437.5	12.5	100	537.5	– 87.5
500	475.0	25.0	100	575.0	– 75.0
550	512.5	37.5	100	612.5	– 62.5
600	550.0	50.0	100	650.0	– 50.0
650	587.5	62.5	100	687.5	– 37.5
700	625.0	75.0	100	725.0	– 25.0
750	622.5	87.5	100	762.5	– 12.5
800	**700.0**	**100.0**	**100**	**800.0**	—
850	737.5	112.5	100	837.5	12.5

they will spend some part of this additional income for consumption goods and services. There will be, in other words, *induced* changes in consumption expenditure. These induced changes can be described as a *secondary* effect flowing from the increased spending for investment goods.

We have been able to isolate and describe two major effects associated with an increase in expenditure of the kind that leads to an increase in output and increased incomes for the producers of the output. These effects are a *primary*, or initial, effect, which is associated with the initial change in income, and a *secondary*, or induced, effect, which arises out of the fact that the original recipients of the increased income will in turn spend some portion of this increase for consumer goods and services. It is in this secondary effect that we have the real key to the multiplier process, for in the absence of any induced or secondary changes in spending, the impact of increased investment expenditure (or any other form of spending) on the income level could be no greater than the amount of the initial change in income. The multiplier effect results from the sum of the initial and induced changes in expenditure (and output) that ensue from a change in the rate of expenditure for any of the component parts of the aggregate, demand structure.

What, however, determines the amount of induced spending? The answer is quite simple: the *marginal propensity to consume*. Once we know what proportion of an increment of income will be spent for consumption goods and services, we are in a position to determine how great will be the secondary or induced effects resulting from autonomous increases in expenditure. The marginal propensity to consume thus provides the analytical key to the increases in secondary spending and, consequently, to the numerical value of the multiplier.

The Formal Multiplier Process

To understand the multiplier process clearly, the first step is to trace in detail the effects of the increase in investment expenditure of $25 billion. The hypothetical consumption function presented in Tables 6–2 and 6–3 is constructed in such a way that it has a slope of .75, which means that the marginal propensity to consume, a, is .75; out of every $1.00 increment of income $.75 will be spent for consumption. On the basis of this and given our assumed increase in investment outlays of $25 billion, we have constructed Table 6–4 to show how this initial increment in investment expenditure will generate a whole chain of respendings. The first column, which contains only the figure of $25 billion, represents the *initiating* increase in expenditure. The second column represents groups of income recipients, designated by numbers, while the third column records the increments of income that accrue to each of these groups as a result of

TABLE 6–4. The Multiplier: With a Single Initiating Increase in Investment Expenditure (in billions of constant dollars)

(1) *Initiating Increase in Expenditure* ΔI	(2) *Income Recipients*	(3) *Income Changes* ΔY_{np}	(4) *Induced Consumption* ΔC	(5) *Algebraic Derivation of* ΔC
$25.00	1st Group	$25.00	$18.75	ΔIa
	2nd Group	18.75	14.06	ΔIa^2
	3rd Group	14.06	10.55	ΔIa^3
	4th Group	10.55	7.91	ΔIa^4
	5th Group	7.91	5.93	ΔIa^5
	6th Group	5.93	4.45	ΔIa^6
	7th Group	4.45	3.34	ΔIa^7
	8th Group	3.34	2.50	ΔIa^8
	9th Group	2.50	1.86	ΔIa^9
	nth Group	1.86	1.40	ΔIa^n
25.00		$\Sigma = 100.0$*	$\Sigma = 75.0$*	

*After an infinite number of spendings and respendings.

successive rounds of spending. The fourth column shows the *induced* consumption spending that results from the income increases experienced by each successive group. The fifth column shown the algebraic derivation of the change in consumption for each group, based upon the initiating increase in investment expenditure of $25 billion. Breaking the process of income change down into separate groups of income recipients is an artificial simplification, but it does enable us to analyze clearly how an initial increase in spending has multiple effects.

The initial increase in investment expenditure accrues as income to the first group, which then increases its consumption expenditures by $18.75 billion (75 percent of $25 billion). The spending will accrue as income to the suppliers of these consumption goods and services, namely, the second group, which also increases its consumption expenditures by 75 percent of the rise in its income, providing additional income for yet a third group. And so forth. We can thus see that the initial increase in expenditure will generate a series of spendings and respendings, which, if carried far enough, will raise income by some multiple of the original increment. The data in Table 6–4 show that ultimately the sum of induced consumption expenditure will total $75 billion, which, with the original increase in investment expenditure of $25 billion, will add up to a total increase of income of $100 billion or four times the initiating increase. The value of the multiplier in this case is 4. Students familiar with mathematics will recognize that the total change in income (ΔY_{np}) involves a geometric progression of infinite sequence in which the change in investment (ΔI) is the first term and the marginal propensity to consume (a) is the common ratio or fixed number by which each preceding number in the sequence is multiplied.

Two further aspects of Table 6–4 should be noted. First, the multiplier has a time dimension, since it would be quite impossible in reality for the whole series of spending and respending to occur simultaneously. This point is stressed because in theoretical analysis we often ignore, for reasons of simplicity, the time element in the multiplier process. Second, the data of Table 6–4 show only what happens with a single, nonrecurring increment of investment expenditure. If we extended our example over a greater time span, income, which at first rose, would gradually fall back to its original level. The total increase in income spread over the whole time period in which the multiplier process was at work would, of course, equal the $100 billion shown in Table 6–4, but this would not be a permanent change. In order for the equilibrium income level to rise permanently to a new and higher level—which is the situation depicted in Table 6–3 and Figure 6–5—the increase in expenditure that initially triggers the expansion must be a *sustained* increase. Investment expenditure would have to expand from $75 billion to $100 billion and remain at that level if an enduring increase in the income level from $700 to $800 billion were to be brought about.

The nature of the multiplier process, given the assumption of a sustained increase of $25 billion in investment expenditure, is shown in Table 6–5. The data shown for Period 0 pertain to the equilibrium existing prior to the increase in investment expenditure by $25 billion. In Period 1 investment expenditure increases by $25 billion, a development which amounts to a shift upward in the aggregate demand schedule from $700 billion to $725 billion. In this table we are operating on the assump-

TABLE 6–5. The Multiplier: With a Sustained Increase in Investment Expenditure (in billions of constant dollars)

(1) Period	(2) Aggregate Demand $C+I$	(3) Aggregate Supply Y_{np}	(4) Actual Increase in Output ΔY_{np}	(5) Planned Consumption C	(6) Induced Consumption ΔC	(7) Planned Investment I	(8) = (3) − (5) Actual Investment I'
0	$700.00	$700.00	—	$625.00	—	$ 75.00	$75.00
1	725.00	700.00	—	625.00	—	100.00	75.00
2	743.75	725.00	$25.00	643.75	$18.75	100.00	81.25
3	757.18	743.75	18.75	657.81	14.06	100.00	85.94
4	768.36	757.81	14.06	668.36	10.55	100.00	89.45
5	776.27	768.36	10.55	676.27	7.91	100.00	92.05
6	782.20	776.27	7.91	682.20	5.93	100.00	94.07
7	786.65	782.20	5.93	686.65	4.45	100.00	95.55
8	789.99	786.65	4.45	689.99	3.34	100.00	96.66
∞	800.00	800.00	—	700.00	—	100.00	100.00

tion that output cannot respond instantaneously to an increase in expenditure; consequently, output does not rise to the level of aggregate demand of Period 1 until Period 2. In Period 2 the actual increase in output of $25 billion—Column (4) in the table—induces additional consumption expenditure in the amount of $18.75 billion as shown in Column (6). This is because the assumed value for the marginal propensity to consume is .75. Aggregate demand in Period 2, therefore, is equal to the total of planned consumption expenditure ($625 billion plus $18.75 billion) and planned investment expenditure ($100 billion). Output in this period has risen in response to the level of aggregate demand of the previous period, but aggregate demand has risen even higher because of the phenomenon of induced consumption expenditure. Gradually, though, the increments of induced consumption become smaller and smaller as the new equilibrium level of $800 billion is approached. In theory, this level will be reached only at the expiration of an infinite number of income periods, but, as a practical matter, the increments of both income and consumption expenditure will become insignificantly small after a finite number of periods. Once the new equilibrium income level has been attained, consumption expenditure will total $700 billion and investment expenditure will be $100 billion. There has been a multiplier effect of 4, because the initial increase of $25 billion in investment expenditure has brought about a total increase in income of $100 billion.

Algebraic Statement of the Multiplier

Now that we have examined by means of a numerical example the multiplier process, let us formalize the concept by stating it in terms of some relatively simple algebraic formulas. From our investigation of the multiplier process we have discovered that the magnitude of the multiplier effect depends upon the sum of initial and secondary effects. We saw that the key to the magnitude of the secondary effect is the marginal propensity to consume. Let us begin our algebraic analysts with the basic identity.

$$Y_{np} = I + C = Y_d \tag{6–8}$$

The above equality is true because we are assuming neither taxes nor transfer payments (see footnote 7). In the following algebraic discussion, the multiplier is defined in relation to net national product, which is the same as disposable income, given the foregoing assumption.
From the above identity it follows

$$\Delta Y_{np} = \Delta I + \Delta C \tag{6–9}$$

In the preceding analysis it was concluded that induced consumption expenditures depend upon the value of the marginal propensity to consume. In Equation (6–3) the marginal propensity to consume out of disposable income ($\Delta C/\Delta Y_d$) was designated as a. Since Y_d and Y_{np} are assumed to be equal, we can substitute $a\Delta Y_{np}$ for ΔC in Equation (6–9). We now have

$$\Delta Y_{np} = \Delta I + a\Delta Y_{np} \qquad (6\text{–}10)$$

Let us manipulate this equation albegraically as follows:

$$\Delta Y_{np} - a\Delta Y_{pn} = \Delta I \qquad (6\text{–}11)$$

$$\Delta Y_{np}(1-a) = \Delta I \qquad (6\text{–}12)$$

$$\Delta Y_{np} = \Delta I \times \frac{1}{1-a} \qquad (6\text{–}13)$$

$$\frac{\Delta Y_{np}}{\Delta I} = \frac{1}{1-a} \qquad (6\text{–}14)$$

The left-hand side of Equation (6–14) is what was defined in Equation (6–7) as the multiplier, the ratio of a change in income to a change in investment. From this we may conclude that in a formal, mathematical sense the multiplier is equal to *the reciprocal of 1 minus the marginal propensity to consume.*[13] In our simple and hypothetical economy the multiplier would also be equal to the reciprocal of the marginal propensity to save, for as long as saving and consumption are viewed as the only alternatives for the disposition of income, it is a simple matter of arithmetical truth that one minus the marginal propensity to consume, $1 - \Delta C/\Delta Y_d$, equals the marginal propensity to save, $\Delta S/\Delta Y_d$. But one must be careful here not to generalize that the value of the multiplier is always equal to the reciprocal of the marginal propensity to save. It is equal to this only in the absence of taxes and foreign trade.

Now that we have defined the multiplier algebraically, we shall review the process and apply the formula to the data of our hypothetical economy. Originally, the income equilibrium level was $700 billion, given the consumption function and a level of investment expenditure of $75 billion (Table 6–2). The marginal propensity to consume is .75, which yields a numerical value for the multiplier of 4. All that is necessary is to apply this coefficient to the change in investment expenditure, $25 billion. A change of investment expenditure of this amount will cause income to rise by $100 billion ($k \times \Delta I = 4 \times \$25$ billion $= \$100$ billion). As a result of this $100-billion increase in income, consumption expenditure will rise by $75 billion.

13. The theoretical limits to the value of the multiplier are 1 and infinity (∞). If the value of the marginal propensity to consume is zero (0), then the multiplier will have a value of 1; if, on the other hand, the value of the marginal propensity to consume is 1.00 (100 percent), the multiplier will have a value of infinity (∞). The reader should work out the simple arithmetic to convince himself that it is true.

Summary Remarks on the Theory of the Multiplier

Before we discuss other important aspects of consumption theory, it is important to summarize the salient features of the multiplier concept.

First, the multiplier is a device for explaining why a change in spending may have cumulative effects upon the income level. The multiplier is associated with any autonomous change in expenditure in the economic system; it is not limited, as in our example, to changes in investment expenditure.

Second, the multiplier is properly regarded as an aspect of consumption theory, since its value depends upon induced consumption spending.[14] The amount of induced, or secondary, consumption spending that will ensue depends upon the marginal propensity to consume, the slope of the consumption function.

Third, the magnitude of the multiplier effect is inversely related to the total of *leakages* from the current income stream. Income that is not spent for currently produced consumption goods and services may be regarded as having *leaked out* of the income stream. Most economists regard the marginal propensity to consume as normally having value of less than 1, because it is felt that some leakages are bound to be present. In this chapter saving represented the only form of leakage from the income stream. In reality, though, there are other forms of leakages. Tax collections and expenditures for imported goods and services can be considered as leakages, as we shall see subsequently. A leakage is anything that reduces the tendency toward the spending or respending of income on currently produced domestic goods and services; the greater such leakages, the smaller will be the multiplier effect. It is for this reason that we cannot claim that the multiplier is always equal to the reciprocal of the marginal propensity to save. If we could determine and measure all leakages as marginal propensities, then we could state comprehensively that the multiplier has a value equal to the reciprocal of the sum of all leakages.

Finally, we must be very careful to note that the computation of a numerical value for the multiplier depends upon accurate knowledge of the economy's consumption function and marginal propensity to consume. The empirical data examined earlier suggest that consumers tend to behave in the fashion indicated by the consumption function hypothesis, but this does not mean that it is easy to construct a statistical consumption function which will determine the exact value of the multiplier for the economy. In the mid-1960s, the Council of Economic Advisers estimated a value of two for the multiplier effect of a contemplated tax cut. This estimate turned out to be approximately correct. In essence, we are

14. It should be noted that consumption expenditure is not the only type of expenditure that may be induced through a change in income. It is possible for investment expenditure, too, to be induced. This is a matter that we shall discuss in the following chapter.

cautioning against an overly simple interpretation of the multiplier phenomenon. If we recognize and understand this limitation, we are still left with a concept of great value for analysis of the process of change in the income and employment level.

Income, Consumption, and Saving in the Long Run

There is another aspect of the income-consumption relationship which has intrigued economists for a number of years. The consumption function depicted in Figure 6–1 is one in which the average propensity to consume falls as the income level rises. The slope of a function of this type is such that it intersects both the aggregate supply function and the vertical axis. Since this schedule pertains to the behavior of consumption expenditure over relatively short periods of time, it is usually described as a short-run, or cyclical, function. The statistical data shown in Table 6–1 and plotted in Figure 6–3 tend to confirm the existence of this type of relationship.

A dilemma is created by the fact, however, that statistics on income, consumption, and savings for very long periods of time show that the consumption-income ratio, C/Y, tends to be constant. In some path-breaking studies published just after World War II, Nobel laureate Simon Kuznets showed that for approximately 60 years (1869 to 1929), the ratio between consumption and income tended to be constant.[15] Kuznets's data are shown in Table 6–6. Also shown in this table are data for two post–World War II decades, 1950–59 and 1960–69. These more recent data are not strictly comparable with the earlier data developed by Kuznets, primarily because he employed different definitions of both the net national product and consumption expenditures than those currently used by the Department of Commerce. Nevertheless, the post–World War II data also show a constant ratio between consumption spending and income (net national product). The only exception to this for data in the table is the decade 1929–38, when the ratio of consumption to income rose to nearly 100 percent, the reason being that this period included years of the Great Depression.

The upshot of all this is that over the long run, consumers spend about the same proportion of their income, even though they have experienced a steady rise in the level of real income. As a matter of fact, in the 60

15. Simon Kuznets, *Uses of National Income in Peace and War* (New York: National Bureau of Economic Research, 1942), p. 31, table 2, and p. 35, table 6. See also Kuznets, *National Product since 1869* (New York: National Bureau of Economic Research, 1946), p. 119. Similar results were found by Raymond Goldsmith. See his *A Study of Savings in the United States* (Princeton: Princeton University Press, 1955), pp. 22, 78.

TABLE 6–6. Net National Product and Consumption Expenditures in the Long-Run (in billions of 1929 dollars)

(1) Decade	(2) Net National Product	(3) Consumption Expenditures	(4) Average Propensity to Consume (3) ÷ (4)
1869–78	$ 9.3	$ 8.1	87.1
1874–83	13.6	11.6	85.2
1879–88	17.9	15.3	85.5
1884–93	21.0	17.7	84.2
1889–98	24.2	20.2	83.5
1894–1903	29.8	25.4	85.2
1904–1913	45.0	39.1	86.9
1909–18	50.6	44.0	86.9
1919–28	69.0	62.0	89.8
1924–33	73.3	68.9	94.0
1929–38	72.0	71.0	98.7
1950–59*	520.5	384.3	73.8
1960–69*	740.2	546.4	73.8

SOURCE: Decades for 1869–78 through 1929–38 from Simon Kuznets, *National Product Since 1869* (New York: National Bureau of Economic Research, 1946), p. 119. Decades 1950–59 and 1960–69, *Economic Report of the President* (Washington, D.C., U.S. Government Printing Office, 1977), pp. 190, 206.

*1950–59 and 1960–69 data are for national income rather than net national product and are in 1972 dollars.

years covered by Kuznets's data when the propensity to consume remained practically constant, *real* income rose nearly eightfold. Diagramatically, the long-term (or *secular*) consumption function appears as a straight line whose slope is such that the marginal and average propensities to consume are equal. Such a consumption function is shown in Figure 6–6. The Kuznets data are also shown in this figure. It is called a secular function because it pertains to the behavior of consumption expenditures in relation to income over long periods of time.

The dilemma faced by economists is how to reconcile statistical evidence on the long-run constancy of the average propensity to consume with equally worthy statistical evidence which shows that in the short run the consumption-income ratio is not a constant. Actually, we have already suggested the one solution to this dilemma, for in our earlier discussion of the empirical validity of the consumption function hypothesis we pointed out that the short-run data on income and consumption suggest that over time the consumption function may actually be shifting upwards. The secular upward "drift" of the consumption function, as it has been called,

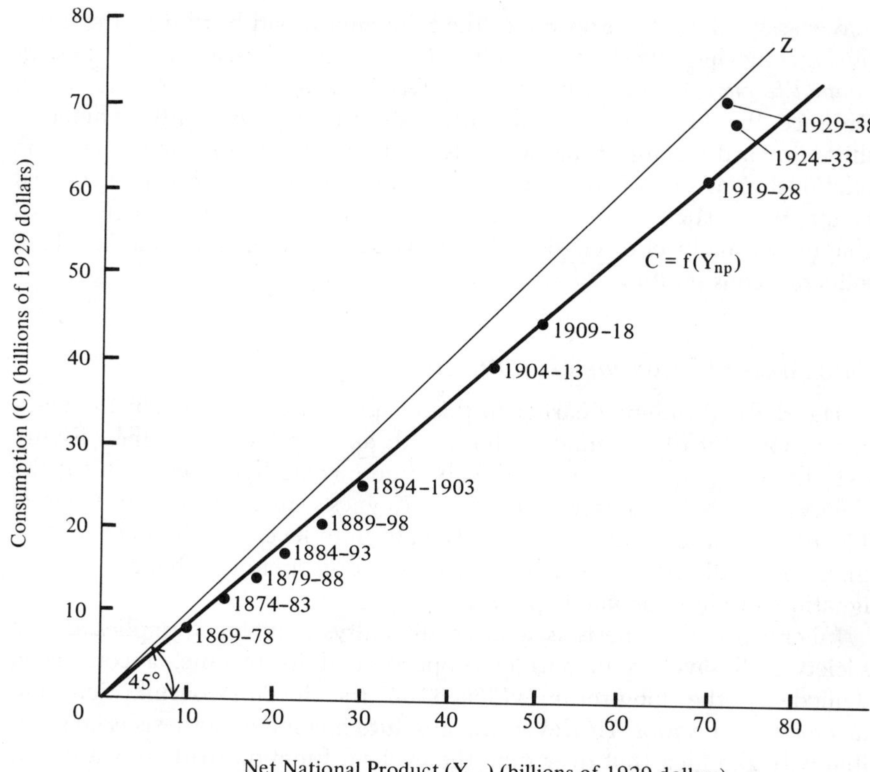

FIGURE 6–6. The Secular Consumption Function

is clearly seen in Figure 6–3, when we extrapolate data from earlier periods into later periods. In each instance the extrapolated curve (the dotted line extensions in Figure 6–3) lies below the curve which fits the measured data in the next period. Thus, it may be argued that the measured consumption function has shifted upwards.

This, however, is not the only possible explanation of the observed differences between the consumption-income ratio in the long run as compared to the short-run. It may also be argued logically and convincingly that the *real* relationship between consumption and income is one of proportionality (as revealed by the long-term data), but that short-term—or *cyclical*—factors distort this relationship, giving us the kind of consumption-income pattern displayed in Figure 6–3. What is the proper explanation for these differences in empirical findings? Unfortunately, contemporary income theory does not have a precise answer to this question. Rather, there has emerged from the research of the last several decades three general hypotheses—or theories—which seek to explain the ratio of consumption to income and what happens to this ratio through time. We may classify these theories under the following broad headings: the *absolute* income hypothesis; the *relative* income hypothesis; and the *permanent (life-cycle)* income hypothesis. The first two are hypotheses which embrace the idea that the measured short-term consumption function shifts upward through time, whereas the third hypothesis views the basic relationship as one of proportionality, distorted by short-term or cyclical factors.[16] We shall examine each of these theories, and then conclude this chapter with a brief discussion of some variables other than income which influence consumption.

The Absolute Income Hypothesis

The thesis developed earlier in this chapter to the effect that the average propensity to consume declines with an increase in income (Figure 6–1) has come to be known as the absolute income hypothesis. This is the theory that stems most directly from Keynes's analysis in *The General Theory.* Its basic tenet is that it is the absolute level of a family's income that, above all else, determines its consumption spending; hence, the designation absolute income hypothesis.

Inherent in this thesis is a basic difficulty; namely, it implies that a society will save an increasing proportion of its income, a conclusion denied by the long-term evidence on the income-consumption and income-saving ratios. However, the absolute income hypothesis is compatible with the idea that over time the cyclical function drifts upward, but as theory it does not offer an explanation for this phenomenon.

What this means is that we must look to a change in one or more variables other than income to account for this shift. In the analysis of consumer spending, the general practice is to treat all influences on consumption other than income as *parameters,* whose values determine the level and slope of the consumption function.[17] If there are changes in the parameters, then the position of the consumption function will shift. What kinds of influences might account for the secular upward drift of a consumption function of the type $C = C_o + aY_d$?

Several such factors have been identified by economists as capable of exercising this kind of influence, although no conclusive statistical evi-

16. Strictly speaking the third category involves two separate theories, the *permanent* income hypothesis *and* the *life-cycle* hypothesis, but their basic ideas are so similar that there is ample justification to put them into a single category for purposes of explanation and exposition.

17. Parameters are magnitudes whose values are assumed to be constant. As such they determine the position of the function. The parameters of the consumption function are C_0 and a; changes in other factors influencing the consumption decision operate to change the value of these constants.

dence exists showing a strong correlation between them and consumer spending. Among the most important of these parameters are household wealth, the distribution of income, the introduction of new consumer goods, urbanization, changes in the age structure of the population, and a decline in the number of self employed persons in the economy. For example, with an increase in household wealth, there might be a greater willingness to spend out of current income, thus raising the average propensity to consume. Urbanization might have the same effect because thee is some evidence that saving propensities are higher among farmers than for city-dwellers. In like fashion, a more equal distribution of income could raise the propensity to consume because of the fact that family budget studies generally show a decline in the income-saving ratio as income declines. Goods that were once regarded as luxuries sooner or later become necessities, another development which would tend over time to keep the income-consumption ratio constant. The same effects might result from an increase in the proportion of people in the retirement age category in the population, simply because their incomes are likely to decline much more rapidly than their consumption patterns change. Self-employed persons normally save a higher proportion of their income than do wage-earners, so a decline in the proportion of self-employed in the working population would also tend to raise the average propensity to consume.

Changes in some of these parameters will be analyzed more fully in the closing section of this chapter. Here it suffices to stress again that changes of the kind just described in these parameters may have sufficient force to keep the income-consumption ratio constant through time, assuming that the absolute income hypothesis has validity. Empirical evidence on this point, though, is inconclusive.

The Relative Income Hypothesis

An alternative to the absolute income hypothesis was developed initially by Professor James S. Duesenberry of Harvard University and a former member of the President's Council of Economic Advisers.[18] Unlike the absolute income hypothesis, this theory does not depend upon changes in the value of parameters to account for the long-term stability of the C/Y ratio. Duesenberry's relative income hypothesis is based upon two key ideas: First, consumer preferences are interdependent, which

18. James S. Duesenberry, *Income, Saving and the Theory of Consumer Behavior* (Cambridge, Mass.: Harvard University Press, 1949), pp. 17–46. See also Duesenberry, "Income-Consumption Relations and Their Implications," in *Income, Employment and Public Policy: Essays in Honor of Alvin H. Hansen*, (New York: Norton, 1948), pp. 54–81.

means that the level of consumption of a family or household depends upon its income *relative* to other families and households. Consumption spending, in other words, is *emulative*, which is to say that it depends upon the spending of families on a higher rung of the income distribution ladder. Second, consumer spending does not depend upon the level of current income alone, as the absolute income hypothesis views it, but on a relationship between current income and the highest income that the family or household has previously experienced. Let us examine by means of a diagram the relative income hypothesis as developed by Professor Duesenberry.

In Figure 6–7 the curve labeled C_s is the secular, or long-term, consumption function, whereas the curves labeled C_1, C_2, and C_3 represent a series of cyclical, or short-term, consumption functions. Let us assume that initially the income level is given by Y_1, and that this represents the

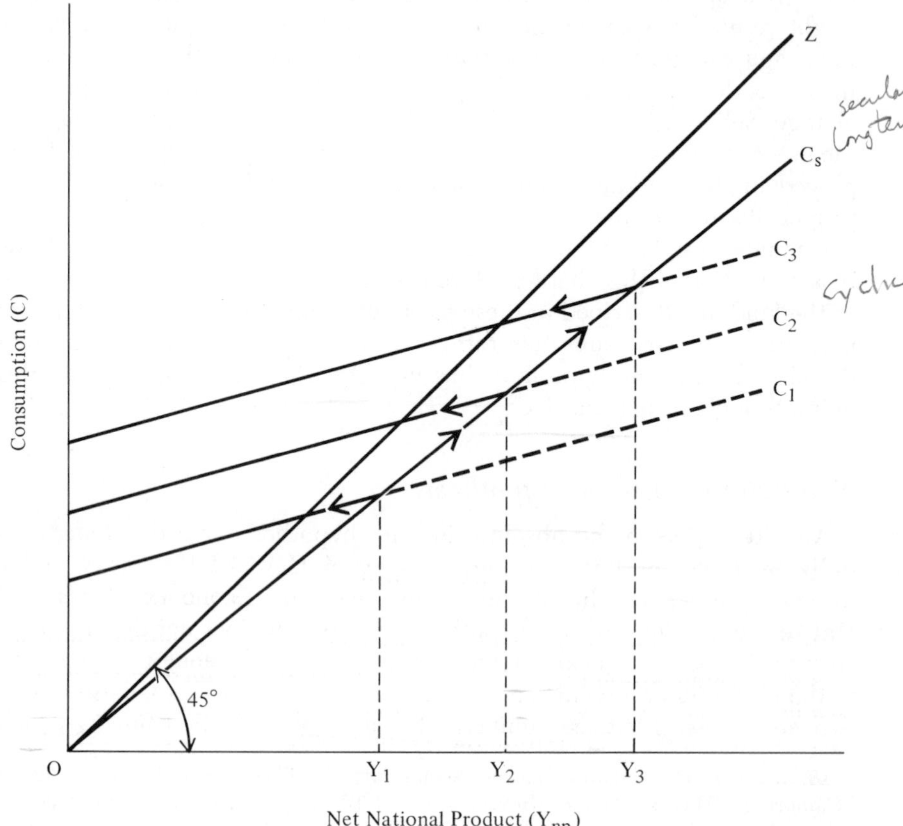

FIGURE 6–7. The Upward Drift of the Cyclical Consumption Function

highest level of income yet achieved in the economy. We are at the peak of a cycle. What will happen now if income falls from the level of Y_1? On the diagram this is, of course, a movement to the left. According to Duesenberry's theory, consumption will move along the short-run path represented by the function C_1, because the most immediate and strongest influence on consumption will be the recent experience of achieving an income level equal to Y_1. Consumers, having become accustomed to this level during the boom will strongly resist any reduction in their standard of consumption. Consumption will decline, of course, but more slowly than income. This is exactly the kind of behavior pattern envisaged by Keynes, since the most important influence at work is the consumer's habitual standard of life. The movement of consumption spending along the C_1 curve also means that the average propensity to consume will rise and the average propensity to save will fall. As the income level moves back to its original position, which will come about as the economy moves out of a recession, consumption will rise again along the path of C_1, at least until restoration of the previous high peak of income is achieved. As the income level moves back toward its prior peak, consumers will want to restore the earlier relationship between consumption and saving, and consequently the saving-income ratio, S/Y, will rise and the consumption-income ratio, C/Y, will fall.

What will happen once the economy regains the level Y_1 and, in a surge of growth, moves on toward Y_2, a new and higher income level? In this instance, consumption will rise along the path of the secular function, C_s, until the new peak level, Y_2 is achieved. Consumption increases proportionally to income. Why? For one thing, the prior income peak, Y_1, no longer exercises its influence over consumer behavior, since the economy is moving toward a new peak. In such a situation increments to income will be allocated between spending and saving in a constant ratio, the latter being the ratio regarded as normal at the prior highest income level. The relative income hypothesis holds that the average propensity to consume for the economy as a whole will not change as long as the distribution of income does not change. During the period when the economy is moving toward a new peak income level, there is no reason why the pattern of income distribution should change. All spending units will enjoy a higher absolute level of income because the income level of the whole economy has risen, but the *relative* position of each group will not necessarily change. Therefore, the average propensity to consume for the whole economy will not change. One important implication of the relative income theory is that there is a *ratchet effect* at work, tending to boost consumption spending to ever-higher levels of what consumers come to regard as normal.

Much the same conclusion concerning the relationship between the cyclical and secular consumption functions was reached independently by another economist, Professor Franco Modigliani.[19] He also suggests that the ratio between income and saving (or consumption) has to be linked not merely to current income but to a ratio or index that embodies both current income and the highest income level previously reached. In this respect his analysis is quite similar to Duesenberry's. In the Modigliani analysis, consumption will also follow a Keynesian path when the income level goes below the highest level yet achieved. He attributes this not only to consumer resistance to a reduction in acquired consumption habits, but to the growth in unemployment in the downward phase of the cycle and to the redistribution of income that occurs when the income level falls. With respect to the growth of unemployment, Modigliani's thesis asserts that even if there is a long-run tendency for employed persons to consume a constant proportion of their income, the ratio of consumption to income will rise when there is growing unemployment because unemployed persons consume even though they have no incomes. The redistribution of income that occurs in the downward phase of the cycle is likely to be in favor of groups having the highest propensity to consume. This is because the greatest income squeeze in a recession or depression is on profits. All these factors taken together account for the rise in the average propensity to consume when the income level falls, and the reverse when the income level is rising. With respect to the long-run picture, Modigliani agrees with Duesenberry that a constant proportion of income will be consumed once the economy moves beyond the highest income level previously achieved. But he explains this by the continuous appearance of new products and the improvement of old commodities. Portions of the income increments that accrue to all groups as a result of the long-term rise in the real income of the whole economy are absorbed by new goods and services that gradually become available. This is the basic reason offered by Modigliani for the long-term constancy in the consumption-income or saving-income ratio.

The Permanent (Life-Cycle) Income Hypothesis

The two major theories which belong in this category have in common the primary idea that the consumer plans his income *not* on the basis of income received currently, but on the basis of long-term or even lifetime income expectations. Thus, the fundamental theoretical relationship between consumption and income is one of proportionality, although short-term (or cyclical) factors can cause departures of the average pro-

19. Franco Modigliani, "Fluctuations in the Saving-Income Ratio: A Problem in Economic Forecasting," in *Studies in Income and Wealth,* vol. 11 (New York: National Bureau of Economic Research, 1949), pp. 379 ff.

pensity to consume from the long-term norm. We shall now examine these ideas.

The best known exposition of the permanent income hypothesis is that developed by Professor Milton Friedman of the University of Chicago, also the foremost proponent of the modern monetarist approach to the determination of the level of economic activity (See Chapter 11).[20]

The key concept in Friedman's hypothesis is that of *permanent income*. Permanent income is roughly akin to lifetime income, based upon the real and financial wealth at the disposal of an individual plus the value of one's human capital in the form of inherent and acquired skills and training. The average expected return on the sum of all such wealth at the disposition of an individual would be his permanent income.

The foregoing is the concept. Measurement is something else. The income that an individual actually receives in a year is what Professor Friedman calls *measured* income. Over a lifetime, measured income ought to coincide with permanent income, but in any one year measured income as a result of cyclical fluctuations and because of other random changes may depart from permanent income. But the best way to measure permanent income, according to this hypothesis, is through a weighted average of past and present measured income, with less weight being attached to measured income the further it lies in the past. In any one year the difference between measured income and permanent income is called *transitory* income. It may be positive or negative, but over an individual's lifetime it is necessarily zero.

Professor Friedman's essential thesis is that an individual's permanent consumption is proportional to his permanent income. In other words, the consumer or household expects over its life to save a fixed proportion of its lifetime—or permanent—income. Practically, this thesis means that saving will increase (or decrease) whenever there is an increase (or decrease) in the transitory component of income. This is what accounts for short-term fluctuations in the saving income (or consumption-income) ratio as depicted in the short-term, or cyclical, function. The idea that all transitory increases in one's income are saved may seem contrary to ordinary observation, as people often use windfall gains in current income to buy some kind of a durable consumer good, such as a car, color TV set, or stereo outfit. But, in concept at least, this difficulty disappears if durable goods purchases are viewed as additions to private wealth and their services viewed as consumption.

The essential idea of the permanent income hypothesis may be illustrated with a simple diagram, like that in Figure 6–8. In the diagram, Y_p represents permanent income, C_p permanent consumption, and Y_m mea-

20. Milton Friedman, *A Theory of the Consumption Function* (Princeton: Princeton University Press, 1957).

sured (or current) income. The difference between Y_p and Y_m is transitory income. The diagram shows the path over time of these three variables. Starting at the point in time t_1, current or measured income expands. As it rises from its starting level to a peak at time t_2, the ratio between permanent consumption C_p and measured income will decline. This is the ratio that may be observed from actual or current data. As measured income starts a decline from this peak, the measured (or observed) propensity to consume will increase. This will continue until measured income bottoms out at time period t_3, following which it will begin to climb once again. Thus, over the course of cyclical fluctuations in measured income, the average propensity to consume derived from observed data will follow the pattern found in the cyclical consumption functions discussed earlier. It is the assumption that consumption expenditures are tied in proportional fashion to permanent income and, thus, do not fluctuate as measured (or observed) income fluctuates.

Why should people behave in this fashion? The roots of Professor Friedman's theory trace back to the ideas of one of America's greatest economists from an earlier era, Irving Fisher.[21] Given the fact that households may desire to build up their stock of wealth through saving and

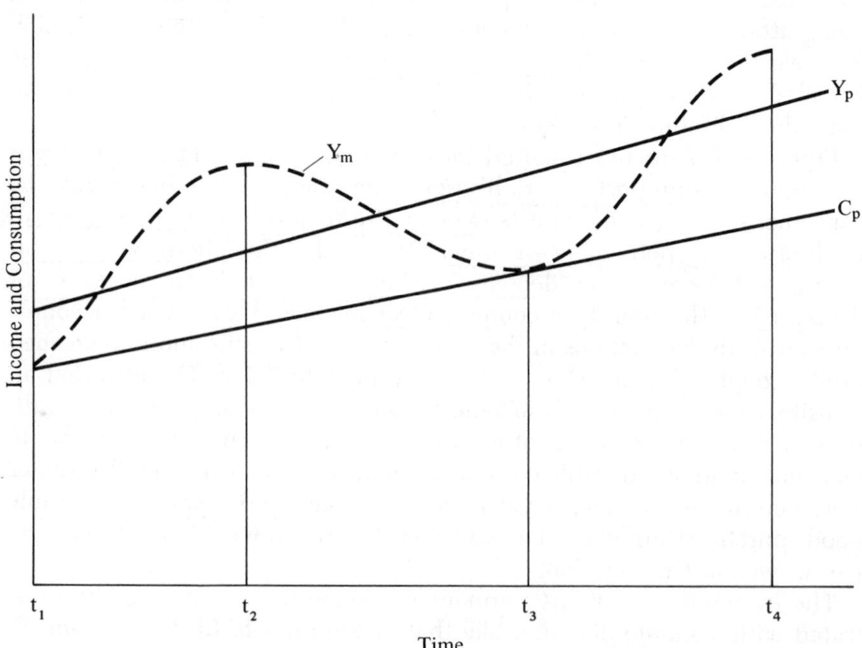

FIGURE 6–8. The Permanent Income Hypothesis

21. Irving Fisher, *The Theory of Interest* (New York: August M. Kelly, 1961), chaps. 4, 5.

given, too, the fact that people may save because of uncertainty and for anticipated future needs, how will they manage the relationship between saving and income over their lifetimes? A rational household seeking to maximize the utility it gets from both consumption and saving for the aforementioned objectives would try to arrange its affairs so that over its life it neither saved more nor less than the desired amount. This means, though, that the household would have to save any income that was above its lifetime average—or permanent—income and dissave when its income fell below this figure. This is essentially what the permanent income hypothesis says will happen.

Both the life-cycle hypothesis and the permanent income theory suggest that the consumer adjusts his consumption patterns to the total resources which he can draw on for spending over his life. These resources consist of both his wealth and the present value of his expected income (the value of the human capital at his disposal.)[22] The life-cycle hypothesis differs from the Friedman theory, however, in that the propensity to consume of an individual will vary with age as well as wealth. The basic relationship in the hypothesis is one of proportionality between the individual's lifetime income as determined by his total resources (material wealth and human capital), but the observed relationship between consumption and income at any time will depend on the age of the consumer. Since the individual consumer's observed income is relatively low at the beginning and end of his or her life, the proportion of income consumed out of measured income will be high at these times. In his or her middle years, income will be high and the propensity to consume will be lower. Over the consumer's lifetime, however, consumption will be a fixed proportion of total income. The essential point of both theories is that the long-term proportion of permanent income consumed is independent of the consumer's income in a particular period. Transitory income changes do not have any significant impact upon current consumption. Thus, short-term changes in the observed consumption-income ratio are the result of transitory shifts in income.

Which Theory?

Which of the above theories offers the best—or most appropriate—explanation of consumer behavior? Unfortunately, no precise answer can be given to this question, as each represents a hypothesis that is reasonably in accord with observed experience. There are elements of truth in all

22. For details of the life-cycle hypothesis see F. Modigliani and Richard Brumberg, "Utility Analysis and the Consumption Function: An Interpretation of Cross-Section Data," in K. Kurihara, ed., *Post Keynesian Economics* (New Brunswick, N.J.: Rutgers University Press, 1954), and A. Ando and F. Modigliani, "The Life-Cycle Hypothesis of Saving," *The American Economic Review*, March 1963.

these approaches to understanding the relationship between income and consumption (or savings). Probably what is most crucial is the realization that both theoretical analysis and empirical observation point strongly to the conclusion that income is the dominant factor in explaining consumption behavior in the national economy. Further, the *observed* relationship between income and consumption seems to adhere to a Keynesian-type path over over the short-term, even though this relationship is a proportional one when a longer span of time is taken into consideration.

Other Influences on Consumption

In the discussion of the support which empirical data concerning income and consumption offer the consumption function hypothesis, we pointed out that few economists believe that income is the only determinant of consumption spending. Let us now briefly examine some other variables that influence consumer expenditures. As already stressed, the general practice in analysis of consumer spending is to treat variables other than income as *parameters*, whose values determine the level and slope of the consumption function. Analytically, this means that changes in the value of any of these parametric factors will result in a shift in the position of the entire schedule, rather than a movement along it. While parametric factors are generally recognized to influence the level of consumption expenditure, many of them are not subject to quantification and precise measurement. This being the case, we have to depend in part upon deduction to arrive at dependable conclusions concerning the way in which such variables influence consumer expenditures.

Attitudes toward Thrift

In a general way, we can group together in the category of thrift the psychological attributes of human nature which lead people to save rather than spend some part of current income, as well as various business practices and institutional arrangements of a society that make for saving. In connection with the former, Keynes suggested that there are at least eight motives of a subjective nature that lead individuals to refrain from spending out of their incomes. These include the following desires: (1) to build a reserve for unseen contingencies (Precaution); (2) to provide for anticipated future needs, such as old age, education of children, or the maintenance of dependents (Foresight); (3) to obtain a larger future income through investment at interest of funds saved from current income (Calculation); (4) to enjoy a gradually increasing expenditure and standard of life as a result of saving some of current income (Improvement); (5)

to enjoy the sense of independence and power that comes from sustained saving (Independence); (6) to secure a *masse de manoeuvre* to carry out speculative or business projects (Enterprise); (7) to bequeath a fortune (Pride); and (8) to satisfy pure miserliness (Avarice). The reader will readily recognize the highly subjective character of these motives; yet their existence is real enough. The most we can say is that if these motives are strong in a society, then the society will be favorably predisposed toward thrift, which, other things being equal, will lower the consumption function or raise the saving function.

Cultural factors that condition a society's attitudes toward thrift and spending are deeply rooted in its past and not readily subject to change. In the United States the Puritan tradition with its stress on the intrinsic virtues of work and frugality operated in times past to create a social climate more favorable to saving than to spending. Today, though, developments such as consumer credit and time-payment plans have a countereffect, although the impact of such phenomena on the position of the consumption function is by no means a simple or one-way affair.

Installment purchasing and other forms of borrowing that raise the propensity to consume are to some extent offset by developments of modern life which tend to raise the propensity to save. The twentieth century, in fact, has witnessed a powerful tendency toward the institutionalization of saving through commitments of income to life insurance, private pension plans, and long-term mortgages on private homes. Since saving is the nonexpenditure of current income for currently produced goods and services, these institutional arrangements create a continuous flow of quasi-compulsory saving that does not change simply because the income level has changed. The average person does not usually think of premiums on the life insurance, payroll deductions for a pension plan, or monthly amortization of home loans as forms of saving, yet they represent saving from the viewpoint of the whole economy. Moreover, most saving of this type is contractual in nature, and thus cannot readily be changed.

Asset Holdings by the Consumer

Another factor believed by many economists to exercise a powerful influence on consumer spending patterns has to do with assets held by the consumer, including both financial assets in the form of cash on hand, bank accounts, bonds, stocks, and other claims and physical assets in the form of stocks of durable goods in possession of the consumer.

Financial Assets · The most plausible hypothesis that we can advance regarding the influence of financial assets on expenditures is simply that spending will vary directly with the value of private holdings of financial assets. Such holdings, particularly if they are easily converted into purchasing power, constitute a reserve of spending power which the consumer can draw on in emergencies. As a consequence there is less need to save out of current income in order to build such a reserve. This means that an increase in holdings of liquid assets by consumers would, other things being equal, shift the consumption function upward. Moreover, households possessing stocks of liquid assets are more willing and more able to finance consumption spending by borrowing.

The hypothesis of a direct relationship between consumer spending and holdings of financial or liquid assets is subject to some reservations. For one thing, the distribution of ownership of liquid assets will have a bearing upon their over-all impact on consumer spending. If, for example, ownership is concentrated in the upper-income groups, it is doubtful that the size or value of such holdings will have much influence upon the level of consumption for the whole economy, since high-income earners as a group tend to save a large proportion of their income at all times. If this viewpoint is valid, then holdings of liquid assets will not necessarily tend to raise the consumption function. It appears that existing empirical evidence does not show conclusively that holdings of liquid assets exert an influence on consumer spending in one direction or another.[23]

In addition to the distribution of ownership, changes in the real value of liquid assets may exercise an influence on the consumer's spending-saving decisions. For example, if the general price level rises, the real value of financial assets in the form of bank deposits, bonds, and other types of debt instruments will decline. This is not necessarily the case with equities, as they may appreciate in value along with the rise in the general level of prices. However, if there is a decline in the real value of the consumer's stock of liquid assets, this may induce him to save more out of his current income in order to recoup a desired position with respect to his holdings. The possibility of a unique relationship between the real value of the stock of liquid assets, the general level of prices, and the position of the consumption function is known as the *Pigou effect,* after A.C. Pigou, a noted British economist.[24] Pigou argued that a fall in the general level of prices would stimulate the economy by tending to shift the consumption function upward. The price drop would increase the real value of the consumer's financial assets and thereby lessen his need to save. We shall encounter the Pigou effect again in our later discussion of the general

23. See Lawrence R. Klein, "The Empirical Foundations of Keynesian Economics," in Kenneth K. Kurihara, ed., *Post Keynesian Economics* (New Brunswick, N.J.: Rutgers University Press, 1954), p. 293; and also Robert Ferber, "Research on Household Behavior," *American Economic Review*, March 1962, p. 37.

24. A. C. Pigou, "The Classical Stationary State," *Economic Journal*, December 1943; and "Economic Progress in a Stable Environment," *Economica*, August 1947. The latter is reprinted in *Readings in Monetary Theory* (Philadelphia: Blakiston, 1951), pp. 241–51.

price level, but it is doubtful if many economists today take it very seriously. It is more in the nature of an exercise in abstract logic than an attempt to deal with forces that operate in the real-world economy.

Stocks of Durable Goods · The second type of asset that may affect the spending-saving pattern of the consumer consists of the stock of durable goods in his possession. As a general proposition, a large stock of durable goods in the hands of consumers may, other things being equal, have a tendency to depress consumption spending. For the consumer such goods represent a capital investment which provides him with a stream of services as long as the good is in existence. The man who owns an automobile, for example, need not spend much of his income for other forms of transportation. Similar results flow from the ownership of other types of durable goods, such as television sets and radios, home laundry equipment, and various other household appliances. It should be recognized, though, that ownership of durables may stimulate other expenditures. The owner of an automobile, for example, must purchase large quantities of gasoline, new tires, and spare parts. He is, moreover, a purchaser of insurance and other services that stem directly from his ownership of an automobile. On balance, it is difficult to say which of these influences is the strongest, and the objective evidence pertaining to this point is inconclusive.

The chief conclusion we can draw concerning the influence of the stock of consumer durables on consumer spending is that such goods by their very durability introduce elements of uncertainty into consumer spending. Beyond this it is difficult to say more with certainty because economists have yet to accumulate sufficient empirical data to indicate any precise relationship between the stock of consumer durables and consumption expenditure.

Asset Holdings and Living Standards · One interesting line of analysis has suggested that consumption expenditure should be related to the *standard of living*.[25] According to this thesis, the standard of living includes the consumer's assets, both financial and durable, as well as in his current purchases of goods and services. In order to achieve a desired standard, the consumer at times may be primarily interested in increasing his stock of consumer durables, which leads temporarily to more consumption spending and less saving; at other times, his primary objective may be to enlarge his stock of liquid assets, which will have the contrary effect. An analysis of the behavior of the consumption-income ratio in the early post-World War II era lends some support to this hypothesis but

25. See John P. Lewis, "The Lull That Came to Stay," *Journal of Political Economy*, February 1955.

more research needs to be done before the standard of living (however defined) can be viewed as a determinant of consumption expenditors equal in importance to income.

A consequence of this hypothesis is to introduce a further element of instability into the consumption-income relationship. Shifts in the consumption function may come about as a result of changes in the desires of consumers to build up one type of asset at the expense of the other. Such shifts may be either upward or downward, depending upon the relative strength of the consumer's desire to increase his holdings of durable goods or liquid assets. Whether it is possible to determine the direction of future shifts in the consumption function following the interplay of these two forces remains problematical.

The Distribution of Income

Economists regard the distribution of money income of a society as one of the important parametric determinants of the consumption-income relationship. This particular influence on consumption is thought to be stable, as the pattern of income distribution in any society is determined by a complex of institutional factors, including the structure of property rights, the distribution of ownership of productive assets, the tax system, and the social security system, all of which appear to change with relative slowness.[26] Insofar as the pattern of income distribution has an influence upon the level and slope of the consumption function, some economists believe that, other things being equal, a movement toward more equality in the distribution of income will raise the level—and possibly, too, the slope—of the consumption function, whereas any movement toward greater inequality in the distribution of income will have the opposite effect. This deduction is based on the fact that studies of income and its disposition at the level of the household show that families in the lower-income brackets have a higher average propensity to consume than families in the upper-income brackets. Such studies are less conclusive with respect to the marginal propensity to consume of the two income groups, although economists have tended to assume on *a priori* grounds that the marginal propensity to consume would be low for the upper-income groups and high for the lower-income groups.

Let us consider the presumed relationship between differences in the average propensity to consume for families in different income brackets, the over-all distribution of income, and the level of the consumption function. If the distribution of income in a society is relatively unequal, families in the upper-income brackets receive a large proportion of the total

26. Available statistical evidence indicates little change in the United States in the pattern of personal income distribution since 1929.

income. If this is the case, the average propensity to consume for the whole society will be low, irrespective of the level of total income of the society, since the upper-income groups tend, on the average, to consume a comparatively low percentage of their income. On the other hand, if the distribution of income is relatively equal, families or spending units in the lower-income brackets will receive the largest proportionate share of the income total. Since the average propensity to consume for these groups is high, the ratio for the society as a whole will also be high, regardless of the level of total income. Thus, greater equality in the distribution of income tends to raise the level of the consumption function, while more inequality has the opposite effect.

This analysis, buttressed by the assumption that the marginal as well as the average propensity to consume is higher for spending units in the lower income brackets, leads to the conclusion that the consumption function could be raised if steps were taken to bring about a greater degree of equality in the distribution of money income. Taxation and transfer expenditures are the policy means by which the federal government could achieve this goal, assuming that it was desirable to increase the proportion of income spent. For example, if group A with an assumed marginal propensity to consume of .50 had its disposable income reduced by $100 through taxation, and this sum was transferred to group B, which has a marginal propensity to consume of .75, the result would be a net increase in consumption spending of $25. Note that this argument is concerned with changing the average propensity to consume by changing the distribution of income; it is not addressed to the question of whether the distribution of income should be more or less equal.

This means of bringing about an upward shift in the consumption function has been challenged in two ways. First, some statistical evidence exists to suggest that the differences in the marginal propensity to consume between the upper- and lower-income groups are much smaller than differences in the average propensity to consume. If this is the case, a redistribution of income from the upper- to the lower-income groups might not appreciably affect consumption spending. The decline in consumption spending resulting from a reduction in the disposable income of households in the upper brackets would approximately equal the increase in spending that would occur as households in the lower-income brackets experienced an increase in their disposable income. This would be the initial effect, but if redistributional measures were continued, a permanent alteration would occur in the pattern of income distribution in the direction of greater equality. Once this has taken place, the average rather than marginal propensity to consume should hold sway.

The idea that the consumption function can be raised by fiscal and other measures that bring about a redistribution of personal income faces a second challenge. It is argued that income redistribution theory is valid only upon the assumption of the absolute income hypothesis, which let us recall, asserts that a consumer's preferences for goods and services are formed independently of the preferences of other consumers. If a family moves into a different income bracket—as a result, say, of measures designed to redistribute income—they will assume the income-consumption pattern of prior occupants of the bracket.

But the relative income hypothesis, which holds that consumer preferences are interdependent, implies that the level of consumption of a family depends upon its income relative to other families. This means that consumption standards are emulative, in that the amount an individual spends upon consumption does not depend simply on his own income, but also on the consumption patterns of families or spending groups on a higher rung of the income distribution ladder. If consumer preferences are interdependent and consumption standards emulative, this leads to the conclusion that a redistribution of income in the direction of greater equality may not increase consumption expenditure; on the contrary such a redistribution could even lower consumption. In an interdependent and emulative society, reduction in the income and consumption of groups in the upper-income brackets might tend to reduce the pressure toward consumption spending for groups situated at lower levels on the income distribution scale. The standards of consumption that the latter groups emulate have been lowered, and thus their own consumption standards will follow suit.

In the face of these arguments, any conclusion about the probable effects of income redistribution measures on the level of the consumption function cannot be anything but nebulous. Most economists agree that the prevailing pattern of income distribution is an important determining factor of the level and slope of the consumption function. But economists do not agree upon either the extent to which income distribution can be changed in the short run or the immediate effects, if any, of such changes on the level of the consumption function.

The Rate of Interest

At one time many economists would have been inclined to list the rate of interest as probably the most important determinant of consumption and saving. According to classical thought, to save is to exchange present satisfactions (gained from consumption) for future satisfactions, but a price must be paid to persuade people to make such an exchange. This price is interest. The higher the price, the greater the willingness of people to postpone consumption; the lower the price, the smaller their willingness. As a consequence, in classical thought, interest came to be regarded as a prime determinant of the amount that famillies and spending units would save out of their income.

Today many economists do not believe that the rate of interest exercises any appreciable effect one way or the other on the level of consumption or saving. No statistical or empirical evidence of significance exists to lend support to the classical view,[27] while from a deductive point of view it is possible to show that increases in the level of interest rates may actually reduce saving. For one thing, a rise in interest rates means that if people save in order to amass a sum designed to yield them some specific annual income, a smaller absolute sum would yield an identical annual income at higher interest rates as a larger sum at lower rates. If, for example, the rate of interest rose from 6 to 9 percent, a saver would have to amass only $22,222 rather than $33,333 in order to obtain an annual interest income of approximately $2,000. A rise in the rate of interest also may tend to reduce some types of contractual saving, such as life insurance. At higher interest rates a *fixed* amount of life insurance requires smaller premiums.

Price Changes and Consumer Expectations

Changes in the general level of prices and shifts in consumer expectations for the future are two additional and related factors that economists recognize as potential influences on spending and saving levels. Our knowledge of the impact of these particular variables is more speculative than empirical. There is a presumption that a rise in the level of all prices will raise the average propensity to consume, assuming (somewhat tenuously) that money income does not change in the same degree. The increase in prices leads real income to decline, causing a higher consumption-income ratio. The reader should note, however, that a change in the average propensity to consume resulting from a change in real income does not necessarily imply a shift in the function; it might take place as a movement along the consumption function. It is also possible, in the face of a fall-off in real income, that consumers will attempt to maintain the same absolute level of real consumption. This would result in a shift upward of the consumption function, for consumption spending would absorb a higher proportion of an absolutely lower real income level.

A few pages back, we touched briefly on the Pigou effect, which concerns a shift in the consumption function brought about by a change in the real value of the consumer's liquid assets. This suggests that a rise in the general level of prices would tend to shift the consumption function downward rather than upward, the reason being the fall in the real value of assets increases the propensity to save. This is exactly the opposite outcome from that discussed in the preceding paragraph.

Consumer expectations concerning future prices may also influence the

27. Klein, p. 292.

position and slope of the consumption function. It is possible, for instance, that widely held expectations that prices will continue to rise, will lead consumers to devote a higher proportion of their current income to consumption purchases than would otherwise be the case. However, the propensity to save out of disposable income actually rose during 1973 and 1974, years in which the inflation rate was accelerating (inflation was in excess of 10 percent in 1974). Thus, there is no clear-cut statistical support either way for the effect that future price expectations may have on current income-consumption relationships.

Consumer expectations concerning future income may also be of significance, affecting not so much the level as the slope of the consumption function. The slope of the function is the marginal propensity to consume, which specifies the way in which consumers react to a change in their incomes. Logically, one would expect that an individual (or spending unit) would react differently to an increase (or decrease) in income, depending upon whether or not the change was expected to be permanent. Recent research carried out by the Survey Research Center at the University of Michigan indicates that expectations do condition spending and saving behavior. Research into consumer attitudes holds promise for enlarging our understanding of consumer behavior, but it has not yet developed any new, powerful, and widely accepted hypotheses concerning this behavior.

Consumer Credit

The significance of consumer credit on consumption is readily apparent; the availability of credit permits more spending for consumption purposes than would be possible if current income were the only source of purchasing power. The practical importance of consumer credit as a factor in consumer expenditure in the United States is enormous. In 1976 the volume of outstanding consumer credit of all types was nearly 186 billion, an amount that had risen by about 71 percent since 1969.[28] Moreover, the volume of credit extended to consumers has increased in nearly every post-World War II year, irrespective of the recessions of 1949, 1954, 1958, and 1970. The only exception was 1974 (a recession year) when the total fell slightly.

The obvious fact concerning consumer credit is that borrowed funds represent additional financial resources that can be used for current consumption expenditures. If consumers borrow sufficiently so that the total of their indebtedness increases—i.e., new borrowings exceed repayments—the consumption function would tend to shift upward. Total consumption spending would rise relative to income, since borrowing has given

28. Joint Economic Committee, *Economic Indicators*, February, 1977.

the consumer control over financial resources greater than the amount represented by current income. It is interesting to note that ever since 1946 consumers have added to their borrowings at a greater rate than they have repaid their obligations. Consumer credit in this period thus created upward pressure on the consumption component of aggregate demand.

While it is true that an initial extension of credit to the consumer tends to raise the propensity to consume, it is equally true that the subsequent effects of such credit extension may depress consumption expenditure. Such loans must be repaid. If Mr. Jones, for example, borrows $2,500 to help finance the purchase of a new automobile, his expenditure of the proceeds of the loan will take an item of current output off the market. Subsequently, though, a portion of Mr. Jones's current income will no longer be available to spend for currently produced goods and services, since he must repay the loan. If he arranges to repay the $2,500 at the rate of $83 a month, then for a period of thirty months (ignoring interest and other charges connected with the loan) the amount of current income that he can spend for currently produced goods and services will be $83 less than usual.

What lesson does this hypothetical example hold for the economy as a whole? Unless there are new borrowings sufficient to offset the repayment of old borrowings, any stimulus to consumption expenditure that came from an extension of credit to the consumer will be short-lived. If borrowing by the consumer tends to raise the level of the consumption function, repayment of loans has the opposite effect. Economists interested in the influence of consumer credit on consumption expenditure are more concerned with the relationship between the rate of new borrowing and the rate of repayment than with the absolute amount of consumer credit outstanding at any particular time.

The rate at which consumers increase their indebtedness is no doubt in some way tied in with expectations. Again there is scant empirical evidence to help us determine the precise nature of this relationship. It does not require any great feat of the imagination to see how disastrous it could be for the economy if consumers decided all of a sudden to reduce drastically their rate of new borrowing. The result would be a precipitate fall in the level of the consumption function.

A Concluding Comment

In this chapter we have examined in detail the findings of modern economic analysis with respect to the determinants of consumption expenditure. The impetus for study and analysis of this key component in the structure of aggregate demand comes from Keynes's *The General Theory*. Keynes's belief in the existence of a functional relationship between real income and real consumption has been formalized in the concept of the consumption function. This has become one of the key analytical tools of modern income and employment theory. In retrospect, we can say that while economists are no longer as sure as they once were of either the stability or simplicity of the consumption-income relationship, they do regard its embodiment into the formal body of economic analysis as one of the major achievements of economic science within the last several decades.

APPENDIX

Formal algebraic proof that the value of the multiplier k is equal to 1/1—a

The value of the multiplier depends upon the sum of the initial injection of funds into the system plus the ensuing induced expenditures. The multiplier effect of an additional $1 of investment expenditure can be expressed in equation form as shown below. In the equations, a is the marginal propensity to consume and n represents the number of income periods.

(1) $k = 1 + a + a^2 + a^3 + a^4 + \ldots + a^n$
(2) $ak = a + a^2 + a^3 + a^4 + a^5 + \ldots + a^{n+1}$
(3) $(k - ak) = (1 - a^{n+1})$ [Equation (2) subtracted from Equation (1).]
(4) $k(1 - a) = 1 - a^{n+1}$
(5) $k = \dfrac{1 - a^{n+1}}{1 - a}$

(6) When the number of income periods, n, is very large, the value of a^{n+1} will be so small as to be negligible, if $0 < a < 1$. Therefore, we conclude that

$$k = \frac{1}{1 - a}$$

Algebraic proof that a equals the marginal propensity to consume

(1) $C = C_o + aY_d$
(2) $C + \Delta C = C_0 + a(Y_d + \Delta Y_d)$
(3) $C + \Delta C = C_0 + aY_d + a\Delta Y_d$
(4) $\Delta C = a\Delta Y_d$ [Equation (1) substracted from Equation (3).]
(5) $a = \dfrac{\Delta C}{\Delta Y_d}$

Algebraic determination of the equilibrium income level

(1) $Y_{np} = C + I$ The basic identity
(2) $C = C_o + aY_d$ The consumption function
(3) $C = C_o + aY_{np}$ This follows because $Y_d = Y_{np}$ when taxes and transfers are zero
(4) $I = I_o$ Autonomous investment
(5) $Y_{np} = C_o + aY_{np} + I_o$ Substitution of Equations (3) and (4) into (1).
(6) $Y_{np} - aY_{np} = C_o + I_o$
(7) $Y_{np}(1 - a) = C_o + I_o$
(8) $Y_{np} = \frac{1}{(1 - a)} (C_o + I_o)$
(9) $Y_{np} = k(C_o + I_o)$

Using the data from Table 6–2 in which $C_o = 100$ and $I_o = 75$ we can find the value of Y_{np} as follows. The multiplier $k = 4$.[1]

(1) $Y_{np} = 4(100 + 75) = \$700$

1. $k = \frac{1}{1 - a} = \frac{1}{1 - .75} = 4$

7

Investment Spending and Finance

In this chapter we turn to the second major category of expenditure entering into aggregate demand: investment expenditure. There are three basic reasons why investment expenditure occupies a highly significant role in the functioning of the economy. First the demand for investment goods is a large and important part of the total demand picture. In 1976, for example, gross private domestic investment was $243.3 billion, an amount equal to 14.3 percent of GNP. Investment expenditures play an especially strategic role in the economy, because changes in both income and employment are more likely to result from fluctuations in spending for capital goods than from fluctuations in spending for consumer goods. Changes in spending for consumer goods generally come about as a result of changes in the income level, rather than the other way around. In *The General Theory* investment is the key variable—the driving force which explains why output and employment are so prone to fluctuation.

Second, investment expenditures are volatile. Students of change and growth have long been aware that fluctuations in capital goods production are more violent than fluctuations in the production of consumer goods and services. This is true both in a relative sense and in an absolute sense. Investment expenditures not only initiate change in income and employment levels, but also act to exaggerage the effects. As Keynes saw it, the basic reason for the volatility of investment is that it depends upon our expectations about the future. But the future is something about which we know very little.[1]

1. John Maynard Keynes, "The General Theory of Employment," *Quarterly Journal of Economics*, February 1937, p. 221.

Finally, investment expenditures are significant because of their impact on the economy's productive capacity. Investment expenditures involve the acquisition of capital goods, the procreative element in an industrial society. Their function is to produce other goods and services. This means that even though investment expenditures play a key role in determining current levels of income and employment, their influence reaches beyond the present by means of their impact upon capacity. Investment expenditures thus are vital factors in economic growth, which depends to a great extent upon how rapidly productive capacity is being enlarged.

The Investment Decision

There is one basic fact about investment spending in a market system that one should never forget: business firms invest in equipment and buldings in order to make money. It is as simple as that. All investment expenditure is undertaken in the expectation of profit. In actuality it is often difficult in an enterprise to separate expectations of profit from actual (or current) profitability, which is dependent upon current levels of output, sales, and costs. Expected profits obviously will be influenced by current profits, as well as other variables. This is good common sense. But it does not mean that investment will take place only when current profits are satisfactory, because in many instances firms with low profit margins will invest in money-saving equipment in an effort to reduce costs.[2]

Generally speaking, there are two ways in which investment in capital will improve the profitability of the firm's operations. First, investment in new and improved equipment is a means of reducing production costs. Capital equipment is productive partly because it can supplement or take the place of other resources, particularly labor. Capital goods are tools. Through their use the effectiveness in production of both labor and natural resources may be enormously enhanced. It is estimated, for example, that machines in a modern factory supply from thirty to seventy times as much energy as could be provided by human muscle.[3] Capital is also productive because it frequently represents the means by which new methods or techniques of production are introduced into the economic process.

The second way in which investment in capital equipment may improve the profitability of the firm's operations centers on market conditions. Frequently, the firm will be confronted with an opportunity to increase its profits either by introducing a new product or by expanding

2. Walter W. Heller, "The Anatomy of Investment Decisions," *Harvard Business Review*, March 1951.

3. A. J. Brown, *Introduction to the World Economy* (New York: Rinehart, 1959), p. 51.

the output and sales of existing products. In either case, added capacity may be required if the firm is to exploit fully the profit potential of a favorable market situation; investment in new equipment and plants is necessary to provide this added capacity. In the quest for greater profitability, many firms engage extensively in product research and sales promotions. Both these activities frequently force a firm to invest in more plant and equipment.

Now that we have examined briefly the reasons why investment expenditure cannot be separated from profitability in the operation of the firm, let us examine the nature of the investment decision. How does the entrepreneur look upon an item of capital equipment? What factors does he have to take into account when he is contemplating the purchase of additional capital equipment? These questions lie at the heart of the investment decision, and investment theory, if it is to be meaningful, must provide at least tentative answers to them.

Investment and Expected Income

Since the entrepreneur undertakes investment expenditure in the expectation that it will be profitable, he sees an item of capital equipment essentially as a stream of expected income, or, as Keynes described it, "a series of prospective returns, which he expects to obtain from selling its output, after deducting the running expenses of obtaining that output, during the life of the asset.[4] To the businessman, the value of a capital good lies in the stream of net income that the asset is expected to yield over its life. What the businessman does in essence is convert money (his own or borrowed money) into capital goods (equipment and buildings) which are expected to generate a cash flow over their lifetime. The investment process in a market society is one which moves from money to goods and back to money. The stream of income—or cash flow—is an *expected* stream primarily because capital is durable and thus yields value to its user only over a relatively long period of time. The size of the expected income stream depends upon, first, the physical productivity of the capital instrument; second, the price at which the output produced with the aid of the capital equipment can be sold (which is primarily a matter of future demand and market conditions); and finally, the nature and amount of other expenses in the form of wages and material costs that may be incurred from the use of additional amounts of equipment. These expenses, too, depend upon future market conditions. Keynes said that the considerations upon which "expectations of prospective yields are based are partly existing facts . . . and partly future events which can only

4. John Maynard Keynes, *The General Theory of Employment, Interest and Money* (New York: Harcourt, Brace & World, First Harbinger ed., 1964), p. 135.

be forecasted with more or less confidence. . . . The *outstanding fact is the extreme precariousness of the basis of knowledge on which our estimates of prospective yields have to be made.* Our knowledge of the factors which will govern the yield of an investment some years hence is usually very slight and often negligible."[5] Here in a nutshell is why investment spending is so much less stable than consumption spending, why expectations are subject to sudden and frequent change.

In analyzing the investment decision the usual practice is to think of the stream of expected income associated with the use of additional amounts of capital as being net of all other expenses that the firm may incur as a result of using more capital. Added expenditures for labor and materials, as well as any other additional operating expenses, are deducted from the contemplated income stream or prospective returns on the capital good. This is done because the entrepreneur is primarily interested in what the equipment will yield him in the way of income over and above any additional expenses that may be involved in its operation.

Having stripped the stream of expected income of all costs incidental to the process of producing additional output, the entrepreneur is faced with the question of whether the investment is worthwhile. Will it, in other words, be profitable? As has just been stressed, the businessman in modern industrial society obtains a profit by converting money, which is the most liquid of all assets and which can always be loaned out at interest, into a less liquid form, that of a capital asset. Through the sale of its output, the capital asset is converted back to monetary form. This movement from money to capital asset and back to money will be profitable to the entrepreneur only if the asset yields him more than the cost of its acquisition. Here is the nub of the investment decision. The entrepreneur will find an investment worthwhile if it yields him a stream of income greater than what he must pay to acquire the asset. The investment decision involves balancing expected gain against the costs of acquiring the gain.

The Costs of Investment

What are the costs that the entrepreneur has to take into account in estimating the profitability of an investment expenditure? If we ignore momentarily the element of risk present in the acquisition of any capital asset, we can distinguish two fundamental types of costs that enter into the investment decision: the cost under current market conditions of the capital asset itself and the cost involved in the use of money or funds to acquire the asset.

The cost of the capital good under current market conditions is called

5. Ibid., pp. 147, 149. [Italics added.]

the *supply price of the asset*. This is the price which would induce the manufacturer of any particular type of capital asset to produce one additional unit of the capital asset in question. The supply price for a particular capital asset is not the current market price of existing assets of that kind, but, basically, the cost of producing a new unit. It is the price that lies somewhere on a supply curve for the kind of capital equipment under discussion. From a monetary standpoint this represents what the entrepreneur must spend in order to acquire the asset. It also represents the absolute, irreducible minimum that the entrepreneur expects to get back from the purchase and utilization of a capital good. In a world dominated by the profit motive no entrepreneur would contemplate the purchase of a new capital asset unless he believed that the asset would yield a stream of income whose present value, in the very least, would be equal to the supply price of the asset. In actuality, he would expect more, but this notion of a kind of irreducible minimum gives us a point of departure.

The above statements would be wholly correct if the use of money did not involve any costs. Then we could say that it would be profitable to acquire a capital asset whenever the value of the stream of expected income was greater than the current supply price. This, though, is not the case, for in a monetary society there is always a cost involved in the use of money. The entrepreneur contemplating the acquisition of a capital asset has two choices open to him. Since he cannot obtain the asset without money, he must either borrow the necessary funds to finance its purchase or else draw upon his own accumulated reserves. If he borrows, he must pay the current market rate of interest appropriate to a loan of the type and duration necessary. The interest rate reflects the *financial cost* of the investment decision. Even if the entrepreneur uses his own funds to finance his purchase of capital equipment, the interest rate reflects financial cost. In this event, the financial cost is implicit, since by using his own funds for the purchase of a capital instrument, the return on which is uncertain, the entrepreneur foregoes the possibility of securing a return on these funds equal to the current market rate of interest, which he could get by lending his funds. It is only proper for the entrepreneur to treat such foregone interest income as a cost element in the acquisition of a capital asset. The market rate of interest is a measure of the opportunity cost involved in the use of funds to purchase an item of capital in preference to lending such funds to someone who is willing to pay the going rate to secure their use.

The essential point of the foregoing paragraph is that capital assets no matter what their physical nature or durability must be financed, which is to say that business firms have to acquire money before they can acquire more capital assets. Where do firms get the money? Essentially they may get it from their earnings (ploughing a part of profit back into new capital), by selling additional shares in the stock market (equity financing), or by borrowing (through bank loans or by issuing bonds or other types of debt instruments). In all three cases the current rate of interest represents either the implicit or explicit cost to the firm in using money however obtained to purchase additional capital assets.[6] Borrowing to obtain funds is not only a common practice, but presents for the business firm problems of a different sort than it may encounter when it uses its own resources or sells shares to obtain money.[7] The reason is that a loan arrangement sets up a stream of cash payments which have to be met in order to pay off the loan. Normally this cash flow of required payments is contractual in nature, which means the firm is legally committed to make payments to its creditors until the loan is paid off or refinanced with a new loan. When funds are obtained internally or by the sale of shares, no such contractual pledge exists, although the owners will expect a return on the money (i.e., dividends) they have put into the firm by the purchase of its shares. As we shall see subsequently, the size of the contractual flow of payments which confronts a firm as a result of debt financing of new capital assets may affect significantly its willingness to invest in such assets.

The Keynesian Framework

Now that we have examined the essential character of the investment decision, let us turn to the formal framework of investment theory that Keynes postulates in *The General Theory*. In the preceding discussion the point was emphasized that an excess of expected revenues from the use of a capital good over its supply price means that the good yields a prospective profit. This is true, regardless of the financial costs of the investment, as long as the expected income stream is greater than the supply price. The excess of the expected yield over the cost of the capital can be expressed as a rate; more specifically, a *rate of return over cost*, in which the net return per unit of time is shown as a percent of the original cost. For example, a machine might cost an entrepreneur $10,000 and yield him a net annual return of $1,000. Without at this moment considering

6. In the case of the use of internal funds, the firm would expect to get back through the profitability of the capital a return at least equal to what the firm could have obtained by lending. If shares are sold, the purchasers will also expect a return in the form of dividends which also is at least equal to what they could have obtained by lending their money. There is no guarantee that the firm will earn such a return from the capital assets so acquired, but this is the expectation.

7. It is estimated that approximately three-quarters of investment expenditure (equipment, buildings, and inventories) which is financed externally is financed by borrowing.

the question of the useful life of the machine, we can say that such a machine yields *an annual rate of return over cost* of 10 percent.

The rate of return over cost relates the expected yield of a capital good to its supply price. It is this relationship that Keynes calls the *marginal efficiency of capital.*

> The relation between the prospective yield of a capital asset and its supply price or replacement cost, i.e., the relation between the prospective yield of one more unit of that type of capital and the cost of producing that unit, furnishes us with the *marginal efficiency of capital* of that type. More precisely, I define the marginal efficiency of capital as being equal to that *rate of discount* [italics added] which would make the present value of . . . the returns expected from the capital asset during its life just equal to its supply price.[8]

The above definition emphasizes the word *marginal.* We are interested in the expected rate of return on additional units of capital, not the rate of return now being earned on existing capital. Keynes defines the marginal efficiency of capital as a rate of discount; specifically, as the rate of discount which will make the present value of the income stream derived from the capital good just equal to its supply price. What is a rate of discount? It is a rate used to determine the *present value* of a sum that will not be received until sometime in the future. For example, $100 due one year from today is worth less than $100 now on hand, the reason being $100 on hand can be loaned at interest. Thus in one year the $100 will be worth more than $100 because of interest. Therefore, $100 due in a year must be worth less than $100 in hand. When we allow a sum to grow over time at a fixed rate of interest this is known as compounding—that is, growing at a constant rate. Discounting is just the opposite of compounding. It means shrinkage at a constant rate.

The Discount Formula

There exists a mathematical formula for finding the present value of an expected future income. The discount formula applies a rate to some expected future sum that will cause it, as it were, to shrink in value. The usual procedure for determining the present value of some expected income stream is to discount it at the current rate of interest. To see how this works, let us assume that we have an asset that will yield an income of $3,000 per year for a three-year period ($9,000 over its total life span). We want to know the present value of this asset. The discount formula for finding the present value of a future income is

$$V_p = \frac{R_1}{(1+i)} + \frac{R_2}{(1+i)^2} + \ldots + \frac{R_n}{(1+i)^n} \qquad (7\text{–}1)$$

8. John Maynard Keynes, *The General Theory,* p. 135.

In the equation, V_p is present value; R_1, R_2 . . . R_n is the expected income stream in absolute amount; and i is the current rate of interest. The numerical subscript appended to each R represents the year in which each of the specific sums that are a part of the total is due. If we assume that the current rate of interest is 5 percent, we can apply the above formula to find the present value of our asset.

$$V_p = \frac{\$3{,}000}{(1.05)} + \frac{\$3{,}000}{(1.05)^2} + \frac{\$3{,}000}{(1.05)^3}$$

And clearing fractions,

$$V_p = \$2{,}857 + \$2{,}721 + \$2{,}592 = \$8{,}170$$

The present value of the series is thus \$8,170, an amount less than the sum of the absolute amounts to be received in the three years. The process we have just described is also called *capitalization*. When we use the rate of interest to find the present value of an income stream we are said to have "capitalized" the income stream. Present value is found, in other words, by capitalizing expected future cash flows.

Our example shows that the more remote the date in the future at which the income is expected, the less its present value; \$3,000 due in three years, for example, has a lower present value than \$3,000 due in one year. Again leaving aside any question of uncertainty, simple arithmetic tells us that if we lend the sum of \$2,857 for a period of one year at a rate of interest of 5 percent, we will get back \$3,000, which includes the original sum and interest. This being the case, no one would be willing to pay more than \$2,857 for an asset that would yield a total return of \$3,000 one year hence. By the same reasoning, if we lend \$2,721 for a period of two years at a rate of interest of 5 percent we will get back \$3,000, for \$2,721 compounded at a rate of 5 percent for two years equals \$3,000. Thus no one would be willing to pay more than \$2,721 for an asset that yields a total return of \$3,000 two years hence. The same reasoning applies to the third sum in our series, namely \$2,592, if it is made available as a loan for a three-year period at the rate of 5 percent.

Examination of the process of discounting shows that there must be a *rate of discount* which will make the present value of prospective returns from a capital good equal to its supply price. This is the rate that Keynes calls the marginal efficiency of capital, which we shall designate by r. Let us now modify the foregoing discount formula by substituting the current supply price of the capital instrument for present value, V_p, and also by substituting the marginal efficiency of capital, r, for the current rate of interest, i. The formula now appears as

$$K_s = \frac{R_1}{(1+r)} + \frac{R_2}{(1+r)^2} + \ldots + \frac{R_n}{(1+r)^n} \qquad (7\text{–}2)$$

The expected income stream (or series of *R*s) is the same as in Equation (7–1). The current supply price, K_s, is a known value in contrast to the unknown present value, V_p, in the earlier equation. In the above formulation the unknown is the marginal efficiency of capital, *r*, or discount rate, which will make the present value of the expected income stream $R_1, R_2 \ldots R_n$ equal to th supply price, K_s. The equation must be solved for the unknown *r*.

As long as the computed value of the marginal efficiency of capital is positive, we know that the capital asset in question will yield some rate of return. This means the income stream expected from the use of the capital asset is at least large enough to cover the supply price. But, the current supply price of the asset represents only a part of the cost of acquiring an added unit of capital. In addition to the supply price, there is the financial cost that arises from the use of money funds in the acquisition of the asset. Since this cost element is measured by the current rate of interest, we can compare it directly with the marginal efficiency of capital; both are rate phenomena.

If such a comparison is made and we find that the marginal efficiency of capital is greater than the current rate of interest, the situation is favorable to investment. The income stream expected from the use of an additional unit of capital exceeds the costs of acquiring the capital. Consequently, the capital instrument will be purchased. Of course, an entrepreneur may use his resources to purchase a financial asset rather than an item of capital equipment, and presumably he will do so whenever the marginal efficiency of capital falls below the current rate of interest.

The idea that, other things being equal, investment expenditure will take place whenever the marginal efficiency of capital is greater than the current rate of interest is the key element in the theory of investment. It is the formal, theoretical expression of the view that profitability is the dominant factor in the investment decision. Unless the prospects are such that the expected yield of a new item of capital exceeds its supply price plus financial cost, it will not be purchased by the business firm. When we say that the marginal efficiency of capital, *r*, is greater than the rate of interest, *i*, we are also saying that the present value, V_p, of the capital asset (which is obtained by discounting its expected income at the current rate of interest) is greater than its supply price K_s.

The Investment Demand Schedule

The key point in the foregoing discussion is that investment will take place whenever the marginal efficiency of capital exceeds the rate of interest. But what happens after that? When investment does take place it means that the business firm will increase its stock of capital assets of a particular type. Investment by its very nature means adding to the firm's holdings of physical capital—equipment, buildings, or inventories. But when this happens, the expected rate of return for each successive quantity of capital added must necessarily decline. In *The General Theory*, Keynes explained this process as follows:

> If there is an increased investment in any given type of capital during any period of time, the marginal efficiency of that type of capital will diminish as the investment in it is increased, partly because the prospective yield will fall as the supply of that type of capital is increased, and partly because, as a rule, pressure on the facilities for producing that type of capital will cause its supply price to increase; the second of these factors being usually the more important in producing equilibrium in the short run, but the longer the period in view the more does the first factor take its place.[9]

To understand what Keynes means let us refer back to Equation (7–2), in which the supply price for new capital (K_s) and prospective returns ($R_1 + R_2 + \ldots R_n$) are linked together by the marginal efficiency of capital (r). Through the formula it can be seen that, *ceteris paribus*, an increase in the supply price (Keynes's second factor) will lower the marginal efficiency, or, again *ceteris paribus,* a reduction in expected returns (Keynes's first factor) will have the same effect. Since the rate of return on any capital asset is in part a function of its scarcity relative to other resources, investment in capital of a particular type can be expected to reduce the returns that will be expected from further investment in capital of that type. This is what Keynes meant by saying that prospective yield will fall as the supply of a particular type of capital increases and that this effect works primarily in the longer run.

Once the principle was established that increased investment in any given type of capital asset was associated with a falling marginal efficiency for that type of capital, Keynes went on to argue that for each type of capital it is possible to build up a schedule which will show precisely how much investment in that type of capital will have to increase for its marginal efficiency to fall to any given level. When Keynes said it was possible to "build up a schedule" as just described he was speaking in an abstract, theoretical sense, not in a literal quantitative sense. Theoretically, then, "We can then aggregate these schedules for all the different types of capital, so as to provide a schedule relating the rate of aggregate investment to the corresponding marginal efficiency of capital which that rate of investment will establish.[10] Such a schedule is shown in Part A of Figure 7–1. It shows that the marginal efficiency of

9. John Maynard Keynes, *The General Theory*, p. 136.
10. Ibid.

capital curve is one which slopes downward to the right. Technically, this means that the marginal efficiency of capital (r) is a function of the volume of investment (I). Thus

$$r = f(I) \qquad (7\text{–}3)$$

The relationship is an inverse one.

But this curve is readily transformed into an investment demand schedule. The reason is, as Keynes phrased it, " . . . it is obvious that the actual rate of current investment will be pushed to the point at which there is no longer any class of capital-asset of which the marginal efficiency exceeds the current rate of interest. In other words, the rate of investment will be pushed to the point . . . where the marginal efficiency of capital in general is equal to the rate of interest."[11] What this means is that, *ceteris paribus*, the rate of interest becomes the prime determinant of the level of investment. Investment, in other words, is a function of the rate of interest. As with investment and the marginal efficiency of capital, the relationship is inverse; hence the investment demand curve slopes downward to the right, In algebraic terms we have:

$$I = f(i) \qquad (7\text{–}4)$$

Thus we have the substance of Keynes's theory of investment, which, in its conceptual framework is much like the classical theory discussed in Chapter 4. But as we shall see, Keynes adds elements to his analysis not present in classical thinking.

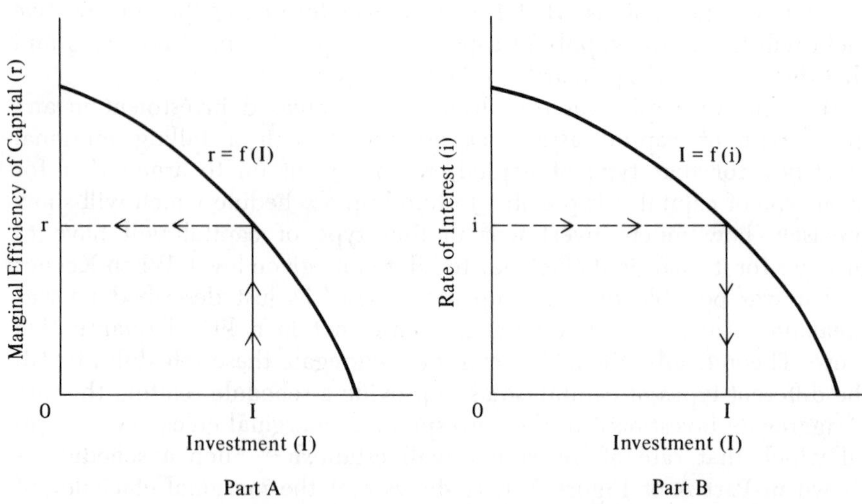

FIGURE 7–1. The Marginal Efficiency of Capital Schedule and the Investment Demand Schedule

11. Ibid.

Note the similarity of our treatment of investment expenditure to the earlier analysis of consumption expenditure. What we have done is to make investment a function of a single variable—interest—much in the same manner that consumption is a function of a single variable—income. This does not mean, however, that other variables are unimportant as determinants of the aggregate level of investment expenditures. Rather, as was done with the consumption function, other variables have been treated as parametric factors whose values determine the shape and level of the investment demand function. As we shall see these other variables are often far more important than interest in determining what happens to investment spending in a market economy. To complete the analogy with the analysis of the consumption function, the formal algebraic statement of the relationship embodied in the investment demand schedule is given by the following equation:

$$I = I_0 - ci \qquad (7\text{–}5)$$

In this equation I_0 is the amount of investment which will take place at a zero rate of interest (In Figure 7–1, Part B, it is equal to the distance from the origin to the point at which the investment demand curve intersects the horizontal axis), and c is the coefficient relating investment expenditure to the rate of interest. The fact that it is negative reflects the inverse correlation between investment and the rate of interest—the greater the value of i, the smaller will be the value of I.

Shifts in the Investment Demand Schedule

As is true for any demand schedule, the investment demand curve depicted in Figure 7–1 (Part B) is subject to either upward or downward shifts. These shifts are to be explained in terms of the fundamental determinants which lie behind the schedule. To clarify this, let us refer once again to Equations (7–1) and (7–2). They serve to underscore the two major sources of a shift in the investment demand schedule. When we speak of a shift in a demand curve it means that there will be more or less of the variable shown on the horizontal axis associated with any specific value for the variable shown on the vertical axis. In the case of investment demand, it means more investment spending for a given rate of interest if the demand schedule shifts upwards, and less when it shifts downwards.

The two major sources of a shift in the curve are a change in the expected yield of capital (the R series in Equations (7–1) and (7–2)), and a shift in the supply curve for capital goods. Suppose there is a sharp decrease in expected yields for new capital (the R series in the equations), the result of a wave of pessimism sweeping over the business community. In terms of Equation (7–1) this would reduce the present value of any capital asset a firm contemplated acquiring, assuming no change in market rates of interest, and in terms of Equation (72) it would reduce the marginal efficiency for that type of capital. But since it is assumed interest votes are unchanged, this latter change would cause the marginal efficiency of capital schedule (Part A of Figure 7–1) to shift to the left. Since the marginal efficiency of capital schedule transforms into an investment demand schedule, the latter curve also shifts to the left as a result of an unfavorable change in the expected yield for new capital. Similar results would follow from a shift in the supply curve for newly produced capital goods. A shift in the supply curve means that the schedule of prices for all possible quantities of capital the capital goods industry can produce will change, either upwards or downwards. If the supply curve shifts upwards, it means in terms of Equation (7–2) a rise in the value of K_s, the current supply price. But with no change in the expected income stream (the series of R's), the marginal efficiency of capital must decline. This, then, is tantamount to a shift to the left of the marginal efficiency of capital schedule as well as the investment demand schedule. At any given rate of interest, there will be less investment.

This then, is the formal model of investment spending found in Keynes's *The General Theory*. But it doesn't quite capture the full spirit of this classic work. What really counts is the volatility of the investment demand schedule—it is a highly unstable function, depending on expectations of the yield to be derived from capital goods whose useful life may stretch far into an uncertain future. As was pointed out earlier, Keynes believed that the basis of the knowledge on which the businessmen form their expectations of prospective yields is extremely precarious, subject to sudden and unforeseen changes as the climate of business opinion fluctuates. In *The General Theory* Keynes devoted an entire chapter to this theme,[12] a chapter in which he reminds us that "human decisions affecting the future, whether personal or political or economic, cannot depend upon strict mathematical expectation, since the basis for making such calculations does not exist; and that it is our innate urge to activity which makes the wheels go round, our rational selves choosing between the alternatives as best we are able, calculating when we can, but often falling back for our motive on whim or sentiment or chance."[13] Developing a schedule in which we link investment spending to a single variable like the rate of interest is a highly useful analytical technique, but we must not allow our preoccupation with the technique itself to cause us to lose sight of the more fundamental economic forces at work in any economic situation. Often the latter are not readily reduced to a quantitative, functional relationship.

12. Ibid., Chapter 12, "The State of Long-Term Expectation," pp. 147–64.
13. Ibid., p. 162.

The Shape of the Investment Demand Schedule

Even though the Keynesian investment demand schedule may be subject to frequent and unpredictable shifts, economists are also interested in its shape. Technically, this is a matter of the *interest elasticity* of investment expenditure, by which we mean the responsiveness of aggregate investment expenditure to a change in the rate of interest. Specifically, the interest elasticity of the investment demand schedule, which we shall designate as e_i, is equal to the ratio of a percentage change in investment expenditure to a percentage change in the rate of interest. In algebraic terms the interest elasticity of the investment demand schedule is given by the following formula:

$$e_i = \frac{\Delta I/I}{\Delta i/i} = \frac{\Delta I}{I} \times \frac{i}{\Delta i} \qquad (7\text{–}6)$$

An investment demand schedule that is relatively *elastic* will have a coefficient of elasticity whose absolute value is greater than 1, whereas an investment demand schedule that is relatively *inelastic* will have a coefficient of elasticity whose absolute value is less than 1.

The question of how investment spending responds to a change in the rate of interest is an important one, especially for policy purposes. Monetary policy, for example, works through changes in the money supply which, in turn, may effect the rate of interest. Whether investment spending responds to such changes is, therefore, an important policy consideration. Basically, two sets of circumstances determine how responsive investment spending may be to changes in the rate of interest, one of which is external to the business firm and the other internal. Let us examine these, using Equations (7–1) and (7–2) as our frame of reference. We shall assume a decline in interest rates.

A decline in interest rates, *ceteris paribus* will favor more investment spending because after the decline, the marginal efficiency of capital momentarily becomes greater than the rate of interest. A decline in interest rates also increases the present value (V_p) of any capital asset which the firm contemplates purchasing (Equation 7–1). Thus investment spending should increase, but how much investment spending actually increases depends in part upon a factor external to the business firm. This is the elasticity of the supply schedule for the production of new capital assets (structures, equipment, and inventories). As the demand for capital rises, the supply price (K_s) normally rises also. But as Equation (7–2) shows, a rise in the supply price (K_s) will, *ceteris paribus*, cause the marginal efficiency of capital (r) to fall. This is where the elasticity of the supply schedule for capital goods becomes crucial. The more *elastic* this schedule, the more the production of capital assets can be increased without a sharp rise in their price. Therefore, the more investment spending can respond to any given decline in the rate of interest. On the other hand, if the supply schedule for capital goods is *inelastic*, then any increase in demand for such goods will cause their prices to move up sharply, thus limiting the effectiveness of a decline in interest rates on investment spending. In sum, elasticity in the supply schedule for capital assets makes for elasticity in the investment demand schedule, and inelasticity in the supply schedule for capital assets makes for inelasticity in the demand schedule for capital.

The other factor which governs the elasticity of the investment demand schedule is essentially internal in that it pertains to the physical life of the capital asset which the firm contemplates purchasing. The effect of physical life on investment spending can readily be seen by examining the variables in Equation (7–1). The longer the physical life of a unit of capital, the smaller will be the expected net return on the asset in any single year (R_1 in the equation, for example). But the smaller the net return in a single year, the more pronounced is the impact on present value (and hence the marginal efficiency of capital) of a given change in the rate of interest. It follows from this that the more durable the capital asset—that is, the longer its expected physical life—the more sensitive investment spending for that type of asset will be to changes in the rate of interest. The less durable the asset, the less will be the response of investment spending to any change in the rate of interest.

The practical import of this is that business structures and residential construction, being quite long-lived, are the types of investment spending most sensitive to changes in the rate of interest. Equipment is normally less long-lived than structures, and inventories the least durable of all forms of business investment. Thus, it follows that the demand schedule for investment in either equipment or inventories is significantly less elastic than the demand schedule for investment in structures. Given the fact that the interest sensitivity (elasticity) is likely to vary significantly for each of the three major types of investment expenditure—structures, equipment, and inventories—it is difficult to generalize accurately about the sensitivity of over-all investment spending to changes in the rate of interest. Among economists the prevailing opinion seems to be that the interest elasticity of the investment demand schedule, though greater than zero, is not large, especially in the historically relevent range of 3 to 10 percent interest rates which apply to investments in capital assets.[14]

14. E. Kuh and J. R. Meyer, "Investment, Liquidity, and Monetary Policy," in *Impacts of Monetary Policy*, Commission on Money and Credit (Englewood Cliffs, New Jersey: Prentice-Hall, Inc., 1963), pp. 340–41. See also M. J. Hamburger, "The Impact of Monetary Variables: A Survey of Recent Econometric Literature," in W.L. Smith and R.L. Teigen, *Readings in Money, National Income, and Stabilization Policy*, rev. ed. (Homewood, Ill.: Richard D. Irwin, Inc., 1970), pp. 414–33.

An Alternative Approach: The Demand Price for Capital

There is an alternative—and in some respects a simpler—approach to the problem of the theory of investment spending. This approach too has its roots in Keynes's *The General Theory*,[15] although most contemporary thinking about investment spending is cast within the more traditional framework of a demand for investment schedule. We may term it the "demand price for capital" approach. It draws upon the same fundamental ideas which explain the concept of an investment demand schedule but stress is placed upon the present value of a contemplated capital asset rather than its marginal efficiency.

Present value, as we have seen, is obtained by discounting the expected yield—the stream of expected income—of a capital asset at some interest rate. The rate used to determine present value we may term the *capitalization* rate; it may or may not be equal to the current interest rate, depending on factors having to do with how a firm obtains the funds necessary to buy a new capital asset (See section on the financing of investment, p. 227). Present value (V_p) is the same thing as the demand price for a new capital asset. This can readily be seen by looking again at Equations (7–1) and (7–2). If the present value of an expected income stream as derived by applying a capitalization (discount) rate to the stream (Equation 7–1) is greater than the current supply price for the capital asset expected to yield the income stream (K_s in Equation (7–2)), then the marginal efficiency of the capital asset (r) is greater than the interest rate used to calculate present value (i). The latter will necessarily reflect the costs to the firm of getting the necessary funds to buy the asset. Thus, it follows that present value must be the demand price for the capital asset —that is, the price which the firm is willing to pay to get an additional unit of the kind of capital in question. It is analogous to the supply price, which, let us recall, is the price which will just induce the manufacturer to produce one additional unit of the capital.

Conceiving of the demand for a capital asset in this sense permits us to construct a demand curve (or schedule) for capital as seen by the business firm. This is done in Figure 7–2. In the diagram, the vertical axis measures present value (V_p)—the demand price for capital—and the horizontal axis the quantity of capital (K) that a firm would demand at different possible prices. In this respect, the demand curve for capital is no different from the demand curve for any commodity or service. It shows that, *ceteris paribus*, a firm will buy more capital assets as the price of the latter declines. The fundamental explanation for the negative slope of any single demand curve for capital lies in the principle of diminishing pro-

15. Hyman P. Minsky, *John Maynard Keynes*, (New York: Columbia University Press, 1975), p. 96.

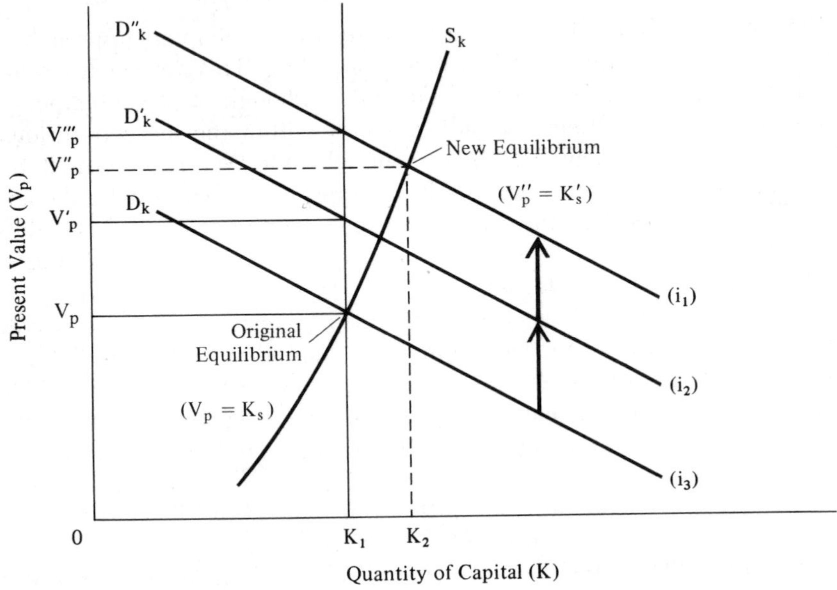

FIGURE 7–2. The Demand and Supply of Capital

rate of interest is to increase the capital intensity of production, i.e., to ductivity. Given the rate of interest, and with all else held constant, including demand for the final product, the expected profitability of each successive increment to the capital stock must decline. In the terms of the variables of Equation (7–1), the expected income stream will decline as firms acquire more capital assets. But as this happens the present value of each added unit declines, which means they will acquire more capital only at a lower price.

But more is involved. For each possible level of the rate of interest there exists a single down-sloping demand curve for capital. In Figure 7–2 three curves are shown. It should be noted that other things being equal, the lower the rate of interest, the higher will be the level of the demand curve. The reason for this can be seen by reference to Equation (7–1); for any given income stream ($R_1, R_2 \ldots R_n$), present value must be larger the lower is the rate of interest. This is a matter of mathematics. Thus, the effect of a change in the rate of interest is to shift the position of the demand curve for capital. If the rate of interest is lowered, the curve will be shifted upward. The economic reason for this is that a fall in the rate of interest will increase the present value of the firm's marginal unit of capital, making it more profitable for the firm to utilize additional capital. From the viewpoint of the firm, the consequence of a fall in the cause firms to use more capital per unit of labor and other resources. If all firms in the economy are affected in similar fashion by a decline in interest rates, what will be the over-all result? It will be to increase the demand for capital assets and thus cause more investment spending to take place. In this context, as in the context of the investment demand schedule discussed earlier, a fall in the rate of interest is associated with more investment spending. A rise in interest rates will have the opposite effect.

How a change in the interest rate affects the business firm with respect to its use of capital is depicted in Figure 7–2. Assume initially that the firm's demand curve for capital is given by D_k, the level of which is associated with the interest rate i_3. Given this interest rate the quantity of capital used by the firm will be K_1, a quantity determined by equality between the demand price for capital (V_p) and the supply price K_s). In the diagram the curve labeled S_k represents the supply schedule for capital assets. A decline in the rate of interest to i_1 shifts the demand schedule for capital upwards to the level represented by the schedule labeled D''_k. Since supply cannot respond instantaneously to increased demand, the demand price (present value) of capital jumps initially to the level V''_p. The higher price will in time evoke a supply response—more investment spending, in other words—which will tend to bring the price back down. Eventually, a new equilibrium for the firm will be established at which the demand for and supply of capital are once again in balance. This will involve a quantity of capital equal to K_2, and equality once again between the demand price for capital (V''_p and the supply price (K'_s).

The relationship between the demand for capital and the investment demand schedule approaches to investment spending is illustrated most effectively by reference once again to Equations (7–1) and (7–2). In the foregoing discussion the key point is that equilibrium in the use of capital is attained once the demand price (V_p) and the supply price (K_s) for more units of capital are equal. But if V_p and K_s are equal for any given series of expected returns (the *R*'s of our two key equations), then the rate of interest (i) and the marginal efficiency of capital (r) must also be equal. It cannot be otherwise arithmetically. What we have, in effect, are two different ways to approach the same basic Keynesian idea, namely that investment will take place (or firms will add to their stock of real capital assets) as long as it is worth while for them to do so. The latter notion can be expressed either as a situation in which the marginal efficiency of capital (r) exceeds the rate of interest, or the demand price for capital (V_p) is greater than the current supply price (K_s).[16]

16. There is an aspect of this analysis which is troublesome, both in theory and in reality. This stems from the fact that the demand for capital approach (Figure 7–2) involves equilibrium in terms of a *stock*—that is, the quantity of capital being used by all firms in the economy. The investment demand schedule approach in-

Although it is basically correct that the marginal efficiency of capital and the demand for capital approaches to investment behavior are in concept quite similar, there are some advantages found in the latter which are not present in the former. As one writer puts it, the demand price for capital technique is a "more natural" way to approach the problems of fluctuating investment.[17] This is because the stream of expected income (or cash flow) which is so crucial to the investment decision does not get lost from sight as tends to happen when the problem is cast in the marginal efficiency of capital frame of reference. This approach also allows us to put greater stress on the rate used to capitalize the income stream, paying particular attention to the factors which may cause this rate to vary from the market rate of interest on safe and secure loans.[18] When we examine later in this chapter the way in which the financing of investment expenditure influences investment spending this point becomes quite important.

Current Income and Investment Expenditure

Although the central idea in Keynes's theory of investment is the inverse relationship between investment expenditure and the rate of interest, many economists argue that *income* is a major determinant of investment expenditure. This approach involves the phenomenon of *induced* investment, which we shall designate as I_i. In the algebraic terms $I_i = f(Y)$. This equation should be interpreted to mean that investment outlays will

volves equilibrium in terms of a *flow*—namely, the quantity of investment spending. This presents a knotty problem because as long as any net investment spending exists, the economy's total stock of capital will continue to grow, a condition which is incompatible with the equilibrium condition described in Figure 7–2. Since, however, the stock of capital (K) is one of the "givens" necessary to drawing an investment demand function (Figure 7–1), one solution to the problem is to allow the investment demand curve to shift as the stock of capital increases. This fits in with the point made earlier to the effect that the Keynesian investment demand schedule is inherently unstable. This, as the stock of capital expands as a consequence of investment spending, the schedule will drift downward to the left, such a drift continuing until the schedule intersects the vertical axis at a rate of interest which leads to an equilibrium between the demand for capital and the supply of capital. In Figure 7–2 this would be the rate of interest i_1 and the stock of capital K_2. What this means is that a fall in the rate of interest will cause *net* investment spending to rise at first, and then gradually fall back to zero, once a new equilibrium has been reached with respect to the economy's over-all stock of capital. For a complete and relatively advanced treatment of this problem, see James G. Witte, Jr., "The Microfoundations of the Social Investment Function," *Journal of Political Economy*, October 1963, pp. 441-56.

17. Minsky, p. 100.
18. Ibid.

Ii = f(Y)

Induced Investment

increase as income increases. The income measure appropriate to this relationship is the net national product.[19]

In Equation (7–3), it was stated that $I = I_o - ci$. Let us designate $I_o - ci$ *as* I'_o and define it as all investment expenditure which is autonomous with respect to the income level. We can then postulate the following identity:

$$I = I'_o + I_i \tag{7–7}$$

This equation simply states that total investment consists of the two major categories of autonomous and induced investment. Since the latter is a direct function of income, we can transform the Equation (7–7) into the following form:

$$I = I'_o + bY_{np} \tag{7–8}$$

In the above expression b is the *marginal propensity to invest*, which algebraically we may define as:

$$b = \frac{\Delta I_i}{\Delta Y_{np}} \tag{7–9}$$

The student will note that we defined the marginal propensity to invest in a fashion analogous to the marginal propensity to consume and the marginal propensity to save, namely as the ratio of a change in investment to a change in income (net national product). The marginal propensity to invest concept implies that some portion of any increased income will be directed toward investment expenditure, a logical outcome of the assumption that current investment expenditure is linked functionally to the current income level. The marginal propensity to invest also measures the slope of the schedule which relates induced investment to income. A schedule of this type is displayed in Figure 7–3. Net national product is measured on the horizontal axis and investment on the vertical axis. Because investment is an increasing function of income the schedule slopes upward to the right. The level at which the schedule intersects the vertical axis equals I'_o, investment which is independent of the income level.

The assumptions embodied in this relationship are, first, that investment depends upon profitability, and second, that profitability is directly linked to the current income level. If these are correct assumptions, then a rising level of income will be accompanied by rising profit margins. As businessmen project current profit experiences into the future, expectations will be favorable and, consequently, investment expenditure will rise in response to the rising income level. This, of course, is an oversimplifi-

19. Net national product Y_{np} and disposable income Y_d remain equal because we are still assuming neither taxes nor transfer payments are present in the system.

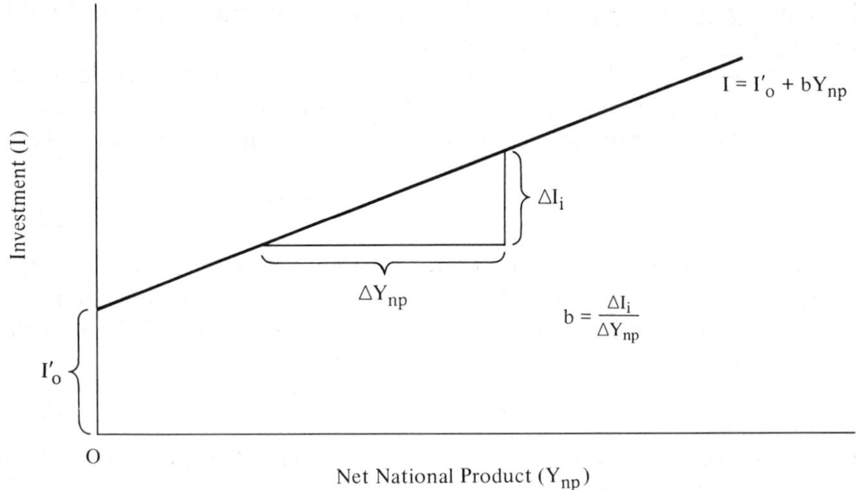

FIGURE 7–3. Investment and the Income Level

cation of a complex relationship. But the proposition that investment is a direct function of income enables us not only to deal with the phenomenon of induced investment in a direct way, but also to incorporate investment expenditure into the equilibrium income determination process and the theory of the multiplier far more readily than when we consider investment expenditure as a function of the rate of interest.

The Marginal Propensity to Invest and Equilibrium Income

Let us examine how the concept of the marginal propensity to invest may be incorporated into our formal equilibrium diagram. In Figure 7–4 the 45° line OZ again represents the aggregate supply function; the schedule labeled C is the consumption function. The basic difference between this figure and Figure 6–4 (p. 160) is that the aggregate demand schedule does not lie parallel to the consumption function; investment expenditure is not autonomous with respect to the income level, but increases as the income level increases. We construct the aggregate demand schedule by adding an investment schedule of the kind shown in Figure 7–3 to the consumption function. Equilibrium is attained at the point of intersection of the schedules of aggregate demand and aggregate supply. However, because we have included induced investment, the equilibrium level is higher than otherwise would be the case.

This can be clearly seen by contrasting an aggregate demand schedule, constructed with an autonomous investment function, with the aggregate demand schedule constructed with a function involving induced investment. In Figure 7–4 the dotted line $C + I'_o$ is an aggregate demand schedule of the former type, while schedule $C + I'_o + I_i$, on the other hand, incorporates the phenomenon of induced investment. $C + I'_o + I_i$ intersects the aggregate supply schedule at a higher income level than $C + I'_o$, and it should be noted that the slope of $C + I'_o + I_i$ is greater than the slope of $C + I'_o$. The slope of $C + I'_o + I_i$ is equal to the sum of the marginal propensity to consume and the marginal propensity to invest; the sum of these two marginal propensities can be defined as the *marginal propensity to spend*, a concept particularly relevant to multiplier analysis because, as was shown earlier, the value of the multiplier depends upon the amount of additional spending that is *induced* by an exogenous change in spending.

Induced Investment Expenditure and the Multiplier

Let us explore briefly the manner in which induced investment expenditure may be incorporated into multiplier theory. In order to facilitate the exposition, we shall break the investment component of the aggregate

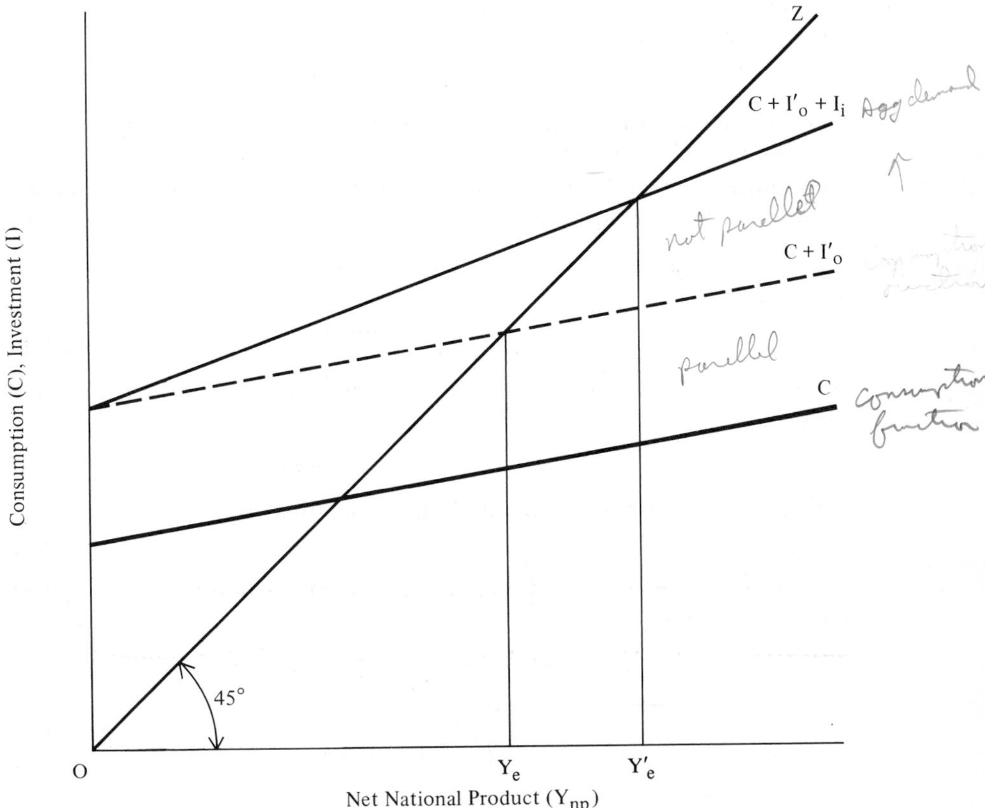

FIGURE 7–4. Induced Investment and Aggregate Demand

demand schedule into two subcategories: autonomous investment, which we have already designated as I'_o in Figure 7–4, and induced investment, represented symbolically by I_i. We assume that investment and consumption are the only expenditure categories, and that changes in the income level are initiated as the result of shifts in the autonomous investment function. Given these basic assumptions, we can postulate the following two definitional equations:

$$Y_{np} = I'_o + I_i + C \tag{7–10}$$

$$k' = \frac{\Delta Y_{np}}{\Delta I'_o} \tag{7–11}$$

Equation (7–10) is the basic identity equation which states that income (net national product) is equal to the sum of consumption and investment, except that investment is broken down into its two subcategories. Equation (7–11) is the basic definition of the multiplier, *i*, except that in this instance we are using the symbol k' to indicate the multiplier because we incorporate into it the phenomenon of induced investment.

From Equation (7–10) we get the following identity pertaining to a change in the income level:

$$\Delta Y_{np} = \Delta I'_o + \Delta I_i + \Delta C \tag{7–12}$$

Since the change in induced investment expenditure, ΔI_i, depends upon the value of the marginal propensity to invest, *b*, and since the change in consumption expenditure depends upon the value of the marginal propensity to consume, *a*, we have

$$\Delta I_i = b \times \Delta Y_{np} \tag{7–13}$$

and

$$\Delta C = a \times \Delta Y_{np}\text{[20]} \tag{7–14}$$

If we substitute the above values for ΔI_i and ΔC in Equation (7–12) we have

$$\Delta Y_{np} = \Delta I'_o + b\Delta Y_{np} + a\Delta Y_{np} \tag{7–15}$$

This equation can be manipulated algebraically as follows:

$$\Delta Y_{np} - a\Delta Y_{np} - b\Delta Y_{np} = \Delta I'_o \tag{7–16}$$

$$\Delta Y_{np}(1 - a - b) = \Delta I'_o \tag{7–17}$$

$$\Delta Y_{np} = \Delta I'_o \times \frac{1}{1 - a - b} \tag{7–18}$$

$$\frac{\Delta Y_{np}}{\Delta I'_o} = \frac{1}{1 - a - b} \tag{7–19}$$

20. $\Delta Y_{np} = \Delta Y_d$ when taxes and transfers are zero.

Thus, we can define k', the effective multiplier, as the reciprocal of 1 minus the marginal propensity to consume and the marginal propensity to invest. A quick examination of the algebra shows that by introducing an additional kind of induced spending into our analysis—namely, induced investment spending—we will obviously get a larger, ultimate increase in spending for any initial exogenous increase in spending. As a parenthetical note, k' is sometimes called the supermultiplier.

In the foregoing discussion we assumed a constant value for the marginal propensity to invest, b, which in turn enables us to compute an exact value for the multiplier k'. Reality, of course, is not so accommodating, and it is most unlikely that the marginal propensity to invest will have a constant value for any significant length of time. This particular approach to induced investment rests on the assumption that current profits are sufficient to engender favorable expectations with respect to the profitability of additional capital equipment. If the current profit picture is not satisfactory, however, there is no reason to believe that any amount of investment expenditure will be induced by the current income level. Thus, there is no real assurance that the value of the marginal propensity to invest will remain stable, and, for that matter, there is no positive assurance that it will remain above zero.

The Acceleration Principle

A much more complex and dynamic analysis of the phenomenon of induced investment is based on the *acceleration principle.* This principle asserts that net investment is a function of the rate of change in final output rather than of the absolute level of output. This is an important distinction. The earliest complete formulation of the acceleration principle was made in 1917 by Professor John Maurice Clark in a renowned article, "Business Acceleration and the Law of Demand: A Technical Factor in Economic Cycles."[21] Clark set out to show, first, that a special and technical relationship exists between the demand for a final product and the demand for the capital equipment necessary to produce the final product, and second, that this technical relationship is of such a character that it can be employed to explain not only the nature of the demand for new capital instruments, but also why the demand for capital fluctuates much more violently than the demand for final goods. Since the publication of Clark's historic article, many economists have analyzed and refined this principle, using it to explain the apparent cyclical nature of much economic activity.

In our discussion of the acceleration principle we shall use the income symbol Y to designate *output of final goods and services,* and the symbol

21. Reprinted in *Readings in Business Cycle Theory* (Philadelphia: Blakiston, 1944).

K to designate the capital stock. The technical relationship existing between a given level of output and the quantity of capital necessary to produce that output is defined as the *capital-output ratio.* We shall designate this ratio by the capital letter A. Thus we have

$$A = \frac{K}{Y} \tag{7–20}$$

If we assume no change in the technical condition under which resources are combined in order to obtain a given output, it is reasonable to assume that an increase in output once full capacity has been achieved will require additional capital equipment in the proportion indicated by the capital-output ratio. For example, if we find that, on the average, it requires capital equipment in the amount of $3.00 for each $1.00 of output, then as long as there is no change in the technical conditions under which capital is combined with other resources in the productive process, every $1.00 increase in output above the level of existing capacity will require $3.00 worth of additional capital equipment. We can draw the formal generalization that, given constant technical conditions of production, the marginal capital-output ratio will equal the capital-output ratio proper. The latter is generally designated as the *average* capital-output ratio when we are discussing the technical relationship between capital and output for the whole economy. In any event, when the average and the marginal capital-output ratios are equal

$$A = \frac{K}{Y} = \frac{\Delta K}{\Delta Y} \tag{7–21}$$

By definition though, the change in the capital stock, ΔK, is the same thing as net investment in the economy, I_n. Substituting I_n for ΔK in the algebraic formula and transposing ΔY to the left-hand side of the expression, we have the following:

$$A = \frac{I_n}{\Delta Y} \tag{7–22}$$

$$I_n = A \times \Delta Y \tag{7–23}$$

Equation (7–23) is the formal algebraic expression of the acceleration principle, as it tells us there exists some coefficient A which, when multiplied by the change in output will give us net investment expenditure. To put the matter the other way around, we can say that the formula tells that if output is to increase by an amount equal to ΔY, then additional capital equipment in the amount I_n is required. This is necessary because, as it can readily be seen from the formula, the larger the absolute change in output, the larger the amount of induced investment.

If we set this analysis within a time sequence, it is relatively easy to see why the acceleration principle makes induced investment expenditure a function of the rate at which output is increasing (or decreasing). Net investment in the current income period (designated by the symbol t) is equal to the difference between the capital stock of the current period, K_t, and the capital stock of the previous period, K_{t-1}. Thus

$$I_t = K_t - K_{t-1} \tag{7–24}$$

The change in income in the current period, ΔY_t, is equal to the difference between current income, Y_t, and the income of the previous period, Y_{t-1}. Therefore, we have

$$\Delta Y_t = Y_t - Y_{t-1} \tag{7–25}$$

The rate at which income (or output) changes between one period and the next is measured by the ratio of ΔY_t to Y_{t-1}. For example, if income rose by $45 billion between the present and the past income period, and if Y_{t-1} was $900 billion, then the rate of income increase, $\Delta Y_t / Y_{t-1}$, will be 5 percent. The importance of this is that the rate of change in income depends upon the absolute change in income in a period relative to the income level of the previous period. The larger the absolute change relative to income of the previous period, the larger will be the rate of change. But the acceleration formula, Equation (7–23), shows that, given a fixed technical relationship between capital and output, the amount of induced investment will vary directly with the size of the absolute change in output. Consequently, the acceleration principle means *induced net investment in a function of the rate of change of final output.*

Practical Implications of the Acceleration Principle · There are two important implications flowing from the acceleration principle. In the first place, as suggested earlier, we can employ the principle to explain a phenomenon long observed by economists, namely that the output of capital instruments fluctuates much more violently than the output of goods in general. The exaggerated impact of an increase (or decrease) in demand for final output on the demand for capital goods can be illustrated by means of a simple arithmetical example. Let us imagine a hypothetical industry whose output of final goods is 100 units per income period (see Table 7–1). The capital-output ratio for this industry is assumed to be 3, which means 300 units of capital are required to produce this output. These units of capital have an average economic life of 10 income periods, so the normal replacement demand for capital equipment is 30 units per income period. Let us now see what will happen if there is a 10 percent increase in demand for the final product. A 10 percent increase in demand will mean the production of 10 additional units of final product per income period. But if the industry is operating at its capacity level

TABLE 7–1. The Acceleration Effect and the Demand for Capital

Income Period	*Capital Stock*	*Output*	*Replacement Demand*	*Demand for New Capital*	*Total Demand*
1	300.0	100.0	30.0	0.0	30.0
2	330.0	110.0*	30.0	30.0	60.0
3	346.5	115.5†	30.0	16.5	46.5
n‡	346.5	115.5	34.6	0.0	34.6

*10 percent increase in final demand.
†5 percent increase in final demand.
‡when capital added in period, 2 and 3 begins to be replaced.

prior to this increase in demand, then the production of 10 additional units of final product per income period will require 30 additional units of capital. Now if this increase in demand of 10 percent for the final product is presumed to take place within the confines of a single income period, the demand for capital goods will increase by 100 percent in this same income period. The reason for this is that the 30 units of capital needed to provide an additional 10 units of output are added to the normal replacement demand of 30 units, thus making a 100 percent increase in demand for capital goods. In the subsequent income period, however, the demand for capital goods will fall back to the level dictated by normal replacement needs,[22] because, according to the acceleration principle, only during the time that the demand for final output is actually changing will there be additional induced investment. The reader should also note that the more durable the capital instrument, the greater will be the fluctuation in the demand for capital instruments relative to the demand for final output. If, in our hypothetical example, the capital units had an average economic life of 20 rather than 10 income periods, a 10 percent increase in demand for final output would have brought about a 200 percent increase in demand for capital instruments (15 replacement units plus 30 additional units of capital). This would be true as long as the capital-output ratio remained equal to 3.

Our hypothetical example demonstrates the most important single fact about the acceleration principle: There will be induced investment expenditure only so long as final demand is increasing. Once the latter stabilizes at a new and higher level, induced investment expenditure will cease. Expressed in formal terms, the absolute level of induced net investment will enlarge as long as final demand is increasing at an increasing rate; once the rate of increase of final demand begins to slow down, the absolute level of induced net investment will decline. To illustrate, let us

22. The normal replacement demand will be 30 units of capital per income period, until the new units added have to be replaced. Eventually, replacement demand will rise to 33 units.

refer once again to our hypothetical industry with its 100 units of output and 300 units of capital. In the first income period a 10 percent increase in final demand, because of the prevailing capital-output ratio, caused a 100 percent increase in the demand for capital goods. In absolute amount this was equal to 30 units. Now let us assume that in the subsequent income period the demand for final output advances by 5 percent, which still is an increase, but at a decreasing rate. This 5 percent increase in demand over the level of the previous period will require production of 5.5 additional units,[23] which, in turn, will require 16.5 additional units of capital. The absolute level of induced investment has fallen from 30 to 16.5 units as the rate of increase in demand for final output fell from 10 to 5 percent (see Table 7–1).

These observations about final demand and the level of investment expenditure lead us to a second practical implication of the acceleration principle. In combination with the Keynesian investment multiplier, the acceleration principle can be used to explain why fluctuations of a cyclical character tend to be an inherent characteristic of a market economy. An exogenous increase in aggregate demand, such as results from an upward shift in the autonomous investment function, will induce additional consumption spending by means of the multiplier process. The rising level of output which results from the combination of the original increment in investment spending and the induced consumption spending may induce additional investment spending by means of the accelerator. It is the combined effect of the induced consumption (via the multiplier) and the induced investment spending (via the accelerator) that can bring about a powerful, cumulative upward movement of income. The multiplier and the accelerator can act together to produce a kind of self-generating cyclical movement of the income level, because the acceleration principle makes induced investment a function of the rate of change in output. When the multiplier process gets under way, induced consumption expenditure will occur, but the increments of added consumption expenditure in each successive round of spending and respending will become smaller and smaller. Since the amount of induced investment varies directly with the absolute change in income (or output), net induced investment will at first rise and then decline. But the multiplier process, it will be recalled, comes into play whenever there is a net change in the rate of spending. Consequently, if the rate of net induced investment begins to decline, a multiplier process in reverse is set in motion. This tends to create the self-generating cyclical movement of the income level.

Table 7–2 provides a simple numerical example of how the combined interaction between the multiplier and the accelerator may produce a self-generating cyclical movement, assuming equilibrium in the system is

23. Five (5) percent of 110 units is 5.5.

disturbed by an outside "shock" of some sort. In this example, the accelerator effect is limited to investment expenditure induced by a change in consumption, and the change in consumption is assumed to depend on the change in income in the prior period. A lag, in other words, is introduced into the example. Initially the system is without investment and is in a state of equilibrium in which both income (Y) and consumption (C) are equal to 100. The outside shock which starts the multiplier-accelerator interaction is an increase in autonomous investment expenditure (I_0) in the amount of 10. What happens after that can be seen by a close examination of the data in this hypothetical example. In accordance with the consumption function hypothesis, the increased income resulting from investment induces in the third period more consumption ($\Delta C = 5$), which in turn causes induced investment spending to rise by an amount equal to the change in consumption multiplied by the accelerator ($\Delta I_i = 5 \times 2 = 10$). There is a buildup in the income level to a peak in the fourth period, but as the rate of change in consumption spending begins to slow down (Column 7) the accelerator effect begins to operate in the opposite direction. Income turns down and continues to drop until once again the process is reversed.[24]

Limitations of the Acceleration Principle · In spite of the usefulness of the acceleration principle as a device for explaining the cyclical movement of income and sharp fluctuations in the output of capital goods, there are some severe limitations inherent in the concept. For one thing, most economists recognize that the acceleration principle is too mechanical to serve as an explanation of such a complex phenomenon as the investment process in a modern economy. One criticism is that the acceleration principle has little or no motivational content. The entrepreneur is presumed to act like a thermostat, noting when capacity is overtaxed and then taking the necessary steps to overcome this deficiency.[25]

24. In a classical article, Professor Paul Samuelson demonstrated that mathematically there are four possible ways in which the economy may respond to an outside "shock." The response depends upon whether or not the shock (such as an autonomous increase in investment expenditures as the example in the text) is continuous, and the values assumed for both the marginal propensity to consume (the multiplier) and the accelerator. The four responses were (1) an initial raise in income followed by a fall back to the original equilibrium level; (2) oscillatory movements of income which are initially large but gradually approach a new and higher equilibrium level; (3) oscillatory movements of income which are explosive, resulting in ever increasing oscillations; and (4) an ever increasing level of income which approaches a compound interest rate of growth. See Paul A. Samuelson, "Interactions between the Multiplier Analysis and the Principle of Acceleration," *Review of Economics and Statistics*, May 1939, pp. 75–78.

25. John R. Meyer and Edwin Kuh, *The Investment Decision* (Cambridge, Mass.: Harvard University Press, 1957), p. 14.

TABLE 7–2. The Combined Multiplier and Accelerator Effect

(1) Period	(2) Y	(3) ΔY	(4) I_o	(5) C	(6) ΔC	(7) $\Delta C/C$*	(8) Ii	(9) ΔIi	(10) $(I_o + Ii)$
0	100	—	—	100	—	—	—	—	—
1	110	10	10	100	—	—	—	—	10
2	125	15	10	105	5	5.0%	10	10	20
3	139	14	10	113	8	7.6	16	6	26
4	144	5	10	120	7	6.2	14	− 2	24
5	139	− 5	10	123	3	2.5	6	− 8	16
6	124	−15	10	120	− 3	− 2.4	− 6	−12	4
7	106	−18	10	112	− 8	− 6.6	−16	− 4	− 6
8	95	−11	10	103	− 9	− 8.0	−18	− 2	− 8
9	98	3	10	98	− 5	− 4.8	−10	8	0
10	114	16	10	100	2	2.3	4	14	14
11	134	20	10	108	8	8.0	16	12	26
12	148	14	10	118	10	9.2	20	4	30
13	149	1	10	125	7	5.9	14	− 6	24
14	134	−15	10	126	1	0.8	2	−12	12
15	108	−26	10	114	− 8	− 6.3	−16	−18	− 6
16	85	−23	10	101	−13	−11.4	−26	− 8	−16
17	75	−10	10	89	−12	−11.8	−24	2	−14
18	84	9	10	84	− 5	5.6	−10	14	0

Note:
I_o = Autonomous Investment
Ii = Induced investment
$C = f(Y)$ (Consumption is a lagged function of income in the prior period)
$\Delta C/\Delta Y = .5$ (The marginal propensity to consume)
$Ii/\Delta C = 2$ (The Accelerator. Limited to the change in consumption, not total income)
$Y = (C + I + I')$ (The basic identity)

Figures have been rounded to nearest whole number

*Rate of change of consumption (Ratio of ΔC in current period to C in past period.)

A more serious criticism and limitation of the principle concerns the matter of productive capacity. In a strict sense, the acceleration principle is effective only when an industry or the economy as a whole is operating at a level of full utilization of existing capacity. Since the principle is based upon a technical relationship between capital and output, it logically follows that additional capital will not be required to make possible additional output unless existing productive capacity is being fully utilized. If surplus capacity exists in the economy, the principle breaks down because added output can be supplied from the untapped capacity. This has led some economists to conclude that insofar as business-cycle analysis is concerned the principle may have validity during the upswing (when rising demand eventually presses hard against existing capacity), but not in the downswing or depression phase of the cycle (when excess and idle capacity is one of the most common features of the economy).

Another and related objection concerns the sticky matter of the definition of capacity. As one economist has pointed out, there is little, if anything, in the voluminous literature that has grown up around the acceleration principle that attempts to define precisely the meaning of such terms as *capacity* and *surplus capacity*.[26] In a literal sense, the acceleration principle asserts that net investment is induced, or more capital is created, because output has risen. Because of the technical relationship between capital and output fundamental to the acceleration principle, additional output can be forthcoming only if the stock of capital has already been increased. This is the dilemma that faces us if we interpret both the acceleration principle and its underlying assumption of full-capacity production quite literally. The only way out of this dilemma is to interpret the notion of capacity somewhat freely and suggest that at some point the entrepreneur will reach the conclusion that his existing facilities will be overtaxed if he attempts to provide for an expected demand without expansion. This, of course, does not destroy the notion of the acceleration principle, but it does make the whole matter much more subjective—and hence less precise—than do mechanical models of the principle based upon a constant technical relationship between capital and output. As has been said, there is "an element of truth in the acceleration principle; but it is an element that is so heavily overlaid by other factors that the acceleration principle by itself is inadequate as a theory of investment."[27]

Theory and Reality

From the foregoing discussion of investment theory since Keynes, three variables emerge as prime determinants of investment spending in the economy. They are, first, the rate of interest; second, the level of income; and third, the quantity of capital required to produce a particular level of output. The most basic idea, of course, is that investment spending is undertaken in the expectation of profit, and that such expectations are always tied to an elusive and unknown future. Formal investment theory attempts to cut through the difficulties involved in dealing with the uncertainties which surround expectations and tie investment spending to variables which are observable and measurable. The basic question, then, is which theoretical approach has the greatest validity?

In spite of the enormous—and growing—volume of economic literature which embodies empirical investigations into the determinants of invest-

26. A. D. Knox, "The Acceleration Principle and the Theory of Investment: A Survey," *Economica*, August 1952.

27. Ibid., p. 296.

ment spending,[28] no definitive answer to this question has emerged. As we found true in the case of different theories of consumption spending, there are elements of value in each of the foregoing approaches to the complex problem of investment behavior. Nevertheless, the empirical evidence now available offers support for at least two of the theoretical ideas discussed in this chapter. In these studies real output emerges as the most important single determinant of investment expenditure. This ties in with the theoretical analysis of induced investment spending. In manufacturing industries, for example, it was found that a 1 percent change in output led to a 1.5 to 2 percent change in investment spending within a two-year period.[29] Further, in practically every empirical study in which the interest rate was included as a variable, interest was found to be significant. There was no agreement in the studies on the elasticity of investment spending in relation to the interest rate, but there was agreement that interest rates are an important factor in determining the level of investment, especially in capital which is long-lived. In manufacturing it was found that a change of one percentage point (say from 4 to 5 percent) in long-term interest rates causes investment to change by 5 to 10 percent over a two-year period, although there may be a lag of a year or more before the interest change has an effect.[30] Evidence on the validity of the accelerator is at best mixed, some studies finding support for such a relationship and others rejecting it. Although it is encouraging that empirical research (to date) tends to support the basic ideas about the determinants of investment spending which emerged from *The General Theory*, it is unlikely that even the most painstaking econometric research will uncover the definitive investment function. The reason is rooted in the uncertainty and precariousness which surrounds *all* efforts to gauge the income stream that a new item of capital will yield. This is unlikely to change, no matter how sophisticated our econometric techniques.

The Financing of Investment

Investment spending, as we have seen, is an unstable component in the structure of aggregate demand in a market economy, the basic reason being the uncertainty which surrounds estimating the present value of an

28. For a recent survey of this literature see Dale W. Jorgenson, "Econometric Studies of Investment Behavior: A Survey," *Journal of Economic Literature*, December 1971, pp. 1111–47. In the bibliography which is a part of this survey, 109 articles and books dealing with the investment question are listed.

29. Michael K. Evans, *Macroeconomic Activity: Theory, Forecasting, and Control* (New York: Harper & Row, 1969), p. 138.

30. Ibid.

expected income stream. This is the essence of the Keynesian view of investment. This basic instability may be exaggerated by how a business firm finances its acquisition of new capital assets. This is the basic reason for paying careful attention to the financing side of the investment decision, a topic to which we now turn.

Earlier it was pointed out that there are basically three sources from which firms can get the money needed to purchase new capital assets. These are (1) retained earnings (the internal cash flow of the firm); (2) selling of shares in the firm (equity financing); and borrowing (issuing of bonds or other forms of debt). Although the first two sources of investment finance are not in any sense "problem-free," it is funds obtained through borrowing which are of major significance in linking finance to the volatility of investment spending. Thus we shall concentrate most of our analysis upon this type of finance. Some idea of the magnitude of debt financing is found in the fact that in 1976 net new security issues of all types of American corporations totaled $40.9 billion, of which $29.9 billion (or 73 percent) were either bonds or short-term notes (promises to pay).[31]

Financial Instruments and Real Capital Assets

Professor Hyman Minsky suggests that it is necessary to adopt a Wall Street perspective if we are to understand fully the crucial role that finance plays in investment behavior.[32] By such a perspective he means that we are dealing not only with a monetary economy with highly sophisticated financial institutions, but one in which money and debts are the key instruments through which ownership or control of *real* capital assets is acquired. Thus the instruments of finance (including money) become in their own right a powerful factor in the investment equation, especially because a market system attaches values—that is, prices—to such instruments just as it does to real capital assets as well as goods and services in general. Keynes described this intermingling of money, the instruments of finance, and real capital as follows:

> There is a multitude of real assets in the world which constitute our capital wealth—buildings, stocks of commodities, goods in the course of manufacture and of transport, and so forth. The nominal owners of these assets, however, have not infrequently borrowed *money* in order to become possessed of them. To a corresponding extent the actual owners of wealth have claims, not on real assets, but on money. A considerable

31. *Federal Reserve Bulletin*, May 1977., p. A-37. This does not measure the amount of debt financing for new capital assets, as it includes borrowings for all purposes by corporations, not just the acquisition on new physical capital.

32. Minsky, p. 73. This section draws heavily upon Professor Minsky's analysis of the role of debt finance in the investment decision.

> part of the "financing" takes place through the banking system, which interposes its guarantee between its depositors who lend it money, and its borrowing customers to whom it loans money wherewith to finance the purchase of real assets. The interposition of this *veil of money* [italics added] between the real asset and the wealth owner is a specially marked characteristic of the modern world.[33]

Keynes wrote that in 1931. If anything it describes more accurately the contemporary paper world of money and finance than it did when first set into print.

What happens when a firm borrows to finance purchase of real capital?[34] Basically by issuing debts (bonds) the firm gets the cash necessary to buy the desired capital asset. By issuing bonds the firm creates for itself a contractual obligation not only to repay the sum borrowed at some future date, but to meet periodically the interest payments on the debt. The firm, in other words, obligates itself to a flow of cash payments which stretch into the future, such payments lasting for the lifetime of the debt. Over and against this cash-flow commitment the firm must balance the expected cash inflow which stems from the assets purchased with the proceeds of the loan. Professor Minsky says that the fundamental speculative decision of a business firm centers on how much of the firm's income from normal operations can be pledged to pay the interest and principal on the liabilities incurred in order to acquire income-producing (capital) assets.[35] The firm, in adding to its liability structure, is "betting that the ruling situation at the future dates (when payments come due) will be such that the cash commitments can be met; it is estimating that the odds in an uncertain future are favorable."[36]

Pricing Financial Assets

To understand how the firm makes this fundamental speculative decision we must look again at the discount (capitalization) process. As we saw earlier, the investment decision in its most basic sense involves comparing the present value of the expected income stream produced by a capital asset with its supply price. When we introduce a contractual cash flow commitment into the picture, the comparison has to be between the present value of the expected income stream and the present value of the contractual cash flow. The latter covers both the supply price of the capi-

33. John Maynard Keynes, "The Consequence to the Banks of the Collapse of Money Values," in *Essays in Persuasion* (New York W.W. Norton & Company, Inc., 1963), p. 169.

34. The analysis to follow applies primarily to investment in long-term capital—plant and equipment. Inventories are normally turned over in a very short time; hence immediate sales prospects are the key factor in the investment in inventories decisions.

35. Minsky, p. 86.

36. Ibid., p. 87.

tal—what the firm has to pay for a newly produced unit and the interest charges on the borrowed money.

Present value, let us recall, is determined by capitalizing a payments flow at *some* rate of interest. Unless a firm experiences a complete financial collapse, its long-term obligation (bonds) are secure because they are contractual. Thus the present value for the debts issued by a firm normally would be found by discounting their contractual cash flows at the prevailing market rate of interest.[37] If the world were free of risk and the future not characterized by uncertainty the same capitalization (or discount) rate could be applied to the stream of income expected from the capital assets whose purchase is being contemplated. Then it would only be necessary to compare two present values: if present value for the expected income stream were greater than present value for the cash-flow commitment from a newly issued debt, then the investment decision could be positive.

But the world is not like this. Risk is present and the future is uncertain. This means that much greater certainty attaches to income derived from a contractual cash commitment such as a bond provides than to income derived from a newly produced item of capital. But the less certain the future income stream, the less its present value. Since greater uncertainty (and risk) attaches to the prospective yield on capital, a higher rate of discount must be used to determine its present value as compared to the going rate for money loans. The difference between these two rates must in logic reflect the state of uncertainty existing at any particular time. The key question thus becomes: what determines this uncertainty?

In *The General Theory* Keynes dealt with this question by distinguishing between two types of risk: borrower's risk and lender's risk. As Keynes phrased it:

> Two types of risk affect the volume of investment which have not commonly been distinguished, but which it is important to distinguish. The first is entrepreneur's or borrower's risk and arises out of doubts in his own mind as to the probability of his actually earning the prospective yield for which he hopes. If a man is venturing his own money, this is the only risk which is relevant.
>
> But where a system of borrowing and lending exists, by which I mean the granting of loans with a margin of real or personal security, a second type of risk is relevant which we may call the lender's risk. This may be due to either a moral hazard, i.e., voluntary default or other means of escape, possibly lawful, from the fulfillment of the obligation, or the possible insufficiency of the margin of security i.e., involuntary default due to the disappointment of expectation.[38]

37. This would also be the rate of interest which the bond pays, since the decision or comparison being discussed is made when new debt is being issued.

38. Keynes, *The General Theory*, p. 144.

Borrower's risk is essentially subjective, existing primarily in the mind of the borrower, never appearing explicitly in a contract. Lender's risk, on the other hand, is objective and shows up in various ways in financial contracts—higher interest rate, shorter terms to maturity, or the pledge of specific assets as collateral for a loan.[39] Borrower's risk is the key to the difference between the discount rate appropriate to a firm's debt structure and the rate used to determine present value for uncertain yields from new capital assets. Borrower's risk, in other words, is the focal point through which uncertainty makes itself felt.

Basically, the process works as follows. As a firm increases the proportion of new capital assets financed by debt relative to either internal funds or equities, the firm's basic financial position becomes increasingly risky. The reason is simply that it finds itself in a situation in which the cash-flow obligations it must meet because of its debt structure grow while the prospective yields become less and less certain as the firm continues to acquire new capital assets. Thus, the discount rate used to determine the present value of expected yields must rise to reflect the increasing uncertainty which follows from a rise in the ratio of debt to other forms of financing. But this means, of course, that the demand price for new capital will decline as uncertainty increases.[40] But as the demand price for capital (the present value of the expected yield) falls, the less favorable are the prospects for continued investment spending, particularly since normally the supply price for new capital assets is positive (Figure 7–2). Since borrower's risk is highly subjective, it may increase quite suddenly, thus causing a collapse in the demand price for capital, followed by a sharp drop in investment spending.

Boom Conditions, Asset Values, and Investment Spending

Boom conditions may provide a setting for this sequence of events. A factor which strongly influences borrower's risk is the past performance of the economy. Thus in the early stages of a boom, when the economy is picking up steam, borrower's risk is likely to be low; furthermore, the debt-financing ratio may be low. In a boom period past estimates of the prospective yield for capital assets may turn out to have been too low—actual yields are higher than anticipated. This leads to capital gains—increases in the value of the firm and the firm's assets because of the favorable higher than anticipated earnings on newly acquired assets. As a consequence both borrower's and lender's risk are reduced, a development which pushes the firm further into debt financing. As the boom proceeds, firms become more and more willing to resort to debt financing. Boom conditions often lead to a "layering" of debt, which means using

39. Minsky, p. 110.
40. Ibid., p. 109.

actual or anticipated capital gains as a source of more borrowing power. But as this process continues the firm's cash commitments due to its liabilities (debts) may begin to mount faster than the income the firm gets from its operations and assets it may own. In terms of the factors which enters into the investment decision, the cash-flow commitments from newly issued debt begin to outpace the proceeds expected from the capital assets financed by the debt. The optimism of the boom often leads a firm to overcommit itself to debt financing, the result being a situation in which its cash-payment obligations exceed the cash receipts flowing in from current operations. If the firm gets itself into this situation, both borrower's risk and lender's risk will rise sharply— especially borrower's risk, the consequence being a drastic fall in the demand price for new capital relative to its supply price and thus a collapse in investment spending. With the latter, the boom will also collapse. A process of debt deflation may follow, a period in which firms attempt to scale down their debt structure, using whatever internal funds they can muster to service existing debts. They will try and reduce their cash-flow commitments by replacing short-term debt with long-term debt as the former matures, a process called refunding. It doesn't reduce the total debt-based cash commitments of the firm, but it can reduce the size of the more immediate, short-term cash obligations confronting the firm. During the debt deflation process borrower's risk remains high, a development which keeps investment spending for new capital low and the economy in a depressed condition.[41]

The Supply Curve for Finance

Before we look briefly at some other factors which may influence the business firm's investment decision, some comments are in order on how firms typically view the costs of alternative forms of finance. The prior

41. The American economy has not experienced a serious debt-deflation induced depression since the 1930s, but Professor Minsky believes the economy has come close on at least three occasions in recent years—in 1966, in 1970–71, and in 1974–75. In each of these periods trouble developed in the financial sector of the economy because too many leading financial institutions had used short-term debt to finance their holdings of longer-term assets which could not be readily sold to meet short-term cash commitments. They engaged, in other words, in speculative finance, expecting to be able continuously to renew ("roll over" is the term the financial community uses) short-term debt as it came due. When this proved difficult, they found themselves in deep trouble. What saved the economy from going through the wringer of a full-blown debt deflation and the ensuing depression was the high level of government spending which sustained incomes and the willingness of the Federal Reserve System to provide the funds necessary to prevent collapse in the financial system. See Hyman P. Minsky, "The Financial Instability Hypothesis: An Interpretation of Keynes and an Alternative to 'Standard' Theory," *Nebraska Journal of Economics and Business*, Winter 1977, pp. 5–16, and "How 'Standard' Is Standard Economics?" *Society*, March/April 1977, pp. 24–29.

discussion centered around debt finance, primarily because this particular type of financing plays a crucial role in the volatility of investment spending. But firms also finance new capital assets from retained earnings and from issuing additional shares of the stock of the firm. The explicit or implicit cost of funds obtained from the three possible sources of finance is an important factor in the investment decision. For the typical firm contemplating the purchase of real capital assets, the supply curve for finance appears as shown in Figure 7–5.

Essentially, the supply schedule for finance has three segments, each one of which relates to the different source of finance. In the figure the first segment (designated A) is retained earnings. There is no lender's risk involved in getting funds from this source, and if we assume borrower's risk is a constant, then the rate appropriate for funds from this source is that interest rate foregone by not lending (i.e., purchasing securities) earnings retained. Thus, this segment of the curve is perfectly elastic (horizontal) at the current rate for outstanding long-term debts (i.e., bonds). The next segment (designated B) represents funds obtained by borrowing. This portion of the curve slopes upwards to the right, reflecting the fact that as the firm borrows more, the cost of borrowing will rise. This is primarily due to lender's risk, since this will get larger the more heavily indebted the firm becomes. Finally, there is a range in which the firm will resort to equity financing, which is to say it will issue new ownership shares to obtain the money needed to finance investment outlays (Segment C in Figure 7–5). This type of financing is generally regarded as more costly than borrowing, even though there is no obligation to pay out dividends to the shareholders. The reason for this is the differential

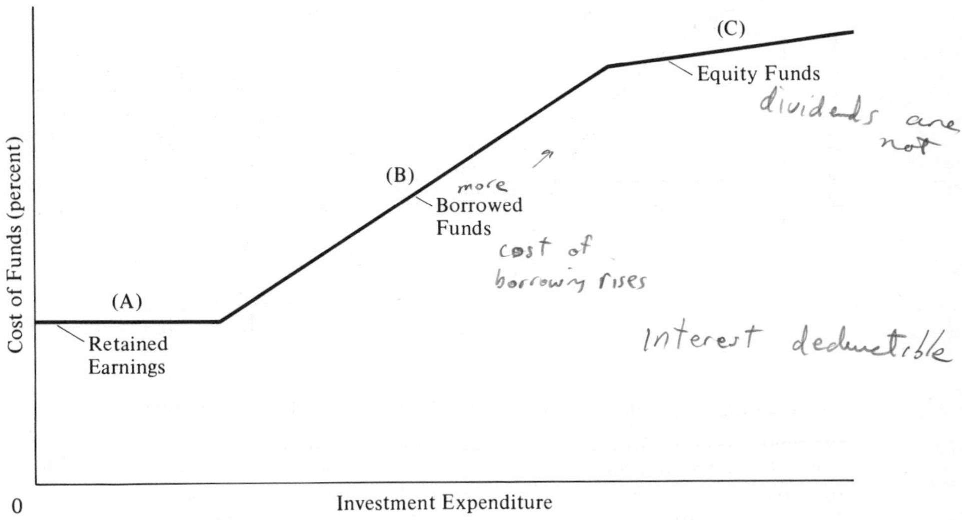

FIGURE 7–5. The Supply Curve for Finance

treatment under the income tax laws for interest and dividend payments. Interest is a deductible expense in computing the tax liability of a business corporation, whereas dividends are not. The equity portion of the finance curve also slopes upwards. This is because if a firm issues new shares, the increased supply of its stock will depress the market price of shares outstanding, thus causing their yields to rise.[42]

If we bring together the supply curve for finance shown in Figure 7–5 and the Keynesian investment demand curve developed earlier (Figure 7–1, Part B) we can show how the interaction between the marginal efficiency of capital and the cost of finance determine the rate of investment. This is done in Figure 7–6, part A. We can also use this diagram to show the impact of a change in both borrower's and lender's risk on the rate of investment. This we find in Part B of Figure 7–6. In this part of the figure the original demand and supply curves shift to the positions indicated by the dotted curves in the diagram. The investment demand schedule collapses because of a rise in borrower's risk. The impact of increased lender's risk is shown by an upward shift in the supply of funds curve. The resulting outcome—investment outlays decline to I'_e—is one in which investment spending is limited by the amount of internal finance available, the reason being firms hesitate about resorting to debt financing of capital outlays until they have reorganized and scaled down their debt structure.

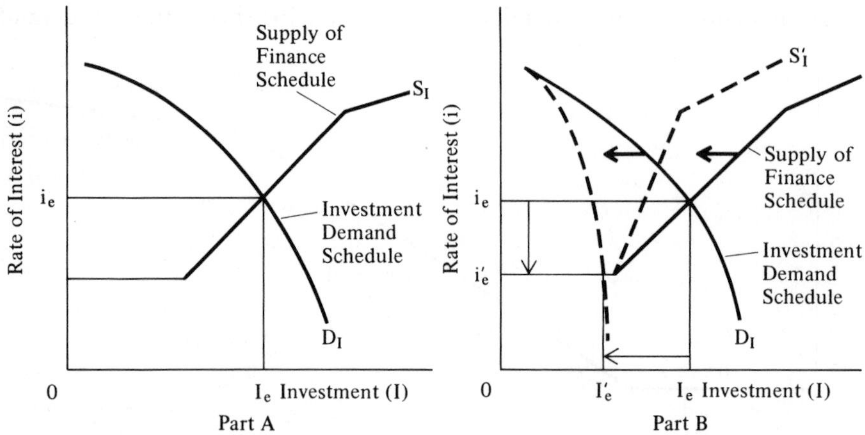

FIGURE 7–6. Investment Demand and the Supply of Finance Schedule

42. The foregoing analysis of the supply schedule for finance is drawn primarily from the approach developed by James S. Duesenberry. See his *Business Cycles and Economic Growth* (New York: McGraw-Hill, 1958), esp. Chapter 4.

Other Influences on the Investment Decision

Within the basic analytical framework of the capital and investment demand schedules, other determinants of investment are treated as parametric factors whose basic role is to determine the position of these schedules. Changes in the value of any of these factors cause a shift in their position or slope. As was true with the consumption function, many of these factors are subjective and hence not capable of exact quantitative measurement. But there is a growing amount of empirical investigation into the investment decision, and many of the conclusions economists have reached concerning determinants of investment expenditure have a sound basis in fact, even though the way in which such determinants are linked to investment expenditure cannot be reduced to a precise mathematical formula. The investment determinants that we shall discuss at this point in no sense represent all the factors other than interest and income that bear on the level of investment; we have selected those that we believe to have the most telling effects.

The Role of Government

There has been an enormous expansion in the role and influence of the public sector in this century, a development which could not help but have far-reaching repercussions on the investment decision and the level of investment expenditure. Governmental units purchase an important part of the final output of goods and services in the economy and, as we have seen, demand for final output has a direct effect on investment outlays.

The public sector may exert a less obvious influence on investment activity through transfer payments. Transfer expenditures and the taxes that finance such expenditures affect both the distribution of personal income in the economy and the pattern of consumption expenditures. Changes in the latter will affect the demand for final goods and services and thus, indirectly, the demand for investment goods.

Probably the most important influence that public activity has on investment expenditure operates through taxes and the tax laws. The marginal efficiency of capital is concerned with the profitability of additional amounts of capital to the business enterprise, so it is to be expected that the businessman or entrepreneur would be acutely aware of the influence of anything as direct as taxation on the expected rate of return on capital assets. Investment expenditure depends upon the expected rate of return over cost, and it can thus be presumed that taxes, because they lower the expected returns, will lower investment expenditures. High taxes, to put it differently, impinge on incentives, and therefore adversely affect the investment decision.

Specifically, two techniques have been used by the federal government in recent years to influence investment spending in the economy. These are accelerated depreciation accounting, and the investment tax credit. We shall examine each of these briefly.

Accelerated depreciation is an administrative technique which permits a firm to depreciate a capital asset at a more rapid pace than usual. Since the Internal Revenue Service allows business firms to treat depreciation as an expense of doing business, acceleration will reduce the taxable income of the firm during the earlier years of the asset's life. Overall, taxes should not be changed, only deferred. But this will have two advantages for the firm. First, it will get for a time the use of money that would otherwise go to the government. Second, reduced taxes in the early years of the asset's life will increase its present value during those years, the reason being its net after-tax income will be higher. Later, of course, the net after-tax income will go down, but since a dollar of expected income in the near future is worth more than a dollar due in the more distant future, the present value of the asset should be greater. Thus, accelerated depreciation should stimulate investment spending.

The investment tax credit as a device to stimulate investment spending was first introduced in 1962 by the Kennedy administration. An investment tax credit allows a firm to deduct a certain percentage of its investment outlays from its income tax liability. What this does, in effect, is to lower the supply price for a new item of capital, thereby raising its effective marginal efficiency (the r of Equation (7–2)). When first introduced the tax credit was 7 percent. The investment tax credit was suspended in 1966, put back into effect in 1967, terminated by the Tax Reform Act of 1969, and reinstated again in 1971. In the spring of 1975 the rate was raised to 10 percent for a two year period as part of a tax package designed to bring the economy out of the 1974–75 slump.[43]

The Role of Technology and Innovation

Among the possible factors that enter into the investment process, probably a majority of economists would rate changing technology and innovation near the top in terms of influence and importance. This is true even though technology and innovation are concepts that cannot be measured with precision or clearly distinguished from one another. More-

43. Perhaps the most recent highly publicized case involving the investment tax credit concerned President Carter. Because of tax credits against investments made during 1976 in his Georgia peanut business, the President wound up not owing any taxes for 1976. The President made a voluntary contribution of $6,000 to the government because he thought all citizens ought to pay something in support of the government.

over, there is much obscurity in economic analysis with respect to the specific manner in which the investment decision is affected by these forces.

The concept of innovation as a significant force in economic life is most closely associated with the work of the late Professor Joseph A Schumpeter. As a result of his analysis, innovation has come to be connected with the idea of change and the introduction of new commodities and resource combinations into the economic process. In his classic work, *The Theory of Economic Development*, Schumpeter defined innovation in terms of a change falling into one or more of the following categories:

1. The introduction of a new good, or of a new quality of an existing good.
2. The introduction of a new method of production.
3. The opening of a new market.
4. The conquest of a new source of supply.
5. The establishment of a new organization of industry.[44]

Technology as a concept is generally construed as dealing more with the productive process than with the introduction of new goods or substantial changes in the quality and style of an existing good. The usual definition of *technological change* is a change involving a shift in the production function.[45] The production function, it will be recalled from Chapter 4, concerns the technical relationship between inputs of economic resources in the form of land, labor, and capital, and the output of product. Any particular combination of economic resources will embody a particular level of technology, and a change in technology means either more product from the same quantity and combination of resources, or else the same amount of product with a smaller quantity of resources. If a change in technology involves a shift in the production function, it follows that innovations which lead to a reduction in costs and new ways of producing old goods cannot, in practice, be distinguished from changes in technology. On the other hand, innovations that have to do with the introduction of new goods may not involve new or different production techniques, and thus need not necessarily be construed as a change in technology. In any event, the reader is reminded that any real distinction between innovation and technological change is a subtle thing. In reality it is difficult to imagine a change in techniques of production that will not, sooner or later, affect at least the quality of existing goods, and thus ultimately become innovational in character. In our discussion of the impact of these two phenomena on the investment decision, we shall try

44. Joseph A. Schumpeter, *The Theory of Economic Development* (Cambridge, Mass.: Harvard University Press, 1951), p. 66.

45. Yale Brozen, "Determinants of the Direction of Technological Change," *American Economic Review*, May 1953.

to keep them separate; but the student should keep in mind that this is an arbitrary procedure, done primarily for analytical purposes.

Innovation and Investment · Introduction of a new product or development of a new market may or may not require new investment; there is no inherent reason why these kinds of innovation should require a drastic change in the physical quantity of any particular resource, such as capital. As Schumpeter points out, economic development results primarily from the employment of existing resources in a different way, or in doing new things with them rather than in increasing their quantity.[46] Thus, innovation may simply lead to a readjustment in existing capital equipment rather than an increase in the physical quantity utilized by the firm. If this happens, it is necessary to look to conditions affecting the demand for the product in question before we can say anything about the probable effect of the innovation on investment expenditure. One possibility, of course, is that the introduction of a new product will be followed by such a rapid rise in demand for the product that the original introducer of the product, as well as his imitators, will have to expand capacity. In this case more investment will be forthcoming. In general, we can say that the manner in which the introduction of a new product or development of a new market will affect investment demand will depend largely upon the competitive character of the industry or market involved. Other things being equal, we might expect that the firm which introduces a new product in a highly competitive industry would gain a momentary advantage over its rival that could lead to more investment.

Technological Change and Investment · How does technological change affect the demand for capital instruments? The traditional view is that technological change is highly favorable to investment spending. Some would argue that because capital goods are the physical embodiment of new production techniques, the latter cannot be introduced without at the same time creating more capital. It is also maintained that the adoption of techniques which shift the production function requires that the ratio of capital to other resources be increased, and that technological change renders existing capital goods obsolete. Both of these tendencies, if present in the economy, would link the demand for capital very closely to the rate of technological change.

While many economists would agree that technological change is an important factor in the investment decision, there are reasons to doubt that the relationship between technological change and the investment decision is as simple and as direct as suggested by the traditional view.

46. Schumpeter, p. 68.

Howard R. Bowen, for example, questions the view that technological change will require more capital relative to other resources and that technologically induced obsolescence will increase the demand for capital.[47] Does technological change raise the capital-output ratio? If it does, then clearly technological change will increase the demand for capital. But, as Bowen points out, many innovations of a technological character are capital saving in the sense that they reduce the capital-output ratio. If technological change tends to be capital saving rather than capital using, its effects on the demand for capital may be reduced.[48] Bowen also argues that a rapid rate of technological change may be inimical to a high level of investment expenditure because it increases the risk of obsolescence. If technological change makes existing capital obsolete, it may create a demand for new capital. But because obsolescence raises the element of risk in all investments, the entrepreneur may demand higher rates of return from prospective capital investments than otherwise would be the case. Thus, it is entirely possible that technological change can inhibit, as well as spur, investment expenditure.

Some studies cast doubt upon the assumption that technological change must necessarily be embodied in new capital instruments. These studies sought to determine the relative importance of different types of resource inputs—labor, capital, etc.—and of technological change in determining the nation's economic growth over the long run. For example, Benton F. Massell found that 90 percent of the increase in output per man-hour between 1915 and 1955 in the United States should be attributed to technological change and only 10 percent to an increase in the physical quantity of capital employed per man-hour.[49] Studies like Massell's should not be interpreted to mean that technology and technological change have no impact on investment expenditure, but rather that a distinction can be

47. Howard R. Bowen, "Technological Change and Aggregate Demand," *American Economic Review*, December 1954,

48. If the amount of capital required per unit of output is reduced, it does not necessarily follow that the demand for capital has been reduced. A reduction in the capital output ratio means that the productivity of capital has been increased, and this may lead to an increase in the demand for capital. On this point see especially the article by Robert Eisner, "Technological Change and Aggregate Demand," *American Economic Review*, March 1956. See also John LaTourette, "Sources of Variations in the Capital-Output Ratio in the United States Private Business Sector, 1909–1959," *Kylos*, fasc. 4, 1965.

49. Benton F. Massell, "Capital Formation and Technological Change in United States Manufacturing," *Review of Economics and Statistics*, May 1960. See also Robert M. Solow, "Technical Change and the Aggregate Production Function," *Review of Economics and Statistics*, August 1957; and Edmund S. Phelps, "Tangible Investment as an Instrument of Growth," in *The Goal of Economic Growth* (New York: Norton, 1962), pp. 94–105.

made between changes in technology and changes in the capital stock. They suggest that economists should give close attention to the factors that govern the rate at which new technological developments take place within the economic system.

The Role of Market Structures

The term *market structures* is used in reference to the kind and degree of competition characteristic of the industrial environment within which the firm functions. Traditionally, economists have argued that a competitive economic environment is highly conducive to both economic progress and a high rate of investment expenditure. This view rests upon the assumption that, since business firms seek to maximize profits, a major way of achieving this objective is to reduce production costs. In an environment of rigorous competition firms will be forced, if they are to survive, to seize every opportunity for the introduction and exploitation of cost-reducing innovations. Since innovation may lead to investment expenditure, it follows that a competitive market structure may be favorable to a high level of investment activity.

The reasons for the belief that monopoly is inimical to both investment expenditure and economic progress are summarized in a classic article by Evsey Domar.[50] When the business firm is confronted with a technological or innovational change that requires additional investment in capital equipment, it must reach a decision with respect to two different and possible developments. In the first place, investment in new equipment often leads to the scrapping of older equipment which has become obsolete; the firm must balance the gain from the introduction of new equipment against the capital losses involved in scrapping older equipment. If the industry is competitive, the individual firm really has no choice. Inevitably, other firms in the industry will introduce the new equipment, and the individual firm faces capital losses because its equipment has become outmoded. A monopoly, on the other hand, can avoid the capital losses involved in the acquisition of new equipment by introducing new production techniques at a more leisurely pace and financing the necessary investment from internal sources. The capital losses that result from the scrapping of obsolete equipment are part of the price that a competitive economy must pay for both a rapid rate of technological change and a high rate of capital formation.

The second possibility confronting the firm concerns its market position. Domar argues that a technological or innovational development that leads to a reduction in costs or the introduction of a new product may

50. Evsey D. Domar, "Investment, Losses, and Monopolies," in *Income, Employment, and Public Policy* (New York: Norton, 1948), pp. 33–53.

present the firm with the opportunity to enlarge its share of the total market. This is most likely in oligopolistic industries. In the purely competitive type of industry, such as exemplified by agricultural production, no single firm can ever command more than a negligible portion of the total market. But in markets which are dominated by a relative handful of firms (the automobile industry is perhaps the best example), the share of each particular firm in the over-all market is a subject of concentrated and continual interest on the part of management. Under these circumstances, innovation and investment may be a particularly attractive means for enlarging the firm's share of the total market. Monopoly would not lead to this result, for the monopolist does not have to worry about his firm's relative position in the market.

Some economists maintain that monopoly may be just as conducive as competitive oligopoly to innovation, technological change, and a high rate of investment expenditure. The ability, for example, of a firm to innovate and invest depends to a large degree on its entrepreneurial and managerial capacity and its financial power. If this is true, the monopolistic firm will be better off than the typical small firm in a highly competitive industry, the small firm having neither the ability to attract outstanding entrepreneurial talent nor the financial power to undertake the investment that is often necessary for the introduction of new techniques. It can be argued that only financially powerful firms, found in industries characterized by monopoly and oligopoly, can afford to underwrite the extensive, formalized research that is the necessary prelude to new developments in production and products in a world of rapid technological change.

We can best sum up this discussion of market structures and investment by pointing out that the traditional view that an economy dominated by the competition of many small units is most conducive to economic progress is not particularly appropriate in a world in which research and technological change have become dominant factors in the competitive position of the firm. Competition remains necessary and desirable, but it is a different type of competition than that envisaged in the model of a purely competitive market economy. It is, rather, the competition of a relatively few large economic units with the ability and power to bring together the human talent and other resources necessary for performing the increasingly specialized functions of research and introduction of the fruits of research into the economic process.

A Summary View

We have sought in this chapter to examine and analyze the most important things that contemporary economic theory has to say about the determinants of investment expenditure. The investment decision remains one of the most involved problems relating to the operations of the modern economy, chiefly because the factors that enter into it are more varied and less predictable than, say, those that enter into the consumption-saving decision. In the area of consumption theory the economist has at least the solid fact of income upon which to build his analysis; no matter what other influences may be involved, it is impossible to ignore or overlook the dominant role that income plays as a determinant of consumption expenditure. In investment theory, however, there is no such prime determinant to provide a foundation for analysis. In the early days of Keynesian analysis, economists believed that the rate of interest could occupy the same role in investment theory that income occupies in consumption theory, but research into the mechanics of the investment decision has tended to undermine faith in this view. Modern investment theory is cast in the framework of the capital and investment demand schedules. But, at best, this approach is a device to organize our thinking, a means of getting started, not a complete theory that adequately explains the fluctuating phenomenon of investment. Many of the more important determinants are to be found in the area that we have labled "other influences" and the major difficulty here is not that their existence and importance go unrecognized, but that they are highly subjective. Most of the time these other determinants cannot be measured quantitatively, and there is no easy way to assess their relative impacts on the level of investment expenditure.

APPENDIX

Algebraic determination of the income level with the inclusion of induced investment

(1) $Y_{np} = C + I'_o + I_i$ The basic identity

(2) $C = C_o + aY_d$ The consumption function

(3) $C = C_o + aY_{np}$ This is correct when taxes and transfers are zero

(4) $I'_o = (I_o - ci)$ Investment expenditure which is independent of the income level

(5) $I_i = bY_{np}$ Induced investment

(6) $Y_{np} = C_o + aY_{np} + I'_o + bY_n$ Substitution of Equations (3) and (5) into Equation (1)

(7) $Y_{np} - aY_{np} - bY_{np} = C_o + I'_o$

(8) $Y_{np}(1 - a - b) = C_o + I'_o$

(9) $Y_{np} = \frac{1}{1 - a - b}(C_o + I'_o)$

(10) $Y_{np} = k'(C_o + I'_o)$ (k′ = the supermultiplier)

8

Public Expenditures, Taxes, and Finance

In this chapter our focus is on how government expenditures, taxes, and other sources of finance for the government's activities affect income and employment. As before, we approach this problem through the structure of the economy's aggregate demand function. Government purchases of goods and services exert a direct influence on the level of the aggregate demand schedule because they are a part of the demand for final output; government transfer expenditures and taxes exert an indirect influence as their impact is on the nongovernmental components of the schedule, consumption and investment.

Government Purchases of Goods and Services and the Income Level

To show how the purchase of goods and services by governmental units enters into the structure of aggregate demand, let us again make use of data pertaining to a hypothetical economy, as was done in Chapter 6.[1] These data for our hypothetical economy are shown in Table 8–1. Our economy is still closed, which is to say it has no economic ties with any other nation, but now we have assumed that there are three, rather than

1. Chapter 6, pp. 159–61.

TABLE 8–1. A Closed Economy with Three Categories of Output (in billions of constant dollars)

(1) Net National Product Y_{np}	(2) Consumption C	(3) Investment I	(4) Government Expneditures	(5) Aggregate Demand (C + I + G)
0	100	40	60	200
350	275	75	60	410
400	300	80	60	440
450	352	85	60	470
500	**350**	**90**	**60**	**500**
550	375	95	60	530
600	400	100	60	560
650	425	105	60	590
700	450	110	60	620
750	475	115	60	650
800	500	120	60	680
850	525	125	60	710
900	550	130	60	740

merely two, categories of output (or expenditure): consumption, *C*, investment, *I*, and government, *G*. The consumption function is given in Column (2) and shows the intended consumption expenditures at income levels ranging from 0 to $900 billion. The marginal propensity to consume of this schedule is 0.5 or ½. Investment expenditure, shown in Column (3), includes both autonomous and induced investment outlays. The marginal propensity to invest is 0.1 or $\frac{1}{10}$. Government purchases of goods and services are shown in Column (4). For the sake of analytical simplicity we assume that government expenditures are autonomous with respect to the income level. Although it is likely that government expenditures increase as income increases, the nature of any such relationship is not known exactly.

Once we have assumed values for the investment function and autonomous government expenditures, the aggregate demand schedule is obtained by adding these to the consumption function, the position and slope of which is given by the parameters C_0, consumption at zero income, and *a*, the marginal propensity to consume. The parameters for the investment function are I'_0, investment expenditure which is autonomous with respect to the income level, and *b*, the marginal propensity to invest.[2] The results of this addition are given in Column (5) which now shows the aggregate demand schedule, $C + I + G$.

We have done this graphically in Figure 8–1. The aggregate demand schedule, $C + I + G$, or *DD*, is derived by adding to the consumption

2. Chapter 6, p. 152, and Chapter 7, p. 215.

function the appropriate values for investment and government expenditures. The process of income determination that results from the construction of an aggregate demand schedule which includes government expenditures is identical to the process discussed in earlier chapters. Equilibrium income is at the point of intersection of $C + I + G$, the aggregate demand schedule, and OZ, the aggregate supply schedule. In this instance, equilibrium is at \$500 billion. This is the only output level at which the three major expenditure categories will add up to an amount identical with aggregate supply. At any output level greater than \$500 billion $C + I + G$ would fall short of output, and we would have a disequilibrium situation in which aggregate supply, OZ, would be greater than aggregate demand, DD. Consequently, the income level would fall. At

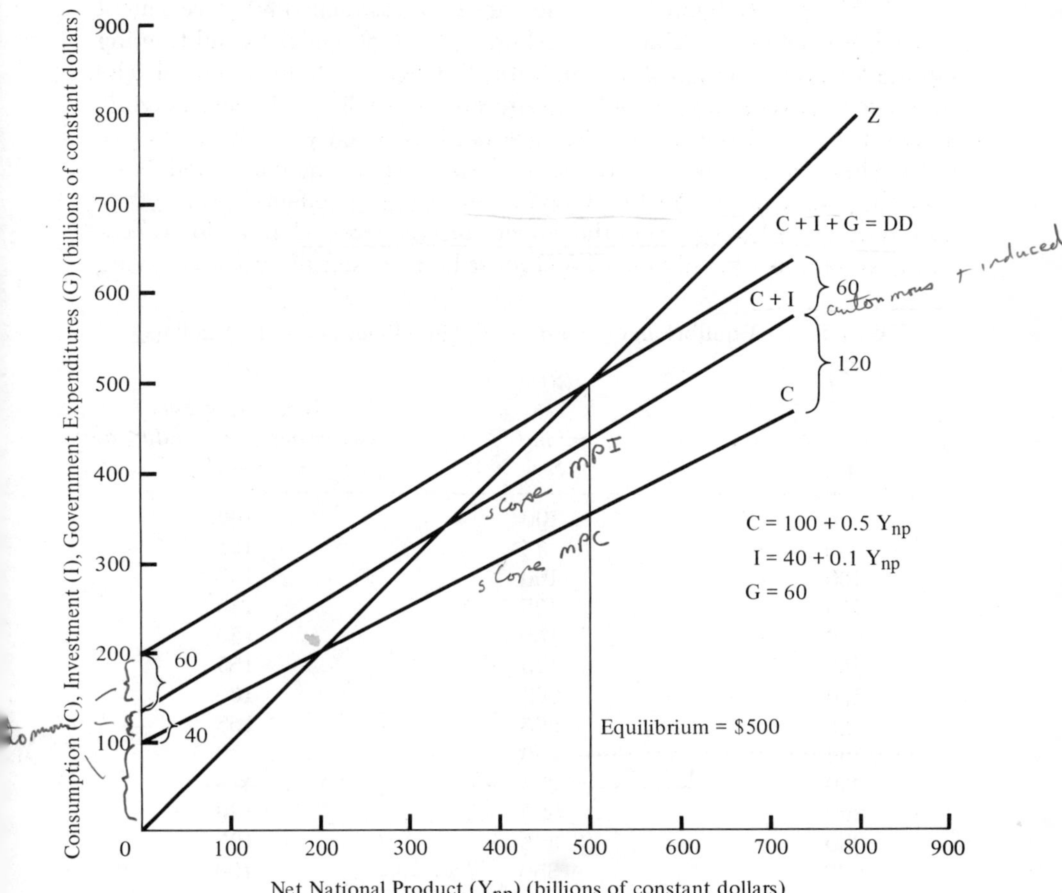

FIGURE 8–1. The Process of Income Determination: Government Expenditures and Aggregate Demand

any income level below $500 billion the reverse would be the case. Aggregate demand, *DD*, would run ahead of aggregate supply, *OZ*, and the income level would rise.

The reader will recall that an income equlibrium is defined not only in terms of an equality between aggregate demand and aggregate supply, but also as a situation in which saving and investment *ex ante* are equal.[3] It is possible, given the data assumed for our hypothetical economy, to construct saving and investment schedules and show why the point at which they intersect must necessarily be the equilibrium income level.[4] When we include government purchases of goods and services in the analysis, the definition of an equilibrium in terms of equality between saving and investment must be modified to take into account these purchases. This is done in Table 8–2.

In Table 8–2, Column (3) is the sum of investment and government expenditure totals of Table 8–1. Column (2) is obtained by subtracting intended consumption as shown in Table 8–1 from each income level. The difference between income and consumption we shall still define as saving, simply because at the moment we are not concerned with the matter of taxes. They will be brought into our analysis shortly. It may be noted, however, that taxes are similar to saving in their economic effects because they also represent a leakage from the current income stream.[5] In a closed economic system income not consumed must be disposed of either as saving

TABLE 8–2. Equilbrium of S and $I+G$ (in billions of constant dollars)

(1) Net National Product Y_{np}	(2) Saving S	(3) Investment plus Government Expenditures $I+G$
0	−100	100
350	75	135
400	100	140
450	125	145
500	**150**	**150**
550	175	155
600	200	160
650	225	165
700	250	170
750	275	175
800	300	180
850	325	185
900	350	190

3. Chapter 6, p. 161.
4. See Figure 6–4, p. 160.
5. Chapter 6, p. 172.

or as taxes. Consumption, saving, and taxes are the only three alternatives for the disposition of income in a closed economy. In an open economy the purchase of imported goods and services is a fourth alternative. Returning to Table 8–2, we find the sum of investment and government purchases of goods and services in Column (3). Equality between S and $I + G$ exists when income is $500 billion.

The data of Table 8–2 are plotted graphically in Figure 8–2. The equilibrium level of income is determined by the intersection of the two schedules. At the equilibrium income level of $500 billion, $I + G$ *ex ante* is equal to S *ex ante.* Leakages out of the current income stream through saving are just being offset by expenditures for investment goods and government purchases of goods and services. This being the case, income must be in equilibrium.[6]

Government Expenditures and the Multiplier

Since the public sector buys a part of the national output in the same manner as consumers and business firms, the economic impact of government expenditures for goods and services is essentially the same as that associated with either consumption or investment expenditure. Conse-

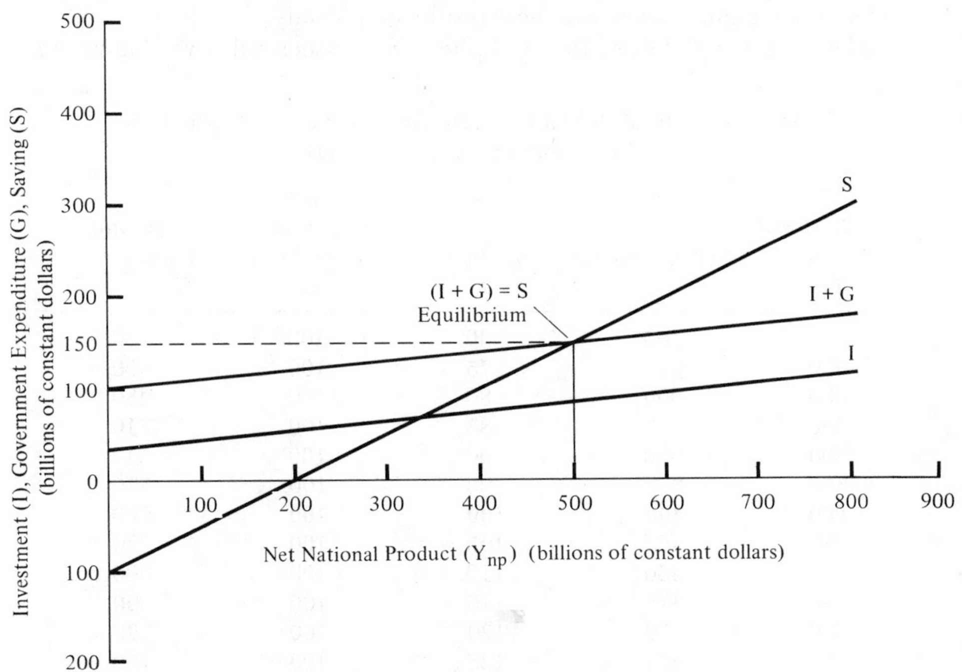

FIGURE 8–2. Equilibrium of $I + G$ and S

6. The manner in which G is financed is discussed later.

quently, a change in government purchase of goods and services will shift the level of the aggregate demand function in exactly the same manner as either an autonomous change in investment spending or an autonomous shift in the consumption function. It follows logically that there will be a multiplier effect associated with a change in government expenditures that is identical in concept with the general multiplier effects discussed earlier.

In Table 8–3 we have assembled another set of data pertaining to our hypothetical economy. The only difference between these data and those of Table 8–1 is that the level of autonomous government expenditures, G, has risen from \$60 billion to \$100 billion. It is now labeled G'. We leave aside temporarily the question of how these increased government expenditures are being financed; for the moment it suffices to point out if, prior to this change, saving was equal to the sum of investment and government expenditures, the expansion of government expenditures by the amount of \$40 billion means that new funds are being injected into the income stream. The data of Table 8–3 show that the increase in government expenditure by this amount has, *ceteris paribus*, brought about a rise in the equilibrium level of income to \$600 billion. There is an increase of \$100 billion in the income total as a result of an autonomous change in government expenditures of \$40 billion. Thus we have a multiplier of 2.5. Figure 8–3 shows these results graphically.

The underlying logic of the multiplier effect associated with changes in

TABLE 8–3. Results of an Expansion in Government Expenditures (in billions of constant dollars)

(1) *Net National Product* Y_{np}	(2) *Consumption* C	(3) *Investment* I	(4) *Government Expenditures* G'	(5) *Aggregate Demand* $(C+I+G')$
0	100	40	100	200
350	275	75	100	450
400	300	80	100	480
450	325	85	100	510
500	350	90	100	540
550	375	95	100	570
600	**400**	**100**	**100**	**600**
650	425	105	100	630
700	450	110	100	660
750	475	115	100	690
800	500	120	100	720
850	525	125	100	750
900	550	130	100	780

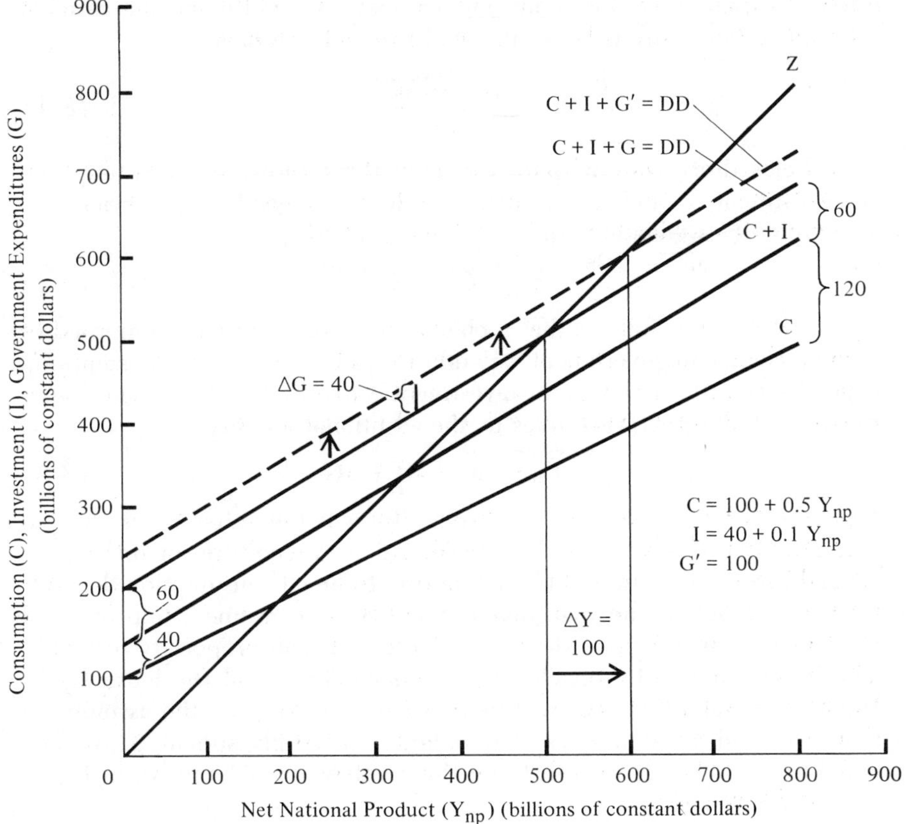

FIGURE 8–3. Increase in Government Expenditure

government expenditures is the same as that of the multiplier effect in conjunction with changes in investment expenditure or autonomous shifts in consumption.[7] The multiplier effect results from the combined impact of the initial (or primary) change in spending (which in this instance is the amount by which government purchases of goods and services have increased) and the induced (or secondary) spending that is a consequence of the increased income resulting from the original increase in expenditures. Induced spending is in the form of purchases of consumer goods and services and additional investment outlays.

The multiplier effect associated with the change in government expenditures can be explained through a series of simple algebraic formulas. In a formal sense, and as was the case with investment changes, we define the multiplier as the ratio of a change in income, ΔY_{np}, to a change in gov-

7. Chapter 6, especially p. 165.

ernment expenditures for goods and services, ΔG. As the income variable relevant to our analysis is net national product, we have

$$k' = \frac{\Delta Y_{np}}{\Delta G} \quad (8\text{–}1)$$

In a closed economy output consists of three categories: consumption, C, investment, I, and government purchases of goods and services, G. Consequently, we begin with the following identity:

$$Y_{np} = C + I + G \quad (8\text{–}2)$$

From the above it follows that a change in income must be composed of either a change in government expenditures, ΔG, a change in consumption expenditures, ΔC, a change in investment expenditures, ΔI, or some combination of all three. This gives us the additional identity:

$$\Delta Y_{np} = \Delta C + \Delta I + \Delta G \quad (8\text{–}3)$$

Since the change in government expenditures is the autonomous change, it follows that changes in either consumption expenditures or investment expenditures will be of an induced nature. Induced consumption depends upon the value of the marginal propensity to consume while induced investment depends upon the value of the marginal propensity to invest. The former, it will be recalled is designated by a and the latter by b[8] Induced consumption, ΔC, will be equal to $a \times \Delta Y_{np}$, on the assumption that taxes and transfers are still zero, and induced investment, ΔI_i will be equal to $b \times \Delta Y_{np}$. If we substitute these values for ΔC and ΔI_i in Equation (8–3) we have

$$\Delta Y_{np} = \Delta G + a\Delta Y_{np} + b\Delta Y_{np} \quad (8\text{–}4)$$

This expression may now be manipulated algebraically as follows:

$$\Delta Y_{np} - a\Delta Y_{np} - b\Delta Y_{np} = \Delta G \quad (8\text{–}5)$$

$$\Delta Y_{np}\,[1 - (a + b)] = \Delta G \quad (8\text{–}6)$$

$$\Delta Y_{np} = \Delta G \times \frac{1}{1 - (a + b)} \quad (8\text{–}7)$$

$$\frac{\Delta Y_{np}}{\Delta G} = \frac{1}{1 - (a + b)} = k' \quad (8\text{–}8)$$

Equation (8–8) tells us that the value of the multiplier in a closed system, with investment and government spending for goods and services, is equal to the reciprocal of 1 *minus* the marginal propensity to consume plus the marginal propensity to invest. It should be noted at this

8. See footnote 2, this chapter, p. 244.

point that the mathematical expression $1 - (a + b)$ is a measure of leakages expressed as marginal propensities. The formal mathematical statement of the multiplier relationship just developed underscores once again the fundamental idea that the over-all magnitude of the multiplier effect associated with any shift in the aggregate demand function depends upon the total secondary spending induced by such a shift.

Transfer Expenditures and the Income Level

Unlike government purchases of goods and services which are a part of the aggregate demand function, transfer expenditures exert an indirect influence on aggregate demand. It is primarily by their impact on the volume of consumption expenditures that transfer payments influence the level of aggregate demand. To a lesser degree they may affect investment expenditures as well, but our analysis is directed basically toward the manner in which they affect expenditures for consumer goods and services.

To understand the influence of transfer expenditures on aggregate demand, it is necessary, first, to recall that the crux of the income-consumption relationship is that the amount of spending for consumption purposes is determined by the income level. In our discussion of the empirical validity of the consumption function hypothesis, we concluded that the most meaningful income measure appropriate to this relationship is that of *disposable income*[9] Since we assumed a linear relationship between income and consumption, the consumption function in equation form is as follows:

$$C = C_o + a(Y_d) \qquad (8\text{–}9)$$

The reader will recall that disposable income was defined in Chapter 6 as the net national product less taxes (direct and indirect) paid by the owners of economic resources plus transfer payments received by individuals and households. Since we assumed that all saving (other than capital consumption allowances) originates with individuals or households and that government is the only source of transfer payments, disposable income was defined as follows:

$$Y_d = Y_{np} - TX + TR \qquad (8\text{–}10)$$

In Equation (8–10), Y_{np} is the net national product; TX, the total of all taxes, including indirect taxes; and TR the total of all transfer expenditures. The consumption function can now be written as

$$C = C_o + a(Y_{np} - TX + TR) \qquad (8\text{–}11)$$

9. Chapter 6, p. 147.

It is apparent from Equation (8–11) that transfer expenditures influence consumption expenditure and thus indirectly the level of aggregate demand by affecting the amount of disposable income in the hands of individuals and households. A change in transfer expenditures will bring about a change in disposable income which in turn will induce a change in consumer spending, since the amount of disposable income constitutes the point of origin of spending for consumer goods and services. Schematically, the chain of causation appears as follows:

$$\Delta TR \longrightarrow \Delta Y_d \longrightarrow \Delta C$$

Let us refer once again to the data of the hypothetical economy for a demonstration of how this chain of causation may work out in actuality, To show the relationships involved, we shall turn to Table 8–4 and Figure 8–4, confining the analysis initially to the impact of transfer

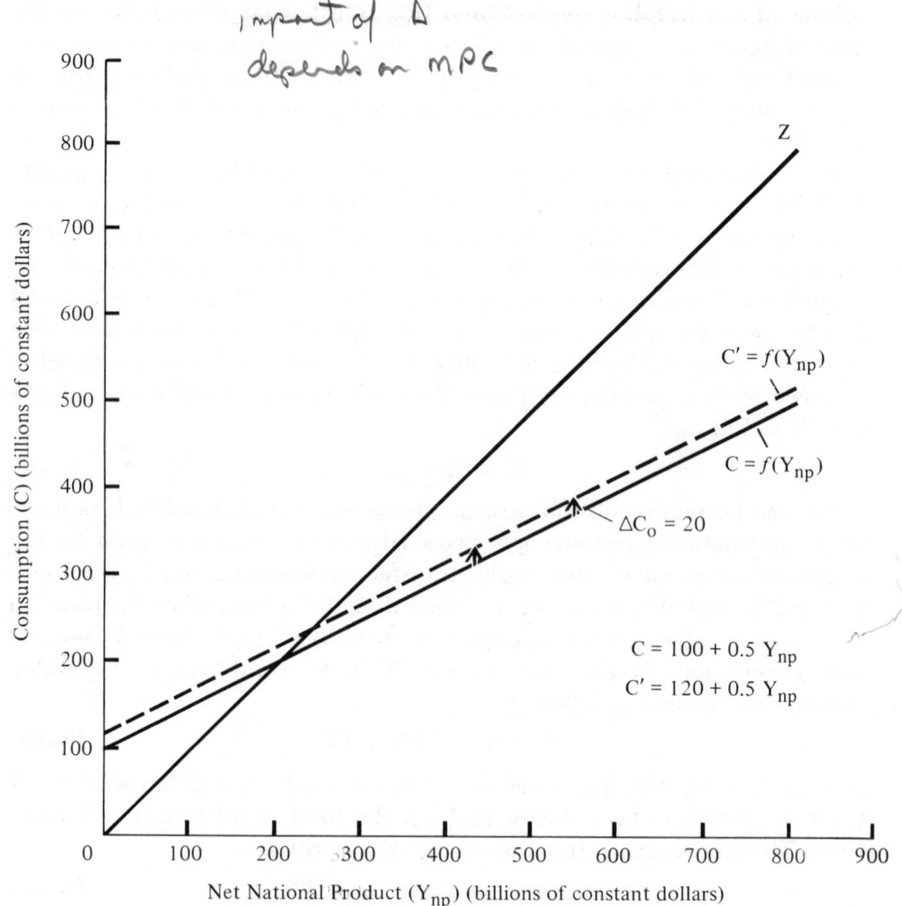

Figure 8–4. Shift in the Consumption Function

expenditures on the consumption function. In Column (2) of Table 8–4 the consumption function for the hypothetical economy is as set forth in Table 8–1. This schedule appears as the solid line C in Figure 8–4. We may note that Table 8–1 contained no transfer expenditures, and consequently net national product and disposable income were the same. In Table 8–4 net national product and disposable income are equal prior to the introduction of transfer expenditures. They appear in Column. (1).

What impact does the introduction of transfer expenditures into the analysis have on the level of consumption? Let us assume that the government of our hypothetical economy undertakes transfer expenditures of $40 billion. (We shall not concern ourselves at this point with the manner in which this new expenditure is financed.) The immediate effect of this new expenditure is to increase disposable income at all possible income levels, as shown in Column (4) of the table. This is the same at all income levels because the assumed increase in transfer expenditures of $40 billion must have the same effect on disposable income *irrespective of the actual income level.* The impact of this increase in disposable income on consumption expenditure depends upon the value of the marginal propensity to consume. Our original consumption function was drawn with a

TABLE 8–4. Results of an Increase in Transfer Expenditures (in billions of constant dollars)

(1) *Net National Product** Y_{np}	*(2)* *Consumption* C	*(3)* *Change in Disposable Income†* ΔY_d	*(4)* *Disposable Income* Y_d	*(5)* *Change in Consumption‡* C	*(6)* *New Level of Consumption* C'
0	100	40	40	20	120
350	275	40	390	20	295
400	300	40	440	20	320
450	325	40	490	20	345
500	350	40	540	20	370
550	375	40	590	20	395
600	400	40	640	20	420
650	425	40	690	20	445
700	450	40	740	20	470
750	475	40	790	20	495
800	500	40	840	20	520
850	525	40	890	20	545
900	550	40	940	20	570

*Net National Product = Disposable Income when taxes and transfers are zero.

†This is equal to the increase in transfer expenditures.

‡The marginal propensity to consume is 0.5.

slope such that the marginal propensity to consume has a value of 0.5. If we assume that the introduction of transfer expenditures into the analysis in no way affects the slope of the schedule, it follows that consumption expenditures at each and every possible level of income will increase by $20 billion, one-half of the increase in disposable income. This change is shown in Column (5) of Table 8–4. The overall impact of the introduction of transfer expenditures may be described *as a shift in the position of the consumption function*. The consumption function has shifted upward because of the added factor of transfer expenditures. As a consequence, consumption expenditures are higher at all levels of the net national income. This shift is shown graphically in Figure 8–4. The new and higher consumption function is labeled C'. Thus, transfer expenditures constitute one of the key factors that influence the level of the consumption function. In a technical sense transfers exercise their influence through the parameter C_0, which determines the level of the function. A change in transfer expenditures will, therefore, bring about a shift in the position of the schedule, and in this way affect consumption spending and the level of aggregate demand.[10]

Let us refer once again to the data of Table 8–1 and the income equilibrium level associated with these data. On the assumption that government expenditures for goods and services totaled a constant $60 billion, the equilibrium income is $500 billion, given the original position of the consumption function as shown in Column (2) and the investment function shown in Column (3) of Table 8–1. What will happen to the equilibrium income if an additional $40 billion in government transfer expenditures are injected into the picture? The immediate result is to shift the consumption function upward as we have done in Table 8–4. This means, in turn, an equal upward shift of the aggregate demand schedule. The immediate (or initial) increase in spending that this change entails is equal to the amount by which both the consumption function and the aggregate demand schedule have shifted upward. This is $20 billion, and if we multiply this change by the general multiplier of 2.5, we find that the new equilibrium level will be $50 billion higher than previously. This value of 2.5 for the general multiplier is based upon our assumed value of 0.5 for the marginal propensity to consume and 0.1 for the marginal propensity to invest. The effect on the income level of a change in transfer expenditures is shown numerically in Table 8–5 and graphically in Figure 8–5. In the table the original position of the consumption function is given by Column (3); its position after the introduction of transfer expenditures by Column (7). The aggregate demand function, $C' + I + G$, at the new and higher level of the consumption function is shown in Column (8). The new equilibrium income level is $550 billion.

10. It is possible, too, that a change in transfers may affect the slope of the function, but this is precluded in our example.

TABLE 8–5. Transfer Expenditures and Aggregate Demand (in billions of constant dollars)

Before Transfers				After Transfers*			
(1) Net National Product Y_{np}	*(2) Dispos-able Income* Y_d	*(3) Consump-tion* C	*(4) Aggregate Demand* $C+I+G$†	*(5) Net National Product* Y_{np}	*(6) Dispos-able Income* Y_d	*(7) Consump-tion* C'	*(8) Aggregate Demand* $C'+I+G$†
0	0	100	200	0	40	120	220
350	350	275	410	350	390	295	430
400	400	300	440	400	440	320	460
450	450	325	470	450	490	345	490
500	**500**	**350**	**500**	500	540	370	520
550	550	375	530	**550**	**590**	**395**	**550**
600	600	400	560	600	640	420	580
650	650	425	590	650	690	445	610
700	700	450	620	700	740	470	640
750	750	475	650	750	790	495	670
800	800	500	680	800	840	520	700
850	850	525	710	850	890	545	730
900	900	550	740	900	940	570	760

*Transfers = $40

†$I + G$ are the same as in Table 8–1.

Transfer Expenditures and the Multiplier

There is a multiplier effect associated with a change in the level of transfer expenditures similar in a fundamental conceptual sense to all the multiplier effects previously discussed. An increase (or decrease) in transfer expenditures will lead to an increase (or decrease) in the income level that is some multiple of the initial change in consumption resulting from the change in transfers. This is identical to what takes place when there is an autonomous change in investment outlays or government purchases of goods and services. But there is an important difference between the multiplier effect associated with transfers and that associated with the *G* or *I* components of the aggregate demand schedule. Normally, the multiplier effect associated with transfer expenditures will be smaller than the multiplier effect of a change in either investment or government expenditures. Let us see why this is true.

The multiplier phenomenon results from the combination of initial and induced changes in spending. But a change in transfer expenditures does not operate directly on the aggregate demand function in the same way as does a change in either investment expenditures or government pur-

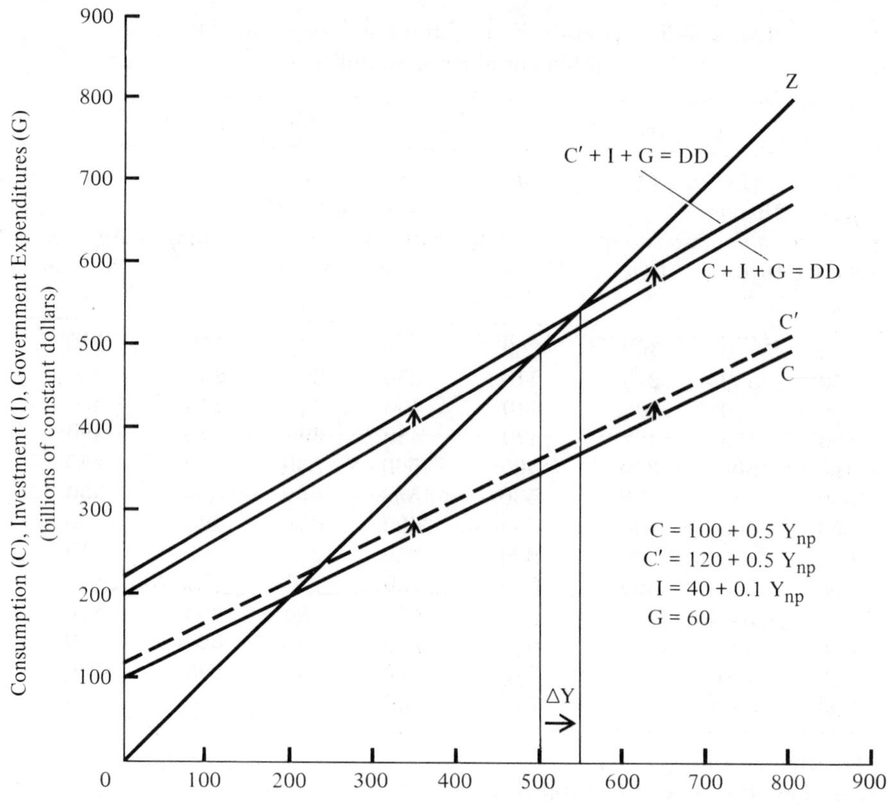

FIGURE 8–5. Aggregate Demand and a Shift in the Consumption Function

chases of goods and services. Additional transfer expenditures trigger, first, a change in disposable income, then, via the marginal propensity to consume, a new level of consumption spending. But so long as Keynes's fundamental psychological law holds true—that is, that normally the marginal propensity to consume is less than 100 percent—consumption cannot rise (or fall) by the full amount of the change in transfer expenditures. Consequently, *the shift in the aggregate demand function,* which is the initial or primary change in spending that gives rise to the multiplier process, *must always be smaller than the change in transfer expenditures.* It follows that, if the initial effect of any given change is smaller, then the induced effect will also be smaller. Thus, the multiplier effect will be smaller for transfers than for investment or government expenditures.[11]

11. See the Appendix to this chapter for an alternative treatment which develops a multiplier that can be applied directly against the entire change in transfer expenditures (or taxes) to derive the total change in income.

Taxes and the Income Level

Our detailed analysis of the way in which transfer expenditures affect the income level by their influence on disposable income and consumption spending makes it relatively easy for us to consider the impact of taxes on the income level. Once we realize that taxes are, in a sense, nothing more than negative transfers, it can be seen that they will affect the income level in a manner exactly the reverse of transfers. Taxes, *ceteris paribus*, have the effect of reducing disposable income, as we saw in Equation (8–10). Thus an increase in taxes would tend to reduce consumption spending because it woud reduce disposable income. On the other hand, a decrease in taxes would have the opposite effect of increasing consumption spending because it would increase disposable income. The foregoing remarks apply primarily to a situation in which taxes increase (or decrease) by a specific amount. Changes in taxation that may accompany changes in the income level present a more complex problem, as we shall see shortly.

In view of the above similarities between the impact of transfers and taxes on the income level, let us assert as a general principle that the absolute level of taxes is a factor which, like the absolute level of transfer expenditures, influences the level of the consumption function. This statement applies to that part of the tax total that is independent of income level. Given this general principle, it follows that any increase in taxes that is autonomous with respect to the income level will, *ceteris paribus*, shift the cosumption function downward. On the other hand, an autonomous reduction in the level of taxation will, *ceteris paribus*, shift the consumption function upward. As is the case with transfer expenditures, the amount by which the consumption function shifts as a result of a change in taxation depends upon the value of the marginal propensity to consume. Taxes change disposable income, and consumption spending will change in accordance with whether the value of the marginal propensity to consume is high or low.

Let us refer once again to the data of our hypothetical economy to analyze the impact of an introduction of taxes into the system. We shall assume that a flat total of taxes in the amount of \$80 billion is imposed. The effect of this change on disposable income and the consumption function is shown in Table 8–6. Essentially, the effect of new taxes in the amount of \$80 billion is to reduce, first, disposable income by a like amount at all levels of the net national product, and, second, to reduce consumption spending in accordanc with the value of the marginal propensity to consume. This value is 0.5, which means, in effect, that at all levels of the net national product consumption spending will decline by $0.5 \times \Delta TX$. This is \$40 billion; thus, we have an autonomous downward shift in the consumption function in the amount of \$40 billion. The new position of the consumption function is shown in Column (6) of Table 8–6.

The data contained in Table 8–7 indicate the effect of the introduction of taxes into the system upon aggregate demand and the equilibrium income level. Prior to this change, the equilibrium income was $550 billion and the position of the consumption function was given by Column (7) of Table 8–5. The initial impact of the added taxes is to reduce autonomously the consumption function by $40 billion—as we have just seen—and, if it assumed that no change in either government purchases of goods or services nor the investment function follows, this means, too, that the aggregate demand function shifts downward by $40 billion. When the general multiplier of 2.5 is applied against this shift, the ultimate decline in the net national product is $100 billion. Thus, the new equilibrium position is depicted in Table 8–7 as being at the $450 billion level. These changes are depicted graphically in Figure 8–6.

In Table 8–7 the concept of net taxes is introduced. The reader should carefully note this concept, as it is crucial to a clear understanding of the algebraic derivation of the multiplier in a system which incorporates changes in *both* taxes and transfer expenditures as the net national product changes. Net taxes are defined as total taxes less transfer payments; they represent the net withdrawal of income from the income stream as a

TABLE 8–6. Results of the Introduction of Taxes (in billions of constant dollars)

(1) *Net National Product* Y_{np}	(2) *Consumption** C'	(3) *Change in Disposable Income†* ΔY_d	(4) *Disposable Income* Y_d	(5) *Change in Consumption* C	(6) *New Level of Consumption* C''
0	120	−80	−40	−40	80
350	295	−80	310	−40	225
400	320	−80	360	−40	280
450	345	−80	410	−40	305
500	370	−80	460	−40	330
550	395	−80	510	−40	355
600	420	−80	560	−40	380
650	445	−80	610	−40	405
700	470	−80	660	−40	430
750	495	−80	710	−40	455
800	520	−80	760	−40	480
850	545	−80	810	−40	505
900	570	−80	860	−40	530

*Same as Column (6) of Table 8–4.

†This is equal to the increase in taxes ($80 billion). This is applied against the disposable income shown in Column (6) of Table 8–5.

TABLE 8–7. Taxes and Aggregate Demand (in billions of constant dollars)

(1) Net National Product Y_{np}	(2) Net Taxes T*	(3) Disposable Income Y_d†	(4) Consumption C'	(5) Aggregate Demand $C''+I+G$‡
0	40	−40	80	180
350	40	310	255	390
400	40	360	280	420
450	**40**	**410**	**350**	**450**
500	40	460	330	480
550	40	510	355	510
600	40	560	380	540
650	40	610	405	570
700	40	660	430	600
750	40	710	455	630
800	40	760	480	660
850	40	810	505	685
900	40	860	525	715

*T = *Net Taxes* = $(TX - TR)$.
†$Y_d = Y_{np} - T$.
‡$I + G$ is the same as in Table 8–1.

result of the combined effect of both taxes and transfer payments. In symbolic terms we have:

$$T = (TX - TR) \tag{8–12}$$

From this it follows that the consumption function can be written:

$$C = C_o + a(Y_{np} - T) \tag{8–13}$$

Earlier in this chapter we pointed out that taxes are a leakage from the income stream in the same sense as saving. This being true, equilibrium requires that leakages in the form of net taxes plus saving must be offset by investment expenditure and government purchases of goods and services. Now that net taxes have been introduced into our analysis, we can plot schedule—or *ex ante*—values for $I + G$ and $S + T$ and show that equilibrium obtains at the intersection of these schedules. This is done in Figure 8–7.

Transfers, Taxes, and the Multiplier

We shall now proceed to derive algebraically the multiplier in a system which includes both transfers and taxes, as well as induced investment. In Equation (8–12) we defined net taxes T as the difference between total taxes and transfer payments. We may also define net taxes as follows:

$$T = T_o + tY_{np} \tag{8–14}$$

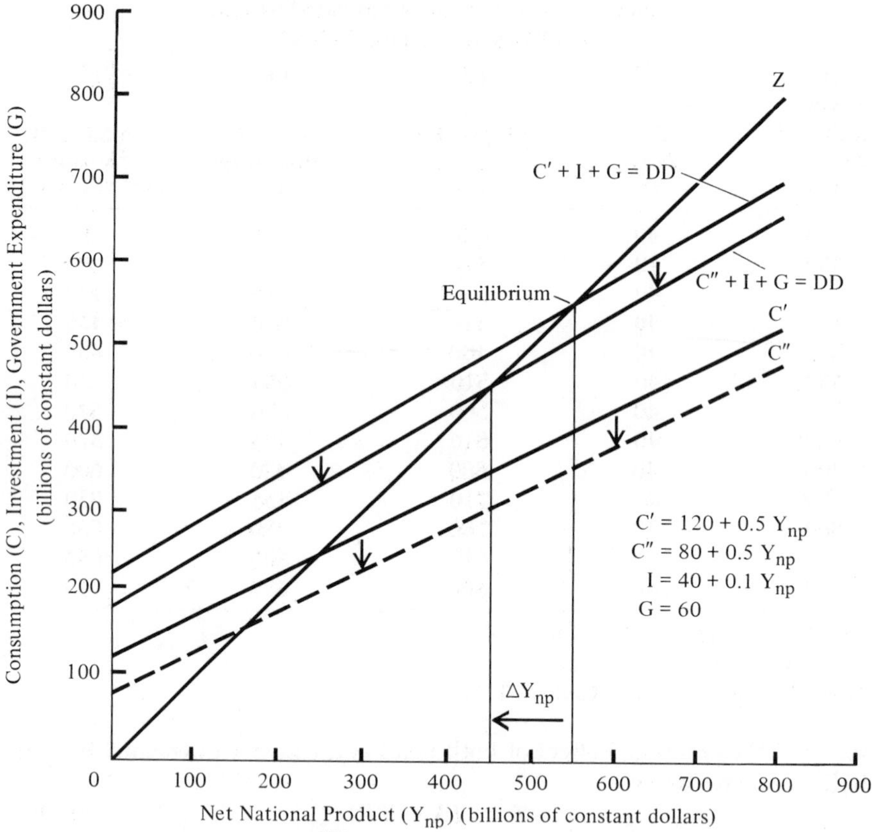

FIGURE 8–6. Effect of Taxes on the Aggregate Demand Schedule

In this equation T_o represents net taxes which are independent of the income level, while t may be defined as the net marginal propensity to tax out of net national product. It is equal to $\Delta T/\Delta Y_{np}$. The value of t may increase, remain the same, or decline as Y_{np} rises, depending upon the nature of the rate structure for the tax system, a topic we shall discuss shortly. Equation (8–14) is the net tax function.

The consumption function shown in Equation (8–13) can be further modified by the substitution of the net tax function given above for T in the equation. This gives the following:

$$C = C_o + a[Y_{np} - (T_o + tY_{np})] \tag{8–15}$$

$$C = C_o - aY_{np} - aT_o - atY_{np} \tag{8–16}$$

$$C = C_o - aT_o + (a - at)Y_{np} \tag{8–17}$$

We shall designate $(C_o - aT_o)$ as C'_o. This represents consumption that is independent of the level of the net national product. The expres-

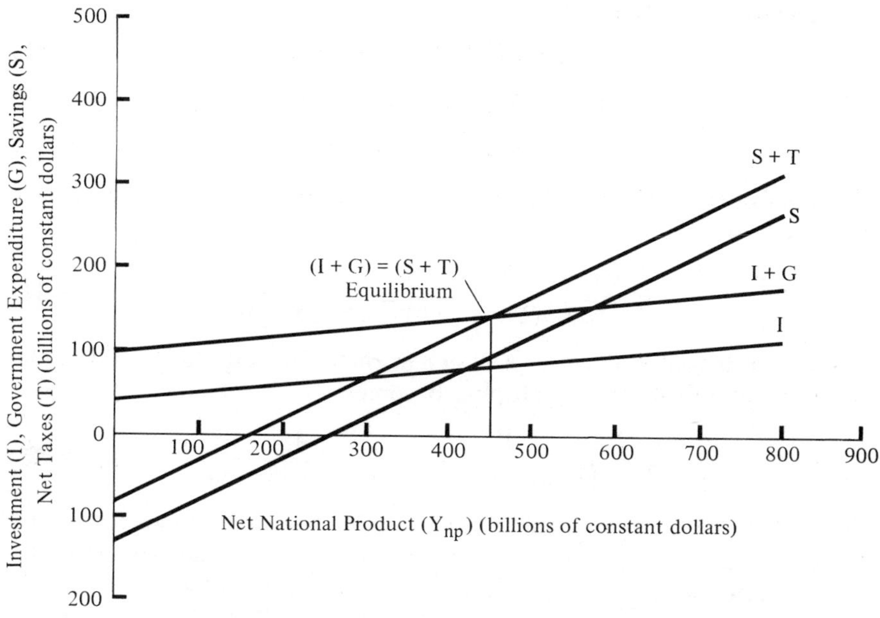

FIGURE 8–7. Equilibrium of $I + G$ and $S + T$

sion $(a - at)$ is the marginal propensity to consume out of the net national product.[12] We shall designate this as a'. We now have the equation:

$$C = C'_0 + a'Y_{np} \tag{8–18}$$

Since both transfer payments and taxes have been introduced into our analysis, there no longer is equality between disposable income and the net national product. The multiplier formula must take this into account. We shall continue to designate the multiplier which reflects the effect of both transfers and taxes as well as induced investment, as the *effective* multiplier, again using k' as the symbol for the multiplier. Recall, too, that k' is sometimes called the super multiplier. Algebraically, the effective multiplier is

$$k' = \frac{\Delta Y_{np}}{\Delta D} \tag{8–19}$$

In the equation, ΔD refers to any autonomous shift in the aggregate demand function. To complete our analysis, let us assume that it is an increase in government purchases of goods and services which is the source of an autonomous shift in the aggregate demand function. Then $\Delta G = \Delta D$. If this happens, it follows that

$$\Delta Y_{np} = \Delta G + \Delta C + \Delta I \tag{8–20}$$

12. See the Appendix for algebraic proof that $a' = (a - at)$.

By substitution we have

$$\Delta Y_{np} = \Delta G + a'\Delta Y_{np} + b\Delta Y_{np} \quad (8\text{–}21)$$

$$\Delta G = \Delta Y_{np} - a'\Delta Y_{np} - b\Delta Y_{np} \quad (8\text{–}22)$$

$$\Delta G = \Delta Y_{np}(1 - a' - b) \quad (8\text{–}23)$$

If we substitute the right-hand portion of Equation (8–23) for ΔD in Equation (8–19) we get

$$k' = \frac{\Delta Y_{np}}{\Delta Y_{np}(1 - a' - b)} = \frac{1}{(1 - a' - b)} \quad (8\text{–}24)$$

When a' is replaced with $(a - at)$ in the above expression, the equation defining the effective multiplier becomes

$$k' = \frac{1}{1 - (a - at) - b} = \frac{1}{1 - a + at - b} \quad (8\text{–}25)$$

By careful examination of the above equation the student can see clearly the effect of both transfer payments and taxes on the value of the multiplier and hence on income changes as a result of an autonomous shift in aggregate demand. Any development which increases the value of the net marginal propensity to tax, t, will have the effect of reducing the size of the effective multiplier; any development that reduces t will have the opposite effect.

Putting Theory into Practice

Several times in recent years the federal government has resorted to changes in taxes as a means of altering the over-all level of economic activity. These changes, which represent application of the foregoing theoretical ideas, are examples of the "limited number of experiments" in economics of which John Stuart Mill spoke (Chapter 1).

By far the best-known of these "experiments" in demand management by tax changes was the 1964 tax cut pushed through by the Kennedy-Johnson administration. Originally proposed to Congress by President Kennedy in 1963 to stimulate a sluggish economy, the reduction legislation was not passed until the spring of 1964, some months after President Kennedy's assassination. It is worth noting that the 1963 *Economic Report of the President* contains a textbooklike explanation of the way in which a tax cut would work, including an analysis of its expected multiplier effects.[13] Interestingly enough, the Council of Economic Advisers concluded that for each additional dollar of *direct* spending generated by the

13. *Economic Report of the President* (Washington, D.C.: U.S. Government Printing Office, 1963), pp. 45–51.

tax cut, there would be an additional $0.50 of induced consumption spending. In other words, the CEA estimated that the marginal propensity to consume out of the GNP was .5, a value similar to the one assumed in the numerical examples developed earlier in this chapter.

Did the 1964 tax cut work? Three years later, the Council of Economic Advisers concluded that the overall impact (original stimulus of about $11 billion plus the multiplier effects) was around $30 billion.[14] In the eyes of many economists the 1964 tax cut was a watershed event, as it seemed to demonstrate quite conclusively that tax cuts could be used successfully to move the economy out of a sluggish state and toward full employment. The 1964 "experiment" also was taken as proof of the public acceptance of one of the key ideas of Keynesian economics, namely that through fiscal policy (changes in taxes and/or expenditures) the government could affect aggregate demand and thereby the general level of economic activity, especially the employment level.

Later actions involving tax changes have been less certain in their economic effects. Belatedly, in 1968 the Johnson administration and the Congress raised taxes in an effort to stem the inflationary pressures which began to build up following the rapid growth in military outlays after the 1966 escalation of the Vietnam war. Professional economic opinion was nearly unanimous that taxes should have been raised in 1966, once the war buildup began, but neither the administration nor the Congress was willing to act until two years later.[15] The 1968 tax increase was a fiscal counterpart to the tax reductions of 1964, but its overall effectiveness was less clear-cut. Prices did not stop going up after the tax increase was enacted, but it may have caused enough of a slowdown in consumer spending to help nudge the economy into a recession in late 1969. Arthur M. Okun, former Chairman of the Council of Economic Advisers, concluded in a 1971 study that the tax increase did put the brakes on consumer spending, but not sufficiently to end the inflation.[16]

In the spring of 1975 and again in the spring of 1977 taxes were cut once again as a stimulative measure. In 1974 the economy had plunged into its worst slump since the 1930s, a recession in which unemployment reached a post-World War II high of 8.9 percent of the labor force. In late March 1975 the Congress passed tax cuts proposed by the Ford administration, a package bill involving rebates on 1974 personal income taxes, tax credits for nearly all taxpayers, and reduction in corporate tax

14. *Economic Report of the President* (Washington, D.C.: U.S. Government Printing Office, 1966), p. 34.

15. The tax increase took the form of a 10 percent surcharge on personal and corporate income taxes. The rate dropped to 5 percent during the first half of 1970, and expired completely on June 30, 1970.

16. Arthur M. Okun, "The Personal Tax Surcharge and Consumer Demand, 1968–70," *Brookings Papers on Economic Activity*, No. 1, 1971.

liabilities. Overall, the cuts contained in the Tax Reduction Act of 1975 amounted to about $15 billion, or an estimated 5 percent of the federal government receipts that would have been forthcoming in the absence of a tax cut.[17] Once again the results were not clear-cut. Probably the tax cut helped as the economy began to recover in the second half of 1975, but all through 1976 the recovery was sluggish and unemployment remained stubbornly high, standing at 7.7 percent of the labor force at year's end. High unemployment and the nation's slow economic recovery were key issues in the presidential contest, as candidate Carter continuously attacked the economic record of the Ford administration. As president, Jimmy Carter initially proposed an array of tax cuts for consumers and business which was to total about $30 billion over a two-year period. As inflationary fears mounted in the spring of 1977 the reduction finally approved by the Congress was about half the sum originally proposed.

Built-in Stabilizers

The foregoing discussion pertains to recent experience with *deliberate* changes in taxes as a technique for economic management by the federal government. But there is another way in which both taxes and transfer payments may play an important role in the functioning of the economy. This stems from the fact that both taxes and transfer payments may vary (or change) as a consequence of changes in the income level. This is the basis for *built-in stabilizers,* also called automatic fiscal stabilizers. The term *stabilizers* is used because these features of the economic system operate in a manner that counteracts fluctuations in economic activity. They are described as built-in because they come into play automatically as the income level changes. These built-in stabilizers do not depend, in other words, upon discretionary action by the monetary and fiscal authorities.

To illustrate, taxes may act as a stabilizing influence upon the economic system if the tax structure is designed so that the amount of taxes collected by the government rises with an increase in the net national product. If this is the case the effect will be to lessen the expansion in disposable income that accompanies any autonomous shift in the aggregate demand function. From a stabilizing point of view the consequence of this will be a less rapid rise in induced consumption spending than would be the case in the absence of a tax system possessing this character. If the tax system is constructed so that the percentage of income going to taxes increases with an increase in net national product the stabilizing impact will be even greater. This situation will prevail if the rate structure for

17. *Economic Report of the President* (Washington, D.C.: U.S. Government Printing Office, 1976), p. 51.

the tax system is progressive, because then the effective rate at which income is taxed increases as the level of income increases. In terms of the analysis in the preceding section such a system is one in which the value of the net marginal propensity to tax is an increasing function of the income level. Stabilizing effects of a reverse character come into play when the income level declines. The fiscal system, in short, operates in a countercyclical or stabilizing fashion if its over-all effect is to insulate to a degree disposable income from changes in the net national product.

The foregoing analysis is predicated on prices being reasonably stable, for sharp and continued inflation can cause the stabilizers to work in a perverse fashion. One of the unhappy consequences of the serious inflation the nation experienced in the 1970s (annual rates from 6 percent to double-digit levels) was to thrust many families into a higher tax bracket, even though their money incomes were not rising any faster than the price level. Thus, the combination of inflation and a progressive tax structure brought them an actual decline in *real* income, not just a slowing down in the rate at which their income was rising. Many economic observers were in agreement that a major cause of the 1974 slump was the blow to the consumers *real* income brought on by excessive inflation.

The effect of different tax structures on net taxes, disposable income, and consumption spending is indicated by the hypothetical data contained in Tables 8–8 and 8–9. In these examples transfer expenditures are assumed to be constant, but net taxes are determined on the basis of three different types of tax systems. In a regressive tax system the rate of taxation (TX/Y_{np}) declines as the tax base—the net national product—increases.[18] A second system is proportional taxation, in which taxes are a constant percent, or proportion, of the net national product. The rate in this example is 20 percent. Finally, we have progressive taxation, which is a system in which the rate increases as the tax base increases.

Table 8–8 shows what the amount of net taxes T will be at each possible level of the net national product, given a constant volume of transfer expenditures of $40 billion and the different tax structures described above. Regressive taxation will obviously not have any stabilizing effect, as net taxes remain constant irrespective of the level of net national product. Proportional taxation will lead to an absolute increase in the amount of net taxes as net national product increases [Column (6)], but the absolute increase is not nearly so large as it is with the progressive taxation [Column (10)]. Table 8–9 shows how both disposable income and consumption expenditures will be affected by the different tax systems. The important point to note is that consumption increases (or decreases)

18. In the hypothetical example shown in Table 8–8 total taxes, TX, are shown as a constant $80 billion only for the sake of simplicity in exposition. Taxes in absolute amount will normally increase as Y_{np} increases, even if the rate structure is regressive.

TABLE 8–8. Alternative Tax Structures (in billions of dollars)

	Regressive			Proportional			Progressive		
(1) Net National Product Y_{np}	(2) Transfer Payments TR	(3) Taxes TX	(4) Net Taxes TT	(5) Tax* Rate TX/Y_{np}	(6) Taxes TX′	(7) Net Taxes T′	(8) Taxes TX″	(9) Tax* Rate TX''/Y_{np}	(10) Net Taxes T″
0	40	80	40	0%	0	−40	0	0%	−40
350	40	80	40	23	70	30	42	12	2
400	40	80	40	20	80	40	56	14	16
450	40	80	40	18	90	50	72	16	32
500	40	80	40	16	100	60	90	18	50
550	40	80	40	15	110	70	110	20	70
600	40	80	40	13	120	80	132	22	92
650	40	80	40	12	130	90	156	24	116
700	40	80	40	11	140	100	182	26	142
750	40	80	40	11	150	110	210	28	170
800	40	80	40	10	160	120	240	30	200
850	40	80	40	9	170	130	272	32	232

*Rounded

much less rapidly with the progressive tax structure than is the case with either the proportional or regressive system.

The consumption function shown in Column (10) not only yields a higher volume of consumption expenditures at the lower income levels, but its slope is such that the marginal propensity to consume out of net national product declines as the income level rises. The latter has the effect of exerting a greater dampening effect for either an autonomous shift upward or downward in the aggregate demand function than is possible with either of the other schedules shown in the table [Columns (4) and (7)].

This brief discussion of built-in stabilizers has concentrated on taxes, but the reader should be aware that various forms of transfer expenditures affect the economy in a similar countercyclical fashion. If transfer payments are to have a stabilizing effect, they must decrease in absolute amount when the net national product (or national income) increases and increase when the reverse happens. Transfers in the form of unemployment compensation payments provide a good example of this kind of behavior. When output and employment are falling, payments to the unemployed automatically increase, thus insulating disposable income to a degree from a decline in earned income—i.e., net national product and the national income. When unemployment declines with a recovery from a recession or depression, transfer payments fall off and, thus, disposable income does not raise as rapidly as would be the case otherwise.

An important question is: How effective are the built-in stabilizers? It

TABLE 8–9. Alternative Consumption Schedules (in billions of dollars)

	Regressive			Proportional			Progressive		
(1) Net National Product Y_{np}	(2) Net Taxes T	(3) Disposable Income Y_d	(4) Consumption C	(5) Net Taxes T'	(6) Disposable Income Y'_d	(7) Consumption C'	(8) Net Taxes T''	(9) Disposable Income Y''_d	(10) Consumption C''
0	40	−40	80	−40	40	120	−40	40	120
350	40	310	255	30	320	260	2	348	274
400	40	360	280	40	360	280	16	384	292
450	40	410	305	50	400	300	32	418	309
500	40	460	330	60	440	320	50	450	325
550	40	510	355	70	480	340	70	480	340
600	40	560	380	80	520	360	92	508	354
650	40	610	405	90	560	380	116	534	367
700	40	660	430	100	600	400	142	558	379
750	40	710	455	110	640	420	170	580	390
800	40	760	480	120	680	440	200	600	400
850	40	810	505	130	720	460	232	618	409

is instructive to look at some figures from the two most recent recessions, 1969–70 and 1974–75. These are in Table 8–10, which shows the percentage changes in both federal tax receipts and transfers to persons for the period 1968 through 1976. They are derived from current dollar figures, not data corrected for changes in the price level. According to the theoretical propositions set forth in this chapter, we should expect the rate of tax collections to fall off and the rate of transfer outlays to rise during a recession. This is exactly what happened. There was a mild recession in 1969–70 (unemployment rose to 4.9 percent of the labor force in 1970 as compared to 3.6 in 1968) and again in 1974–75, when unemployment hit a post World War II peak of 8.9 percent. In 1970 and 1975, for example, federal tax revenues actually declined, whereas transfers payments jumped sharply. For the nonrecession years in the period shown, transfers grew at an annual average rate of 13.2 percent and taxes at an annual average rate of 12.6 percent. Compare these averages with the figures for the recession years, both for taxes and transfers.

The behavior of the built-in stabilizers has been analyzed by many economists. One study of the experience of the 1950s concluded as follows:

> On the average a fall in national income has led to a rise in transfer payments and a fall in tax collections, totaling a swing of approximately 50 percent of the decline in national income. During upswings the automatic stabilizers have exhibited a swing to increases in national income of slightly less than 30 percent on the average. Thus, assuming a $10 billion increase in national income, disposable income will rise by $2.8 billion less than it would have had automatic stabilization been inoperative. Had

TABLE 8–10. Changes in Federal Tax Receipts and Transfer Payments to Persons: 1968–76 (annual percentage change)

Year	*Tax Receipts*	*Transfers to persons*	
1968	16.1%	14.7%	
1969	12.6	10.0	
1970	– 2.5	21.1	Recession
1971	3.3	18.6	
1972	14.6	10.6	
1973	13.5	15.8	
1974	11.6	22.6	Recession
1975	– 0.6	27.5	Recession
1976	15.4	9.1	

SOURCE: *Economic Report of the President*, 1977.

national income fallen by $10 billion, the induced drop in disposable income would have been $5.1 billion less as a consequence of the presence of automatic stabilizers.[19]

Another study estimated the extent to which the stabilizers reduced the potential change in income during three recessions and three expansions. In this instance it found that the stabilizers are capable of reducing declines in the national income by about 50 percent, if the values for the marginal propensity to consume out of disposable income and the marginal propensity to invest out of retained corporate earnings are close to 0.9 and 0.5 respectively. (Note that the higher the value of the marginal propensity to consume out of disposable income, the greater is the impact of transfer expenditures in maintaining disposable income in the face of a decline in the national income.) It was also found that during expansions the stabilizers would prevent over 40 percent of the potential increase in income if the values for the marginal propensity to consume out of disposable income and the marginal propensity to invest out of retained corporate earnings were as above, and if, further, government spending upon goods and services remained unchanged.[20]

In 1963 the Council of Economic Advisers had the following comments about built-in stabilizers:

> Thus the tax-and-transfer 'response narrows fluctuations in income caused by irregularities in the strength of demand. The sharper the response of tax collections to changes in GNP, the stronger the stabiliza-

19. M. O. Clement, "The Quantitative Impact of Automatic Stabilizers," *Review of Economics and Statistics*, February 1960, p. 60.

20. Peter Eilbott, "The Effectiveness of Automatic Stabilizers," *American Economic Review*, June 1966, p. 463. See also George E. Rejda, "Unemployment Insurance as an Automatic Stabilizer," *Journal of Risk and Insurance*, June 1966, pp. 195–208.

> tion effect. Although the tax-and-transfer response cannot prevent or reverse a movement in GNP, it can and does limit the extent of cumulative expansions and contractions. At least with respect to contractions, this is clearly an important service to the economy.
>
> Automatic fiscal stabilizers have made a major contribution in limiting the length and severity of postwar recessions. Each of the four postwar recessions—1948–49, 1953–54, 1957–58, and 1960–61—has been both short and mild.[21]

Few economists would argue that the stabilizers by themselves can smooth out fluctuations in income and employment in the complex economy characteristic of a modern nation, but most would probably agree that they are a vital and effective complement to discretionary action.

The Role of Finance

In our earlier discussions in this chapter of the impact upon output and employment of an increase in government expenditures (or the reverse) or a decrease in taxes, questions pertaining to how the government finances added expenditures or how it responds to a revenue loss following a tax cut were deferred. Now it is appropriate to deal with these questions. If government expenditures are increased and the added expenditures are financed by an equal increase in taxes, there will be some impact on output and employment, but the effect will be minimal (see the following section on the balanced budget thesis). Much the same will be true if a tax cut is accompanied by an equal reduction in government expenditures, leaving the over-all budget position of the government unchanged.

Finance enters the picture when the government either increases its expenditures without an offsetting tax increase or reduces taxes without cutting back on its outlays. Then a deficit is created, or an existing deficit is enlarged. In either event the government will have to resort to more borrowing—the deficit must be financed. This is the crucial point, for the ultimate impact of the fiscal action—increasing government expenditures or cutting taxes—will depend on how the deficit is financed.

Assuming that the government will simply not resort to the printing press to finance its deficit, it has basically two choices: one, it can borrow from the public (this is done by selling government bonds to the public),[22] or, two, it can borrow directly from the central bank (the Fed-

21. *Economic Report of the President* (Washington, D.C.: U.S. Government Printing Office, 1963), p. 67.

22. The term "public" includes banks, insurance companies, other firms, as well as persons.

eral Reserve System in the United States). We shall examine each of these alternatives. When the government obtains funds by borrowing directly from the public the effect may be to lessen the stimulative impact of either an increase in spending or a reduction in taxes. This may happen either because households and business firms decrease some of their spending for goods and services in order to buy government bonds—the bonds are not purchased at the expense of either household or business saving—or else increased demand by government for credit causes interest rates to rise. This would lead to a reduction in private borrowing with a subsequent decline in private spending. It is possible in principle that private spending would fall sufficiently to nullify wholly the economic impact of more public spending or a tax cut.

The Crowding Out Phenomenon

If this happens, then the economy will have experienced the phenomenon known as "crowding out." This is a term which refers to the failure of any expansionary fiscal action by government (spending increases or tax cuts) to stimulate overall the level of economic activity. The "crowding out" thesis orginated with a paper published in 1968 by the Federal Reserve Bank of St. Louis.[23] Essentially, the thesis argues that, overall, the level of aggregate demand remains unchanged, the reason being that the stimulus coming from government action (more spending or a tax cut) will be offset by unplanned reductions in private spending elsewhere in the economy. As suggested above, the latter may result from higher interest rates or a decrease in spending slowing down the sale of bonds to the public. In either case, the expansionary effects are nullified. Since it was first formulated about a decade ago, the "crowding out" thesis has generated considerable controversy among economic theorists, plus no small amount of empirical research, but no agreement has been reached on either the magnitude or certainty of this effect.[24]

Monetizing the Debt

A different picture emerges if the government chooses to finance its deficit by borrowing from the central bank (the Federal Reserve system). Technically, the U.S. government is limited by law in the amount the treasury can borrow directly from the Federal Reserve system—the limit is $5 billion. But there is a way around this because there is no limit

23. See "Crowding Out and Its Critics," *Review*, Federal Reserve Bank of St. Louis, December, 1975.

24. For full details on the development and course of the controversies surrounding the "crowding out" effect see the Federal Reserve Bank of St. Louis article just cited.

on the amount of Treasury debt (bills and bonds) that the Federal Reserve can buy in the open market for government securities. When the Federal Reserve purchases treasury obligations in the open market this, of course, increases the supply of money and credit. In effect, the Federal Reserve is indirectly financing the government's deficit through an expansion of the money supply. If the deficit is financed in this fashion—this is described as "monetizing" a part of the government's debt—there will not be the same pressure on interest rates as occurs when the government borrows directly from the public. In fact, the added supply of money and credit could cause lower rates, thus leading to an increase in private spending. The upshot of all this is that private spending is much less likely to be curtailed if this is the route chosen by the government for the financing of its deficit.

To this point the discussion has centered on the financing problems associated with a deficit which results from either increased public expenditures or a tax cut. But, as the analysis undertaken earlier in this chapter suggests, fiscal action may move in either direction. That is, the government also may reduce its expenditures or increase its taxes. If expenditures are reduced without a corresponding cut in taxes, or taxes increased without an increase in expenditures, the government will have a surplus.[25] A surplus obviously does not pose a financing problem as does a deficit, but it may have consequences for the general level of economic activity. Other things being equal, a surplus tends to be deflationary, the reason being its existence means the government through taxes is taking more out of the income stream than it is putting back in through expenditures. But the impact of the surplus on aggregate demand will depend on the disposition the government makes of its surplus.

In principles, two options are available to the government. First, it may elect to use the surplus to retire debt held by the public. If it does this, it is, in effect, transferring the surplus revenues received to the public, which may or may not spend them. If the funds received by the public when debt is retired are spent, then the deflationary impact of the government's surplus is reduced. It is not too likely that this will happen, however, as many of the holders of government obligations are in the upper income brackets; they will probably use the checks they receive from the government to purchase other securities. The alternative to debt retirement is for the government simply to continue to hold the surplus funds idle; then there cannot be any offsetting private expenditures at all. This is possible in principle, but the chances that it would actually happen are exceedingly remote.

25. Discussion of the economic effects of a budget surplus may seem academic, as there have been only four years since 1960 when the federal government had a surplus. These years were 1960, 1963, 1965, and 1969. This applies to the deficit or surplus calculated on the national income accounts basis (See Chapter 2).

The Balanced Budget Thesis

Discussion of the impact of government expenditures, taxes, deficits, and surpluses on the level of output and employment would not be complete without consideration of a special case in which an increase (or decrease) in government expenditures for goods and services is matched by an equal increase (or decrease) in taxes. This is a special situation because, contrary to what one might think at first glance, a tax-financed increase in such expenditures may be expansionary. This possibility has come to be known as the *balanced budget thesis*. It is derived from the fact that the multiplier effect associated with changes in both taxes and transfers is normally smaller than the multiplier effect associated with changes in government expenditures for goods and services.

To illustrate the nature of this thesis, let us refer once again to the data of Table 8–3. We made the assumption there that government exhaustive expenditures had increased by $40 billion. Let us now assume further that taxes are simultaneously increased by an equal amount so that the new and higher level of government expenditures can be financed. Our problem is to determine how the combined impact of the increase in both government expenditures and taxes will affect the income level. Contrary to what might be assumed at first glance, a change of this type is not neutral in its effects on the income level.

The effect of simultaneous change in both government expenditures and taxes depends upn the combined impact of the increase in government expenditures and the increase in taxes upon the aggregate demand function. In our example let us assume, as earlier, that the marginal propensity to consume out of disposable income, a, is 0.5; the marginal propensity to invest, b, is 0.1; and the marginal propensity to tax, t, is 0.2. The value of the effective multiplier, according to Equation (8–25), is thus 2. The shift in the aggregate demand function will equal the increase in government expenditure, ΔG, less the autonomous shift downward in the consumption function which results from the tax increase. This latter shift is designated as ΔC_o. In algebraic terms we have

$$\Delta D = \Delta G - \Delta C_o \qquad (8\text{–}26)$$

But ΔC_o depends upon the value of the marginal propensity to consume (out of disposable income) and the change in disposable income. The latter is the same as the increase in taxes. Thus we have

$$\Delta C_o = a\Delta Y_d = a\Delta TX \qquad (8\text{–}27)$$

Given a value of 0.5 for a, we find that ΔC_o is equal to $20 billion. The combined effect of the increase in government purchases of goods and services and the increase in taxes will be to shift the aggregate demand function upward by $20 billion. When the effective multiplier of 2 is applied against this increment in aggregate demand, the final change in the net national product is $40 billion, which is just equal to the amount by which government expenditures for goods and services increased. The significant point to note is that the expansion of these expenditures, even though accompanied by an equal increase in taxes—the balanced budget thesis—was not neutral with respect to its impact upon the output level. In other words, an expansion of government purchases of goods and services under balanced budget conditions may cause a rise in the output level; if the expansion were to occur with full employment conditions the result would be a significant increase in pressure on the price level.

In the foregoing example the student will note that the net national product increased by an amount just equal to the increase in government expenditures, namely $40 billion. If the marginal propensity to tax, t, were zero rather than 0.2 the increase in the net national product would have been $50 billion rather than $40 billion. On the other hand, if the value of the marginal propensity to tax is greater than 0.2 the increase in the net national product will be less than $40 billion, but will still be greater than zero. It would be a useful exercise to compute, assuming different values for the marginal propensity to consume out of a disposable income, a, how large a tax increase would have to be to prevent any increase in the net national product, given a $40 billion increase in government outlays. The student should note carefully, too, that the shift in the aggregate demand function, given the amount of the tax increase, is governed by the value of the marginal propensity to consume out of disposable income while the size of the ultimate change in the net national product, given both the increase in taxes and the value of a, depends upon the value of the marginal propensity to tax, t.

APPENDIX

Transfers, Taxes, and the Multiplier: An Alternative Treatment

Some writers prefer to treat the multiplier effects associated with both transfer payments and taxes in a different fashion. Rather than develop, as done in the text of this chapter, a general multiplier which can be applied against a shift in the aggregate demand function, and which, too, embodies the effect of both transfers and taxes, they prefer to speak of a transfer or tax multiplier as such. This multiplier coefficient, when multiplied by the change in either transfer payment or taxes, yields the resulting change in income (net national product). The student should understand clearly that in no sense does this approach involve a different type of multiplier than discussed to this point; rather, it is simply a different way of approaching the multiplier effects associated with either transfers or taxes. To illustrate this we shall derive algebraically a transfer expenditures multiplier. A tax multiplier could be derived in identical fashion, except that its value would be negative.

(1) $k_{tr} = \dfrac{\Delta Y_{np}}{\Delta TR}$ = a formal definition of the transfer multiplier

(2) $\Delta Y_{np} = \Delta C_o + \Delta C_i + \Delta I$ [The increase in the net national product will be equal to the increase in autonomous consumption, ΔC_o, plus the induced changes in consumption and investment. This equation is an identity.]

(3) $\Delta C_o = a\Delta TR$ [The increase in autonomous consumption–i.e., the shift in the consumption function–depends upon the increase in transfers and the value of the marginal propensity to consume out of disposable income, a.]

(4) $\Delta Y_{np} = a\Delta TR + \Delta C_i + \Delta I$ [By substitution.]

(5) $a\Delta TR = \Delta Y_{np} - \Delta C_i - \Delta I$ [From (4) above.]

(6) $\Delta TR = \dfrac{\Delta Y_{np} - \Delta C_i - \Delta I}{a}$ [From (5) above.]

(7) $k_{tr} = \dfrac{\Delta Y_{np}}{(\Delta Y_{np} - \Delta C_i - \Delta I)/a} = \dfrac{a\Delta Y_{np}}{\Delta Y_{np} - \Delta C_i - \Delta I}$

(8) $k_{tr} = \dfrac{a}{1 - \dfrac{\Delta C_i}{\Delta Y_{np}} - \dfrac{\Delta I}{\Delta Y_{np}}} = \dfrac{a}{1 - a' - b}$

$\dfrac{\Delta C_i}{\Delta Y_{np}} = a'$ = the marginal propensity to consume out of net national product

(9) $k_{tr} = \dfrac{a}{1 - a + at - b}$ since $a' = (a - at)$

Since a (the marginal propensity to consume out of disposable income) is normally less than unity, this formula for the transfer multiplier means that its numerical value will be smaller than the effective multiplier developed in the text. The tax multiplier can be derived in the same fashion, but its value will be negative.

Formal proof that $(a - at) = a'$, the marginal propensity to consume out of net national product

(1) $a = \dfrac{\Delta C}{\Delta Y_d}$ = the marginal propensity to consume out of disposable income

(2) $a' = \frac{\Delta C}{\Delta Y_{np}}$ = the marginal propensity to consume out of net national product

(3) $t = \frac{\Delta T}{\Delta Y_{np}}$ = the net marginal propensity to tax out of net national product

(4) $(1-t)\frac{\Delta Y_d}{\Delta Y_{np}}$ = the net marginal rate of retention of income. This is derived as follows:

(a) $Y_{np} = Y_d + T$

(b) $\Delta Y_{np} = \Delta Y_d + \Delta T$

(c) $1 = \frac{\Delta Y_d}{\Delta Y_{np}} + \frac{\Delta T}{\Delta Y_{np}}$ /Divide both sides of (b) by ΔY_{np}

(d) $\frac{\Delta Y_d}{\Delta Y_{np}} = 1 - \frac{\Delta T}{\Delta Y_{np}} = (1-t)$

(5) $(1-t) \times a = \frac{\Delta C}{\Delta Y_{np}} = a'$ /This is derived as follows:

(a) $\frac{\Delta Y_d}{\Delta Y_{np}} \times \frac{\Delta C}{\Delta Y_d} = \frac{\Delta C}{\Delta Y_{np}} = a'$ [By substitution.]

(b) Therefore: $a' = a(1-t) = (a - at)$

Algebraic determination of the equilibrium income level using the effective multiplier

(1) $Y_{np} = C + I + G$ = the basic identity

(2) $C = C'_o + a'Y_{np}$ = the consumption function

(3) $I = I'_o + bY_{np}$ = the investment function

(4) $Y_{np} = (C'_o + I'_o + a'Y_{np} + bY_{np} + G)$ [Substitution of (2) and (3) into (1).]

(5) $Y_{np} - a'Y_{np} - bY_{np} = (C'_o + I'_o + G)$

(6) $Y_{np}(1 - a' - b) = (C'_o + I'_o + G)$

(7) $Y_{np} = \frac{1}{(1 - a' - b)} \times (C'_o + I'_o + G)$

(8) $Y_{np} = \frac{1}{1 - a + at - b} \times (C'_o + I'_o + G)$

(9) $Y_{np} = k'(C'_o + I'_o + G)$

9

International Transactions and Aggregate Demand

Up to this point in our analysis we have assumed a "closed" economy, an economy that does not have any economic transactions with other nations. In this chapter we shall drop this assumption and undertake an analysis of the manner in which the international economic transactions of a nation interact with income and employment levels in the domestic economy. Specifically, we shall examine, first, how changes in the international economic position of a nation affect its internal economy, and, second, how internal economic changes may affect the nation's international economic position. Our approach will be primarily in terms of relationships existing between international economic transactions and the aggregate demand function. Before we begin, however, it is necessary to sketch out the essential elements which enter into a nation's international transactions and how they are measured. This we do in the following section.

The Nature of a Nation's Foreign Balance

A nation's international economic balance involves all of the economic transactions that residents of the nation enter into with residents of all other nations during some specific period of time. The most important tool for analysis of the internal economic position of a nation is the balance-of-payments statement.[1] This accounting statement records (in principle) all the economic transactions that residents of one country make with residents of foreign countries during a given period of time, normally the calendar year. Since an economic transaction generally consists of a payment or a receipt in exchange for a good, service, or some type of financial asset, the balance-of-payments statement constitutes a record of payments made by residents of a country to foreigners and payments made by foreigners to residents of the country in question.

In balance-of-payments accounting practice, transactions that require foreigners to make payments to residents of the domestic economy or, alternatively, provide residents of the domestic economy with the means to make payments to foreigners are treated as *credit* entries in the balance-of-payments statement. Thus an export of merchandise by an American firm to the United Kingdom and a loan extended by a British bank to American residents would be credit entries in the American balance-of-payments statement. On the other hand, transactions that require residents of the domestic economy to make payments to foreigners or, alternatively, provide foreigners with the means to make payments to residents of the domestic economy are treated as *debit* entries in the balance-of-payments statement. Imports and loans extended to foreigners would fall into the category of debit transactions in the balance-of-payments statement of the domestic economy.[2] Balance of payments accounting is often confusing and complex. However, if the following key rule is kept in mind, it will be easier to understand:

> A credit (+) is any transaction which results in a receipt from residents in the rest of the world (foreign residents) and a debit (−) is any transaction which requires a payment be made to residents in the rest of the world.

The Structure of the Balance of Payments Statement

A nation's balance of international payments statement normally consists of several component parts, sometimes called accounts. There are basically two major "accounts" plus one or more measures of the nation's external balance. The latter vary with individual governments and the

1. For the purpose of balance-of-payments accounting the word "residents" is interpreted to mean not only physical persons, but also business firms, governments, and international agencies. Persons are considered residents of the country in which they normally reside. Residents are not necessarily or always citizens. In the United States balance of payments statistics are compiled by the Department of Commerce.

2. For a more extended discussion of the mechanics of balance-of-payments accounting see Richard E. Caves and Ronald W. Jones *World Trade and Payments* (Boston: Little, Brown and Company, 1977), Chapter 17.

particular national purposes which balance of payments statements may be designed to serve. In the United States the most important parts of our balance of payments statement consist of the *current* account, the *capital* account, and the *balance of official reserve transactions* segment of the statement.

The Current Account

The current account section of the balance of payments records all *current* transactions, which are transactions that involve either the export or import of goods (i.e., merchandise) and services. Under "services" are grouped income from transportation, banking, and insurance; income in the form of interest and dividends from various financial assets; and expenditures by tourists. Transactions involving services are described as *invisible* items, whereas transactions in goods or merchandise are classified as *visible* items. In general, goods and services exported by the domestic economy are a part of the national output, but goods and services imported constitute a form of disposition of the national income. There are exceptions to this principle, but they are for the most part of minor significance.

The difference between the export (or credit) items and the import (or debit) items in the current account represents its net balance. If the credit transactions exceed the debit transactions, it is customary to describe the current account balance as *active*. On the other hand, an excess of debit over credit transactions is usually spoken of as a *passive* balance on the current account. In Chapter 2 we pointed out that the net foreign investment component of the national output (GNP) can be *approximately* defined as the net difference between a nation's exports of goods and services and its imports of goods and services, because any excess of receipts from exports over payments for imports—or vice versa—reflects a net change in the international asset position of the nation concerned. The world "approximately" is emphasized because the Department of Commerce defines net foreign investment as the difference between exports and imports *plus* transfer payments to foreign residents.

The current account has special significance for the purposes of this text. This is because the transactions recorded in this portion of the balance of payments statement are linked closely to the determination of the national output and the employment level. Exports of goods and services enter directly into the aggregate demand schedule and hence become one of the determinants of output in an open economy. Imports of goods and services are, on the hand, a form of disposition of the national income, analogous in their economic effects to saving and transfers.

Special mention needs be made of one type of transaction normally found in the current account. This is the category of "unilateral transfers."

Included in this category are all transfers, gifts, or donations, both public and private, made either by U.S. residents to the rest of the world, or by foreign residents to the United States. The United States, for example, gives military and economic aid to some foreign nations. This is a unilateral transfer (government) from this country to the rest of the world. In the current account, the amount of such a transfer in any one year would be recorded as a debit (−) item, and the goods or services which were exported because such a transfer was made would be recorded as a credit (+) item. The latter presumes the proceeds of the transfer were spent by the recipient country.

The Capital Account

The capital account represents the financial counterpart of transactions involving currently produced goods and services that are recorded in the current account. Let us assume, for example, that a nation has in the current income period an excess of exports (of goods and services) over imports. Since exports generate payment claims against foreign residents and imports generate payment claims by foreigners against domestic residents, it can readily be seen that the export surplus increases the claims of the domestic economy against the rest of the world. An import surplus would, of course, have just the opposite effect. Within the context of the current income period, settlement of the net export surplus can be effected in a number of ways. Foreigners, for example, may borrow the needed funds from residents of the domestic economy. If this is done, there will be a net increase in the foreign claims or internationally held assets of residents of the domestic economy. A transaction of this type is called a *capital export*, and in the balance-of-payments statement of the domestic economy it is recorded as a debit item since it provides foreign residents with the means to make payments to residents of the domestic economy. Alternatively, it is possible that foreign residents may finance the aforementioned export surplus of the domestic economy by drawing down bank balances they may hold in the banks of the domestic economy. If this is done, it means there has been a *net decrease* in the liabilities owed by domestic residents to foreign residents because a bank deposit is a liability of the bank.

The capital account section of the balance-of-payments statement basically reflects the net change during the accounting period in the claims and liabilities (real and financial) of the domestic economy *vis-a-vis* the rest of the world. But this net change can take the form of a capital export, an increase in claims (or decrease in the liabilities) of domestic residents relative to foreign residents; conversely, it can take the form of a capital import, a decrease in the claims (or increase in the liabilities) of domestic residents relative to foreign residents.

International Equilibrium and the Balance of Payments

As an accounting instrument, the balance-of-payments statement must necessarily be in balance; for every credit entry there has to be an offsetting debit entry. But this does not mean that an *equilibrium* exists with respect to a nation's international economic position. While there is no clear-cut and universally accepted method of determining economic equilibrium with respect to a nation's international payments position, the state of a nation's international "reserves" is a good indication of its international economic situation. For the nation, international reserves consist primarily of gold, national currencies widely accepted as money in international transactions (the U.S. dollar has been such a currency throughout most of the post-World War II period), Special Drawing Rights and other borrowing rights in the International Monetary Fund.[3] An important measure of the international economic position of the United States is the *balance of official reserve transactions*, the third important component in the nation's balance of international payments structure. This indicates the net change in the country's international reserves, including its holdings of gold, foreign currencies, and borrowing rights in the International Monetary Fund.

The common sense meaning of an international equilibrium for a nation is that it is "paying its way" internationally, which is to say that it is obtaining sufficient foreign exchange on a sustainable basis to meet its needs to make payments abroad. Normally a nation obtains foreign exchange through its exports or by borrowing abroad on a long-term basis. But increasingly since World War II, grants by governments and international agencies have become important as sources for certain currencies, particularly the dollar. Disequilibrium in a nation's balance of payments implies a condition that is not sustainable; one or more items in either the current account or capital account must undergo change if an equilibrium condition is to be restored, and this can affect income and employment levels in the domestic economy.

Changes in the current or capital account may be described as either autonomous or induced. An *autonomous* change in the current account is one that is not the consequence of a change in the capital account; an *induced* change in the current account is one which follows from a change in the capital account. For example, a nation may find as a result of events abroad that its exports increase, and an export surplus develops in the current account. If imports remain unchanged, then this development requires an offsetting transaction in the capital account. This offset-

3. For the United States, of course, dollars would not count as a part of its international reserves, but they would for other nations because the dollar is widely accepted as an international medium of exchange. Foreign currencies held by the United States do count, however, as a part of the nation's international reserves.

ting transaction, which will take the form of an outflow of capital, is properly described as *induced* because it is a consequence of a change that has already taken place in the current account. On the other hand, a nation may undertake lending operations abroad (i.e., a capital export) quite independently of any current account developments. If such *autonomous* capital transactions take place, they must be followed by offsetting transactions in the current account. In this event, changes in the current account would be of an induced nature. From an examination of the statistical data contained in a balance-of-payments statement it is not always possible to determine whether the recorded changes are autonomous or induced, but these concepts are nonetheless useful for economic analysis.

The Exchange Rate

Besides knowledge of the balance of payments, some understanding of foreign exchange rates is needed for a full appreciation of the manner in which international economic transactions interact with the domestic economy. The rate of exchange is simply the price of one national currency measured in terms of another national currency. For example, the dollar-pound rate of exchange in late May, 1977 was $1.71 = £1, which meant that it cost American residents $1.71 to obtain one unit of British currency. The exchange rate is important because exports, imports, and all possible financial transactions are affected not only by the levels of real income and prices which prevail in different countries, but also by the prices at which their currencies exchange for one another. To illustrate, Americans might increase their imports from Great Britain because, for one reason or another, the prices for certain goods in Britain were lower than in America. Or they might buy more from the United Kingdom because British currency had fallen in price in terms of American dollars.

Exchange rates may be either *fixed* or *flexible* (floating). A fixed exchange rate system is one in which the rate—or price—at which different currencies exchange for one another simply does not change, or at most changes infrequently. The gold standard system of the nineteenth century worked in this way.[4] For most of the post-World War II period, exchange rates between the major world currencies were relatively fixed. This was the Bretton Woods system, so named because of the 1944 wartime conference held in Bretton Woods, New Hampshire, which led to the establishment of the International Monetary Fund. The workings of the Bretton Woods system are easily understood. Under the initial agreement, exchange rates were set using the U.S. dollar as the key—or benchmark—currency. Signatories also agreed to rather stringent conditions for

4. Caves and Jones, pp. 287–90.

changes in exchange rates, the latter to be carried out under the auspices of the International Monetary Fund. The individual currencies were linked to gold by virtue of the fact that the U.S. dollar maintained a basic gold parity ($35 per ounce), and the U.S. government agreed to convert dollars held by foreign "official" holders (foreign central banks and international organizations like the IMF) into gold at this price. Thus, dollars were regarded as "good as gold" and for much of the post-World War II period, nations were content to hold their international monetary reserves as dollars.

The alternative to a fixed exchange rate system is one in which rates are free to fluctuate (or float) on the basis of the interplay of demand and supply forces for different currencies. This is the system currently in force in most of the world economy. It came into existence not by design, but because of the gradual breakdown of the Bretton Woods system of fixed exchange rates caused by imbalances in the international economic accounts of the United States throughout the post-World-War II period. During most of this period the outflow of dollars from the United States due to the combined impact of our import purchasing, our lending, and our unilateral transfers (one-way grants) exceeded the inflow derived from exports and loan repayments. In the 1950s—the era of the worldwide "dollar shortage"—most nations were content to have dollars as international reserves and see their dollar holdings grow. But not so in the 1960s. As the dollar outflow continued because of international economic disequilibrium, more and more nations became uneasy, worrying about the convertibility into gold of their growing stock of U.S. currency. Thus, they increasingly exercised their right to convert official holdings into gold, the result being a drastic drain of gold from the United States. From a peak of $29 billion in 1949, the U.S. gold stock dropped to near $10 billion at the end of the 1960s. The continued pressure on the dollar and unceasing gold loss led President Nixon on August 15, 1971 to abandon all convertibility of the dollar into gold. Thus, the cornerstone of the Bretton Woods system crumbled. From there it was but a short step to the present system of fully *flexible* exchange rates. In December, 1971 the dollar was devalued in terms of gold (its official price was raised from $35 to $38 an ounce), and most of the major currencies were revalued in terms of the dollar. But this arrangement lasted only until February, 1973, when once again the dollar was devalued in terms of gold (the price went to $42.22 per ounce), and shortly thereafter all efforts to maintain fixed exchange rates between the major currencies were ended.

Our backdrop is now complete, and we can turn our attention to the main theme of this chapter. This is to analyze how changes in a nation's international economic position affects its domestic economy and vice versa.

Exports, Imports, and the Structure of Aggregate Demand

To analyze the manner in which exports and imports of goods and services fit into the structure of aggregate demand, let us begin by a review of the basic identity equations appropriate to an open economy. In an open economy, exports of goods and services enter directly into the aggregate demand function because they represent the portion of the demand for the national output that originates abroad. The demand for a nation's exports, X, is as much a part of the demand for its output as is the demand for consumption goods and services, C, investment goods, I, or social goods, G. Thus, in an open economic system the origin and component parts of the net national output can be summed up in the following identity equation.[5]

$$Y_{np} = C + I + G + X - M \tag{9-1}$$

What determines the level of exports for a nation? We shall not try to answer this question at this point, but only make the assumption that expenditures for exports are autonomous with respect to output and employment levels in the domestic economy. This is not an unrealistic assumption, although we shall need to modify it later in the analysis. Since export expenditures constitute demand for domestic output originating outside the nation, their level will not be significantly affected by changes in the domestic income and employment levels. Thus the export function may be shown as a horizontal line, as in Figure 9–1.

A nation's imports of goods and services do not represent expenditure for any part of the domestic or national output, but they do represent a form of disposition of the money income created as a consequence of current productive activity—specifically, the part of the domestic income that is directed toward the purchase of the output of other nations. In this sense, imports are a form of leakage from the domestic income stream and analogous in their economic effects to saving and taxes.

With respect to the level of imports, M, we are on somewhat surer ground than with exports. Since imports are a form of disposition of domestic income, the most reasonable hypothesis that we can advance is that the level of imports of a nation is basically a function of the general level of economic activity within the nation. Specifically, this means that imports are a function of the income level, as in the following equation:

$$M = f(Y_{np}) \tag{9-2}$$

In most societies an important share of the import total will consist of

5. See the earlier discussion on identities in Chapter 2, p. 53.

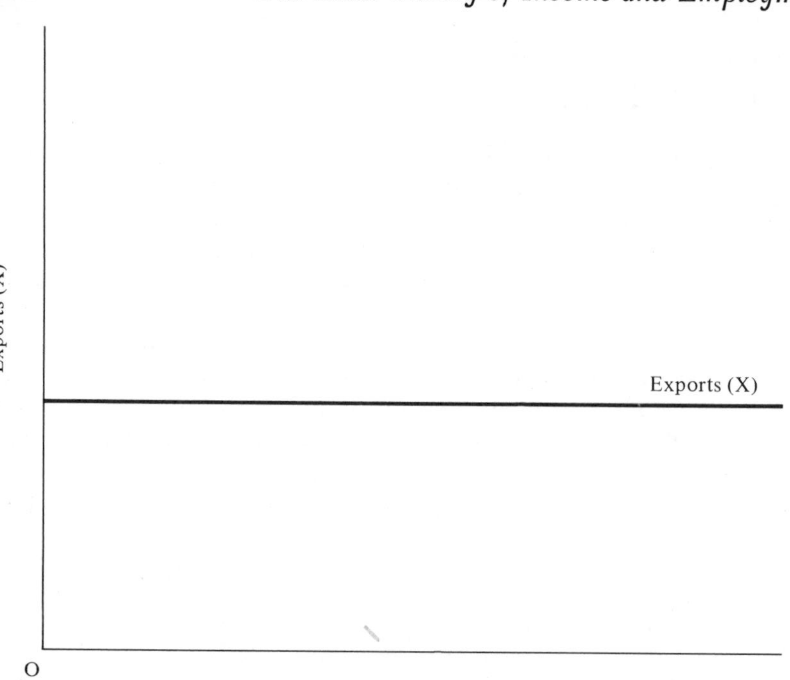

FIGURE 9–1. The Export Function

consumer goods and services. Given this, we would expect a society's expenditures on imported consumption goods to rise as its income level rises. Equation 9–2 is therefore nothing more than an extension of consumption theory to the situation of an open economy. Beyond this it is not unreasonable to expect that expenditures for imported goods which enter into the investment and government expenditures components of aggregate demand will rise along with rising levels of income and employment.

Since imports are analogous in their economic effects to saving and taxes, it follows that the import-income relationship can be expressed as a schedule. This is done in Figure 9–2. Income is shown on the horizontal axis; and imports on the vertical axis. For the sake of simplicity the import function, $M = f(Y)$, is presented as a straight line, although in reality the relationship between imports and the national income is not necessarily linear. The point at which the import function crosses the vertical axis indicates the amount of expenditures on imports at a zero income level. This, of course, is primarily a theoretical rather than a practical proposition. Algebraically the import function may be defined as:

$$M = M_o + mY_{np} \tag{9–3}$$

The technical attributes of this function are conceptually similar to those

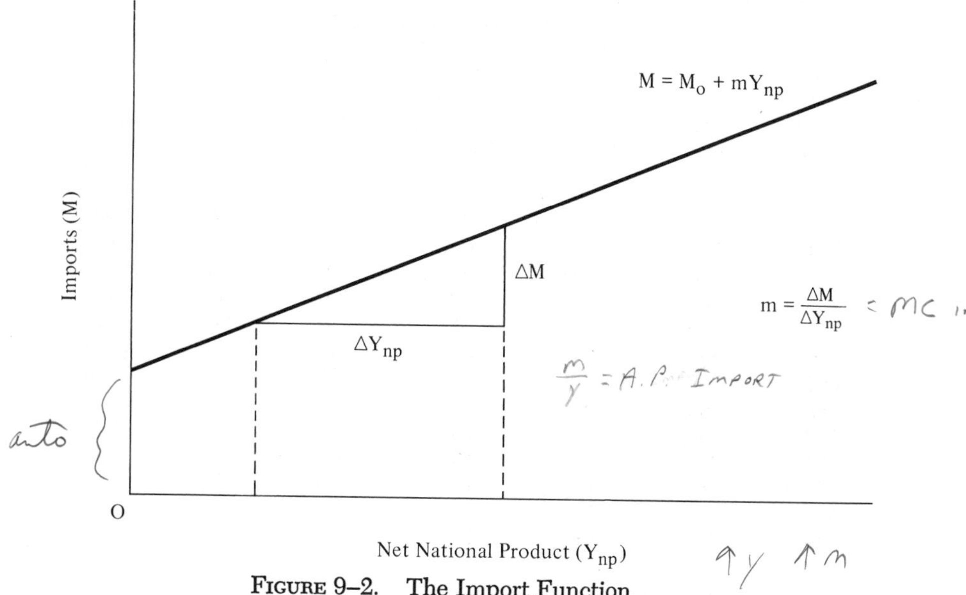

FIGURE 9–2. The Import Function

associated with both the consumption and the saving function. M_o represents import expenditures at zero income. The ratio between the level of imports, M, and the level of income, Y, at any and all possible income levels is the *average propensity to import*. This ratio shows the proportion of any given income level that is being spent for imported goods and services. Like the average propensity to consume and its counterpart, the average propensity to save, the ratio M/Y will vary as the income level varies. The ratio of a change in imports, ΔM, to a change in the income level, ΔY, is the *marginal propensity to import*. This ratio measures the slope of the import function (as shown in Figure 9–2) and indicates how (in percentage terms) imports will vary as the income level shifts. From the standpoint of the impact of changes in the export-import balance on the level of income and employment in the domestic economy, the marginal propensity to import, m, is a vital concept.

Income Equilibrium in an Open Economy

Determination of the equilibrium level in an open economy is essentially a matter of fitting both exports and imports into the kind of analytical structure that we have developed in earlier chapters. In Table 9–1 are found data pertaining to a hypothetical economy. These data are similar

TABLE 9–1. Exports, Aggregate Demand, and Equilibrium Income (in billions of constant dollars)

(1) *Net National Product* Y_{np}	(2) *Consumption** C''	(3) *Investment* I	(4) *Government Expenditures* G	(5) *Aggregate Demand* $(C'' + I + G)$	(6) *Exports* X	(7) *Aggregate Demand* $(C'' + I + G + X)$
0	80	40	100	220	20	240
350	255	75	100	430	20	450
400	280	80	100	460	20	480
450	305	85	100	490	20	510
500	330	90	100	520	20	540
550	**355**	**95**	**100**	**550**	**20**	**570**
600	**380**	**100**	**100**	**580**	**20**	**600**
650	405	105	100	610	20	630
700	430	110	100	640	20	660
750	455	115	100	670	20	690
800	480	120	100	700	20	720
850	505	125	100	730	20	750
900	530	130	100	760	20	720

*From Table 8–7, Chapter 8.

to those in Chapter 8, except that now included is a column representing the value of the economy's exports. For the moment we shall assume that imports are zero. The export figures shown in Column (6) are the same for all income levels because of the autonomous nature of exports relative to the net national product. Investment and government purchases of goods and services are the same as in Table 8–3, while the consumption function is drawn from Table 8–6. The aggregate demand function for this hypothetical—and open—economy is obtained by adding the stated values for investment, government expenditures, and exports to consumption at each indicated level of the net national product. This result is shown in Column (7). Given this aggregate demand schedule, we find that the equilibrium income level for this open system is \$600 billion. The reader should observe that Table 9–1 also contains an aggregate demand schedule for a closed economic system—that is, no exports or imports. This is shown in Column (5). In the absence of exports, the equilibrium level of the net national product is \$550 billion. The upward shift of the aggregate demand function by \$20 billion—the amount of the exports—has the effect of increasing the equilibrium value of the net national product by \$50 billion. Thus, a change in the foreign balance can exercise a multiplier effect upon the domestic economy. We shall discuss shortly the operation and value of the multiplier in an open system.

The process of income determination is shown graphically in Figure 9–3. The aggregate demand schedule, *DD*, now includes exports, *X*, as well as the other components of output included heretofore. As in our previous analysis, the income equilibrium is determined at the point of intersection of the aggregate demand, *DD*, and aggregate supply, *OZ*, functions. This, according to the figure, is an income level of $600 billion. Given the position of the aggregate demand schedule, it is the only possible income level at which our four major expenditure categories will add up to an amount equal to aggregate supply.

For simplicity's sake we assumed in the foregoing example that imports were zero. We can now make our hypothetical model more realistic by introducing an import function into the analysis. This is done in Table 9–2, in which the import function is shown in Column (5). In our example, imports, *M*, are equal to $3 billion plus 0.02 Y_{np}. M_o, in other words, is equal to $3 billion and the marginal propensity to import, *m*, equals 2

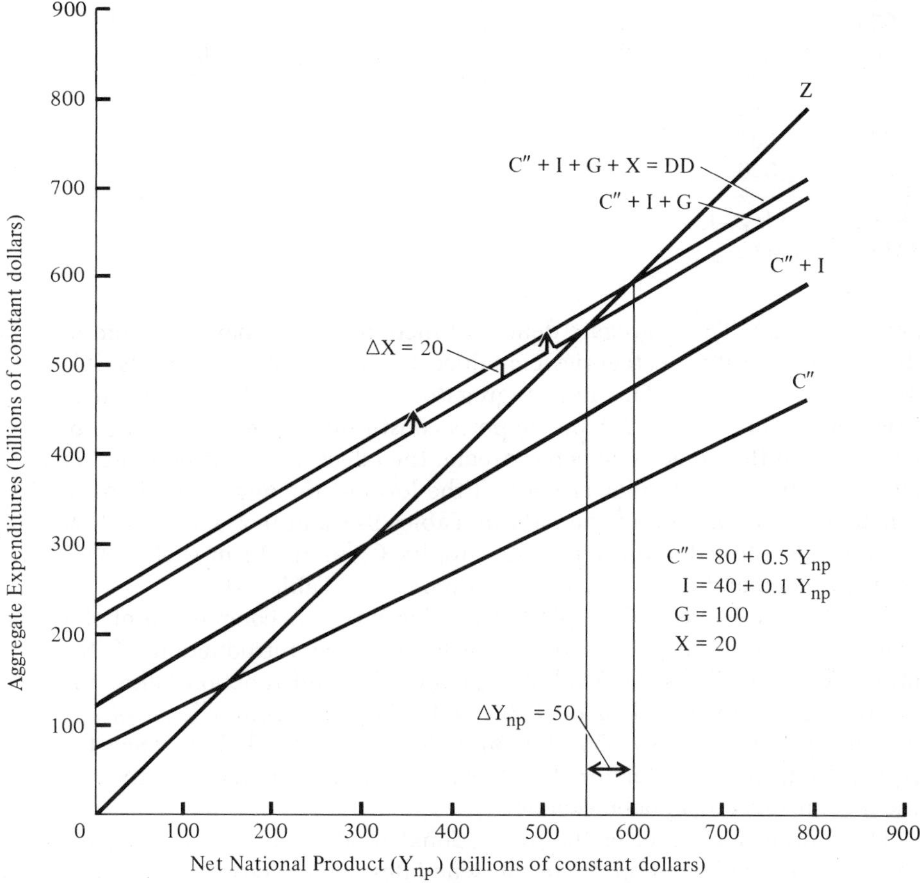

FIGURE 9–3. Exports and Aggregate Demand

TABLE 9–2. Exports, Imports, Aggregate Demand, and Equilibrium Income (in billions of constant dollars)

(1) Net National Product Y_{np}	(2) Consumption* C''	(3) Investment and Government Expenditure $I+G$	(4) Exports X	(5) Imports† M	(6) Aggregate Demand $(C''+I+G+X-M)$	
2	80	140	20	3	237	
350	255	175	20	10	440	
400	280	180	20	11	469	
450	305	185	20	12	498	
500	330	190	20	13	527	equilib-
550	355	195	20	14	556	rium
600	380	200	20	15	585	at $564
650	405	205	20	16	614	billion
700	430	210	20	17	643	
750	455	215	20	18	672	
800	480	220	20	19	701	
850	505	225	20	20	730	
900	530	230	20	21	749	

*Same as Table 9–1.
†$M = 3 + 0.02\,Y_{np}$.

percent (0.02). The aggregate demand function now becomes the sum of the four expenditure categories contained in Table 9–2 less imports ($C'' + I + G + X - M$). This new aggregate demand schedule is shown in Column (6) of Table 9–2. Since imports constitute, in effect, a leakage of income from the domestic income stream, the effect of the introduction of an import function is to lower over-all the level of the aggregate demand function. A comparison of the data in Tables 9–1 and 9–2 will show that at each possible value for aggregate supply—Column (1) in each table—aggregate demand is less in Table 9–2 than it is in Table 9–1.

The data of Table 9–2 are plotted in Figure 9–4. A comparison of this diagram with Figure 9-3 shows clearly that the introduction of the import function shifts the level of aggregate demand function below the position given by the data of Table 9–1. The equilibrium level of net national product is now $564 billion rather than $600 billion. (See the Appendix to this chapter for the algebraic formula for determination of the income level in an open economy.)

The equilibrium level of the net national product in our open system can also be explained in terms of schedules which represent *ex ante* values for expenditures other than consumption (investment, government

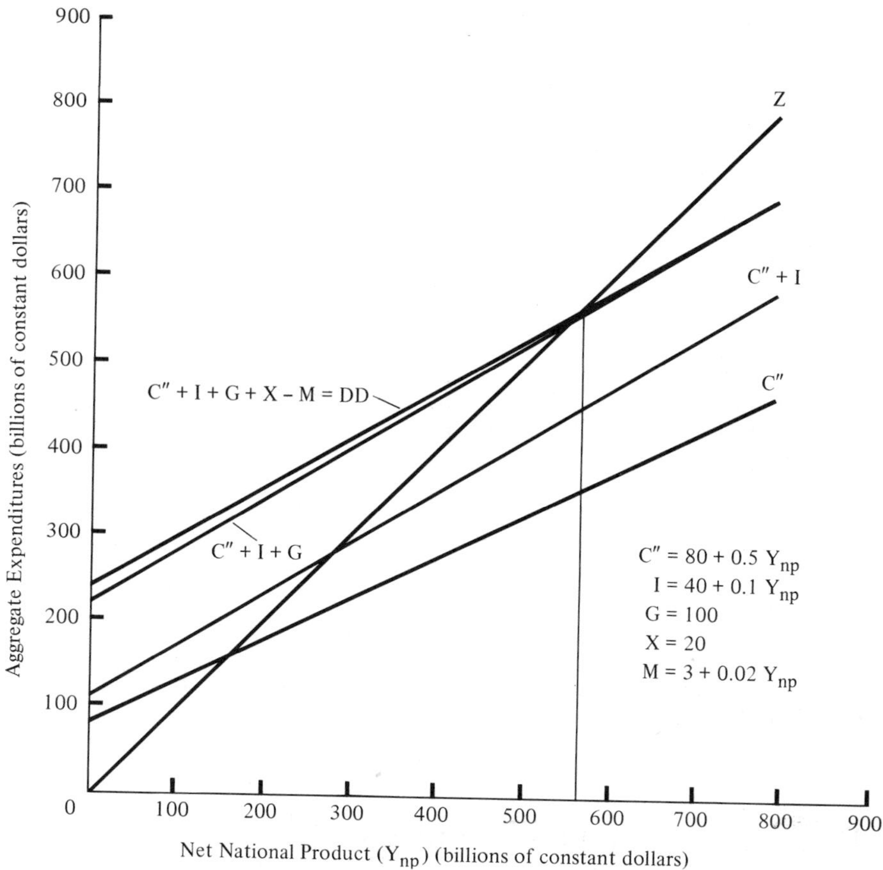

FIGURE 9–4. Exports, Imports, and Aggregate Demand

purchases of goods and services, and exports), and leakages out of the domestic income stream (saving, net taxes, and imports). Equilibrium exists at the point at which these expenditures $(I + G + X)$ just offset the leakages from the current income stream $(S + T + M)$. The sum of the expenditures items $(I + G + X)$ is shown in Column (2) of Table 9–3 and the sum of leakages $(S + T + M)$ is given in Column (3) of the same table. Equality between the two exists at the $564 billion level of the net national product. Individual schedules for each of these variables are plotted and summed in Figure 9–5, which depicts graphically the determination of the equilibrium level of the net national product in terms of the schedule values for $(I + G + X)$ and $(S + T + M)$. Income equilibrium requires that *ex ante* values for all leakages be offset by *ex ante* expenditures. At any level of the net national product at which $(S + T + M)$ is greater than $(I + G + X)$, aggregate supply

TABLE 9–3. Equilibrium of $(I + G + X)$ and $(S + T + M)$ (in billions of constant dollars)

(1) *Net National Product* Y_{np}	*(2)* *Investment, Government Expenditures, and Exports* $(I + G + X)$	*(3)* *Saving, Net Taxes, and Imports* $(S + T + M)$
0	160	− 77
350	195	105
400	200	131
450	205	157
500	210	183
556	215	209
564	**217**	**217**
600	220	235
650	225	261
700	230	287
750	235	303
800	240	339
900	250	391

will be in excess of aggregate demand, and output will fall. If the reverse situation prevails, output and employment will rise.

Foreign Trade and the Multiplier

An important implication of the preceding analysis is that income equilibrium in an open economy also means that equilibrium exists in the nation's balance of payments situation. Equilibrium in the nation's international economic position does not require that exports and imports be exactly in balance, but it does require that any imbalance between exports and imports be offset by other international transactions, such as loans or grants. (See the discussion of the role of the capital account in the discussion of the balance of payments in the beginning of this chapter). A change in a nation's international economic position affects the export-import balance either directly or indirectly. When this happens the position of the aggregate demand function is altered. As we know from our previous study, a change in the position of the aggregate demand schedule will have a multiplier effect upon the income and employment levels within the domestic economy. Since a change in the export-import balance affects the position of the aggregate demand function, there will be a multiplier effect associated with such a change. Some writers prefer to talk of the *foreign trade*, or the *open system* multiplier when discussing

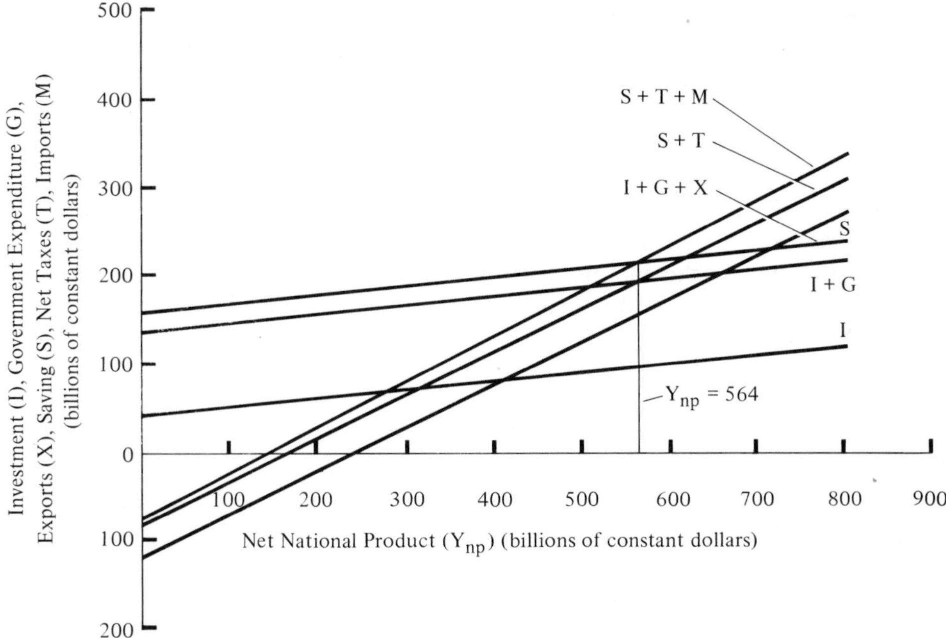

FIGURE 9–5. Equilibrium of $(I + G + X)$ and $(S + T + M)$

this phenomenon, but actually what is involved is nothing more than the application of the general theory of the multiplier to shifts in the aggregate demand function which have their origin in a change in the nation's international economic position. We saw in Table 9–1 that an autonomous increase in exports in the amount of \$20 billion led to an ultimate increase in the net national product of \$50 billion. Of course, an autonomous increase in imports—i.e., an upward shift of the import function—would have the opposite effect.

To derive algebraically the multiplier in an open system, let us begin, as in Chapter 8, with our basic definition of the effective multiplier, k'. This is

$$k' = \frac{\Delta Y_{np}}{\Delta D} \tag{9–4}$$

In an open economy it follows from Equation (9–1) that

$$\Delta Y_{np} = \Delta C + \Delta I + \Delta G + \Delta X - \Delta M \tag{9–5}$$

By substitution we then have

$$\Delta Y_{np} = a'\Delta Y_{np} + b\Delta Y_{np} + \Delta G + \Delta X - m\Delta Y_{np} \tag{9–6}$$

If we assume that $\Delta G = O$, we then have

$$\Delta X = \Delta Y_{np} - a'\Delta Y_{np} - b\Delta Y_{np} + m\Delta Y_{np} \tag{9–7}$$

$$\Delta X = \Delta Y_{np}(1 - a' - b + m) \tag{9–8}$$

Since the change in aggregate demand, ΔD, is the same as the change in exports, ΔX, we can substitute the right-hand portion of Equation (9–8) for ΔD in Equation (9–4). We thus get

$$k' = \frac{\Delta Y_{np}}{\Delta Y_{np}(1 - a' - b + m)} = \frac{1}{(1 - a' - b + m)} \tag{9–9}$$

Equation (9–9) gives us the value of the multiplier in an open system. It includes, the reader should note, not only the marginal propensity to import, but also the marginal propensity to tax. The latter is the case because $a' = a - at$. By further substitution we can define the multiplier in an open system as

$$k' = \frac{1}{(1 - a + at - b + m)} \tag{9–10}$$

Graphic Illustrations of the Multiplier in an Open System

Figure 9–6 depicts the effects on the net national product and imports which result from an autonomous change in exports. We assume, a simplified economy which has neither investment and saving, nor government expenditures and taxes. In such a system the necessary condition for equilibrium is that exports *ex ante* and imports *ex ante* be equal, because only when they are equal will leakages, represented by imports, M, be just offset by expenditures originating outside the economy i.e., exports, X. In Figure 9–6 the equilibrium income level is determined by the intersection of the schedule of *ex ante* exports (depicted by the lower horizontal line) and the import function, $M = M_o + mY_{np}$. At this income level exports and imports are in balance.

A shift upward in the export function from X to the new level X' causes a movement of the equilibrium net national product from Y_{np} to Y'_{np} The magnitude of this change depends upon the value of the multiplier, which in this instance is determined solely by the value of the marginal propensity to import, m. The important point to note is that, as the multiplier process works itself out and the income level rises, the volume of imports will also continue to rise. This is true because we have assumed a positive value for the marginal propensity to import. In our hypothetical system, in which there are no leakages other than expenditures for imports, the import level will have to continue to rise until once again it is equal to the volume of exports. The autonomous increase in exports disturbed a pre-existing balance in the current account of our hypothetical economy, but the increase in income that was generated by

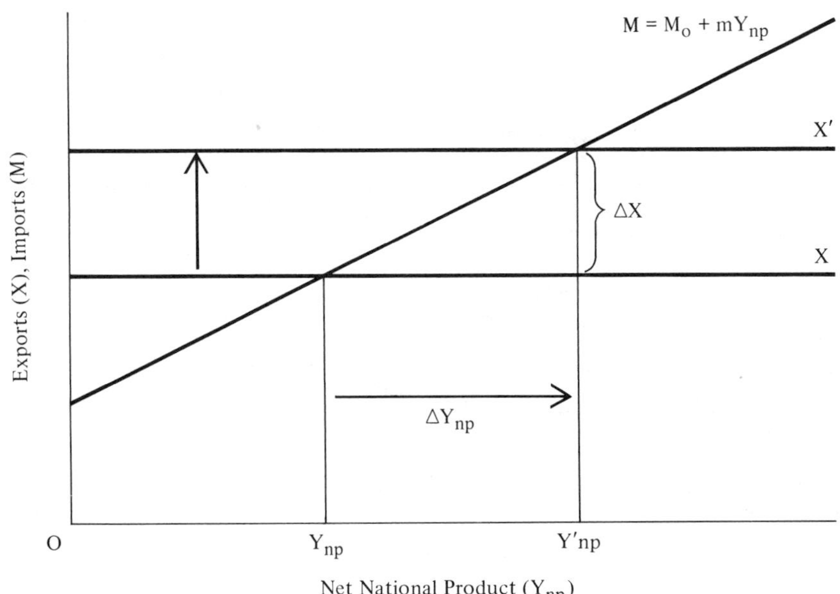

FIGURE 9–6. Foreign Trade and the Multiplier (*I, G, S,* and *T* omitted)

the change in exports induced a sufficient rise in imports to restore the export-import balance. At the new equilibrium income level, exports and imports are once again in balance. Changes in the opposite direction would, of course, take place if the economy experienced a decline in exports.

A more realistic picture results if we reintroduce both investment and saving as well as government expenditures and taxes into the analysis. This is done in Figure 9–7. The initial income equilibrium, Y_{np}, is at the point of intersection of the $I + G + X$ schedule and the $S + T + M$ schedule. The diagram is so drawn that at the initial equilibrium income level exports X and imports M are in balance, although the reader should note that this does not necessarily have to be the case. From the standpoint of the income equilibrium all that is required is that $I + G + X$ *ex ante* be just equal to $S + T + M$ *ex ante*, not that I be exactly offset by S, G be exactly offset by T, or X be exactly offset by M.

Let us examine the impact on the economy of an increase in exports. This change will shift the entire $I + G + X$ schedule upward. The new position of the schedule is given in Figure 9–9 by the line labeled $I + G + X'$. The increase in exports, ΔX, will, via the multiplier process, drive income to the new and higher equilibrium level of Y'_{np}. The rise in the income level brought about by the increase in exports also induces in this instance not only an increase in imports, but additional saving and taxes as well. At the new and higher income equilibrium Y'_{np}, the sum of $I +$

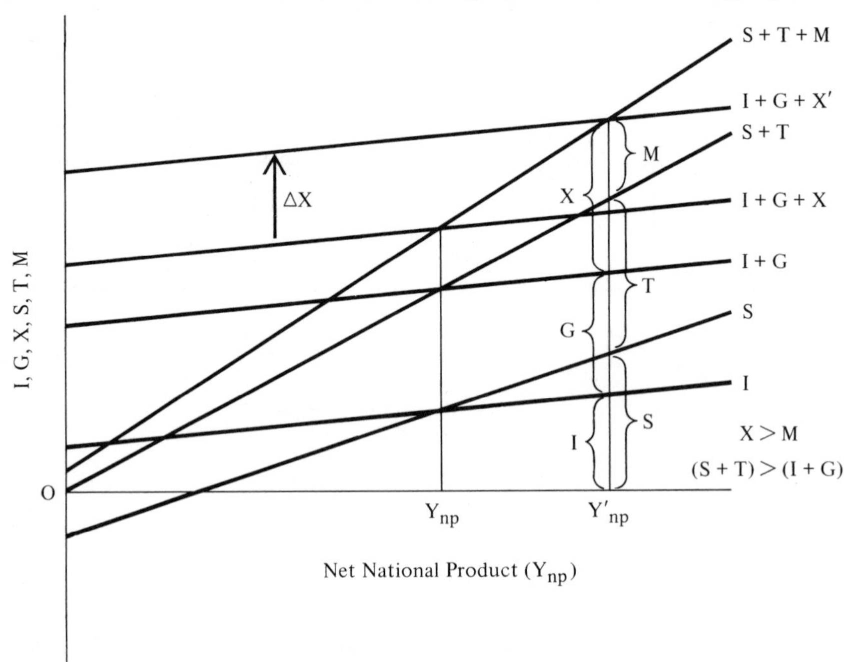

FIGURE 9–7. Foreign Trade and the Multiplier (*I, G, S,* and *T* included)

$G + X'$ is again in balance with the sum of $S + T + M$. Imports have not risen sufficiently to restore equality in the nation's export-import balance because leakages in the form of both taxes and saving also rise as the income level rises. The amount by which exports and imports differ at the new and higher income level will be just offset by the difference between domestic investment and saving or government expenditures and taxes, or both. Since $X > M$, then $S + T$ must be greater than $I + G$ by a like amount.

The Foreign Repercussion Effect

Up to this point we have not been concerned with the impact of a change in the international balance of the domestic economy upon foreign economies. This is a possibility that must be considered, because the imports of one nation are the exports of another. Consequently, the levels of income and employment in different economies may be linked together through their international economic transactions. The possibility that a change in the international economic position of the domestic economy can have repercussions abroad which, in turn, reverberate back to the domestic economy is described as the *foreign repercussion effect.* Such an effect exists only when the economy of one nation is relatively large as compared to the economy of other nations. Changes in the export-import balance of a very small nation are not likely to affect significantly the income and employment levels of other nations. However, a change in the imports of the United States, for example, could significantly affect the national income of one or more countries because of the sheer size of the American economy.

The nature of the foreign repercussion effect can readily be described. For the sake of simplicity in the analysis we shall assume only two countries. We shall call the domestic economy *A*, the foreign economy *B*. Let us assume, first, that there is an autonomous shift upward in the investment demand schedule in *A*. This will start the usual multiplier sequence in motion and bring with it not only an increase in income, but also induce additional imports as well as saving and taxes. For our present purposes the important point is that the rise in income in the domestic economy, *A*, will cause imports to rise as well. The sequence of events is as follows:

$$\Delta I_A \longrightarrow \Delta Y_A \longrightarrow \Delta M_A$$

The foreign repercussion is concerned primarily with the effect that this change has on income and employment levels in the domestic economy. The increase in imports in *A* consequent to the increase in *A*'s income is, given our assumption of only two countries, the same thing as an increase in the exports of *B*. But if *B* experiences an increase in its exports, its domestic income and employment level will be affected by the foreign trade multiplier. Further, the increase in income in *B* can be expected to increase its imports as well. Thus, for country *B* the sequence of events will be

$$\Delta X_B \longrightarrow \Delta Y_B \longrightarrow \Delta M_B$$

The above increase in *B*'s imports will reverberate back to the economy of *A* and cause its income to rise more than would be the case if domestic investment alone had changed. More exports by *A* will further stimulate its economy. The economy of *A* is linked to the economy of *B* through its exports; in identical fashion the economy of *B* is linked to the economy of *A*.

The essential character of the foreign repercussion effect can be demonstrated by a relatively simple geometric diagram such as Figure 9–8.[6] The income of the domestic economy, *A*, is shown on the horizontal axis; the income of the foreign economy, *B*, on the vertical axis. The curve $A = f(B)$, which slopes upward to the right, shows how the income level of *A* will vary directly with changes in the income level in *B*. The position of

6. Romney Robinson, "A Graphical Analysis of the Foreign Trade Multiplier," *Economic Journal*, September 1952, pp. 546–64.

the curve depends on the strength of the other determinants of income within the domestic economy, such as domestic investment, government expenditures, and the consumption function. The curve $B = f(A)$ shows the same thing for the foreign economy, that is, the manner in which the income level in *B* will vary with changes in the income level in *A*.

The point of intersection of the two schedules represents a condition of equilibrium with respect to the income levels of the two nations and their trade with each other. At this point neither the export-import balance nor the income level of *A* or *B* shows any disposition to change. There is equilibrium in both nations. The foreign repercussion is demonstrated in the diagram through a shift to the right in the schedule representing the income level in *A*. The new position of the schedule for *A* is: $A' = f(B)$. The shift is the result of a change in any of the internal determinants of the income level in *A*, such as a shift upward in either the investment or government expenditures component of the aggregate demand function. The effect of this is to move the equilibrium income level upward in both *A* and *B*, from Y_A to Y'_A in *A*, and from Y_B to Y'_B in *B*. The nature of the foreign repercussion effect is indicated by the fact that in the domestic

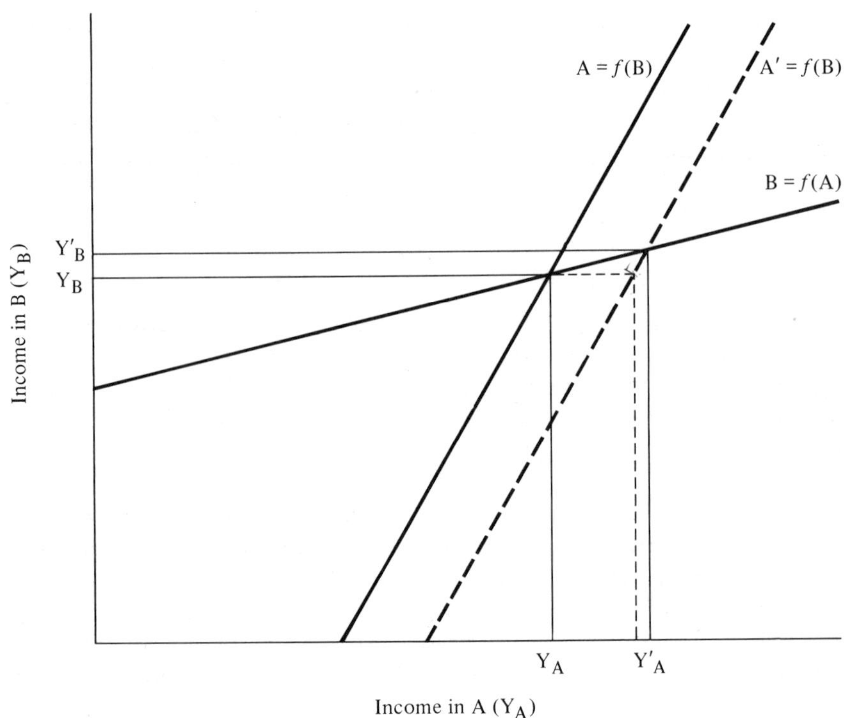

FIGURE 9–8. The Foreign Repercussion Effect

economy the change in the income from Y_A to Y'_A is greater than the difference between old schedule $A = f(B)$ and new schedule $A' = f(B)$. The amount of the change in income in the economy of A that is due solely to internal factors is indicated in the figure by the distance from Y_A to the vertical dotted line.

What determines the size or significance of the foreign repercussion effect? Since it involves the relationship between exports and the national income of the countries involved, the size of the foreign repercussion effect is determined largely by those factors that influence the size of the foreign trade multiplier. For example, the smaller the marginal propensities to save, tax (net), and import in the domestic economy, the larger will be the foreign repercussion effect. When these marginal propensities are small, the multiplier is large; thus the effect on the domestic income level of any given change in exports will be considerable. In the foreign economy a high marginal propensity to import will, *ceteris paribus,* make for a greater foreign repercussion effect in the domestic economy, although this lowers the value of the multiplier effect abroad. On the other hand, if the marginal propensities to save, tax, and import are low abroad, this will raise the value of the multiplier in the foreign nation and thus cause income to rise quite rapidly as a result of an increase in its exports. But for this increase in income abroad to reverberate back to the domestic economy to any significant degree requires a high value for the marginal propensity to import in the foreign economy. Thus, from the standpoint of the foreign nation no simple generalization concerning the factors making for a strong foreign repercussion effect in the domestic economy is possible.

Income Changes and the Export-Import Balance

Our analysis has been largely directed toward the effect of a change in exports or imports on income and employment levels in the domestic economy. It is appropriate that we look at the other side of the coin and analyze how internal changes in the income level may affect a nation's export-import balance.

Income equilibrium in an open economy may be defined in terms of an equality between $I + G + X$ *ex ante* and $S + T + M$ *ex ante*. For the sake of simplicity let us assume that government expenditure, G, and net taxes, T, are equal (and therefore eliminate them from the foregoing equality). Thus, in our equilibrium condition, $I + X = S + M$. Transposing the terms in this equation, we get the following:

$$X - M = S - I \qquad (9\text{–}11)$$

The meaning of the above equation is that *ex ante* the current account balance must be equal to the difference between saving and investment if an income equilibrium is to exist. Since the values that we have been discussing in this context are *ex ante* in nature, we can express $X - M$ and $S - I$ in the form of schedules that link both of these to the income level. This is done in Figure 9–9.[7] Net national product is measured on the horizontal axis; the net differences between exports and imports, $X - M$, and between saving and investment, $S - I$, are measured on the vertical axis. The $X - M$ schedule slopes downward to the right because, even though the level of exports is presumed to be autonomous with respect to the domestic income level, the level of imports will rise as the domestic income level rises. Thus, as the economy moves from a lower to a higher income level, the export-import balance will shift from a positive to a negative value. The $S - I$ schedule slopes upward to the right because saving increases as the income level rises at a rate greater than investment.

To illustrate the impact of a change in domestic income on the export-import balance, let us start the analysis with equality between exports

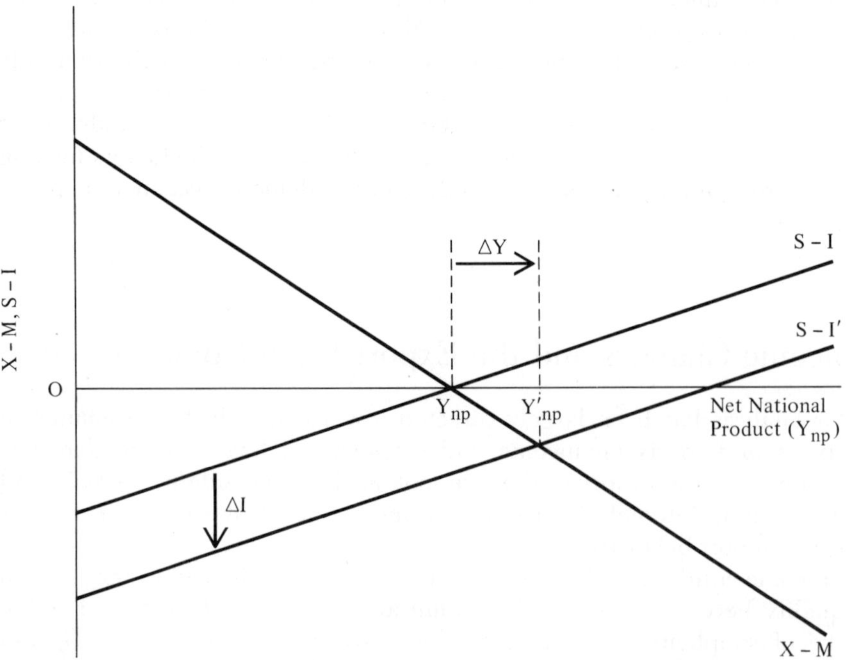

FIGURE 9–9. Income Changes and the Foreign Balance

7. Charles P. Kindleberger, *International Economics*, 5th ed. (Homewood, Ill.: Irwin, 1973), p. 349.

and imports. This is shown in Figure 9–9 at the income level Y_{np}. The $X - M$ curve and the $S - I$ curve intersect so that the net difference between exports and imports, $X - M$, and saving and investment, $S - I$, is zero. The effect on the domestic income level as well as the balance of trade of an *increase* in the level of autonomous investment is depicted by a shift downward in the $S - I$ schedule.[8] The new and higher equilibrium income level occurs at Y'_{np}, a point determined by the intersection of schedule $X - M$ and the new and lower schedule $S - I'$. The point of intersection of these two schedules now lies below zero on the vertical axis, which means that $X - M$ is now negative, or that imports exceed exports. We can therefore conclude that a change in the domestic income level—in this instance an increase—has induced an increase in imports sufficient to cause an adverse balance to develop in the nation's balance of trade. Our analysis ignores the foreign repercussion effect which would shift the $X - M$ schedule upward, thus raising the income level even more, but reducing the balance of trade deficit.

The preceding discussion of the impact of a change in the domestic income level on the balance of trade position has been worked out on the assumption of an increase in the income level, leading to a worsening of the export-import balance. This, of course, is not the only possibility ,as study of Figure 9–9 will reveal. The income level may fall, for example, as a result of a shift upward in the saving function. This will raise the $S - I$ curve, and cause it to intersect with the $X - M$ curve at a lower income level. This change, on the assumption that the foreign repercussion effect can be ignored, will lead to an export surplus in the current account. In reality, though, it is unlikely that such a surplus could be maintained for long because the decline in imports will have repercussions abroad which are likely to be felt in the domestic economy. In this instance, the foreign repercussion would take the form of a shift downward in the $X - M$ schedule that would further lower the domestic income level.

Starting from a balanced trade position, an increase in the domestic income level will, *ceteris paribus*, lead to an import surplus and weaken the nation's international payments position. If the trade deficit can be financed on a sustaining basis, no serious problem results. If not, the disequilibrium in the nation's international accounts may sooner or later force a downward adjustment in the domestic income level. What will happen if, starting from a balanced position, the domestic income level falls? Precisely the opposite of what we have just described.

8. The reason for this is that at every income level, $(S - I)$ will be less than it was prior to the increase in autonomous investment. This presumes, of course, that the saving function is unchanged.

Exchange Rates and the Export-Import Balance

It is now time to include foreign exchange rates in the analysis, as it makes a great deal of difference to a nation and its international economic position whether it operates with a system of fixed or flexible exchange rates. We shall consider the consequences of each of these alternatives.

A system of fixed exchange rates not only ties a nation's domestic situation closely to its international economic position, but also makes it difficult to secure simultaneously a full employment equilibrium in the domestic economy and equilibrium with respect to its international economic transactions. A review of the situation shown in Figure 9–9 will clarify this.

As already pointed out, a rise in domestic investment (depicted by a shift downward in the $S - I$ schedule in Figure 9–9) causes a disequilibrium in the nation's export-import balance. If the nation is able to borrow at long-term (experience a capital inflow), no serious problems result and the exchange rate can remain fixed. But if long-term capital inflows are not forthcoming, the situation is quite different. As long as the exchange rate is fixed and in the absence of induced (or accommodating) capital transactions, the nation will experience a loss of its international reserves (foreign exchange and drawing rights in the International Monetary Fund). There is no other way in which a nation can get the necessary foreign exchange to finance an excess of imports or exports.

The continued loss of international reserves by a nation ultimately will force changes in its international economic position.[9] This so because sooner or later a nation will exhaust its international reserves, including its drawing rights in the International Monetary Fund. What then? The most likely result would be an official devaluation of its currency—a reduction in its price as measured in other national currencies. This was the remedy nation's generally opted for during the Bretton Woods era—1944 to 1973. Since a currency devaluation makes a nation's exports cheaper (in terms of other currencies) and its imports more expensive, exports should rise and imports should fall, thus tending to restore balance in the nation's international economic position. Refer once again to Figure 9–9. If devaluation works as just described, the $X - M$ schedule will shift upwards, a change which has the effect of not only increasing the net national product, but also restoring international economic equilibrium. But there is a catch: as the national income rises, imports will also rise,

9. There is no generalization about the link between international reserves and a nation's money supply which is valid for all countries. For some nations, especially those which have used the U.S. dollar as a reserve currency, the link may be quite close, as the central banks of such countries are likely to loosen or tighten the money supply on the basis of changes in the nation's inventory of international reserves. For other nations, this is not the case. The United States is in the latter category.

thus tending to nullify somewhat the impact of the devaluation. Further, these developments can take place *only* if the economy is at less than full employment when devaluation takes place. In Figure 9–9, in other words, Y'_{np} must be a less than full employment net national product. If this were not the situation, an increase in export demand would cause output to bump up against the full capacity ceiling, after which prices would rise. But a rise in the price level would also nullify the effect of the devaluation (in whole or in part), since it would make the nation's exports more expensive. Imports would become more attractive for the nation's residents.[10]

The upshot of all this is that a system of fixed exchange rates makes it largely a matter of chance whether or not simultaneous equilibrium for a full employment output and the balance of international payments is attained. The two simply may not be compatible, which means the nation will have to choose one at the expense of the other. Of course, if all prices —including the prices of factors of production as well as for goods and services—were flexible both upwards and downwards, the foregoing conclusion would not hold. Any shift in demand in a nation away from domestic output toward imports would cause the price of the former to fall relative to the latter, thus tending to restore balance between exports and imports. But the real world is simply not like this; most prices are flexible in only one direction—up! Thus, the basic problem remains with a fixed exchange system the nation may have to choose between the pursuit of domestic stability and full employment at the cost of international imbalance, or balance of payments equilibrium at the cost of full employment at home. Since most Western nations have committed themselves to maintaining full employment (e.g., the American Employment Act), the realities of politics mean they select the first alternative.

If exchange rates are fully flexible the situation is quite different. In principle, it is impossible for there to be an imbalance between imports and exports, save as a result of lags and other imperfections in the market. The reason is that the rate of exchange would be continuously adjusting to changes in the demand and supply of exports and imports. Thus, if a nation increases its demand for imports relative to the foreign demand for its exports, the foreign exchange value of its currency will fall, causing an immediate increase in the price of imports and a corresponding decrease in the price (for foreigners) of its exports.

Turn once again to Figure 9–9. A fully flexible exchange rate system means that the $X - M$ line becomes horizontal; it coincides with the horizontal axis in the diagram. If this were the situation, then an increase in

10. If devaluation fails to correct a trade imbalance, then a nation may have to resort to more direct, restrictive measures, such as tariffs or quotas. Most economists prefer devaluation to quantitative restrictions on imports (such as quotas) because the former acts through price and permits more scope for consumer choice.

domestic investment (depicted by the downward shift of the $S - I$ schedule) would cause the net national product to rise without any impact on the foreign balance. Under such circumstances equilibrium in the output level would be restored at the point of intersection of the $S - I'$ schedule and the horizontal axis. The multiplier effect of a change in investment is much greater in this situation, simply because none of the increase in income is drawn off into imports purchases. This is well and good if the new equilibrium is at or below the full employment level of net national product, but if beyond it then prices will be up.

The practical consequence of a system of fully flexible exchane rates is to loosen the major ties between the domestic ecpnomy of a nation and its international economic situation. A nation's trade balance, in other words, is less affected by domestic disturbances than is the case with fixed exchange rates. It is also true that the domestic economy is more insulated from income and monetary disturbances originating abroad, disturbances which under a system of fixed exchange rates are transmitted from one country to another through their impact on a nation's exports or imports. It also means there is less interdependence with respect to domestic's policies pursued by different countries. If country A, for example, wants to pursue a vigorous policy of domestic expansion it may do so without fear that its actions will cause balance of payments problems abroad.

A Summary Comment

In this and the three preceding chapters our concern has been with analysis of the component parts of the economy's structure of aggregate demand. As was stressed in Chapter 5, the central thesis of modern employment theory is that in the short run, when the economy's capacity to produce is relatively fixed, the key to both the income and employment level is demand for the economy's whole output or, more simply, aggregate demand. Expectation of demand leads to the creation of output—and income. Thus, if we can analyze what determines the level of demand for the output of the whole economy, we learn something about the determination of income and employment.

As a result of theoretical developments stemming from the work of Keynes and others and of advances in the field of national income accounting, it is possible to identify the four major components of the economy's aggregate demand structure: consumption, investment, government purchases of goods and services, and the export-import balance. Our purpose has been not only to tie these four forms of demand together into a single integrated structure representing the demand for the economy's total output, but to analyze, too, the determinants of the level of each of these individual parts of the aggregate demand function. Moreover, we have sought to show how changes in the income (and employment) level are linked to changes in the economy's aggregate demand function, and how changes in this function are the result of shifts in any or all of its component parts.

APPENDIX

Algebraic determination of the income level in an open economy

(1) $Y_{np} = C + I + G + X - M$ = the basic identity
(2) $C = C'_o + a'Y_{np}$ = the consumption function
(3) $I = I'_o + bY_{np}$ = the investment function
(4) $M = M_o + mY_{np}$ = the import function
(5) $Y_{np} = C'_o + a'Y_{np} + I'_o + bY_{np} + G + X - M_o - mY_{np}$
(6) $Y_{np} - a'Y_{np} - bY_{np} + mY_{np} = (C'_o + I'_o + G + X - M_o)$
(7) $Y_{np}(1 - a' - b + m) = (C'_o + I'_o + G + X - M_o)$
(8) $Y_{np} = \frac{1}{(1 - a' - b + m)}(C'_o + I'_o + G + X - M_o)$

III

Money, Interest, and Income

10

Money and Interest

We turn now to the role that money and interest rates play in the determination of income and employment levels in modern society. Two major streams of thought dominate the relationship between money and the general level of economic activity, one associated with Keynes and his work, the other stemming from the provocative ideas of Professor Milton Friedman of the University of Chicago.

Specifically, in this chapter we shall concentrate on Keynesian ideas about money, interest, and their economic significance. In the next chapter we shall take up the key ideas in what is now known as the monetarist—or modern quantity—approach to money and economic activity. The most important thread running through these diverse analyses is the notion of the demand for money and the way in which this demand affects the general level of economic activity. By the term "demand for money" economists mean a functional relationship between the quantity of money that people want to *hold* and the variables which determine that quantity. The latter may be income, interest rates, wealth, or something else, as economic analysis does not offer an explanation of this particular type of demand in terms of a single variable. Nevertheless, demand for money equations have become extremely important in the development of theoretical models which purport to explain the behavior of the whole economy. We shall not in this chapter neglect the supply side of the money equation, although it is generally of less importance in contemporary analysis than is the demand side. In Chapter 12 a general model of the economic system is created by merging the ideas advanced concerning money with the observations in Part Two on income and output determination. In Chapter 13 this model (plus criticisms of it) becomes the basis for an appraisal of stabilization policies in the post-World War II era.

The view that money possesses certain peculiar attributes which may be distinguished from its role as a medium of exchange can largely be traced back to the thinking of John Maynard Keynes. In an essay prior to *The General Theory*, Keynes developed the outline of the theory of a monetary economy. This is the theory of an economy in which money is more than simply a device for facilitating the real economic process of production and exchange. In a monetary economy, according to Keynes, "money plays a part of its own and affects motives and decisions and is, in short, one of the operative factors in the situation, so that the course of events cannot be predicted, either in the long period or in the short, without a knowledge of the behavior of money between the first state and the last."[1] In such a world, money is not a neutral phenomenon, as Keynes argued was true of the classical theory, but rather a phenomenon governed by principles very different from those that hold sway over the process of production and exchange.

In the modern *market economy* there are two spheres of economic activity. There is, on the one hand, the real, or goods, sphere of activity, which has to do with the forces of aggregate demand and supply and the conditions under which an equilibrium of output and employment is achieved. On the other hand, there is the monetary sphere in which the economic forces at work are those centering around the demand for money. These latter forces are subject to principles of behavior quite different from those that govern activity in the economy's goods sector. According to the contemporary view, the existence of a separate monetary sphere of activity is a fact of profound significance; what takes place in the monetary sphere may suddenly and dramatically influence the level of both output and employment.

The method by which Keynes introduces money into the operation of the economy is through development of a theory of interest in which the demand for money is dominant. He sees the rate of interest[2] as the link between the real sphere and the monetary sphere. It is the factor around which investment theory is constructed; investment outlays, let us remember, comprise one of the strategic determinants of the level of income and

1. Quoted in Kenneth K. Kurihara, ed., *Post-Keynesian Economics* (New Brunswick, N.J.: Rutgers University Press, 1954), p. 6. This essay is reprinted in the *Nebraska Journal of Economics and Business*, autumn 1963.

2. It is an oversimplification to talk of the rate of interest, for in actuality there is not a single interest rate in the economy, but a whole series of different rates. It is meaningful to speak in generalized terms about the rate of interest. The reader should remember, though, that such a term really refers to the entire structure of interest rates characteristic of the modern economy.

employment. In the opinion of Keynes, interest is a monetary phenomenon which must be related to the demand for and the supply of money. To get a full appreciation of the flavor of Keynes's thinking on the unique role that the demand for money plays in the determination of the national output, we shall begin with a brief review of some of the essential characteristics of money, the money supply, and monetary equilibrium, followed by a short analysis of classical ideas on the role that money plays in the operation of the economy. This procedure should place Keynes's ideas about the importance of money in an appropriate historical perspective, as well as help set the stage for analysis of more recently developed views of the modern monetarists in Chapter 11.

The Nature of Money

There is one fact about money on which there is nearly universal agreement: it is neither easily nor simply defined. More than three-quarters of a century ago an economist made the following observation:

> It is a singular and, indeed, a significant fact that, although money was the first economic subject to attract men's thoughtful attention, and has been the focal centre of economic investigation ever since, there is at the present day not even an approximate agreement as to what ought to be designated by the word. The business world makes use of the term in several senses, while among economists there are almost as many different conceptions as there are writers upon the subject.[3]

The situation is not quite that bad today, although the Federal Reserve System regularly publishes data for five different measures of the nation's money stock, the reason being a lack of agreement on a single, all-inclusive definition of money.[4] Probably the best place to start is with the fundamental characteristic of money; it is a generalized *claim* that can be exercised against all other goods, services, and claims of whatever kind and irrespective of their origin. Thus the essential nature of money does not lie in the physical properties of whatever material substance may happen to fulfill the role of monetary exchange in a society at any particular time; it springs from the fact that the material substance in question is universally accepted as a generalized claim against all other things that possess economic value. The modern demand deposit, a major form of money in many highly developed economic systems, can hardly be said to

3. A. P. Andrew, "What Ought to be Called Money," *Quarterly Journal of Economics*, January 1899, p. 219.

4. These five measures are discussed subsequently in the section on the supply of money.

possess physical properties of value. It consists of nothing more than notations in the ledger of the bank, yet it is something that is almost universally accepted in payment for goods and services, or in the settlement of claims.

Given the nature of money as a generalized claim against all things or entities that possess economic value, it follows that money is the most *liquid* of all assets. *Liquidity* relates to the ease or convenience with which an asset can be converted from one form to another *without loss of value*. Money meets this requirement better than any other type of good or claim. Further, the costs of money are negligible as compared to the carrying costs that may be involved if one's assets are held in some other form. It cannot be stressed too strongly that understanding the notion of liquidity is a key to understanding Keynes's unique contribution to the theory of a monetary economy.

Although money is the asset with the highest degree of liquidity, it suffers from the disadvantage that it does not yield its holder any return—as normally is the case with other kinds of assets. This is a matter of basic importance in modern interest theory, as will become apparent in our analysis of interest rate determination.

The Functions of Money

Economic analysis traditionally states that money performs four major functions. First, money serves as a *standard for the measurement of value*. Without some such standard it would be impossible to reduce the vast and heterogeneous activity of the modern economy to anything meaningful and comprehensible. Unfortunately, money is not a perfect measuring rod because its value will fluctuate as the general price level changes, although this defect can be compensated for (to some extent) by statistical techniques for eliminating the effect of price changes on our measurements.[5] Second, money acts as a *medium of exchange*. In this sense, money is extremely important to the efficient functioning of the economy, for without some medium which everyone is willing to accept in exchange for any good, service, or asset, the economy would have to operate on a barter basis, which would be clumsy and inefficient. Third, money serves as a *store of value*. Since money is essentially a generalized claim to all forms of economic value, this means that economic value can be kept intact over time in the form of money. Of course, any claim or form of wealth that is not highly perishable can serve to store value over time, but money is best suited for performing this function. Finally, money can function as a *standard of deferred payments*. It is customary to measure a debt or promise for future payment in terms of money, rather than some commodity or service.

5. Chapter 3, p. 68.

Of the four functions of money we have outlined, the second and third —money as the medium of exchange and as a store of value—are most germane to the analysis in this chapter.

Alternatives to Money: Debt and Equity Instruments

In a broad sense, each form of wealth represents a claim against every other form of wealth, for it is usually possible to convert items of wealth into money (through sale) and then reconvert the money into a different form of wealth (through purchase). The ease with which this can be accomplished without a loss of economic value varies widely, depending on the nature of the specific items of wealth in question. Of immediate significance to our analysis are certain financial instruments which are in the nature of claims, although of a less generalized character than money. One of the most important of these is the *debt instrument.* A debt instrument is any kind of a note that legally obligates an individual, a business firm, or a governmental unit to make repayment at some date of a sum borrowed. Normally most debt instruments are interest bearing; the borrower agrees to pay to the lender a sum over and above the specific sum borrowed.

Two types of debt instruments are especially important to economic analysis. First, there is the *bill,* basically a short-term document (usually three months) which promises to pay a specific sum at a future date. The bill normally does not contain an explicit statement about interest; instead, interest is paid through the procedure of promising to pay a larger sum at the bill's maturity than the amount borrowed. This is called discounting. The lender, in effect, deducts the interest in advance. Treasury bills, which are short-term obligations of the U.S. Treasury, often are used by business firms as a form of wealth-holding for very short periods. Such bills are almost as liquid as money, and they have the advantage of yielding the holder a return in the form of interest.

The second form of debt instrument of special interest to us is the *bond.* Basically, the bond is a document that promises to pay to the holder (that is, the lender) a fixed sum of money as interest at stated intervals and repay the sum initially borrowed at a specific future date.[6] Bonds are considered as long-term debt instruments, because they normally have a life of more than one year. In actuality, most bonds are drawn for periods of from ten to twenty or more years. There is an unusual type of bond we should mention. This is the *consol,* a bond issued in perpetuity—that is, it does not have a maturity date. It is not used in

6. This is not true with the savings bonds issued by the U.S. Treasury. Bonds of this type, which are the kind most people are familiar with, do not entitle the holder to receive interest at periodic intervals; rather interest is accumulated over the life of the bond and at the time it is cashed the holder receives back his original sum plus the accumulated interest.

the United States, but has been common in Great Britain. It is mentioned because using a consol type bond in our exposition is a big help in understanding the relationship between the price of bonds and the rate of interest (see pp. 331–32). This relationship is of key importance to Keynes's theory of interest.

In most developed economies active markets exist for the purchase and sale of debt instruments in the form of both bills and bonds. Through these markets the original holder may sell his debt instrument long before its date of maturity. Markets for the purchase and sale of debt instruments provide a supply of interest-bearing claims of various types for individuals and others seeking to hold wealth in relatively liquid form for short or long periods of time. These markets, in other words, make debt instruments relatively liquid alternatives to money as means for storing wealth. There is, of course, a risk involved in storing wealth in the form of debt instruments rather than money because the current market value of any debt instrument is subject to sudden and unpredictable changes. This fact has a vitally important bearing on contemporary interest theory.

A second financial claim that is important in economic analysis is the *equity instrument.* In contrast to a debt instrument, which involves a promise to pay, an equity instrument is a claim involving the ownership of wealth. The most important type of equity instrument for our purposes is the *share,* or certificate of ownership in a joint-stock company. As most readers are aware, the stock market is the place in which equity instruments in the form of shares are bought and sold. In the modern economy, shares are easily acquired or disposed of because a ready market exists for them. But since the current market value of equities is probably even more volatile than that of debts, there is a definite risk element involved in holding equities in preference to money.

The Supply of Money

There must be an adequate supply of money in an economy to perform the four functions discussed earlier. By the *supply of money* we mean essentially *all those things that are generally acceptable in payment of debt and as payment for goods and services.*[7] Since we are dealing with a stock phenomenon, the existing supply of money must be held at all times by someone or some entity in the economy. This is a point of some significance in our analysis because it is necessary to make a distinction between the amount of money that is actually being held at a point in

7. Lester V. Chandler, *The Economics of Money and Banking,* 6th ed. (New York: Harper, 1973), p. 12.

time and the amount that people and institutions may, for various reasons, want to hold. The amount held and the amount wanted do not necessarily coincide.

Deposit Money and Reserve Money

What types of exchange media constitute the economy's stock or supply of money? In modern societies the money supply consists of: (1) metallic coins, (2) paper money issued by governments, and (3) checking deposits or checkbook money.[8] For economic analysis it is useful to classify the money supply into the two major categories of *deposit* (or commercial bank) money, and *reserve* (or central bank) money. Deposit money consists primarily of demand deposits, although sometimes and for some purposes it may be desirable to include time deposits as a part of the money supply. In recent years it has become customary to label the money supply defined as currency plus demand deposits (adjusted to exclude government and interbank deposits) as M_1. This is the definition of money generally used by the Federal Reserve System. Professor Milton Friedman and other monetarists prefer to add time or savings deposits in the large commercial banks to M_1 to get a definition of the money supply. This is called M_2. The reason for including savings deposits is Friedman's belief that they are so easily converted into cash that they should be counted as money. The demand deposit portion of the money supply grows when the assets of the commercial banks increase and shrinks when these assets decrease. Commercial bank assets consist of cash, loans, and investments.

The Federal Reserve System has three other definitions for money, not surprisingly labelled M_3, M_4, and M_5. A brief explanation of each of these is in order, although the concept generally employed through this text is M^1. M_3 is equal to M_2 plus deposits at mutual savings banks, savings and loan associations, and credit unions. M_4 is equal to M_2 plus large negotiable Certificates of Deposit (CDs). A Certificate of Deposit is a short-term (usually) fixed interest note used mostly by nonfinancial corporations as a way to earn interest on idle funds (i.e., excess liquidity). Normally they are issued after negotiations between the firm and a bank. Often they are negotiable, which means that the bank can resell them to other banks. M_5 is equal to M_3 plus large, negotiable Certificates of Deposit.

At this point you may wonder—and rightly so—why are there so many different definitions of money? To some extent these different definitions reflect relatively greater emphasis on a particular function of money. The

8. Ibid., pp 20–42, for an explanation in greater detail of the different forms of money.

definition of money used at the start of this section—those things acceptable in payment of debt or as payment for goods and services—clearly mirrors the medium of exchange function. Currency and demand deposits (M_1) readily fit this approach. Milton Friedman, however, has suggested that money ought to be considered as any asset which serves as a "temporary abode for purchasing power." By this he apparently means assets held for relatively brief periods when a business firm or an individual has receipts in excess of expenditures. The other definitions of money—M_2 through M_5—perhaps fit this definition, albeit somewhat loosely for some.[9]

All of the foregoing represent various categories of deposit money (or bank money). The other crucial part of the money supply is reserve or central bank money. In the United States this consists of Federal Reserve notes and the reserve balances of member banks. Federal Reserve notes are, of course, a part of the money supply in active circulation, but the reserve balances of member banks on deposit in the Federal Reserve Banks are not in circulation. While the money supply is generally interpreted to mean money actually in circulation, the idea of including the reserve balances of member banks in the concept of the money supply is useful for analysis of the impact of changes in the money supply on economic activity. Reserve money will fluctuate in accordance with changes in the assets of the central bank—primarily, government securities, and private securities in the form of discounts and advances to the commercial banks. The reserves of the commercial banks on deposit in the Federal Reserve System are often described as high-powered money because changes in these reserves have the power to produce multiple changes in the volume of demand deposits outstanding.

We need not at this point undertake a complete review of the process of bank credit and expansion, but some summary comments on the key principles involved in this process may prove helpful. These comments apply to M_1, the concept of money most appropriate to the theme of this text—understanding output and employment in the modern market economy. Since M_1 consists primarily of demand deposits,[10] the key principle for understanding changes in the money supply is the *principle of fractional reserves*. This principle simply asserts that, normally, a commercial bank need only keep a fraction of its total deposit liabilities on hand to meet withdrawals of deposits by its customers. Reserves not needed for this purpose become *excess reserves*; as such they become the basis for the bank to make new loans. Commercial banks, of course, are in business to make money, and they do so primarily by lending money, most of

9. For an interesting and clear discussion of changing views on money, see Carl M. Gambs, "Money—A Changing Concept in a Changing World," *Monthly Review*, Federal Reserve Bank of Kansas City, January 1977.

10. In March 1977, 74 percent of active money in circulation (currency plus demand deposits) consisted of demand deposits.

which is "created" by the process of lending out the banks excess reserves.

There is, of course, a catch to this. Any single bank in the system is limited in its lending—and hence, money-creating—power to its excess reserves. But for all banks together, the increase in the money supply through creation of new demand deposits is a *multiple* of the reserves banks are required to keep on hand to meet their obligations. The actual amount of reserves banks are required to have on hand in the United States is established by the Federal Reserve System. What is important to understand, however, is that the fractional reserve principle permits the commercial banking system to expand its deposit liabilities by some multiple of the total reserves in the system. It is this that makes it appropriate to describe reserve money as "high powered" money. Every dollar of reserve money can support four or five dollars more of added demand deposit money.

We can illustrate the effect of reserves with a simple set of equations. Let R_r represent the required reserve ratio for the banking system, R_a the actual reserves in the system, and D_a the deposit liabilities of the system. If the banking system is fully "loaned up," it follows that

$$\frac{R_a}{D_a} = R_r \qquad (10\text{–}1)$$

Equation (10–1) simply shows that the banking system has no excess reserves, for the ratio of actual reserves to deposit liabilities is equal to the required reserve ratio. This is the meaning of being "loaned up." There cannot be any further expansion in the money supply (via demand deposit creation) until more reserves are put into the system.

Equation (10–1) can be rearranged as follows

$$D_a = \frac{R_a}{R_r} \qquad (10\text{–}2)$$

What this equation tells us is that deposits in a fully loaned up system are equal to reserves of the system divided by the required reserve ratio. This is important because it also follows that an increase in reserves (ΔR_a) will lead to the following increase in deposits, (ΔD_a) assuming all banks in the system are able to maximize their profits by lending out all newly acquired excess reserves. Thus

$$\Delta D_a = \frac{\Delta R_a}{R_r} \qquad (10\text{–}3)$$

By a slight rearrangement equation (10–3) will appear as follows

$$\Delta D_a = \Delta R_a \times \frac{1}{R_r} \qquad (10\text{–}4)$$

But $1/R_r$ is the reciprocal of the required reserve ratio. We may term it the money multiplier. In the above formulation ΔR_a represents additional reserves—or more high powered money—put into the system. The equation shows that the maximum expansion in the money supply will be equal to the increase in reserves times the money multiplier. To illustrate, if the required reserve ratio is .20 (20 percent), its reciprocal is 5 (the money multiplier). Consequently, every dollar of high powered money in the system can support $5 in demand deposits.

It is through excess reserves that the central bank (the Federal Reserve System in the United States) gets its leverage over the nation's monetary system. By pumping reserves into or out of the banking system it creates the necessary conditions for either an expansion or contraction of the money supply. Note carefully that the Federal Reserve System cannot force an *increase* in the money supply. It can put more reserves into the banking system, but this does not mean that the public will increase its borrowings. Only if the latter happens will demand deposits (and the money supply) increase. Contraction is a different story. If the Federal Reserve System puts the squeeze on the reserves of the commercial banks of the system, they will be forced to reduce their liabilities—call in loans when possible and not renew loans as they are paid off—which will reduce the money supply. Thus, the powers of the central bank to force a contraction in money are greater than its powers to force an expansion.

There are three basic means by which the Federal Reserve can affect reserve money in the banking system. They are changing the required reserve ratio, R_r, changing the rate it charges commercial banks when it makes loans to them (the discount rate), and through open market operations, the buying and selling of government securities by the Federal Reserve System. When the Federal Reserve buys government securities the effect is to pump more reserves into the system; when it sells in the open market the effect is the opposite.[11] Open market buying and selling is by far the most frequently used control instrument. Lending by the Federal Reserve (discount rate policy) has been especially important during periods of financial crisis, such as those which occurred in 1966, 1970, and again during the 1974–75 recession, at which time the Federal Reserve was called upon at times to "open the discount window" and play the role of lender of "last resort."[12] Changes in the reserve requirements

11. Students interested in the details of management techniques used by the Federal Reserve System to influence the size of the reserves of the banking system are urged to consult any recent text in money and banking. For example, see Dudley G. Luckett, *Money and Banking* (New York: McGraw Hill Book Company, 1976), Chapter 15.

12. The "lender of last resort" concept refers to the ultimate responsibility of the Federal Reserve System for the health of the nation's financial system. Thus, when the Franklin National Bank of New York, with assets of over $5 billion, failed in late December, 1973, the Federal Reserve provided emergency loans to other financial institutions whose financial health was threatened by the Franklin National collapse. It is a matter, essentially of providing emergency credit. This is what is meant by the phrase, "opening the discount window."

are the least used of the means available to the Federal Reserve System to influence the size of the commercial banking system's reserves of high powered money.

The Money Supply: Exogenous or Endogenous?

Quite frequently in income and employment analysis the money supply is considered as an exogenous variable, on the assumption that the size of the money stock is determined by administrative action of the central bank. This is a convenient simplification and one which we shall adhere to when we examine the liquidity preference theory of interest. As we have just seen, government influence over the money supply is largely achieved through the control over the reserves of member banks of the Federal Reserve System, the high-powered money discussed above.

But it is not necessary to assume that the money supply is exogenous; that is, unrelated functionally to other variables in the economic system. The trend of post-Keynesian analysis is to treat the money supply as a variable functionally related to other variables in the income system. For example, Professor Ronald Teigen has developed a money supply function which reflects both profit maximizing decisions of the commercial banks and the policy actions of the Federal Reserve System[13] His theory of the money supply is based upon the view that

> commercial banks act in a profit-maximizing way in response to changes in the return from lending relative to the cost. Both the return and the cost are represented by short-term interest rates: in principle, the return is the yield on loans, and the cost is measured by the cost of acquiring the reserves necessary to support the new loans. When it becomes more profitable to make loans, banks are assumed to be willing to supply more deposits and to increase the money stock. However, member banks are constrained in supplying deposits by the reserve requirements imposed by the Federal Reserve System, and if excess reserves are scarce, member banks will tend to increase their borrowings.

In formal terms this hypothesis is expressed as an equation in which the ratio of the existing money supply to money based on unborrowed reserves is equated to the rate of return on loans and the cost of acquiring reserves. Specifically, Teigen's money supply function is:[14]

$$\frac{M}{M^*} = f(r - r_d) \qquad (10\text{–}5)$$

13. Ronald L. Teigen, "The Demand for and Supply of Money," in *Readings in Money, National Income, and Stabilization Policy,* Warren L. Smith and Ronald L. Teigen, eds. (Homewood, Ill.: Irwin, 1965), p. 60.

14. Ibid., p. 62. Professor Teigen's use of (r) should not be confused with our earlier use of this letter to stand for the marginal efficiency of capital.

In the equation, M is the existing stock of money (currency plus demand deposits) and M^* is defined as the amount of money which could be supported by unborrowed reserves, given the reserve requirements and other institutional characteristics of the Federal Reserve System.[15] Unborrowed reserves are reserves created at the initiative of the Federal Reserve System rather than from member bank borrowing. The significance of M^* in the equation is that it represents the monetary policy variable through which the central bank can affect the money supply. An increase in M^* as a result of Federal Reserve open market operations will lead ultimately to an increase in the money supply (M), assuming no change in either the rate of return from lending (r) or the cost of borrowing from the Federal Reserve by the commercial banks (r_d). This presumes, of course, that the commercial banks are profit maximizers seeking to increase their loans whenever excess reserves become available. The variables on the right-hand side of the equation reflect market forces which operate directly upon the commercial bank's willingness to expand or contract the money supply. An increase in the return (r) on lending, *ceteris paribus,* should lead the banks to expand their loans—and hence the money supply—while a rise in the cost of borrowing (r_d) from the Federal Reserve, *ceteris paribus,* should have the opposite effect.

Overall, the general tenor of Professor Teigen's analysis is to suggest that if the supply of money responds positively to the rate of interest, the multiplier effect associated with any shift in the aggregate demand schedule will be larger than it would be with a fixed money supply. This is so because any increase in aggregate demand, *ceteris paribus,* tends to raise interest rates, a development which will normally depress investment spending and dampen the multiplier effect. But if the money supply also increases as interest rates rise, the ultimate increase in the rate of interest will be smaller and thus the adverse effect upon investment spending—and the multiplier—will be lessened. A full explanation of the restrictive effect of the money supply on the rate of interest must await our analysis later in this chapter of the liquidity preference theory of interest.

Monetary Equilibrium

Before we review classical analysis of money and the economy, it is desirable to introduce the concept of *monetary equilibrium.* By now the reader is well aware that equilibrium as used in economic analysis refers to a situation that shows no disposition to change. We therefore define monetary equilibrium as a situation in which the amount of money in existence—the money currently being held by individuals, firms, or governments—is just equal to the amount that these entities want to hold. In

15. Ibid., p. 60.

short, monetary equilibrium exists when the demand for money is just equal to the current supply. Such a condition may or may not exist at any particular moment of time. When actual holdings and desired holdings are not in balance, we have *monetary disequilibrium.* The concept of monetary equilibrium or disequilibrium is essential to understand how money as a phenomenon in its own right may significantly influence the level of income and employment.

Money in Classical Theory

Classical thinking about money and its role is largely summed up in the quantity theory, which the reader will recall, is essentially a theory of price level determination.[16] Reduced to its simplest form, the quantity theory asserts that the general level of prices varies directly in proportion to the quantity of money.

Classical analysis focuses primarily on the medium of exchange function of money. People want money only as a means of facilitating the real process of exchanging goods for goods; they do not in any sense want to hold money as such. But if the only important function of money is that of a medium of exchange, and if, too, money possesses no intrinsic characteristics, which lead people to desire it for its own sake, then the only thing that can really be done with money is to pass it on as soon as possible through purchase of goods and services. The normal thing to do with money is to spend it.[17]

This view of money as something essentially neutral insofar as the economic process is concerned, together with the classical view of the economy's tendency toward full employment, provides the real explanation of the quantity theory. If money exists only to be spent, and if resources are normally fully employed, then any change in the quantity of money in circulation can only have an impact upon the general level of prices. In this simplified version of the quantity theory it is assumed that the velocity of circulation of the money supply is a constant. Only if this assumption is made does the more rigid version, in which the price level varies directly and *proportionally* to the money supply, hold good. It is not essential to the quantity theory that the velocity of money be assumed constant, but it is essential that the general price level vary *directly* with the quantity of money, even though the relationship between money and prices may not be one of strict proportionality.

16. Chapter 4, p. 113.

17. In the classical view, even if money is saved, it is spent in the sense that it is used to purchase some kind of an income bearing asset such as a bond or share of stock. Money is simply not held as money.

A more elaborate and sophisticated version of the quantity theory was developed by Alfred Marshall. In this approach, known as the Cambridge version of the quantity theory, emphasis is shifted to the desire of individuals to hold a definite quantity of cash balances. Marshall put the matter as follows:

> In every state of society there is some fraction of their income people find it worthwhile to keep in the form of currency; it may be a fifth, or a tenth, or a twentieth.[18]

While Marshall and later classical economists recognized that individuals may want to hold money as such, exploration of the motives for holding money had to wait on the appearance of *The General Theory.* Nevertheless, the Cambridge version of the quantity theory represents an important advance over the earlier and more rigidly orthodox concept primarily because it is a step away from the overly simplified classical assumption that money is of real importance only as a medium of exchange.

The essential nature of the Marshallian or Cambridge theory is summarized in the following equation:

$$L = \phi(pY) \qquad (10\text{–}6)$$

In this equation L is the demand for nominal money balances, p the price level, Y real national income, and ϕ the coefficient which brings the two sides of the equation into balance. Essentially the equation says that society's demand for nominal money balance is linked to its nominal income (the money value of real output).[19] It also follows that the demand for real money balances is linked to real income. This is apparent if Equation 10–6 is rearranged as follows:

$$\frac{L}{p} = \phi Y \qquad (10\text{–}7)$$

L/p is, of course the demand for real money balances.

Superficially, ϕ may appear to be nothing more than the reciprocal of the income velocity of money. It will be recalled from Chapter 4 that the equation of exchange may be written as:

$$M^o v = pY \qquad (10\text{–}8)$$

But this can be rearranged as:

$$M^o = \frac{1}{v}(pY) \qquad (10\text{–}9)$$

If ϕ is mathematically equal to the reciprocal of velocity $(1/v)$, then Equations 10–6 and 10–9 seem essentially the same, assuming monetary equilibrium $(L = M^o)$. They may be the same mathematically, but they

18. Alfred Marshall, *Money, Credit, and Commerce* (New York: Macmillan, 1923), p. 45.

19. Nominal values are values not corrected for changes in the price level, whereas real values are corrected for such changes.

are not the same in an economic sense. The reason is that ϕ is simply not a numerical coefficient. It represents something else. It is the proportion of the national income (nominal or real) that the residents of a nation wish to hold as cash balances. As such it is basically a psychological propensity that may change. Over the long run the value of ϕ was thought to remain reasonably stable, but in the short run it might shift in a sudden and unpredictable manner as a result of changes in the public's state of coinfidence. It is this possibility that brings the Cambridge version of the quantity theory much closer to modern thinking on the subject of money.

The distinction between the original classical version of the quantity theory with its emphasis upon money as something to be spent and the more sophisticated Cambridge version with emphasis upon cash balances (real or nominal) may be clarified by using a diagram. This is done in Figure 10–1. Let us begin this analysis with the basic classical assumption that there is full employment. This means that real output, Y, is constant. It then follows that the nominal quantity of money people want to hold, L, is proportional to the general price level, p. Thus we can say:

$$L = \phi(p) \tag{10–10}$$

In Figure 10–1 both the money supply M^o and the quantity of money that people want to hold, L, are shown on the horizontal axis, while the general price level, p, is shown on the vertical axis. The curve sloping upward to the right and labeled $L = \phi(p)$ is the geometrical expression of the notion of functonal relationship between L and p. The value of the

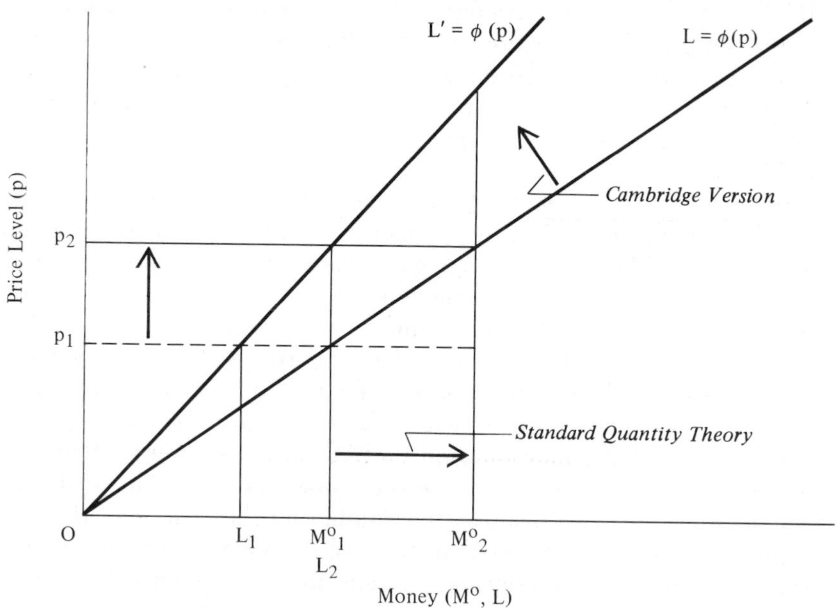

FIGURE 10–1. The Quantity Theory of Money

coefficient ϕ is equal to the reciprocal of the slope of this curve. Line M_1^o depicts the money supply. M_1^o is shown as a vertical line because the amount of money in circulation (the distance from the origin to the point where M_1^o meet the horizontal axis) is assumed to be autonomously determined by the monetary authorities. Monetary equilibrium exists at the point of intersection of the money supply schedule and the $L = \phi(p)$ schedule. The price level at this point is p_1.

In the earlier and more rigid version of the quantity theory a change in the general price level could come about only as a result of a change in the money supply. Such a change would disrupt a pre-existing monetary equilibrium and result in either more (or less) spending with a consequent rise (or fall) in the general price level. To illustrate, let us assume that the money supply curve in Figure 10–1 shifts to the right. Its new position is given by the schedule labeled M_2^o. This injection of additional money into the economy upsets the prior equilibrium between L and M^o. As a result the amount of money actually in existence is now greater than the amount the people want to hold, L_2, at the existing price level p_1. Since the rigid version of the quantity theory views money as only a medium of exchange, the new money injected into the economy will be spent. As this happens, prices will rise because of the assumption that real output is a constant. Prices will continue to rise until the normal relationship between the price level, p, and the demand for money to hold, L, is once again restored. This is at a higher level of prices, p_2, and is depicted at the point of intersection of the new and larger money supply curve, M_2^o and the $L = \phi(p)$ schedule. Opposite effects would ensue if the money supply schedule were shifted to the left. This analysis is properly described as the more traditional version of the quantity theory because the initiative for a change in the price level comes from a change in M^o There is no question of any change in the value of ϕ. The sequence is $\Delta M^o \rightarrow \Delta p$.

In the Cambridge version of the quantity theory the general price level may rise from p_1 *to* p_2, but the manner in which the rise is brought about is altogether different. This is demonstrated in Figure 10–1 by a shift upward in the $L = \phi(p)$ schedule to the level indicated by $L' = \phi(p)$. What is the significance of this shift? Essentially it means a change in the value of ϕ, which is to say a change in the psychological propensity of the public to hold some portion of national income in the form of money. If the $L = \phi(p)$ schedule shifts upward the value of ϕ has declined. Given the new position of $L' = \phi(p)$, the amount of money people want to hold at the price level p_1 *is equal to* L_1. This is the lesser amount than L_2. This disturbs the equilibrium because now the money supply, M_1, is again greater than the cash balances people want to hold L_1. At this point the Cambridge version falls back upon the notion that money is basically wanted as a medium of exchange, and, as a consequence, the surplus of money, $M_1^o - L_1$, will be spent as people seek to rid themselves of excess balances. Again this will only serve to drive up the general level of prices because of our assumption that real output is a constant. Thus equilibrium between the money supply and the amount of money people want to hold will be restored when prices climb to the level p_2.

In the Cambridge analysis, a shift downward in the $L = \phi(p)$ function would mean that the public had decided to hold a larger proportion of national income in the form of money balances. In view of this and on the continuing assumption that real output is a constant, the restoration of equilibrium between M^o and L requires a fall in the general price level. In the rigid version of the quantity theory, this same result requires a reduction in the supply of money.

The Role of Money in Keynesian Theory

The Cambridge version of the quantity theory represented an important advance in our understanding of the economic significance of money because it shifted analytical emphasis from the supply of money per se to the idea that people desire and need to hold money as such. But the Cambridge theorists did not push the analysis deeply into the reasons why people may want to hold money. The Cambridge ϕ implies a desire to hold cash balances, but it does not offer any clear explanation of the reasons for this desire. Keynes, however, fashions an explanation in *The General Theory* through development of the concept of *liquidity preference.* His approach to the role of money in the economy is accepted by many contemporary economists. It differs from the classical analysis primarily because it focuses attention on the demand for money rather than on the supply of money. From this approach a theory of interest is developed that provides the crucial link between money, income, and the employment level, as we will discover in Chapter 12.

Motives for Holding Money

The liquidity preference concept forms the core of the modern analysis of money and its role in the economy. Keynes used the term *liquidity preference* to mean the demand for money *to hold.*[20] The demand for a commodity or a service is conceived in terms of the amount of money that a person is willing to give up in order to obtain the commodity or service.

20. John Maynard Keynes, *The General Theory of Employment, Interest and Money* (New York: First Harbinger ed., Harcourt, Brace & World, 1964), p. 166.

But this notion of demand cannot apply to money, since money is obviously not exchanged for money. The demand for money to hold is a demand for objectives which are one step removed from the act of holding money itself. As a consequence of Keynes's pioneering analysis, modern income and employment theory postulates three major reasons why individuals and business firms want to hold money balances: the transactions motive, the precautionary motive, and the speculative motive.

The Transactions Motive · The transactions motive relates to the need to hold some quantity of money balances to carry on day-to-day economic dealings. Practically all transactions in a money-using economy involve an exchange of money, and, since the receipt of income is not synchronized exactly with all transactions involving money outlays, it is necessary that some money be held in order to meet this need.

Money held to satisfy the transactions motive is related primarily to the medium of exchange function. Money balances held idle in response to this motive provide a means of payment for transactions which will take place in the future. The amount of money in relation to income that people and business firms find it necessary to hold to satisfy the transactions motive depends on the time interval within which income is received relative to the income. To illustrate with a simple example, let us assume an individual has an annual income of $9,600. If this individual is paid only once a year and further, if he spends his whole income during the year, his money balance will be $9,600 at the beginning of the year and zero at the end of the year. His *average* holding of money during the year will be $4,800, or 50 percent of his income. Thus a person paid in this fashion would have to hold, on the average, 50 percent of his annual income in the form of money balances to satisfy the transactions motive. This assumes that income is spent at a uniform rate. Now let us consider what happens if this individual's employer decides to pay him twice a year. Every six months he will receive $4,800 and he will spend the whole of this before the beginning of the next pay period. His money balances will total $4,800 at the beginning of the six-month period and zero at the end. Thus his average money balance will total $2,400 in each pay period during the year. This means that a person paid twice a year must, on the average, hold but 25 percent of his annual income as money balances in order to satisfy the transactions motive. The more frequent the pay period, the smaller is the proportion of an individual's annual income that must be held to carry on day-to-day transactions.

The Precautionary Motive · The precautionary motive is the desire to hold some quantity of money balances to meet unforeseen emergencies or contingencies. It is, in other words, a desire to set aside some money balances to provide for a "rainy day." The need to hold money to satisfy this particular motive arises out of the fact that we do not have certain knowledge concerning future transactions; a situation may arise in which the need for money balances is much greater than the amount required to carry on normal day-to-day transactions. For the individual this may be the result of unemployment, illness, or some other form of economic misfortune, although it should be stressed that all unforeseen developments that require extraordinary expenditures on the part of either individuals or business firms are not necessarily of an adverse character.

The Speculative Motive · The speculative motive is the most complex and the most important of the three major sources of demand for cash balances postulated by Keynesian theory. It is the key to an understanding of interest theory and the manner in which money may powerfully affect the operation of the economy.

Fundamentally, the speculative motive relates to the desire to hold a part of one's assets in the form of cash in order to take advantage of future market movements. It involves, according to Keynes, holding money balances with the objective of "securing profit from knowing better than the market what the future will bring forth."[21] The speculative motive shifts emphasis from the medium of exchange function of money, which dominated classical thinking, and which underlies the transactions and precautionary motives, to the store of value function. Under the speculative motive, money is wanted as an asset rather than as a medium of exchange that can be drawn upon as needed at some future date. Money is being held in preference to holding assets in some other form.

Since idle money balances do not, like debt or equity instruments, yield income, why would an individual or a business firm wish to hold on to them? Let us let Keynes answer:

> Money, it is well known, serves two principal purposes. By acting as a money of account it facilitates exchanges without it being necessary that it should ever itself come into the picture as a substantive object. In this respect it is a convenience which is devoid of significance or real influence. In the second place, it is a store of wealth. So we are told without a smile on the face. But in the world of the classical economy, what an insane use to which to put it! For it is a recognized characteristic of money as a store of wealth that it is barren; whereas practically every other form of storing wealth yields some interest or profit. *Why should anyone outside a lunatic asylum wish to use money as a store of wealth?*
>
> Because, partly on reasonable and partly on instinctive grounds, our desire to hold money is a barometer of the degree of distrust of our own calculations and conventions concerning the future. Even though this feeling about money is itself conventional or instinctive, it operates, so to

21. Ibid., p. 170.

speak, at a deeper level of our motivation. It takes charge at the moments when the higher, more precarious conventions have weakened. *The possession of actual money lulls our disquietude; and the premium which we require to make us part with money is the measure of our disquietude.*[22]

The Transactions Demand for Money

Now that we have defined the three major forms of demand for money to hold, let us direct the analysis to the problem of the determination of the actual amounts of money (idle balances) held to satisfy each of these motives.[23] For this purpose it is logical to lump the transactions and precautionary demands together, since both are related primarily to the medium of exchange function of money. Let us call the combined demand for money to satisfy the transaction and precautionary motives the *transactions demand* and designate it by the symbol L_t.

Given the existence of some kind of a normal ratio with respect to the *proportion* of income that the public wants to hold as idle money balances in response to L_t, the actual amount of money held to satisfy this motive will vary directly with income. Thus L_t is, *ceteris paribus*, a function of income. Algebraically we have

$$L_t = f(Y) \qquad (10\text{–}11)$$

The fundamental reason for this is not difficult to see. In a complex society the volume of economic transactions of all kinds varies directly with the income level. Consequently, the absolute quantity of money balances needed to carry on these transactions also varies directly with the income level. The amount of money that can be held strictly in response to the precautionary component of the transactions demand schedule is for most people a residual sum which will vary with income. The higher the income level, the easier it will be for individuals and firms to hold idle balances to meet unforeseen contingencies.[24]

The functional relationship between the transactions demand for money L_t and the income level is depicted in Figure 10–2. The transac-

22. John Maynard Keynes, "The General Theory of Employment," *Quarterly Journal of Economics*, February 1937, pp. 215, 216. [Italics added.] No better example of what Keynes meant exists, perhaps, than the "run" on American banks during the early months of 1933, a crisis which finally led to the temporary closing of the banks. Because their fears about the continued solvency of the banking system were so great people panicked and sought to withdraw their funds.

23. The analysis which follows is cast in real terms, which is to say the demands for money are for real quantities. This follows because it is presumed that any change in the price level will cause the demand for nominal money balances to change in the same proportion. Thus, it is ultimately real changes which are significant.

24. This should not be confused with saving. Funds held idle to satisfy the precautionary motive may represent one way in which savings are disposed of, but they are not to be mistaken for the act of saving itself.

tions demand, L_t is shown on the vertical axis; the income level, Y, on the horizontal axis. The transactions function is the curve labeled $L_t = f(Y)$. The function is a straight line, drawn so that its slope is less than 45°. This indicates, first, that the ratio of money balances held for transactions purposes to income, L_t/Y, is normally less than unity (100 percent), and second, that this ratio is assumed constant. Given these assumptions, the figure shows that the amount of money demanded for transactions purposes, L_t, varies directly with the income level, Y. For example, at the income level Y_1 the transactions demand is L_{t_1}, and at the income level Y_2, the transactions demand is L_{t_2}.

Since idle money balances do not yield any income, should not the amount of money people are willing to hold as balances be related to interest rates? As a matter of fact this is the crucial relationship insofar as the demand for money to satisfy the speculative motive is concerned. But most economists believe the transactions demand is relatively unresponsive to the rate of interest, except at high interest levels.

Figure 10–3 shows the likely relationship between the transactions demand, the rate of interest, and income. The transactions demand, L_t is depicted on the horizontal axis, and we measure the rate of interest, i, on the vertical axis. The demand for money balances for transactions purposes at a given income level is represented by a straight line parallel to the vertical axis up to the interest rate i_a. This is the crucial level at which the transactions demand for money balances becomes responsive to

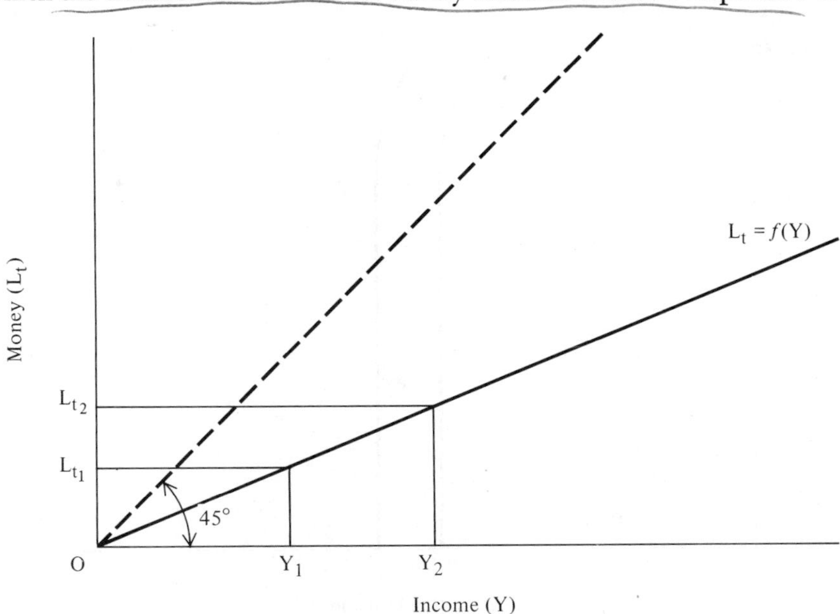

FIGURE 10–2. The Transactions Demand for Money: Idle Balances as a Function of the Income Level

an increase in the rate of interest; thus the curve begins to bend backward at this point. At high interest rates individuals and business firms will economize in the use of money. They seek to make each unit do more work, thus freeing some of their balances for lending under the high-interest conditions prevailing in the economy. This is tantamount to an increase in the velocity of circulation of the money supply.

The distance between the vertical axis and the vertical portion of the transactions demand curve is determined by the income level. Thus in Figure 10–3, the distance OL_{t_1}, as measured on the horizontal axis, is equivalent to the distance OL_{t_1} in Figure 10–2. This being the case, it is appropriate to designate this transactions demand curve of Figure 10–3 as Y_1. If there is an increase in the income level, the transactions demand for money will increase. In Figure 10–2 this is depicted by the change from L_{t_1} to L_{t_2} on the vertical axis. In Figure 10–3 this same change must be shown by a *shift to the right of the curve* representing the transactions demand for money. At the higher income level the position of the curve is given by Y_2 and the demand for money balances corresponding to this income level is given by the distance OL_{t_2}.

The Asset Demand for Money

The other type of demand for idle money balances stems from the speculative motive. The essential feature which distinguishes this demand

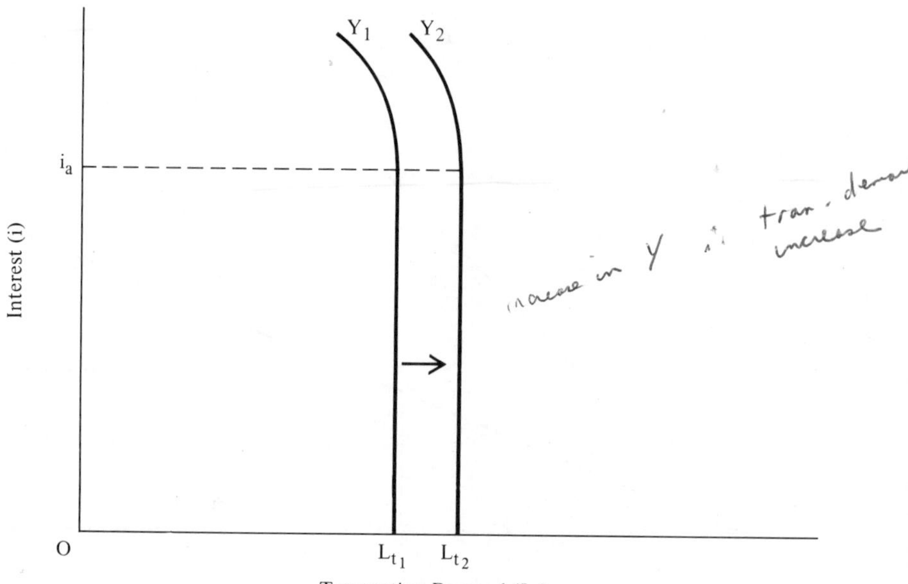

FIGURE 10–3. The Transactions Demand for Money and the Rate of Interest

from the categories considered previously is that it represents demand for money to hold *as an asset.* In our analysis we will call this demand the *asset demand* and designate it by the symbol L_a.

The essence of the asset demand for money is that money is regarded as a way of holding economic value over time, which is preferable to debt instruments and equity instruments.[25] Debt instruments normally yield the holder a fixed income in the form of interest, while equity instruments yield the holder an uncertain income in the form of a profit. Although profit can be expressed as a rate of return and thus compared directly with the income derived from a debt instrument, we will simplify our analysis at this stage by assuming that the person who wants to hold economic value over time considers only two alternatives, holding money or holding debt instruments. We shall use the bond to represent debt instruments.[26]

Why would an individual hold money, which yields no return, in preference to a fixed-income debt instrument? The answer, as Keynes pointed out, lies in the fact of uncertainty with respect to the future market value of the debt instruments. The corollary of this is that the income foregone by holding money in preference to a fixed-income obligation such as a bond becomes the *opportunity cost* of holding money. If we limit the alternative forms in which economic value may be held to money and bonds, then the rate of interest is the cost of holding money as an asset in satisfaction of the speculative motive, since interest is the income foregone when one chooses to hold money in preference to bonds. This implies that the amount of money held as an asset is a function of the rate of interest, although an *inverse* one. Thus we have algebraically

$$L_a = f(i) \tag{10–12}$$

The higher the rate of interest, the more costly it becomes to hold money

25. A person holding either a debt or equity instrument may experience either a capital gain or capital loss because of unforeseen changes in the current market value of the asset. The possibility of a capital loss is a risk a debt or equity instrument-holder assumes.

26. Equity instruments involve considerations of future values for the rate of return over cost (the marginal efficiency of capital) as well as for the rate of interest. If persons and firms turn to equities as a means of holding economic value over time they will have to make judgments about the future yields of capital assets and compare these expected yields with the anticipated return from bonds. Holding equities means, too, that economic value may be tied up in real capital assets; thus, in principle, wealth-holders should take into account the future value of such capital assets as well as the current rate of return in reaching a decision as to the form in which they want to hold economic value through time. Highly organized markets for buying and selling equities such as the New York Stock Exchange tend to blur the distinction between debts and equities. Nevertheless, a rational wealth-holder would allocate his holdings between the three basic forms in which economic value can be held through time—money, debts, and equities—so that at the margin he would get the same money return, or satisfaction in the event he holds money, from each type of holding.

rather than bonds and, consequently, the smaller will be the amount of money held as an asset.[27]

The functional relationship between the asset demand for money and the rate of interest is shown as a schedule in Figure 10–4. The asset demand L_a, appears on the horizontal axis, while the rate of interest, i, is on the vertical axis. The curve $L_a = f(i)$ shows the quantity of money that persons and firms want to hold as an asset at different rates of interest. The reader should note that the asset demand schedule tends to become perfectly elastic—that is, horizontal—at very low levels of the interest rate. This characteristic will be explained when we introduce expectations into our analysis.

The asset demand function is also termed the liquidity preference schedule because, given the fact that money is the most liquid of all assets, the demand for money as an asset is necessarily a demand for liquidity. Keynes used liquidity preference to mean the total demand for money in response to all three motives discussed, not just the demand for money to satisfy the speculative motive. In the economic literature that has appeared since Keynes first offered his own ideas on the subject of money, the term *liquidity preference* is generally used in the more restric-

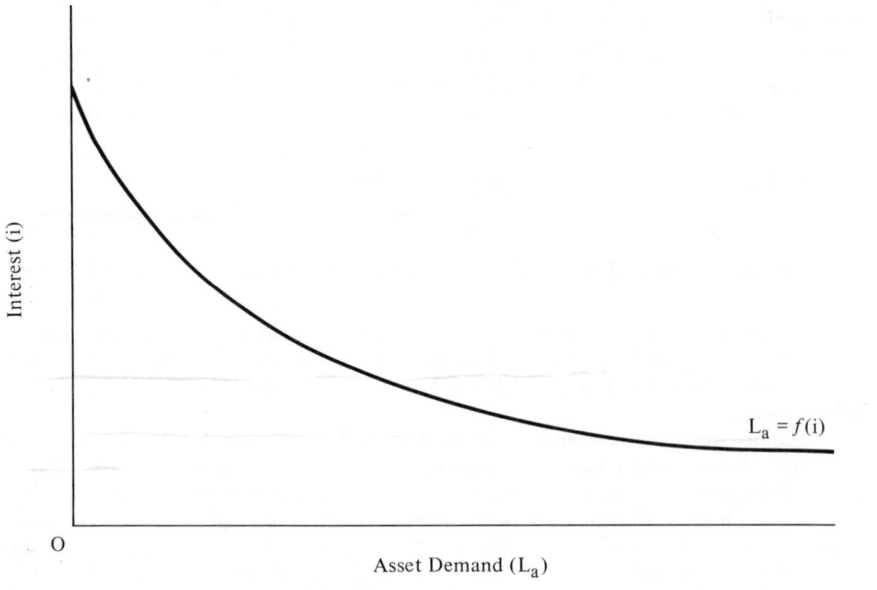

FIGURE 10–4. The Asset Demand for Money

27. In reality the asset demand for money involves more than the simple fact that interest foregone is the opportunity cost of holding money. We shall analyze this relationship more fully after we establish the basic framework for Keynesian interest theory.

tive sense to mean simply the asset demand for money. This matter of terminology is stressed because the interest theory based upon the asset demand for money is usually described as the liquidity preference theory of interest.

Bond Prices and the Rate of Interest

In the preceding section, reference was made to holding bonds as an alternative to holding money. To comprehend fully the rationale for such an alternative the student must understand the relationship between the current market price of bonds and the rate of interest. A bond is a promise to repay at some future date a sum of money which represents the amount borrowed initially by the issuer of the bond. In addition, a bond normally embodies a contractual obligation to pay interest on the amount borrowed. The amount of contractual interest is determined by prevailing market conditions at the time the loan is first made. To illustrate, let us assume that a business corporation issues a series of $1,000 bonds at a time when the market rate for similar long-term bonds is 9 percent. Every individual who purchases one of these bonds—that is, lends the corporation $1,000—is entitled to receive $90 per year until such time as the bonds mature and as long as he retains ownership of the bonds. (Most bonds, both private and public, can be sold prior to the maturity date.) Let us assume that one of the original purchasers wishes to recover the funds he invested in the bonds before they mature. To do so the bondholder can dispose of his holdings in the bond market. If there is a brisk demand for these particular bonds, he may be able to sell his holdings, at a unit price of more than $1,000. If the market is not particularly active, he may be forced to accept less than $1,000. Consider now what takes place if he sells at a price above $1,000, let us say $1,020. The purchaser of the bond is buying a promise on the part of the business corporation to pay $1,000 at some future date; he also stands to receive $90 per year as interest on the bond. But the new holder of the bond has paid $1,020—the current market price of the bond—for an asset which will yield him the same interest, $90 per year, as the original owner received on an investment of $1,000. Thus the current rate of interest has fallen below 9 percent. On the other hand, if the new owner of the bond had been able to purchase it in the market for a price less than $1,000, say, $980, this would mean that the current rate had risen, because for $980 he obtains an asset which will yield him an annual income of $90, which as a rate is better than 9 percent.

Another way to understand the inverse relationship between bond prices and interest rates is to use the example of a consol, the peculiar type of bond without a maturity date (see pp. 311–12). Recall from Chapter 7 that the present value for an asset is given by the discount formula. If that asset is expected to yield income in perpetuity (as in the case of a consol), the formula for determining the present value of that asset becomes:

$$V_p = \frac{R}{i} \tag{10–13}$$

In this formulation R equals the fixed annual income from the consol and i is the current and appropriate (long-term) rate of interest. A simple examination of this formula shows that as long as R is fixed, an increase in the rate of interest (i) must lead to a decline in the present value of the consol, thus causing its market price to decline. If the rate of interest declines, the opposite will take place. Thus, we reach the same conclusion as in the example of bonds issued by a firm, namely, the market price for a bond and the appropriate market rate of interest will move in opposite directions.

The Total Demand for Money

Up to this point we have considered the transactions demand for money, L_t, and the asset demand for money, L_a, as separate functions. This is logical because the determinants of the amount of money held are, in the first instance, income, and in the second, interest. It is possible, though, to combine these two demand functions and obtain a total demand for money. First, we posit the following identity:

$$L = L_t + L_a \tag{10–14}$$

This equation states that the total demand for money is equal to the sum of the transactions demand and asset demand. This being true, we can posit the following functional relationship:

$$L = f(Y,i) \tag{10–15}$$

In this equation the total demand for money, L, is a function of both the income level, Y, and the rate of interest, i.

The combined transactions and asset demand for money is illustrated in Figure 10–5. The rate of interest is measured on the vertical axis; the total demand for money on the horizontal axis. Income as a variable influencing the level of the over-all demand for money is introduced by adding the transactions demand L_t *appropriate to each income level* (see Figure 10–3) to the asset demand function $L_a = f(i)$. The result is a total demand function for money, $L = f(i, Y)$, which combines the asset and transactions demands. As income rises we shall get a series of demand curves for money balances, each one of which is associated with a different level of income. The student should note that the L curves shown in Figure 10–5 are drawn so that they begin to bend backwards at

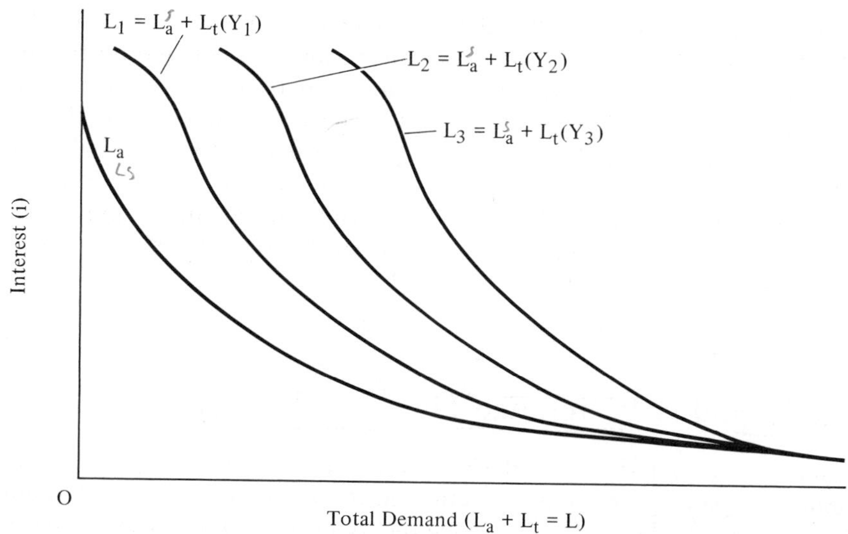

FIGURE 10–5. The Combined Asset and Transactions Demand for Money

the upper ranges of the interest rate. This is because even the transactions demand for money becomes sensitive to the rate of interest at high interest levels.

Some Empirical Findings

Essentially the foregoing analysis tells us that the real demand for money will vary inversely with the rate of interest and positively with the level of output. Does the demand for money behave in this fashion? Since Keynes's *The General Theory* first appeared, there have been a vast number of empirical investigations into the demand for money relationship. No study has yet been able to come up with an exact statement of this relationship, one that could be used without question for predictive purposes. But most of the studies which have appeared do tend to confirm the general theoretical statements made about the demand for money. They show, first, that the demand for money balances is linked positively to the level of real income, and, second, that the relationship between changes in interest rates and the demand for money is an inverse one.

Technically, the magnitude of these relationships is a matter of the elasticities of the demand for money with respect to the two key variables, namely income and interest. The income elasticity of the demand for money is the ratio of the percentage change in money demand to the percentage change in income, and the interest elasticity of the demand for money is the ratio of the percentage change in money demand to the percentage change in the rate of interest. Recent studies suggest that this ratio has ranged between .66 and 1.0 for income and −.33 to −.5 for the rate of interest. To illustrate, if the income elasticity of demand for money were 1.0, this would mean the demand for money balances would grow in direct proportion to the growth in real output. An interest elasticity of demand for money equal to −.5 means that the demand for idle balances will *decline* by one-half a percent for every one percent increase in interest rates. In general, the estimates derived from recent studies pertain to M_1 (currency and demand deposits) and short-term interest rates, such as those for three-month Treasury bills.[28]

The Liquidity Preference Theory of Interest

Keynesian interest theory is derived from the idea that money may be wanted as a store of value just as much as it may be wanted as a medium of exchange. The liquidity preference theory of interest is based primarily upon the asset demand function, although, as we shall see later, a complete theory of interest is not possible without consideration of the transactions demand function.

Fundamental to an understanding of the liquidity preference approach is the concept of interest that is embodied in the analysis. In the classical theory, interest is regarded as the price which equates the supply of and demand for saving; it is considered a phenomenon related to flows rather than stocks. Moreover, interest is seen primarily as the price that is paid for abstinence—the necessary price that must be paid to persuade people not to consume some portion of their current income. The essence of the classical view is that interest is a reward for waiting.

But it is precisely this concept of interest as a reward for saving that Keynes challenges in *The General Theory*. Interest, he argues, cannot be a reward for saving as such because if a person hoards his savings in cash, he will receive no interest, although he has, nevertheless, refrained from consuming all of his current income. Instead of a reward for saving, interest in the Keynesian analysis is *a reward for parting with liquidity*.[29] Interest is the price that must be paid to persuade those who hold idle

28. Interested students should consult the following recent studies on this question. H. Latane, "Income Velocity and Interest Rates: A Pragmatic Approach," *Review of Economics and Statistics,* November 1960; C. Christ, "Interest Rates and Portfolio Selection Among Liquid Assets in the U.S.," in Christ *et al., Measurement in Economics* (Stanford, Calif.: Stanford University Press, 1963); R. Teigen, "The Demand for and Supply of Money"; H. R. Heller, "The Demand for Money: The Evidence from Short-Run Data," *Quarterly Journal of Economics,* May, 1965; Tong H. Lee, "Alternative Interest Rates and the Demand for Money," *American Economic Review,* December 1967; and Stephen Goldfield, "The Demand for Money Revisited," *Brookings Papers on Economic Activity,* 1973:3.

29. Keynes, *The General Theory,* p. 167; author's italics.

money balances in response to the speculative motive to part with the liquidity inherent in such balances. This particular view of the nature of interest takes us back to the question we broached earlier: Why should anyone wish to hold money as an asset in preference to some other form of asset which will yield an income? As we have indicated, the answer is fear and uncertainty with respect to the future value of assets held in forms other than cash. It is necessary to pay people a premium in the form of interest to compensate for the insecurity and diminished liquidity involved in holding assets in other than monetary form at a time of uncertainty. The greater the degree of uncertainty with respect to future economic values, the higher will be the rate of interest.

As stated in *The General Theory*, the rate of interest is "the 'price' which equilibrates the desire to hold wealth in the form of cash with the available quantity of cash."[30] Since we defined the desire to hold wealth in the form of cash in terms of the asset demand function, we can say that the rate of interest is determined by the intersection of the schedule representing the demand for money as an asset—the L_a function—and a schedule representing that portion of the total money supply which is available to hold as an asset. The latter we shall designate with the symbol M_a. This approach to the determination of interest embodies demand and supply concepts, but it is oriented toward stocks rather than flows. For the sake of simplicity in the analysis to follow we shall assume that the money supply is independent of the interest rate. Assuming, however, that the money supply schedule is a positive function of the rate of interest would not change in any way the essentials of the analysis.

The mechanism through which the rate of interest is determined in the liquidity preference theory is demonstrated in Figure 10–6. Interest is on the vertical axis, while the demand for money for asset purposes, L_a, and the supply of money for asset purposes, M_a^o, are shown on the horizontal axis. The asset demand function, $L_a = f(i)$, slopes downward to the right, as suggested previously, and the money supply function, M_a^o, is shown as a straight line drawn parallel to the vertical axis. This signifies that the supply of money for asset purposes is autonomous with respect to the rate of interest. The reason for this is that the liquidity preference analysis assumes that the supply of asset money, M_a^o is given the total supply of money, M^o, a *residual* which is determined by subtracting the quantity of money required to satisfy the transactions demand, L_t, from the total money supply. Given this assumption, the rate of interest is determined by the intersection of the M_a and L_a schedules, for only at this point will the demand for money as an asset be in balance with the quantity of money available to satisfy the speculative motive. This rate is the equilibrium rate and it is designed in the figure as i_e.

In order to understand more fully why the demand for L_a and the

30. Ibid.

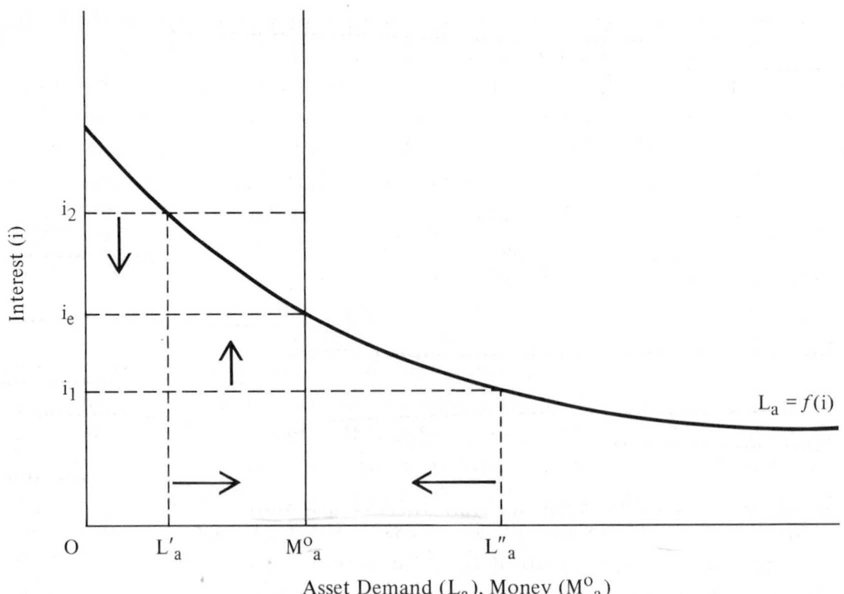

FIGURE 10–6. The Liquidity Preference Theory of Interest Rate Determination

supply of M_a^o must be equilibrated at this particular level of interest rates, let us analyze what will transpire if, momentarily, some other level of the interest rate prevails. For example, what will happen if the interest rate is at the level of i_2, which is higher than the equilibrium rate i_e. At this particular level the asset demand for money L'_a is smaller than the available supply. M_a^o, and, consequently, the rate of interest must fall. Why must it fall? Because at the rate i_2 there exists a situation in which the current price for the surrender of liquidity is so high that people do not want to hold all the asset money that is available. There is, in other words, a surplus of money to hold as an asset, and under such circumstances it is to be expected that the price necessary to persuade people to part with liquidity will come down. This price will continue to fall until a level is reached at which the surplus of asset money is no longer available. This is the equilibrium rate i_e.

The reverse will be true if the rate of interest is below the equilibrium level. Thus at the rate i_1, the demand for money for asset purposes, L''_a, is in excess of the available supply, M_a^o. The rate of interest i_1 is therefore a disequilibrium rate and must rise, because as long as people want to hold more money as an asset than is currently available for this purpose, they will bid up the price for the surrender of liquidity in an effort to persuade some holders to part with their asset money. This process will continue until once again the demand for and supply of money balances are again in equilibrium.

The Bond Market and the Asset Demand for Money

The liquidity preference theory of interest rate determination cannot be fully understood until we see how the asset demand function, or schedule of liquidity preference, is linked to the market for the purchase and sale of bonds.

The essential character of the bond market is shown in Figure 10–7. This is an ordinary demand and supply diagram in which the price of bonds is measured on the vertical axis, and the quantity demanded and supplied is measured on the horizontal axis. *DD* depicts the demand for bonds, and it has the typical negative slope of a demand curve which shows, *ceteris paribus*, that the quantity demanded varies inversely with the price. This curve tells us that buyers are willing to purchase more bonds at a lower price than at a higher price. *SS* represents the supply schedule. This curve ultimately becomes inelastic with respect to price, because if the price goes high enough all bond-holders will want to dispose of their holdings. It is the existing supply of fixed-income assets in the form of bonds that is crucial to the determination of both bond prices and interest rates. Newly issued bonds may have some influence in this connection, but by and large their influence is small in comparison to that exercised by the existing supply.

In Figure 10–7, equilibrium in the bond market exists at the point of intersection of the *DD* and *SS* schedules. The price P_e is the equilibrium price which equates the demand for and supply of bonds. Let us assume that, momentarily, the actual market price is at the level of P_2. This is clearly a disequilibrium situation because at P_2 the quantity of bonds offered (the distance *OM* in the figure) is in excess of the quantity of bonds demanded (the distance *ON*). Why is this so? Since we assumed that bonds and money are the only means to hold economic value over time, and since, too, the existing supply of bonds must be held by someone, the situation shown at the price level P_2 is one in which some bond-holders want to exchange their bonds for the alternative asset form—money. These bond-holders fear that if they continue to hold bonds they may suffer capital losses. This is because they expect that future prices for bonds may be lower than current prices. They see the current price level, P_2 as being "too high;" prudence dictates that they shift to holding cash in anticipation of a decline in the price of bonds. Fear and uncertainty are at work again. But if some bond-holders want to shift from bonds to cash, this is the same as saying that the demand for money as an asset is in excess of the available supply. Why? First, the existing supply of asset money is fixed, and second, if some bond-holders prefer to shift to money as an asset, the demand for money inevitably becomes greater than the existing supply.[31] The counterpart of the situation shown in Figure 10–7, in what the quantity of bonds supplied, *OM* exceeds the quantity demanded, *ON*, is to be found in Figure 10–6 at the rate of interest i_1, for at this rate (which is below the equilibrium rate) the demand for money for asset purposes, L_a, is in excess of the available supply M_a^o.

Once it is understood that Figures 10–6 and 10–7 refer to the same basic phenomenon, it is easy to see why the rate of interest must rise whenever the asset demand for money is in excess of the current supply. Since the situation shown in Figure 10–6 at i_1 is merely a different way of describing a disequilibrium situation in the bond market wherein the current supply of bonds exceeds the current demand at an existing price, then it is inevitable that the rate of interest will rise. As some bond-holders try to shift from bonds to money, current prices for bonds will decline. But a decline in the current market prices of bonds leads to a rise in current interest rates. This process of adjustment will continue until a level of bond prices is reached at which no further attempts are made by present bond-holders to shift from bonds to money. This is the price P_e in Figure 10–7, and it corresponds to the equilibrium rate i_e in Figure 10–6. If no further attempts are made on the part of bond-holders to

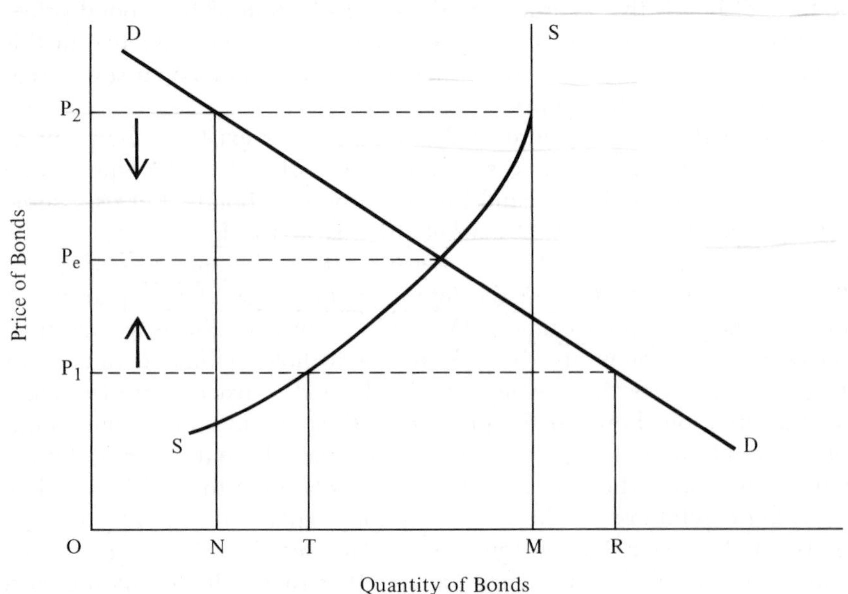

FIGURE 10–7. The Bond Market

31. The reader should note carefully that both Figure 10–7 and 10–6 refer to "stock" phenomena—namely a fixed quantity of bonds (save for the relatively minor influence of new issues) and a fixed quantity of "asset" money.

shift to money, the demand for money as an asset has been brought into balance with the available supply.

A situation exactly the opposite is shown in Figure 10–7 by assuming bond prices to be at the level P_1. At this price the quantity of bonds demanded (the distance OR in the figure) is in excess of the quantity currently available (the distance OT). If the demand for bonds is in excess of supply, this situation is the equivalent of one in which the demand for asset money L_a, falls short of the current supply M_a^o. Consequently, this kind of disequilibrium situation in the bond market is identical to the situation shown in Figure 10–6 at the level of rate of interest represented by i_2. At this level, the asset demand for money, L'_a, is smaller than the available supply M_a^o. Thus the rate of interest will fall; the excess of demand for bonds over the existing supply drives up the current price of bonds and the rate of interest comes down.

Expectations and the Rate of Interest

Our understanding of the liquidity preference theory of interest is not complete without consideration of the role of expectations, specifically the expectations held by both individuals and business firms concerning future economic values. Certain peculiarities of the asset demand function which are of critical economic significance can only be understood through reference to expectations. We saw earlier that uncertainty with respect to the future is the basic reason why some persons prefer to hold money rather than an income-earning asset. This is perfectly sound and logical, but it is not enough. Expectations as to future economic values provide the basic explanation of why individuals and firms shift from money to debt or equity instruments, and vice versa.

Let us return to our model of the bond market in Figure 10–7. At the price level P_2 the available supply of bonds in the market OM is in excess of the quantity currently in demand ON. This leads to a fall in price of bonds. But the disequilibrium situation existing at the price level P_2 means that market conditions are such that there is a general shift from holding bonds to holding money because of fear and uncertainty with respect to future economic values. In the context of this particular market situation, there are more bondholders who expect future bond prices to fall (interest rates to rise) than there are who expect future bond prices to rise (interest rates to fall). At the level of prices represented by P_2 the preponderance of opinion in the market is *bearish*. A pronounced movement from bonds to cash gets under way, and will continue until bond prices in the market have fallen to a level at which the expectations of those who anticipate further declines in bond prices are exactly offset by the expectations of those who anticipate price increases.

Expectations concerning future prices and the kind of behavior that is the consequence of such expectations has meaning only in relation to notions about what constitutes a normal level of bond prices (or interest rates). The balance of opinion in the market is bearish at the price level P_2 only if the majority of traders in the market believe that there does exist some normal level for bond prices, which in this instance must lie below the current price, and to which level current prices will return. As the current price level declines, opinion in the market concerning future prices will becomes less and less bearish. Equilibrium will be reached when bearish opinion in the market is counterbalanced by opinion that is *bullish*.

The foregoing analysis of the shift from bonds to cash can be formulated just as readily in terms of the liquidity preference theory of interest. The situation represented by a price level P_2 for bonds is one in which the rate of interest is at a level such that the demand for money for asset purposes, L_a, is larger than the quantity of money currently available to meet this need, M_a^o. In Figure 10–6 this is the rate of interest represented by i_1. Within the framework of interest rate theory, this situation is one in which the weight of opinion in the market is *bullish* with respect to future interest rates. The majority of traders currently active in the market expect future interest rates to be higher, which is another way of saying that the market anticipates lower prices for bonds. From this situaton there arises the excess demand for cash over the available supply. Again it must be underscored that both current and future interest rates can be interpreted meaningfully only in relation to some concept of normality. The current rate i_1 must be thought of as being below what the market has come to regard as a normal, or safe, rate. Keynes emphasized most emphatically that it is not the *absolute* level of the interest rate which matters, but the divergence of the current rate from what market opinion has come to regard as a *safe* rate.[32] Since the current rate i_1 is thought to be below the safe rate, it follows that expectations that future rates will be higher outweigh expectations that they will be lower. As the current market rises, however, the preponderance of favorable sentiment in the market with respect to future interest rates will subside until eventually an equilibrium rate is reached, at which favorable and unfavorable opinion is again in balance. In Figure 10–6 this gradual shift in the climate of opinion of the market is reflected in a movement upward along the asset demand schedule from the point representing the asset demand for money at the rate of interest i_1 to the point of equilibrium given by the rate of interest i_e.

The introduction of both the bond market and expectations with respect to future value into our analysis provides us with a much fuller

32. Keynes, *The General Theory*, p. 201. For Keynes's complete discussion of these relationships see pp. 170 ff. and 201 ff. in *The General Theory*.

explanation of the shape of the asset demand function than is embodied in the idea that interest is the cost of holding money in preference to some other asset form. Once we understand the relationship between the asset function, the bond market, and expectations, it is possible to see that more is involved in the demand for money than simply the cost of holding it. To illustrate, if the current rate of interest is high relative to what is generally regarded as a normal level, not only will the current cost of holding money be high, but expectations with respect to future prices of bonds will be such that the majority of participants in the market believe that these prices will be higher rather than lower. Thus there is little incentive to hold money in order to take advantage of future market movements. At very high levels of the interest rate, the weight of market opinion will be so overwhelmingly bullish with respect to bond prices that the demand for speculative balances or asset money will be zero. In Figure 10–6 this is of course, the point at which the asset demand function intersects the vertical axis.

Precisely opposite conditions will prevail at interest rates which are low relative to what the market regards as normal. Not only does the cost of holding money become more and more negligible as the rate of interest declines, but, more important, the lower the rate of interest, the greater will be the number of participants in the market who expect future bond prices to be lower rather than higher.As long as some notion of normality exists with respect to both bond prices and interest rates, low levels of the interest rate mean high bond prices and a bond market that is increasingly bearish with respect to future values for bonds. Thus the demand for money for speculative or asset purposes will inevitably grow as the interest rate sinks more and more below levels believed to be normal.

This relationship provides the basis for an explanation of an interesting phenomenon called the *liquidity trap.* In Figure 10–6 this is the point at which the asset demand function becomes perfectly elastic with respect to the rate of interest. Keynes described this as a situation in which liquidity preference may "become virtually absolute in the sense that almost everywhere one prefers cash to holding a debt."[33] The practical meaning of the "liquidity trap" is that it suggests a situation in which the monetary authorities have lost effective control over the rate of interest. Expectations with respect to *future* values for income-earning assets have become so pessimistic that any attempt by the banking authority to lower interest rates by increasing the money supply will fail. All that will happen is that any new money pumped into the system will spill over into idle balances, leaving the interest rate unaffected. Hence, a policy designed to stimulate investment by lowering the rate of interest through monetary means

33. Ibid., p. 207.

would fail if expectations are so darkly pessimistic. Under these circumstances, monetary policy will remain ineffective until there is a change in outlook.[34]

Alternative Explanations of the Demand for Money

The classical and Keynesian ideas about money and its demand traced out in the preceding pages are essentially macroeconomic in character, which is to say they are put in the context of the overall (or total) demand for money. Since Keynes's pathbreaking work on the speculative demand for money, there have been theoretical refinements to the general subject to the demand for money which are closer to the spirit of microeconomics. That is they begin with the individual (business firm or wealth-holder) and treat the demand for money as a theoretical question similar to the demand for any good or service. The results are then generalized to apply to the economy as a whole. Two economists who have made important contributions to our understanding of the demand for money through this approach are Professors James Tobin of Yale and William Baumol of Princeton. Interestingly, their findings are generally in harmony with Keynes's views.

One basic difficulty inherent in the Keynesian explanation of interest in terms of the schedule of liquidity preference and the available supply of money for asset purposes is that it presupposes that persons in the money market will either hold bonds if their expectations are bullish with respect to future bond prices, or cash if their expectations are bearish. Individuals will behave in this fashion if their expectations concerning future movements of bond prices (interest rates) are *certain*. But if not, what then? The fact that there may be uncertainty about what may happen to bond prices (interest rates) in the future may lead an individual to hold both bonds and money—he may be led to diversify his portfolio. As a matter of fact, this is the reality, for the personal wealth portfolio of most people includes at any one time both money and other types of financial assets.[35] What is needed is an explanation for this fact, as well as an explanation of why people shift from holding one type of asset to another.

34. Actually the *liquidity trap* is more a theoretical curiosity than a real possibility for the contemporary economy. In the Great Depression of the 1930s and during World War II, however, interest rates fell to very low levels at the same time that cash balances increased. See James Tobin, "Liquidity Preference and Monetary Policy," *Review of Economics and Statistics,* May 1947, pp. 124–31; and Lawrence R. Klein, "The Empirical Foundations of Keynesian Economics," in Kenneth Kurihara, ed., *Post-Keynesian Economics* (New Brunswick, N.J.: Rutgers University Press, 1954), pp. 277–319.

35. Equities, too, may be included in an individual's portfolio. For purposes of the exposition, though, we will continue to assume the choice is between money and bonds (consols).

Professor Tobin utilizes the concept of risk to explain, first, how it is possible that an individual's asset portfolio may be divided between bonds and cash, and second, why the liquidity preference function (the asset demand) is negatively sloped[36] Tobin reaches virtually the same conclusion as Keynes with respect to the shape of this function, but his explanation is formulated primarily in terms of attitudes toward risk rather than expectations with respect to future bond prices. Tobin's analysis, unlike that of Keynes, does not depend upon the notion of a normal rate of interest for understanding why people may choose to hold money rather than bonds (or vice versa). This aspect of Keynes's analysis has been criticized on the grounds that in time the current rate—assuming it is reasonably stable—may come to be regarded as "normal." If this happens, then a key motive for holding assets in money form disappears. Tobin shows that the asset demand for money will still be inversely related to the rate of interest even if the concept of a normal rate is discarded.

In Tobin's view the world of wealth-holders consists of two kinds of people: risk-lovers and risk-averters. These terms come from the fact that whenever a person holds bonds in preference to cash, he incurs the risk of a capital loss or gain because of uncertain knowledge concerning future bond prices. The larger the proportion of assets held as bonds in preference to money, the greater the risk. The risk-lovers do not have to be induced by higher interest rates to hold bonds instead of cash; they will maximize both risk and interest income by holding all their assets in bonds.[37] If all participants in the money market were risk-lovers an asset demand schedule of the kind shown in Figure 10–4 (p. 330) could not exist.

It would appear, however, that more people in the market are risk-averters than risk-lovers. The risk-averter will first of all, diversify his asset holdings. More important, he will assume more risk—i.e., hold a greater proportion of his portfolio in bonds—only as the rate of interest increases. Higher interest rates are necessary, in other words, to compensate for the additional risk assumed when more bonds and less cash are held. Since this is the case, the asset demand function assumes the shape shown in Figure 10–4. In reality both attitudes toward risk and expectations with respect to future movements of bond prices—or interest rates—constitute

36. James Tobin, "Liquidity Preference as Behavior towards Risk," *Review of Economic Studies*, February 1958, pp. 65–86; see also David E. W. Laidler, *The Demand for Money: Theories and Evidence* (Scranton, Pa.: International Textbook, 1969), pp. 67ff.

37. This is an oversimplification, even though useful for understanding Tobin's basic ideas: It has been shown, however, that even risk-lovers would hold both money and bonds when confronted with uncertainty with respect to both prospective income and expenditures flows. See Roger N. Waud, "Net Outlay Uncertainty and Liquidity Preference as Behavior Toward Risk," *Journal of Money, Credit, and Banking*, November, 1975, pp. 499–506.

forces at work which determine the nature of the asset demand for money.

Professor Baumol's analysis is addressed to the transactions demand for money. Keynes, as did his classical predecessors, treated the transactions demand (including money held in response to the precautionary motive) as determined essentially by the general level of economic activity (See pp.324). Baumol, however, approaches the matter as a problem in inventory management, the inventory being the stock of money the individual or business firm chooses to keep in hand for transactions purposes.[38] It costs something to hold any inventory, including an inventory of money. Thus, what the firm or individual will attempt is to minimize the cost of holding money in response to the transactions demand.

The amount of money an individual needs to hold for transactions purposes depends on the total values of transactions undertaken over a period of time and the frequency of those transactions. Since the receipt of income for an individual or a business firm does not coincide exactly with expenditures, there must be an inventory of cash on hand. This inventory can be obtained fom either holding some portion of income received in the form of cash balances—that is, saving and holding the savings in the form of "immediate liquid command" over goods and services—namely money. Or else it can be obtained by coverting an interest-earning asset (a bond or consol) into cash. These two sources for the cash inventory needed for transactions purposes can be related directly to the costs for maintaining such an inventory—costs which the individual or firm seeks to minimize.

First there is an opportunity cost involved in holding an inventory of cash. This is represented by the current rate of interest, i. This cost exists simply because cash held idle foregoes the opportunity to earn an income through lending at the current rate (purchase of a bond or consol). The larger the inventory of cash held, the greater will be this part of the overall costs for such an inventory. But there are also noninterest transactions (withdrawal) costs which occur each time an income-earning asset is converted into cash. These are broker's fees, as well as any other noninterest cost which may be associated with a conversion to cash transactions (postages, telephone bills, bookkeeping charges, etc.). The more frequently conversion transactions to obtain cash for the inventory are undertaken, the greater will be this aspect of the overall inventory cost. Thus, the total cost for the inventory of cash held for the transactions motive is the sum of interest (opportunity) and transactions (withdrawal) costs.

Now we get to the nub of the problem. If the firm or an individual

38. W. J. Baumol, "The Transactions Demand for Cash: An Inventory Theoretic Approach," *Quarterly Journal of Economics*, November 1952, pp. 545–56. In his analysis, money held in response to both the speculative and precautionary motive is not considered.

holds large cash balances, then there will be few withdrawals to get more cash and, hence, transaction costs will be small. But the opportunity costs of foregone interest become large. On the other hand, the latter are reduced by holding down the size of the cash inventory, but this may necessitate more frequent withdrawals, thus raising the transactions part of total inventory cost. To solve the problem, Baumol developed a formula to determine the size of cash withdrawals (conversion of bonds to money) which would minimize the total cost of maintaining an inventory of cash large enough to finance the volume of transactions over a stipulated period of time.[39] Essentially, the formula shows that the demand for cash balances for transactions purposes will vary positively with both the volume of transactions and transactions costs, but inversely with the opportunity costs (the rate of interest). This finding is also in harmony with earlier conclusions about the nature of the transactions demand (p. 326). The Baumol formula also implies that the demand for cash balances will rise less than in proportion to the increase in transactions, a finding which suggests there are economies in scale in the use of money. The meaning of this is that the richer or more prosperous an individual or business firm is, the greater is their ability to economize in the use of cash. This should not be confused with the tendency of individuals and firms to reduce their cash holdings in response to a rise in interest rates. Both effects may be at work in the modern economy.

Changes in the Rate of Interest

Within the framework of the liquidity preference theory, two types of changes in the level of interest rates may be envisaged.[40] One kind of change involves movement of the interest rate toward an equilibrium position, given the L_a function and the quantity of money available for asset purposes. The mechanics of a change of this type were fully described in the sections which dealt with the liquidity preference theory of interest and the relationship of the bond market to the asset demand for money.

The other type of change involves movement of the rate of interest from one equilibrium level to another. This movement will result from either a shift in the position of the liquidity preference function $L_a = f(i)$, or a change in the quantity of money available for asset purposes. The latter can be brought about either by autonomous action on the part

39. The formula for the optimum size of withdrawal is: $C = 2bT/i$. C is the optimum withdrawal of cash. T is the total transactions in the period, b the costs associated with conversion of earning-assets into cash, and i the appropriate market rate of interest.

40. The analysis here is analogous to that discussed in connection with changes in the equilibrium income level in Chapter 5, p. 142.

of the monetary authorities, changes in the income level, assuming the total money supply responds positively to income, or by a once-over shift in the velocity of circulation. Changes in the income level affect significantly the total demand for money (see Figure 10–5) and consequently the rate of interest, but we shall delay consideration of this until after discussion of the effect upon interest rate of shifts in the liquidity preference schedule.

Figure 10–8 shows a change in the equilibrium interest rate as a result of a once-over change in the position of the asset demand schedule. The shift is from $L_a = f(i)$ to $L'_a = f(i)$. A change of this type will drive the equilibrium rate from the level i_e to the level i'_e. It is best described as a shift in the over-all climate of opinion which affects all participants in the market in the same way. In our earlier discussion of a downward movement of the interest rate level i_2 to level i_e, everyone in the market did not change their expectations about future movements of the rate of interest; only enough had to switch from a bearish position (with respect to interest rates) to a bullish position to make an equilibrium possible at the rate i_e. But the upward shift of the asset demand function is interpreted to mean that the market as a whole expects interest rates to be higher (or bond prices to be lower). Hence there is engendered a general and widespread increase in the demand to hold money as an asset that will lead to a new and higher equilibrium level of the interest rate, i'_e, as long as the supply of money available as an asset is unchanged. A pronounced

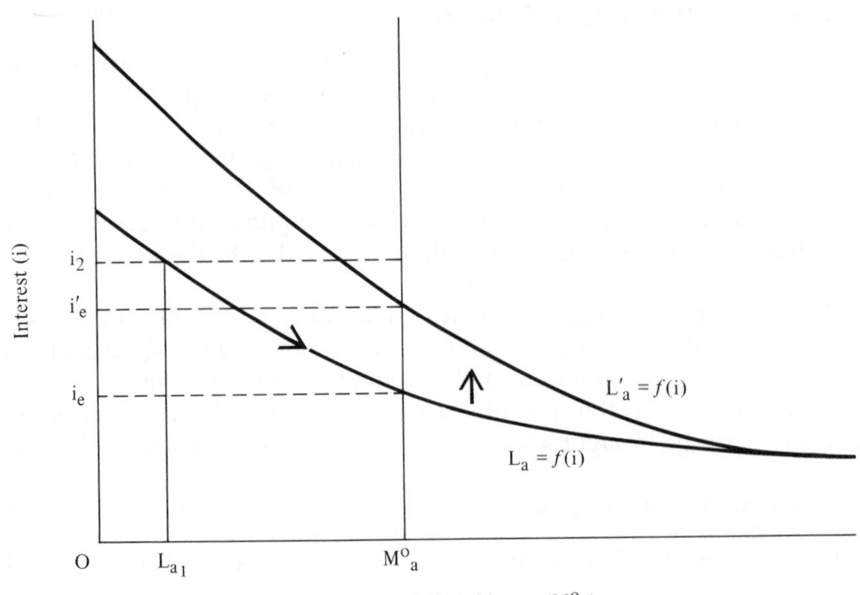

FIGURE 10–8. Shift in the Asset Demand Function

shift in the overall position of the asset demand function means, too, that there has been a change with respect to what is regarded as the normal level of interest rates (or bond prices).

It is difficult to explain precisely what factors cause sudden shifts in the general climate of opinion of the market, although it appears that changes of this type are most likely to be associated with sudden and sharp movements of the economic system from prosperity and expansion into crisis and recession. The demand for money as an asset is likely to be unusally high in such circumstances, thus bringing about a sharp upward movement in the entire schedule of liquidity preference. Downward shifts of the liquidity function, on the other hand, are more likely to be associated with a recovery from recession or depression lows and the return of confidence in future economic values.

The Total Demand for Money and the Rate of Interest

Keynes's liquidity preference theory of interest would be a relatively simple and acceptable theory of interest rate determination, as well as a practical alternative to the classical supply and demand for saving upon theory, if we did not have to take into account the impact of income upon the total demand for money and the relationship of the latter to the rate of interest. Introduction of income into the analysis not only complicates the theory, but makes it impossible to derive a determinate theory of the interest rate apart from a general theory involving the simultaneous determination of income and the rate of interest.[41]

The reader will recall that we constructed the total demand for money by adding the transactions demand prevailing at a given income level to the asset demand. This is shown in Figure 10–5 (p. 333). The significance of this is that we do not have a single curve which relates the demand for money to the rate of interest and which is independent of the income level. The asset demand part of the total money demand curve may be independent of income, but the transactions demand part is not. Thus, we have a series of demand schedules, the position of any one of which is determined by the level of income. What this means for the theory of interest can best be seen by adding a total money supply schedule to our analysis; this is done in Figure 10–9.

Monetary equilibrium, as explained earlier, requires that the total demand for money be just equal to the supply. If we have a series of demand schedules as depicted in Figure 10–9, then there is no single equilibrium rate of interest, but several such rates, each one of which will be associated with a different level of income. Thus, an equilibrium value for the interest rate cannot be determined unless the position of the total demand curve is known. The latter depends, however, upon the income

41. A general theory of the economic system is developed fully in Chapter 12.

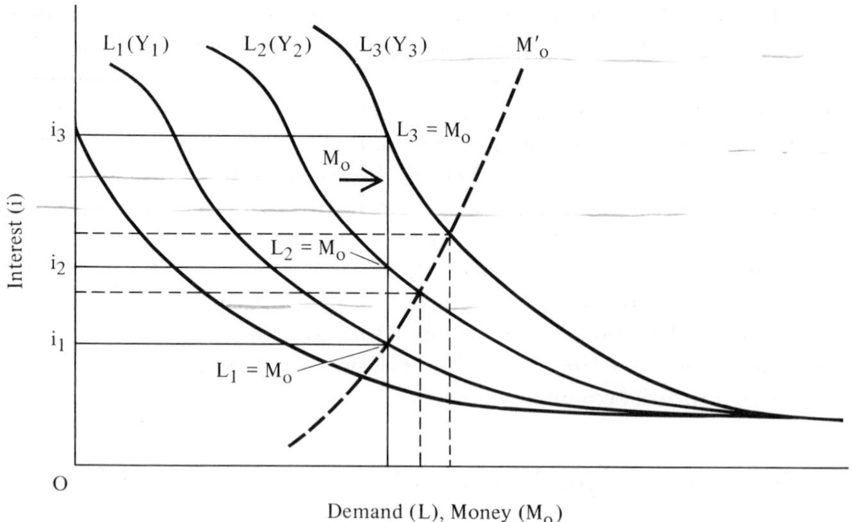

FIGURE 10–9. The Demand for Money, the Supply of Money, and the Rate of Interest

level, and the income level, in turn, depends upon the level of investment, given the consumption function. Investment outlays cannot be determined without knowledge of the interest rate. We are therefore confronted by a chain of interlocking variables, and, our system of income determination cannot be complete until we can construct on the basis of the relationships developed thus far in our text a general theory showing not only the simultaneous determination of both income and the rate of interest, but the manner in which all the key variables are related to one another. This task is undertaken in Chapter 12.

Superimposed upon the basic diagram in Figure 10–9 are a series of dotted lines, including a curve labeled M'_o which is a money supply curve showing a positive link between money and the rate of interest. Introduction of this curve alongside the perfectly inelastic (with respect to interest) money supply schedule designated as M_o does not change the essentials of the foregoing analysis. What it does is show that if the money supply increases when interest rates rise in response to a higher total demand for money, the final equilibrium values for interest rates associated with different income levels will be lower (and the money supply greater) than is the case if the total money supply is assumed to be fixed.

The Significance of the Keynesian Interest Theory

The significance of Keynes's liquidity preference theory of interest does not lie in the fact that it is simply an alternative to the classical theory, an alternative which casts the analysis in terms of stocks rather than flows. The Keynesian theory of interest is important for two major reasons. First it spells out precisely the nature of the monetary sphere of the economic system. Keynesian interest theory makes it clear that monetary equilibrium is the product of different forces than those which produce equilibrium in income and employment. The demand for money as an asset is a major economic force in its own right, but the principles which govern this demand are significantly different from those which govern the demand for goods and services.

Second, Keynes's interest theory provides the necessary theoretical framework to demonstrate that money is not neutral. In the classical theory, money is unimportant precisely because it is neutral, which is to say that money has no role to play in the determination of output and employment. It functions simply as a medium of exchange, in no way affecting the underlying real process of production, exchange, and consumption. Keynes called an economy which uses money merely as "a neutral link between transactions in real things and real assets and does not allow it to enter into motives or decisions . . . a *Real-Exchange Economy*."[42] But in the Keynesian analysis this is not the case. Money, operating through the liquidity preference function, is capable, under the right set of circumstances, of exerting a powerful influence upon the level of both output and employment. Keynes went on to suggest that the non-neutrality of money was the major source of the failure of a market economy to attain continuous full employment without the intervention of government.

Let us examine more fully the meaning of this contention. Because we lack precise knowledge about the future, a market economy, as Keynes never tired of pointing out, is frequently wracked by fear and uncertainty with respect to the future worth of assets of all sorts. But, Keynes goes on to say, the "possession of money lulls our disquietude; and the premium which we require to make us part with money is the measure of the degree of our disquietude."[43] This premium is, of course, the rate of interest and the reason that money "lulls our disquietude" is that it is the asset form that normally has the highest degree of liquidity. When uncertainty and fear predominate, what wealth-holders seek most of all is the security of liquidty.

But here precisely is the rub. A market economy in Keynes's view is geared to produce practically anything in response to demand, save liquidity. The reason lies in the fact that, although money may be demanded

42. John Maynard Keynes, "On The Theory of a Monetary Economy," reprinted in the *Nebraska Journal of Economics and Business*, autumn 1963, pp. 7–9. For a comprehensive discussion of Keynes's views on the significance of money, see Dudley Dillard, "The Theory of a Monetary Economy," in Kurihara, ed., *Post-Keynesian Economics*, pp. 3–30.

43. John Maynard Keynes, "The General Theory," *Quarterly Journal of Economics*, February, 1937, p. 216.

in order to satisfy a need—i.e., that of liquidity—that is just as real as any other human need, it is not produced by the market process in the same manner as are other goods and services. This is because of its other roles, especially that of serving as a medium of exchange. Thus decisions as to the amount of money supplied to the economy are essentially social rather than market decisions. What this means, though, is that, when the demand for liquidity rises, its price, which is the rate of interest, also rises, barring any supply response. The consequence of a sharp rise in interest rates following an increased demand for liquidity is likely to be a drop in investment spending with consequent adverse effects upon output and employment. This is the crux of Keynes's notion that the nonneutrality of money is the key to the inability of a market system to maintain continuous full employment without government intervention.[44]

This view, that the inability of the economy to supply liquidity in response to sudden and unforeseen increases in demand represents a kind of geologic fault inherent to a market system, is less relevant now than when *The General Theory* first appeared. The reason is the emergence over the last third of a century of a broad array of *near monies*, which frequently satisfy the demand for liquidity and respond as well to market forces. Two American economists, Professors John G. Curley and Edward S. Shaw, have been primarily responsible for development and documentation of the thesis that near monies in the form of time deposits, shares in saving and loans institutions, and short-term obligations such as U.S. Treasury bills have many of the same liquidity characteristics as money but also yield an interest return.[45] According to the Gurley-Shaw thesis, near monies are largely created by nonmonetary financial intermediaries, i.e., the mutual savings banks, savings and loan associations, insurance companies, credit unions, and government lending agencies such as Federal Land Banks. The economic importance of these intermediaries lies not only in the fact that they transmit loanable funds from lenders to borrowers, but the kind of debt instruments they create frequently serves as

44. The views embodied in the above discussion about the neutrality or nonneutrality of money should not be confused with the controversy that developed among economists in the late 1950s and during the 1960s over whether money matters. The latter largely had to do with the effectiveness of monetary versus fiscal policy as means to control the general level of economic activity plus the emergence of the modern monetarist—or quantity theory—approach to the role of money in the modern economy, a topic discussed in detail in Chapter 11. For a good review of the "money matters" controversy, see Lawrence S. Ritter, "The Role of Money in Keynesian Theory," in M. G. Mueller, ed., *Readings in Macroeconomics,* 2d ed. (New York: Holt, 1970).

45. John G. Gurley and Edward S. Shaw, "Financial Intermediaries and the Saving-Investment Process," *Journal of Finance,* March 1966. See also by the same authors *Money in a Theory of Finance* (Washington, D.C.: Brookings, 1960); and John G. Gurley, *Liquidity and Financial Institutions in the Postwar Economy,* Study Paper 14, Joint Economic Committee, U.S. Congress, 1960.

a highly liquid asset for the holder. Further, for some of these instruments, such as Treasury bills, the risk of capital loss in holding them as a liquid asset is almost nil by virtue of their short life. Such assets can be held to maturity (a period three to six months) and turned into cash without loss at their face value.

The economic significance of this development for the Keynesian view of liquidity and interest is twofold. First, it suggests that through emergence of the contemporary array of financial intermediaries and near monies, that the market system has developed some acceptable liquidity instruments which are not only alternatives to money, but which also respond to changes in market forces. If this is a correct interpretation, it follows that interest rates are not as sensitive to the demand for liquidity as originally envisaged by Keynes which means, in turn, that the demand for liquidity, powerful as it may be at times, has less of a disruptive potential than heretofore was thought to be the case. Second, the Gurley-Shaw analysis suggests that the existence of near monies reduces the ability of the central bank to engage in a restrictive monetary policy which attempts to raise interest rates as a means of dampening inflationary pressures. The reason is that higher interest rates will stimulate growth in the supply of money substitutes, thereby negating the effect of central bank policy.

11
The Modern Quantity Theory

For nearly half a century the income expenditure—or Keynesian—approach to output determination has dominated income and employment analysis. Keynesianism is now the reigning orthodoxy, just as was the classical theory in the era prior to the Great Depression of the 1930s. But the commanding position that the Keynesian revolution established in macroeconomics has not gone unopposed. Beginning in the 1960s a formidable challenge to the Keynesian orthodoxy surfaced in the form of a modernized version of the classical quantity theory. While the "Monetarist Counter Revolution," so described by one critic,[1] has not succeeded in displacing Keynesian theory as the dominant approach in contemporary macroeconomic analysis, it ranks, nevertheless, as probably the most important theoretical development in aggregate economic analysis since publication of *The General Theory*. This chapter will review the essentials of the modern quantity theory, including analysis of its major points of difference with the more standard income expenditure approach.

Origins of the Modern Quantity Theory

The appearance of a significant challenge to the income expenditure analysis has followed a pattern somewhat similar to the one involved in the more successful Keynesian displacement of the classical orthodoxy. First,

1. Harry G. Johnson, "The Keynesian Revolution and the Monetarist Counter-Revolution," *American Economic Review*, May 1971, pp. 1–14.

an important social problem emerged which appeared invulnerable to solution by established theory; and, second, an alternative body of theoretical ideas came into prominence at approximately the same time. In the case of the Keynesian revolution the critical social problem was, of course, mass unemployment, and the body of theoretical ideas waiting in the wings to displace classical thinking was the system of thought Keynes brought together in *The General Theory.*

To some critics the issue which justifies the search for a new theory is the resistance of rapid and persistent inflation to control by conventional policy measures derived from the Keynesian income expenditure approach to the economy's management. For example, between 1968 and 1976 consumer prices rose 63.6 percent, even though the economy slid through two recessions in this period. In spite of the Johnson administration surtax in 1968, and in spite of restrictive fiscal and monetary policies pursued by the Nixon and Ford administrations, inflation continued unchecked, even reaching the double-digit rate of 10.9 percent in 1974. The combination of rising unemployment and continued inflation gave birth to the unlovely term *stagflation* to describe the condition of the economy.[2] Even the Nixon administration's experiment with comprehensive wage and price controls failed to crush the inflation.

There are, however, a couple of points worth noting about our present situation which weakens the analogy with the 1930s. For one thing, many economists are not convinced that the policy prescriptions which flow from the Keynesian analysis are fundamentally flawed. It may be argued with considerable justification that our current malaise (excessive unemployment and excessive inflation) resulted not from a basic error in theory, but from a failure to apply the policy prescription at the appropriate time. The 1968 surcharge is a case in point. Professional economic opinion was nearly unanimous that the tax increase was needed in 1966, once it became apparent that a massive military buildup was being imposed on a fully employed economy. In 1966, for example, military outlays jumped \$11 billion, a year in which the unemployment rate stood at 3.8 percent. No better formula for economic and social disaster could have been devised than to have stepped up unproductive military outlays under full employment conditions without a corresponding (and offsetting) increase in taxes.[3] The story of the 1970s might have been quite dif-

2. In the 1967–70 recession, for example, unemployment reached 4.9 percent of the labor force and the inflation rate (rise in the consumer price index) was 5.9 percent. In the more serious 1974–75 recession (the worst economic downturn since the 1930s), unemployment climbed to 8.5 percent of the labor force and the inflation rate hit a peak of 10.9 percent.

3. Recall the discussion on the balanced budget thesis in Chapter 8. This suggests that taxes should have been increased by even more than the increase in government outlays if inflationary consequences were to be avoided.

ferent if the Johnson administration and the Congress had been willing to apply Keynesian restraints before the economy became overheated and hard-to-control inflationary forces were unleashed.

There is a second point to consider. In the 1930s there was no doubt that mass unemployment was the single, critical economic problem which confronted the economy. Among professional economists there was probably as much unanimity on this as there has ever been on any single subject. But this is not true as respects inflation. Many economists, of course, view persistent inflation as an important social and economic problem, but not necessarily a more serious social evil than unemployment, even when the latter does not approach the magnitudes experienced in the 1930s. The larger society also reflects this ambivalence. Both the Nixon and Ford administrations tended to view inflation as the more serious problem, but neither was willing to put the economy through the wringer of a massive, 1930s style depression in order to break the upward spiral of prices. No administration could do this today and survive politically, a fact which suggests that unemployment is still viewed as the more serious problem.[4]

Nobel laureate Milton Friedman of the University of Chicago is one of those critics who believe that the Keynesian income expenditure approach is not only an inadequate theoretical instrument for dealing with inflation, but is, perhaps, a cause of continuous inflation. In Friedman's view many "Keynesians"—though not necessarily Keynes himself—came to believe that "money didn't matter,"[5] the reason being the alleged low interest elasticity of investment spending (See Chapter 7). This led many "Keynesians" to advocate a policy of cheap money—that is rapid expansion of the money supply to push interest rates down and expand investment. But this also led, in Friedman's view, to the persistent inflation which has plagued too many countries in the post-World War II era.[6]

Thus for about a quarter of a century Friedman and his followers in the Chicago school have been working on both theoretical and empirical levels to develop a modernized version of the quantity theory of money, capable of explaining fluctuations in income, employment, and the price level. The labels, the modern quantity theory, or monetarism, are attached to Friedman's work mainly because he believes that change in the money supply is the single most important determinant of change in

4. In the 1976 president campaign candidate Carter continuously hammered at the theme of excessive unemployment during the Nixon and Ford administrations.

5. See Chapter 10, pp. 348–51 (The Significance of Keynesian Interest Theory) for discussion of why Keynes believed money was extremely important.

6. Milton Friedman and David Meiselman, "The Relative Stability of Monetary Velocity and the Investment Multiplier in the United States, 1897–1958," in Commission on Money and Credit, *Stabilization Policies* (Englewood Cliffs, N.J.: Prentice-Hall, Inc., 1963) p. 168.

the level of aggregate money income.[7] Until the late 1960s the modern quantity theory was viewed seriously only by Professor Friedman and his most ardent disciples; but since then, it has won at least partial acceptance within the economic profession. Another factor in this development has been a heavy flow of empirical research in support of monetarism from the staff of the St. Louis Federal Reserve Bank.[8] This does not mean that monetarist analysis has succeeded in displacing the income expenditure approach as the primary theoretical frame of reference for macroeconomics, for such is clearly not the case. But it does mean that it represents an important addition to the economic theorist's kit of intellectual tools for analyzing and understanding the economy's total performance.

The Nature of the Monetarist Challenge

A basic point common to the Keynesian and monetarist analyses is the view that in the short-run the economy's output and variations in that output must be explained in terms of total expenditure and changes in expenditure. In this sense it may be said that both approaches operate within a common Keynesian framework. But, aside from this common point of departure, the monetarists believe that the modern quantity theory explains both variations in the price level and money income. The Keynesian income-expenditure approach often assumes constant prices, as its focus has been on such "real" values as output and employment. As we shall see, the price level is a variable which can be readily incorporated into a general equilibrium model of the economic system, a model which is essentially Keynesian in its roots (Chapter 12).[9]

7. Professor Friedman's views on monetarism have appeared in a wide variety of publications, including his regular coulmn in *Newsweek* magazine. Probably the most authoritative statement of his position is the well-known article, "The Quantity Theory of Money: A Restatement," in Milton Friedman, ed., *Studies in the Quantity Theory of Money*, (Chicago: University of Chicago Press, 1956).

8. See especially Michael W. Keran, "Monetary and Fiscal Influences on Economic Activity: The Historical Record," *Review*, Federal Reserve Bank of St. Louis, November 1969; Darryl R. Francis, "Has Monetarism Failed? The Record Examined," *Review*, Federal Reserve Bank of St. Louis, March 1972; and Leonall C. Andersen, "The State of the Monetarist Debate," *Review*, Federal Reserve Bank of St. Louis, September 1973.

9. The constant price approach is followed in Part II in which we developed the basic elements in the income expenditure approach to determination of the output and employment level. The reader will recall that in Chapter 5 an aggregate supply schedule was developed which incorporated the price level, but for the sake of simplicity in explanation the analysis was first formulated in real (constant price) terms (Chapters 5 through 9).

The really crucial difference, though, between monetarism and Keynesianism centers on the issue of what causes changes in expenditures. In the Keynesian model, changes in expenditure—that is, aggregate demand—may be brought about by a variety of factors, including autonomous shifts in the consumption function, increases or decreases in investment as a result of varying interest rates, and, tax and public expenditure changes deliberately engineered by public policy measures. But in modern monetarist theory what really matters are changes in the quantity of money. Money is the key variable. The central idea in the monetarist thesis, in other words, is that changes in the money supply more than any other kind of change explain changes in money income, real output (in the short-run), and the price level. To the modern quantity theorist, the notion that such Keynesian relationships as the consumption function, the investment demand schedule, or the combined transactions and asset demand for money function may shift exogenously and thereby cause changes in output and employment is unacceptable. On the contrary, they hold to the view that any such changes are necessarily endogenous, triggered by prior changes in the quantity of money. The belief that there exists a direct—and causal—link between changes in the quantity of money and changes in money income has been the focus of a major portion of empirical research by contemporary monetarists, including the massive *A Monetary History of the United States, 1867–1960* by Professor Friedman and his coworker Anna Jacobson Schwartz.[10] It is also their contention that monetary influences are much stronger than fiscal ones—i.e., tax and public expenditures changes—in causing changes in the general level of economic activity.

Some of the other differences between the monetarist and income-expenditure approaches are more subtle, but important, nevertheless. The monetarist analysis is cast in terms of the nominal value, that is the current money value, of the relevant variables. This is in contrast to the emphasis in Keynesian analysis upon changes in the underlying real variables of the economic system, especially output and employment. We touched upon this earlier, pointing out that, while the income expenditure approach does not ignore the price level, employment and output fluctuations as well as real economic growth have generally received more attention from Keynesians than has inflation.

In practical terms, the basic meaning of monetarism is that the impact of money is upon such nominal (or monetary) aggregates as the gross national product in current prices, the price level, money wages, or market rates of interest. Thus, the modern quantity theory is essentially short term, for in the long-run monetarists do not believe that real eco-

10. Milton Friedman and Anna Jacobson Schwartz, *A Monetary History of the United States, 1867–1960* (Princeton: Princeton University Press, 1963). See also Anna Jacobson Schwartz, "Why Money Matters," *Lloyds Bank Review,* October 1969.

nomic aggregates such as output and employment are much influenced by the money supply. In the long run what counts are changes in such real factors as the labor force, supplies of natural resources, investment in capital goods, and technology.[11] But in the short run, in the monetarist view, the money supply can be—and is—a "powerful lever for determining income, employment, and the price level."[12] This may happen under two sets of circumstances. If the output can be expanded, then the increase in money expenditures triggered by an increase in the money supply may expand both output and employment. On the other hand, if output cannot be expanded, then money changes will affect only the price level, not such real values as output or employment. How the monetarists explain these relationships is the matter to which we must now turn our attention. What, in other words, is the theoretical framework through which Professor Friedman and other monetarists explain the how and why of the impact of changes in money upon the performance of the economic system?

The Structure of Monetarist Theory

In a nutshell we may characterize Keynesian theory as a theory of the demand for output as a whole cast in the framework of the aggregate demand function ($C + I + G$, in a closed economy). By analogy, the modern monetarist theory can be characterized as a similar theory cast in the framework of a demand for money function that explains how the money supply affects the performance of the economic system. The demand for money is the fundamental behavioral relationship in monetarist theory.

We shall proceed, first, to an examination of the process by which changes in the money supply affect money income and the price level; and we shall follow this with a detailed analysis of Professor Friedman's demand for money function, the key to the entire process, since the monetarists believe that the functional relationship between the quantity of real money people want to hold and its determinants—primarily income and wealth—is highly stable. Two other assumptions are needed, though, to complete the general picture of how changes in the money supply can influence the current level of economic activity: (1) that the velocity of money is also stable and (2) that the central bank (the Federal Reserve System in the United States) can control the quantity of money. It is

11. Leonall C. Andersen, p. 3.

12. David I. Fand, "Monetarism and Fiscalism," *Banca Nazionale Del Lavoro, Quarterly Review*, September 1970.

interesting to note that Professor Friedman believes that the relationship between the quantity of money demanded and the variables that determine it in the modern quantity theory is more stable than the relationship between consumption and its determinants in the income expenditure—i.e., Keynesian—theory. The practical meaning of this is that the velocity of money is believed to be consistently more stable than the Keynesian multiplier k, the consequence being that there is a much more close and consistent relationship between changes in the stock of money and changes in consumption and income than there is between changes in investment outlays (and other autonomous expenditures) and consumption and income.[13]

What then will happen if there is a change in the money supply? Suppose the Federal Reserve creates more money through its open market operations. The initial effect will be to increase money balances in the hands of individuals in the economy. But because an increase in the amount of money will not change the quantity of money that people want to hold in relation to such fundamental determinants as income and wealth, they will seek to readjust their money balances back to the relationship that existed before the Federal Reserve expanded the money supply. To do this they must dispose of the excess money balances, either by spending them or by lending them. As they do this the added spending will bid up prices, expand output, or do both, a process that will continue until the desired balance is restored between money being held and the general level of economic activity. The process just described would, of course, be reversed if the Federal Reserve System chose to reduce the money supply. It is generally agreed by proponents of the modern quantity theory that a lag of six months to a year exists between the initiation of a change in the money supply and its ultimate effects upon money income and the price level.

The essential difference between the Keynesian—or income-expenditure—approach and the modern quantity theory approach to the impact of a change in the money supply on the economy can be illustrated with the aid of a simple diagram, Figure 11–1. In the figure it is assumed that the Federal Reserve is the initiating force for a change in the money supply, a change that in both models works its way into the economic system via the effect of open market operations on the reserves of the commercial banks. Beyond this point, however, the two models display decidedly different *transmission* mechanisms. In the Keynesian model the increase in the money supply operates through the liquidity preference function (see Chapter 10) to influence the rate of interest. Changes in the rate of interest, in turn, impinge upon investment spending via the investment demand function. The ultimate change in total spending—and hence the

13. Friedman and Meiselman, p. 186.

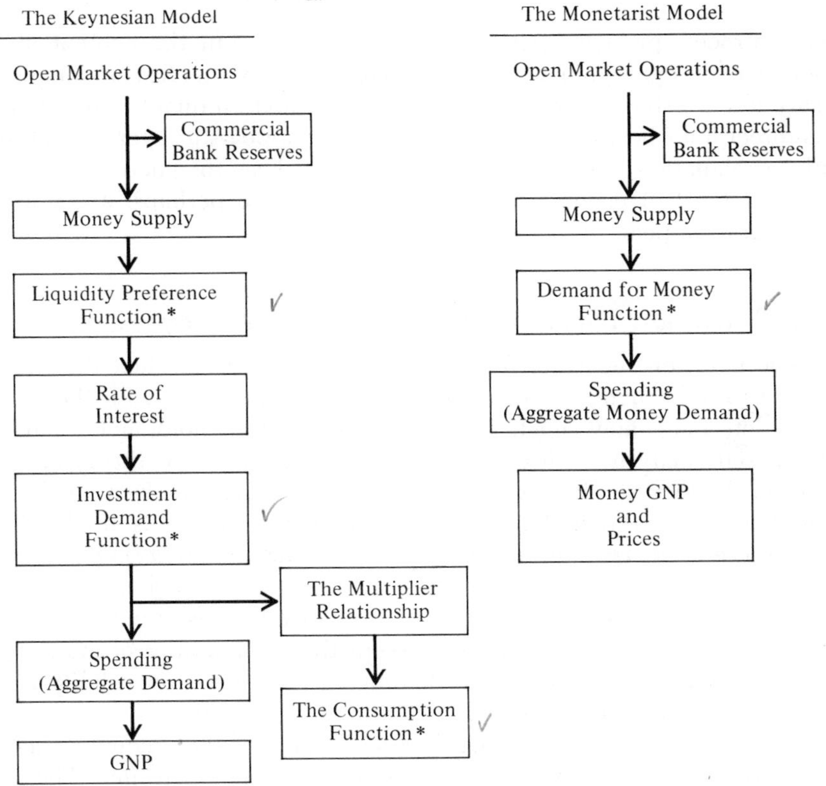

FIGURE 11–1. Keynesian and Monetarist Models Compared

output level—will depend upon the value of the multiplier (whose size depends upon the consumption function) and the amount by which investment spending changes. A key to the way in which the transmission mechanism works in the Keynesian model is the sensitivity of interest rates to the demand for cash. More money will prompt firms and households to exchange some of the excess money for income-earning assets, a process which pushes down interest rates. Indirectly, then, the demand for real output may be stimulated. But the latter cannot take place in the Keynesian model without a prior adjustment in the financial portfolio of the firm or household.

Monetarism tells a different story, one involving a much shorter transmission mechanism with respect to changes in the money supply and aggregate spending for output. In a nutshell, the monetarist's position is that any increase in the money supply spills over directly into the market for goods and services. Understanding the how and the why of this process must wait until we analyze in the next section the nature of Friedman's theory of monetary demand. There is, however, a portfolio adjustment process present in the monetarist's model, but the content of the portfolio differs significantly from that found in the Keynesian model. This, too, we shall explore. In any event, the modern quantity theory with its direct links between money and spending appears to offer a much simpler explanation than does the Keynesian analysis for fluctuations in the general level of economic activity, a fact which, perhaps, accounts for some of its appeal.

The Friedman Theory of the Demand for Money

The point of departure for Friedman's analysis is the fact that people desire to hold money. Friedman is concerned primarily with the factors that determine how much money people want to hold, not, as in the Keynesian analysis, with their motives for holding it. His theory also differs in another significant way from the Keynesian analysis in that he employs a special definition of money. In his view money is anything that will serve as a *"temporary abode for generalized purchasing power,"* a definition that may cover some types of earning assets such as time deposits that do not serve as a medium of exchange.[14] This is not a matter of basic importance for our purpose, except that some critics of monetarism claim that Friedman's empirical findings attesting to the validity of his analysis depend upon his special definition of money.[15]

Friedman identifies three major determinants of the amount of money that households and business firms will hold at any given time. These are (1) the total wealth in all forms of the household or business firm, (2) the opportunity cost of holding money, and (3) the tastes and preferences of the wealth-holding unit. Money in his analysis is viewed like any other commodity or good which yields some utility through its possession. Consequently, the gain—or utility—to be gotten from its possession has to be balanced against the utility forgone by not holding other forms of wealth. In a conceptual sense this view is quite similar to the Keynesian idea that money, through its liquidity, offers utility to its possessor; where it differs significantly is in its specification of the variables which determine the amount of money held.

To flesh out this bare-bones explanation of the quantity of money that households and business firms will hold at any one time, we need to look at all the variables which enter into the three major determinants Professor Friedman postulates. This we can do with the aid of Figure 11–2, which presents in schematic form a formal structure of the variables which determine the demand for money.

14. Stephen W. Rousseas, *Monetary Theory* (New York: Knopf, 1972), p. 161.

15. Dwayne Wrightsman, *An Introduction to Monetary Theory and Policy* (New York: Free Press, 1971), p. 112.

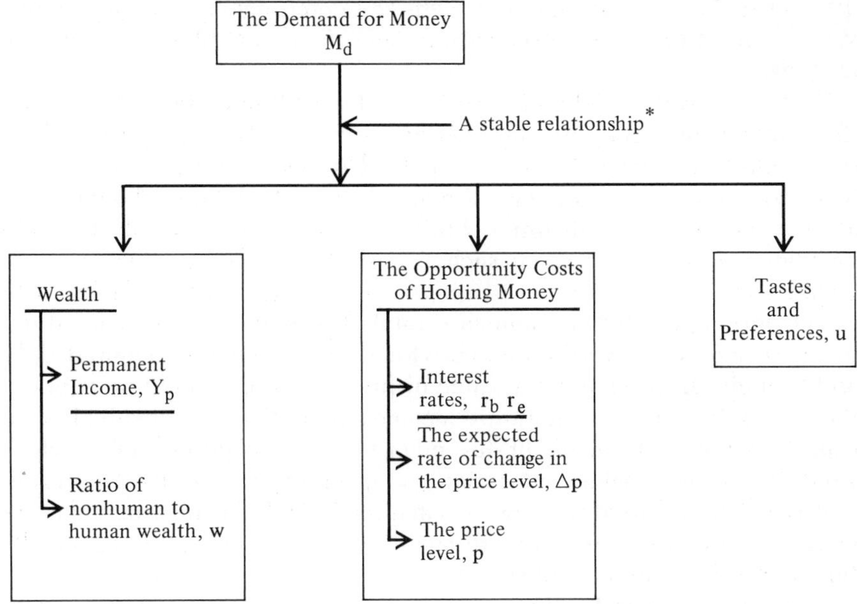

*In equation form the relationship is: $M_d = f(Y_p, w; r_b, r_e, p, \Delta p; u)$

FIGURE 11–2. The Friedman Demand for Money Function

The meaning of these variables may be stated as follows:

1. M_d = the demand for nominal money balances. Although the basic functional relationship is expressed in nominal terms, this does not mean that the holders of money are subject to the money illusion. Monetarists view the demand for money balances as ultimately a demand for real balances, which means that nominal balances must be adjusted for changes in the price level.[16]
2. Y_p = money income in Professor Friedman's permanent sense (see Chapter 6).
3. w = the ratio of nonhuman wealth to human wealth.
4. r_b = the rate of return on bonds.
5. r_e = the rate of return on equities.
6. p = the general price level.
7. Δp = the expected change in the price level.
8. u = the tastes and preferences of the wealth-holding units.

Essentially Professor Friedman holds that, first, the above variables which determine the amount of money that people want to hold do not change much in the short run; and, second, the relationship between the

16. In some versions of Friedman's basic equation (shown in the figure) the demand for money is shown as a demand for real balances, which can be done by dividing both sides by p.

demand for money balances and these key determinants is highly stable. We now need to see more specifically how these variables enter into the analysis.

First, there is the matter of wealth. Total wealth in all forms enters into the demand for money function because it represents the upper limit to the amount of money that can be held. No one, in other words, could hold more money than an amount equivalent to the total of the individual's financial worth in all forms. Professor Friedman's concept of wealth includes more than just assets such as cash, bonds, and equities. He also includes in it various types of tangible capital (such as producer and consumer durable goods) and human capital. The latter, as was pointed out in Chapter 6, is the worth of an individual's inherited and acquired skills and training. In principle, the value of human capital would be equal to the discounted value of the future income stream that an individual could expect to obtain from all of his inherited and acquired skills, which would, obviously, include education and training in all forms. The reader will recall from our discussion in Chapter 7 that the present value—or worth—of any asset is found by discounting its expected future income by the appropriate rate of interest.

In Friedman's words, "From the broadest and most general point of view, total wealth includes all sources of 'income' or consumable services."[17] Included in the latter is the productive capacity of human beings, as well as various physical and financial assets (nonhuman wealth) that an individual may own. The rub in this is the extreme difficulty involved in the measurement of human wealth. Therefore, Friedman uses permanent income (Y_p) as a proxy for wealth in his demand for money function. As the reader will recall from the discussion in Chapter 6, permanent income is defined as the expected average annual return that an individual would get from the sum of all his or her wealth, including human capital.[18]

Given the foregoing, how does the demand for money vary with the stock of wealth? Professor Friedman believes that the holding of money balances should be regarded as a luxury, much like the demand for education and recreation. Consequently, he maintains that the amount of money the public wants to hold not only will increase as wealth—i.e., permanent income—increases, but it will increase more than in proportion to the increase in the stock of wealth. This means in technical terms that the income elasticity of demand for real cash balances is greater than one. In

17. Friedman, "The Quantity Theory of Money," p. 4.

18. Recall, too, from the discussion in Chapter 6 that there is no precise and readily available practical measure of "permanent income." Friedman uses a weighted average of past and present measured income (the income an individual actually receives in a year), with less weight being attached to measured income the farther it lies in the past.

testimony before the Joint Economic Committee of the Congress, Professor Friedman suggested that past experience in the United States (at least prior to World War II) indicates that 1 percent increase in real income per capita tends to be accompanied by nearly a 2 percent increase in the quantity of real cash balances held.[19] In his analysis of the demand for money balances, Professor Friedman clearly regards wealth as a factor which overshadows all the other determinants.

One may ask at this point why is there included in the analysis a variable w representing the ratio of nonhuman to human wealth? Since we do not provide a market for human capital that would establish a rate of return on such capital (this would be possible in a slave society, but we, fortunately, do not live in such a society), there is no simple way in which you can include in the analysis a variable that represents any direct measurement of human wealth, a point of difficulty mentioned earlier. But the individual has some opportunity through education and training to substitute human capital for nonhuman capital (and vice versa) in his total stock of personal wealth. This, though, is a process that takes place only with a considerable lapse of time; hence, in the short term the ratio w will be relatively stable. Since as a practical matter it is difficult to turn wealth in the form of human capital into cash—one cannot easily borrow on the strength of future earning power—Friedman argues that this will be compensated for by a greater demand for cash as the human component in the total stock of an individual's wealth increases. Thus, the relationship between M_d and w is an inverse one.

What is the cost of holding money? This portion of Friedman's demand function for money is remarkably similar to the Keynesian liquidity preference function, except that Friedman introduces changes in the price level into the analysis in addition to the rate of interest. Basically in Friedman's analysis, the cost of holding money is twofold: (1) the rate of interest that could be obtained if bonds or equities were held instead of money, and (2) the effect of changes in the price level on the demand for nominal money balances. The underlying theoretical relationship is inverse, which is to say, when the cost of holding money rises less will be held and when it falls more will be held.

How this works with respect to the rate of interest should be clear from our earlier discussion of the liquidity preference function. In the income expenditure approach, it will be recalled, the demand for money for asset purposes (the speculative demand) varies inversely with the

19. Milton Friedman, "The Supply of Money and Changes in Prices and Output," in *The Optimum Quantity of Money and Other Essays* (Chicago: Aldine, 1969), p. 175. Friedman's views do not agree with other and more recent findings. For example, a 1973 Brookings Institution study found that the income elasticity of demand for money was less than unity. See Stephen M. Goldfeld, "The Demand for Money Revisited," *Brookings Papers on Economic Activity*, 1973:3.

rate of interest. Moreover, the interest elasticity of the demand for money balances is relatively high. As a consequence, as we saw in the previous chapter, any change in the money supply will significantly affect the rate of interest and, indirectly, the level of investment spending. Professor Friedman and other monetarists do not deny that interest rates have an influence upon the amount of money held, but unlike the Keynesians, they maintain that the effect is relatively small.[20] The monetarists, in other words, argue that the interest elasticity of demand for money balances is quite low. Further, they do not make the distinction found in the income expenditure approach between money held as an asset and money held for normal transactions purposes.

What about expected changes in the price level? They work in a different fashion. An expected increase in the price level, for example, has the effect of making it more costly to hold money, since both the real value of nominal money balances will be lessened and the market value of other assets will rise. Thus, there will be a smaller demand for nominal money balances. The reverse would take place if the price level were expected to fall.

The matter is quite straight-forward as respects the price level. Since the demand for money function as shown in Figure 11–2 (see also footnote 16) is formulated in nominal terms, an increase in the price level, p, will result in a proportionate increase in M_d. This must occur if money balances in real terms are to remain constant. Professor Friedman believes that this factor is not particularly significant when price changes are small —a few percent a year—but it becomes of major importance when changes in the general price level are large and continue for a long period of time.

The third major determinant is designated as u in the basic schema presented in Figure 11–2. As Friedman says, "The tastes and preferences of wealth-owning units . . . must in general simply be taken for granted in determining the form of the demand function. . . . it will generally have to be supposed that tastes are constant over significant stretches of space and time."[21] The meaning of this is that no significant change in the amount of money people wish to hold can be expected in the short term as a result of any basic change in their attitude toward holding money as compared to other forms of holding wealth.

As a practical matter, Professor Friedman's theory of the demand for nominal money balances can be reduced to the proposition that there are really four major determinants of this demand. These are (1) wealth or permanent income, (2) the price level, (3) the rate of interest, and (4) the rate of increase in the price level. In its most elementary form, his theory holds that the demand for money varies directly with the first two

20. Ibid, p. 176.
21. Friedman, "The Quantity Theory of Money," p. 8.

and inversely with the latter two. If we transpose his theory into a demand for real balances, it says, in effect, that this demand varies positively with wealth (permanent income) and inversely with the cost of holding money (interest and expected inflation rates).

Now that we have analyzed the essentials of Friedman's theory of the demand for money, we are in a position to examine more carefully how the modern quantity theory works—how, in other words, we get from changes in money to changes in spending for output. The first point to note is the presumed stability of the money demand relationship; this means that if (for any reason) this relationship is disturbed, an effort will be made by persons and firms to restore the relationship. Since the money demand relationship concerns the amount of real cash balances people and firms desire to hold, anything that increases or decreases these holdings will cause them to try and get back to the level of holdings desired on the basis of the enumerated determinants of these holdings. This is why velocity becomes so important. The stability of the Friedman demand for money relationship requires that the velocity of money be stable. If velocity is not stable, then it is quite possible that a disturbance to the existing cash balances position (more or less money becoming available) may be offset by a change in velocity. If this were to happen, then the close link between the demand for money balances and the other variables—particularly income—is broken. This point can, perhaps, be more clearly seen if it is put in the context of the original quantity theory based upon the equation of exchange ($MV = pY$). If we think of the quantity theory as a theory of the demand for money (as Friedman does) rather than a theory of the price level, we have the following equation:

$$M = 1/V\,(pY) \tag{11-1}$$

In this equation, the reciprocal of velocity ($1/V$) is a coefficient which links the demand for nominal money balances to nominal income. If there is to be a stable relationship between the demand for money and the general level of economic activity, then V must also be stable. If it is not, then there is no possibility for the kind of relationship suggested by the modern quantity theory, a point to which we shall return subsequently.

A second basic point concerns monetarism's concept of what should be included in the portfolio of persons and firms. It differs from the ideas found in the Keynesian approach. The reason is because Friedman in his theory of the demand for money balances defines wealth to include *all* assets held, including both producer and consumer durable goods. In contrast, the Keynesian approach limits the portfolio of a person or firm to idle money balances and financial assets (primarily bonds). This is why Friedman's point about the low interest elasticity of demand for money balances becomes crucial. A low interest elasticity of demand for money balances simply means that the willingness of people to hold money as an asset is not especially responsive to the rate of return being obtained on other financial assets, especially bonds (consols). In Keynesian analysis, however, this is a key point, because it is the sensitivity of the demand for money balances to the rate of interest that accounts for the action people or firms take when their monetary equilibrium is disturbed. But if the quantity of money that people want to hold as an asset is not particularly sensitive to changes in the yield on bonds, then excess cash balances are just as likely to be spent for goods and services as for bonds. As a matter of fact, Friedman and the monetarists believe that any excess money balances will spill over directly into the spending stream for goods and services, primarily because the substitution effect between money and the range of financial assets available to the firm or the household is small. Critics of monetarism maintain that they—the monetarists—have not yet demonstrated conclusively the sequence of events whereby excess money finds its way into spending channels. This issue is unresolved.

Policy Implications of the Modern Quantity Theory

While the theoretical differences between the Keynesian income expenditure approach and the monetarist position are subtle and complex, the policy implications of these two visions of how the economy really works are, perhaps, even more important.

The modern quantity theory not only has a deep kinship with classical economics because of its stress on the importance of the money supply, but also because it reverts back to the classical idea that a market economy is not inherently unstable, which is to say that it is not subject to abrupt and wide fluctuations in employment and output. One of the leading proponents of the monetarist point of view has succinctly summarized the monetarist position on this point as follows:

> A central monetarist proposition is that the economy is basically stable and not necessarily subject to wide variations in output and employment. In other words, the economy will *naturally* move along a trend path of output determined by growth in its productive potential. Exogenous events such as wars, droughts, strikes, shifts in expectations, changes in preferences, and changes in foreign demand may cause variations in output around the trend path. Such variations will be mild and of relatively short duration. This basic stability is brought about by market forces which change rates of return and the prices of goods and services in response to these exogenous events.[22]

22. Leonall C. Andersen, "A Monetarist View of Demand Management: The United States Experience," *Review*, Federal Reserve Bank of St. Louis, September 1971.

But are exogenous events the only cause of fluctuations in output and employment? The answer is no, for the monetarists—and here their view contrasts most sharply with the Keynesian outlook—hold that the major source of short-run economic instability is mismanagement of the money supply by the monetary authorities, which in the United States is, of course, the Federal Reserve System. In sum, exogenous events over which we have no control emerge in the monetarist view as the explanation of long-term fluctuations in output and employment, while government action is seen as the cause rather than the cure for short-term economic instability. It almost goes without saying that this is a point of view 180 degrees out of phase with the Keynesian vision of what the economy is really like. Since the 1930s the fundamental thrust of aggregate theory has been that the private market economy is inherently unstable, primarily because of the volatility of investment spending. Accordingly, government should play a stabilizing role, not only by varying its taxes and expenditures to offset fluctuations in private spending, but also by actions which will influence both private spending for consumption and investment in ways favorable to stabilization.

The monetarist's faith in the underlying stability of the economic system stems from a point already mentioned, their belief that significant variations in real economic variables such as output and employment cannot take place if the trend line of growth for the underlying real determinants—labor, capital, and technology—is stable. And monetarists think this is the case. Professor Friedman stressed essentially this idea in his 1967 presidential address to the American Economic Association in speaking of the "natural rate of unemployment," a rate determined by relationships among such underlying real factors as real wages, the rate of capital formation, and technological change.[23] The clear implication of his analysis is that changes in any of the important real aggregates of the economy are beyond the reach of the short-term policy instruments of government, fiscal or monetary.

But if this is the case, what policy is appropriate? Given the stable demand function for money, and given, too, the strong belief that only such nominal variables as money GNP and the price level are affected by the money supply, then money alone becomes the appropriate policy instrument for affecting economic activity. Central bank control of the money supply is, in the monetarist's view, the single most powerful means we have to influence the over-all level of economic activity, far more powerful in their view than fiscal measures involving changes in taxes or public expenditures.

How should the central bank proceed in the conduct of monetary

23. Milton Friedman, "The Role of Monetary Policy," *American Economic Review*, March 1968, p. 8.

policy? As the monetarist's basic theoretical proposition—the demand function for money—indicates, the price level is clearly something that the monetary authority can control. But Professor Friedman and the monetarists reject using the price level as a guide for policy, partly because the link between policy decisions by the central bank and the price level is more indirect than the link between these policy decisions and the quantity of money.[24] The more important reason is the existence of time lags of an unpredictable length between changes in the money stock and the variables affected by such changes, including the price level. Therefore, in Professor Friedman's words, "We cannot predict at all accurately just what effect a particular monetary action will have on the price level and, equally important, just when it will have that effect. Attempting to control directly the price level is therefore likely to make monetary policy itself a source of economic disturbance because of false stops and starts."[25]

The time lags are the real rub and, because they exist, the central bank should not attempt to pursue a countercyclical stabilization policy of varying the money supply in response to its reading of current economic conditions. What the monetary authority should do is adopt a rule that would allow the money supply to grow at a rate of between 3 and 5 percent a year and adhere strictly to this rule, ignoring the current state of the economy. Professor Friedman has never ceased to argue for this policy, and has even gone so far as to suggest that there should be a legislated rule requiring the Federal Reserve System to increase the money supply at a specified rate. *This has been and remains the essence of the policy recommendations of the modern quantity theory.*

The Outcome of the Monetarist Challenge

What has been the outcome of the monetarist challenge to the essentially Keynesian structure of modern income and employment theory? In answering this question, it is important to caution the reader that many of the issues raised by the resurgence of the quantity theory in a modern guise have by no means been settled. The exact and proper role of money in modern theory remains in an unsettled state.

The issues raised by the monetarist challenge are both theoretical and empirical, although Professor Friedman believes they are more empirical than theoretical. In any event, there has been a rash of empirical studies since the mid 1960s that aim either to refute or uphold the contention that the modern quantity theory offers a better guide to the explanation and

24. Ibid., p. 15.
25. Ibid.

determination of the income level than the more standard income expenditure analysis.

Out of the swirl of controversy which has engulfed the economics profession for more than two decades, several major issues have emerged and been clarified, if not resolved—issues important to both the monetarist and the Keynesian positions. These include (1) the question of whether changes in money or changes in autonomous expenditures in the Keynesian sense are most important in explaining short-term changes in output, employment, and the price level; (2) the basic stability of the demand function for money, a matter primarily of the stability of velocity; (3) the interest elasticity of the demand for money; and (4) the ability of the central bank to control the supply of money. We shall examine each of these.

Aside from the massive *A Monetary History of the United States, 1867–1960*, Friedman's most important attempt to find empirical verification for his best argument is the study[26] he completed in collaboration with David Meiselman for the Commission on Money and Credit, a body established in 1957 by the Committee for Economic Development, a private research organization. The basic purpose of the Commission was "to initiate studies into the United States monetary and financial system." Among economists this research has come to be known widely as the Friedman-Meiselman study.

What the authors attempted in this study was to test empirically the validity of the Keynesian and monetarist theories, using in each case highly simplified one-equation models.[27] Having established the two models, they proceeded to "test" them by using regression analysis to fit actual data to the equations for the years covered by the study. What did they find? As between the two theories (the Keynesian and the monetarist), Friedman and Meiselman reported:

> The empirical results are remarkably consistent and unambiguous. The evidence is so one-sided that its import is clear without the nice balancing of conflicting bits of evidence, the sophisticated examination of statistical tests of significance, and the introduction of supplementary information that the economic statistician repeatedly finds necessary in trying to decide questionable points. . . .
>
> The income veocity of circulation of money is consistently and decidedly stabler than the investment multiplier except only during the early

26. Friedman and Meiselman, op. cit.

27. The monetarist equation was $Y = a + V'M$, and the Keynesian equation was $Y = \alpha + K'A$. In these equations Y represented income over time. The monetarist equation expresses income as a linear function of the stock of money, M. V' equals income velocity. The Keynesian equation expresses income as a linear function of autonomous expenditures, A. K' is the multiplier. These equations were their departure point. They were modified before having actual statistical data fitted to them.

> years of the Great Depression after 1929. . . . Moreover, such relationship as there is between autonomous expenditures and consumption seems simply to reflect the influence of money in disguise. . . .[28]

As expected, the Friedman-Meiselman study aroused a storm of controversy in the economics profession, one which has not yet settled down. Basically, two major criticisms were leveled against Friedman and Meiselman. First, the fundamental basis for the comparison was challenged on the grounds that their one equation model of the Keynesian system was a wholly inadequate representation of the Keynesian explanation of how income is actually determined. As a result, the findings were held to be "essentially worthless."[29] As we have seen in the earlier chapters, the Keynesian model of income determination is quite complex, involving construction of an aggregate demand schedule by trying to explain how its major components (consumption, investment, government spending, and net exports) are determined. Such a model cannot be represented by a single, simple equation of the type used in the Friedman-Meiselman study.

The second point of challenge is, perhaps, even more fundamental. It involves a point raised in the first chapter of this text, namely the difficulty of determining causation even though there is correlation. In the Friedman-Meiselman study this has been described by critics as the problem of reverse causation. It is true that changes in the money supply and changes in income are closely correlated. But it is just as plausible to argue that changes in income caused changes in money—after all more money is needed when income goes up—as it is to argue that changes in money caused the changes in income. Statistical correlation does show how two variables may move together, but it can't tell which variable is the cause and which is the effect. As one critic has said, "theoretical issues cannot be resolved by playing the game of 'correlation, correlation, who's got the highest correlation?' "[30]

A second major effort to demonstrate the validity—as well as the superiority—of the monetarist model came a few years after the Friedman-Meiselman study appeared. This was by the staff of the Federal Reserve Bank in St. Louis. In 1968 two economists from this staff, Leonall C. Anderson

28. Friedman and Meiselman, p. 186.

29. Albert Ando and Franco Modigliani, "The Relative Stability of Monetary Velocity and the Investment Multiplier," *American Economic Review*, September 1965, p. 693. In their article Ando and Modigliani also argue that a properly constructed income expenditure model meets the test of statistical correlation just as well as does the more simple monetarist model. See also Michael de Prano and Thomas Mayer, "Tests of the Relative Importance of Autonomous Expenditure and Money" in the same issue of *American Economic Review*. There were also responses by Friedman and Meiselman in this issue.

30. Rousseas, p. 185.

and Jerry L. Jordan, published a study similar in design to the Friedman-Meiselman study in which they sought to do two things: first, test the relative effectiveness of monetary and fiscal policies; and, to develop a basic monetarist model for predicting aggregate demand.[31] What they found was the monetary (as compared to fiscal) actions were generally larger, more predictable, and faster, findings which they believe vindicated the monetarist position. Unfortunately for the state of economic science, the controversy was not so easily settled. Other studies involving econometric models reached different conclusions. One of the most widely used of such models is the one developed jointly by the Federal Reserve System and the Massachusetts Institute of Technology, generally known as the FR/MIT model. In contrast to the monetarist position, in which critics say the transmission mechanism is ill-defined (a sort of "black box" whose workings are hidden from view), the FR/MIT model identifies three channels through which monetary policy works.[32] These include the cost of capital, which affects primarily spending for equipment, business structures, and housing; the net worth of consumers, which affects consumer spending; and, finally, credit rationing, which refers to a situation in which lenders ration credit by various nonprice means.[33] It emerges whenever interest rates are sluggish and fail to respond quickly to market forces. Credit rationing was found to be especially important with respect to the link between savings institutions and the housing market. Figure 11–3 below is a flow chart developed by the Federal Reserve to show how the first round effects of monetary policy work in the FR/MIT model. The view incorporated in this flow chart is basically Keynesian, since it shows that changes in money affect spending flows primarily through their impact upon interest rates.

Not only is the FR/MIT econometric model different in structure from the one developed by the St. Louis Federal Reserve Bank, but the results from use of the model are also decidedly different. Essentially, simulation experiments with the FR/MIT model show that the economy will respond as the Keynesian analysis suggests to an expansion of government expenditures which is sustained. It also shows that the impact of changes in the money supply is much smaller than the impact shown in the Andersen-Jordan (St. Louis Federal Reserve) studies, and that monetary policy works more slowly than fiscal policy, the reason being that it takes time before open market operations are reflected in changes in long-term inter-

31. Leonall C. Andersen and Jerry L. Jordan, "Monetary and Fiscal Actions: A Test of Their Relative Importance in Economic Stabilization," *Review*, Federal Reserve Bank of St. Louis, November 1968.

32. For a detailed account of the structure of the FR/MIT models see Frank de Leeuw and Edward M. Gramlich, "The Channels of Monetary Policy," *Federal Reserve Bulletin*, June 1969, pp. 472–91.

33. Ibid.

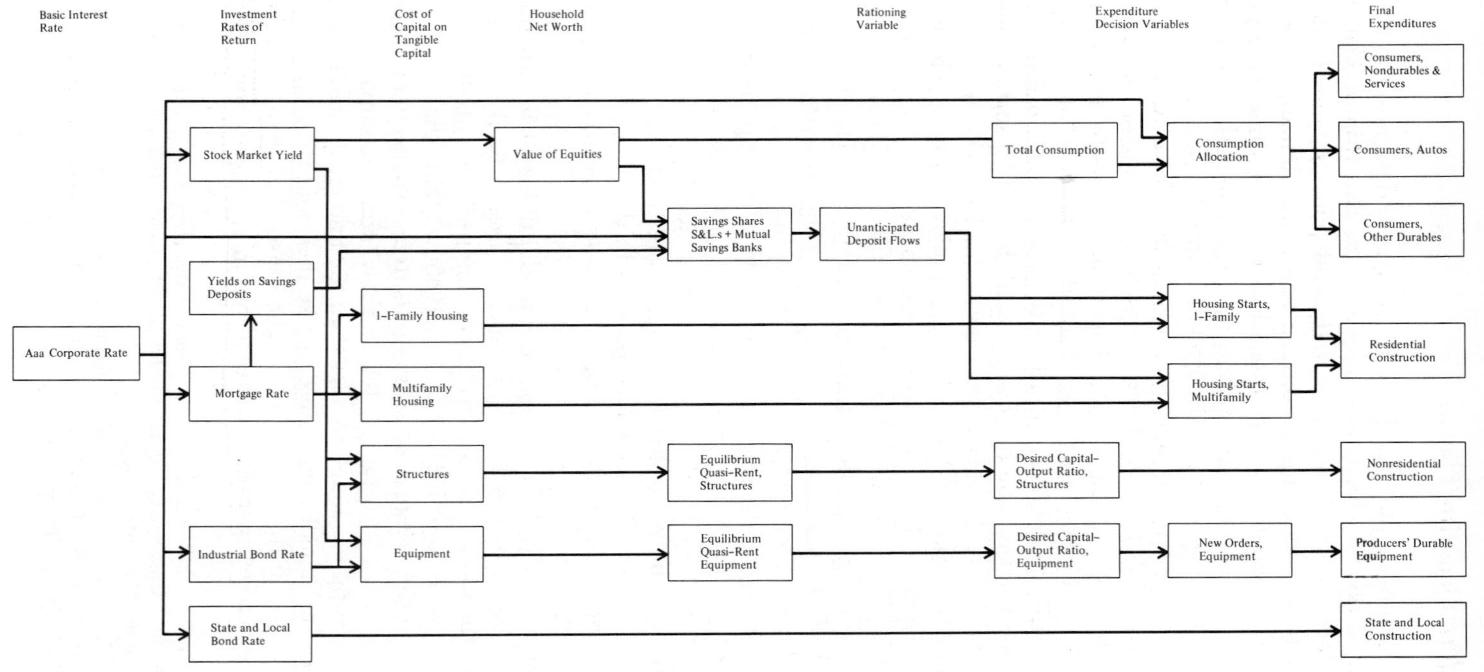

FIGURE 11–3. Flow Chart: First-round effects of monetary policy

est rates.[34] In another study which made use of the same measures of fiscal influence used originally in the Andersen and Jordan study, Professor Roger N. Waud of the University of North Carolina found that fiscal measures were as significant as monetary measures in influencing the level of economic activity.[35] The fiscal influences used in the Waud analysis were high-employment federal expenditures and high-employment federal tax receipts. In order to avoid the problem of reverse causation, Waud developed a disaggregated model in which he examined the demand for production workers' man-hours in several durable goods industries. It was assumed that the demand for production workers in these industries would accurately reflect the general level of economic activity over the period of his study, 1953–68. His basic finding was that "*fiscal influences on economic activity, as measured by the employment of production worker man-hours in durable goods manufacturing industries, are significant and operate in the directions conventionally assumed.*"[36]

Where does all the above leave the matter? Basically still unresolved, as the econometric and empirical tests devised to date have not been able to demonstrate conclusively that either the money supply or the Keynesian autonomous variables are the most important determinants of changes in output, employment, and the price level. Certainly the debate will continue, as the monetarist school strongly believes that money is the key to these changes but Keynesian economists—no doubt still a majority in the profession—believes that money has a role to play, but its importance is vastly overrated by the modern quantity theory approach to economic stabilization and management. Perhaps we can put the controversy into somewhat better perspective if we keep in mind that *neither* fiscal nor monetary policies in isolation (or taken together) have yet proved adequate to cope with the serious and persistent problem of *stagflation*. Finding an answer to the chronic malaise of excess unemployment *and* excess inflation is the most pressing problem which modern macroeconomic analysis confronts.

Let us turn now to the other issues between modern monetarism and the Keynesian analysis. The second point (p. 369) involves the basic stability of the demand function for money, an issue which ultimately involves the question of the stability of the income velocity of money

34. For further details on the findings based upon the FR/MIT model see Frank de Leeuw and Edward Gramlich, "The Federal Reserve-MIT Model," *Federal Reserve Bulletin*, January, 1968, pp. 11–40; Richard G. Davis, "How Much Does Money Matter? A Look at Some Recent Evidence," *Monthly Review*, Federal Reserve Bank of New York, June, 1969, pp. 119–31; and de Leeuw and Gramlich, "The Channels of Monetary Policy."

35. Roger N. Waud, "Monetary and Fiscal Effects on Economic Activity: A Reduced Form Examination of Their Relative Importance," *Review of Economics and Statistics*, May 1974, pp. 177–87.

36. Ibid., p. 186 [Italics in original].

(GNP/M_1). Friedman has said that this does not mean that the velocity of circulation of money has to be numerically constant over time; rather the stability involved in the monetarist position " . . . is in the functional relations between the quantity of money demanded and the variables that determine it."[37] The import of this is not that velocity cannot change, but that the change be gradual and predictable. This seemed to be the case until relatively recently—between the end of World War II and 1974, velocity rose at a relatively steady rate of about 3 percent per year, but beginning in 1975 the rate of increase nearly doubled. Figure 11–4 shows the path of the income velocity of money since 1968.

The sudden upsurge shown in Figure 11–4 has raised serious doubts about the stability of the demand function for money, doubts which did not exist a few years ago, even among economists not sold on the over-all validity of contemporary monetarism. Professor Stephen M. Goldfeld of Princeton University said in a recent study[38] that ". . . the U.S. economy is once again experiencing an apparent shift in the demand for money function. . . . when money-demand functions that have been successfully fitted to pre-1974 data are extrapolated into the post-sample period, they consistently and significantly overpredict actual money demand." For example, Goldfeld found that for all of 1975 the actual demand for money was $15.8 billion less than the predicted demand, and for the first two quarters of 1976 the actual demand was $22.3 billion below the prediction. He also found that using an equation of the type developed in the St. Louis Federal Reserve Bank model to predict GNP understated the actual growth in GNP by more than $100 billion. Perhaps J. Charles Partee, a member of the Board of Governors of the Federal Reserve System, summarized the situation correctly when he said, "Velocity is another element of uncertainty in setting money growth targets. There never was all that much certainty between money and GNP, and now there is less."[39] The upshot of this aspect of the monetarist-Keynesian controversy is simply that if the money demand function is not stable, then the monetary authority (the Federal Reserve System) has—and will continue to have—great difficulty in determining just how much money is needed to keep the economy functioning.

If no consensus has been reached among economists on either the relative importance of fiscal vs. monetary measures, or on the basic stability of the demand for money function, this is not the situation with respect to the link between the rate of interest and the demand for money. On the issue of the interest elasticity of the demand for money, the evidence, as one critic puts it, is overwhelmingly "in favor of the proposition that the

37. Milton Friedman, "The Quantity Theory of Money—A Restatement," p. 5.

38. Stephen M. Goldfeld, "The Case of the Missing Money," *Brookings Papers on Economic Activity*, 1976:3, pp. 683, 728.

39. Quoted in *Business Week,* May 30, 1977.

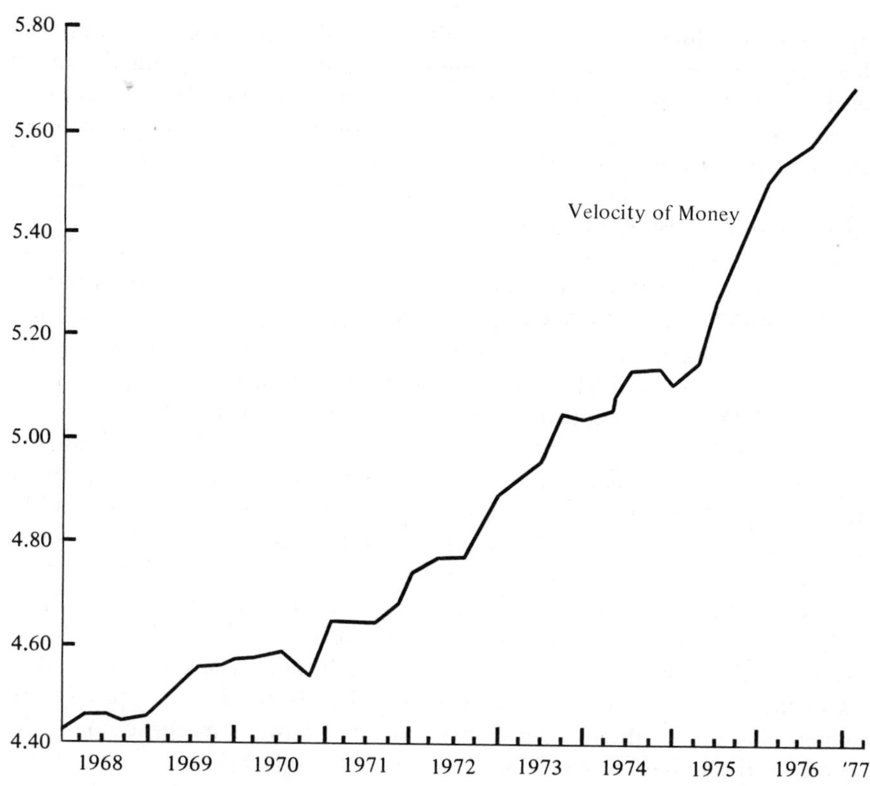

FIGURE 11–4. Income Velocity of Money (GNP/M_1): 1968–1976

demand for money is stable and negatively related to the rate of interest. Of all the issues in monetary economics, this is the one that appears to have been settled most decisively.[40] This finding tends to weaken the monetarist argument that the demand for money is not significantly affected by interest rates. On the other hand, the evidence from the same empirical studies casts doubt on the Keynesian notion that at very low rates of interest, the demand for money balances becomes highly elastic. There is no empirical support for the idea of a liquidity trap, in other words. In sum, the evidence suggests that the demand for money is sensitive to the rate of interest, but not nearly so sensitive as the early Keynesian analysis indicated.

Finally we turn to the money supply. The weight of the evidence is that the total money supply can be controlled with reasonable accuracy by the monetary authorities, although this does not mean that it is wholly

40. David E. W. Laidler, *The Demand for Money: Theories and Evidence* (Scranton, Pa.: International Textbook, 1969), p. 97.

autonomous. Such control is established and maintained through the leverage the central bank has on high-powered money, a point discussed earlier. On the other hand, as we have seen (Chapter 10), the money supply also responds positively to the rate of interest; the implication of this is that the money supply can accommodate itself to changes in level of money GNP, as well as influence money GNP, a point not viewed with favor by the monetarist school.

Before concluding this chapter a few comments are in order on the theoretical aspects of the controversy over the modern quantity theory. One distinguished economist has said that Professor Friedman's elaborate formulation of the modern quantity theory is really nothing more than "a most elegant and sophisticated statement of modern Keynesian monetary theory."[41] Once the special meanings that Professor Friedman gives to wealth and the costs of holding money are understood, the basic similarities between his demand function for money and the Keynesian demand for money relationship (see Equation 10–15 and Figure 10–5) should be apparent. Of greater importance and theoretical interest was the attempt Friedman made in the early 1970s to develop a theoretical framework which would explain what he believed that he had demonstrated empirically was true—namely that there is a close and direct link between money and nominal values for the GNP.[42] All along the chief contention of critics of the modern quantity theory has been that the process by which changes in money get translated into changes in the demand for goods and services is much too vague. Although Friedman's statement helped clarify points which were disputed or unclear in his earlier—and more empirically oriented—statements of the monetarist position, it did not succeed in putting an end to the controversies which surround the modern quantity theory—even at the theoretical level. Even some monetarists were disturbed, as they thought Friedman's effort to clarify the transmission mechanism inherent in monetarist theory only brought him closer to the Keynesian view of this process. Friedman's discussion, they said, is ". . . either misleading or a complete reversal of his often stated position."[43] A strong partisan of Keynesian economics charged that Friedman basically did not really understand the essential character of Keynes's analysis, especially the role that uncertainty plays in the Keynes-

41. Don Patinkin, "The Chicago Tradition, the Quantity Theory and Friedman," in Don Patinkin, *Studies in Monetary Economics* (New York: Harper & Row, 1972), p. 108.

42. Milton Friedman, "A Theoretical Framework for Monetary Analysis," in Robert J. Gordon, editor, *Milton Friedman's Monetary Framework: A Debate With His Critics*, (Chicago, Ill.: The University of Chicago Press, 1974), pp. 1–62.

43. Karl Brunner and Allan H. Meltzer, "Friedman's Monetary Theory," in Robert J. Gordon, op. cit., p. 72.

ian system.[44] The debate seems destined to go on—both empirically and theoretically.

Perhaps the most appropriate note on which to conclude this discussion of the modern quantity theory is by reference to a comment to the effect that the real differences between Friedman and the Keynesians are more ideological than theoretical.[45] And this is probably true, for in a fundamental sense the monetarist counterrevolution is an attack upon the basic Keynesian notion that a market economy is inherently unstable and if it is to work at all well, government must play a stabilizing role, using to the best of its ability monetary and fiscal means to attain this objective. The Keynesian attack on the classical theory demolished the intellectual foundations for *laissez faire* as acceptable public policy; the monetarist counterrevolution seeks to restore these foundations.

44. Paul Davidson, "A Keynesian View of Friedman's Theoretical Framework for Monetary Analysis," in Robert J. Gordon, op. cit., p. 91.

45. Rousseas, p. 196.

12

General Equilibrium and the Neoclassical Synthesis

This chapter has three objectives. First, we shall develop a general equilibrium model of the aggregate economy which is based upon explicitly Keynesian ideas, namely aggregate demand (as developed in Part II) and the liquidity preference theory of money and interest.[1] Second, this model will be expanded by introducing into it a labor market sector and the price level. The labor market sector is essentially classical in spirit and concept, which is what gives this expanded model of the Keynesian system the name, the "neoclassical" synthesis.[2] In Chapter 13 we shall use

1. This model of the economic system was originally developed by J. R. Hicks. See his article, "Mr. Keynes and the Classics: A Suggested Interpretation," reprinted in *Readings in the Theory of Income Distribution*, (Philadelphia: Blakiston, 1946) pp. 461–76.

2. The phrase "neoclassical synthesis" appears to have been invented by Professor Paul Samuelson to describe the combination of Keynesian and classical economic principles which he thought provided an adequate basis for policy measures (primarily monetary and fiscal actions) for managing the modern economy at a high level of employment. Interestingly enough, this phrase appeared in the 6th and earlier editions of his famous text (*Economics*, New York, McGraw Hill), but has been dropped from later editions. Many economists use the term "a complete Keynesian model" to describe the model enlarged by the addition of the labor market and price level, since it has become the dominant post-World War II interpretation of Keynes. But "neoclassical synthesis" is perhaps more accurate, especially in view of the criticisms being directed against this version of Keynes.

these models to examine contemporary policy issues. Finally, the chapter will conclude by introducing the reader to a growing body of economic literature which dissents from the neoclassical interpretation of Keynes on the grounds that it is a misinterpretation and misreading of *The General Theory*.

The Keynesian Model of General Equilibrium

Aside from its usefulness as an integrating device for all the important elements entering into the theory of income determination, the Keynesian general equilibrium model shows clearly the essential differences between the monetary and goods spheres of activity in the economic system. The stress on the distinction between these two segments of the economy is one of the most fundamental contributions of the Keynesian analysis. This general equilibrium model also provides a simple and effective means to contrast the effects of fiscal and monetary policy actions. Another important use of the model is to demonstrate through the concept of general equilibrium the manner in which the two spheres of the economy are linked together. The rate of interest provides a bridge between forces affecting the demand for money balances and those which revolve around the demand for goods and services.

The interdependence of the rate of interest and the level of income makes the model truly general; the underlying system of functional relationships operates in such a manner that it is not possible to determine the equilibrium income level without simultaneously determining the rate of interest. The model illustrates this clearly.

The approach that we will use in the development of the Keynesian general model is to show the necessary conditions under which equilibrium may obtain in the monetary and goods spheres of activity taken separately, and then, the conditions under which equilibrium may exist in both spheres simultaneously. The latter analysis will provide us with the model which demonstrates the nature of equilibrium in the economic system as a whole.

Equilibrium in the Monetary Sphere

The *monetary sphere* refers to the economic activities which center around the demand for and the supply of money to hold. These activities are also lumped under the phrase the *money market* because they include the different forms in which wealth-holders seek to hold economic value over time.

Monetary equilibrium exists when the total demand for money to hold,

L, is equal to the current supply, M^o.[3] The Keynesian demand for money, as we have seen, breaks down into two major components, the transactions demand, L_t, and the asset demand, L_a. Thus, $L = L_t + L_a$. The money supply can also be broken down into the quantity needed for transactions purposes, M_t^o, and a residual amount available for holding as an asset, M_a^o. Consequently, $M^o = M_t^o + M_a$. Therefore the following equation gives us a symbolic statement of the essential condition for monetary equilibrium:

$$L_t + L_a = M_t^o + M_a^o \qquad (12\text{–}1)$$

The total demand for money, L, is a function of both income and the rate of interest because one of its components, the transactions demand, is a function of income, while its other component, the asset demand is a function of the rate of interest. This means that equilibrium with respect to the transactions demand is linked to income, and equilibrium with respect to the asset demand is linked to the rate of interest. Consequently, general equilibrium in the monetary sphere must be defined in terms of both the income level and the rate of interest.

Part A of Figure 12–1 is a series of L functions, each representing a combined transactions and asset demand function. Each function is associated with a different level of income. M^o is a schedule representing an endogenous money supply curve.[4] The figure yields a series of monetary

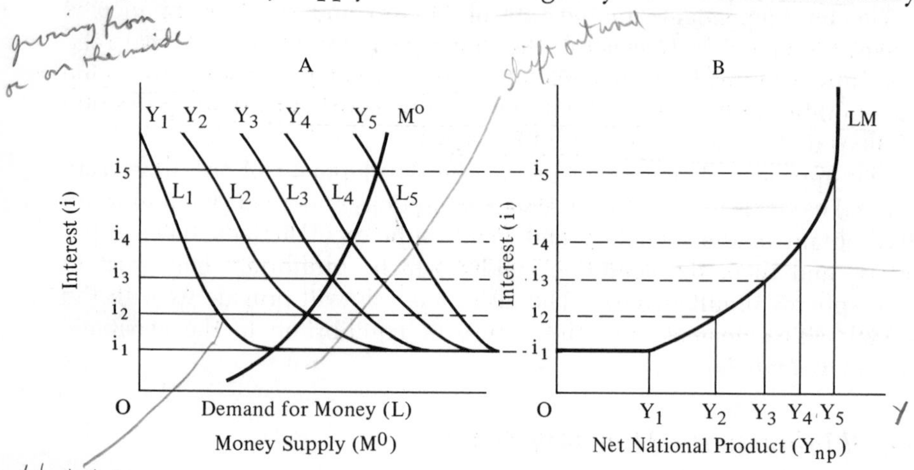

FIGURE 12–1. Equilibrium in the Monetary Sphere

3. Remember the analysis is cast in real terms, which is to say L is the demand for real balances and M the real money supply. Price level considerations will be dealt with later.

4. See Chapter 10, pp. 314-16, for a review of the process of bank credit expansion and a discussion of the theoretical reasons why the money supply curve is endogenous; that is, responds to changes in the rate of interest.

equilibria; each equilibrium is associated with a particular income level and a particular rate of interest. To illustrate, if the economy's income level is equal to Y_1, the money demand function, L, will be at the level of the curve labeled L_1. Given this particular function, and given the money supply, M^o, monetary equilibrium exists at the point of intersection of the L_1 and the M^o schedules. This is at the rate of interest i_1. Now if the income level rises to Y_2, the money demand function will necessarily shift upward. Its new position is given by the curve L_2. With the money demand function at this level, monetary equilibrium again prevails at the point of intersection of the money demand and money supply curves, but it will be at the higher rate of interest i_2. As long as the income level is rising, this process continues and monetary equilibrium exists only at higher and higher rates of interest.

The explanation for the series of L functions in Figure 12–1 was given in Chapter 10. If the money supply is less than perfectly elastic, additional amounts of money needed to sustain more transactions can be obtained only by drawing them out of idle balances or through an expansion of bank credit. But interest is the price that must be paid to persuade people to surrender the liquidity inherent in holding money balances; therefore, the only way to draw more and more funds out of inactive holdings is through higher and higher interest rates. The general lesson of our analysis should be quite clear: a rising level of real income will almost inevitably lead to higher interest rates unless the money supply is increased sufficiently to offset the continuous upward shift of the money demand function. The latter does not happen in the example shown, even though there is a positive response of the money supply to higher interest rates. Actually the only way in which the interest rate could be held constant would be for the money supply curve to be perfectly elastic—that is, horizontal. But this is an unrealistic assumption, as it means the banking system would supply the economy with unlimited quantities of money (credit). The real world is not like this.

The LM Schedule

The essential nature of equilibrium in the monetary sphere and the manner in which it is linked to both the income level and the rate of interest are shown graphically in Part B of Figure 12–1, which is derived directly from Part A. The income level, Y, is measured on the horizontal axis; the rate of interest, i, on the vertical axis. Using the data from Part A we can plot a series of points, each point representing a particular rate of interest and income level at which monetary equilibrium, $L = M$, prevails. Thus, at the income level Y_1 monetary equilibrium exists at a rate of interest equal to i_1: at the income level Y_2, at the rate of interest i_2; and so on. When we connect all these points together, we obtain a smooth curve known as the *LM* schedule, since it describes a series of equilibria between the demand for money, L, and the supply of money M^o, in terms of a relationship between the income level and the rate of interest.

In Figure 12–1 it will be noted that at relatively low income levels the *LM* schedule lies flat or, in technical terms, is perfectly elastic with respect to the rate of interest. On the other hand, at relatively high income levels the *LM* schedule becomes vertical or perfectly inelastic with respect to the rate of interest. What are the reasons for this? The *LM* curve is constructed, it will be recalled, on the assumption that the total supply of money is relatively fixed. This being the case, at low levels of income, the transactions demand for money, L_t, will also be relatively low. Therefore a large portion of the total money supply will be available for holding as idle balances. But any increase in the quantity of money available to hold as an asset, M_a^o, drives the rate of interest down. There is a limit to the extent that the rate of interest can fall, for as we saw in the analysis in the last chapter the asset demand function becomes perfectly elastic at relatively low rates of interest. This is the liquidity trap. Once we reach the critical level at which interest rates do not respond to any further increases in the quantity of money available for holding as idle balances, then the *LM* curve must become perfectly elastic with respect to the rate of interest. A further decline in income will not, in other words, cause any further decline in interest rates through the impact of money balances released by a declining transactions demand. As pointed out in Chapter 11 there is little empirical evidence to support the idea that the demand for money may become perfectly elastic.[5] We include this possibility in our discussion, however, for the sake of theoretical completeness and to point up later the differences at the extreme between the policy implications of Keynesianism and a pure classical analysis. The latter involves a total absence of a speculative demand for money balances.

The vertical character of the upper reaches of the *LM* curve is explained by the fact that without action by the monetary authorities to increase bank reserves, the money supply curve will ultimately become inelastic with respect to the rate of interest. Thus there is some maximum income level that can be financed with a fixed quantity of money.[6]

5. Even Keynes who invented the concept of the liquidity trap recognized its rarity in the real world. In *The General Theory* (p. 207) he said, "There is the possibility . . . that after the rate of interest has fallen to a certain level, liquidity-preference may become virtually absolute in the sense that almost everyone prefers cash to holding a debt which yields so low a rate of interest. . . . *But whilst this limiting case might become practically important in the future, I know of no example hitherto.* Indeed, owing to the unwillingness of most monetary authorities to deal boldly in debts of long term, there has not been much opportunity for a test." [Italics added.]

6. Hicks, p. 470.

Money, in other words, can become a bottleneck that will choke off an expansion of income beyond some given level. As the income level rises, the transactions demand for money will obviously increase. A higher level of income means more transactions, and more money will be needed to sustain the larger volume. But if the total money supply does not grow as rapidly as transactions increase, additional quantities of money for transactions purposes can be obtained only by drawing them out of idle balances.[7] The cost of doing this is a higher rate of interest, and, as the income level rises, interest rates must rise higher and higher. Eventually the economy will reach a critical level at which any further expansion in the income level becomes impossible because the entire money supply is now held in transactions balances, and M^o is no longer responsive to increases in the rate of interest. In Figure 12–1 (Part B) Y_5 is assumed to be the maximum income that an amount of money, M^o, can sustain.

The effect of an increase in the money supply function on the position of the *LM* curve is shown in Figure 12–2. The initial position of the *LM* curve is shown by the solid line LM_1. The dotted line LM_2 represents a shift in the position of the curve. This type of shift would reflect action by the central bank to increase the money supply, presumably by putting more reserves into the commercial banks. The reason why an increase in the money supply will shift the curve to the right can be easily understood by referring once again to Figure 12–1 (Part A). The existence of a fixed money supply schedule meant that monetary equilibrium at each and every possible income level was uniquely associated with a particular rate of interest. An increase in the money supply shifts this curve to the right, thus making possible monetary equilibrium at any particular income level at a lower rate of interest than heretofore. To show this situation in terms of the *LM* curve, it is necessary to shift this curve to the right as is done in Figure 12–2. Each point on the LM_2 curve represents a particular income level that is uniquely correlated with a rate of interest that is lower than the rate correlated with the point representing the same income level on curve LM_1. The effects of a decrease in the money supply would be just the reverse, that is, the *LM* curve will shift to the left.

7. This assumes, of course, that the income velocity of money is unchanged. An increase in velocity can have the same effect as an increase in the money supply. As pointed out in Chapter 11, velocity did increase sharply, beginning in 1975, a development which cast doubt on the stability of the demand for money function, the centerpiece of the modern quantity theory. But this increase in velocity also enabled GNP (in current prices) to grow at a more rapid pace than the money supply. For example, in two years (1975 and 1976) nominal *GNP* grew by 19.8 percent, whereas the money supply (M_1) grew by only 10.2 percent. Our purpose, though, is to analyze the effect on the monetary sphere—particularly interest rates—of a rise in the output level, assuming velocity is relatively constant and the supply of money is not perfectly elastic.

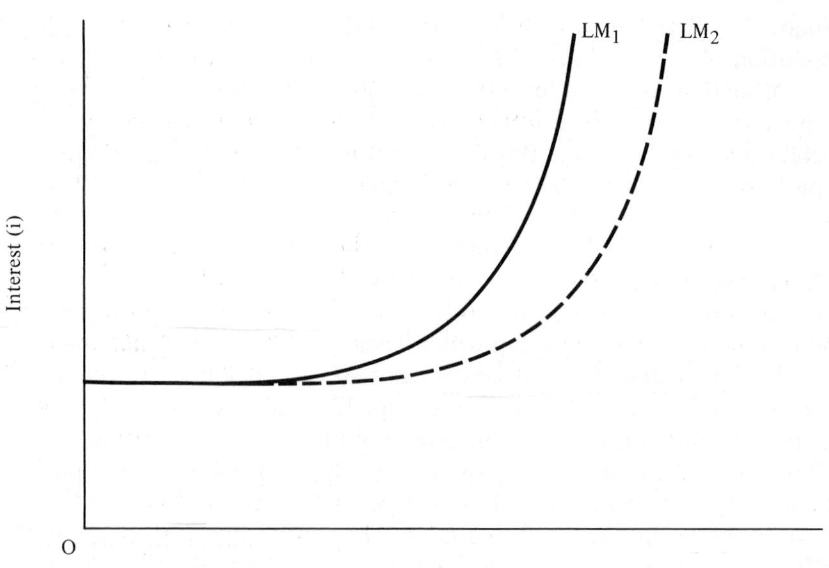

FIGURE 12–2. Shift in the LM Curve

Equilibrium in the Goods Sphere

The *goods sphere* refers essentially to those economic activites involving the production and use of goods and services. Our concern here is with the forces that center in aggregate demand and supply and with the conditions under which an equilibrium exists with respect to the demand for and the supply of goods and services for the economy as a whole.

The major portion of the analysis pursued prior to this chapter has aimed at defining the various conditions under which income equilibrium exists in the economy. Thus if we postulate a simple economy without government and without foreign transactions, the necessary condition for equilibrium is that investment and saving *ex ante* be equal (see Figure 6–4). If we introduce government into the analysis, but retain the assumption that there are no international transactions, the necessary condition for equilibrium becomes one in which *ex ante* investment plus government purchases of goods and services, $I + G$, is equal to *ex ante* saving plus net taxes, $S + T$ (see Figure 8–7). Finally, the introduction of international transactions into the analysis means that the necessary condition for income (and output) equilibrium is one in which the sum of *ex ante* investment plus government purchases of goods and services plus exports, $I + G + X$, equal the sum of *ex ante* saving plus net taxes plus imports, $S + T + M$ (see Figure 9–5).

In constructing our general equilibrium model, we shall assume for the sake of simplicity a closed economy, although the inclusion of foreign transactions changes in no way the basic principles involved. In a closed economy, the basic condition for equilibrium is the *ex ante* equality of saving and net taxes $(S + T)$ and investment plus government purchases of goods and services $(I + G)$. Saving and net taxes are a function of income in the model, whereas investment expenditures are an inverse function of the rate of interest, and government purchases of goods and services are assumed to be autonomous with respect to both income and the rate of interest.[8]

The IS Schedule

The interaction of schedule values for $(I + G)$ and $(S + T)$ in the determination of an equilibrium value for income is shown in Figure 12–3. In Part A of the figure, an investment demand schedule relating investment outlays inversely to the rate of interest is shown. To this schedule at all possible levels of the interest rate is added a fixed amount representing autonomous government expenditures for goods and services. The result is the schedule $(I + G)$, showing an inverse relationship to the rate of interest for the combined total of I and G. In Part C of the figure, the combined saving plus net taxes function is shown, both of which vary directly with income. By means of the schedules shown in Part A and Part C, we can link income and the rate of interest in the goods sphere.

To illustrate, let us assume that initially the rate of interest is at the level i_4. This rate will yield a combined total of I plus G expenditure equal to $(I + G)_1$. The latter is measured on the horizontal axis of the diagram in Part A. Part B in Figure 12–3 shows $(I + G)$ on the horizontal axis and $(S + T)$ on the vertical axis; the 45° line bisecting the figure in Part B thus represents equality between $(I + G)$ and $(S + T)$. By projecting vertically from $(I + G)_1$ in Part A until we intercept the 45° line in Part B and projecting horizontally from the point until we intercept the $(S + T)$ function in Part C, it is possible to determine graphically the specific equilibrium value for the net national product that will result from an interest rate equal to i_4. This equilibrium value is Y_1 on the horizontal axis of the figure in Part C. Essentially our analysis to this point shows that, given the $(S + T)$ function, a high value for the rate of interest will mean a low level of combined $(I + G)$ expenditures, and, hence, a low income level. If we lower the rate of interest, this will increase $(I + G)$ and push the income level higher. Each successively higher equilibrium value for the net national product which results from successive cuts in

8. To simplify the construction of the graphic model, we shall not explicitly take into account investment expenditures induced by a change in the income level, although the phenomenon of induced investment is built into the model in its graphic form (Figure 12–3) and the equation system which underlies the model (See the appendix to this chapter).

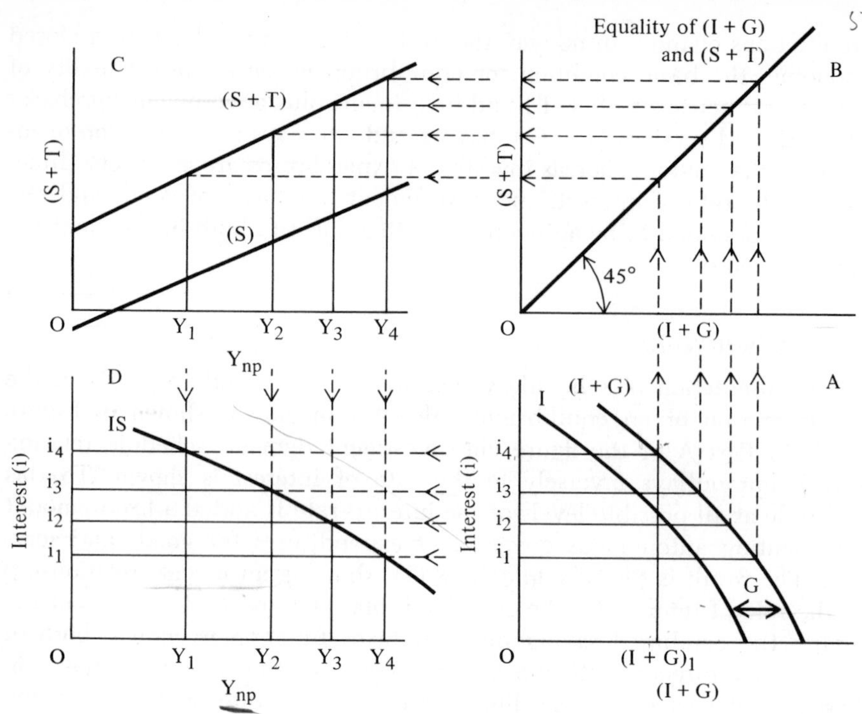

FIGURE 12–3. Equilibrium in the Goods Sphere

the rate of interest is one which will prevail after the multiplier effects have worked themselves out.

The main point is that, given both the $(S + T)$ function and the $(I + G)$ function, equilibrium in the goods sphere of the economy is achieved at higher and higher income levels only as the rate of interest declines. This relationship between the rate of interest, the level of income, and successive equilibrium positions in the goods sphere can be expressed in schedule form in a manner analogous to the construction of the *LM* curve. In Part D of Figure 12–3 net national product Y_{np}, is measured on the horizontal axis and the rate of interest, i on the vertical axis. Since an equality between $(S + T)$ and $(I + G)$ at successively higher income levels results only as the rate of interest declines, the curve that links income and the rate of interest in terms of the $(S + T) = (I + G)$ equilibrium will slope downward to the right. This curve is labeled the *IS* schedule because each point on it relates equilibrium in the goods sphere to income and the rate of interest.

The shape of the *IS* schedule depends upon the essential character of the $(S + T)$ function and the investment demand function. If, for example, the investment demand function is assumed to be relatively *interest inelastic,* then it logically follows that the *IS* curve, too, will be relatively interest inelastic because any given changes in the rate of interest will have only a modest effect on the volume of investment spending. As a consequence, the income level will also be little affected by changes in the rate of interest. A change in the position of either the $(S + T)$ function or the $(I + G)$ schedule shifts the over-all position of the *IS* curve. For example, an upward movement in the investment demand schedule will shift the *IS* curve to the right, and makes possible an equilibrium between $(S + T)$ and $(I + G)$ at a higher level of income than heretofore. A shift of this type is depicted by the dotted IS_2 curve in Figure 12–4.

Including exports and imports in our analysis does not materially change the nature of the curve describing the relationship between income and the rate of interest in terms of the necessary conditions for equilibrium in the goods sphere. The curve would simply lie further to the right, and our conception of it would have to be enlarged to see each point on it as representing a condition in which $I + G + X$ was equal to $S + T + M$ at specific levels of both income and the rate of interest. Since it can be assumed that G *and* X are autonomous with respect to both income and the rate of interest, the $I + G + X$ curve would still slope downward to the right; including G and X in the aggregate demand function does not change the inverse functional relationship between investment and the rate of interest.

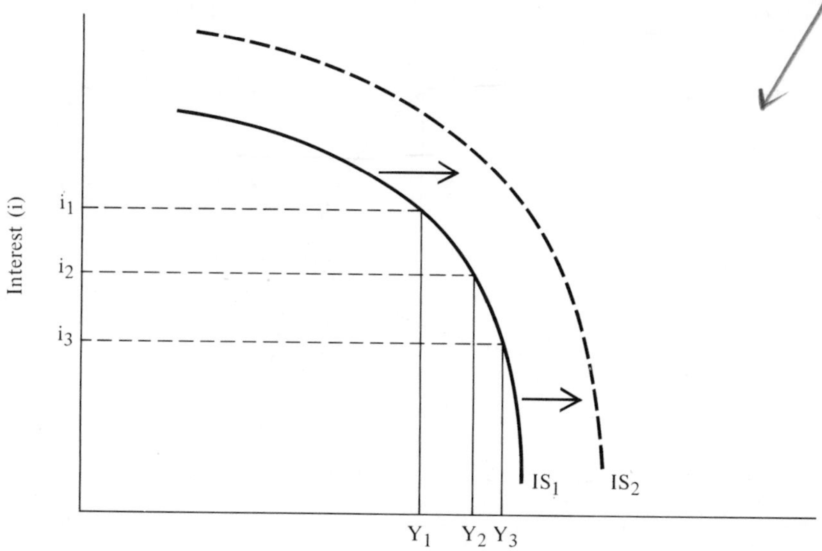

FIGURE 12–4. Shift in the IS Curve

General Equilibrium

By combining the *LM* and *IS* curves in a single diagram we are able to construct in graphic form a Keynesian general model of the economic system which shows, particularly, the manner in which the monetary sphere and the goods sphere are linked together through the rate of interest. Such a graphic model is shown in Figure 12–5. This model can be employed to demonstrate how the rate of interest and the income level are mutually determined in the Keynesian system, and to show a number of different and important situations that may be characteristic of the economic system.

In Figure 12–5 the *IS* and *LM* curves intersect at a point where net national product is at Y_e and the rate of interest is at i_e. These are equilibrium levels with respect to income and the rate of interest, both of which are mutually determined by the intersection of the *IS* and *LM* schedules. At the point of intersection of these curves, the output level, Y_{np}, and the rate of interest, i, are such that $(S + T)$ and $(I + G)$ are in equilibrium, and the demand for money, L, and the supply of money, M°, are also in equilibrium. There are any number of levels of both the rate of interest and income that are compatible with equilibrium of either $(S + T)$ and $(I + G)$ alone, or the demand for and supply of money also considered alone, but there is *only* one rate of interest and one level

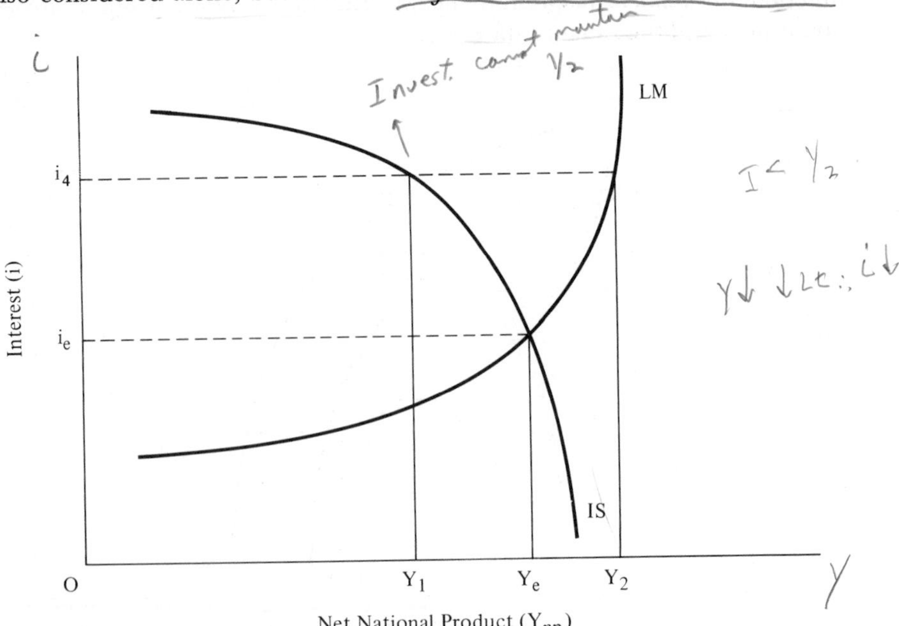

FIGURE 12–5. The Keynesian General Equilibrium Model of the Economic System

of income that is consistent with equilibrium in both the monetary and the goods sphere. The actual level of both income and interest that is consistent with equilibrium in the two spheres depends upon the shape and level assumed for the *LM* and *IS* curves, and this, in turn, is dependent upon the characteristics of the functions which lie in back of these schedules.

The reasons why the point of intersection of the *IS* and *LM* schedules depict a condition of general equilibrium for the whole economy can best be seen if we imagine that income and the rate of interest are, momentarily, at a level different from Y_e *and* i_e.

Let us assume for a moment that the rate of interest and income are actually at levels represented by i_4 and Y_2, as shown in Figure 12–5. This represents a disequilibrium condition in the system as a whole, for while these values for both income and the rate of interest are compatible with equilibrium in the monetary sphere, they are not compatible with income in the goods sphere. At the interest rate i_4, for instance, income would have to be at the level of Y_1, to bring equilibrium in the goods sphere, as determined by the *IS* curve. The system will of necessity move toward an equilibrium point; at the interest rate i_4, investment expenditure will not be sufficient to maintain an income level of Y_2, and hence the latter will decline. But as the income level declines, a portion of the money supply is released from use in response to the transactions motive, and as this happens the rate of interest declines, thereby making possible equilibrium in the monetary sphere at successively lower rates of both interest and income. This adjustment process will continue until a level of interest rates and income is reached that is compatible with equilibrium in both spheres of economic activity. Then, and only then, will a general equilibrium condition for the whole economy prevail.

Changes in the Equilibrium Values of Income and Interest

A change in the equilibrium level of the net national product and the rate of interest comes about within the framework of our graphic model of the economic system as the consequence of a shift in the position of either the *IS* or *LM* curve. It should be noted carefully that all shifts in equilibrium values for income embody the multiplier process; which is to say, every equilibrium value for income shown in the model is arrived at after the multiplier process has worked itself out.

For convenience in our analysis, we can describe changes which affect the equilibrium values for both income and the rate of interest as being either *real* or *monetary* in origin. By *real* changes we mean those that originate in the goods sector, and that thus come about because the *IS* curve has shifted. *Monetary* changes, on the other hand, refer to developments emanating from the monetary sphere and, consequently, manifest themselves through a change in position of the *LM* schedule.[9] Examination of the major sources of shifts in both the *IS* and *LM* schedules will provide us with the necessary background for a discussion of contemporary economic policy and its application to fluctuations in income and employment.[10]

Shifts in the IS Curve

The fundamental explanation for a rightward shift in the *IS* curve is an increase in the aggregate demand function. Four major explanations for an upward movement of the aggregate demand function can be distinguished. First, there may be an autonomous increase in the investment demand function. In this instance, schedule I in Part A of Figure 12–3 shifts to the right, indicating a higher level of investment spending at all ranges of the interest rate. Second, there may be an autonomous increase in government spending for goods and services. If such an increase takes place with no increase in taxes, the maximum shift in the aggregate demand schedule will be obtained. However, even if taxes are increased in an amount equal to an increase in government spending for goods and services, the balanced budget theorem examined in Chapter 8 indicates tha the aggregate demand function will still be displaced upward. Third, there may be an autonomous upward shift in the consumption function. This could come about because of an increase in transfer payments, a reduction in personal income taxes, or a general tax reduction with no change in the level of either government expenditures or investment outlays. It might also result from changing attitudes toward thrift, which would have the effect of reducing the propensity to save at all income levels. Finally, the aggregate demand function may shift because of an increase in exports relative to imports. This may result from an absolute increase in exports or a downward shift in the import function. (Refer again to Figure 12–3 and determine how each of the foregoing changes affects the position of the aggregate demand function and, consequently, the position of the IS curve. Keep in mind at all times that the IS curve is a schedule showing a series of equilibrium values for the output level at alternative values for the rate of interest, given all the underlying rela-

9. One should be careful not to confuse this use of the terms "real" and "monetary" with the distinction drawn earlier (Chapter 10, p.308) between real and nominal values. In the above discussion we are using real and monetary as a way to distinguish between the two spheres of the economy found in Keynesian analysis. In the other usage, the term real refers to values corrected for changes in the price level, whereas nominal refers to values not so corrected. It is well continually to be aware of this distinction.

10. In the discussion that follows we shall focus our attention on shifts to the right in both the *IS* and *LM* schedules. The same reasoning and explanations apply with respect to shifts in the opposite direction.

Autonomous

tionships which enter into determination of the level of aggregate demand.)

Within the framework of our Keynesian general equilibrium model the effect upon income of an upward shift in the aggregate demand schedule depends upon (1) the extent to which the *IS* curve is displaced to the right (the distance *ab* in Part A of Figure 12–6), and (2) the impact that a rising rate of interest will have upon forces which determine equilibrium in the goods sphere (the distance *cd* in the same figure). The factors which govern the magnitude of the shift in the *IS* curve are those which influence the size of the multiplier effect, given an increase (or decrease) in aggregate demand. These latter are the array of factors which determine the extent of leakages from the income stream. If there is no change in the position of the *LM* schedule with a given shift to the right in the *IS* curve, the result will be a rise in the rate of interest. This is due to the fact that the increase in the transactions demand which accompanies the rightward shift in the *IS* schedule can be met only by drawing money out of the asset sphere, a development which necessarily entails higher interest rates. The over-all impact of the rise in the interest rate is to dampen down the income-increasing effect of the rightward shift in the *IS* curve. The magnitude of this dampening effect depends upon both the steepness of the *LM* curve at the point of shift in the *IS* schedule, and the interest elasticity of the investment component of the aggregate demand function. In later discussions of policy, we shall return to this point.

Shifts in the LM Curve

The effect of a rightward shift in the *LM* curve upon both equilibrium income level and the equilibrium value for the rate of interest is depicted in Part B of Figure 12–6. This shift could take place because of

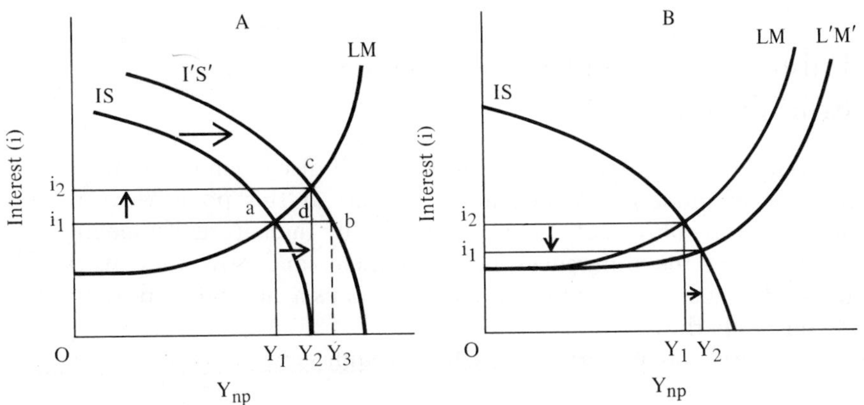

FIGURE 12–6. Shifts in the IS and LM Curves

an autonomous increase in the money supply. The reasons why an increase in the money supply shifts the *LM* curve were touched upon in the discussion in conjunction with Figure 12–2. A change in the money supply is most likely to be the source of a shift in the *LM* schedule. The *LM* curve might shift to the right because of a downward shift in the asset demand component, L_a, of the total demand for money. This would be the result of a general decline in the demand for liquidity throughout the economy. The effect of a downward shift in the liquidity preference function is to release funds from idle balances, which spill over into the bond market, pushing up the prices of the latter and, thereby, reducing interest rates. It follows from this that monetary equilibrium in relation to any given income level will be achieved at a lower rate of interest.[11]

In general, the effect upon the equilibrium income level of a shift to the right in the *LM* curve depends upon (1) the extent to which the rate of interest declines as a result of the shift in the *LM* schedule, and (2) the responsiveness of forces in the goods sphere to a decline in the rate of interest. The latter is primarily a matter of the interest elasticity of the investment demand schedule, although other components of aggregate demand may be affected by a change in the rate of interest. We shall elaborate further upon this in our subsequent discussion of policy and its application.

In connection with shifts in the *LM* curve, one additional point should be noted: With the exception of changes taking place in the range of interest rates equal or below the horizontal portion of the *LM* schedule, a shift to the right in the *LM* schedule will always reduce the rate of interest. The significance of this is that the full multiplier effect will follow; there will be, in other words, no offsetting changes in the rate of interest as is the situation confronting the economy when the *IS* curve shifts.

Public Policy and the Keynesian General Equilibrium Model

Although we shall defer to Chapter 13 a full discussion of the theory and practice of modern macroeconomic policy, at this point we can draw upon the foregoing analysis to describe brefly the nature of monetary and fiscal policy, the differences between them, and how they work. The Keynesian general equilibrium model offers us a succinct and useful vehicle for doing this.

Monetary policy works primarily through controls exercised over the

11. A third possibility involves a decline in the general price level, a possibility which will be explained in the section on the neoclassical synthesis.

supply of money. In an advanced economy this basically means control over the volume of bank lending. In the United States the Federal Reserve System is the chief agency through which such control is exercised. The objective in controlling the money supply, including bank lending, is indirectly to control spending. More specifically, and within the Keynesian framework, changes in the money supply will result in changes in interest rates, which, in turn, will have an impact on spending. The brunt of this impact will be borne by investment expenditure, as neither the consumption nor the government expenditures component of aggregate demand is readily linked to the rate of interest. Thus, the question of the efficacy of monetary policy as an instrument of economic stabilization largely turns on the issue of the shape of the investment demand schedule, about which economists are not in full agreement. To modern monetarists, though, this is not the relevant question, for, as we saw in Chapter 11, they argue that monetary policy works through the impact of changes in the money supply on money balances and the further impact of this on spending for output. Furthermore, the real public policy issue in their view is, in the final analysis, one of persuading the monetary authorities to allow the money supply to grow at a constant rate and do nothing more.

Fiscal policy, on the other hand, involves deliberate changes in government expenditures and taxes as a means of controlling economic activity. The budget of the national government is the key instrument through which fiscal policy is effected. Government expenditures for goods and services directly affect the level of economic activity because such expenditures are a component part of the aggregate demand function; transfer expenditures and taxes, on the other hand, affect disposable income and thus indirectly influence the other two major components of aggregate demand, consumption and investment spending. Fiscal policy therefore works through changes in the government's budget which, in turn, increase or decrease the level of spending in the economy.

Figure 12–7 shows how the economy can move from an underemployment equilibrium by the application of either fiscal or monetary policy or a combination of the two. Let us assume that initially the economy is at an underemployment equilibrium given by the intersection at point *a* of *IS* and *LM* schedules designated as IS_1 and LM_1. Fiscal policy measures have the effect of shifting the *IS* curve to the right. If fiscal policy alone is used to get the economy to the full employment income level of Y_3, the *IS* curve must shift to the position designated in the diagram as IS_3.

The extent to which the *IS* schedule shifts as a result of a given change in either government expenditures, *G*, or net taxes, *T*, depends upon the value of the multiplier. It is the multiplier in combination with the shift in the aggregate demand schedule that determines, *ceteris paribus*, the amount by which equilibrium income changes (see Chapter 8). However,

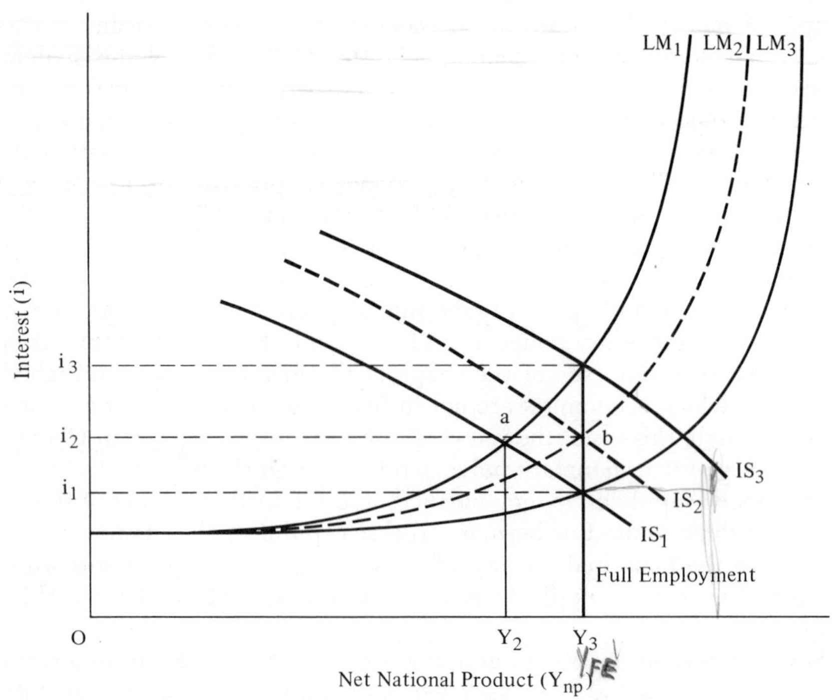

FIGURE 12–7. Fiscal Policy, Monetary Policy, and Full Employment

the shift in the *IS* schedule is not the only factor to be taken into account. If there is no change in the money supply curve, then the interest rate will increase as a consequence of a higher level of real output. At IS_3 and LM_1 the equilibrium interest rate has risen to i_3. A rise in the interest rate, *ceteris paribus*, tends to reduce investment outlays and offsets to some extent the effect of more government expenditures for goods and services or of lower taxes on the economy's equilibrium position. Thus, policy-makers must take interest rate changes as well as the value of the multiplier into account in trying to estimate the net effect of a fiscal change on output and employment.

If monetary rather than fiscal policy is chosen as the means to move the economy to the full employment output Y_3, then the *LM* curve must shift to the position designated as LM_3 in Figure 12–9. This can be brought about by a rightward shift in the money supply curve (see Figure 12–1). For any given shift to the right in the *LM* curve, the response of real output is governed by the interest elasticity of the *IS* curve. This depends primarily on how investment expenditures respond to a change in the rate of interest. If they are sensitive to such changes, then a shift to the right of the *LM* curve will, via the investment multiplier, have a highly favorable effect upon real output. It should be noted, too, that the interest rate effects of monetary policy are the opposite of those associated with fiscal policy changes. Thus, in Figure 12–7, a full employment equilibrium resulting from the intersection of IS_1 and LM_3 will lower the rate of interest to the equilibrium value of i_1.

The examples just cited show the effects in isolation of fiscal or monetary policy upon real output. Reality is more complex; it may involve a combination of both monetary and fiscal action. It is possible, in principle, at least, to move the economy to the full employment output of Y_3 without any change in the rate of interest. This outcome is shown by the intersection of the dotted curves IS_2 and LM_2 at point *b*. A combination of fiscal and monetary action means that less stringent measures of either type have to be taken than would be the case if either policy approach is applied separately and in isolation. For the sake of simplicity in the exposition we have assumed that the *IS* and *LM* schedules are independent of one another. In reality this may not be true, a fact which complicates the application of either fiscal or monetary policy. We shall return to this point in Chapter 13.

The Neoclassical Synthesis

Professor Samuelson used the term "the neoclassical synthesis" to describe an economic world in which the classical principles of demand and supply forces operating in competitive markets would apply, once Keynesian principles had been employed to insure a level of aggregate demand sufficient for full employment. Monetary and fiscal policy would be used to attain this condition.[12] In modern macroeconomic analysis this synthesis has been attained by grafting a classical model of the labor market onto the Keynesian general equilibrium model (the IS–LM framework), followed by the introduction of flexible prices into the enlarged model. This version of the Keynesian system is also called the neoclassical model. We shall proceed in this section to explain how the general IS–LM model is expanded in this fashion.[13]

Introduction of the labor market into the IS–LM general equilibrium model begins with the aggregate production function, a concept discussed

12. Paul Samuelson, *Economics, An Introductory Analysis*, 6th edition. (New York: McGraw Hill, 1955), p. 337.

13. An elegant though somewhat terse exposition of the complete neoclassical model of general equilibrium is found in Martin J. Bailey, *National Income and the Price Level: A Study in Macroeconomic Theory*, 2nd edition (New York: McGraw Hill, 1971), Chapter 2, pp. 3–42. This section also draws on Hyman Minsky's study, *John Maynard Keynes* (New York: Columbia University Press, 1975). Professor Minsky is one of the leading critics of the neoclassical synthesis.

initially in Chapter 4.[14] It will be recalled that in its most basic form, the production function shows the technical relationship between the use of labor and output in the economy.This basic version of the production functions assumes that the stock of capital (K'), the quantity of natural resources (R'), and the level of technology (T) are all *givens* (see pp. 89–94). Labor then becomes the key variable resource, and the relationship between labor used (employment), N, and output is expressed as:

$$Y = f(N) \tag{12–2}$$

In graphic form the production function is shown in part A of Figure 12–8. What the curve shows is that the level of output increases as more labor is employed, but that the rate at which output increases gradually slows down. This is because of the operation of the economic law of *diminishing returns*. At some point output attains a maximum value, which is to say that no more output can be attained even if more labor is employed. The main reason for the operation of this law is that more and more labor is being spread over a fixed quantity of other resources (capital and natural resources), the result being that each successive unit of labor employed is a bit less efficient than prior units. Hence output cannot grow in the same proportion as the input of labor.

The fact of diminishing returns is also reflected in a falling *marginal* product for labor. The curve which depicts the declining marginal product of labor is shown in part B of Figure 12–8. The *marginal product of labor* is the extra output provided by each additional unit of labor used. But if each additional unit of labor used is a bit less efficient than prior units (diminishing returns), then the marginal product associated with each unit used must decline. Hence the downward slope of this curve as shown in Figure 12–8, part B.[15]

Technically, the marginal product for labor for the entire economy is $\Delta Y/\Delta N$, as dividing the increase in total output by the increase in total employment will show how much, on the average, output increases with each additional worker employed. This, of course, is by definition the marginal product of labor. If we assume a competitive economy (Chapter 4, pp. 99–102), all firms will use labor up to the point at which the *value* of output associated with added labor is just equal to its *cost*. When the firm–and by aggregation all firms in the economy–reaches this point it

14. At this point it would be desirable for the reader to review the material on the production function (pp. 92–93 in Chapter 4), as well as the material also developed in Chapter 4 on the classical demand for labor and supply of labor schedules (pp. 101–4). These concepts are essential for understanding how the IS–LM model can be enlarged and have a labor market sector incorporated into it.

15. For a thorough discussion of the production function and related concepts, see Edwin Mansfield, *Microeconomics: Theory and Applications*, 2nd edition (New York: W. W. Norton & Company, Inc., 1975), pp. 122–49.

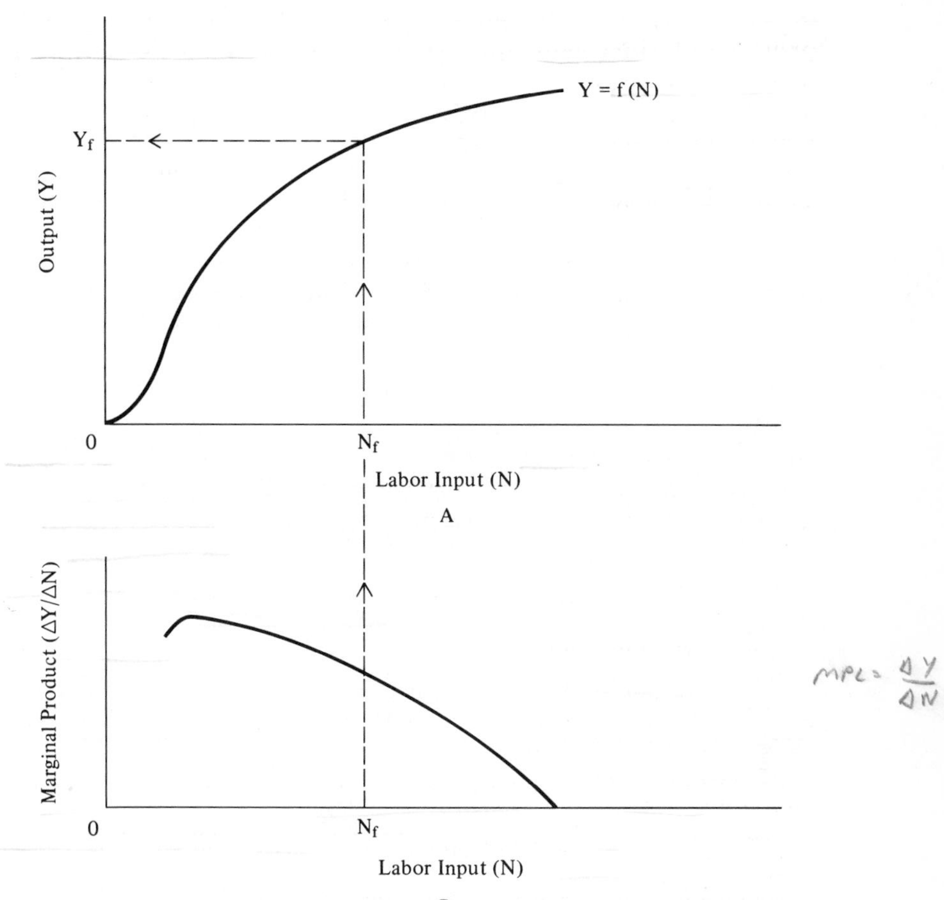

FIGURE 12–8. The Aggregate Production Function and the Marginal Product of Labor Curve

will both maximize its profits and be in equilibrium with respect to the employment of labor. In equation form the necessary condition for profit maximization is (Chapter 4, p. 101).

$$\Delta Yp = \Delta Nw \tag{12–3}$$

In the equation p is the price level and w is the money wage. By rearrangement of 12–3 we get the following:

$$\frac{\Delta Y}{\Delta N} = \frac{w}{d} \tag{12–4}$$

But w/p is the real wage. Thus equation 12–4 says that in equilibrium and with the assumption of profit maximization, the real wage and the marginal product of labor must be equal. What this means, of course, is that the demand for labor becomes a function of the real wage, a view that Keynes accepted. Thus, we have the basic macroeconomic demand curve for labor expressed as follows:[16]

$$N = f(w/p) \qquad (12\text{–}5)$$

All that is now needed to complete the labor market and describe conditions for equilibrium in this market is to bring in the labor supply curve. In the neoclassical synthesis the aggregate labor supply curve is a classical one in that it is assumed that the supply of labor N' varies positively with the real wage. In equation form, the labor supply is shown as a function of the real wage:

$$N' = f'(w/p) \qquad (12\text{–}6)$$

We should remind ourselves at this point that Keynes objected vigorously to the classical concept of labor supply, arguing that the actual behavior of workers in the labor market does not agree with the classical view that the amount of labor services offered in the market rises and falls with changes in the real wage.[17] Nevertheless, proponents of the neoclassical general equilibrium approach to macroeconomics favor such a schedule, believing that it does reflect the long-run behavior of the labor force.[18]

Bringing the demand schedule and the supply schedule together gives us the equilibrium level of employment, a level that is also a full employment level. This is shown in Figure 12–9, which is essentially identical with Figure 4–7 in Chapter 4. (To review the reasons why the equilibrium depicted in this fashion is one of *full* employment see Chapter 4, p. 106.)

The significance of the labor market equations shown above is not only that they determine the equilibrium employment level, but given the production function output is simultaneously determined. At this point let us refer back to Figure 12–8. The equilibrium employment level determined by the intersection of the aggregate demand and supply schedules for labor is shown as N_f on the horizontal axis of the marginal product curve (part B). Projecting upward via the dotted line we reach the production function curve in part A; from this point the line is projected horizontally to the vertical axis to determine the full employment output derived from equilibrium in the market. This is indicated as Y_f.

16. This is the same equation as shown in Chapter 4 (p. 101), except there W was used as a symbol of the real wage. $W = w/p$.

17. John Maynard Keynes, *The General Theory of Employment, Interest and Money* (New York: Harcourt, Brace & World, First Harbinger ed., 1964), p. 12. See Chapter 4, p. 120.

18. For a rigorous theoretical proof that labor behaves in this way, assuming (as classical economics does) that the behavior of workers is utility-maximizing, see William H. Branson, *Macroeconomic Theory and Policy* (New York: Harper & Row, 1972), pp. 103–106.

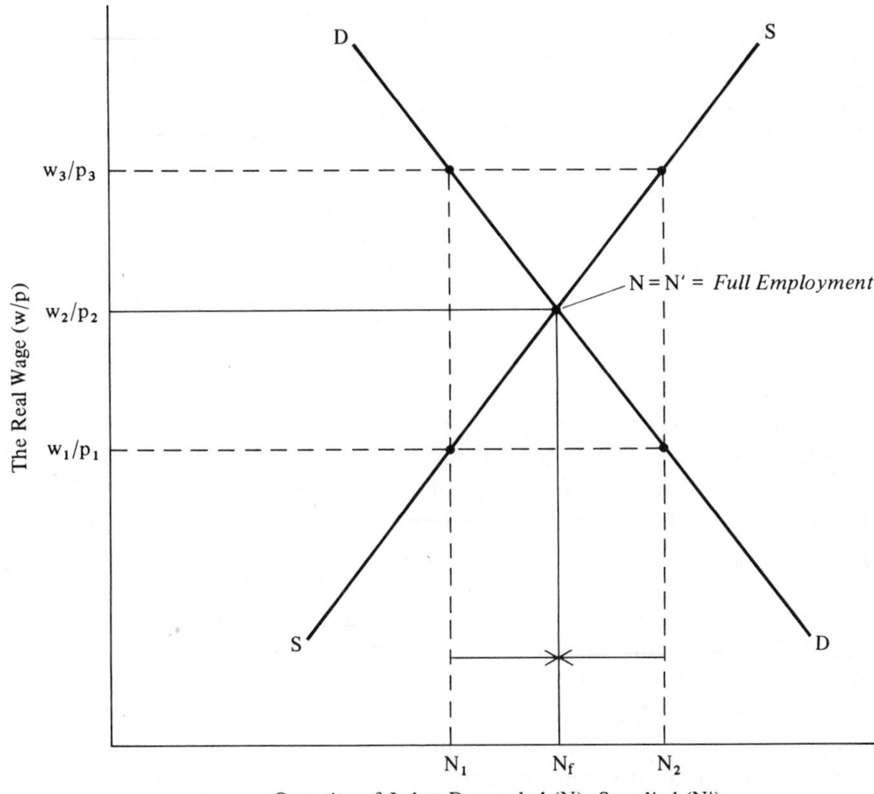

FIGURE 12–9. The Equilibrium Level of Employment

The next step is to incorporate the output level as determined by forces at play in the labor market into the IS–LM Keynesian general equilibrium model of the aggregate economy. This is done in Figure 12–10. What we do is add a vertical line to the standard Keynesian IS–LM diagram at a point on the horizontal axis which is equal to the equilibrium income level (Y_f) determined by the labor market model (Figure 12–9). In Figure 12–10, the labor-market determined full employment line is shown for three different sets of circumstances. In part A of the figure, the vertical line Y_f is so drawn as to pass through the intersection of the *IS* and *LM* curves. In part B it lies to the left of this point of intersection, whereas in part C it lies to the right.

What does Figure 12–10 show us? In part A we have a situation in which the three sets of forces at work in the economy—those which pertain to the goods market, those pertaining to the money market, and those pertaining to the labor market—happen to coalesce in such a way that equilibrium in each of the three spheres of the economy is compatible

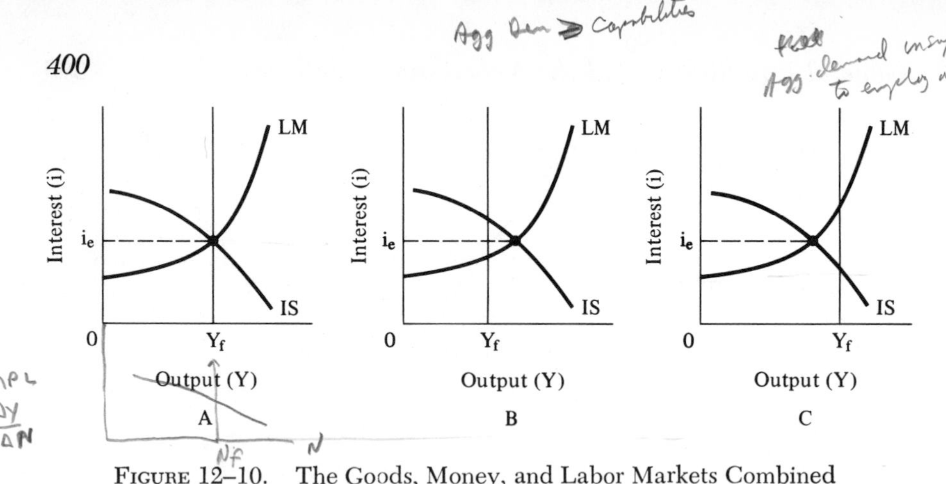

FIGURE 12–10. The Goods, Money, and Labor Markets Combined

with full employment. But parts B and C are different. In part B the intersection of *IS* and *LM* lies to the right of the full employment output (Y_f), a situation which implies that the combination of real and monetary forces which lie behind the *IS* and *LM* curves add up to a level of aggregate demand which exceeds the real capabilities of the economy. Part C, however, shows just the opposite, as the full employment output (as determined in the labor market) lies beyond the intersection of *IS* and *LM*. What this means is that there is insufficient aggregate demand to get the economy to full employment.

From the standpoint of effective economic performance the only acceptable situation is the one depicted in part A, a level of aggregate demand equal to full employment as determined in the labor market sphere. The thrust of Keynesian analysis essentially is that there is *nothing* inherent in the structure of a market economy which will bring the economy to this situation. On the contrary, Keynes believed that if the economy got to such a situation *without intervention by government*, it would not only be a rare occurrence, but completely fortuitous. The more normal condition of the market economy under a policy of *laissez faire* was that depicted in part C of the diagram, a situation in which aggregate demand is chronically deficient.

The foregoing, however, is not the conclusion reached by the neoclassical synthesis. Rather, it embodies an attitude similar to that found in the modern quantity theory, namely that the economy is inherently stable and market forces can be depended upon to push it to either a short-term full employment output or to the output path determined by the growth of its productive potential (Chapter 11, p. 367). Thus, although the neoclassical model admits of the possibility of the economy being in the situation depicted by either part B or C, it does not admit that it can remain there long. Market forces will push it to the situation shown in part A. The crucial question is—how? As developed up to this point there is no mechanism in the neoclassical synthesis to bring this about. It is now time to introduce such a mechanism. It is the price level.

The Price Level and General Equilibrium

Introducing the price level into the analysis involves two problems. The first is to show how in a theoretical sense the price level is related to output (Y), and the second is to explicitly introduce the price level into the expanded *IS–LM* framework. Only when we do the latter will our construction of the neoclassical synthesis be complete.

To solve the first problem we shall again make use of the production function concept and the aggregate demand for labor schedule. Figure 12–11 shows how output can be related to the price level, assuming a given money wage. Part A in the figure presents a production function of the type discussed earlier in this chapter; here, though, the axes are reversed, showing labor inputs, N, on the vertical axis and output Y_{np} on the horizontal axis. Part B shows the demand curve for labor, the quantity of labor being a function of the real wage (W). Again, though, the axes are transposed, the quantity of labor appearing on the vertical axis and the real wage on the horizontal axis.

Part C contains a curve which ties the price level, p, to the real wage, W, by means of the current money wage, w_1. If money wages are given, then the real wage will vary inversely with the price level. This is what the curve W_1 shows. When we combine values for real output (derived from the relationship between the production function and the demand for labor) with the price level (derived from the relationship between real wages and the price level) we obtain in Part D a supply schedule for

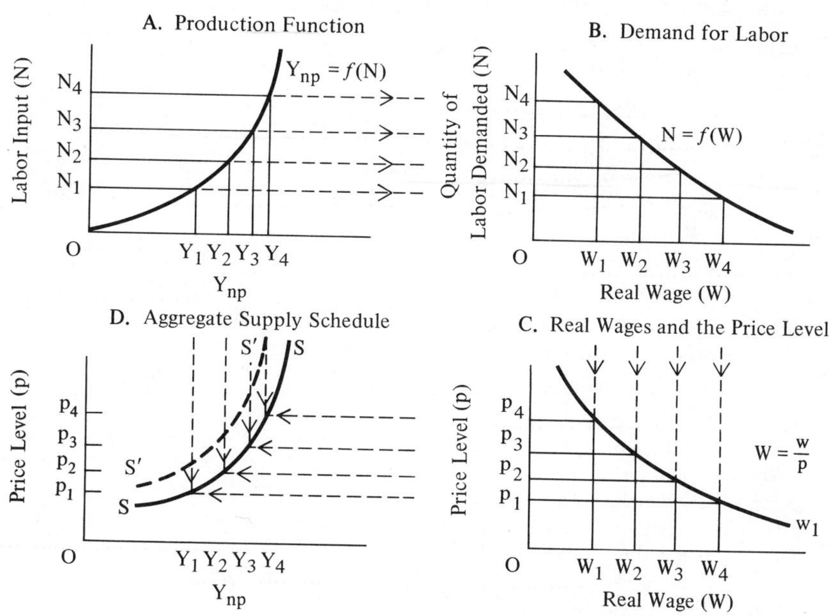

FIGURE 12–11. Real Output and the Price Level

aggregate output, *SS*, which relates Y_{np} to the price level. What this schedule says, in effect, is that, given a fixed money wage and underlying technical conditions of production, more output will be supplied only as the price level rises. A rising price level is needed to bring about the fall in real wages which must take place to induce producers to use more labor. The reader should recognize the conceptual similarity of *SS* to the ordinary supply curve.

What the foregoing analysis establishes is that the price level may vary with output, rising as output expands and falling as output contracts. This assumes prices in general are flexible, upwards and downwards, an heroic assumption indeed in today's world, but one essential nevertheless to development of the full neoclassical model of the Keynesian system.[19] But we also need to recognize that the price level may change without any change in real output (Y_{np}). This can be depicted by a shift in the aggregate supply schedule, *SS* in Figure 12–11, to the level *S′S′*. As we shall see subsequently, this kind of a change in the price level may come about because of a change in the money supply. It is just such a change that the neoclassical synthesis incorporates into the *IS-LM* model. Let us now examine how this may be done.

Let us make one more simplifying assumption, which is that when the price level changes all prices change in the same proportion. This is not always true in reality, but with such an assumption we can trace through in the most direct fashion how a change in the price level will affect the *IS* and *LM* curves. All the key variables which lie behind the *IS* curve—consumption, investment, government spending, and net exports—are measured in real terms, the assumption being that households, business firms, and governments do not suffer from the money illusion (Chapter 4, p. 00). This being the case, there is no reason why a rise or fall in the general price level should shift any of the underlying real functions which determine the position of the *IS* curve.[20] Consequently, we shall assume that the *IS* curve will not shift as a result of a change in the general price level.

It is a different story as respects the *LM* schedule. The demand for money balances is, as we have seen, a demand for real balances, but the amount of money in existence (which is money being held) can only be denominated in nominal terms, as money is the basic unit in which all else is measured. The really important question is what happens to the real

19. We shall examine subsequently in this chapter and in greater detail in Chapter 14 (The Economics of Inflation) some of the consequences of price rigidity, especially downward rigidity in both prices and wages.

20. This is not quite correct, as it is possible that a change in the price level will affect the real value of assets held by consumers—their net wealth position—and this may affect the position of the consumption function. This effect is known as the "Pigou effect," and we shall explore it shortly.

value (their purchasing power, in other words) of such balances when the price level changes, all else remaining constant? If prices go up, this means that the *real* value of nominal money balances has declined. But this will be the same in an economic sense as a decline in the money supply, since persons and firms find themselves with less money available to meet their transactions and other monetary needs. Thus, an increase in the price level, *ceteris paribus*, will pull money out of idle balances into active circulation, thereby causing an increase in the interest rate. There is no difference in this effect between an increase in the price level and a decrease in the money supply, *ceteris paribus*. Since this takes place at any or all values for net national product, the *LM* curve will lie to the left of the position it would occupy at a lower price level. An increase in the price level, in other words, shifts the *LM* curve to the left. A fall in the price level, on the other hand, has the same effect, *ceteris paribus*, as an increase in the money supply. Thus, introduction of a price level variable into the analysis results in a series of *LM* schedules, each one associated with a different price level. These are depicted in Figure 12–12 as *LM* (p_3), *LM* (p_2), and *LM* (p_1).

What we now have in our general equilibrium model is not a single set of equilibrium values for interest and income, as shown earlier in Figure 12–5, but a series of equilibrium values, each one uniquely associated

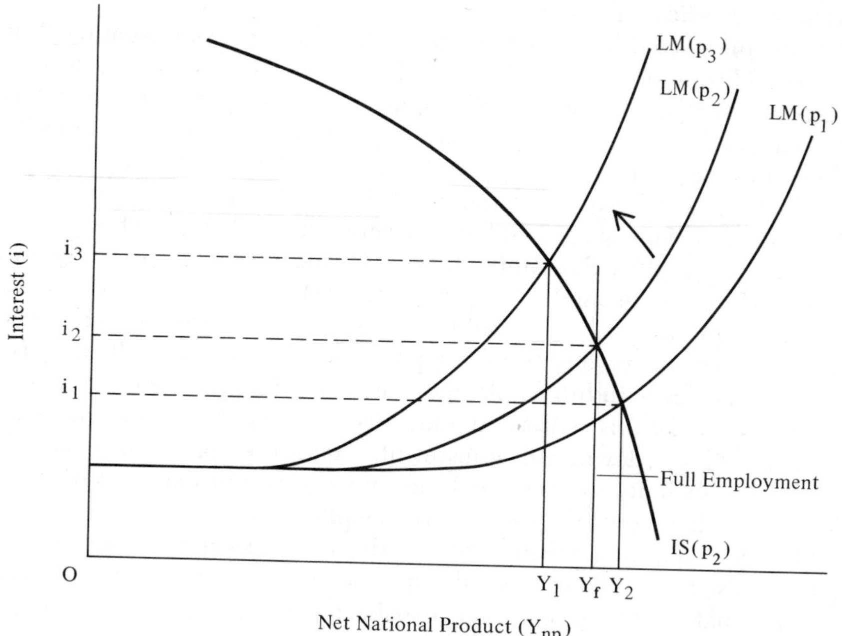

FIGURE 12–12. General Equilibrium and the Price Level

with a different level of prices. But we have something more than this. We now have the mechanism to insure that equilibrium in the goods market (*IS*) and in the money market (*LM*) is brought into balance with the full employment equilibrium determined in the labor market ($N = N'$). This mechanism is the price level, assuming *flexibility* in both money wages and prices.

Turn again to Figure 12–12. If we assume that Y_f is the full employment output level as determined by the labor market (Figure 12–9), and that momentarily the price level is at p_1, we now have a disequilibrium condition in terms of the model. This is because, given the price level p_1, the *IS* and *LM* curves will intersect at an income level equal to Y_2. But this is not possible, assuming Y_f is the full employment real income. Consequently, in this situation, the adjusting factor must be a rise in the price level from p_1 to p_2, assuming no changes in the underlying determinants of the system. The income expenditure model shows, in other words, that if conditions in the monetary and goods sphere are such that the *IS–LM* equilibrium output will be beyond the full employment level, then rising prices are inevitable. The excess level of aggregate demand reflected in the intersection of *IS* and *LM* at the income level Y_2 also implies that at the existing real wage, the demand for labor will exceed its supply. Thus money wages must rise even faster than the price level, for only in this way can the real wage level rise sufficiently to reach the equilibrium real wage level indicated in Figure 12–9.

If the price level happens to be p_3 we have an opposite situation. Now the equilibrium output for *IS* and *LM* is Y_1, which represents a level of aggregate demand below the full employment output level, Y_f. Now what will happen? Just the reverse of what took place in the opposite situation. Both prices and money wages will drop, the latter more rapidly than the former, as the real wage must fall if more labor is to be employed. The fall in money wages follows because the deficiency of aggregate demand reflected in the intersection of *IS* and *LM* at Y_1 also implies a deficiency in the demand for labor at the existing real wage (Figure 12–9). Prices and money wages will continue to fall until the system reaches a full employment equilibrium, a point of intersection of *IS* and *LM* which coincides with full employment as determined by the labor market. In Figure 12–12 this will be at the price level p_2. If money wages are rigid, resisting a downward adjustment, then full employment cannot be attained. Flexibility in prices and money wages insures an automatic adjustment of the economic system to full employment.

One final question remains before the neoclassical synthesis is complete. This is, what determines the specific level of the SS curve (Figure 12–11)—that is, the price level associated with any particular output level? The money supply provides the answer. Let us see how.

Earlier in this chapter monetary equilibrium was defined as a situation in which the total demand for money to hold, L, was equal to the current supply of money. M^o. These represent real balances (p. 382). If we allow L' to represent the total demand for nominal money balances and $M^{o\prime}$ the nominal money supply, then monetary equilibrium in nominal terms is equal to $L' = M^{o\prime}$. In Chapter 10 (p. 332) the total demand for money was defined as $L = f(Y, i)$, an equation derived by combining the Keynesian transactions and asset demand functions for money. We may convert this to a demand for nominal money balances by adding in the price level. The resulting equation is:

$$L' = f(pY, i) \tag{12–7}$$

Since in equilibrium the demand and supply for money balances are equal, we can say that the right-hand side of equation (12–7) must be equal to the nominal money supply. Thus we have:

$$M^{o\prime} = f(pY, i) \tag{12–8}$$

Now if we divide both sides of this equation by the price level, p, we have the following:

$$\frac{M^{o\prime}}{p} = f(Y, i) \tag{12–9}$$

This equation is an expression which says, in equilibrium, the real supply of money balances is equal to the real demand, our original point of departure. But we may rearrange this equation algebraically as follows:

$$p = \frac{M^{o\prime}}{f(Y, i)} \tag{12–10}$$

Now we have the neoclassical answer to the question of the price level. It is essentially that the price level is determined by the money supply, given the demand function for money. One of the key points in the modern quantity theory is that the demand for money function ($f(Y,I)$) is highly stable. If this is the case, then Equation (12–9) shows that the price level will vary directly with the money supply, rising when money is increased, and falling when it is reduced. Thus, the neoclassical model brings us full circle back to the earlier classical position that the money supply is the primary determinant of the price level.

The Keynes and Pigou Effects

Before we conclude this chapter with discussion of dissent from the neoclassical synthesis, some comments are in order on two important elaborations of the idea that, in theory at least, it is possible for a full employment output to be reached by the mechanism of a falling price level. In the literature of economics these have come to be known as the 'Keynes effect' and the 'Pigou Effect.'[21]

The idea that a falling price level might increase output through the impact of lower prices upon the economy's real money supply (M^o/p) is called the Keynes effect. Introduction of the price level into the general equilibrium model permits us to illustrate in simple fashion the special nature of this effect, as is done in Part A of Figure 12–13. Essentially, this is similar to Figure 12–12, except that the assumption of a liquidity trap —the flat portion of the *LM* curve—imposes an absolute limit to expansion of output by reducing prices. This is the income level Y' in Part A of Figure 12–13. Since at this income level, the *IS* curve intersects the *LM* curve in that flat range of the latter, a further reduction of the price level from p' to p_2, for example, will not lead to any additional increase in income, even though it pushes the portion of the *LM* curve above the horizontal section further to the right. Keynes opposed wage and price deflation as a means of increasing output and employment, believing on practical grounds that an increase in the money supply would achieve the same result with less resistance and friction. In any event, the notion of a liquidity trap—even though empirical evidence for its existence is scanty —provided some theoretical ammunition for Keynes's attack in the 1930s on the classical view that the proper cure for the depression was to slash wages and prices.

The argument embodied in the Pigou effect is of a different sort and, in principle at least, does not run into any limit on the extent to which output can be expanded by reducing the general level of prices. As pointed out initially in Chapter 6, the Pigou effect asserts that a falling price level will shift the consumption function upward, the reason being that lower prices increase the real value of the consumer's stock of liquid assets and thus lessen the need to save. Hence, real consumption will be higher at all income levels. In terms of the general equilibrium model, this means that the *IS* curve will shift to the right—or upward—as the price level drops. Thus, as shown in Part B of Figure 12–13, the Pigou effect postulates a series of *IS* schedules, each associated with a different level of prices.[22] As a theoretical proposition, the Pigou effect is entirely logical, but most economists do not believe it has any great practical value. Certainly the experience of past depressions and recessions does not offer any convincing evidence that a falling price level will stimulate demand in this fashion.

21. See Chapter 6, p. 186.

22. For the sake of simplicity and clarity, the Keynes effect is abstracted from Part B of Figure 12–8. In principle, both effects could be present simultaneously in the economy.

A. The Keynes Effect

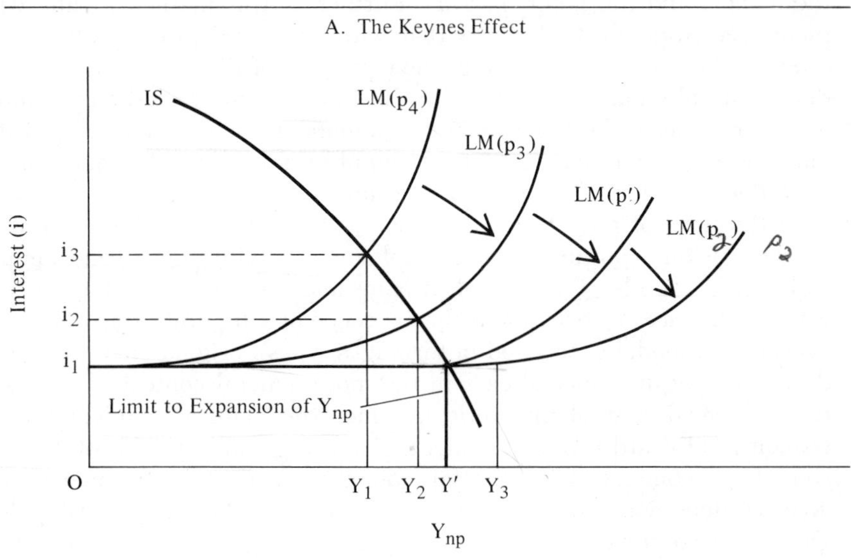

B. The Pigou Effect

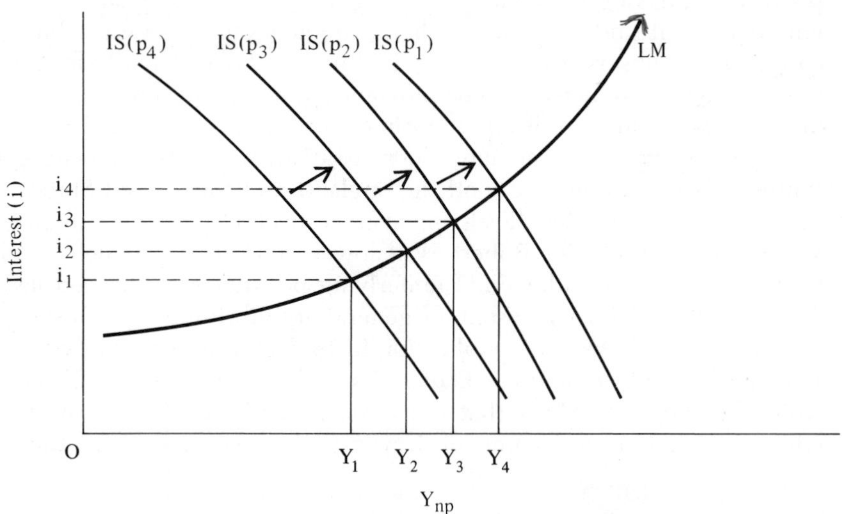

FIGURE 12–13. The Keynes and Pigou Effects

Dissent from the Neoclassical Synthesis

Intellectually the neoclassical interpretation of Keynesian economics has had a strong appeal to many economists, the reason being it provided a complete theoretical model which integrated equilibrium in the goods, the money, and the labor markets. Further, it was mathematically complete (see Appendix). It shows that with wage and price flexibility, the economy becomes self-adjusting; the equations of the labor market insure that eventually market forces will push the economy to full employment. As we have seen, the labor market dominates in determining output; the more purely Keynesian *IS* and *LM* equilibrium adjusts to conditions in the labor market, not the other way around.

At the level of pure economic theory, the meaning of the neoclassical synthesis is that continuing underemployment equilibrum becomes impossible, except under the special circumstances of downward rigidity in wages and prices or because of the existence of a liquidity trap. Thus, the neoclassical model succeeded in turning Keynes's original analysis upside down, making it a special case in the more general context of an essentially classical view of the world in which the "natural" tendency of the economy is toward full employment, given wage and price flexibility. We should not conclude from the foregoing, however, that the neoclassical analysis does not allow room for an active monetary and fiscal policy. Quite the contrary. It is recognized that wages and prices are often sluggish—especially downward—and thus the process through which the economy will adjust automatically toward a full employment condition may, politically speaking, take much too long to attain. Consequently, Keynesian style fiscal and monetary policies are not only necessary but welcome. As one observer has phrased it, "the neoclassical synthesis permits the advocacy of an active full-employment policy to be consistent with an in-theory belief in the self-equilibrating nature of the economy."[23]

Beginning roughly in the late 1960s dissatisfaction with the neoclassical synthesis began to emerge, both in England and the United States. The theoretical roots for this development trace back in part to an influential, key article by Professor Robert W. Clower of UCLA in which he challenged one of the fundamental underlying postulates of the neoclassical synthesis, the Walrasian system of general equilibrium.[24] Another significant development was the publication in 1968 of a massive study by Axel Leijonhufvud, *On Keynesian Economics and the Economic of Keynes*, in which he sought to show that the basic post-World War II theoretical edifice erected in the name of Keynes (the neoclassical synthesis as

23. Minsky, p. 53.

24. Robert W. Clower, "The Keynesian Counterrevolution: A Theoretical Appraisal," in F. Hahn and F. Brechling eds, *The Theory of Interest Rates* (London: Macmillan, 1965), pp. 103–25. Professor Clower uses the term "Keynesian Counterrevolution" to refer essentially to the neoclassical synthesis. Walrasian general equilibrium system refers to the analysis by the great French economist, Leon Walras, in which he demonstrates mathematically the theoretical possibility that in a market system with flexible prices all markets will clear simultaneously. Any excess of supply or demand in any one market is corrected by the price system through deficiencies of supply or demand in other markets.

K— sluggish downward so not effective means of stabilization

described earlier) did not, in fact, adhere to the main thesis found in Keynes's *The General Theory*.[25]

Critics of the neoclassical synthesis are in agreement on a number of areas in which they believe important ideas found in Keynes's *The General Theory* have been neglected, but they have not yet succeeded in developing an agreed-upon macroeconomic model of the economy. Thus, our comment upon this latest series of developments in the continued evolution of modern macroeconomic theory is necessarily limited to a review of the main themes which have emerged from this growing chorus of dissent. To repeat, these themes are ones which the critics believe are either ignored totally or barely mentioned in the neoclassical model, even though they are crucial for understanding the behavior of the economy.

Perhaps the key idea is uncertainty. It is possibly the most important single idea in *The General Theory*, being, as one observer says, "the very bedrock of Keynes's theory of employment."[26] Why this stress on uncertainty? The reason is that we cannot know the future. We cannot know the future because the economy exists in real time, because it cannot be separated from history. Keynes was quite emphatic on this point, saying simply that we have no scientific basis whatsoever to determine, for example, "the price of copper and the rate of interest twenty years hence. . . . We simply do not know."[27] It follows, too, because the economy exists in real, historic time, the system is in a sense indeterminate, the reason being that history itself is indeterminate. What this means essentially is that the economic system cannot be accurately described as a self-contained equilibrium system. Uncertainty means, too, that our expectations with respect to the future (recall the important role expectations play in the determination of investment spending) rest upon flimsy foundations. Keynes, speaking about the investment decision, said, "The outstanding fact is the extreme precariousness of the basis of knowledge on which our estimates of prospective yield have to be made. Our knowledge of the factors which will govern the yield of an investment some years hence is usually very slight and often negligible."[28]

What emerges from this stress on uncertainty, real time, and fragile

25. Axel Leijonhufvud, *On Keynesian Economics and the Economics of Keynes: A Study in Monetary Theory* (New York: Oxford University Press, 1968). Other leading economists who have contributed to the growing body of economic literature critical of the neoclassical synthesis include Roy W. Harrod, Nicholas Kaldor, Hyman P. Minsky, Joan Robinson, Paul Davidson, G. L. S. Shackle and Sidney Weintraub. Readers are referred especially to Hyman P. Minsky's *John Maynard Keynes*, and Paul Davidson's *Money and the Real World* (New York: John Wiley & Sons, 1972).

26. G. L. S. Shackle, *The Years of High Theory* (Cambridge: Cambridge University Press, 1967), p. 112.

27. J. M. Keynes, "The General Theory of Employment," *The Quarterly Journal of Economics*, February 1937, p. 214.

28. John Maynard Keynes, *The General Theory*, p. 149.

expectations is a different view of the economic process than one finds in the neoclassical synthesis. There is no tendency toward equilibrium; in fact some critics argue that the whole idea of an equilibrium needs to be challenged. Joan Robinson has said, "Once we admit that an economy exists in time, that history goes one way, from the irrevocable past into the unknown future, the concept of equilibrium based upon the mechanical analogy of a pendulum swinging to and fro in space becomes untenable. The whole of traditional economics needs to be thought out afresh."[29] But if the system does not tend toward equilibrium, what does it do? The answer suggested by the dissent from the neoclassical synthesis is that cyclical instability and continuous motion is the normal economic state. If we wish to use the language of equilibrium economics, then *disequilibrium* is the norm. Stability, it has been suggested, may be an unattainable goal, since at any given time the condition in which the economy finds itself—boom, crisis, depression, or recovery—carried the seeds of its own destruction.[30] Nothing stands still, the system moves on, and the future is always different from the past. Uncertainty and the institutions of capitalism which reflect this fact (money and money-related financial practices) is the fundamental explanation for this view.

Other seminal ideas flow from the foregoing view of the economic process. One centers on the extreme importance Keynes attached to money, a topic already discussed in considerable detail in Chapter 10. Money is important not only because it provides the necessary link between the present and an uncertain future, but also because the rules which govern money are different. It is not like other commodities. It does not obey the "normal laws" of the market, increasing in supply when the demand for it goes up or having other things substitute for it when its price (the rate of interest) goes up.[31] Money is not neutral. Keynes saw in its institutional peculiarities a source of the fundamental instability of the economy, an instability which tended much of the time toward excessive unemployment.

Closely related to money is the elaborate financial system of the modern economy, another source of systemic instability according to some

29. Joan Robinson, "What Has Become of the Keynesian Revolution?" *Challenge,* January/February 1974, p. 8.

30. Minsky, p. 61.

31. Keynes, in an important article which appeared before *The General Theory* was completed, said he was trying to develop a "monetary theory of production." By this he meant the theory of an economy in which money "plays a part of its own and affects motives and decisions and is, in short, one of the operative factors in the situation, so that the course of events cannot be predicted, either in the long period or the short period, without a knowledge of the behavior of money. . . ." See John Maynard Keynes, "On the Theory of a Monetary Economy," *Nebraska Journal of Economics and Business,* Autumn 1973, p. 7.

critics of the neoclassical synthesis.[32] The modern financial structure is a complex phenomenon, one which involves banks, savings and loan associations, insurance companies, and other institutions which are sources of money and credit. In good times the financial structure is too readily overextended, creating a vast and vulnerable debt structure which exists alongside the *real* output-producing sectors of the economy. If the latter falter, then the debt structure becomes vulnerable to collapse, a situation that happened with catastrophic results in the 1930s. Several times in the post-World War II period the nation teetered on the brink of a serious debt deflation, avoided only by large-scale intervention by the Federal Reserve System.[33]

Finally, the critics of the neoclassical analysis argue that it has almost wholly neglected the theory of the price level found in *The General Theory*, preferring to cling to a modernized version of the quality theory to explain the general level of prices. But the message from Keynes is quite different.[34] Keynes said that in the long run it is the trend of money wages in relation to productivity which determines the stability or instability of the prive level, a view which points to the role that trade unions play in the economy as a factor in inflation.[35] This view also opens the door to bringing in corporate power over prices as well as the continued struggle over the distribution of output (See Chapter 17) as factors which also enter into the determination of the general price level. Market power exercised by trade unions and corporations is not, unfortunately, readily controlled by fiscal and monetary policy, a fact which critics of the neoclassical synthesis say helps account for its inability to cope with continuing inflation and unemployment.

A Concluding Comment

Not too many years ago there existed a large amount of agreement among economists on the basic content of modern macroeconomic theory—Keynesian economics, in other words. Essentially this agreement encompassed the aggregate demand model—or income-expenditure approach—developed in Part II of this text (Chaps. 4–9). This consensus no longer

32. This view is associated primarily with Professor Hyman Minsky of Washington University.

33. Hyman P. Minsky, "The Financial Instability Hypothesis: An Interpretation of Keynes and An Alternative to 'Standard' Theory," *Nebraska Journal of Economics and Business*, Winter 1977, pp. 5–16.

34. Keynes's theory of the price level is discussed in detail in Chapter 14.

35. John Maynard Keynes, *The General Theory*, p. 309.

exists. We have had the development of the modern quantity theory with its underlying philosophical attack on the basic Keynesian notion that a market (capitalistic) economy is inherently unstable. We have had, too, as shown in this chapter, a grafting of basically classical ideas onto the basic income-expenditure model of Keynes (the IS–LM framework) to give us what has come to be known as the "neoclassical synthesis." Finally, we have underway a strong reaction to this synthesis, the results of which are not fully known. For the reader this may be somewhat disconcerting, but he or she should not despair. These disagreements are healthy, forcing economists (as Joan Robinson suggests) to think out afresh the whole of traditional economics. Out of this process will come a better body of theoretical ideas, a system of macroeconomics more able to cope with an economic world in which time and power and uncertainty are among the most important variables.

APPENDIX

Algebraic presentation of the general equilibrium model

Equilibrium in the Goods Sphere in an Open Economy.

(1) $Y_{np} = C + I + G + X - M$ = the basic identity

(2) $C = C'_o + a'L_{np}$ = the consumption function

$a' = (a - at)$ = the MPC out of net national product

$C'_o = (Co - aT_o)$ = consumption that is independent of the income level. Taxes are reflected in both a' C'_o

(3) $I = I'_o + bY_{np}$ = the investment function

$I'_o = (I_o - ci)$ = investment as an inverse function of the rate of interest. I'_o equals investment which is independent of the income level.

(4) $M = M_o + mY_{np}$ = the import function

(5) G = autonomous government expenditures for goods and services

(6) X = autonomous exports

(7) $Y_{np} = C'_o + a'Y_{np} + I'_o + bY_{np} + G + X - M_o - mY_{np}$ [Equilibrium in the goods sphere.]

Equilibrium in the Monetary Sphere

(1) $M^{o\prime}$ = the nominal autonomous money supply

(2) $L_t = f(pY_{np})$ = the transactions demand function

p = the price level

(3) $L_a = f'(i)$ = the asset demand function

(4) $L = L_t + L_a = f(pY_{np}) + f'(i)$ = the total demand function

(5) $\dfrac{M^{o'}}{p} = f(Y_{np}) + f'(i)$ [This defines equilibrium in the monetary sphere in real terms]

Equilibrium in the Labor Market

(1) $Y = f(N)$ = the production function

(2) $N = f(w/p)$ = the demand for labor function

w = the money wage

p = the price level

(3) $N' = f'(w/p)$ = the supply of labor function

(4) $N = N' = N_f$ [Equilibrium in the labor market.]

General equilibrium thus depends upon the solution of three equations—Equation (7) in the goods sphere, Equation (5) in the monetary sphere and Equation (4) in the labor market—in three unknowns, namely Y_{np}, N_f, and i.

13

Stabilization Policy: Overview and Appraisal

There is a dual purpose in this chapter. First, we shall draw together and discuss in greater detail than heretofore the major policy instruments at the disposal of modern governments. Our concern is with those policy instruments which can be used to deal with broad problems involving fluctuations in output, employment, and the price level. To do this we shall make extensive use of the Keynesian general equilibrium model ($IS = LM$) developed in the previous chapter.[1] Second, we shall review and appraise the effectiveness of some of the major policy actions our government in Washington has taken in the post-World War II era, the object being to provide the reader with a candid and up to date understanding of the strengths and weaknesses of contemporary macroeconomic policy.

1. Policy is not a new topic, as we have discussed both fiscal and monetary policy at previous points in the text. In Chapter 8, for example, recent applications of fiscal measures were extensively discussed (pp. 262-63). In a sense the whole of Chapter 11 (The Modern Quantity Theory) is concerned with the subject of monetary policy, as the essential point of modern monetarism is that it is through the money supply (monetary policy) that we can best control the aggregate economy. Formal statements on the nature of both fiscal and monetary policy were made in Chapter 12. What we are doing in this chapter is to develop in a more complete sense the basic principles which govern the application of policy.

The Principles of Economic Policy

The formation of economic policy is a difficult and subtle art, and involves, as Edwin G. Nourse, first chairman of the President's Council of Economic Advisers has said, choice among conflicting values and judgment as to what is best in a total situation.[2] To be effective, economic policy must be grounded in sound economic theory. Therefore we need to understand the policy implications which flow out of the theoretical analysis developed in prior chapters.

Economic stabilization is a major social goal believed to be within the control of government in modern society. The economic power inherent in the public sector puts government in a position to promote stability, full employment, and maximum production. In the United States, the Employment Act of 1946 gave congressional sanction to the idea that the national government has a responsibility for income and employment levels in the economy. Although neither price stability nor economic growth—nor full employment *per se*—are mentioned in the Act, the tacit assumption is often made by economists as well as the federal government that these goals, too, are a part of the intent of the Act.

As we have seen, monetary and fiscal measures are the two chief instruments at the disposal of the central government for attainment of economic stabilization. Since in the Keynesian analysis, fluctuations in income and employment are primarily matters of too much or too little spending in relation to existing supply or capacity, stabilization policy involves the exercise of influence on the economy's over-all expenditure level. Both monetary and fiscal policy measures must therefore be evaluated in terms of their impact on expenditure levels, which is to say in terms of their impact upon aggregate demand. To put the matter somewhat differently, the goal of policy is full employment with stable prices, a goal which governments strive to reach by pulling on the levers marked "monetary" or "fiscal" policy. Difficulty since the mid-1960s in getting to full employment without pushing the price level up at too rapid a pace has given rise to a third type of policy, generally known as *incomes policy*. The term refers to the development of mechanisms whereby money wage and price increases can be held within tolerable limits as the economy approaches a full employment level of output.[3] We shall defer discus-

2. Edwin G. Nourse, *Economics in the Public Service* (New York: Harcourt, Brace, 1953), p. 18.

3. The idea of an incomes policy as a complement to fiscal and monetary policies grew out of the experience of the Kennedy-Johnson administration in the mid-1960s. At that time noninflationary wage-price "guideposts" were adopted. They were persuasive, not mandatory, a feature of the policy which gave rise to the rather derisive term "jawboning" to describe them. Later the Nixon administration experimented with both mandatory and voluntary wage-price controls.

sion of incomes policy to Chapter 14 in which the entire subject of inflation will be examined.

Monetary Policy and Its Application

As we have seen, (Chapter 12), monetary policy involves changing the money supply with the expectaton that such changes will influence total spending and thus output, employment, and the price level. The central bank, which in the United States means the Federal Reserve System, is the body responsible for carrying out monetary policy. From a strictly Keynesian viewpoint, monetary policy works indirectly through the impact of money on the rates of interest, whereas the monetarists hold that changes in money affect aggregate demand directly. These points have been discussed previously. There are, however, other matters to consider.

To begin, monetary policy operates through two broad sets of controls. First, there are general or indirect controls, which include changes in the reserve requirement of the commercial banks, changes in the rediscount rate, and open market operations by the central bank—that is, the Federal Reserve System. Second, there are selective or direct controls aimed at specific types of credit, such as installment credit, mortgage credit, or credit extended for the financing of stock market transactions. Indirect controls are used to alter the over-all volume of credit available to the economy; they do not seek to influence the allocation of credit (that is, money funds) among alternative uses. As discussed in Chapter 10, the primary instruments for the exercise of indirect monetary controls are open market operations, changes in the discount rate, and control over reserve requirements. The locus for these powers is the Board of Governors of the Federal Reserve System. General (or indirect) credit controls have been by far the most important policy instrument used by the Federal Reserve System. Thus any general discussion of monetary policy must be directed primarily toward the use and effectiveness of these controls.

The foregoing is but a part of the story. In order to carry out monetary policy, the monetary authority (the Federal Reserve System in the United States) must depend upon some economic variable as a policy guide, as an *indicator* which will signal the necessity for a policy change. Such a policy guide or indicator ought to tell the monetary authority something of what is going on in the economy currently. But it ought to do more than that. It should be a variable which has an impact upon the goals of policy (i.e., full employment or price stability) and it should be one which changes in response to changes in policy. In practice two such guides have been important in recent years. These are the money supply itself (or a variable closely related to the money supply, such as the volume of commercial bank reserves), or the general state of credit conditions, often represented by one or more rates of interest. To put the matter as succinctly as possible, the question is: should the Federal Reserve as the custodian of monetary policy pay the most attention to the money supply (however defined) or interest rates as a guide to its policy decisions? The answer is neither obvious nor simple. Figure 13–1 shows the linkages involved in this question.

If either the money supply or interest rates are to be used as guides to monetary policy, two things are essential. First, changes in either should lead to changes in total spending (and hence output, employment, and the price level), and second, they (money and interest rates) should be subject to control by the Federal Reserve System. The difficulty is that there is no agreement among monetary specialists—as well as economists in general—on either of these points. Take the matter of Federal Reserve control over either the money supply or interest rates. Proponents in favor of using the money supply as the basic policy guide (usually monetarists) argue that in the short term the Federal Reserve does not have good control over interest rates, the primary reason being that credit markets are quite sensitive to other factors besides actions taken by the Federal Reserve (open market operations, for example). On the other hand, advocates of the interest rate as a policy guide (generally Keynesians) say essentially the same thing about the money supply, namely that the money supply is not under control of the Federal Reserve System to the degree required to make it a good policy indicator. One reason for this is the existence of *near monies* (Chapter 10, p. 350).[4]

As a practical matter, the choice of a policy guide really comes down to the question of how the transmission mechanism works, which is, in effect, a question of which monetary theory is valid—contemporary monetarism or Keynesianism. Since monetarists believe that there is a close,

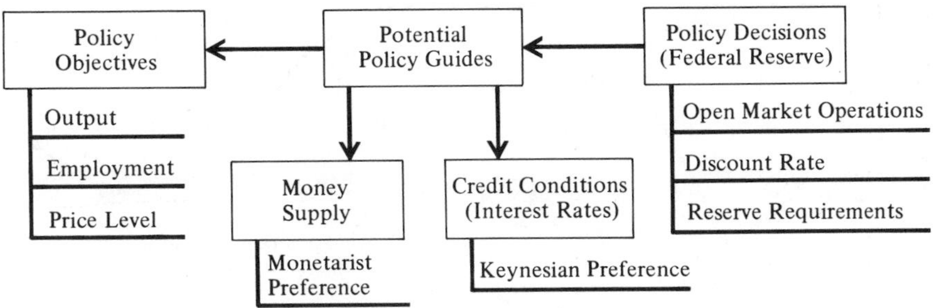

FIGURE 13–1. Policy Guides and Monetary Policy

4. For a complete discussion of various types of money supply and credit conditions policy guides, including criticisms of each, see Dudley G. Luckett, *Money and Banking*, (New York, McGraw Hill Book Company, 1976), pp. 538–543.

causal link between the money supply and the general level of economic activity, their preference is for using money as the primary policy indicator. As the matter of fact, Friedman and other monetarists fear that use of interest rates as an indicator may actually be destabilizing rather than stabilizing. For example, if interest rates are rising because of high employment and rapid economic expansion, any attempt by the Federal Reserve System to stabilize or bring interest rates down by *adding* to the money supply would be self-defeating. More money, in their view, would fuel more spending, which would cause interest rates to go up even faster. Nonmonetarists, on the other hand, adopt what is essentially a Keynesian position, namely that the link between money and the general level of economic activity is through the interest rate (See discussion in Chapter 11 on the Keynesian view of the channels of monetary policy, pp. 358–59). Thus, the preference of Keynesians is for using interest rates as a policy guide. Prior to the early 1970s the Federal Reserve System relied almost exclusively on credit conditions (interest rates) as a policy indicator, but since then more attention has been paid to the money supply, a consequence of the growing influence in policy matters of the monetarist position. It has not, however, even come close to adopting the monetarist view that the money supply ought to expand at a fixed rate in the 3 to 5 percent range. A glance at Figure 13–2 confirms this, as the annual rate of expansion of the money supply (M_1) has been quite erratic over the past dozen years.

There are other concerns in the application of monetary policy. One of these is the matter of lags. This involves the length of time between a

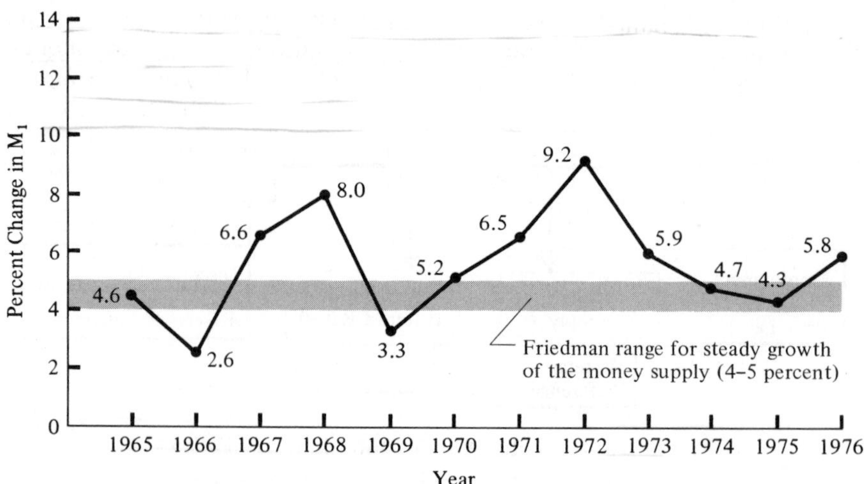

FIGURE 13–2. Annual Percentage Rate of Change in the Money Supply (M_1): 1965–76

change in policy and its effect upon the economy. The problem is that there is no exact statistical information on the length of such lags—what information we do have suggests, further, that they may be highly variable, ranging, perhaps, from a few months to nearly two years. The lack of precise information on the length of policy lags is another reason why monetarists such as Friedman prefer that the monetary authority adhere to a fixed rule for expansion of the money supply. Two basic types of lags are important, *inside* lags and *outside* lags. The former refers to the length of time which passes between the need for action and the actual taking of action by the Federal Reserve System. The latter pertains to the time involved between the taking of action by the Federal Reserve and the effect of that action on the goals of policy, namely the employment or price levels.

Another problem affecting monetary policy is that its ultimate impact may be both uneven and unfair. A large corporation often has adequate financial reserves, and thus is not forced to go into the money market to get funds for expansion. On the other hand, the small firm has fewer internal financing resources, and must depend upon bank credit for some of its operations. Consequently in a period of tight money, the pressure of monetary policy may be felt most acutely by small business, leaving large corporations relatively unaffected by central bank policies. Since the spending decisions of large corporations generally have more impact on the economy than those of small businesses, some of the effectiveness of monetary policy may be lost. Industrial concentration—the tendency for industries to be dominated by a handful of large firms—may also be furthered under these circumstances.

Economists recognize that different investment expenditures differ significantly in their sensitivity to a change in the rate of interest. For example, expenditures for buildings, including residential housing, are much more sensitive to a change in the rate of interest than are business expenditures for inventories, or even new equipment. Table 13–1 below shows mortgage interest rates and new (private) housing starts for the twelve year period, 1965 through 1976. Note the sharp downturn in new housing construction in the years in which money "tightened"—1966, 1969, and 1973–75. Thus, a stringent monetary policy which leads to a sharp rise in the rate of interest affects investment spending unevenly. Whether such uneven effects are desirable from the standpoint of a social policy is a matter of key importance.

Monetary policy has also been criticized because if it is applied with sufficient vigor in a period of inflation to bring about a contraction in investment spending, it will push the economy into a recession. The unhappy experience of the Nixon administration with its first "game plan" lends credence to this view. In 1969 the money supply was tightened, interest rates rose sharply, and in 1970 gross investment spending dropped. The

TABLE 13–1. Interest Rates and New Housing: 1965–76

Year	*Mortgage Rates (in percent)*	*Housing Starts (in thousands of units)*
1965	5.81	1,473
1966	6.25↑	1,165↓
1967	6.46	1,292
1968	6.97	1,508
1969	7.81↑	1,467↓
1970	8.45	1,433
1971	7.74	2,052
1972	7.60	2,357
1973	7.95↑	2,045↓
1974	8.92↑	1,338↓
1975	9.01↑	1,160↓
1976	8.99	1,538

SOURCE: *Economic Report of the President*, 1977.

most recent recession—1974–75—was also preceded by a period of tighter money, although there is a less clear-cut relationship between this and the subsequent recession than in the earlier period, the reason being that most economists agree that the inflation itself was a major factor in explaining the 1974 downturn. Higher prices cut into real income, which in turn led to spending cutbacks.

On the other hand, monetary policy cannot be relied upon to bring the economy out of a serious depression, because even a drastic change in the interest rate is not enough of an incentive to stimulate investment spending when aggregate demand is at a low level. Proponents of monetary policy are likely to point in reply to the indirect character of monetary policy as one of its chief virtues because the government is not involved directly in the regulation of economic activity. Monetary policy can be said to possess the virtues of speed and flexibility since normally it is administered by central banks and thus does not require legislative action.

To sum up, economists are by no means in agreement with respect to either the effectiveness or desirability of monetary policy. From roughly the end of World War II to the mid 1960s a clear majority of economists held that fiscal policy was the more powerful, the more effective instrument for the overall control of economic activity. No longer is this the case, primarily because of the impact that the monetarist "Counter-Revolution" has had on economic thinking. But it would not be accurate, either, to suggest that a majority of economists now regard monetary policy as a more effective control instrument. Rather, modern macroeconomic theory sees *both* fiscal and monetary policies as having important roles to play in any stabilization program. They should not be regarded as rivals, but complementary approaches to the problem of economic stabilization. No doubt an even more accurate view is that a growing number of economists believe that, as the economy is presently structured, neither monetary nor fiscal instruments seem well suited for the control of inflation.

Fiscal Policy and Its Application

Fiscal policy, as we have seen, involves *deliberate* changes in the taxes government collects and the money it spends as a means to influence the economy. Taxes and spending are the means and the government's budget is the instrument through which fiscal policy is carried out In the definition the word deliberate must be stressed. Governments collect taxes and spend money for a variety of purposes, ranging from building highways to providing for the common defense. Only when they deliberately change their spending or taxes to try and affect the economy's performance is it correct to speak of fiscal policy. In the United States, the locus of fiscal policy is in the administration in power (the president) and the Congress. Usually, the president initiates fiscal policy—a tax or spending change—but nothing can happen until such changes are approved by the Congress.

Prior to the 1960s two widely different viewpoints held sway among professional economists as to the proper role and scope for fiscal policy. At one extreme was the concept of *functional finance* which asserted that the primary consideration of the government in all its operations should be the effects of its actions on income and employment levels.[5] Advocates of functional finance argue for example, that government should raise (or lower) taxes not because it needs more (or less) money, but because it wants to decrease (or increase) consumption spending. Proposals embodied in the notion of functional finance rest upon the assumption that economic stabilization is the one really important function of the modern government, a point of view that will be disputed by those who are keenly interested in the problem of an adequate supply of social goods and services in an expanding and affluent society. We may note parenthetically that here is a point of potential conflict and contradiction because a growing need and demand for social goods may make it difficult if not impossible, at times to adjust the tax and expenditure budgets of the public sector to the requirements of stabilization policy.

5. Abba P. Lerner has been the chief proponent of this idea. See his *The Economics of Control* (New York: Macmillan, 1949), pp. 302 ff.

At the other extreme were proposals which suggested that the budget of the federal government ought to be so constructed that taxes and expenditures would be automatically in balance at an income level somewhat below that of full employment. If this were done, and if, further, tax rates and government expenditures remained constant, then a budgetary surplus would automatically be generated as the economy approached the full employment level. But if income fell below the level at which taxes and expenditures were in balance, an automatic deficit would ensue.[6] A budgetary policy which leads to a surplus in prosperity and a deficit in recession or depression is generally recognized as countercyclical because the surplus draws funds out of the current income stream and the deficit adds funds to the income flow. Such a policy relies entirely upon the built-in characteristics of the tax structure that cause taxes automatically to rise in periods of income expansion and to fall in periods of income contraction. It allows no room for discretionary fiscal action by either the executive or legislative branch of the government. The similarity of this sort of arrangement to Professor Friedman's desire for a fixed rate of growth in the money supply should be recognized. What both approaches have in common is a distaste for discretionary action and a faith that somehow the economy can be made to perform automatically if only the proper, self-regulating instrument can be discovered. The real world economy is unlike this, though. It is untidy, irregular, and requires some form of public intervention if it is to function well. This is the fundamental viewpoint of Keynes.

If a poll had been taken among economists in the 1940s and 1950s the view of a majority on the proper scope of fiscal policy probably would have been bound to lie midway between the extremes of functional finance and the notion of an automatic countercyclical budget. A point, though, upon which there would have been near unanimity of opinion is that there is no sound economic reason why the budget of the national government should be balanced on annual basis. It is only desirable, according to the rules of modern fiscal policy, that deficits incurred during a depression or recession be offset by surpluses acquired in subsequent periods of prosperity. The economy's track record on this point is not especially good. In nineteen of the last twenty-eight years (1949–76) the federal government has had a deficit, even though many of these years were marked by prosperity. Even so there is no general consensus among economists on the proper mix of automatic stabilizers and discretionary action by appropriate authorities. The last year in which there was a surplus in the accounts of the federal government was 1969. That was a

6. This idea is generally credited to the Committee on Economic Development. For further details see the studies issued by the CED: *Taxes and the Budget*, November 1947; and *Monetary and Fiscal Policy for Greater Economic Stability*, December 1948.

year of highly restrictive monetary and fiscal policies, resulting in a recession the following year.

Beginning in the 1960s, though, the focus of fiscal policy shifted away from the idea of minimizing the ups and downs of cyclical fluctuations in both income and employment. Largely because of the persuasive influence exerted by Professor Walter Heller of the University of Minnesota who served as Chairman of the Council of Economic Advisers in the Kennedy administration, the primary emphasis became one of using discretionary fiscal policy, especially changes in individual and corporate tax rates, as a means of keeping the economy growing at its full potential. Heller described this shift as follows:

> As part of the reshaping of stabilization policy, then, our fiscal policy targets have been recast in terms of "full" or "high" employment levels of output, specifically the level of GNP associated with a 4-percent rate of unemployment. *So the target is no longer budget balance every year or over the cycle*, but balance . . . at full employment. And in modern stabilization policy, as we will see in a moment, even this target does not remain fixed.[7]

The budget of the federal government is the primary instrument for the implementation of fiscal policy. The mechanics of this are relatively simple. If the federal government at full employment spends more for goods and services, G_f, than it receives in net taxes, T_f, then it will be operating at a deficit, which is to say that it will be putting more into the income stream via its expenditures than it is pulling out through net taxes.[8] Consequently, the over-all effect of the federal budget will be expansionary. On the other hand, a surplus would have a contractive economic effect, since it entails an excess of net taxes, T_f over spending for goods and services, G_f, which in turn means the federal government is pulling more out of the income flow than it is putting in. The over-all expansionary or contractive effect of the federal budget depends, of course, on the absence of offsetting changes in the private sector, such as a fall in private investment when a federal deficit emerges.

The way of looking at the federal budget which Heller described above has come to be known as the *full employment budget.* It offers a different and presumably more meaningful way of looking at the economic effects of a surplus or deficit in the federal budget. It is, in other words, a better guide to the real economic impact of the federal government's fiscal be-

7. Walter W. Heller, *New Dimensions of Political Economy* (New York: W.W. Norton & Company, Inc., 1967), p. 66. [Italics added.] What Heller meant by the full employment target not being fixed was that the economy would grow over time, since a growing labor force and a rising productivity for the labor force would increase continuously the output level associated with a 4 percent unemployment rate.

8. The subscript f is used to denote spending and taxes at the federal level.

havior than the state of balance of the budget in any given year. Essentially, the full employment budget attempts to estimate the federal deficit or surplus that would emerge if the economy were operating at the full employment level, a procedure that not only involves estimating the economy's full employment output potential (see Chapter 4), but the federal tax revenue this level of output will generate, as well as the amount of expenditures that will be forthcoming. Table 13–2 shows the actual and estimated full employment surplus and deficit for 1970–76.

The basic rationale for this budget concept is that the true inflationary or deflationary potential of the federal budget is apparent only when the economy is at full employment. The reasoning behind this is quite simple. If the economy is at full employment, and if, too, there is a deficit ($G_f > T_f$), then the government's fiscal activities (tax and expenditure policies) are clearly inflationary. The reverse is, of course, the case if there is a surplus ($T_f > G_f$). On the other hand, the situation is not clear-cut for the real effects of either a current surplus or deficit when the economy is not at full employment. To illustrate, suppose in the current year the federal government runs a deficit. But if this deficit happened because of a recession and the resulting fall off in taxes, it would mean that the

TABLE 13–2. Actual and Full Employment Federal Government Receipts and Expenditures: 1970–76 (billions of current dollars)

Calendar Year	*Receipts*	*Expenditures*	*Surplus or Deficit (−)*	
			Amount	*Change*
Actual				
1970	192.1	204.2	−12.1	−20.6
1971	198.6	220.6	−22.0	−9.9
1972	227.5	244.7	−17.3	4.7
1973	258.3	265.0	−6.7	10.6
1974	288.2	299.7	−11.5	−4.8
1975	286.5	357.8	−71.2	−59.7
1976	330.6	388.9	−58.3	12.9
Full-Employment				
1970	201.0	203.6	−2.6	6.3
1971	210.0	219.1	−9.2	−6.6
1972	222.1	243.6	−21.5	−12.3
1973	257.5	265.4	−7.9	13.6
1974	311.8	297.7	14.1	22.0
1975	337.6	350.1	−12.5	−26.5
1976	371.6	381.9	−10.3	2.2

SOURCE: *Economic Report of the President*, 1977.
NOTE: Detail may not add to totals because of rounding.

deficit was an induced consequence of changing economic conditions rather than a force deliberately designed to change economic conditions. The figures in Table 13–2 for 1974 illustrate clearly these two situations. In this year the actual budget was in deficit by $11.5 billion. This was the year in which the economy was sliding downhill into a recession, and, as expected, the deficit increased over the previous year. But the full employment budget for 1974 shows a surplus of $14.1 billion, a figure which indicates that the federal budget in this year was basically a restrictive force, being, therefore, a factor in the downturn. Even though there are serious limitations inherent in the concept of a full-employment budget—especially because of difficulties involved in estimating and measurement—many economists believe it is a much better tool for indicating the probable impact of discretionary fiscal policy than a simple calculation of the current surplus or deficit of the federal sector.

Toward New Budgetary Policies

Prospects for the efficient administration of fiscal policy improved when the Congress passed the Congressional Budget and Impoundment Control Act of 1974, a historic piece of legislation which is designed to help the Congress—in contrast to the administration—develop an over-all budget policy. For the first time in our history, the Congress will be required to look at the federal budget in total, both with respect to expenditures and receipts. Heretofore, both spending proposals and appropriation measures were considered separately, not only for the spending and taxing totals, but for their component parts. It was a piecemeal process that never permitted the Congress to view the budget in its taxing and spending aspects as an entity in relation to its impact on the economy. That has now changed. The 1974 Budget Act provides, first, that the entire Congress adopt in May of each year spending and revenue targets. This is done by a concurrent resolution. Later in September, just prior to the beginning of the new fiscal year on October 1, a second concurrent resolution is adopted which either affirms or revises these targets. This second resolution becomes binding. The reform act also established committees on the budget in both houses of the Congress, committees which have the responsibility for developing a comprehensive budget policy each year. To help in doing this, the 1974 legislation also established the Congressional Budget Office, a body roughly designed to serve the Congress in the same way that the Council of Economic Advisers serves the president.

Even if fiscal policy is a powerful instrument for economic stabilization it, like monetary policy, is subject to difficulties and limitations. First, fiscal policy measures which involve changes in public expenditures may conflict with the long-term character of many governmental expenditure programs. It is not possible continually to adjust expenditures for basic social goods and services to meet the shifting exigencies of economic stabilization. Second, the political process through which changes in expenditures and taxes are effected is so long drawn out and fraught with so many uncertainties that it is nearly impossible in a democratic society to obtain the necessary speed and flexibility that fiscal policy requires if it is to be successful as an instrument for economic stabilization. This is probably true in spite of the passage of the Budget Reform Act in 1974. This act will undoubtedly give the Congress a better understanding of the economic consequence of the budget, but it probably won't speed up the political process significantly. The exception to this view, perhaps, is tax reduction, as the Congress has shown it can act with a fair amount of speed when tax cuts are involved. It took about two months for the Congress to pass the Ford administration's tax reduction proposals in 1975, but a somewhat longer period before it acted on the Carter administration requests in 1977. Our limited experience to date suggests two to three months appears to be the norm for Congressional action involving a tax reduction. This should be contrasted to the possibility that the Federal Reserve can literally act within a week if necessary.

To give fiscal policy the same speed and flexibility characteristic of monetary policy, it has been suggested that the president be given limited authority to vary tax rates within limits laid down by the Congress, and subject, as well, to a congressional veto.[9] Both the Kennedy and Johnson administrations made such a recommendation. In his last budget message, President Johnson proposed that the President have the authority to vary rates on personal and corporate income taxes (up or down) by 5 percent. To date the Congress has resisted strongly the idea of giving the president authority to vary tax rates within guidelines laid down by the legislative body. Since Watergate the surge of hostility toward any more delegation of legislative power to the president makes the possibility of an arrangement of this type even more remote.

Finally, it is averred that one concept of modern fiscal policy, the cyclically balanced budget at the national level, simply won't work politically. There is no serious objection to a governmental deficit in a recession or depression, because nearly everyone will benefit from the stimulus this brings to the economy. But opposition to the kind of tax policy necessary

9. The president is not without some power to act without congressional approval. He can in a small way vary the timing for expenditures within the budget limits set by the Congress. This works in either direction, which is to say he can speed up or slow down spending. President Nixon attempted to "impound" funds already appropriated by the Congress, his object being to cut back on spending. This involved him in an ongoing battle with the Congress over its constitutional right to control the "purse strings," and was a factor that led to the passage of the 1974 Congressional Budget Act.

to generate a surplus may be so strong that the required budgetary surplus fails to appear in period of prosperity.[10] As already pointed out, deficits appear to be the norm, no matter what the state of the economy happens to be.

The Application of Fiscal and Monetary Policy

It is now appropriate that we turn to a more in depth analysis of the workings of fiscal and monetary policy. For this purpose we shall use the Keynesian general equilibrium model as our primary expository device. In a brief introduction to this topic in the previous chapter (pp. 379–83), it was pointed out that the workings of either fiscal or monetary policy or both in combination can be demonstrated by shifts in either the *IS* or *LM* curves. We shall continue in this vein. Initially we shall disregard changes in the general price level, as our first objective is to concentrate on the effects of monetary and fiscal policy actions on real output (and employment). After we have done this, we can introduce price level changes into the analysis and see how the effectiveness of various policies is affected.

In *The General Theory* there is a statement by Keynes which most appropriately describes the procedure we shall be following. In economic analysis we have to consider various relationships in isolation from one another, and then after we understand them, bring other relationships into the picture. In doing this, Keynes said:

> The object of our analysis is, not to provide a machine, or method of blind manipulation, which will furnish an infallible answer, *but to provide ourselves with an organized and orderly method of thinking out particular problems*; and after we have reached a provisional conclusion by isolating the complicating factors one by one, we then have to go back on ourselves and allow, as well as we can, for the probable interaction of the factors amongst themselves. *This is the nature of economic thinking.*[11]

Theoretical Limits to Fiscal and Monetary Policy

As a backdrop to our subsequent discussion of the practical workings of both fiscal and monetary policy measures, an explantion of the theoretical limits to the effectiveness of either policy approach is in order. In reality,

10. This difficulty is dramatically illustrated by the obvious reluctance of the Johnson administration to request a tax increase at any time during 1966, even though the rising level of military expenditures for the war in Vietnam put the economy under strong inflationary pressures. The Nixon administration was equally unwilling to raise taxes to combat inflation.

11. John Maynard Keynes, *The General Theory of Employment, Interest, and Money* (New York, Harcourt, Brace & World, First Harbinger ed., 1964), pp. 297. [Italics added.]

it is unlikely that the economy will get into a situation in which these theoretical limits are actually present; yet we may approach them, and thus some knowledge of them is important for understanding the circumstances under which one policy approach may be more effective than the other.

In the post-World War II literature of macroeconomics these possible limits to the effectiveness of either fiscal or monetary policy have come to be known as the Keynesian range (or case) and the Classical range (or case). The Keynesian general equilibrium model offers an ideal vehicle for dramatizing these two alternatives. Figure 13–3 illustrates these extremes of viewpoint. In the figure IS_1 intersects the *LM* curve in the range in which the latter is perfectly elastic with respect to the rate of interest (the Keynesian range) and IS_2 intersects the *LM* curve in the range at which this curve becomes perfectly inelastic with respect to the rate of interest (the classical range).

If the *IS* curve intersects the *LM* schedule in the range at which the latter is perfectly elastic with respect to the rate of interest, certain significant policy implications follow. Such a situation might arise because the economy is in a deep depression, with both income and the rate of interest declining to relatively low levels. In this situation monetary policy involving an increase in the money supply will be completely ineffective. An increase in the money supply shifts the *LM* curve to the right, and this will, *ceteris paribus*, tend to raise the income level, but only if the rate of interest lies above the critical level at which the *LM* schedule is perfectly elastic. The point of intersection of IS_1 and the *LM* curve typifies a situation in which the demand for liquidity is so great that any increase in the money supply simply is added to existing idle balances. The increase, in other words, drops into the *liquidity trap*; consequently no change in either the rate of interest, investment expenditure, or the income level will ensue. Under these circumstance it might be said that "money doesn't matter." A rise in the income level must wait upon a higher position of the *IS* curve which would require an upward shift in the aggregate demand function. The obvious implication of this analysis is that fiscal rather than monetary policy measures are needed.

A situation quite the opposite of the one just described prevails if the *IS* curve intersects the *LM* curve at a point at which the latter is perfectly inelastic with respect to the rate of interest. This is shown in Figure 13–3 by the intersection of IS_2 and the *LM* schedule in the inelastic range of the latter. This is a classic case of a situation in which the only effective means to increase income is through monetary policy. Hence, we might say that "only money matters." If the money supply is increased, the interest rate will fall, and the income level will rise as investment expenditure responds to a lower rate of interest. If the intersection of the *IS* and *LM* curves in the range in which the latter is perfectly interest inelastic

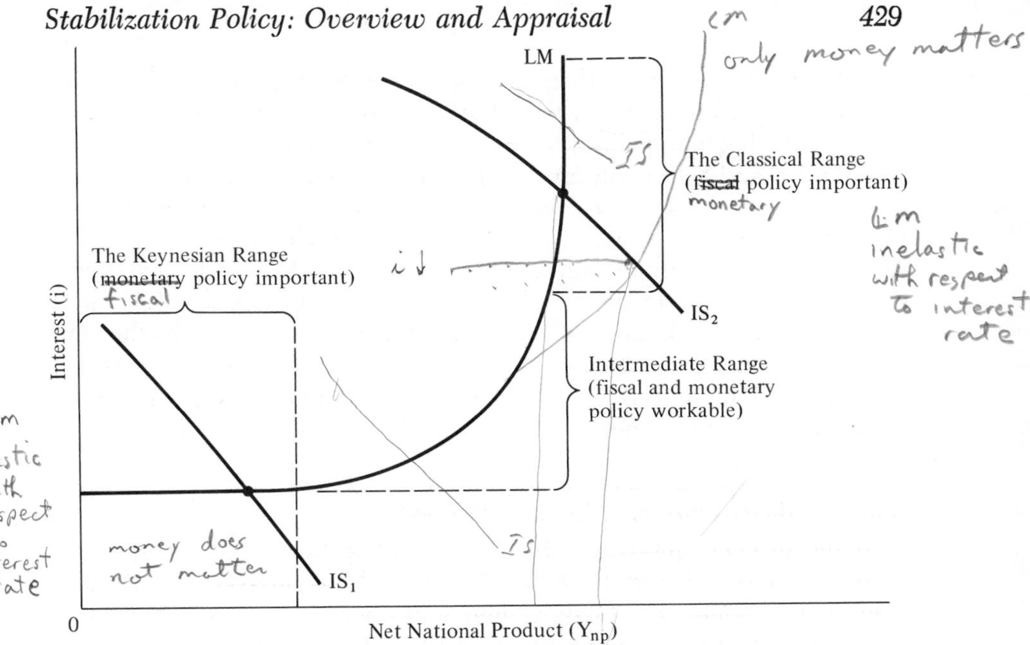

FIGURE 13–3. Theoretical Limits to Fiscal and Monetary Policy

implies the desirability of monetary policy, it is equally true that intersection in this range implies the complete unworkability of fiscal policy. Fiscal policy measures that induce an upward shift in the aggregate demand function without any corresponding change in the money supply are bound to be self-defeating. The only consequence of fiscal action is an increase in the rate of interest. An upward shift in the aggregate demand function, assuming no change in the money supply, merely drives interest rates higher because of the rising transactions demand induced by the original shift in the aggregate demand function. The net result ultimately is no change in the income level, but equilibrium of saving and investment at a higher rate of interest.

As a practical matter it is the area which lies between the extreme Keynesian and Classical positions which is important for policy in the real world. In terms of the diagram, this is the area in which *both* fiscal and monetary policy are workable in the sense that they can affect the level of real output—net national product (Y_{np}) in the diagram. The closer the economy lies to the Classical position the greater is the relative effectiveness of monetary policy, whereas the closer it is to the Keynesian range, fiscal policy becomes relatively more effective. When we speak of the economy being close to either of these extremes it is not meant literally. We don't have any machines which can tell us the exact state of our economic health or where we stand at any particular time. Policy-makers, in the final analysis, exercise their own judgment on these matters, deciding the proper mix of fiscal and monetary actions to reach desired ends. As stated at the beginning of this chapter, the formulation of economic policy is a difficult and subtle art, involving choice among conflicting values and judgment as to what is best in a total situation. The reader should not forget that our discussion and analysis pertain to what takes place within the confines of a graphic model of the economy, and thus the conclusions offered with respect to the effectiveness of both monetary and fiscal policies should not be thought of as providing definitive answers to the complex problems of policy that exist in the real economic world. At best they represent insights into the workings of the economy and suggest only the broadest sort of guidelines to actual policy formulation.

Fiscal and Monetary Policy Compared

Let us now compare the effectiveness of the fiscal and the monetary approach to economic stabilization. Since fiscal policy involves changes in government spending or taxes, its impact is upon the basic components of aggregate demand—government spending for goods and services, consumption spending, and investment spending. In the framework of the Keynesian general equilibrium model, the effect of fiscal policy is shown by shifts in the *IS* curve. Monetary policy centers on increases or decreases in the money supply; consequently it works thrugh changes in the *LM* curve, again within the context of the Keynesian general equilibrium model. All this is not new, but it is of such fundamental importance that it bears repeating. In making these comparisons we shall, initially, assume *pure* fiscal and monetary policies. A *pure* fiscal action changes the spending stream without directly affecting the money supply curve, while a *pure* monetary action changes the money supply curve without directly affecting the spending stream. If fiscal and monetary policies are *pure* in this sense, then either the *IS* or *LM* curve can shift without affecting the position of the other curve. The curves become independent of one another, in other words. Later we shall drop the *pure* assumption. Resorting to such an assumption is another example of what Keynes meant when he said that after reading a "provisional conclusion by isolating the complicating factors one by one, we have to go back on ourselves and allow . . . for the probable interaction of the factors amongst themselves."

Figure 13–4 shows graphically the basic differences between fiscal and monetary policy, assuming the objective is to raise real national income. Part A of the diagram illustrates the *pure* fiscal policy case and part B the *pure* monetary policy case. We shall examine each of these in turn.

Initially the economy is at Y_1, a level of income determined by the intersection of IS_1 and the *LM* curve. Assume now that we have a shift to the right (upwards) in the *IS* curve, the reason being either an increase in government expenditures or a cut in taxes. The extent to which the *IS* curve shifts depends upon the value of the Keynesian multiplier and the amount by which the aggregate demand schedule changes because of either the increase in government expenditures or the cut in taxes. As analyzed in Chapter 8 (p. 257), a tax cut has a smaller initial impact upon aggregate demand than an increase in government expenditures, the reason being that it (the tax cut) affects aggregate demand indirectly. In any event, the new equilibrium income level will be determined by the intersections of IS_2 and the *LM* curve. This shift takes place in the Keynesian range of the model, which means that the rate of interest doesn't rise. If the economy is in a liquidity trap situation, potential spenders—governments, business firms, and even consumers—presumably have idle balances which they can activate to sustain higher levels of spending. For a while then, more borrowing would not be necessary to permit output to expand. Under these circumstances the economy will experience the full multiplier effect from either an increase in government spending or a cut in taxes. The closest our society has actually come to this situation was in the depths of the Great Depression, in 1932 and 1933.

Much more normal is the situation depicted by the intersection of IS_3 and the *LM* curve, where income is at the level Y_3, a level presumably less than full employment. The rightward shift of the *IS* curve is the same in magnitude as in the prior instance, but the impact on the income level will be less (the difference between Y_4 and Y_3 is smaller than the difference between Y_2 and Y_1). The reason for this is that some of the increased government spending (or added private spending induced by a tax cut) will be offset by the rise in interest rates from i_2 to i_3. Some spending (private) has been "crowded out" by the fiscal stimulus, a

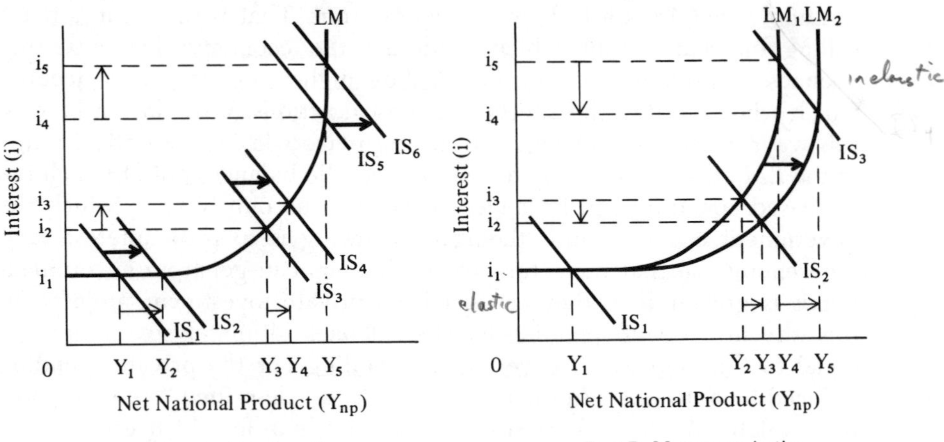

FIGURE 13–4. Fiscal and Monetary Policy Compared

development which means that the overall impact is less than it was in the prior instance when the interest rate was unaffected by increased spending. As pointed out in Chapter 8, "crowding out" is associated with the financing of a government deficit. In the example being considered, the rise in interest rates could result from the sale by the government of new securities to the public—that is government borrowing—an act which would depress existing security prices (bonds or consols), thereby forcing up the rate of interest. This process may be viewed as involving either an addition by government to the supply of bonds, or an offer of higher rates of interest to persuade some wealth-holders to switch from holding money to holding bonds. In either case the result is the same—higher interest rates and some offsetting declines in private investment (and consumption) spending. In a purely Keynesian perspective all that needs happen is for interest rates to rise and pull some money out of inactive balances into active circulation. But more is involved because wealth-holders have to be persuaded to hold their wealth in some form other than money. This is why lending and borrowing has to come into the picture. The "crowding out" which occurs in this example is only partial, as the stimulus to output resulting from more government spending (or a tax cut) is not wholly offset by induced declines in private spending.

A completely different situation exists when the economy's initial position is shown by the intersection of IS_5 and the *LM* curve. At this point this equilibrium income level is Y_5. Once again the *IS* curve shifts in response to fiscal actions, a cut in taxes or an increase in government spending for goods and service. But the output level does not change. In terms of the diagram the increase in the rate of interest is great enough to cause a fall in private investment (and consumption) spending which just offsets the effects of the fiscal stimulus. Note carefully this analysis does not imply that Y^5 is a full employment output. That is to say, it is not a ceiling on real output which confronts the economy, but offsetting declines in private spending induced by higher interest rates—declines which wholly nullify the effects of the fiscal actions. Why does it happen this way? Since these changes are taking place within the vertical range of the *LM* curve, it means that there are no idle balances out of which the increased spending can be financed. Hence, the only way in which the government can get funds thourgh borrowing is to push interest rates high enough so that the return wealth-holders can get from government bonds is greater than they can get from private investment projects. In this way investment spending will be cut back ultimately by an amount equal to the increase in government spending (or the private spending induced by a tax cut). In the circumstances just described "crowding out" is complete. We have a "pure" classical case, one in which fiscal policy has become totally ineffective. What will happen, however, is a change in the composition of output; the application of fiscal measures under these circumstances means there will be more public spending and less private spending, but the overall output level will be unchanged.

Let us now turn to the monetary side of the question as illustrated by Part B in Figure 13–4. We shall start again with the intersection of IS_1 and LM_1 which gives us a low level equilibrium income level Y_1. Monetary policy works by changing the money supply, which in the framework of the Keynesian general model is reflected through shifts in the LM curve. In our analysis we shall be concerned only with an increase in the money supply; thus the LM curve shifts from LM_1 to LM_2. But in this instance nothing happens. The reason is that the economy has sunk into the liquidity trap, a situation in which the demand for money has become perfectly elastic. There is so much uncertainty—and fear—about future bond prices, that the public (wealth-holders) is quite willing to exchange the bonds it is now holding for additional cash without the price of bonds having to increase. When the government pumps more money into the economy, all that happens is that the public winds up holding more cash and fewer securities. Monetary policy cannot drive down the rate of interest further, and therefore it has no effect upon the level of aggregate demand. Parenthetically, let us note that the situation just described—one in which monetary policy is wholly ineffective—is not recognized as valid by monetarists. It exists only within a Keynesian perspective. This requires that the demand for liquidity (money) may become absolute and that changes in the money supply always be transmitted to aggregate demand through the interest rate, propositions rejected by monetarism.

Turn now to the intersection of IS_2 and LM_1. Equilibrium income is Y_2. Now the economy is operating in a range in which monetary policy is effective. The analysis is quite straightforward. As the money supply is increased, the LM curve shifts to the right (LM_2), which brings the rate of interest down from i_3 to i_2. The mechanism for doing this is the purchase of securities (bonds or consols) by the central bank, an action which drives up their prices and pushes down the rate of interest. Since the economy is in the range in which the LM curve is neither wholly horizontal nor wholly vertical, some of the new money will be absorbed into speculative balances and some into active (transactions) balances. As long as any of the money spills over into idle balances, the increases in aggregate demand will be less than the increase in the money supply, assuming no change in velocity. The increase in income in measured by the distance from Y_2 to Y_3.

The last situation we shall examine is depicted by the intersection of IS_3 and LM_1, which gives us an equilibrium income equal to Y_4. As we pointed out earlier, the vertical segment of the LM curve means a condition in which there are no idle or speculative balances—all money is in active circulation. Interest rates are extremely high ("extremely" in this case means relative to general perceptions of what is a "normal" level for the rate of interest). The rightward shift in the *LM* curve means, once again, that the government is buying securities, an action which will increase the money supply in the hands of the public and drive down the rate of interest. In the diagram IS_3 intersects LM_2 in the vertical range of the former. This means that the rate of interest will have to fall far enough to absorb *all* the new money into active circulation, since the economy is still in a "pure" classical world in which no balances are being held for speculative purposes. If this happens, the increase in aggregate demand will be equal to the increase in the money supply, again assuming no change in velocity. Thus, monetary policy will be totally effective.

In the foregoing analysis we traced out the income effects of policy induced shifts in either the *IS* or *LM* curve. There is one final point to consider. If we assume the two curves are independent of one another (as we have done), then the extent to which income responds to a shift in either the *IS* or *LM* curve depends upon the shape of the other curve. This becomes a matter of the interest elasticity of the curves—that is the sensitivity of the underlying determinants of the two curves to changes in the rate of interest. For example, for any given change in the *IS* curve, the income effect will be greater as the *LM* curve approaches the horizontal—as it becomes more interest elastic. Further, the "crowding out" effect of interest rate changes will be minimized the *less* responsive investment (and consumption) spending are to changes in the rate of interest—or the more interest inelastic is the *IS* curve. For a change in the *LM* curve, on the other hand, the income effect will increase as the *IS* becomes more interest elastic—as its slope becomes more horizontal. Further, the effectiveness of monetary policy becomes greater as the *LM* curve becomes less interest elastic—as it approaches the vertical. The overall effectiveness of fiscal and monetary policy and the cross relationships between these two important curves—*IS* and *LM*—are summarized in the matrix arrangement shown in Figure 13–5. It should be studied carefully in relation to the analysis developed in connection with Figure 13–4.

Effectiveness of:	INTEREST ELASTICITY	
	High	Low
Fiscal Policy	LM Curve	IS Curve
Monetary Policy	IS Curve	LM Curve

FIGURE 13–5. Interest Elasticity and Effectiveness of Fiscal and Monetary Policy

Crowding Out Once Again

In the foregoing comparison of fiscal and monetary policy, the phenomenon of crowding out was discussed under the assumption that the *IS* and *LM* curves are independent. Except for the extreme classical case (which is not likely to be encountered in reality), crowding out would only be partial most of the time (see p. 270). This, however, does not satisfy advocates of the crowding out thesis (monetarists primarily). It is argued that if a wealth effect is taken into account, or if the assumption of stable prices is dropped, then crowding out may occur even if the economy is operating between the extremes of the Keynesian and classical ranges. Figure 13–6 examines how this may come about.

In part A of Figure 13–6 the economy is originally at income level Y_1, a result of the intersection of IS_1 and LM_2. Now it is assumed that through fiscal policy the *IS* curve is shifted to the right to the position IS_2. To understand how complete crowding out may occur, let us recall Friedman's theory of the demand for money (Chapter 11, pp. 360–66). The demand for money varies positively with the quantity of wealth people hold. Included in such wealth will be government bonds which are newly issued to finance the added government expenditures (or a tax cut). But this means that the demand for money will increase. In the context of the Keynesian general equilibrium model, an increase in the demand for money envisaged in this way shifts the entire series of money demand curves upwards (See Figures 10–5, 10–9. and 12–1), assuming no change in the money supply curve. The consequence of this will be an upward (leftward) shift in the *LM* curve to the position of LM_1 in Figure

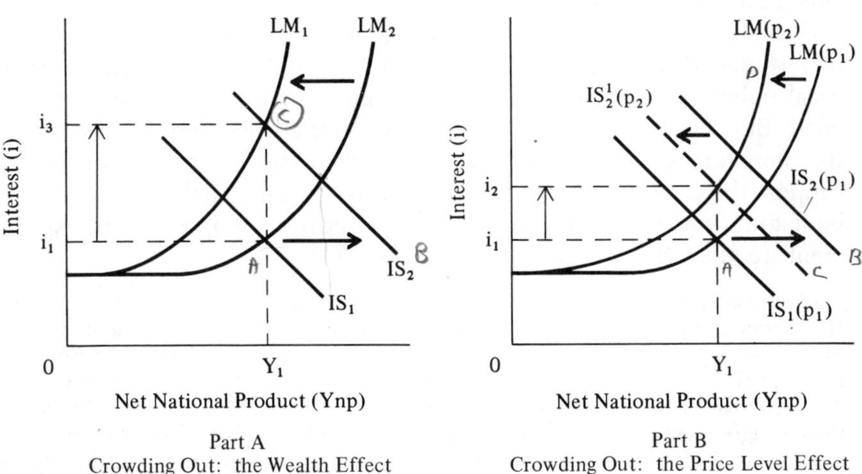

Part A
Crowding Out: the Wealth Effect

Part B
Crowding Out: the Price Level Effect

FIGURE 13–6. Crowding Out: Wealth and Price Effects

13–6. In the example shown, the *LM* curve has shifted sufficiently to just offset the effect of an increase in government spending (or a tax cut). Crowding out is complete, and the only change of consequence is a rise in interest rates from i_1 to i_3. Friedman characterizes the changes which result from a shift in the *IS* curve as "first round effects." Changes which show the impact of increased wealth upon the demand for money and subsequently the position of the *LM* curve represent the "ultimate effects." Friedman believes that the latter are in the final analysis, stronger than the first round changes, although they have not been put to empirical testing.[12]

There is yet another way in which crowding out may occur. This requires dropping the assumption of stable prices, an approach illustrated in Part B of Figure 13–6. As before the *IS* curve shifts to the right, a result of either more government spending or increased private spending because of a tax cut. The shift is from IS_1 (p_1) to IS_2 (p_1). Now however, the increased aggregate demand pushes the price level up (See Figure 12–11). This has two consequences. First, higher prices reduce the real value of the assets people hold, causing the consumption function to shift downward, a "Pigou effect" in reverse. This is shown in Figure 13–6 by a second shift of the *IS* curve to the level shown by the dotted line IS_2 (p_2). But higher prices also have the same effect as a decrease in the money supply (Figure 12–12); thus the *LM* curve will shift upward (leftward) to the position of *LM* (p_2). The combined consequence of these two changes is to leave the income level unchanged, but cause interest rates to rise from i_1 to i_2. Interest rates have not increased as much in the situation in which crowding out is induced by the wealth effect, but they have gone up, nevertheless.

Crowding out is obviously an issue of both theoretical and empirical importance. If it occurs on any appreciable scale, then the effectiveness of fiscal policy as an instrument for economic expansion is seriously weakened. But the controversy is by no means settled. As matters now stand, the monetarists have failed to develop adequate empirical evidence to support the crowding out hypothesis, even though a theoretical case can be made for its existence. History has not yet thrown up sufficient experiments to allow the controversy to be decided.[13]

12. Robert J. Gordon, ed. *Milton Friedman's Monetary Framework: A Debate with His Critics* (Chicago: University of Chicago Press, 1974), p. 147. See also Alan S. Binder and Robert M. Solow, "Does Fiscal Policy Matter?" *Journal of Public Economics*, 2 (1973), pp. 319–37; W. Silber, "Fiscal Policy in IS–LM Analysis: A Correction," *Journal of Money, Credit, and Banking,* November 1970, pp. 461–72. Note: there is agreement among both Keynesians and monetarists that a deficit financed by printing money (or direct sale of government bonds to the treasury) will be expansionary.

13. For a concise survey and analysis of the current state of the crowding out controversy, see Keith M. Carlson and Roger W. Spencer, "Crowding Out and Its Critics," Federal Reserve Bank of St. Louis *Review,* December 1975, pp. 2–17.

Stabilization Policy in Perspective

In this section we shall take a broad look at some of the major policy decisions made during the post World War II era. Our intent is not to examine these in detail,[14] but to convey to the reader some sense of the major developments which required policy dcisions, some feel for the political and economic climate in which these decisions were made. We shall conclude the chapter with some comments on the present state of stabilization policy, including some suggestion for changes in the economy.

The Truman-Eisenhower Years

In the 15 years from the end of World War II to the election of John Kennedy as president in 1960, the nation experienced four measurable recessions,[15] although the period in retrospect is generally viewed as one of prosperity and rising real income for most Americans. The latter is true to a degree, although not to the extent that the 1970s nostalgia for the less turbulent 1950s has made it seem. In the period *real* GNP grew by 31.8 percent, a figure which translates into an annual average rate of growth of 2 percent. This is well below the long-term historic average for the American economy (See Table 15–1, Chapter 15). *Real* per capita disposable income grew by 11.4 percent in this period—a solid though not spectacular gain. In spite of the Employment Act being passed in 1946, and in spite, too, of the obvious example of World War II as a successful application of Keynesian ideas, little effort was made during the Truman-Eisenhower years to apply the lessons of the Keynesian "Revolution" to the peacetime management of the economy. Four recessions—mild though they may have been in comparison to the Great Depression of the 1930s —attest to this.

In the spring of 1948 the Congress passed a substantial reduction in the personal income tax over President Truman's veto, an act which was in no sense aimed at the state of the economy, but which turned out fortuitously to be the right thing to do. The reason was that later in the year the economy slid into the first of the mild postwar recessions it was to undergo between 1946 and 1960. President Truman believed at the time that inflation was a much more serious threat than deflation, so much so that he asked for a substantial tax increase in his 1949 budget message, even

14. The annual *Economic Reports of the President* which contain the president's annual economic message to the Congress and the much lengthier *Annual Report* of the Council of Economic Advisers are the best source for details of key policy decisions each year.

15. Technically a recession exists when *real* gross national product declines for two successive quarters. For more details see Chapter 16.

though by then the economy had definitely turned down. It was not until mid-year that the administration recognized that a recession was under way. In its mid-year economic report the request for a tax increase was withdrawn. The president also gave up his hope for a balanced budget, suggesting that a deficit would be a source of support against the factors making for decline in the economy.[16] The deficit was the result of the recession, not a policy-inspired deficit. No major fiscal policy measures were called for to deal with the recession, which reached a trough in the fourth quarter of 1949. Expansion got under way in the spring of 1950 and the Korean War boosted the economy into boom conditions through 1953.

The Eisenhower administration which took office in January 1953 was even more committed to a balanced budget philosophy than its predecessor. In his 1960 *Economic Report*, President Eisenhower said that the appropriate budget policy is one that "not merely balances expenditures with revenues, but achieves a significant surplus for debt retirement."[17] This statement fairly well sums up the budget philosophy characteristic of the Eisenhower years. Behind this view appears to have been a persistent fear of inflation coupled with a belief that budget deficits were the prime source of inflation. There simply is not any evidence that the Eisenhower administration understood—or wanted to understand—how Keynesian ideas might be used for effective economic management. The result was three more recessions— 1953–54, 1957–58, and 1960–61—of which at least the first was probably the direct result of the administration's near-continuous preoccupation with a balanced budget. In an effort to cut down on the deficits incurred during the Korean War (1950–53), the new Eisenhower administration sharply curtailed federal spending in 1953–1954. As a result the federal budget as measured on a full employment basis became sharply restrictive and the economy in mid-1953 dropped into a second post-war recession. Unemployment rose from a Korean war low of 2.9 percent in 1953 to 5.5 percent in 1954. Once again a fortuitous development helped bail the economy out, as both individual and business taxes were cut in 1954. But these tax reductions were not put into effect as an anti-recession measure; they had been planned and scheduled earlier as a part of the administration's efforts to reduce the size of the federal budget.[18] In the last two recessions of the Eisenhower years, primary blame for the recessions cannot be laid at the door of the federal government. The administration did not, however, initiate vigorous policy mea-

16. Wilfred Lewis, Jr., *Federal Fiscal Policy in the Postwar Recessions* (Washington, D.C.: The Brookings Institution, 1962), p. 113.
17. *Economic Report of the President* (Washington, D.C.: U.S. Government Printing Office, 1960), p. 54.
18. Lewis, p. 182.

sures in either 1957–58 or 1960–61[19] to get the economy out of the recessions.

The same fear of inflation which dominated the Eisenhower administration's thinking about the budget is apparent in monetary policy during these years. In most of the Truman portion of the 1946–60 period there was, in effect, no possibility of any monetary policy. This was because of the wartime "accord" between the Federal Reserve and the Treasury. In order to hold down interest rates—and with them the financial cost of government borrowing—the Federal Reserve agreed in 1941 to buy an unlimited quantity of government securities in the open market at fixed prices. This, in effect, put a floor under the price of government securities and a ceiling on interest rates. If the price of bonds could not fall, then interest rates could not rise. Thus, it was impossible to have a monetary policy since the "accord" would not allow the Federal Reserve to take action to raise interest rates—that is, enter the open market and sell securities. This accord continued into effect until 1951, when it was abandoned.

From 1951 onwards monetary policy was restrictive. Figure 13–7 shows this clearly. Except for the Korean war years when deficit financing gave it a spurt, the money supply grew very slowly through most of the Eisenhower years. As Figure 13–7 shows, the annual average rate of change in the money supply (M_1) was below the rate of 4 to 5 percent Friedman recommends for policy. During the eight Eisenhower years (1953–60), the money supply grew at an annual average of 1.6 percent. The basic attitude of the Board of Governors at this time is aptly summed up in the statement that the then chairman, William McChesney Martin, made to the Joint Economic Committee of the Congress early in 1961: "The flexible monetary policy that has been in effect for a full decade . . . is one of leaning against the winds of inflation and deflation with equal vigor."[20] Translated, this meant that when inflation threatened, the Federal Reserve System would clamp down on the money supply and when recession loomed, the money supply would be expanded. Although the Board of Governors is not officially on record with respect to its primary objectives, it has traditionally placed more emphasis upon stable prices as a policy goal than any other objective,[21] a point of view that fit in well with the inflationary fears which dominated the Eisenhower years.

19. By 1961 the Eisenhower administration was out of office. In his last budget message, sent to the Congress in January, 1961, President Eisenhower took an optimistic view of the state of the economy (unemployment in 1960 was 5.5 percent), and said that it was essential to maintain fiscal integrity. He continued to argue the need for a budget surplus.

20. Quoted by Sherman J. Maisel in his *Managing the Dollar* (New York: Norton, 1973), p. 63. Dr. Maisel, a former Governor of the Federal Reserve System, is now a professor of economics at the University of California at Berkeley.

21. Ibid., p. 66.

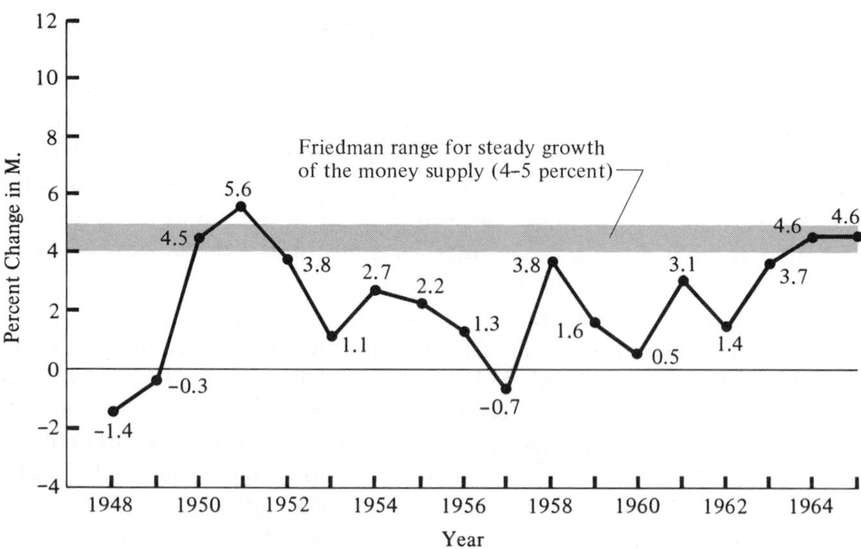

FIGURE 13–7. Annual Percentage Rate of Change in the Money Supply, (M_1): 1948–1965

One final question remains concerning the Truman-Eisenhower years. It does seem clear that neither the Truman nor Eisenhower administrations had either clear understanding of Keynesian principles or a willingness to pursue a virogous anticyclical policy. The question then is why did not any of the four recessions in this fifteen year period turn into a major, post-World War II depression? The answer is not found in the policies followed by either administration—except for the fortuitous fiscal measures—but partly in the effectiveness of the economy's built-in stabilizers, a topic first discussed in Chapter 8 (pp. 264–69). As one observer comments, the "built-in fiscal stabilizers have made a substantial contribution to the stability of the postwar economy. They have pushed the federal budget strongly toward a deficit when that was needed in each postwar recession, thus helping to slow the economic decline."[22] The other relevant factor was the strength of the postwar demand for consumer goods, a carryover from wartime shortages.

The Kennedy Era

When the Kennedy administration came to power in early 1961, the entire intellectual climate as well as the character of economic policy-making changed drastically. Essentially there were two fundamental changes.

22. Lewis, p. 15.

First, the Kennedy administration intended to pursue a policy of aggressive economic management. President Kennedy, after all, had campaigned on the promise to "get the country moving again," and he was determined to carry out this campaign pledge. Second, the new President was a bright man, willing, even eager, to learn what modern macroeconomics had to say about the economy. John Kennedy was not knowledgeable about Keynesian economics when he assumed office, but he was a quick learner. Since the period 1961–65 represents a time when the prestige of economics and economic policy attained a post-World War II high, what happened in this period is worth close analysis.

In January 1961 the major economic problem which confronted President Kennedy and his Council of Economic Advisers[23] was the stagnant state of the economy, still floundering in the fourth recession since the end of the war. During the preceding Eisenhower years, unemployment averaged 4.9 percent of the labor force, a figure judged excessive by the 4 percent minimum which the Kennedy Council regarded as the desirable objective of stabilization policy. Just how the new administration planned to resolve this persistent problem of a sluggish economy and excessive unemployment did not become fully apparent until a year later when the first *Economic Report* of the new administration appeared.

In its first full report, the Kennedy CEA stated that since mid-1955, the rate of growth of actual output was significantly below the economy's potential. The consequence of this lag in economic growth below the potential was a gap of $40 billion between the actual output in 1961 and the value of the goods and services that could have been produced if there had been full employment in 1961.[24] Figure 13–8 reproduces the CEA's charts from the historic 1962 report showing the gap between *actual* and *potential* GNP and unemployment rates (as a percent of the civilian labor force) for 1955 through 1965.

The CEA got its measure of potential output by the simple technique of projecting a trend for the actual GNP in mid-1955 forward at an annual average rate of growth from 3¼ to 3½ percent. Mid-1955 was used as the base year for those calculations because, with unemployment down to 4 percent of the labor force, actual output was equal to potential output. In determining the growth rate to be used to measure the trend of potential output, the CEA took into account the rate of growth in the potential labor force, the annual average rate of labor productivity for the entire labor force and the downward trend in hours worked per year. The reader may wish at this point to review the discussion in Chapter 4 of the

23. Members of the original Kennedy Council at that time were Professor Walter W. Heller, Chairman; Professor Kermit Gordon; and Professor James Tobin.

24. *Economic Report of the President* (Washington, D.C.: U.S. Government Printing Office, 1962), p. 51.

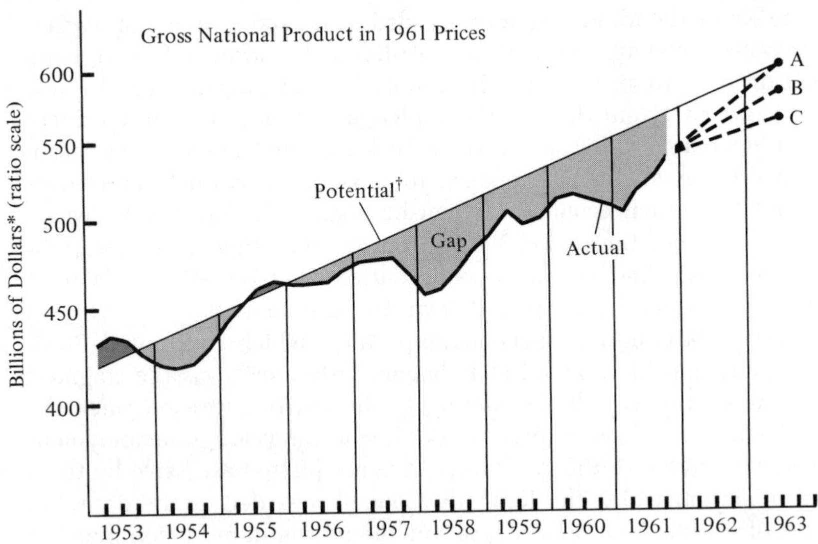

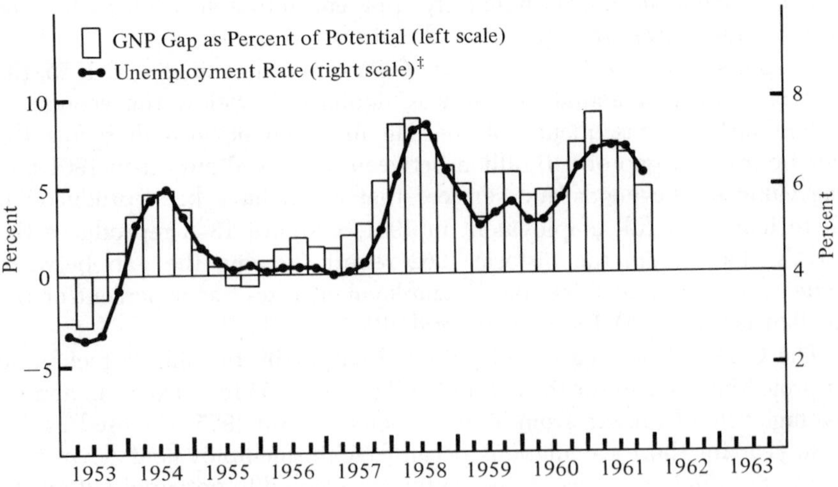

*Seasonally adjusted annual rates

† 3½% trend line through middle of 1955

‡ Unemployment as percent of civilian labor force; seasonally adjusted

Source: Council of Economic Advisers

Note: A, B, and C represent GNP in middle of 1963 assuming unemployment rate of 4%, 5%, and 6% respectively

FIGURE 13–8. Gross National Product (Actual and Potential) and Unemployment Rate

determinants of productive capacity as well as the concept of the output gap (See pp. 94–97).

This concept of an output, or performance, gap emerged in the early 1960s as one of the key tools used by the CEA for analysis of the economy's performance. To explain the serious performance gap which characterized the American economy from mid-1955 onward, the CEA developed a theory of fiscal stagnation. The Council argued that the failure of the economy to expand at a rate sufficient to provide full employment was not due primarily to a deficiency of either private consumption or investment demand, but to the restrictive impact of the federal tax structure on the over-all level of demand.

The major analytical tool utilized by the Council of Economic Advisers to demonstrate the restrictive effect of the federal tax structure upon the economy was the concept of the full employment surplus. Earlier in this chapter we defined the full employment budget. The full employment surplus is a variant of this concept. In the 1962 *Economic Report* the CEA used it to mean the budgetary surplus of the federal government which would be generated by a given budget program under conditions of full employment (a 4 percent unemployment rate). Figure 13–9 is from the 1962 CEA report and illustrates this concept. In the diagram the ratio of actual GNP to potential GNP is shown on the horizontal axis. This axis is labeled the "Utilization Rate"; the 100 percent point represents full employment. It will be recalled that potential GNP is based on projecting a trend which embodies a 4 percent unemployment rate. Thus, when the ratio of *actual* to *potential* GNP equals 100, the economy must be operating at full employment. On the vertical axis, the federal surplus of deficit is measured as a percent of the potential GNP.

Two schedules are shown in the diagram, one of which reflects the tax and expenditure program of the federal government for the fiscal year 1960 and the other for the fiscal year 1962. Both of these schedules slope upward to the right, which indicates that the surplus or deficit associated with any given budget program will depend upon the level of economic activity prevailing in the economy. By a "given budget program" is meant a particular pattern and level of expenditures combined with a particular structure of tax rates. With fixed expenditures and a given rate structure for the tax system, a deficit will decline or a surplus will increase as the economy's utilization rate increases—or as the economy approaches full employment. The height and steepness of the schedule depends upon the character of the budget program which exists at any given time—namely, the level of expenditures, tax rates, and the degree of progression present in the system.

Discretionary fiscal policy—action which deliberately changes the level of government expenditures or tax rates—has the effect of shifting the

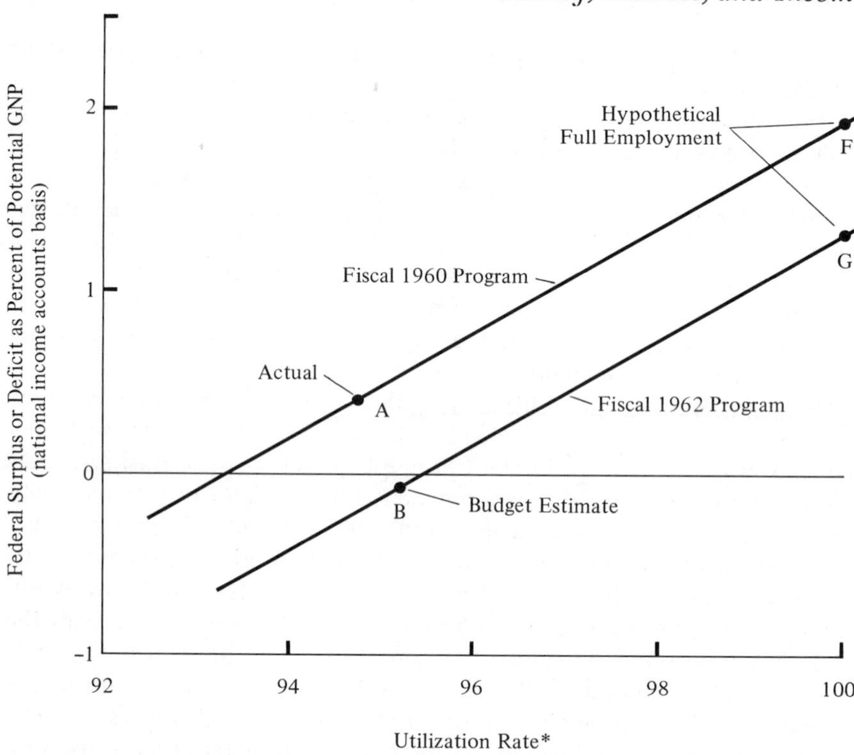

FIGURE 13–9. Effect of Level of Economic Activity on Federal Surplus or Deficit

schedule up or down. For example, a reduction in tax rates would lower the schedule, thus either increasing a deficit or reducing the surplus associated with a specific level of economic activity—the utilization rate shown on the horizontal axis. The effects of built-in stabilizers, on the other hand, are reflected in a movement along the schedule as the level of economic activity changes. A rise in the income level will automatically generate a surplus sooner or later, as long as there is no change in expenditures. It should be noted, too, that if tax rates and expenditure programs remain constant, the full employment surplus will rise over time. The reason for this is that over time the full employment potential GNP grows, simply because a growing labor force which is fully employed and whose productivity is improving inevitably means a larger output. As long as tax rates are unchanged, the absolute volume of tax revenues yielded by a full employment economy must increase over time. This being the case and with expenditures unchanged, the budgetary surplus should grow.

The economic significane of a full employment budget surplus lies in the fact that the actual achievement of full employment requires that gross investment expenditures (including net foreign investment in an open economy) must be large enough to offset the total private saving plus the net surplus of the public sector which the economic system generates at full employment. In equation form $I = S + (T - G)$, in which the variables represent full employment, *ex ante* (or planned) values. The actual situation between 1955 and the early 1960s, according to analysis of the Council of Economic Advisers, was a tendency for full employment saving (including government saving or the full employment surplus) to run ahead of gross investment, including net foreign investment. In symbolic terms, $S + (T - G) > I$.

The Remedy for Fiscal Stagnation

The solution proposed by the Kennedy administration to fiscal stagnation was a massive reduction both personal and corporate income taxes. President Kennedy in a 1963 special message on tax reform requested that the tax rates on personal income be reduced from a range of 20 to 91 percent to a range of 14 to 65 percent, and that the rate on corporate income be reduced from 95 to 47 percent. The Congress did not act on President Kennedy's request, but following his assassination, essentially the same proposals were presented to the Congress in January 1964. Speedy action was forthcoming and the Revenue Act of 1964 was signed into law of February 16, 1964. In its 1965 *Annual Report* the CEA estimated that the total of tax reductions taking effect in 1964 and 1965 would be $11 billion for individuals and $3 billion for corporations.[25]

It was expected that the tax cuts would operate to stimulate both consumption and investment spending, thus bringing output closer to the full employment potential. The reduction in the personal income tax would add directly to the personal disposable income of consumers and since most of this added income would be spent, the multiplier would come into play and generate a cumulative expansion in consumption. Investment spending would rise both because the after-tax profit on new facilities would be increased and because more internal funds would be available to firms for investment purposes.

In its 1963 *Annual Report,* the CEA presented a textbooklike explanation of the multiplier effects which could be expected to flow from the reduction in rate on the personal income tax. After taking into account all the various leakages at work in the economic system, the Council concluded that each additional dollar of GNP generated initially by the tax cut would generate an additional $0.50 of consumption expenditures. In other words, the marginal propensity to consume out of the GNP is 0.50,

25. *Economic Report of the President* (Washington, D.C.: U.S. Government Printing Office, 1965), p. 65. The Excise Tax Reduction Act of 1965 called for a reduction in excise taxes totaling $4.6 billion over several stages through 1969.

which yields a multiplier of 2 to be applied against the initial increase in consumption spending stimulated by the increase in disposable income.[26] The ultimate expansionary effect was expected to be even greater because of the stimulus to investment resulting both from the initial reduction in the corporate rate, and also from the expansion in consumption generated by the cut in personal income tax rates.

The Effectiveness of the 1964 Tax Cut

While there are no absolutely conclusive tests that can be employed to determine the effectiveness of the 1964 tax cut, the available evidence is strong that the tax cuts did, in fact, achieve the results expected. In the first place, the gap between actual and potential output, which reached a peak of $50 billion at an annual rate in the first quarter of 1961, was reduced to an annual rate of $10 billion in the last quarter of 1965. The unemployment rate declined to 4.1 percent by the end of 1965; in September, 1966, the rate stood at 3.8 percent of the civilian labor force. These changes largely took place before the Vietnam military build-up had begun to have much effect upon the economy.

Additional evidence for the effectiveness of the tax cut is to be found in the performance of GNP. In 1964, GNP (in current prices) increased by $41.2 billion, in contrast to an increase of $30.2 billion (in current prices) in 1963. The CEA stated in its 1966 *Annual Report* that statistical analysis of the impact of the tax cut indicates that it was responsible for nearly $10 billion of the gain in the annual increase of the GNP. The increase continued in 1965. With respect to the entire expansion, the CEA estimated that by the end of 1965, the contribution of the tax cut reached $30 billion.[27]

The third piece of evidence that can be cited in support of the effectiveness of the tax cut is the fact from the close of 1964 to the close of 1965, federal revenues increased by $9 billion, in spite of the fact that in this same period tax reductions effected by both the Revenue Act of 1964 and the Excise Tax Reduction Act of 1965 totaled about $16 billion.[28] This experience bears out the claim of the CEA that a tax reduction, if it succeeds in stimulating economic growth, would lead to an increase rather than a decline in revenues. Thus, it is apparent that if the level of government expenditures had remained constant during this period, the federal government would have experienced a substantial surplus by the end of 1965. Actually, total expenditures (including transfers) of the fed-

26. *Economic Report of the President* (Washington, D.C.: U.S. Government Printing Office, 1963), pp. 45–51.

27. *Economic Report of the President* (Washington, D.C.: U.S. Government Printing Office, 1966), p. 34.

28. *Economic Report of the President* (Washington, D.C.: U.S. Government Printing Office, 1977), p. 271.

eral government rose from $118.2 billion in 1964 (on a national income accounts basis) to $123.8 billion in 1965, an increase of $5.6 billion, a figure slightly more than the increase in revenues in the same period. The federal government attained a small surplus of $0.5 billion in 1965.[29]

Vietnam and Its Aftermath

From 1966 to the early 1970s economic effects of the Vietnam war and its inflationary aftermath dominated the economy and economic policy. By the end of 1966 the unemployment level fell below 4 percent, the target figure the Council of Economic Advisers established in the early 1960s as representing full employment. During 1969 unemployment averaged 3.5 percent, the lowest figure in the entire post-World War II year except for the Korean war years. Also in 1966 the GNP gap disappeared, not to reappear until the 1970 recession (See Figure 4–4, p. 94). With reduction of the unemployment rate below the target level and the disappearance of the GNP gap, inflation quickly became the number one aggregate—and domestic—economic problem.

During the Vietnam period economic policy was directed almost totally toward the control of inflation.[30] The major policy moves included imposition of a 10 percent surcharge on corporate and individual income taxes in 1968, the 1969 game plan of the Nixon administration for inflation control, and the experiment with an incomes policy which began in mid-1971. The latter is discussed in detail in Chapter 14. Here we shall discuss the 1968 surtax and the policies pursued to control inflation by the Nixon administration during its preincomes policy phase.

By mid-1966 it was evident to most economists that the heating up of the economy consequent to the escalation in Vietnam required the application of a restrictive fiscal policy,[31] although it was not until two years

29. Monetary policy played a much less dramatic role than did fiscal policy in the Kennedy era. Nevertheless, the Federal Reserve stepped up the rate of growth in the money supply (M_1) in 1963 and 1964, a development which is the basis of the claim of some monetarists that the increase in the money supply rather than the 1964 tax cut was responsible for improved economic conditions in the Kennedy era. This is an issue which will probably never be settled.

30. The major economic stimulus from the war came from 1966 through 1968 in the form of rising military expenditures, but the inflationary aftermath lasted through 1973. Thus, economically, the Vietnam war period runs from 1966 through 1973.

31. In 1966 the purchase of goods and services by the federal government for military purposes jumped by over $10 billion, an increase that took place in a fully employed economy. No new taxes were imposed to finance this vast and sudden increase in federal outlays, a development that caused the federal government's deficit to rise to over $13 billion on a national income accounts basis the following year. It would be difficult to find a more perfect example of irresponsible government action that inevitably would have serious inflationary consequences.

later that the Johnson administration and a reluctant Congress enacted a tax increase. The Revenue and Expenditure Control Act of 1968, signed into law at the end of June, provided for a 10 percent surcharge on personal and corporate income taxes, retroactive to January 1, 1968 for corporate income taxes and to April 1, 1968 for the personal income tax. Through subsequent action by the Congress, the surcharge on personal income was extended at a 10 percent rate through 1969, dropped to a 5 percent rate in the first half of 1970 and allowed to expire on June 30, 1970. The same provisions applied to the corporate income tax.

The 1968 surtax was a fiscal policy counterpart to the tax reductions of 1964, as it was expected via its impact upon disposable income and corporate profits to dampen spending and thus contribute to bringing inflationary pressures under control. Was the 1968 tax increase as successful in holding down aggregate demand as its predecessor tax cut apparently had been in stimulating aggregate demand? The answer, unfortunately, is by no means clear-cut. Consumer prices rose at an annual average rate of 4.2 percent in 1968, 5.4 percent in 1969, and 5.9 percent in 1970. It was not until the economy went into the 1969–70 recession that a slowdown in the inflation rate became evident. This happened in 1971, when the annual rate of price increase dropped to 4.3 percent. Since the surcharge was allowed to expire in mid-1970, we really do not know what might have happened under circumstances in which the tax remained in effect. Further, as critics of the surtax maintain—especially some proponents of the permanent income hypothesis—consumers were well aware of the temporary nature of the tax. Consequently, they adjusted to it by reducing their saving rather than their spending when the tax increase cut into their disposable income. Personal saving as a percent of disposable income did decline from 7.5 in 1967 to 6.5 in 1968 and 5.6 in 1969, and then climbed back to 7.4 in 1970 the year in which the surtax was lifted. But 1970 was also a recession year, marked by a good deal of consumer caution and uncertainty, so the evidence on the saving ratio is not definitive.

A highly comprehensive study of the effectiveness of the 1968 surtax was completed in 1971 by Arthur Okun, former chairman of the Council of Economic Advisers.[32] Professor Okun used four different econometric models to test the hypothesis that the surtax was expected to curb consumer demand, then compared the results obtained with the estimated actual impact on consumption. He did find that, with the exception of the demand for automobiles, the surtax was effective during the 1968–70 period in curbing consumer demand for other durables, as well as nondurables and services. Automobile demand, for reasons that are not

32. Arthur M. Okun, "The Personal Tax Surcharge and Consumer Demand, 1968–70," *Brookings Papers on Economic Activity,* no. 1, 1971.

entirely clear, displayed great strength during this period, as did business investment (including residential construction) in spite of the surtax on corporate income. Professor Okun's general conclusion is that, over-all, consumer demand responded about as expected to the reduction in disposable income, but the expansionary and inflationary forces let loose by the Vietnam war were much greater than recognized at the time. As he says, "The medicine of the personal tax surcharge did lower the patient's fever. To be sure, the patient was more feverish than the doctors recognized and consequently their antifever prescription was inadequate. But don't blame the medicine; it did most of what is should have been reasonably expected to do. In short, the evidence of the surcharge period provides further confirmation of the general efficacy and continued desirability of flexible changes in personal income tax rates—upward or downward, permanent or temporary."[33] The most damaging weakness of the surtax was its application approximately two year too late, a failing of the political system rather than in economic diagnosis.

The stance of the Nixon administration when it assumed power at the beginning of 1969 was that the first priority was to bring inflation under control. This, it was thought, could be done by a gradualist approach which would try and slow down the economy sufficiently to dampen the inflationary psychology that the Nixon economists believed three years of rising prices had engendered. In 1969 the administration was confident that his could be done without bringing on a recession or too much unemployment. Under the leadership of Professor Paul McCracken of the University of Michigan, the Nixon CEA put together a combination of fiscal and monetary restraints designed to accomplish this, a package that came to be known as the administration's "game plan." In 1969 the rate of growth of federal expenditures for goods and services slowed sharply—from 9.8 percent in 1968 to 1.8 percent in 1969—as did the rate of growth in the money supply—dropping from 8.0 percent in 1968 to 3.3 percent in 1969. We shall return to the subject of monetary policy shortly.

What were the results? Since there is a normal lag of six to twelve months between the initiation of economic policy and ultimate results, 1970 was the decisive test year for the effectiveness of the 1969 game plan. By the end of the year, it was apparent that gradualism had not done the job of stopping inflation. It has already been pointed out that consumer prices rose by 5.9 percent in 1970, as compared to 5.4 percent in 1969 and 4.2 percent in 1968. Yet unemployment rose from the 3.5 percent level of 1969 to a rate of 6 percent by December, 1976. The failure of the gradualist approach was abetted by the Nixon administration's strongly voiced unwillingness at the start of 1969 to give any consideration to having an incomes policy. Further, the administration was openly hostile to the sur-

33. Ibid.

charge, making no move to ask the Congress to extend it beyond the planned expiration date of June 30, 1970. During the first half of 1971 the Nixon administration largely marked time in terms of economic policy, uncertain as to how to cope with the growing problem of both unemployment and inflation. Finally in mid-August President Nixon made his bombshell announcement that with a wage-price freeze his administration had embarked on an experiment with a comprehensive incomes policy, an approach the administration had scornfully rejected in early 1969. The results of this phase of the Nixon administration economic policies are discussed in the next chapter.

In the meanwhile, what role did monetary policy play in the Vietnam period? In general the acceleration in the rate of growth in the money supply which began in the Kennedy era continued, but with two important exceptions—1966 and 1969. In late 1965 and early 1966, the Federal Reserve System, worried about the growing inflationary pressures because of Vietnam, slammed on the monetary brakes. The discount rate was raised and growth in the money supply sharply curtailed (in 1966, overall, the rate of monetary growth dropped to 2.6 percent, compared to 4.6 in 1965). The result was a severe credit squeeze, generally known as the "credit crunch" of 1966. Particularly hard hit was the housing industry, because the rise in open market interest rates exceeded the rates which financial intermediaries such as savings and loan association, mutual saving banks, and life insurance companies were able to pay. Consequently, the flow of savings to these intermediaries dropped, which in turn dried up the flow of money into home mortgages.[34] Thus, the construction of new houses slumped badly (new housing starts were off by more than 300,000 in 1966). In many respects 1969 was a repeat of 1966. As part of the Nixon game plan the money supply was tightened—the rate of growth of M_1 dropped to 3.3 percent in 1969 as compared to 8.0 percent the prior year. And again as in 1966 housing was hurt as the flow of savings to financial intermediaries began to dry up. The crunch was not so severe as earlier however, as the Federal Reserve moved to a less restrictive stance early in 1970. The experience in 1966 and 1969 demonstrates dramatically the point made earlier in this chapter about the uneven impact of monetary policy (p. 433).

In the view of one knowledgeable observer, 1966 was a year crucial in significance in the post-World War II development of monetary policy. That year, according to Sherman J. Maisel, former member of the Board of Governors of the Federal Reserve System, marked the end of the "age of innocence" for the system.[35] What he meant was that henceforth the

34. This process is called *disintermediation.* The reason is the financial institutions mentioned above operate essentially as channels for the transfer of funds from savers to borrowers. Hence, they are serving as intermediaries. When the process slows down or stops, we have disintermediation.

35. Maisel, p. 69.

system had to abandon the simplistic view of former Chairman Martin that its main task in an inflationary era was to restrict the money supply; rather, it had to be equally mindful of how its credit and monetary policies would affect the different sectors of the economy, a lesson driven home by the severe—and adverse—effect that monetary restriction during 1966 had on the flow of funds into the housing market.

After 1966, in short, the Federal Reserve recognized that the effective use of monetary policy required that the Board take into account the actual workings of financial markets in terms of traditional channels of lending and borrowing as well as the total quantity of money lending and borrowing as well as the total quantity of money and commercial bank reserves available to the economy.

The 1970s

There is no clear line of demarcation which indicates precisely when the Vietnam war ceased to be the dominating factor in policy-making for the economy. In a sense because of the continued pressure on the price level, we are still feeling the effects of that historic national misadventure. But for practical policy-making, the failure of the 1969 Nixon game plan and the shift to an incomes policy in mid-1971 represents a rough turning point. From then onwards, the fiscal and monetary policies of the ill-fated Nixon administration were geared toward bringing down the unemployment rate, particularly with a presidential election in the offing.

In both 1971 and 1972 fiscal and monetary policy became aggressively expansive. To illustrate, the deficit on the full employment budget rose from \$2.6 billion in 1970 to \$9.2 billion in 1971 and \$21.5 billion in 1972, an \$18.9 billion dollar swing in two years.[36] This resulted from a combination of tax cuts and rising expenditures. Equally expansive was monetary policy, as the money supply (M_1) increased by 6.5 percent in 1971 and a phenomenal 9.2 percent in 1972, a higher rate of growth than any year since 1948. The administration was confident that the system of wage and price controls instituted in mid-1971 (called "The New Economic Policy" in the press) would contain any added inflationary pressures resulting from the fiscal and monetary stimulus.

What were the results of the switch from a policy of restraint (1969) to all out expansion (1971 and 1972)? They were mixed, an outcome which reflects the fact that it is becoming increasingly difficlt to deal adequately

36. In a news conference early in 1971 President Nixon said "I am a Keynesian," a remark widely interpreted as indicating the willingness of his administration to use fiscal measures to stimulate the economy. This view was strengthened by his endorsement of the concept of the full employment budget in his 1971 Economic Message to the Congress.

with either inflation or unemployment in our economy by fiscal and monetary means. The unemployment rate continued to rise through 1971, reaching a rate of 5.9 percent for the year. In 1972 it came down slightly —to 5.6 percent—but the decline was far less than expected in view of the strong fiscal and monetary stimulus applied to the economy. The stubborn resistance of unemployment to improvement by applying the usual Keynesian remedies has turned out to be one of the more persistent and difficult problems of the 1970s. It is rooted in the structure of the labor force, since some groups—minorities and teen-agers especially—benefit only in a marginal way from higher levels of aggregate demand (See Figure 4–1, p. 00). With respect to the price level, there was improvement in both 1971 and 72, a development which appeared to indicate that controls were working. In 1971 the inflation rate dropped to 4.3 percent and it fell further in 1972 to 3.4 percent, a low for the entire post-Vietnam war period. There is some evidence however (See Chapter 14 following) that these gains were nothing more than a lagged consequence of the 1969–70 recession.

When Gerald Ford became president in the late summer of 1974 he inherited fiscal and monetary policies which had once again turned restrictive. The new president, if anything, was even more concerned than his predecessor with an inflation which was accelerating rapidly. In the first half of the year consumer prices rose at an annual rate slightly in excess of 10 percent. Americans began to hear more and more about a new economic menace—"double digit" inflation. Even though the Arab oil embargo in late 1973 and poor crops were in part responsible for the acceleration in the inflation rate, the Ford administration continued to pursue policies which were strongly restrictive. This took place in spite of the fact that the crucial business cycle indicators of the Department of Commerce were pointing downwards (See Chapter 16). In 1974 the money supply (M_1) grew at an annual rate of 4.7 percent, down from the 5.9 growth rate of 1973 and well below the record rate of expansion in 1972. Fiscal policy, too, continued to be restrictive, a fact reflected in the swing of the full employment budget from a deficit of $7.9 billion in 1973 to a surplus of $14.1 billion in 1974. Overall this was a swing in a restrictive direction of $22 billion. Inflation plus the combination of highly restrictive fiscal and monetary policies led to the most severe economic slump since the Great Depression of the 1930s. Real gross national product declined in both 1974 and 1975 and the unemployment rate rose to a post-World War II high of 8.9 percent in May, 1976.

Recovery began in the spring of 1975, coincident with the passage of a tax cut bill proposed by the Ford administration—a package which overall contained tax cuts on the order of $15 billion. Since then events have moved along a path which is becoming distressingly familiar, even though there was a change in administrations at the start of 1977. Real output has been expanding since the turnaround came in the third quarter of 1975, but not rapidly enough to bring the unemployment rate down to even the Ford administration's suggested target of 5.5 percent for "full employment." Two years after the recovery got under way (May, 1977), unemployment was still at the excessively high figure of 6.9 percent of the labor force. Inflation was down from the double-digit range which alarmed so many people in 1974, but the situation was not satisfactory. In the first four months of 1977 consumer prices rose at an annual rate of nearly 10 percent, a development which the Carter administration attributed to bad weather in the early part of the year. Nevertheless, it was fear of a new surge of inflation which caused the administration to slash by about two-thirds the size of the tax cut that it recommended at the beginning of the year as a stimulus for the economy (See Chapter 8, p. 264).

The pattern suggested by developments during the 1970s is one of cyclical swings of growing intensity, swings which leave the economy with a higher residue of both unemployment and inflation—especially inflation. The inflation rate declines following an economic downturn, but it did not decline in 1971–75 to as low a level as in 1969–70, even though the most recent slump was much more severe. Unemployment, too, has been moving upwards; at the peak of the Vietnam war boom it was down to 3.5 percent, but in the 1973–74 boom it fell to only 4.9 percent. Now there is concern as to whether it can get below 5.5 percent without pushing the economy back into an intolerable inflationary situation. The Carter administration hopes to change this, as its long-term prescription calls for bringing the unemployment rate down to about 4.8 percent by 1981 and the inflation rate to 4 percent by the same date. Whether the tools of contemporary macroeconomic analysis are adequate for this task remains to be seen.

Some Summary Comments

What has been learned from the experience with economic policy in the post-World War II period, especially the turbulent years since the onset of the Vietnam war? Several points are important. First, it seems clear that we have the economic knowledge necessary to manage the economy in a manner which will prevent another major depression on the order of the 1930s. None of the six recorded recessions since 1945 has been allowed to develop into a long and damaging depression. That is a plus. What we don't have is the knowledge or skill to "fine tune" the economy. "Fine tuning" is a phrase which came into vogue after the success of the Kennedy tax cut. It meant the continuous use of fine adjustments in fiscal and monetary policy to keep the economy moving on a full employment path of economic growth without excessive inflation. The experiences of the last decade have disabused most economists—not to mention the public—of the notion that through "fine tuning" the business cycle has been banished from our economic life. As we have already indicated, the business cycle is far from dead. We shall examine this fact further in Chapter 16.

Second, it should be quite plain from the experience since 1965 that through fiscal and monetary policies inflation cannot be ended or even brought under control—at least not without costs in terms of unemployment which are wholly unacceptable to our society. Putting on the fiscal and monetary brakes pushes the economy into a recession much faster than it brings down the inflation rate. That is the sad lesson of the failure of the Nixon game plan and the disaster of Ford's 1974 WIN (Whip Inflation Now) campaign. We shall never know, of course, *if* the prompt imposition of a tax increase in 1966 might have held the Vietnam inflation in check. What we do know is that once inflation gets started and persists, then inflationary expectations become built into the economy, expectations which tend to be cumulative in their effects. No doubt a recession (or depression) deeper and more prolonged than anything experienced since World War II would break the back of such expectations, but such a policy might destroy the economy in the process.

Third—and this is a corollary of the above—the social ineffectiveness of a restrictive monetary and fiscal policy stems from wage and price rigidities deeply rooted in the structure of the economy—the power of trade unions and the giant corporations. This makes for a situation in which prices and wages—as well as other costs—are readily flexible upwards, but not flexible downwards. Under such conditions the results that we have been discussing are almost inevitable when the money supply is tightened or taxes are increased. Oligopolistic firms and strong trade unions will react to a fall off in demand by raising prices and wages. Worse yet, the impact of restrictive monetary and fiscal measures may add directly to inflationary pressures because higher interest rates become a part of the cost structure and higher taxes may lead workers to bargain for higher money wages to maintain take-home pay.[37] The foregoing would not work in a highly competitive economic environment, such as Keynes assumed, but it surely works when there is a substantial amount of economic power in the hands of both firms and workers.

As a fourth point, the experience of the last dozen years casts doubt upon our ability as a society to submit to the social discipline necessary to make fiscal and monetary policy work *in both directions*. This is aside from the necessity of creating conditions under which we can "dampen

37. Robert Eisner, "What Went Wrong?" *Journal of Political Economy*, May/June 1971, p. 633.

down" the economy without plunging it into a recession. Admittedly this is more a political than an economic problem, yet it is one which economists cannot ignore. The realities of our political life suggest that policy is one-directional—expansionary in the form of tax cuts. Worse yet, it seems we as a society are unwilling to finance through taxes what we demand out of the national government. In nineteen of the last twenty-eight years the federal government has run a deficit (on a national income and accounts basis); since 1965 there have been only two years in which the federal budget was in balance or registered a surplus. This is not to suggest a return to an outmoded fiscal philosophy which says the budget must be balanced annually,[38] but serious questions are raised about the efficacy of modern fiscal and monetary policies *if* the norm has become one of deficits in good years and bad. Federal red ink is not the sole cause of inflation as many conservative thinkers believe, but when conditions are relatively prosperous and employment high (as has been the case over much of the post-World War II era), they do contribute to inflation.

Finally, we need to realize and keep in perspective just how far we have come in our understanding of the economy as compared to where we were in the early 1930s. Then there was no real understanding of what could and should be done in the face of the collapse that began in 1929, and quickly spread to most of the world. This was so in spite of the impressive body of theoretical analysis which had been developing over the prior century—classical economics. We have not yet found the exact key to the problem which is now most vexing—stagflation—but in modern macroeconomic analysis we do have the necessary theoretical tools to do the job. Further, our policy instruments, imperfect as they may be, are being used to prevent our having to face another bout with mass unemployment 1930s style while we struggle to cure an equally damaging social evil—chronic inflation.

38. It is interesting to note that the Ford administration was much more conservative than Nixon's in its budget philosophy. During 1974 and 75 the administration moved back toward an annually balanced budget policy, largely because of the influence of Treasury Secretary William Simon. In the press this was often described as a "return to the old time religion." It is interesting to note, too, that President Carter also talks strongly about the need to balance the federal budget. The Carter administration has said it wants to attain a budget surplus of $25 billion or more by 1981.

IV
Inflation, Growth, and the Business Cycle

14

The Economics of Inflation

In this chapter we shall consider the forces which determine the general level of prices in the economy. In Part II the analysis was developed largely in real terms—that is, a stable price was assumed. This was done because our primary interest was in changes in output (real GNP) and employment, both of which move closely together. In Chapter 12 the price level was introduced as part of our analysis of the neoclassical synthesis, although in this model it remains largely exogenous because prices depend primarily upon the money supply. Our interest at that point was to show the effect of a change in the general price level on output and employment, an objective served well by the neoclassical synthesis.

Now it is time to reverse the situation and examine how the price level is affected by changes in output and employment as well as money income. More than that, we want to identify the key causal forces at work on the price level. This is an especially challenging problem because most Western nations, including the United States, have had high levels of employment during the more than three decades since the end of World War II, but they have also experienced a persistent—and in some instances, a spectacular—rise in prices during the same interval.

Figure 14–1 shows what has happened to the general price level in the United States.

It is readily apparent that prices have marched upward since 1947; in 30 years prices soared 169 percent.[1] The rate at which prices advanced in this period was by no means even. Except for the last few years, the

1. The price index used is the U.S. Department of Commerce GNP deflator which converts gross national product to real terms. The base year in this case is 1947.

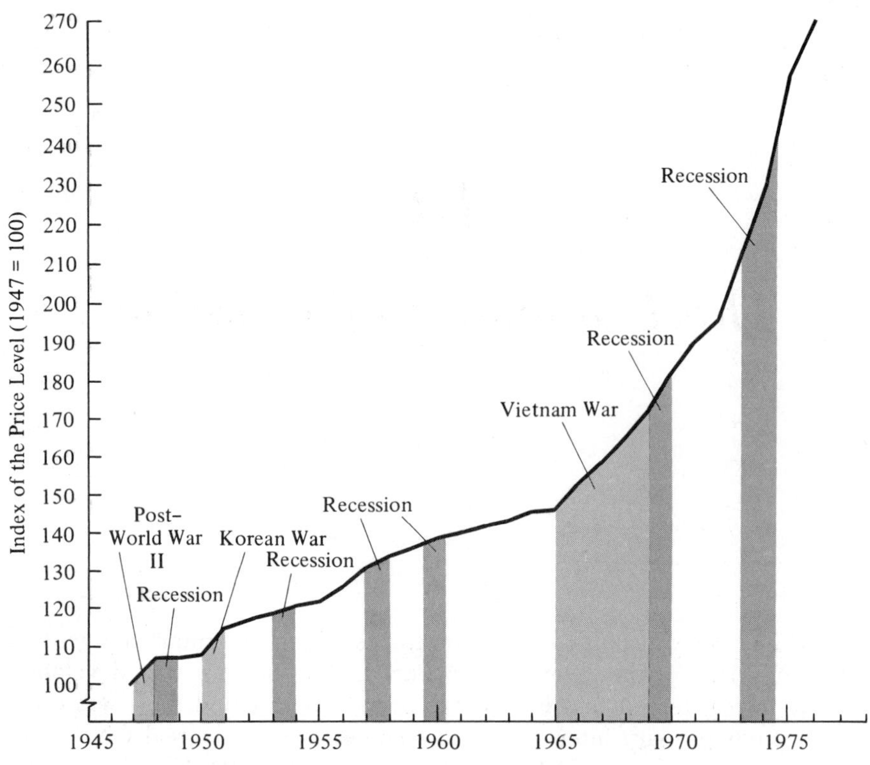

FIGURE 14–1. The Post-World War II Inflation

sharpest increases were the result of war or its aftermath. When price controls were taken off after World War II, prices jumped 21 percent in two years (1946–48). Again during the Korean war the price level shot up (10.3 percent), as also happened in the Vietnam war period (19.3 percent). But the really explosive rise in the price level came in peacetime—in the four years from 1973 to 1976 prices climbed by 33.7 percent, one of the sharpest inflations in our history. Two additional facts should be noted about the post-World War II inflation. First, consumer prices rose in each one of the six postwar recessions, a phenomenon unique in our history. Second, and also unlike past experience, inflation during wartime was *not* followed by a drop in the price level after the war. Prices did not come down after World War II, the Korean war, or the Vietnam conflict, although they did drop after the Revolutionary War, the War of 1812, and Civil War, and World War I.[2]

2. Jim E. Reese, "The New Inflation," *Journal of Economic Issues,* June 1977, pp. 285–97. Professor Reese found that the United States had experienced ten periods of inflation prior to 1939 (not all wartime inflation periods). In every case the inflationary period was followed by an abrupt and often prolonged drop in prices. This has not happened with the post-World War II inflation. He also found that the current inflation has lasted longer than any previous inflation.

There is no single theory of the price level. This point cannot be emphasized too strongly. There are, however, a number of well-established approaches to the problem of changes in the price level. We shall proceed to examine each of these separately, although it is necessary to bear in mind that the inflationary process in the real world economy is exceedingly complex. In any specific period in which prices are rising sharply, forces that reflect one or more of the currently recognized theories of the price level may be at work.

How does the empirical evidence on inflation bear on the Keynesian-monetarist controversy over the role of money? Statistical data on output, the money supply, and the price level show that price level changes correlate closely with both changes in output and changes in the money supply. Figure 14–2 is a scatter diagram of the index of real GNP, using 1947 as the base year, against an index of the general price level with the same base. The period covered is 1947 through 1976. The pattern revealed by the scatter indicates quite clearly that, over time, increases in real GNP are accompanied by significant increases in the price level.

Figure 14–3 is another scatter diagram, although in this case the price

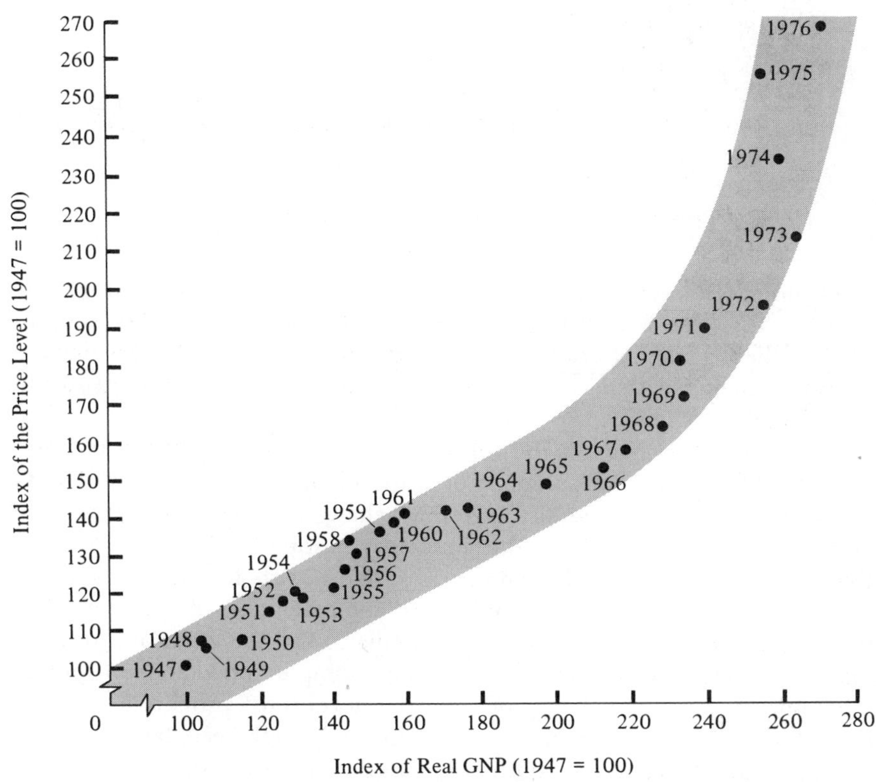

FIGURE 14–2. Real GNP and the Price Level: 1947–1976

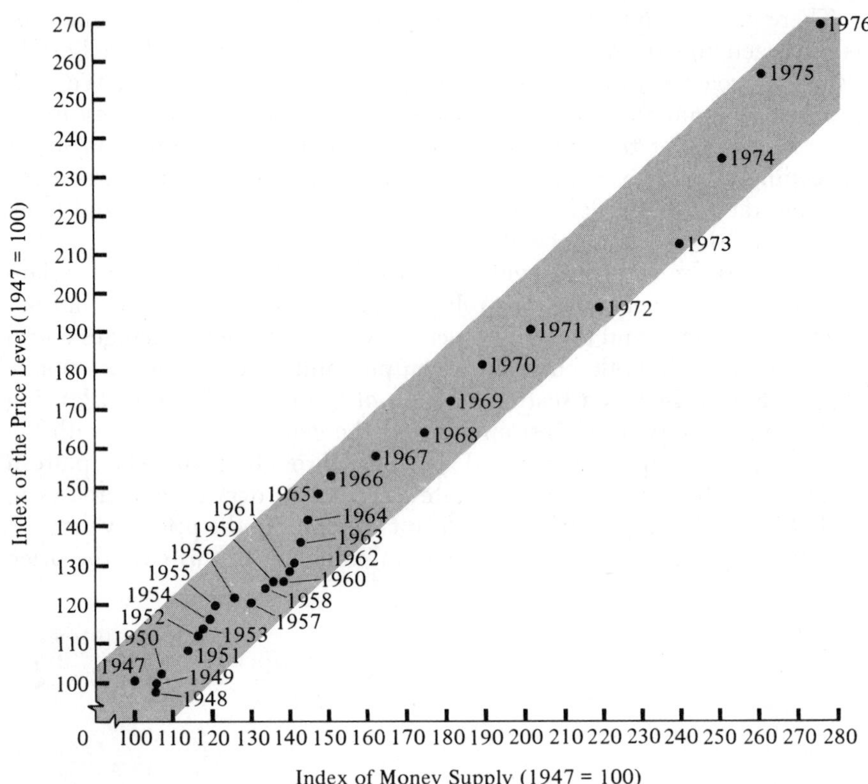

FIGURE 14–3. Money Supply and the Price Level

level index is plotted against an index of the money supply, using 1947 again as the base period for both indexes. This diagram shows, too, an apparently significant relationship between increases in the money supply, which consists of currency plus demand deposits, and increases in the general price level.

What are we to make of the foregoing? If it is presumed that changes in real GNP are the consequence of shifts in the Keynesian $C + I + G$ aggregate demand schedule, and that changes in the money supply largely reflect decisions of the monetary authority—i.e., the Federal Reserve—then it appears that empirical support exists for either a simplistic Keynesian or a simplistic monetarist interpretation of inflation. The former involves an excess of aggregate demand and the latter an excess of money. Actually, inflation is a much more complex phenomenon, but at minimum, any general theory of the price level must provide a satisfactory mechanism for showing how the money supply can be related to aggregate demand and how both are related to the price level.

The Meaning of Inflation

We have used the terms *inflation* and a *rise in the price level* in a manner which suggests they are synonymous. This is not quite correct. While inflation normally involves an upward movement in the general level of prices, all price level increases are not of the same magnitude nor is their economic consequence and duration always the same. This is readily seen if we examine the data in Table 14–1. The periods shown correspond to the broad divisions established in Chapter 13 for our discussion of post-World War II policy actions. They are, of course, arbitrary, but they permit us to be more specific about what the term inflation means.

As data in the table indicate, there were wide variations in the rate at which prices went up during this thirty-year span. Even a year or two may make a significant difference in the average calculated for a sub-period. In 1947, for example, prices rose by 13.1 percent, a consequence of the removal of wartime price controls. If this year is removed from the Truman-Eisenhower years, then the average for this period drops to 2.6 percent, a moderate rate of rise by comparison to what has happened in the 1970s. Many people would say that for all practical purposes we had price stability in the Kennedy era. The rate of increase was a modest 1.6 percent, and given the fact that there was undoubtedly some improvement in the quality of the goods and services produced in these years, inflation in a real sense was probably close to zero. But the more recent data also show that the rate at which prices are going up has accelerated; it is now more than double what it was in the first half of the postwar period. For the period as a whole, prices went up at an annual average rate of 3.8 percent. During these three decades, there were eighteen years in which prices rose at a rate higher than the average for the whole period, and twelve years in which the rate was below the average.

What is the moral of this? Essentially—and in the absence of any techniques whereby price changes can be corrected for quality changes—it is that we cannot define inflation in terms of any *specific* rate of change in

TABLE 14–1. Inflation Rates in the Post World War II American Economy (Annual Average Percentage Increase)

Period	*Inflation Rate*
Truman-Eisenhower Years (1947–60)	3.3
The Kennedy Era (1961–65)	1.6
Vietnam and Its Aftermath (1966–70)	4.2
The 1970s (1971–76)	6.8
30-Year Average (1947–76)	3.8

SOURCE: *Economic Report of the President*, 1977.

the price level. We simply have to fall back on the common-sense idea that inflation is a persistent or sustained rise in the general level of prices. This is a less satisfactory situation than exists with respect to full employment, for at least there is agreement among economists that full employment lies somewhere between a 4 and 5.5 percent unemployment rate. By the standard just enunciated we thus had inflation even during the Kennedy era, although it was much more moderate—and hence easier to live with—than what we have experienced in recent years.

Types of Inflation

Keynes defined true inflation as a condition in which any additional increase in aggregate demand produces no further increase in output.[3] When the economy reaches this point any increase in aggregate demand expends itself wholly in price increases. Inflation such as this is the kind envisaged by the classical quantity theorists, although it should be noted that this definition does not preclude some price increases prior to the point at which the economy has reached the absolute upper limit of its output potential. In speaking of true inflation Keynes meant to emphasize only that there is some point in the short run when the elasticity of output with respect to changes in aggregate demand falls to zero, and it is at this point that it is proper to talk of a true inflationary condition.

Not too many years ago it was fashionable to speak of "creeping" or "gradual" inflation, such as the nation experienced during the Truman-Eisenhower years or the Kennedy era. This was a type of inflation in which there was a slow but persistent upward movement of the general price level, even though the economy was not necessarily operating at full employment. Actually some economists looked with considerable favor on such a situation as it was believed that a mild inflation was not only a good stimulus to output and employment gains, but probably necessary in a society characterized by downward rigidities in prices, wages, and costs in general. No handy tag has been found to characterize or describe the kind of inflation we have experienced in the 1970s, an inflation too rapid to be described as "creeping" and yet not so out of control as to warrant the adjective "hyper" (see below). It is perhaps premature to speak of a permanent inflation, although it has been suggested that an underlying, 5 to 6 percent "basic" inflation rate has become built into the economy.[4] This results from a combination of money incomes outrunning productivity and firmly-held expectations that inflation will continue. In any event, the post-World War II inflation is different. Prior to the last three decades —and from the 16th century onward—inflations were temporary and gen-

3. John Maynard Keynes, *The General Theory of Employment, Interest and Money* (New York: Harcourt, Brace, & World, First Harbinger ed., 1946), p. 303.

4. See *Economic Report of the President* (Washington, D.C.: U.S. Government Printing Office, 1976), p. 31.

erally limited in the number of countries affected. Now inflation is persistent and worldwide.[5]

Inflation is sometimes described as suppressed. There is no inflation in the technical sense of the word here, because prices do not rise. Suppressed inflation is a situation in which, by one means or another, the general price level is held down, but at the cost of a buildup of forces that may make for an explosive surge upward in prices at some later date. Suppressed inflation is most common during wartime when controls and rationing limit spending and prevent price increases but do not prevent the public from accumulating large amounts of liquid assets that can be readily turned into purchasing power at some future date. This clearly happened after World War II when prices jumped by 30 percent in 1946 and 1947. It is not so clear that this happened during the wage-price control experiment carried out by the Nixon administration—from August 1971 through April 1974. The reason is that prices began going up long before price controls were removed, even during the more stringent phases of the program (See the last section in this chapter for full details).

Finally, there is hyperinflation, which is best described as a situation in which the value of the monetary unit is totally destroyed. Under conditions of hyperinflation, prices rise to astronomical heights, and the velocity of circulation of money becomes almost infinitely great. Money ceases to serve as a store of value and is used only as a medium of exchange. Money that has become almost worthless is still somewhat more efficient than barter. If the hyperinflation goes far enough, there may be a complete collapse of the monetary system and people will have to resort to barter. Hyperinflation is almost always associated with defeat in war, the revolutionary destruction of an existing government, or some other equally catastrophic event that brings normal productive processes to a halt, forcing a government to resort to uncontrolled use of the printing press to finance its needs.

What Is Wrong With Inflation?

It is not necessary to belabor the point that hyperinflation—an inflation that totally destroys the currency of a nation—is a major social disaster. We only need to recall the great German inflation of the early 1920s, an inflation which many economists believe helped destroy the Weimar Republic and pave the way for Hitler and the ascent of Nazism.[6] However,

5. Irving S. Friedman, *Inflation: A World-Wide Disaster* (Garden City, N.Y.: Anchor Press/Doubleday, 1975), p. 5.

6. For a recent discussion of the link between the German hyperinflation of the 1920s and the rise of Hitler see L. E. Hill, C. E. Butler, and S. A. Lorenzen, "Inflation and the Destruction of Democracy: The Weimar Republic," *Journal of Economic Issues,* June 1977, pp. 299–313.

ever, this is not the kind of inflation we face. Even so, we need to understand why, next to persistent unemployment, persistent inflation is a social evil of major proportions. Keynes has said that "there is no subtler, no surer means of overturning the existing basis of Society than to debauch the currency. The process engages all the hidden forces of economic law on the side of destruction, and does so in a manner which not one man in a million is able to diagnose."[7] Let us examine some of the things Keynes may have had in mind.

We must always be careful about making generalizations on the basis of a limited number of observations. Nevertheless, the experience of the 1970s strongly suggests that persistent inflation looms as a major barrier to high employment and prosperity. An unchecked inflation sooner or later chokes off a business boom because too many people find that their money incomes are not keeping pace with soaring prices. Thus, *real* incomes fall, buying is curtailed, and an economic collapse is triggered. Among expert observers—economists, business forecasters, and corporate executives—there was near unanimous belief that inflation was one of the prime causes of the 1974–75 economic collapse.[8]

What inflation does is to redistribute income and wealth in an arbitrary, capricious, and usually unjust fashion. "Throughout history," it has been said, "inflation, social injustice, and political upheaval have been strongly correlated; this association is neither coincidental nor arbitrary, but has much to do with the impact of inflation on the distribution of income and wealth between the various classes of society."[9] More often than not the redistribution wrought by inflation is from the poor to the affluent, from the ordinary citizen to the government, a fact not widely understood.

Among the groups which suffer the most in an inflation are the aged and the poor. The aged suffer because most of them are on fixed incomes, incomes which are derived from savings, private pensions, insurance, or Social Security benefits. Since 1972 the latter have been "indexed," which is to say that benefits are adjusted upwards along with changes in the consumer price index. But because the income most retired couples get from Social Security is quite low, indexing does not solve the inflation problem for the aged. The aged—and the poor generally—also suffer because in an inflation all prices do not rise at the same rate. In recent years prices for basic necessities—food, shelter, medical care, and transportation—have been going up faster than most other prices. Since families of low or moderate means spend on the average three-fourths of their

7. John Maynard Keynes, *Essays in Persuasion* (New York, W. W. Norton & Company, Inc., 1963), p. 78.

8. *The Wall Street Journal*, April 25, 1975.

9. Sylvia Ann Hewlett, "Inflation and Inequality," *Journal of Economic Issues*, June 1977, p. 353.

budget for such necessities, this aspect of inflation may be especially devastating.

Workers, too, are often among the losers in an inflation, even though some workers through unions may be able to protect themselves somewhat against inflation through "escalator" clauses in their wage contracts. The U.S. Department of Labor estimates there are about 8 million workers in private and public employment covered by such contracts. Usually they provide for automatic wage increases based upon changes in the consumer price index, although escalator contracts don't always allow for increases equal to the full change in the price index. What such clauses do is allow the better organized workers to secure gains at the expense of the less organized, one example of how inflation redistributes income perversely.

But inflation may play a cruel joke on all workers, organized or unorganized, by thrusting them into a "Catch 22" situation. In fact, most families may find themselves in this situation. Because their money incomes go up during inflation, they are pushed into a higher tax bracket. But the increase in their money incomes is not sufficient to keep pace with both rising prices and rising taxes. During the 1974–75 economic slump, the Joint Economic Committee of the Congress reported that taxes calculated as a percent of personal income actual rose from 17.8 percent at the peak of the boom in 1973 to 18.3 percent as the recession reached bottom in late 1974.[10] Rising prices plus increased taxes caused the consumer's *real* take-home or spendable income to drop off more sharply than in any economic downturn since the 1930s. It should be noted that this perverse working of the tax system—a feature of its progressive character—tends to offset the stabilizing effects of built-in stabiilzers. Milton Friedman calls this aspect of inflation the "inflation tax." Inflation, he says, "is the only form of taxation that can be imposed without anybody having to vote for it."[11]

It is not just income which is rearranged in a capricious and usually unjust fashion by inflation. The same thing happens to personal wealth, especially monetary wealth in the form of savings deposits, cash holdings, bonds, the value of life insurance policies, pension rights, and other claims on present and future purchasing power. Basically, inflation redistributes wealth from creditors to debtors, provided debts are stated in fixed money terms, as is usually the case. The reason there is redistribution is that inflation enables the debtor to pay off his obligation in money whose real value has declined.

10. "Inflation and the Consumer in 1974," Joint Economic Committee, Congress of the United States, (Washington, D.C.: U.S. Government Printing Office, February 10, 1974), p. 12.

11. Milton Friedman, *Is Inflation a Curable Disease?* Graduate School of Business, University of Pittsburgh, May 1975, p. 8.

Professor G. L. Bach of Stanford University recently investigated how much redistribution of wealth resulted from inflation following World War II. From the end of the war until the beginning of the 1970s, Bach found there was a massive transfer of wealth from households—ordinary citizens, in other words—to governments and to business. The magnitude of this transfer has been staggering—between one-half to two-thirds of a trillion dollars.[12] The reason why the transfer has been *from* households to government and business is because households have been net creditors in this era. Their assets exceeded their liabilities.

But this is not the whole story. Inflation has also been responsible for significant transfers of wealth *between* households. Bach found these to be of two kinds. First, wealth was transferred from both the very poor and the very rich to households in the middle income range. This happened because the latter are often, on balance, debtors, especially for houses and automobiles. The poor, on the other hand, have few debts and usually do not own assets whose value appreciates in an inflation (land or houses), whereas the rich are usually without debts simply because they are rich. Also their assets are often of a monetary nature (such as bonds), and hence vulnerable to inflation. What few assets the poor have are also in monetary form. Second, there was a large transfer of wealth from the old to the young, the reason being that young families are often heavily in debt. They borrow to set up a household, to buy houses and cars, and to finance education. On balance, a large proportion of the assets of the old are in a fixed value form.

The foregoing represent concrete, measurable ways in which inflation is damaging. But its ultimate threat is more intangible, more subtle, though nonetheless real. It arises out of the fact that modern society is a future-oriented society. No individual, no family, no business, or no government lives wholly in the present, disregarding the future. More perhaps than many realize, money and assets valued in money are our link which the economy has to the future. This, perhaps, is the most insidious danger of inflation. Between 1939 and 1976—37 years—the U.S. dollar lost 75 percent of its purchasing power. In the 1970s alone (1970–76) the value of the dollar shrunk by 32 percent.

Destruction of the value of a nation's currency is serious. Besides being a link to the future, money is part of the glue holding a society together. When confidence in the value of money erodes, a pernicious and corrosive element enters into the nation's economic life. People are robbed of a dependable yardstick for understanding and evaluating what is happening around them. Further, there tends to be within a society a subtle but dangerous tilt away from productive activities toward those which are pri-

12. G. L. Bach, "Inflation: Who Gains and Who Loses?" *Challenge*, July/August 1974, pp. 48–55.

marily speculative. Inflation provides an ideal milieu for the fast-buck operator—often more money can be made by dealing in things which already exist than by producing new wealth. It is also true that inflation exacerbates the struggle over the distribution of income. As individuals and families catch on to the adverse effects that inflation has on relative income positions, they become aroused, aggressive, and angry, ready to deploy all the economic power they command to protect or enlarge their share of the income pie. A vicious circle ensues. Inflation worsens income distribution, but the struggle over distributive shares which it unleashes feeds the inflationary spiral.

Theories of Inflation

Since the end of World War II there has been much discusson concerning the cause and cure of the persistent inflationary trend that has characterized the economies of most nations. As a consequence of such discussions, as well as extensive analysis and empirical research, three broad theoretical explanations for the phenomenon of inflation have emerged. These may be described as the *demand-pull* hypothesis, the *cost-push* hypothesis, and the *structural* hypothesis. We shall examine each of these in turn, but the reader is cautioned at the outset that postulating three theories of the inflationary process does not mean that they are mutually exclusive or that any one of them will suffice to explain the inflationary process. The upward trend of the general price level that appears to be an important characteristic of most modern economies is neither wholly understood nor readily controlled.[13]

The Demand-Pull Hypothesis · The demand-pull hypothesis relates to what may be called the traditional theory of inflation. The theory holds that inflation is caused by an excess of demand (spending) relative to the available supply of goods and services at existing prices. In both the traditional and modern quantity theories the factor of key significance is the money supply; only an increase in the money supply is capable of driving the general price level upward. In income-expenditure theory, demand-pull is interpreted to mean an excess of aggregate money demand relative to the economy's full-employment output level. This is similar, the reader will note, to the Keynesian definition of true inflation, although the demand-pull hypothesis should not be interpreted to mean that no upward movement in the general level of prices is possible prior to the point of full employment. The basic idea is that whatever upward pressure may exist on the price level emanates from demand. The theory fur-

13. The development of incomes policies as a technique for the control of inflation is discussed in the latter part of this chapter.

ther presumes that prices for goods and services as well as for economic resources are responsive to supply and demand forces, and will thus move readily upward under the pressure of a high level of aggregate demand.

The presumed cure for inflation in the demand-pull category is quite obvious; if there is an excess of spending, it must be cured by the vigorous pursuit of monetary and fiscal policies that will reduce total spending and thus lessen the upward pressure on the price level. The demand-pull thesis presumes, too, that prices and other costs are flexible downward as well as upward, and therefore, that policy measures necessary to reduce total spending will not adversely affect employment levels. However, if money wages and prices are not flexible downward, then it is not possible to control excess spending without significant reductions in employment. This point was verified by the experience in 1969–70 again in 1974–75 when the fiscal and monetary brakes were applied by the Nixon and Ford administrations. The result were recessions but continued inflation.

The Cost-Push Hypothesis · The cost-push explanation of the source of inflation has come into favor since World War II, especially in the 1970s.[14] This theory finds the basic explanation for inflation in the fact that some producers, groups of workers, or both, succeed in raising the prices for either their products or services above the levels that would prevail under more competitive conditions. Inflationary pressure originates, in other words, with supply rather than demand, and spreads throughout the economy. An inflation of this type is possible in theory because in the aggregate prices and wages are not only costs as seen from the standpoint of buyers, but also income when viewed from the standpoint of sellers of goods and labor. For any single commodity or factor service an increase in its price will reduce the quantity of the good or services demanded, but this is not necessarily true for the whole economy.

Inflation of the cost-push variety is most likely to originate in industries which are relatively concentrated, and in which sellers can exercise considerable discretion in the formulation of both prices and wages. Competitive conditions must be such that either business firms or trade unions have some control over the prices of their products or services. Cost-push inflation would not be possible in an economy-characterized by pure competition. If recent inflationary pressures in the United States and other economies can really be attributed to cost-push factors, serious and difficult problems of policy are raised. An inflation caused by cost-push is not susceptible to control by traditional monetary and fiscal measures directed at the level of aggregate demand and spending because adminis-

14. This type of inflation is also described as market power inflation, income share inflation, and administrative inflation.

tered prices and wages by their very nature are insensitive to changes in demand. Thus measures that reduce over-all demand may not affect prices, but can affect quite adversely the economy's real output and employment level. On the other hand, policy measures that involve direct controls over either wages or prices are strongly resisted by both organized labor and the business community under peacetime conditions. Although initially there was broad public support for the Nixon administration's program of wage-price controls (introduced in August 1971), business groups, organized labor, and the general public became increasingly disillusioned with such controls the longer they were in effect.

The Structural Hypothesis · The structural thesis was developed by Charles Schultze to explain the inflation experienced by the American economy in the late 1950s,[15] a time when considerable slack existed in the economy. Schultze is a former professor of Economics at the University of Maryland and currently Chairman of President Carter's Council of Economic Advisers.

It shows that inflation may be the consequence of internal changes in the structure of demand, even though over-all demand may not be excessive and there are no undue concentrations of economic power within the economy. This particular theory of inflation has its origin in the fact that in many areas of the economy wages and prices are flexible upward in response to increases in demand, but not flexible downward when demand declines. If this is the situation, it follows that inflationary pressure can be generated by internal changes in the composition of demand alone. In a dynamic economy such changes are an inherent part of the economic process, consequent upon continuous changes in the structure of consumer tastes and desires. The mechanism by which such changes can generate inflationary pressure in the absence of any marked excess of aggregate demand or aggressive exploitation of positions of market power is relatively clear-cut. The expansion of demand for the output of particular industries or sectors will lead to wage and price increases in these areas because wages and prices have an upward sensitivity when demand is rising. But the contraction of demand in other sectors will not lead to any coresponding downward movement of prices. Thus, over-all, the average level of prices will necessarily rise. The structural thesis makes price inflation inherent in the process of resource allocation, if wages and prices are flexible upward but not downward.

15. Charles L. Schultze, *Recent Inflation in the United States,* Study Paper no. 1, Joint Economic Committee, Study of Employment, Growth, and Price Levels (Washington, D.C.: U.S. Government Printing Office, 1959). This is also described as intersectoral or demand shift inflation.

The Inflationary Process

No single explanation will suffice when we deal with a phenomenon as complex as inflation in the modern economy. The theories just described should not be construed as alternatives in any absolute sense, but rather as approaches that lay stress on one factor relatively more than another. In the inflation characteristic of the contemporary American economy, elements present in each of the theories have been at work. Thus, it is not much the question of one theory being better, or more valid, than another, as it is of the emphasis that should be placed on demand, cost, or structural factors.

Except for the convinced monetarists, most economists do not see the problem of inflation as basically a matter of too much money in circulation. But this does not mean that the money supply is not in the picture. Barring unprecedented shifts in the velocity of circulation, all the theories of the inflationary process that we have discussed predicate increases in the money supply if the inflation is to continue. The income expenditure approach sees these increases in money as a secondary consequence of other changes that in themselves are primarily responsible for the increases in prices, while the classical view (traditional and modern) regards changes in the money supply itself as the basic cause of inflation.

Crucial to any understanding of the nature of the inflationary process, as well as the causes of inflation, is a knowledge of the sensitivity of prices and wages to changes in demand. Two possibilities are present: Wages and prices may be flexible or inflexible. By flexible we mean that both wages and prices respond readily and quickly to changes in demand. Wages and prices that are inflexible, on the other hand, are sometimes said to be *cost determined*,[16] that is, they do not respond to changes in demand. Wages are cost determined in the sense that they are fixed in relation to some index of living costs, such as the consumer price index, and change only as the latter changes. Prices are cost determined in the sense that they are determined on the basis of cost considerations and remain relatively fixed irrespective of demand conditions as long as costs do not change.

Demand-Pull Inflation

Let us begin our analysis of the inflationary process with the assumption that inflation gets under way with an excess of aggregate demand over *current supply at existing prices.* The Vietnam-induced inflation provides an almost perfect textbook example of such a situation. During 1965 the economy was near full employment—at the end of the year the unem-

16. Ibid., p. 5.

ployment rate had dropped to 4.1 percent of the civilian labor force—and the price level was nearly stable. In 1966, however, and as part of the Vietnam military buildup, expenditures for goods and services for military purposes jumped by more than $10 billion, a spending surge that sent the economy on an inflationary surge that was still going strong at the start of the 1970s. Given the type of aggregate supply curve described in Figure 5–3 the excess of aggregate demand will drive the price level up, even if the economy is not initially at the full employment level. The price level rises because the elasticity of output has a value of less than unity, and the elasticity of the price level has a value greater than zero.[17] This initial increase in prices and costs does not mean that all prices and wages are affected equally. There will be some groups that register a net gain from the initial inflationary spurt in the economy because their money incomes have increased more than the prices of things they buy. Other groups find their real position unchanged; their money incomes and the prices of the things they buy have changed in the same proportion. Still others are net losers because prices increase more swiftly than their money incomes.

The extent to which an upward movement in the price level generated initially by aggregate demand continues depends basically upon whether or not all groups in the economy attempt to maintain their real income and expenditure positions. If all groups, in the face of inflation, try to maintain real expenditure positions, real aggregate demand is unaffected by changes in the price level. But real expenditure positions can be maintained only if aggregate money demand—that is, expenditure—continues to rise at the same rate as the general price level. For example, if the groups that initially saw their real economic position adversely affected by the original inflationary spurt succeed in raising either the prices of the things they sell or their money wages, their real income and expenditure position remains intact. But this, of course, will boost prices to still higher levels, and thus require additional upward adjustments in money income and expenditure on the part of still other groups that now seek to maintain intact their real expenditure positions. From the viewpoint of the whole economy, an added increase in the level of aggregate money expenditure is inevitable if the level of real aggregate demand is to remain constant.[18]

17. Technically, the elasticity of output is the ratio of a percentage change in output to a percentage change in aggregate demand and the elasticity of the price level is the ratio of a percentage change in the price level to a percentage change in aggregate demand.

18. In a dynamic setting in which output is rising, aggregate real demand must rise, not remain constant. See Schultze, p. 26. The student should note most carefully at this point that the analysis is attempting to spell out the circumstances under which the price level will continue to rise, given an initial excess of aggregate demand over

The reader should not forget that the level of aggregate demand in real terms—that is, constant prices—is of significance with respect to the employment level. The key to an understanding of the inflationary process lies in the impact that a rising price level has on real aggregate demand. An upward movement of the general price level can continue, irrespective of whether the initial inflationary impulse came from demand-pull, cost-push, or structural factors, only if aggregate real demand remains unchanged, or does not drop too severely. This requires that aggregate money expenditures rise at about the same rate as the general price level. The 1974–75 experience is instructive on this point, as it suggests that under present conditions a severe drop in aggregate real demand—i.e., a deep depression—may be necessary to break the back of an inflation, once it is under way. Such a course of action is not tolerable politically—or morally for that matter.

Some studies indicate that there are a number of possible ways in which a rising price level may have a dampening effect upon aggregate real demand.[19] For example, a progressive tax system could lead to a reduction in real consumption because money income in the hands of the economy's spending units will not rise in proportion to a change in prices. As pointed out in the discussion on the effects of inflation, this clearly happened in the 1974–75 recession. It is possible, too, that a rising price level will reduce the real value of liquid assets held by consumers, and thus lead to a slackening of real consumer demand as households attempt to bring their asset holding back to what they consider a desirable level. This is the Pigou effect at work in reverse. If, in addition, it is assumed that the money supply is fixed, an increase in the price level may have a depressing effect upon real investment outlays because under these circumstance the rate of interest will rise.

Granted that the possibility exists that aggregate real demand may decline—or, alternatively, that aggregate money demand may not rise in proportion to the change in the price level—the significance of this for a continuaton of the inflationary process depends upon the sensitivity of prices and money wages to changes in demand. If we assume, first, that a rising general price level tends to depress the level of real demand, and second, that both money wages and prices are flexible, then the economy contains a kind of built-in corrective factor that makes a continued

---

supply at current prices. A continued expansion of demand is much the simpler case. Recent experience provides empirical verification on the point. Aggregate real demand slowed sharply in 1969 and actually declined in 1970, but money national income continued to rise in both years. The same thing happened again in 1974 and 1975. In both these years real GNP fell, but GNP valued in current prices continued to rise. This happened even though the 1974–75 slump was the most severe since the Great Depression of the 1930s.

19. Schultze, pp. 21–26.

upward movement of the general price level difficult to sustain. More particularly, a cost-push type of inflation is practically impossible under these conditions, because the decline in the level of aggregate real demand means both a decline in the demand for the different categories of output and for the services of different economic resources, particularly labor. In the short run this will lead to growing unemployment of labor and excess plant capacity. But if prices and wages are sensitive to the state of demand, it will be impossible for any upward movement of either to continue. If wage and price sensitivity exists, in other words, the inflationary process will come to a halt unless there is a constant renewal of excess aggregate money demand. This is not likely if restraint is exercised by the government in the face of the downward pressure on the price level that will develop once the force of the initial volume of excess expenditure exhausts itself. Recent experience, though, does not offer much evidence that matters are likely to work out this way. There is certainly no indication that wages and prices are flexible downward, and the ability of the federal government to exercise restraint in spending is doubtful. The initial impetus to inflation from Vietnam war spending was largely exhausted by 1969, when military outlays stabilized, and then dropped to lower levels for four years (1970–73). But total federal expenditures (in current prices) for goods and services continued to mount, going from $207.9 billion in 1960 to $365.6 billion in 1976, a 75.9 percent increase in seven years.

Cost-Push Inflation

The results are different if money wages and prices are not particularly sensitive to a change in demand, even though aggregate real demand is adversely affected by a general upward movement of the price level. Under these conditions the economy no longer contains any kind of internal corrective factor to limit the extent to which an initial excess of aggregate demand may push up the price level. A reduction in real aggregate demand, given inflexible wages and prices, leads chiefly to a reduction in employment and to excess capacity. Prices and wages will not decline, and thus the inflation may continue. If unemployment and idle capacity lead to demands from organized labor and business that the government adopt monetary and fiscal policies which will increase aggregate money demand sufficiently to restore real aggregate demand to its prior level, a cost-push type of inflationary process is possible. This clearly was the case in early 1971, at which time the Nixon administration junked the game plan that called for a gradual slowdown in the pace of economic activity in the hope of containing inflation. The same scenario was played over again in the spring of 1975 when the Ford administration changed its policy stance and called for a tax cut as part of a package to stimulate the economy. The Carter administration did the same in the spring of 1977, even though the economy then was in the recovery stage from the 1974–75 recession. Under such circumstances the stage is set for a continuous upward movement of the price level, particularly because all groups do not share equally in the initial round of price increases. When the price level begins to rise, aggregate real demand may fall. But this does not bring prices down. As a consequence, groups which did not gain from the initial price rise now seek to boost their money incomes so as to maintain real expenditure positions. This creates more upward pressure on the price level, and, indirectly, puts pressure on government to take the necessary steps to sustain aggregate real demand and prevent unemployment. Both the 1970 and 1974–75 recessions and the sluggish recoveries which followed these economic downturns illustrate this process. As Table 14–2 shows, hourly earnings in current dollars continued to rise in the recession years at rates which were only slightly less than they rose in the preceding boom periods. In 1970, for example, gross hourly earnings in private nonagricultural activity increased by 5.9 percent, compared to 6.7 percent in 1969—a year of fiscal and monetary restraint—and 6.3 percent in 1968, a boom year. Again in 1974 and 1975, clear recession years, hourly earnings rose even more rapidly than they did in 1972 and only slightly less than they rose in 1973. The latter two years were boom years.

In the situation described above both the elasticity of the price level, and the elasticity of money wages,[20] have values that are high with respect to any increase in aggregate money demand, but low with respect to a decrease in aggregate real demand. Beyond this, the mechanism must exist through which pressure can be generated to raise the level of aggre-

TABLE 14–2. Annual Average Increase in Hourly Earnings in Nonagricultural Employment: 1968–76 (in percent)

Year	*Economic Conditions*	*Percent Increase in Hourly Earnings*	*Unemployment Rate*
1968	Boom	6.3%	3.6%
1969	Boom + restraint	6.7	3.5
1970	Recession	5.9	4.9
1971	Recovery–slow	6.8	5.9
1972	Boom	6.7	5.6
1973	Boom + restraint	8.0	4.9
1974	Recession	7.7	5.6
1975	Recession + stimulus	7.6	8.5
1976	Recovery–slow	7.3	7.7

SOURCE: *Economic Report of the President*, 1977.

20. The elasticity of money wages is the ratio of a percentage change in money wages to a percentage change in aggregate demand.

gate money demand and thus prevent unemployment and idle capacity from developing. It is clear from recent experience that the political process provides that mechanism.

If we drop the assumption that a rise in the general price level tends to reduce real aggregate demand, then there is less reason to assert that any kind of a built-in corrective factor is present in the economy. Under the assumption that aggregate real demand is not adversely affected by a rise in the general price level, no downward pressure on either prices or wages will develop in the event of an initial rise, irrespective of whether the first impulse toward higher prices resulted from demand-pull or cost-push forces. However, a cost-push type of inflation is much easier to sustain if a rising price level does not depress aggregate real demand. Then, no downward pressure on either prices and wages or employment levels will develop as various groups push prices and costs upward in an effort to sustain real expenditure levels. From the point of view of the whole economy, rising costs (and prices) can generate an equal increase in aggregate monetary demand as long as we assume that aggregate real demand is unaffected by a rise in the general price level. Thus a cost-push inflationary process can, in theory, continue indefinitely without any necessarily adverse effects on the employment level. Under the foregoing circumstances, the degree of flexibility or inflexibility of both wages and prices loses much of its significance, for this is a matter of importance chiefly when we assume that a rise in the price level will depress aggregate real demand.

The phenomenon of inflation in the modern economy cannot be fully explained in terms of either the demand-pull or the cost-push theories. The major distinction between these two theories of the inflationary process centers on the sensitivity of both money wages and prices to changes in demand. Those who believe that significant price and wage flexibility exists in the economy would generally argue in favor of the demand-pull thesis as the basic cause of inflation because such flexibility makes it virtually impossible for any cost-induced inflationary trend to sustain itself if the level of aggregate real demand is sensitive to a rising price level. On the other hand, economists who are skeptical concerning the extent of wage and price flexibility in the economy are inclined to place more emphasis upon the cost-push theory as basic to an explanation and understanding of inflation. Such theorists do not deny the importance of demand factors, but they take the view that the basic insensitivity of wages and prices to demand conditions means that a substantial—and probably intolerable—level of unemployment and idle capacity would be required before the general price level was stabilized. In essence, the cost-push theorists see inflation as a consequence of market power, a phenomenon that cannot be dealt with by traditional fiscal and monetary tools. In a cost-push situation the pressure on the price level does not have to come solely from wages or other costs. It may originate with prices themselves, given the existence of market power in key sectors of the economy. Many large trade unions have the power to push wages up in the face of a falling demand, but many large corporations have the same power with respect to prices. In a 1974 report on the causes of the economy's inflation, the Joint Economic Committee of the Congress said that "increasingly, a significant part of the current inflation can be understood only in the context of administered prices in concentrated industries which typically increase despite falling demand."[21] Concentrated industries, the Committee asserted, have the power to resist competitive forces and achieve a target rate of return on investment in good times and bad. To do this they must have power to control prices. To cope with inflation caused by private market power, administrative and legislative action should be taken to break up such power, and to eliminate, as well, government regulations and practices which restrict competition. This was a key recommendation of the Committee.[22] Among economists, John Kenneth Galbraith and Gardner C. Means are probably the best known advocates of the thesis that concentrated market power in the oligopolistic sectors of the economy is a major factor in the contemporary inflation, particularly inflation when unemployment is high.[23] Both also believe that the basic remedy is for the government to control prices in the few hundred giant corporations which dominate the American economy. In the long run Means is willing to experiment with policies that would reduce market power by breaking up oligopolistic enterprises, but Galbraith is skeptical of this approach.

Structural Inflation

The third theoretical explanation offered for the inflation was described earlier as the structural thesis. As noted, it differs from both the demand-pull and cost-push analyses primarily in that it stresses changes in the composition of demand.

In this analysis the starting point for inflation is a change in the structure of demand which leads to an increase in the demand for the products of particular industries. There is nothing unusual in this, for in a dynamic economy it is presumed that a process of changing demand and resource

21. "An Action Program to Reduce Inflation and Restore Economic Growth," Joint Economic Committee, Congress of the United States (Washington, D.C.: U.S. Government Printing Office, September 21, 1974), p. 3. See also Howard M. Wachtel and Peter D. Adelsheim, "How Recession Feeds Inflation: Price Markups in a Concentrated Economy," *Challenge*, September/October, 1977.

22. Ibid., pp. 10 ff.

23. The best statement of Galbraith's position on this question is found in his *Economics and the Public Purpose* (Boston: Houghton Mifflin Company, 1973), especially Chapters 19 and 26. See also Gardner C. Means, "Simultaneous Inflation and Unemployment," in *The Roots of Inflation* (New York, Burt Franklin & Co., Inc., 1975), pp. 1–30.

reallocation is continuously under way. What is significant, though, is that both money wages and prices in the modern American economy are flexible upward in response to shifts in demand, but rigid downward. Prices will therefore move upward in those industries which experience an increase in the demand for their output, but prices will not fall in those industries where there is either an absolute or relative fall in demand. Not only will prices fail to fall in the industries where demand declines; they may actually rise. The increase in wages and other prices in the industries with an expanding demand will force the demand-deficient industries to pay higher wages for labor and higher prices for other materials in order to get the economic resources they need to continue in production, even though these industries are confronted with a decline in the demand for their output. Wage and price rigidity downward is basically the cause for this type of behavior, for it would not be possible for prices to move significantly upward in the industries which have an increase in demand if wages and prices elsewhere moved downward in response to a declining demand situation. Consequently, wage and price increases in particular sectors gradually spread out and permeate the whole economy.

The most important single implication of the structural explanation of the inflationary process is that monetary and fiscal measures of a general character are not capable of coping with this type of an inflationary situation. General monetary and fiscal measures aim basically at the control of aggregate demand, but this is much too blunt an approach for an inflation that has its origin in changes in the composition of demand. Restrictive measures designed to reduce the over-all level of demand may simply lead to unemployment of labor and idle plant capacity without any significant impact on the price level. Schultze has suggested that an inflation which results from changes in the composition of demand is a means by which an economy characterized by downward rigidities in its cost-price structure brings about the necessary reallocation of resources in response to changing conditions of demand. In the development of any policy measures designed to cope with this type of inflation, care would have to be exercised not to control prices at the cost of blunting the process of resource allocation. The difficulty with this is that there is no way of knowing just how much inflation is necessary and acceptable for this purpose. We cannot distinguish, in other words, between this type of inflation and inflation which results from other causes.

The Microeconomic Roots of Inflation

The theories we have examined, as well as our analysis of the inflationary process, point to the conclusion that, whatever the ultimate explanation for any sustained rise in the price level, the modern market economy experiences significant upward pressure on the price level well before full employment output is reached. Empirical verification for this is to be found in examination of the relationship between the rate of wage and price increases and unemployment rates by means of the Phillips Curve, an analytical technique we shall discuss later in this chapter. In the meantime, though, it is appropriate that we look at some of the forces at work at the microeconomic level—i.e., within the firm and the industry—to help explain this process.

As suggested earlier in this chapter, contemporary income expenditure analysis argues that the relationship between the price level and output takes the form of a curve of the kind shown in Figure 14–4. As output rises toward full employment (Y_f), increases in the price level become more and more pronounced until eventually the curve depicting the relationship of the general price level to income becomes vertical. This happens at Y_f and signifies that at this point any further increase in aggregate demand will not lead to additional output, but simply to an increase in the price level. This is what Keynes designated as true inflation.

In order to understand why the general price level tends to vary in the manner shown in Figure 14–4, we need to analyze the forces that determine prices at the level of the firm and the industry. The behavior of the general price level in response to changing levels of aggregate demand depends upon how individual prices respond to output changes that are

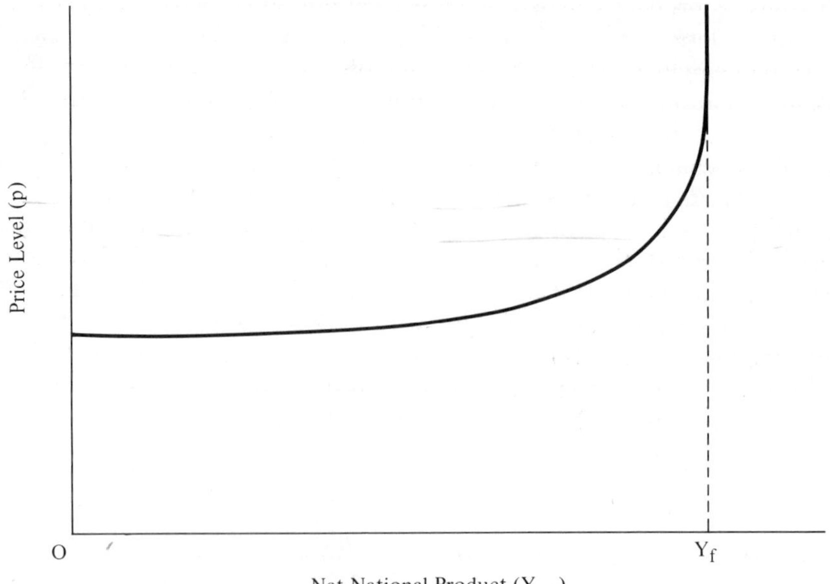

FIGURE 14–4. The Price-Output Relationship

brought about by changes in demand. Therefore we can employ the same key analytical concepts of demand and supply that we use to explain the process of individual price determination to explain the process through which the general price level is determined.

Traditionally, the body of economic analysis called price, or value, theory (microeconomics) teaches that prices are governed by demand and supply conditions. In our analysis we have been concerned primarily with demand for the whole output of the economy. In a conceptual sense aggregate demand represents the sum of all the individual industry (or product) demand schedules that exist in the economy at any given moment. There is associated, in other words, with any given level of aggregate demand an underlying structure of demand schedules for all the different industries that make up the economy. It logically follows that some or all of the individual demand curves will shift when there is a change in aggregate demand, although the individual schedules will not necessarily shift to the same degree as the total demand.[24] If we thus assume some change in an industry demand schedule consequent upon a shift in aggregate demand, our problem reduces itself to one of explaining how output and price will respond at the industry level to such a change.

In Figure 14–5 we present a typical demand and supply diagram showing how market price is determined for some given commodity. Let us call this commodity A. Given the existence of the industry supply curve *SS* and the industry demand curve *DD*, the equilibrium price is P_1 and the equilibrium output is A_1. Since we are interested in the impact of a change in demand on both price and output, let us see what happens if we shift the demand curve to the right, from *DD* to *D′D′*. The result of this shift is an increase in output to the level of A_2, and also an increase in price to the level of P_2. There has been both an output and a price response to the change in demand.

Why has this increase in price accompanied the higher level of output? If we are going to explain the price change depicted in Figure 14–5, it is necessary to go behind the schedules, so to speak, and analyze the factors that underlie supply. With an assumed shift in demand, the manner in which both price and output will change depends primarily upon supply considerations.

The position and shape of a typical supply schedule, such as *SS* in Figure 14–5, reflect the behavior of costs as output changes. From the standpoint of the individual business firm costs are the key determinant of

24. The extent to which the demand for a particular commodity shifts as a result of a change in the aggregate demand function is primarily a matter of the income elasticity of demand, assuming that any increase in aggregate demand is accompanied by an increase in real income. For a discussion of the concept of income elasticity see Edwin Mansfield, *Microeconomics: Theory and Applications*, Second Edition (New York: Norton, 1975), pp. 93–95.

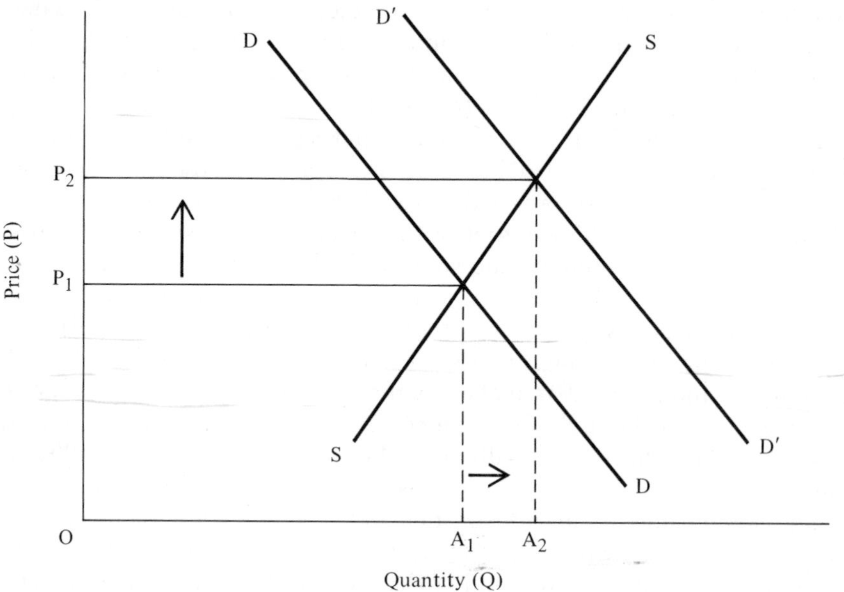

FIGURE 14–5. Determination of Market Price

the supply function. The most important cost element in the short run is *marginal cost*, defined as the cost of producing an additional unit of output. Since marginal cost represents cost associated with changes in output, it is apparent that the behavior of marginal costs is crucial to an understanding of the behavior of prices in response to changes in output. In the short run, with fixed plant capacity, marginal cost is the same thing as a change in variable costs, which are costs that vary directly with changes in output. The most important variable costs are the wages of labor and the cost of materials.

Modern economic analysis asserts that, typically, the costs of the business firm are not constant as output expands toward the capacity level; rather, the presumption is that increases in output eventually lead to increases in variable costs per unit of output—and hence marginal costs—and that this will occur prior to the point at which the absolute upper limit of the firm's productive capacity is reached. The short run is characterized, in other words, by a rising level of both variable and marginal costs. Figure 14–6 depicts the shape of the variable and marginal cost curves for the typical business firm in the short run.

There are three reasons why variable costs may rise prior to the point of maximum capacity. The first of these involves the classic principle of diminishing returns. Even if we assume all resources are homogeneous, additional inputs of a variable resource such as labor eventually lead to a less than proportionate increase in output as long as productive capacity remains fixed. This is the essence of the principle of diminishing returns. If the price of our variable resource, labor, is fixed—that is, money wages are constant—a decline in physical productivity is tantamount to a rise in variable costs per unit produced.[25] Thus diminishing productivity means that ultimately the firm will be faced with rising labor costs per unit of output.

A second major reason for the increase of variable and marginal costs as output expands is the nonhomogeneity of resources that are variable in the short run. This is strongly stressed by Keynes.[26] In reality, labor and other resources are neither homogeneous nor fully interchangeable in the productive process. An expansion of output within the limits of ultimate productive capacity may require the use of labor units that are less and less efficient in relation to the going wage rate. This will cause an increase in the labor cost per unit of output even though the firm's capital equipment is not fully utilized. Rising labor costs may result in spite of the fact that suitable equipment is available for use in conjunction with added labor—if the labor units are not of the same degree of efficiency.

The third explanation for rising costs—and prices—as output expands is simply that the prices the firm must pay for its variable resources are

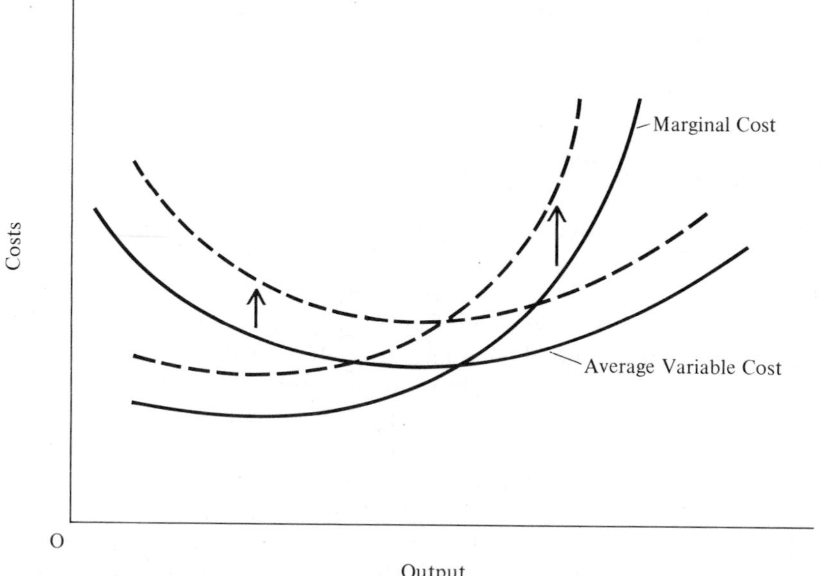

FIGURE 14–6. The Costs of the Business Firm

25. The reader should recognize that this is essentially the same analysis as developed in Chapter 12, where the relationship of the demand for labor and a falling real wage (productivity) to the supply of output and the price level was shown (Figure 12–11). They are different routes to the same objective—showing why prices rise with increased output.

26. John Maynard Keynes, *The General Theory,* pp. 42, 299–300.

unlikely to remain constant as output expands. If an expansion of output is general in the economy, it is most likely that the prices that firms must pay for labor and other resources will rise prior to attainment of the full employment level. There are two reasons for this. First, the elasticity of supply of all commodities and services is not the same; thus for some resources supply may become perfectly inelastic before output as a whole has become perfectly inelastic, that is, before the full employment level for the economy as a whole is reached. The emergence of bottlenecks in particular industries and for particular goods and services will cause the price of various *intermediate goods and services* to rise, and will thus ultimately affect the price of final goods and services. Second, a period of expanding demand and output will lead to increased pressure by organized labor for wage increases. Wages are flexible upward but not downward. If the economic outlook is generally favorable, business firms are not likely to resist these demands very strenuously. Changes in the prices that the business firm must pay for its variable resources will cause a change in its unit costs over the entire range of output possible within the limits of the firm's capacity. Thus changes of the type we have just been describing are subsumed in shifts in the position of both the variable and marginal cost curves of the firm, such as those depicted by the dotted lines in Figure 14–6.

The Keynesian Theory of the Price Level

The foregoing discussion leads us directly into the theory Keynes developed to explain the price level. In a chapter in *The General Theory*[27] which never received from economists the attention it deserves, Keynes attempted to show that the same forces which economists stress in their explanation of how individual prices are determined (see prior section) also determine prices in general. As Keynes put it, one of his objectives was "to bring the theory of prices as a whole back to close contact with the theory of value."[28] What the classical economics had done, according to Keynes, was explain prices at the level of the firm and industry by conditions of supply and demand, but introduce an entirely different kind of explanation into the picture when it came to prices in general—namely, the quantity theory of money. This Keynes viewed as a false division. Keynes sums up his basic argument quite succinctly as follows:

> In a single industry its particular price-level depends partly on the rate of remuneration of the factors of production which enter into its marginal

27. Chapter 21, "The Theory of Prices."
28. Keynes, *The General Theory*, p. 293.

> cost and partly on the scale of output. There is no reason to modify this conclusion when we pass to industry as a whole. The general price level depends partly on the rate of remuneration of the factors of production which enter into marginal cost and partly on the scale of output as a whole, i.e. (taking equipment and technique as given) on the volume of employment.[29]

Here in a nutshell are the essential ideas we discussed in the previous section. By scale of output Keynes means to encompass all those factors which influence the shape of the cost curves (Figure 14–6) as the output level changes. By remuneration of the factors of production, Keynes is pointing to all the forces which may cause the prices businessmen have to pay (wages, interest, rents, etc.) to get resources to rise as they use more resources. In Figure 14–6 these forces influence the level of the cost curves—shown by the dotted lines.

To complete his explanation of how prices in general vary with changes in output, Keynes brought into the analysis all the key elements which enter into his own explanation of income and employment. Starting with an increase in the quantity of money,[30] Keynes asked how and by what process does such a change get to the price level? The answer he gave runs as follows. A change in the money supply will affect, first, the rate of interest. How interest changes depends on the schedule of liquidity preference, which in turn depends upon expectations concerning the future as well as the current level of economic activity. Next a change in the interest rate will lead to a change in investment spending. How much investment spending changes is a matter of the sensitivity of the latter of changes in the rate of interest. This is a question involving *all* the variables which enter into the investment demand schedule (See Chapter 6), including expectations and the state of business confidence. A change in investment spending will lead to a change in aggregate demand, but the magnitude of the latter depends upon the value of the multiplier. This, it will be recalled, is determined by the various "leakages" from the income stream (Chapters 7, 8, and 9). Once aggregate demand has increased, it will exhaust itself either in an increase in output (and employment), an increase in the price level, or both. This brings us full circle to Keynes' basic argument, for how more spending divides itself between higher prices and more output depends on the strength of the underlying forces which operate through the scale of output and which determine the rate

29. Ibid., p. 294.

30. This in a way is a classical stance, but presumably he used this as a starting point in developing his theory because he wanted to show that the link between money and the price level had to take into account not only his basic theory of output determination, but also essentially classical ideas of how individual prices are determined. Only in this way could he bring the "theory of prices as a whole back to close contact with the theory of value."

of remuneration for the factors of production. Figure 14–7 shows these relationships in a diagram.

In the short run Keynes believed strongly that the principle of diminishing returns (or productivity) was a major factor in explaining why marginal and variable costs rise as output expands (See Figure 14–6), the reason being that technique and equipment (i.e., capital) are fixed. In this respect he was very much a classical economist. But in the long run, he believed that the level of money wages and their relationship to changes in productivity are the more important. As he put it, "And the long-run stability or instability of prices will depend upon the strength of the upward trend of the wage unit (or, more precisely, of the cost unit) compared with the rate of increase in the efficiency of the productive system."[31] The British economist Joan Robinson has called the idea that in an industrial economy the level of prices is determined primarily by the level of money wages "the other half of the Keynesian Revolution," the first half being the principle that aggregate demand determines the level of output.[32] She believes that this view seriously undermines the neoclassical belief that the economy is inherently stable, tending toward an equilibrium of full employment. "The level of money wages in any country at any time is more or less a historical accident going back to a remote past and influenced by recent events affecting the balance of power between employers and trade unions in the labor market."[33] Another economist, Professor Sidney Weintraub of the University of Pennsylvania, has drawn upon Keynes's basic analysis to develop a theory which is particularly appropriate to the pricing process in the concentrated industries. Weintraub argues that typically the large firms add a standard "mark-up" to their wage bill, the "mark-up" being large enough to cover all other costs and insure the firm of a target rate of return on its investment.[34] Thus when wages go up as a result of collective bargaining, prices will follow accordingly. This approach presumes that both trade unions and firms have sufficient economic power to push up both wages and prices even when aggregate demand is depressed.

Confirmation of Keynes's view about the longer term relationship between money wages and the price level is found in Table 14–3. This shows in index number form the link since 1965 between increases in

31. Keynes, *The General Theory*, p. 309. By the wage-unit Keynes means the money wage. The cost-unit would be all unit costs. But money wages are of major importance, accounting for two-thirds to three-fourths of production costs.

32. Joan Robinson, "What Has Become of the Keynesian Revolution?" *Challenge*, January/February 1974, p. 9.

33. Ibid., p. 9.

34. Sidney Weintraub, *Classical Keynesianism, Monetary Theory, and the Price Level* (Philadelphia, Chilton Company, 1961), esp. Chapter 3, "The Theory of the Price Level and the Analysis of Inflation."

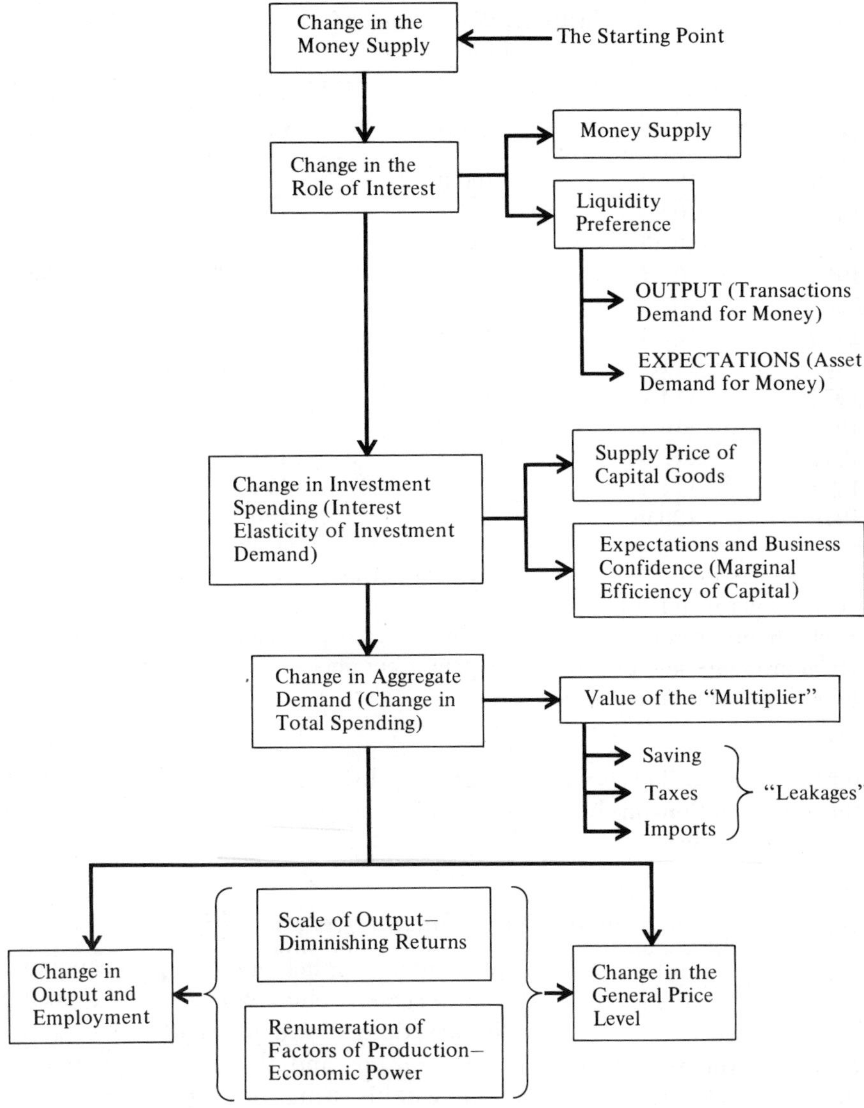

FIGURE 14–7. The Keynesian Theory of the Price Level

hourly compensation (money wages plus employer contributions to public and private benefit programs for workers), productivity, unit labor costs, and the price level. If money wages go up faster than productivity (Keynes's "the rate of increase in the efficiency of the productive system"), unit labor costs will rise. If there is a mark-up factor at work as Weintraub suggests, then prices ought to rise at about the same pace as

TABLE 14–3. Productivity, Wages, Labor Costs, and Prices: 1965–76 (1965 = 100)

Year	*Productivity**	*Wages†*	*Unit Labor Costs*	*Consumer Prices‡*
1965	100.0	100.0	100.0	100.0
1966	102.5	106.1	103.4	102.8
1967	104.5	112.2	107.3	105.8
1968	107.8	120.4	111.5	110.3
1969	107.7	128.2	119.0	116.2
1970	107.8	136.8	126.7	123.1
1971	111.1	145.8	131.1	128.4
1972	114.4	154.2	134.7	132.6
1973	116.4	166.2	142.7	140.8
1974	112.3	181.8	161.8	156.3
1975	114.3	199.4	174.2	170.6
1976	120.0	213.8	180.4	180.4

SOURCE: *Economic Report of the President*, 1977.
*Output per man hour in the private, nonfarm economy
†Total hourly compensation (wages and salaries plus employer contributions to social insurance and private benefit plans) per person.
‡The Consumer Price Index.

unit labor costs. This is what has happened since 1965. Readers should note the close relationship between the index of unit labor costs and the index of the price level.

Nonreversibility of the Price-Output Relationship

It is important to stress a phenomenon much noticed by economists during the postwar period: the *nonreversible* character of the relationship between prices and output. The schedule shown in Figure 14–4 is one depicting the relationship between output and the general price level during a period when aggregate demand is rising. But this curve is not an accurate picture of the relationship between output and the general price level during a downswing in economic activity. When aggregate demand and the level of economic activity decline, the general price level does not move downward as sharply as it moves upward. This is what is meant by the statement that the relationship between output and the price level is nonreversible. In general, prices and costs are much more sensitive to increases in demand than to decreases. This is strongly evidenced by the behavior of prices during five postwar recessions. In 1949, 1954, 1958, and

1974–75 real GNP declined, yet in each of these years consumer and wholesale price indexes either declined hardly at all or rose.[35]

The nonreversible character of the price-output relationship for the economy as a whole is shown in diagrammatic form in Figure 14–8. The S_1 curve describes the behavior of prices as output rises initially toward the full employment level, Y_f, which is determined by existing productive capacity in the first income period. The figure is constructed on the assumption that the boom comes to an end soon after the economy reaches the full employment level. When this happens, aggregate demand and output fall off. But prices do not fall off to the same degree. In the diagram the downward path of the general price level is no longer along S_1; instead, because both prices and cost are strongly resistant to downward declines in demand, the general price level moves along the dotted line S_2. Thus the economy may fall back to a lower level of real income, but the general level of prices and costs is higher than it was at an earlier period when the same real income level prevailed. The actual experience of the 1970s to date confirms we have an even worse situation on our hands, for prices neither fell slightly nor remained stable during two

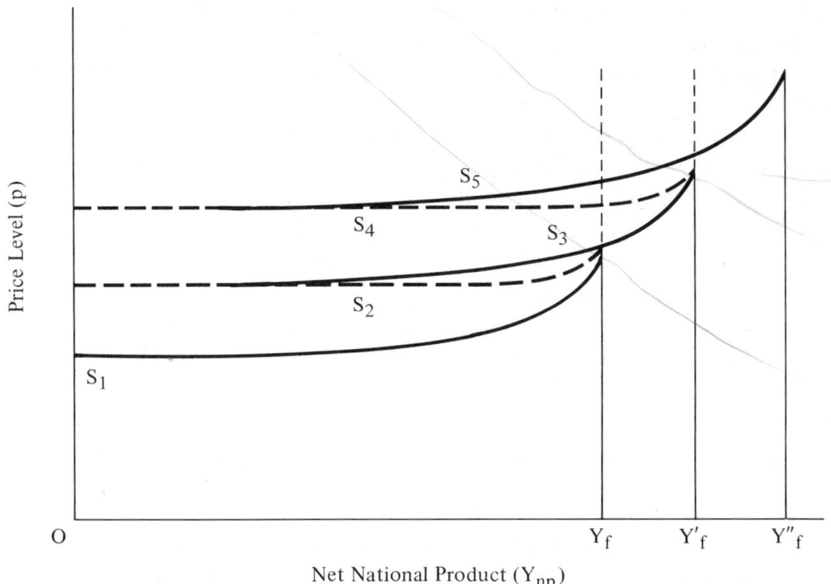

FIGURE 14–8. The Nonreversible Character of the Price-Output Relationship

35. *Economic Report of the President* (Washington, D.C.: Government Printing Office, 1977).

recessions—they actually rose. If the vertical axis in Figure 14–8 is used to depict the rate of inflation, then the diagram would illustrate a point made earlier in Chapter 13 to the effect that the economy has drifted into a cyclical pattern in which an expansion or boom takes off from an inflation rate that is escalating. More on this below.

During the next boom this same process will repeat itself. As a recovery gets under way and the economy moves once again toward a new and higher full employment output level, Y'_f the general price level will move along the S_3 curve. The full employment output level moves further to the right along the horizontal axis because investment and expansion of population and the labor force during the preceding boom will have expanded the economy's productive capacity. But once again the same kind of ratchet effect with respect to the movement of the general price level can be observed. When the economy attains full employment at the peak of a new boom, prices once again will have risen to a new peak. When the boom collapses, prices might decline somewhat, but by not nearly so much as they rose during the preceding boom. Thus they move downward along the dotted line S_4. The same process repeats itself as the economy recovers and begins to move toward a new and still higher full employment income level Y''_f. Thus over the longer run there is pronounced upward trend in the general price level.[36]

The rigidity of prices in the face of declining demand can be accounted for in several ways. In the first place, many markets—particularly those in manufacturing—are oligopolistic in structure; they are dominated by a relatively few, large business firms. As pointed out previously, prices in such markets are frequently *administered*, which means they are set by the seller and normally held constant for a period of time. Since firms in an oligopolistic industry usually operate in an atmosphere of uncertainty with respect to the reaction of their rivals to a shift in prices, they are extremely reluctant to reduce prices when demand falls off. Instead, oligopolistic firms prefer to adjust to shifting demand conditions through output and employment changes.

Many prices also remain stable in the face of a declining demand because wages tend not to yield to the slump in economic activity. Since money wages are a major element in the cost structure of the business firm, it logically follows that rigidities of wage rates will exert an important effect on the behavior of the price level. The chief reason for the rigidity of wages appears to lie in the strong determination of all workers—the unorganized as well as the organized—to resist cuts in money wages, even if such resistance comes at the expense of some employment. One study, for example, found that between 1900 and 1960 there were only

36. This is the ratchet effect at work. To date the avaliable empirical evidence indicates that it is present only when recessions are relatively mild, as for example since World War II. A severe depression would no doubt bring drastic price decreases.

five years in which average money wages in manufacturing industry declined below the average of the preceding year. In all other years the average rose over that of the preceding year. In every year since 1960 money wages in the private economy have been higher than the previous year. Wages exhibited this strong resistance to any downward movement in spite of the fact that during approximately half the year of the 1900–1960 period unemployment was 4 percent or more of the labor force.[37] Since 1960 unemployment has been above 4 percent in thirteen out of seventeen years (1960–76).

The Phillips Curve

Empirical verification of the relationship between the rate of change of money wages and the general level of employment (and output) was presumably established in the late 1950s by the Phillips Curve, so named because the British economist A. W. Phillips first set forth the relationships involved in an article published in 1958.[38] A Phillips curve is shown in Figure 14–9. It is shown as the solid line designated *aa*.

In the diagram the rate of change in money wages is shown on the vertical axis and the unemployment rate on the horizontal axis. The significance of this curve lies in the fact that the unemployment rate can be expected to decline as aggregate demand increases, but a fall in the unemployment rate will be accompanied by a higher rate of increase in money wages.

In the diagram the solid curve is drawn with a slope such that the rate of increase in money wages is 3 percent when unemployment reaches a level of 5 percent of the labor force. If the unemployment rate were reduced to 4 percent through an increase in aggregate demand, the rate of increase in money wages rises to about 5 percent. The extent to which any particular rate of increase in money wages would tend to cause increases in the price level depends upon the annual rate at which the average productivity of labor is increasing. If, for example, this rate were also 3 percent, then it would be theoretically possible for the economy to attain an unemployment rate of 5 percent of its labor force and have money wages increase at an annual average rate of 3 percent without any increase in the general price level. Any reduction of the unemployment rate below the 5 percent level would generate upward pressure on prices.

37. Charles L. Schultze, "Creeping Inflation: Causes and Consequences," *Business Horizons*, Summer 1960, p. 68.

38. A. W. Phillips, "The Relation between Unemployment and the Rate of Change of Money Wages in the United Kingdom, 1861–1957, *Economica*, November 1958, pp. 283–99.

What is the significance of the Phillips Curve? One of the most important conclusions drawn from the establishment of an apparently stable empirical relationship between the rate of change in money wages and the rate of unemployment is the possibility of the simultaneous existence of both unemployment and inflation, a condition that has in fact existed several times in recent years. To illustrate, if 4 percent unemployment is an assumed measure of full employment, and if, too, the actual Phillips Curve occupied the position shown in Figure 14–9, then the economy might be confronted with a significant amount of inflation, even though the unemployment rate climbed to 5 or 6 percent.

The matter can be put in slightly different form. What the Phillips Curve really means is that the policy-makers are confronted with an uncomfortable dilemma—a trade-off between unemployment and inflation. It is impossible, in other words, to have both full employment and price level stability; the two are simply incompatible goals. If full employment is the prime policy objective, then the social cost of attaining this objective is a rise in the price level. The exact inflation rate depends upon

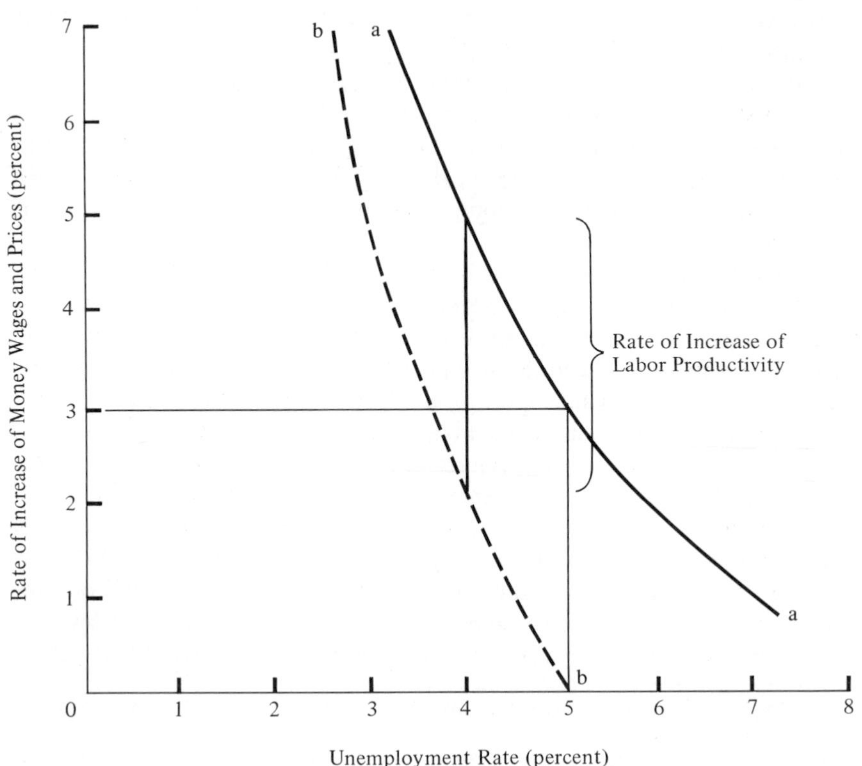

FIGURE 14–9. The Phillips Curve

transforming the rate of the wage increase–unemployment curve into a rate of increase in the general price level–unemployment curve. This can be done quite simply, if we know the annual rate at which labor productivity is growing. For example, if the latter is 3 percent and money wages are increasing at an annual rate of 5 percent, then the rate of increase in the price level will be 2 percent. In Figure 14–9 the rate of increase in the price level–unemployment curve is obtained by subtracting from the curve *aa* at each employment level an amount equal to the annual rate of increase in productivity. The result is the curve *bb*. This curve tells us that an unemployment rate of 5 percent is the necessary trade-off for absolute stability in the general price level, assuming that the rate of increase in labor productivity remains at 3 percent.

As we shall see, events of the 1970s have cast doubt on the idea that there is a stable, trade-off relationship between unemployment and the price level. The controversy over this point has not been settled. But if we accept as a working hypothesis the notion of a stable Phillips Curve, some policy problems of the modern economy can be illuminated. It means, for example, that policy makers must choose betwen more inflation and less unemployment or more unemployment and less inflation, an unhappy combination of choices in any event. Whether reducing inflation is stressed at the cost of rising unemployment or reduced unemployment is preferred over higher prices depends obviously upon the values and social philosophy of the administration in power at any particular time. Presumably, too, an administration will try and develop the right combination of monetary and fiscal policies designed to move the economy along the Phillips Curve in the direction of more or less unemployment or inflation.

There is, though, another difficult problem in public policy that the Phillips Curve analysis helps to illuminate. This stems from the possibility that if the economy succeeds, on the one hand, in bringing the unemployment rate down to an acceptable level, it may be confronted with an unacceptable rate of inflation, and, on the other, if it gets the price level under control, the unemployment rate may be too high. This possibility implies that there are maximum rates for both unemployment and increases in the price level that are socially—or politically—acceptable. Rates above these maxima simply will not be tolerated. If such rates exist, this poses another difficult—or cruel—dilemma for policy-makers.[39]

The situation is illustrated in Figure 14–10. The shaded area represents a "zone of socially tolerable outcomes," derived from the combination of the acceptable rate of inflation and the acceptable rate of unemployment. If the Phillips Curve lies above and to the right of this zone, then there is

39. For an excellent survey of the development of the Phillips Curve analysis, see Thomas M. Humphrey, "Changing Views of the Phillips Curve," *Monthly Review*, Federal Reserve Bank of Richmond, July 1973.

no combination of unemployment and inflation that become politically or socially acceptable. It would seem the economy has been in this fix a good part of the time in recent years. That is what "stagflation" is all about. In the figure this is the situation depicted by the solid line Phillips Curve labeled *aa*. If the inflation rate is brought down to a level that the society is willing to tolerate—point *A* in the diagram—then the unemployment rate rises to an intolerable level, point *C* on the horizontal axis. On the other hand, if the unemployment rate is reduced to the tolerable level, as indicated by point *B* in the figure, then the inflation rate is pushed beyond an acceptable rate to point *D* on the vertical axis.

What is to be done? If it is impossible by means of fiscal and monetary policies to attain an acceptable combination of inflation and unemployment, then different policy alternatives must be found. Monetary and fiscal policies can move the economy along a given Phillips Curve such as *aa*, but they cannot shift the curve downward and to the left into the zone representing an acceptable combination of unemployment and inflation rates. How can such a move be brought about? One approach is through adoption of an incomes policy, a term that has come to refer to measures

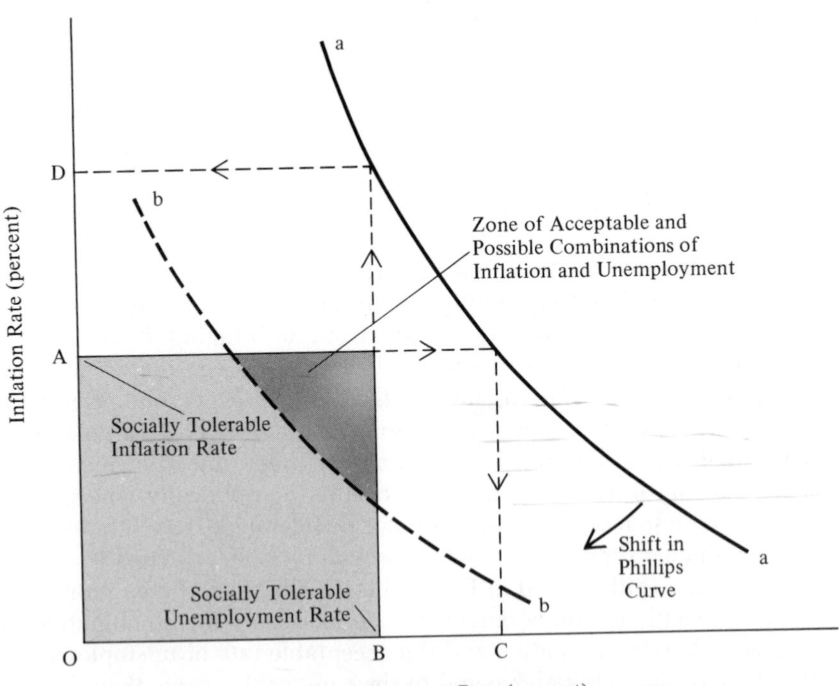

FIGURE 14–10. The Phillips Curve and Socially Tolerable Rates of Inflation and Unemployment

designed to limit the rate at which wages and prices rise as the economy approaches full employment. In the late 1960s the Johnson administration developed an incomes policy in the form of wage-price guideposts, and the Nixon administration had its own incomes policy in the form of direct wage-price controls, beginning in mid-1971. We shall discuss both forms of income policies later in the chapter. Another approach lies in the development of manpower programs to train and retrain unskilled, semi-skilled, and displaced workers so that the economy has a better supply of trained workers as it moves toward higher employment levels. If such policies succeed, the Phillips Curve will be shifted downward and to the left, thus making possible the attainment of some combination of unemployment and inflation that is socially acceptable. The dotted curve *bb* shows this. To date, however, manpower programs have not demonstrated any spectacular successes.

Challenges to the Phillips Curve Analysis

Until the late 1960s the idea that the Phillips Curve reflected a stable trade-off relationship between inflation and unemployment was not subject to serious question. This is no longer the case. For one thing, recent data on both inflation and unemployment cast doubt upon the stability of this relationship. Figure 14–11 contains a scatter diagram relating the inflation rate as measured by the annual rate of change in the GNP price deflator and the unemployment rate for the period 1960 through 1976. The solid line curve *ee* is sketched in to indicate that the data for the years 1960 through 1969 roughly approximate the behavior pattern suggested by the Phillips hypothesis. More specifically, there appears to be a close correlation between falling unemployment and a rising price level from the beginning of the decade through 1966. For the next three years —1967 through 1969—prices rose very sharply with only minimal effects upon the unemployment rate. But the most noticeable—and damaging—departure from the Phillips hypothesis occurred in the 1970 through 1976 period. In each of these years the unemployment rate was much higher for any given inflation rate than it ought to have been, given the relationship shown by the curve *ee*. What, therefore, are we to conclude? One possible explanation is that the data for 1970 through 1976 are to be found on Phillips Curves which lie to the right of and above the curve *ee*. If this is the case, it means that there may not be one basically stable functional relationship between inflation and unemployment, but possibly a series of short-run Phillips Curves of a volatile nature. Another is simply that the curve has shifted steadily upward in recent years. But the data are too erratic to support this view.

Bolstered by empirical findings which indicate a shifting Phillips Curve, monetarists launched a strong theoretical attack in the late 1960s

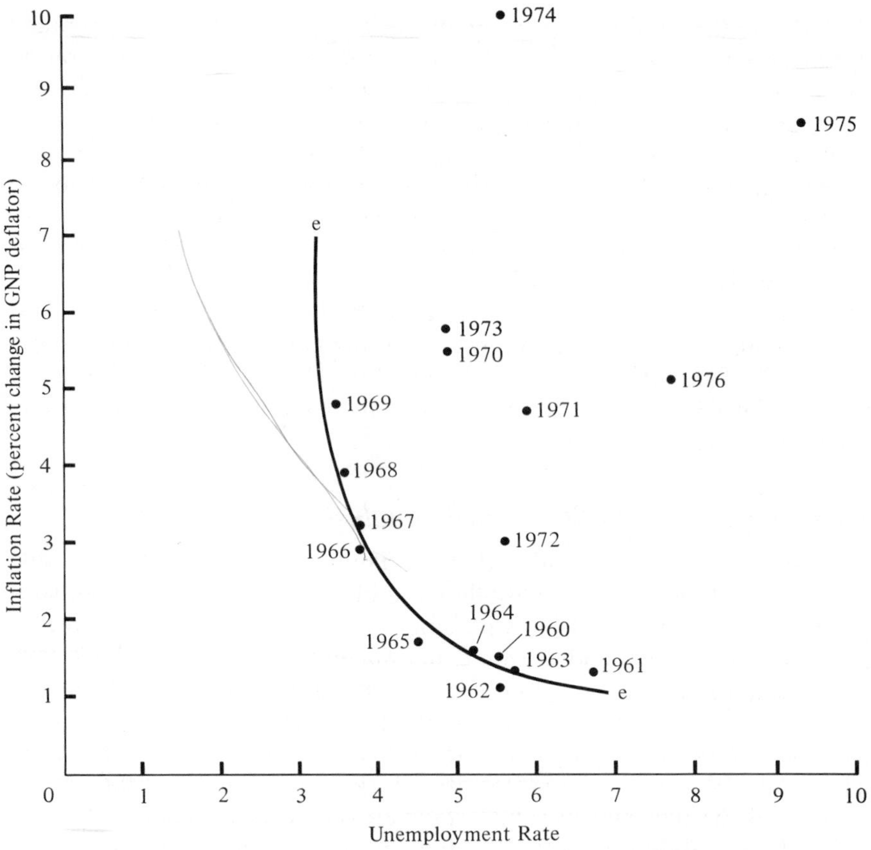

FIGURE 14–11. The Inflation-Unemployment Trade-Off, 1960–76.

on one of the fundamental premises of the Phillips Curve analysis, namely that it is possible to permanently reduce the unemployment rate to some desired level by driving up the price level. On the contrary, according to the monetarists, there is no permanent trade-off between inflation and unemployment. Policy measures based upon such an assumed trade-off will, in the long run, only result in an acceleration in the inflation rate, with no permanent change in the unemployment level.

As in the case of the controversy over the role of money in aggregate economic analysis, this monetarist challenge to the Phillips Curve analysis has been led by Professor Milton Friedman of the University of Chicago. He has argued, first, that there exists a natural unemployment rate, determined by underlying real factors such as capital formation and technological change; and, second, that the Phillips Curve is a short, transitory relationship, valid only so long as the wage-earners adhere to the money illusion and have no expectations prices will continue to rise.

Once wage-earners, though, lose the money illusion and develop expectations about continued inflation, they will begin to bargain for real wages by attempting to take the anticipated inflation rate into account in their wage negotiations. If, under these circumstances, the attempt is made to reduce the unemployment rate by increases in the price level, all that will happen is an acceleration in the inflation rate, but with no effect upon the long-term natural rate of unemployment. It is for this reason that the monetarist critique of the Phillips Curve theory is sometimes called the accelerationist thesis.

The manner in which this works is shown in Figure 14–12. According to the accelerationist thesis the Phillips Curve becomes, in the long run, perfectly inelastic with respect to the rate of change in the price level at the natural rate of unemployment. This is the vertical line labeled the "Long–run Phillips Curve" and which intersects the horizontal axis at the natural rate of unemployment U_n. The curves PC_1, PC_2, etc., represent a series of short-term Phillips Curves, each one of which incorporates a different *expected* rate of inflation. An increase in the expected inflation rate will cause the Phillips Curve to shift upwards. The point at which a particular short-term curve intersects the long-run curve represents equality between the expected and actual inflation rates. Let us suppose that the policy objective is one of reducing the unemployment rate to U_t, a level below the presumed natural rate. If we assume, further, that the economy was in equilibrium with stable prices, then aggregate demand would have to increase to bring the economy closer to the target level of unemployment U_t. The increase in aggregate demand will trigger a rise in prices, which will be reflected in a movement of the economy along the short-term Phillips Curve labeled PC_1. Prices must rise faster than money wages—that is, real wages must fall—if unemployment is to be reduced.

According to the accelerationist thesis, however, the rise in the price level cannot keep the economy permanently at a level of unemployment below the natural rate. This is true for two reasons. First, money wages will begin to catch up with the price level, thus pushing the real wage back toward its original level. This tends to cause the unemployment rate to move back toward the natural rate U_n. But the inflation rate will have accelerated to 4 percent. Second, wage earners soon abandon the money illusion in the face of a rising price level and begin to bargain for money wages which take into account anticipated increases in the price level. If this happens the short-term Phillips Curve will shift upward in response to expectations that inflation will continue. It will now be at the level PC_2, a level which incorporates a new set of expectations (4 percent) about the inflation rate in the future. But the target goal of a reduction of unemployment to the level of U_t has not been reached. If aggregate demand is stimulated once again the process will repeat itself, except this time the movement will be along the curve PC_2, and the inflation rate

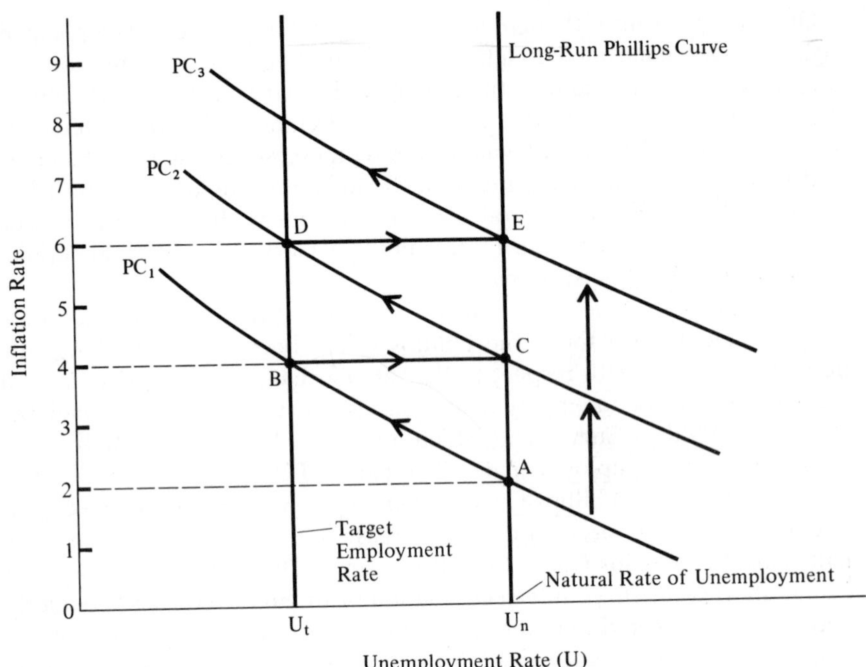

FIGURE 14–12. The Accelerationist Thesis

will rise to 6 percent. Once again employment will sink back to the natural rate as money wages catch up with the rising price level. But 6 percent now becomes the expected rate and the Phillips Curve shifts once more, this time to the level PC_3. The conclusion of the monetarists is quite clear: The unemployment rate can be kept below the natural rate only by a *continuously accelerating* inflation rate. The inflation and unemployment rates will follow the zigzag path marked ABCDE. What Figure 14–12 shows is that the short-term Phillips Curve must move continuously upwards for unemployment to remain at the level U_t. Since it is unlikely that a society will tolerate a continuous acceleration in the inflation rate for the sake of marginal gains in unemployment, the short-term Phillips Curve should eventually stabilize. But when this happens, the unemployment rate will move back to its natural level and the inflation rate will be at a permanently higher level. In the figure this is 6 percent. This is the essence of the accelerationist thesis. In the view of Professor Friedman and other monetarists, the only way in which the unemployment rate can be permanently lowered is through structural changes that reduce the natural unemployment rate. These would include measures to improve the mobility of labor through better information systems relating to labor demand and supply, improved vocational and on-the-job training, less discrimination in hiring, getting rid of legal minimum wages, and the reduction or elimination of import quotas and tariffs. Some of these measures tend to make the labor market more effective and others, such as the elimination of tariffs, put downward pressure on the domestic price level. It may be noted, too, that supporters of the Phillips Curve hypothesis endorse some of these measures, for, as pointed out earlier, improvements in the skill and knowledge of the work force tend to push the curve to the left.

Like much of the controversy surrounding the role of money in the economy, the disputes over the viability of the Phillips Curve hypothesis have not been resolved. Many economists are not ready to accept wholly the accelerationist critique on the basis of the rather erratic behavior of prices and unemployment in the last few years. Evidence accumulated for much longer periods of time supports the thesis of a trade-off between inflation and unemployment, although most economists will now concede that the relationship is probably less stable than they once thought. Professor James Tobin suggests that a Phillips Curve relationship exists which is quite flat at high levels of unemployment, but tends to become vertical as the economy approaches critically low levels of unemployment.[40] His view involves a blending of the original Phillips Curve hypothesis with elements of the monetarist critique, although it does not require the postulate of a natural rate of unemployment.

Incomes Policy in the 1960s

The emergence of the Phillips Curve hypothesis in the early 1960s gave a strong impetus to the development of incomes policies as complements to the older and more traditional fiscal and monetary approaches to influencing the level of output and employment. In its essentials, an incomes policy deals with the development of mechanisms through which money wage and price increases can be held within tolerable levels as an economy approaches full employment. As indicated in the prior discussion, the lesson of the Phillips Curve analysis is that, unless something is done about the matter, the economy cannot expect to get to full employment without high—and probably unacceptable—rates of inflation.

In the United States the first serious attempt to develop an incomes policy was made in 1962, when the President's Council of Economic Advisers established a series of guideposts for noninflationary wage and price behavior.[41] The principles of the guideposts were relatively simple. The Council asserted in effect that if gains in wages and other forms of

40. James Tobin, "Inflation and Unemployment," *American Economic Review*, March 1972.

41. *Economic Report of the President* (Washington, D.C.: Government Printing Office, 1962).

money incomes were to be noninflationary, then they should be no greater, on the average, than the annual average gain in productivity (output per man-hour) for the economy as a whole. If all increases in money income were held within this limit, then factor costs per unit of output for the economy as a whole would be stabilized, thus eliminating any tendency for market forces to bring about an increase in the general price level. In its analysis of the situation the Council of Economic Advisers put primary stress upon increases in money wages, since they account for 65 to 70 percent of the national income. The principle, though, applied to all forms of money income, including profits.

The Council made allowance for appropriate adjustments in individual industries, if their conditions varied from the conditions prevailing in the economy as a whole. For example, if an industry experienced a rate of increase in productivity that was greater than the national average, the prices of its product should decline, because a higher than average rate of productivity increase implies falling labor costs. The reverse would be true if productivity lagged behind the national average. At the time the guidepost policy was proclaimed the Council believed that productivity was rising on the average at a rate of 3.5 to 4 percent a year; hence wages and other forms of income could advance at this rate without being inflationary.

The guidepost policy expressed the view that society should enjoy the benefits of improved productivity through higher money incomes and stable prices rather than through stable money incomes and falling prices. Given the distribution of income, the benefits of productivity gains would spread more evenly over the whole society if stability in money incomes was coupled with a declining price level. But in a world in which prices and costs are generally flexible upward and inflexible downward, such an outcome was not likely. The Council was no doubt being realistic in arguing that the most practical way to translate advances in productivity into improved material well-being is through a policy that permits money income in all forms to increase at the same pace as output per man-hour.

How well did the guidepost policy work? From 1962 through 1965 it was moderately successful, as the data in Table 14–4 indicate. In these years, annual average percentage increases in compensation per man hour (wages and salaries plus employer contributions to social security and private benefit plans) were only slightly higher than the annual average gain in productivity, with consequent mild effects upon unit labor costs. But beginning in mid-1966, when the unemployment rate fell below 4 percent of the civilian labor force and the expenditure buildup for Vietnam accelerated, the guidepost policy broke down as pressures mounted for wage and salary adjustments in excess of productivity gains. Since 1966 wage and salary adjustments have shown very little relationship to productivity changes.

TABLE 14–4. Changes in Productivity, Compensation per Man-Hour, and Unit Labor Costs: 1962–76 (percentage change from previous year)

Year	*Productivity*	*Compensation Per Man-Hour*	*Unit Labor Costs*
1962	4.4	4.1	– 0.3
1963	3.5	3.7	0.1
1964	3.7	4.8	1.0
1965	3.3	3.4	0.1
1966	2.5	6.1	3.4
1967	1.9	5.8	3.8
1968	3.2	7.3	3.9
1969	0.2	6.5	6.6
1970	0.2	6.7	6.5
1971	2.9	6.6	3.5
1972	3.0	5.8	2.7
1973	1.7	7.8	6.0
1974	– 3.5	9.4	13.4
1975	1.8	9.7	7.7
1976	4.1	10.3	6.0

SOURCE: *Economic Report of the President*, 1977.

One reason for the breakdown of the guideposts policy was the fact that the government had no effective means for forcing business and industry to adhere to productivity guidelines in wage and salary settlements. The government's power was largely limited to persuasion and exhortation, which derisively was termed *jawboning*. This apparently worked only so long as organized labor and the management of large and powerful business firms were willing to adhere voluntarily to the guidelines, a condition that rapidly evaporated when the economy began to heat up as a consequence of the expanded war in Vietnam. In view, though, of the relative failure of the incomes policy of the Nixon administration, it remains uncertain whether the policy would have worked much better if the government had had some real enforcement power.

Incomes Policy in the 1970s

Although the Nixon administration came to power in 1969 firmly convinced that an incomes policy was unnecessary and that inflation could be brought under control by the delicate applications of monetary and fiscal policy in mid-1971 it completely reversed its stance. On August 15, 1971 the president announced to a startled nation his New Economic Policy, a program which, among other things, contained a ninety-day absolute freeze on wages, prices, and rents. This date marks the beginning of the nation's most comprehensive and longest experiment with an incomes policy involving strong controls over wages and prices backed by the enforcement power of the federal government, an experiment that ran its full course by April 1974. Authority for the control system cam from the Economic Stabilization Act, first passed in 1970, and extended in 1972 for another two years.

Incomes policy in the Nixon administration evolved through four stages, or phases, as they came to be known to the public. The headline-catching element of Phase I was the ninety-day freeze on wages and prices but the package also included tax cuts, a slowdown in federal spending and employment, and a devaluation of the dollar in the foreign exchange markets. A Cost of Living Council, headed by the secretary of the treasury was created, charged with the task of developing a permanent incomes policy.

In November 1971 Phase II went into effect. The freeze was lifted, but mandatory guidelines were set for wage and price increases. Wage increases of 5.5 percent were to be allowed and price increases of 2.5 percent. Administration of these controls was through a five member Pay Board and a seven member Price Commission, two agencies established at the time the New Economic Policy first went into effect. Phase II lasted until January 1973, at which time it was replaced by a system of voluntary controls. This was the beginning of Phase III. The decision to abandon mandatory controls was nearly as much of a surprise as President Nixon's earlier decision to impose controls in August 1971, as most observers had expected Phase II to continue well into 1973. Although a majority of business firms and trade unions were freed from restraints under Phase II, controls were left in effect in three particularly troublesome areas: food prices, health costs, and the construction industry. Voluntary guidelines for wage adjustments were still pegged at 5.5 percent and price increases were not supposed to exceed cost increases, although the latter were not clearly defined.

The voluntary control program was short-lived, for in June 1973 in another startling reversal of economic policy, the Nixon administration imposed a new sixty-day freeze on prices. The new freeze, which was dubbed by the press Phase III-B or Phase III½, was clearly a stop-gap measure designed both to buy some time as the administration struggled to contain an accelerating price level and work out new policies to control inflation. At the time the new freeze was imposed the consumer price index (CPI) stood at 131.5, more than 10 percentage points above the level of a year earlier. In mid-July the president announced the outlines for Phase IV, which the administration said would take the nation out of the freeze on a sector-by-sector basis. Food prices were exempted from the freeze at the time the Phase IV program was announced. Phase IV in essence, amounted to a return to a tougher system of mandatory controls administered on a selective basis. The key principle for price increases was to permit prices to rise as costs rise, providing there were no increases in profit margins. Standards for wage increases were the same as in Phases I and II. Large firms, defined as those with annual sales in excess of $1 million, were required to notify the Cost of Living Council of intended price increases; such increases could not be put into effect for thirty days, during which time the Council could suspend or deny the increases. The president stated that Phase IV was designed to move the nation back to a control-free economy. Phase IV and with it the nation's first major peacetime experiment with wage and price controls ended in April, 1974. As one observer says, "By the time the controls expired . . . they had outlived their usefulness. Public support, evident throughout Phases I and II, had evaporated."[42]

When Phase IV ended in April, 1974 the nation also ended its first major peacetime experiment with wage and price control. Neither the Ford nor the Carter administration (to date) indicated any interest in a renewal of the experiment. How successful was the Nixon "New Economic Policy"? No definitive answer is possible to this question, given the impossibility of knowing what would have happened to price levels in the absence of a control system during this period. At best, though, the results are mixed, and at worst they suggest that mandatory wage and price controls are not especially effective in peacetime in containing powerful inflationary pressures. Figure 14–13 is instructive in this respect. It contains data showing, on a monthly basis, the percentage change in the consumer price index for the prior six months converted to an annual basis. These data give us a moving average of changes in this index and thus are most useful for showing trends.

Two significant points concerning the effectiveness of the control system are suggested by the data of Figure 14–13. First, it is clearly evident that the peak of the Vietnam induced inflation was reached in January 1970, about twenty months before the first freeze was imposed. At the time the freeze was imposed—August 1971—the trend for the rate of increases in the price level was clearly downward. Inflation was not being eliminated, but it was slowing down. The probable reason for this was the recession in 1970, which followed the economic slowdown measures taken by the Nixon administration in 1969 (Chapter 13). Thus, the imposition of controls was not responsible for the lessened rate of inflation, but did coincide with a reduction in the inflation rate, a reduction that was the lagged response to the 1969 actions. The second point is that these data also indicate that the trend in the inflation rate had moved strongly

42. Jerry E. Pohlman, *Inflation Under Control* (Reston, Va.: Reston Publishing Company, Inc., 1976), p. 218.

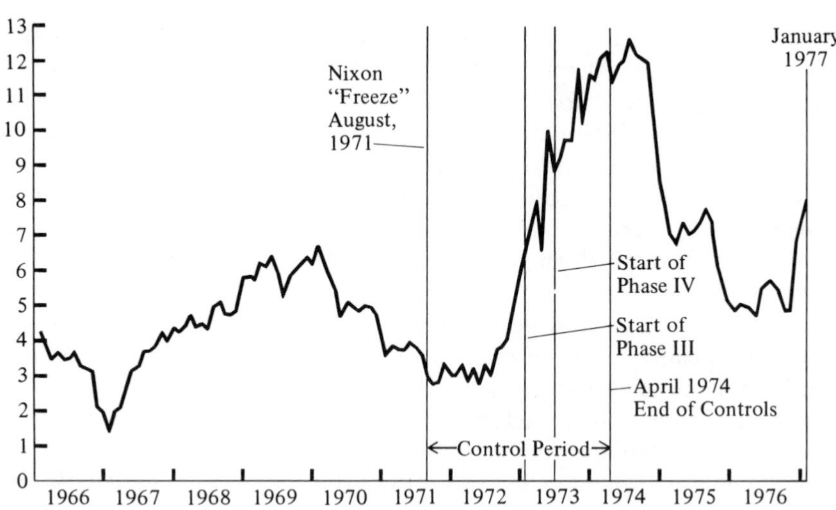

FIGURE 14–13. Consumer Price Index (Annual Rate of Change of Six-Month Intervals)

upward long before Phase II was dropped in favor of the voluntary system of Phase III. Thus, the argument that Phase II was dropped too soon and this is the reason for the wild upsurge in prices during 1973 does not stand up under close scrutiny. A vigorous boom was underway by mid-1972 and this, in combination with such other factors as worldwide economic prosperity, higher exports stemming from successive devaluations of the dollar, bad weather and droughts which hurt food production all over the world, and no strong anti-inflationary fiscal policy, is much more responsible for the record-breaking inflation of 1973 than the premature abandonment of Phase II.

At this writing the future of peacetime wage and price controls in the United States, as in most other industrial nations, remains in doubt. It has been 16 years since the nation began the search for the elements of a successful incomes policy; to date this quest has not been successful. One conclusion seems evident, though, from the economy's turbulent history of the last decade and a half and this is that neither fiscal policy, monetary policy, nor an incomes policy alone has sufficient strength to do the job of controlling inflation. At no time since the beginning of the military buildup for our ill-starred venture in Vietnam, has either the administration in power or the Congress been willing to apply in a strong and coordinated way fiscal and monetary policies *and* an incomes policy for inflation control. If this had been done, perhaps the economic story since 1965 would have been quite different.

15

Principles of Economic Growth

We turn our attention now to some of the principles and problems of a growing economy. Up to this point we have examined output, employment, and the price level under conditions of a relatively fixed productive capacity. Now it is the time to shift from an essentially static to a dynamic approach, analyzing what happens when the economy's productive capacity as well as its aggregate demand function moves upward.

Until quite recently economic growth was a complex but not especially controversial subject. In the late 1950s and early 1960s considerable public debate swirled around the question of whether or not the American economy was growing fast enough. At that time the issue of whether or not the economy ought to grow did not really exist. All this has changed. Within the last dozen years or so the focus of concern has shifted dramatically, in part because of environmental problems which result from unfettered economic expansion, and in part because dwindling stocks of energy resources raise fundamental questions about the economy's ability to grow rapidly. Economic growth has thus become both controversial and emotionally explosive.

The first major objective of this chapter is to sort out the key issues in the growth controversy. Two separate but related questions are included: (1) Is continued economic growth possible? and (2) Is continued economic growth desirable? Our concern is primarily with the first, since it can be tied directly to our analysis of the forces which determine output, employment, and the price level in both the short and the long run.[1]

1. For excellent nontechnical discussions of both these issues see E. J. Mishan, "Growth and Antigrowth: What Are the Issues?" *Challenge*, May/June 1973, and

A second objective of this chapter is to extend the Keynesian income expenditure model of output and employment determination constructed in Part II into the realm of economic growth. The best means for attaining this objective is through a detailed explanation and analysis of what has come to be known in the literature of economics as the Harrod-Domar approach to the problems that advanced market economies such as the United States confront in seeking to maintain full employment and a rising level of real output over time.[2] We shall concentrate on the Harrod-Domar analysis because it grows directly out of Keynesian equilibrium analysis. In an appendix to this chapter the essentials of an alternative approach to the phenomenon of growth will be analyzed, namely the neoclassical theory.

Before we turn though, to a detailed analysis of these objectives, it will be worthwhile to examine briefly some other facets of economic growth. A few comments about the nature of economic growth as well as the process of growth and its relationship to economic theory are in order.

The Nature of Economic Growth

Economic growth can be defined as the expansion of a nation's capability to produce the goods and services its people want. Since the productive capacity of an economy depends basically on the quantitiy and quality of its resources as well as on its level of technological attainment, economic growth involves the process of expanding and improving these determinants of productive capacity.

Although a fundamental definition of economic growth is in terms of the economy's potential for the production of goods and services, this is not a sufficient definition. Productive capacity is crucially important to the concept of economic growth, but actual growth depends not only upon

---

Robert M. Solow, "Is the End of the World At Hand?" *Challenge*, March/April 1973. It is the adverse environmental effects of economic growth that are involved in the question of whether or not growth is desirable. These are also the source of much of the emotion generated by the topic.

2. The name Harrod-Domar comes from the work of two economists who, independently, developed similar analyses to the problem posed above. The economists are Evsey Domar, an American, and Roy F. Harrod, an Englishman. The basic similarity of their analyses as well as the fact that both developed their respective theories within a Keynesian framework gave rise to the label of Harrod-Domar. Professor Harrod developed his ideas in a series of lectures given at the University of London in 1947; Professor Domar's basic model appeared in the *American Economic Review* in the same year. For details, see R. F. Harrod, *Towards a Dynamic Economics* (New York: St. Martin's Press, 1966), especially Lecture Three, pp. 63–100, and E. D. Domar, "Expansion and Employment," *American Economic Review*, March 1947, pp. 34–55.

change in the economy's potential for production, but also upon the extent to which that capacity is utilized. Economic growth involves, in other words, an increase over time in the actual output of goods and services as well as an increase in the economy's capability to produce goods and services.

Interest in economic growth stems in large part from our concern with human welfare. There is, of course, no acceptable set of criteria for measurement of such a subjective matter as welfare, but there is general agreement that material welfare (or well-being) in the last analysis, depends upon the availability of goods and services. A rising level of economic well-being for any society requires an expansion in its output of goods and services.[3]

If we are interested in economic growth because of its significance for our material well-being, then what counts is not just an increase in capacity and output per se, but output per capita. What is important from a welfare standpoint is the availability of goods and services per person; it is reasonable to talk of an improvement in the material well-being of a people only if, over time, each person has a growing volume of goods and services at his disposal. Thus, the measure of economic growth that is most meaningful is the level of real output per capita. Analysis of economic growth on a per person basis requires that we take into account not only changes in a nation's productive potential and its use of that potential, but also changes in its population. If population grows at a faster rate than either output or capacity, no improvement in the average standard of material well-being on a per capita basis is possible (see Table 15–1).

Why is economic growth important? Growth certainly is not an end in itself. It is a means to an end. It provides a society with the means—resources plus goods and services—whereby it can do more things for itself and for its citizens. Growth makes more goods and services available to consumers for their private use, and more resources available to the public sector for its purpose and responsibilities. The ways in which private citizens and governments use the added output may be wise or foolish, but one cannot gainsay the fact that without economic growth prospects for a better life for everyone would be much grimmer. In the developed nations of the West standards of life are affluent enough so that some of the population can afford the luxury of discussing whether or not more growth is desirable. But for most of mankind this is not possible. The overwhelming proportion of the world's people lives on the edge of grinding poverty. For them growth is an absolute imperative if they are to survive.

3. The reader might review at this point the discussion in Chapter 3 of attempts to develop improved measures of welfare and product.

The Growth Record of the American Economy

A brief review of the growth record of the American economy shows that over the long run its performance has been highly impressive. The overall record of growth for the period 1839–1976 is summarized in Table 15–1. The data for 1839 through 1959 are taken from an analysis of the American economy prepared in 1960 for the Joint Economic Committee of the U.S. Congress. Separate data for the period 1960–76 are shown in column 5 of the table. They are taken from the 1977 *Economic Report of the President.*

As the table shows, the data for 1839 through 1959 are broken down into three subperiods, each of forty years' length. The average annual rate of growth for the real GNP of the American economy over the whole 120-year period (1839–1959) was 3.66 percent, a record unmatched by any other country for so long a period. These data also show that there was some slowing down in the rate of total real output in the third period, although when the data are reduced to a per capita basis there does not appear to be any significant change in the long-term trends. Real GNP rose at an annual average rate of 4.31 percent during the first forty-year period (1839–79). In the period 1879–1919 the growth rate fell to 3.72 percent per year, and then for the next forty years (1919–59), declined further to an annual average rate of 2.97 percent. The per capita data do not show the same long-term decline. During the first forty-year period GNP per capita in constant prices increased at an annual average rate of 1.55 percent. This period, though, was the one in which population increased most rapidly; population grew at an annual average rate of 2.71 percent, as compared to 1.91 percent in the second forty-year period, and 1.30 percent in the third forty-year period. The slower rate of population growth is reflected in the fact that real GNP per capita in

TABLE 15–1. Growth Trends in the American Economy, 1839–1976 (percentage increase per year)

	(1) *Entire period*	*(2)*	*(3)* *40-year subperiods*	*(4)*	*(5)*
	1839–1959	*1839–1879*	*1879–1919*	*1919–1959*	*1960–1976*
Price level	1.15	−0.16	1.91	1.40	4.12
GNP in constant prices	3.66	4.31	3.72	2.97	3.41
Population	1.97	2.71	1.91	1.30	1.12
Per capita GNP in constant prices	1.64	1.55	1.76	1.64	2.24

SOURCE: Joint Economic Committee, Congress of the United States, *Staff Report on Employment, Growth and Price Levels,* 1960; and *Economic Report of the President,* 1977.

constant prices actually increased at a more rapid rate in the second and third forty-year periods, even though this was not true for the aggregate GNP. In the period 1879–1919 real GNP per capita rose at an annual average rate of 1.76 percent. During the next forty-year period (1919–59) the rate declined to an annual average of 1.64 percent, although this figure is still above the average of 1.55 percent per year for the first one-third of the whole 120-year period.

And what of the more recent period, 1960–76? The data do suggest some shifts in the long-term trends, although it is, perhaps, premature to say that they are permanent. More likely they reflect in part some of the turbulence of the last decade and a half. Real GNP grew more slowly than the long-term historic average, a development resulting in part from two recessions in the 1970s. The most dramatic change is in the price level, as its rate of growth is significantly above the average for any of the pre-1960 periods covered by the data in the table. This clearly reflects both the severity of the recent inflation and its uniqueness as compared to the nation's historical experience. The trend for population growth continued to decline, a development that is in line with past experience. Since 1970 the rate of growth of population has dropped to less than 1 percent, the actual rate being 0.86 percent for 1970–76. This is close to the zero population growth (ZPG) rate, a development some anti-growth advocates welcome. Finally, real per capita GNP rose at a rate faster than any previous period in span covered by the table. Was this a real gain? Given the fact of an unpopular war and the social turbulence of the 1960s and early 1970s one would, indeed, have to be bold to assert *all* of this increase represented real gains in social and economic welfare.

The Process and Theory of Economic Growth

The process of economic growth has to do with the means by which a nation expands its productive capacity. In any society four factors are of fundamental importance in the growth process. These are (1) the quantity and quality of the labor force, (2) the quantity and quality of natural resources, (3) the quantity and quality of real capital, and (4) the level of technological attainment of the society. These fundamental determinants of economic growth define the potential for production of any economy. As used in our analysis, *technology* is a broad term which refers to the effectiveness with which economic resources in the form of labor, natural resources, and capital are combined in the productive process. As a practical matter, it is difficult to separate technology from the resources themselves, for the quality of the latter is a reflection of a society's level of technological attainment.

Theories that have to do with the process of economic growth are by no means new. Adam Smith and the early classical economists concerned themselves with the probable long-term development of a capitalistic system and Karl Marx was deeply interested in the same problem. What is relatively new, though, is the very rapid development since the end of World War II of a large volume of literature concerned with the theory and the problems of a developing economy. These post-World War II theories are of two distinct types. There is one group of theories oriented primarily toward the problems of growth in the economically underdeveloped nations which attempts to develop a comprehensive theory that accounts for all the important variables, economic and noneconomic, that enter into the process of economic growth. These theories dig deep into the underlying social and cultural structure of a society to identify and explain the forces that are determinants of the four fundamental factors mentioned above. The central problem of the economically underdeveloped nations is a severe shortage of productive capacity; a theory of growth that would be adequate to cope with the real problems of such societies must be broad in scope and extend beyond the usual boundaries of economics. Underdeveloped nations usually cannot increase their productive capacity without far-reaching changes in their economic, political, and cultural institutions and behavior patterns.

The other group of theories centers primarily on the problem of growth and change in developed economies, such as those of contemporary Western Europe or the United States and Canada. These theories are often labeled post-Keynesian partly because they have been worked out entirely within the framework of modern income and employment analysis, and partly because their primary objective is to discover and understand the conditions under which sustained growth is possible in an advanced economy. In an advanced economy the critical problem is not always one of insufficient productive capacity; more often the important problem is to insure a sufficiently high level of aggregate demand so that the existing productive potential is fully utilized. In advanced economies, moreover, productive potential does not remain constant. Growth is inherent in the highly dynamic character of most advanced economies, and thus when we move out of a relatively short-term setting we are confronted with the peculiar type of growth problem faced by the advanced nation.

The post-Keynesian type of growth theory does not attempt to explain change in any of the fundamental determinants of productive capacity. It assumes instead that one or more of these variables (usually the stock of capital) is undergoing change at a steady rate over time. The theories study the effect of a continuous change of this kind on the economy's productive capacity and seek to explain how the level of aggregate demand may be adjusted over time to the resulting changes in productive capacity. Such theories can yield valuable insights into the problems of growth in an advanced economy, even though they may not be able to provide a basic explanation for the phenomenon of growth itself. This is the essential problem to which the Harrod-Domar analysis addresses itself. But before we turn to that, let us examine the recently emerged controversy which revolves around the question of whether continued growth is possible.

The Economic Growth Controversy

Until quite recently there was little quarrel with the idea that economic growth is desirable. But in the late 1960s this viewpoint came increasingly under attack, primarily because of a developing awareness by the public of the adverse spillover effects often associated with a growing economy. Among the most widely recognized of the social costs of economic growth are such disamenities as air, water, and solid waste pollution, the despoliation of the countryside, the destruction of wildlife, overcrowding in the cities, and the rapid exhaustion of vital natural resources. Environmental groups and conservationists, as well as economists, have had a hand in arousing the public's consciousness about the darker side of economic growth. In general the environmental- and conservation-minded focused their fears on the possible exhaustion of the earth's limited supplies of mineral resources, a possibility made dramatically evident to the public by the emerging energy crisis of the 1970s. Economists critical of growth have concentrated more upon analysis of the external diseconomies—or social costs—that growth entails.[4] Both groups have made important contributions to a vigorous and widespread dialogue and debate over the quality of our national life—an issue that has become one of the dominant public policy questions of the 1970s.

Interesting and important as this aspect of the controversy over economic growth is, we must aim our analysis in a different direction, toward the first question we posed about growth: This is not whether growth as such is desirable, but whether its continuation is possible. Irrespective of the ultimate uses made of additional output, the economist must come to grips with the fundamental question of whether or not the economy can continue to grow at rates near or equal to our long-term historic experience (see Table 15–1). How is it possible, in other words, for an econ-

4. E. J. Mishan has been a pioneer analyst and critic of the notion that economic growth is undesirable. See his book, *The Costs of Economic Growth* (New York: Praeger, 1967). See also Robert Lekachman, *National Income and the Public Welfare* (New York: Random House, 1972), esp. chaps. 6 and 7. See also Edward F. Renshaw, *The End of Progress: Adjusting to a No-Growth Economy* (North Scituate, Mass.: The Duxbury Press, 1976). For a different approach which argues that the limits to growth are social and cultural rather than material, see Fred Hirsch, *Social Limits to Growth* (Cambridge, Mass.: Harvard University Press, 1976).

omy to grow by some constant percentage rate when nearly every literate person now realizes that we live on a planet of limited resources—spaceship earth.

The fear that we may soon run up against an absolute limit stems from two facts. These are that growth at a constant percentage rate is exponential growth and that the modern economy uses up finite material resources at a fantastic pace. Exponential growth, as in compound interest, has intrigued and puzzled people for a long while. In any system which grows at an exponential—or constant percentage rate—the absolute increment of growth added in each period becomes ever-larger simply because the rate is continually being applied to a bigger base. Thus, the finite resources consumed by an economy which is growing exponentially will also rise by an absolute amount that accelerates each year. Furthermore, the length of time it takes for the doubling of any quantity that is growing at a constant percentage rate continually shrinks. If there is any kind of absolute upper limit to any system—social or biological—capable of exponential growth, this limit may be approached with astounding suddenness. It is these characteristics of exponential growth, in combination with the incontrovertible fact that the world's material resources are limited, which have given rise to so-called doomsday models—analyses which assert that unless really drastic changes are made in how and what we produce and consume, we face sudden, catastrophic, and ruinous economic collapse.

This question of whether economic growth can continue is not really new, however. One of the reasons why economics in the nineteenth century became known as the "dismal science" was that a number of the classical economists reached the conclusion that an end to economic progress was inevitable. For the pessimistic-minded among the classical thinkers, the end result of the economic process was the stationary state. Examination of classical ideas about the limits to economic growth will help us place the modern doomsday models in perspective, for, in spite of their apocalyptic nature, they have much in common with the earlier classical analysis.

The Classical Model of Economic Growth

Classical thinking on the process of economic growth and its outcome in the form of the stationary state rested upon three basic propositions: (1) the Malthusian law of population, which held that population, unless checked by disease, famine, or war, tends to expand at an exponential rate; (2) the fundamental economic principle of diminishing returns, especially as applied to the scarce resource of agricultural land; and (3) a theory of capital accumulation in which profit is a key variable. David Ricardo was the classical economist most responsible for bringing these key factors together into a basic theoretical system in which the ultimate outcome of the growth process is the stationary state.

The workings of the classical model are best illustrated by means of a diagram such as Figure 15–1.[5] In the figure population and the labor force are shown on the horizontal axis with output and the division of output between wages, profits, and rents represented on the vertical axis. The dynamic element in the classical theory is investment—or capital accumulation—which depends upon profit. Capital and profits, in other words, are the engines of progress. The growth of population—and the labor force—is controlled by the subsistence wage, which is a wage level that just enables the workers and their families to survive. In the early classical thinking the subsistence wage was thought of as a biological minimum, but later under the influence of John Stuart Mill it was regarded as a cultural minimum based upon a voluntary restriction of births. Nevertheless, the dynamics of population growth in the classical model are such that if market wages rise above the subsistence level, population and the labor force will grow. Only when market wages are driven back to—or below—the subsistence level will population growth cease. In Figure 15–1 the

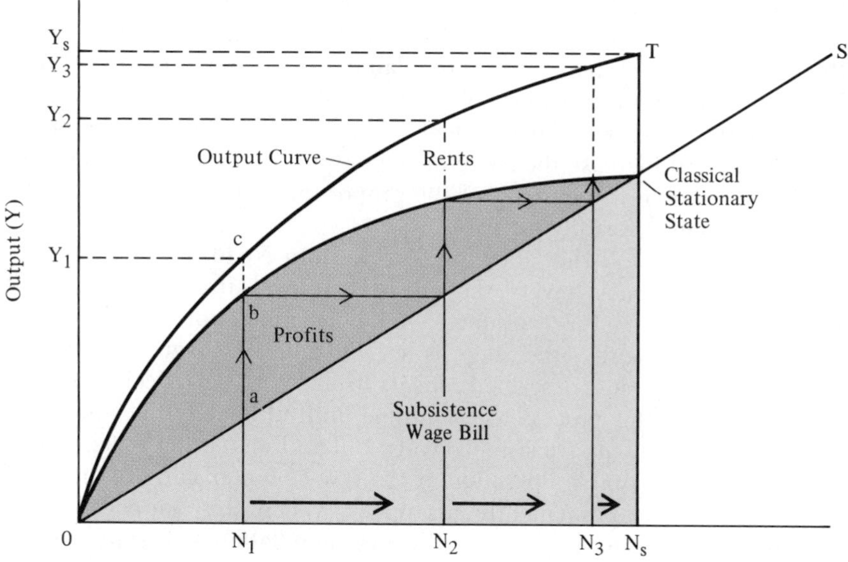

FIGURE 15–1. The Classical Model of Economic Growth

5. This diagram and the exposition of the classical model is largely based upon the treatment found in William J. Baumol's *Economic Dynamics*, 2nd ed., (New York: Macmillan, 1959), chap. 2. For a discussion of some of these classical ideas in a modern context, see Wallace C. Peterson, "The Stationary State in Your Future," *MSU Business Topics*, Summer 1976, pp. 5–11.

area under the line OS is the subsistence wage bill, which is equal to the subsistence wage times the working population.

The process that Ricardo and the other classical economists envisaged begins at an early stage of development when population is small as compared to available arable land and, consequently, profits and the opportunities for capital accumulation are high. In Figure 15–1 this situation prevails with a labor force of N_1. At this time output will be Y_1, the wage bill will be N_1a, profits ab, and rents bc. What will follow? The high level of profits stimulates investment—capital accumulation—which in turn increases the demand for labor, thereby driving market wage rates above the subsistence level. This sets in motion the forces that induce an expansion in population and the labor supply. But as more labor becomes available, output will expand, moving along the curve OT, which is labeled the output curve in the diagram. As depicted in Figure 15–1 labor is the variable input.

As this happens two other developments will take place. First, the rise in market wage rate above the subsistence level will squeeze profits, thus tending to slow down the rate of capital accumulation: and, second, more land must be brought into use to accommodate the food requirements of a growing population. But since arable land is a limited natural resource, the employment of more and more labor on a fixed quantity of land brings diminishing returns into play. What this does is reduce the average productivity of labor, a development reflected in the shape of the output curve, OT, and increase the share of the output total going to the owners of land. As shown in Figure 15–1 the proportion of output being claimed by rent payments steadily increases.

As population and the labor force grow from N_1 to N_2, market wages will tend to fall back toward the subsistence level, thus restoring profits and the motivation for continued capital accumulation. At the output level Y_2, consequently, the stage is set for another surge of growth in which the process just described repeats itself. As the classical economists saw the matter, this process will continue until ultimately the squeeze on profits from a growing subsistence wage bill and increasing rents brought about by the inexorable operation of the law of diminishing returns is so great that profits permanently disappear. When this happens, capital accumulation in any net sense will cease, population will stabilize, and the economy will enter into the classical stationary state.

As depicted in the thinking of the early classical economists this was a fairly grim state of affairs, given their view of the subsistence wage as the biological minimum necessary for survival. The only group which would have anything approaching a comfortable standard of living would be the landowning class, as their ownership of the limited, and scarce land resources enabled them to claim all output in excess of the amount required to maintain the working population at a constant level. As noted earlier, however, John Stuart Mill saw the stationary state as more of a blessing than an evil, since he was hopeful that wages could be stabilized well above the subsistence level, if workers would voluntarily limit population at an optimum rather than a maximum size. Mill, moreover, was not taken with the notion of a pulsating, competing society, pushing ever-harder toward higher and higher levels of output. He believed the stationary state could be a more civilized and humane arrangement, an idea that is echoed today in the thinking of some of the critics of growth and high-pressure economic systems.

What is missing from the classical thinking about the process of economic growth is any notion of technological progress. Their model is dominated by the iron-clad working of the law of diminishing returns because of the finite supply of a critical resource—namely land. This is an outlook that also in its essentials is characteristic of the contemporary doomsday models of economic growth. If technological progress is introduced into the analysis, this has the effect of shifting the output curve *OT* upward, thus offsetting the operation of diminishing returns and pushing the point of the stationary state further into the future. If we view the long sweep of development from the early classical period to the present, this is what has happened. In the developed nations of the West at least, events have not unfolded as the classical theory predicted. Over this long time span productivity and real wages have not been falling, nor has the rate of growth of either output or capital tended to shrink. In sum, the overall impact of technology has been to more than offset the effect of natural resource scarcities upon the economy's ability to grow. Whether this will remain true in the future is uncertain, but it has been our experience to date.

The Doomsday Models of the Growth Process

Within the last few years there has been a revival of classical fears about the end of economic growth with the appearance of doomsday models that predict a sudden and catastrophic collapse of the economy. Unlike the classical model, which foresaw a gradual, though inevitable, movement of the system toward the stationary state, these models foresee a total collapse.

Probably the best-known of these models is the one developed for the Club of Rome. The latter is an informal organization made up of no more than one hundred members representing a variety of national backgrounds and intellectual and scientific disciplines whose purpose is "to foster understanding of the varied but interdependent components—economic, political, natural, and social—that make up the global system in which we all live." An important work of the organization was its 1972 report, *The Limits to Growth*, in which a number of computer models were developed showing the impossibility of continued exponential growth and the inevitable collapse if the world attempted to continue along such a path.[6]

The doomsday models rest upon the same basic assumption as the classical model, that the finite supply of natural resources presents an ultimate, insurmountable barrier to confined growth in output and population. However, they add a new element: pollution. If the present pace of industrialization continues, pollution would grow exponentially. According to the doomsday models, mankind would then be overwhelmed by growing scarcities of natural resources on the one hand, and uncontrollable pollution, on the other.[7]

As in the case of the classical theory, the workings of the doomsday hypothesis can be most easily explained by use of a simplified diagram. In Figure 15–2 the three key elements in this analysis are depicted in an oversimplified manner. Essentially, Figure 15–2 depicts an explosive system in which the exponential growth path of population and output collide with and overshoot the natural resource base barrier, thus causing a rapid downward movement of both. In contrast to the classical model, there is no feedback mechanism in the form of diminishing returns which brings about a gradual slowing down in the rate of growth as the economy approaches its natural resource limit. Collapse appears to be sudden and total. The pollution path shown in the diagram reflects the argument built into the Club of Rome model that even if, for example, the limits to physical resources were overcome by unlimited nuclear power and extensive recyclying, growth still would be stopped by rising pollution.

Economists have been critical of the doomsday type of analysis for several reasons. In the first place, once the models are stripped of their computer mystique, they are seen to be little more than a modernized version of the classical view of a world which tends to consume its limited natural resources at an increasing rate but with no means of avoiding the inevitable exhaustion of its resource base. But like their classical forebears, too

6. Dennis L. Meadows and associates, *The Limits to Growth* (New York: New American Library, 1972).

7. There has been a second "Club of Rome" report issued which holds out more hope that mankind may be able to avoid the disaster of total collapse, but it does not retreat significantly from the basic theme of the earlier report that mankind now is on such a course and if changes are not made in how we manage and develop our limited resources disaster will be the outcome. See Mihajlo Mesarovic and Eduard Pestel, *Mankind at the Turning Point: The Second Report to the Club of Rome* (New York: Reader's Digest Press, 1974).

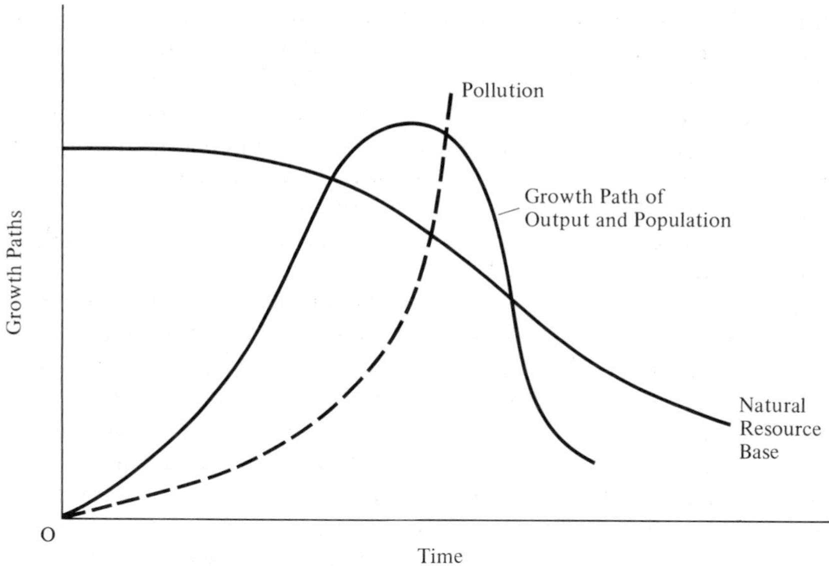

FIGURE 15–2. The Doomsday Model of Economic Growth

little recognition given to the role that technological change and knowledge plays in the growth process. Knowledge and its application to production has tended to expand at an exponential rate without running up against the hard fact of diminishing returns. It may be that this will not continue in the future, but to date the evidence does not bear this out. There is no evidence of permanent decline in the rate of growth in productivity.

Another weakness of both the classical and doomsday types of models is their view of the resource base as something fixed, immutable and thus limited in supply. What this fails to take into account is the fact that through expanding knowledge and technology new resources are created from materials that at one time seemed worthless. Resources are not fixed and unchanging; they are a function of the level of technology that prevails in a society. At the moment, for example, it is not economically feasible to extract the petroleum which geologists tell us exists in enormous quantities in the superbundant shale rock found in the Rocky Mountains. But with advanced technical knowledge, including development of extraction processes that cause minimal damage to the physical environment, utilization of the shale may be possible. We are, perhaps, just on the threshold of exploring even more exotic energy sources, such as the sun itself (solar energy), geothermal energy from the earth's interior, or even energy from the ebb and flow of the ocean's tides. Another glaring defect of the doomsday model is the failure to build into it any price mechanism. As Professor Solow points out, the price mechanism is a key social institution whereby the economic system registers and reacts to relative scarcities of all sorts.[8] The price system provides the necessary feedback mechanism that will bring technological knowledge into play when we confront scarcities of specific commodities. It not only works to spur the development of new resources as supplies of existing and conventional resources near exhaustion, but also stimulates the substitution of one resource for another. The extensive use of plastics in place of metals is a good example.

One should not, however, minimize the seriousness of the problems which confront the economy and its resource base, especially those stemming from pollution in the developed world and the population explosion in the underdeveloped world. They cannot be waved away. But if the longer-term outlook is for a slowdown in growth, which may well be the case, then it is likely to be a gradual process rather than a violent collapse. If we are ultimately destined to reach something like the classical stationary state, then we must depend more than ever upon the continued advance of human knowledge and technology. If and when we do reach some sort of final no-growth state it will be at levels of real per capita output and wealth that make possible the kind of highly civilized and humane condition that John Stuart Mill envisaged.

Post-Keynesian Growth Theories

Let us turn to the second major objective of this chapter, namely analysis of the conditions required for developed, market economies to sustain both full employment and a rising level of output over time. As stressed earlier, this involves a close and critical examination of the growth models developed by Professors Domar and Harrod.

The appropriate point of departure for discussion of these theories is a brief review of the Keynesian full employment equilibrium in a short-run setting. Parenthetically, it is important to remember that the basic Keynesian model as developed in Chapter 5 is static simply because it does not involve any change over time in the fundamental determinants of the economy's productive potential. As Keynes pointed out, his analysis takes as given "the existing skill and quantity of available labour, the existing quality and quantity of available equipment, the existing technique, the degree of competition, the tastes and habits of the consumer."[9] With

8. Solow, "Is the End of the World At Hand?"

9. John Maynard Keynes, *The General Theory of Employment, Interest and Money* (New York, Harcourt, Brace & World, First Harbinger ed., 1964), p. 245.

capacity known and fixed, the central problem is the determination of the level of aggregate demand; in static analysis the level of aggregate demand determines the output and employment level, and shifts in the aggregate demand schedule bring about shifts in both output and employment.

In the simplest version of the Keynesian system aggregate demand consists of consumption and investment expenditure. The basic condition for equilibrium at any level of income and employment is that investment expenditure be sufficiently large to absorb the saving forthcoming at the income level in question. Consequently, the necessary condition for a full employment equilibrium income level is that investment expenditure be sufficient to absorb the saving made at the full employment income.

There is nothing wrong with this analysis since it expresses an idea fundamental to all modern income and employment theory: namely, income paid out or created during the productive process must be returned in one form or another to the income stream if the expectations of producers are to be satisfied and equilibrium maintained. But, as Domar and Harrod have observed, the equilibrium so obtained has meaning only for a relatively short period of time because the *capacity-creating* effects of investment expenditure will cause the income level that is appropriate to the full employment of both labor and other resources to rise over time.

To facilitate our understanding of why a level of income sufficient to achieve full employment of all resources today may not be sufficient to achieve full employment of all resources tomorrow, let us discuss income, investment, and saving in the net sense, that is, after proper allowance has been made for the replacement of capital goods used up in the current production process. If the discussion is cast in net rather than gross terms, it does not change the underlying principle: Full employment equilibrium requires that investment expenditure be equal to full employment saving. The key difference is that now the basic statement describing the necessary condition for achieving and maintaining a full employment income level must be modified to read that *ex ante* net investment must equal *ex ante* net saving at full employment.

But when we put the analysis in net terms and define full employment equilibrium in terms of an equality between net saving and investment, we are faced with a serious dilemma because the analytical system no longer retains its static character. Net saving is a dynamic concept, for if a society steadily saves some portion of its net income and just as steadily invests the income saved in productive capital, it follows that the stock of productive capital equipment, one of the basic determinants of both capacity and output, will change. Static analysis does not concern itself with a situation in which a basic determinant of productive capacity such as the capital stock changes. The paradox of the situation arises from the fact that net investment is by definition an addition to the economy's stock of wealth in the form of productive capital, and thus net investment must logically increase the economy's productive capacity. But if productive capacity is increasing, the analysis can no longer be static.

The Domar Analysis of Economic Growth

The paradox that net investment is, on the one hand, a necessary offset to net saving if full employment is to be maintained and, on the other, an addition to the economy's stock of capital provides a setting for Domar's analysis of the problem of growth in an advanced economy. The dominant theme in his theoretical treatment of economic growth is that net investment raises productive capacity and thus causes the economy to grow. Given the capacity creating impact of net investment, Domar attempts to determine the rate at which income must grow if full employment is to be maintained over time.[10]

To explore this problem, Domar develops an analytical model which seeks to show how growth in capacity over time can be linked to growth in aggregate demand, output, and employment. Domar's analytical framework is essentially Keynesian, although it is placed in a long-run and includes some new elements.

Before we examine Domar's analysis of the growth process, we must define the concepts he employs and state the assumptions underlying the analysis. The key concepts and assumptions are as follows:

1. *The propensity to save.* This is the ratio of saving to income at any given level of income. Domar assumes that S/Y is constant, which means he is working with a long-run saving function. Also, the marginal propensity to save, $\Delta S/\Delta Y$, is equal to the average propensity to save, since mathematically the average propensity to save could not be a constant unless it was equal to the marginal propensity to save. In the analysis both the marginal and the average propensity to save are designated by α. In Domar's analytical system, as in Keynesian economics proper, the significance of the average propensity to save is that it determines the amount of saving that will have to be absorbed by investment for the achievement of a full employment income level, while the significance of the marginal propensity to save is that it is the key to the value of the multiplier.

2. *The capital-output ratio.* This magnitude, which is sometimes called the capital coefficient, is the ratio of the capital stock of the economy, K,

10. Domar, p. 38.

to full capacity output, Y. Basically, K/Y_1 a way of defining the economy's capacity in terms of its capital stock; given an existing level of technology, there will be, on the average, a certain physical quantity of capital required to obtain a given quantity of output. Since both capital (a stock phenomenon) and output (a flow phenomenon) must be measured in terms of their monetary values, the capital-output ratio becomes, as a practical matter, the number of dollars' worth of capital required on the average to get a dollar's worth of output. Domar bases his analysis on the average capital-output ratio for the whole economy, although the actual capital-output ratio may vary widely from industry to industry.

3. *The marginal capital-output ratio.* This ratio represents the relationship between changes in the capital stock, ΔK, and changes in the output level, ΔY. Since a change in the capital stock is the same thing as net investment, $\Delta K/\Delta Y$ tells us how much added capital or investment is needed to get an additional unit of output. The marginal capital-output ratio or capital coefficient may or may not be equal to the average capital-output ratio, but if the marginal ratio is constant and equal to the average ratio, technological change is said to be neutral.[11] Technological change that is not neutral alters both the average and marginal capital-output ratios, but especially the latter, because new developments make themselves felt primarily at the time when additions to the capital stock are being made. Technological change may, moreover, lower or raise these ratios by reducing the amount of capital required to obtain a unit of output. If the capital requirement has been reduced, capital saving is said to have taken place; if it has been increased, the result has been capital deepening.

The nature of the marginal capital-output ratio can be shown by means of a diagram. In Figure 15–3, with output and capacity on the horizontal axis and net savings and investment on the vertical axis, OS represents the long-run saving function, the slope of which is such that the average and marginal propensities to save are equal.[12] If Y_1 is the full employment income, then the full employment requirement is that net investment be equal to saving at this income level. This is the distance Y_1S_1. The marginal capital coefficient is represented by the Y_1U_1, the slope of which is equal to the ratio of an increment of capital to an increment of output. Thus, if investment in the income period proceeds at the rate Y_1S_1, the impact on the economy's productive capacity is shown by projecting a horizontal line from S_1 to the point at which it intersects the Y_1U_1 line (point a in the diagram), and then dropping a vertical line from this point to the horizontal axis. The distance Y_1Y_2 represents the increase in

11. Neutral technological change leaves the capital-output ratio unchanged. See Harrod, p. 83.

12. This diagram was developed by Harold Pilvin. See "A Geometric Analysis of Recent Growth Models," *American Economic Review*, September 1952, pp. 594–99.

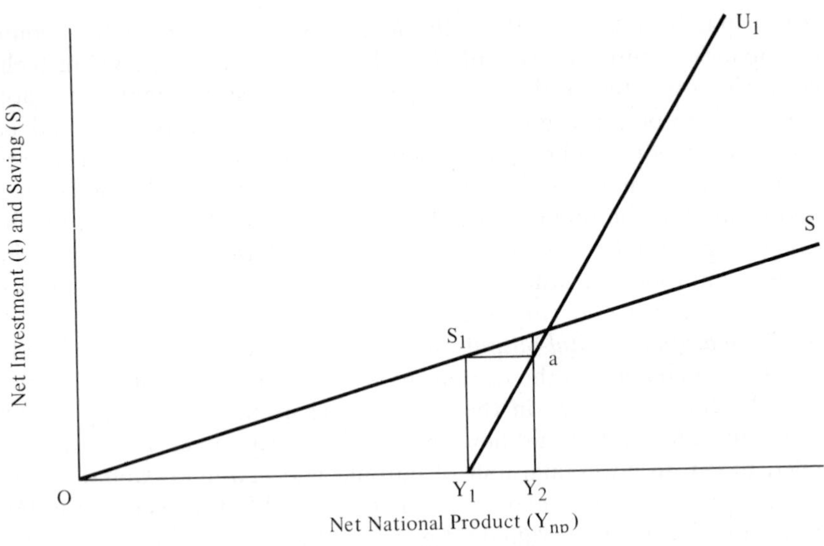

FIGURE 15–3. The Marginal Capital-Output Ratio

capacity that has resulted from net investment in the amount Y_1S_1 in the present income period.

4. *The productivity of capital coefficient.* In Domar's analysis, and in growth economics generally, the ratio Y/K (the reciprocal of the capital-output ratio) is a measure of the average productivity of capital in the same sense that a full employment output, Y divided by the labor force, N', is a measure of the average productivity of labor. The ratio Y/N', which may be called the *average productivity of labor*, has frequently been used to determine the economy's potential for production, as it is only necessary to multiply the average productivity of labor by the assumed labor force to get a measure of potential output. The ratio Y/K shifts the emphasis from labor productivity to capital productivity in the determination of capacity.

In Domar's analysis the ratio of an increment of output, ΔY to an increment in the capital stock, ΔK, is designated by s. If the average and marginal ratios are assumed equal, s is both a measure of the average productivity of capital *ex post* and a measure of the amount by which each dollar's worth of newly created capital, taken by itself, will add to the productive capacity of the economy. Viewed in the latter sense Domar's is simply the reciprocal of the marginal capital-output ratio, because, if, on the average, three dollars' worth of capital equipment is required to produce one dollar's worth of additional output, s will have a value of 0.33. In other words, the average productivity of capital will be 0.33, because each dollar's worth of new capital will increase capacity by this amount.

Although Domar employs the symbol s to describe the immediate and direct effect on capacity that results from added capital, this particular ratio is not the appropriate ratio for the whole economy, because, he asserts, normally some newly created capital goods will be brought into use at the expense of existing capital. Thus the amount by which over-all capacity is increased for each new dollar's worth of capital equipment will be less than s. To designate the amount by which productive capacity for the whole economy is increased for each dollar's worth of new capital Domar employs σ which he calls the *potential social average productivity of investment.* Normally σ is smaller than s. Ae we shall see shortly, σ is the most important single concept employed by Domar in his analysis of the growth process.

5. *Some simplifying assumptions.* The concepts discussed in the foregoing paragraphs constitute the key ideas Domar employs in the construction of his growth theory, but there are some simplifying assumptions that should be made clear before we turn to discussion of the theory itself. In the first place, he assumes an economy in which there is neither government nor international economic transactions. This does not imply that public activity and international transactions have no role to play in the growth process, but simply reflects Domar's desire to concentrate the whole of his analysis on the growth potential embodied in the capacity-creating effect of net investment in the private sector. Second, the analysis assumes there are no lags in adjustment, which is to say that output is assumed to respond immediately to changes in expenditure and expenditure is assumed to respond immediately to changes in income. The absence of lags permits us to see clearly as possible the key relationships involved in the growth process. Finally, the analysis starts with the assumption that a full employment income level has been attained.

The Capacity Creating Process

Having discussed Domar's key concepts, we can now examine the way in which he describes the capacity creating process associated with a given amount of net investment. In Figure 15–3 the full employment income level is assumed to be Y_1, and the amount of net investment required at this income level is given by the distance Y_1S_1. If investment expenditure proceeds during the income period at this rate, we can use σ to determine the effect of this amount of investment on productive capacity. Specifically, if net investment in the income period is equal to I dollars, the subsequent increase in the productive capacity of the whole economy is

$$\Delta Y_Q = I\sigma \tag{15–1}$$

ΔY_Q represents the increase in the *productive potential* of the economy; it does not represent any actual increase in output. The expression $I\sigma$

reflects the supply side of the economic system, for it describes the extent to which productive capacity has been increased as a consequence of a specific amount of net investment. In terms of the Keynesian diagrammatic analysis this means that the full capacity output level has been pushed farther to the right along the horizontal axis. If, to refer back to Figure 15–3, Y_1 represented a full employment income level at the beginning of the current income period, it no longer represents the full employment income level at the end of this period.

The nature of the capacity creating process of net investment can be clearly illustrated by a simple numerical example. Let us assume, first, that σ has a value of 0.3 and, second, that the average (and marginal) propensity to save out of net income is 0.10. Let us assume further that the full employment income in the present period (the Y_1 of Figure 15–53) is $700 billion. Then, for full employment, investment expenditure must equal $70 billion (or 10 percent of $700 billion). If the net investment of the economy is at the rate of $70 billion during the current income period, what effect does this have on productive capacity? The potential social average productivity of investment coefficient, σ, supplies the answer; if, on the average, every dollar's worth of new capital increases productive capacity by $0.30, then $70 billion of new capital will increase the over-all productive capacity of the economy by $21 billion ($70 billion $\times$ 0.3 = $21 billion).

What are the consequences of the above process? Although $700 billion represented the full employment output level at the start of the income period, this is no longer the case. Capacity has grown and with it the full employment output level. This fact underscores the fundamental necessity for output to grow if full employment is to be maintained over time in an economy in which there is positive net saving and positive net investment. What would happen if, in the next income period, income remained at $700 billion? As Domar points out, the creation of new capital will result in one of three possible effects, assuming the level of income remains unchanged:[13] (1) the new capital remains unused, in which case it should not have been produced in the first place; (2) the new capital is used at the expense of previously constructed capital, which also may represent a waste of resources if net investment is large; and (3) the new capital may be substituted for labor, which may lead to a substantial amount of involuntary unemployment if the introduction of the new equipment is not accompanied by a voluntary reduction in either the size of the labor force or the length of the work week. If income remains at the same level in the next period, even though there has been net investment in the present period, the result will be either unemployed labor, unemployed capital, or both.

13. Domar, p. 37.

The Demand Requirement

The key point of the foregoing analysis is that if net investment increases the economy's productive capacity, it is essential that output grow through time to insure that the added capacity created by the investment process is continually absorbed into use. The problem is therefore to determine, first, how output can be made to expand so as to bring into use the added capacity and, second, the necessary rate at which output must expand to achieve the continued full utilization of additional capacity.

Domar's analysis of the growth process is carried out within the Keynesian framework of aggregate demand and aggregate supply, where the most important role played by aggregate demand is to bring capacity into use. Both output and employment result from the use of capacity, and it is the expectation of demand that leads the entrepreneur to make use of the productive capacity at his disposal. It follows that *it is necessary for aggregate demand to rise if added productive capacity is to be brought into use.*

Since we have eliminated government expenditure and international transactions from the analysis, and since consumption is a dependent variable (in that it is a function of income), investment is the key determinant of the level of aggregate demand. Thus investment will have to increase if there is to be an upward shift in the aggregate demand function, the shift must be great enough to bring about an over-all increase in aggregate expenditure sufficient to utilize—and thus justify—the added productive capacity. This aspect of the problem is easy to understand, for the reader need only recall the multiplier analysis to realize that any given total increase in aggregate expenditure depends upon the amount by which investment itself has risen as well as upon the value of the multiplier. The latter, of course, is dependent upon the marginal propensity to save.

If the utilization of additional capacity requires an increase in aggregate expenditure equal to the amount by which capacity has increased, and if changes in investment expenditure are the ultimate source of changes in effective demand, we can express the required increase in effective demand in equation form as

$$\Delta Y_D = \Delta I \times \frac{1}{\alpha} \qquad (15\text{–}2)$$

This equation is simply the multiplier formula applied to an increase in investment expenditure. ΔY_D represents the over-all increase in effective demand or total expenditure brought about by the given increment in investment expenditure. $1/\alpha$ is the simple investment multiplier, since α represents the marginal propensity to save.

In conjunction with the equation depicting the demand side of his system, Domar places great stress on what he terms the *dual nature of the investment process.* By this he means that the capacity creating effects and the demand creating effects of investment expenditure are dissimilar, because all net investment expenditure adds to the economy's capital stock and thus increases the economy's productive capacity, but only increments to investment expenditure, operating through the multiplier effect, raise the level of effective demand. This, in short, is the real paradox of investment; if net investment expenditure simply remains constant through time, the income level will not change—that is, equilibrium will be maintained—but the result will be idle capacity and a growing volume of unemployed labor. Investment and income must grow in each succeeding income period if net investment expenditures in any specific income period are to justify themselves.

The Required Rate of Income Growth

If the maintenance of full employment for both the economy's labor force and stock of productive capital requires that output grow at the same rate at which productive capacity is increasing because of net investment, we can bring together the equations discussed above and compute the necessary rate at which output must grow. The basic condition is that, over time, increments of effective demand must equal increments of capacity. Symbolically, this can be stated as:

$$\Delta Y_Q = \Delta Y_D \qquad (15\text{–}3)$$

In the above definition equation we can substitute the earlier values for ΔY_Q and ΔY_D. Thus:

$$I\sigma = \Delta I \times \frac{1}{\alpha} \qquad (15\text{–}4)$$

$I\sigma$ represents the supply side of the system, for it shows the potential increase in supply that results from current investment, while $\Delta I \times \frac{1}{\alpha}$ represents the demand side, since it depicts the amount by which aggregate effective demand must rise if the added capacity is to be utilized.

Domar solves the above fundamental equation by multiplying both sides by α and then dividing both sides by I. The result of this is the following growth equation:

$$\frac{\Delta I}{I} = \sigma\alpha \qquad (15\text{–}5)$$

The left side of this equation shows the absolute increment in investment expenditure divided by the total volume of investment expenditure.

It is expressive of the percentage rate of growth of investment. Thus, Equation (15–5) means basically that *investment expenditure must grow at an annual rate equal to the product of the marginal propensity to save, α, and the potential social average productivity of investment, σ*, if a state of continuous full employment is to be maintained. Since Domar assumes that the average and marginal propensities to save are equal and that the average and marginal values of σ are equal, it is easy to demonstrate algebraically that income as well as investment must grow at a constant annual percentage rate equal to the product of α and σ.[14] Thus:

$$\frac{Y}{\Delta Y} = \sigma\alpha \qquad (15\text{–}6)$$

The above equation, like Equation (15—5), indicates in a simple and direct way the necessary condition for the maintenance of full employment output over time. It shows, to quote Domar, "that it is not sufficient, in Keynesian terms, that savings of yesterday be invested today, or, as it is so often expressed, that investment offset saving. Investment of today must always exceed savings of yesterday. . . . The economy must continuously expand."[15]

A Numerical Representation of the Growth Process

The nature of this growth process may be illustrated by numerical example. Tables 15–2 and 15–3 contain hypothetical data pertaining to the growth of net national output, consumption, and investment over a five-year period, assuming different sets of values for both α and σ. In Table 15–2, the propensity to save, α, has a value of 0.10, while the value of the productivity of capital coefficient, σ, is 0.30. The required rate of growth is thus 3 percent per year, since $\alpha \times \sigma = 0.03$. If the net national income of the economy is \$700 billion in the first year, a 3 percent annual rate of growth will raise income to the level of \$787.8 billion at the end of five years. The effect of investment upon capacity in each income period is shown in Column (5). The figures in this column are the product of $I\sigma$, for we assume that the net saving of each income period is invested. The amount of such saving is determined by the average propensity to consume. Investment (and saving) remain a constant proportion of income,

14. This can be shown algebraically as follows:
 (1) $I = aY$ [This assumes that the saving of the period is invested.]
 (2) $\Delta Y_Q = \sigma\alpha Y$ [This is from Equation (14–1).]
 (3) $\Delta Y_D = \sigma\alpha Y$ [This on the assumption that the change in aggregate effective demand must equal the change in capacity.]
 (4) $\frac{\Delta Y}{Y} = \sigma\alpha$ [This follows algebraically from above.]

15. Domar, p. 42.

TABLE 15–2. The Required Growth of Income: I (in billions of dollars)

$\alpha = 0.10$
$\sigma = 0.30$
$\sigma\alpha = 0.03/yr.$

(1) Year	(2) Income (Y)	(3) Consumption (C)	(4) Investment (I)	(5) Increase in Capacity ($I\sigma$)
1	$700.0	$630.0	$70.0	$21.0
2	721.0	648.9	72.1	21.6
3	742.6	668.3	74.3	22.3
4	764.9	688.4	76.5	22.9
5	787.8	709.0	78.8	23.6

but the absolute amount of investment is greater in each subsequent income period. This is a clear example of what Domar means when he states, as quoted above, that the investment of today must always exceed savings of yesterday. This simple example offers considerable insight into the dynamic behavior inherent in maintaining full employment over time in an advanced economy; the economy must not only expand continuously in order to avoid unemployment but in order to do this it must constantly find outlets in investment expenditure for a rising absolute amount of saving.

Table 15–3 contains similar hypothetical data, except in this instance we are assuming higher values for both the propensity to save and the productivity of capital coefficient. Specifically, α is assumed to have a value of 0.12, and σ a value of 0.40. This means, first, that this hypothetical economy saves, on the average, a higher proportion of its net income and, second, that the productivity of capital is, also on the average, higher. As a consequence, investment expenditure equal to the saving at any particular income level will have a greater impact on the economy's productive capacity than was the case in the prior example. This is not only because the absolute amount of saving will be greater at each and every income level, but also because the higher value for the productivity of capital coefficient means, in effect, that every dollar of investment expenditure increases productive capacity by a greater amount. Thus, the over-all effect of higher values for both the propensity to save and the productivity of capital coefficient is to increase the necessary growth rate for our hypothetical economy. With the above assumed values for these coefficients, the necessary growth rate for maintenance of full-employment output level over time becomes 4.8 percent. The data of Table 15–3 show that such a growth rate, if sustained for a five-year period, would raise the output level from $700 billion in the first year to $844.4 billion in the

TABLE 15–3. The Required Growth of Income: II (in billions of dollars)

$\alpha = 0.12$
$\sigma = 0.40$
$\sigma\alpha = 0.048/yr.$

(1) Year	(2) Income (Y)	(3) Consumption (C)	(4) Investment (I)	(5) Increase in Capacity ($I\sigma$)
1	$700.0	$616.0	$84.0	$33.6
2	733.6	645.6	88.0	35.2
3	768.8	676.5	92.3	36.9
4	805.7	709.1	96.9	38.7
5	844.4	743.1	101.3	40.5

fifth year. The readers should compare the impact of investment on productive capacity in each period, Column (5) in Table 15–3, with the same data in Table 15–2. In each period I_Q is greater.

A Diagrammatic Representation of the Growth Process

The growth process envisaged by Domar can also be illustrated by means of a diagram. Figure 15–4 is similiar to Figure 15–3; the line OS represents the long-run saving function, and its slope is such that the average and marginal propensities to save are equal.

Let us assume initially the full employment income level is equal to Y_1, and investment expenditure is such as to absorb the saving at this income level. Investment is thus equal to Y_1S_1. Since investment is autonomous with respect to income, the investment function is represented by the schedule labeled I_1. The impact of this amount of investment on the economy's productive capacity is depicted by the line Y_1U_1, the slope of which is equal to the marginal capital-output ratio. Since the marginal capital-output ratio is the ratio of a change in the capital stock (after account has been taken of the displacement of some existing capital by new capital) to a change in the output level, the reciprocal of Y_1U_1 is the productivity of capital coefficient, σ.

If net investment proceeds in the first income period at a rate equal to Y_1S_1, productive capacity will be increased by an amount equal to the distance Y_1Y_2. This distance is determined, in Figure 15–4, by projecting a horizontal line from point S_1 to the point at which it intersects the Y_1U_1 line, and then dropping a vertical line from this point to the horizontal axis. Consequently, Y_2 now represents the economy's full employment income level. But if this is the case, and given the saving function OS, the absolute amount of saving that will be forthcoming at the new full em-

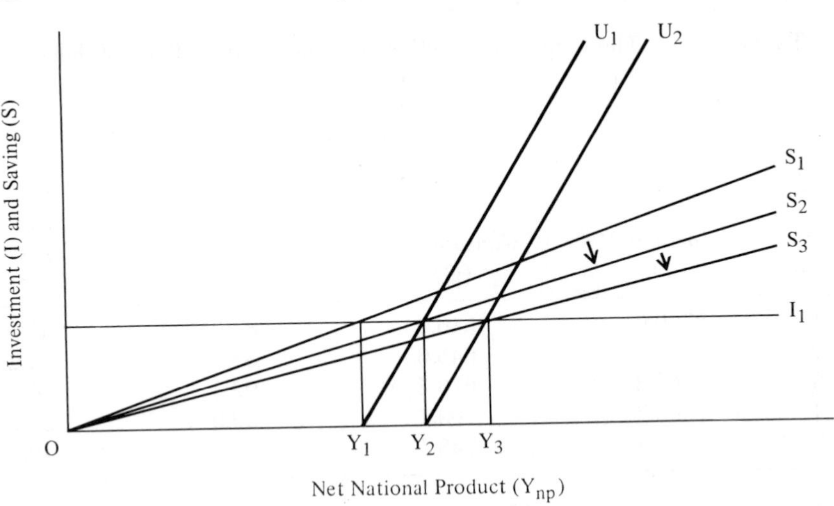

FIGURE 15–4. Net Investment and the Growth Process

ployment income level has risen to the amount Y_2S_2. Since equilibrium in the Keynesian sense requires equality between saving and investment *ex ante*, investment expenditure must rise to the level depicted by the investment schedule I_2 if the economy is to maintain full employment. This shift of the equilibrium income to the level represented by Y_2 requires, too, a shift in the curve representing the productivity of investment coefficient to the position Y_2U_2, because net investment in the amount Y_2S_2 will result in further additions to the economy's capital stock. Since σ remained constant during the time interval involved in raising income from Y_1 to Y_2, Y_2U_2 can be drawn parallel to Y_1U_1. Net investment in the second income period equal to Y_2S_2 will cause productive capacity to rise by an amount equal to the distance Y_2Y_3. Once again investment will have to increase if a full employment income level is to be maintained, because the saving at Y_3 is greater than the saving at Y_2. Investment must now rise to the level shown by the investment function I_3.

Inspection of this model reveals a number of interesting aspects of the growth process. If we assume fixed values for both the propensity to save and the productivity of investment coefficient, not only must investment expenditure rise continuously through time if full employment is to be maintained, but also the absolute increments of investment required in such subsequent income periods must become larger and larger. The logic of this is readily apparent, for if capacity increases through time by increasing absolute amounts, and if the investment multiplier is constant because of a constant marginal propensity to save, effective demand will increase through time in an amount equal to the increase in capacity only if the increments to investment expenditure become absolutely larger in each successive income period. Figure 15–4 clearly shows the difficulties facing an advanced economy which habitually saves some significant portion of its net income. Such an economy must continuously find new outlets for not just a constant but a growing absolute volume of saving. For this reason, advanced economies have frequently found it exceedingly difficult to sustain a constant rate of growth over relatively long periods of time.

The above analysis may strike the reader as unduly restrictive because of the underlying assumption that both the propensity to save and the productivity of investment coefficient have constant values. Different results will ensure with different values of either α or σ. For example, the investment function would not have to shift upward continuously (as shown in Figure 15–4) if the long-term propensity to save were to undergo a decline. This possibility is depicted in Figure 15–5, which shows the saving function, *OS*, pivoting downward with each successive increase in capacity. This decline in the value of the propensity to save does not eliminate the capacity-creating effect of net investment, but means merely that the absolute increases in capacity, ΔY_Q, in each income period would be constant because investment remains constant in each income period. It is scarcely realistic, however, to assume that the secular saving function undergoes a downward shift; this would mean that over time the economy saved a smaller and smaller proportion of its net income, but empirical research indicates that the proportion of net income saved remains constant over the long run.[16]

A final possibility has to do with changes in the value of the productiv-

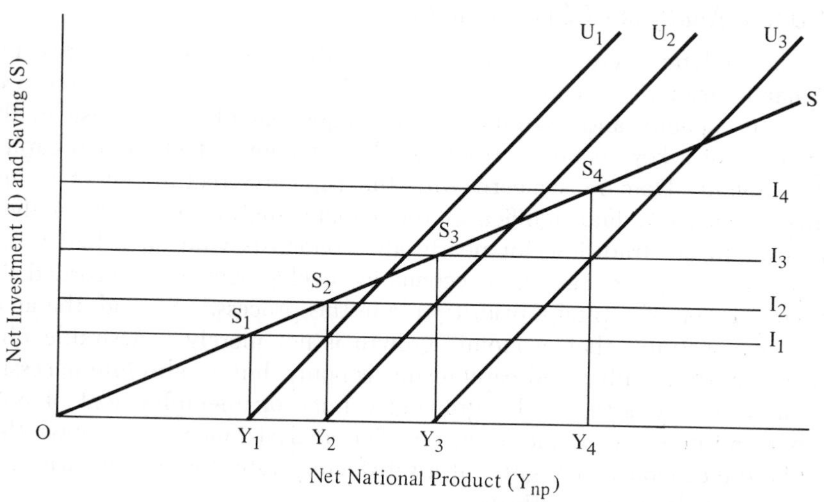

FIGURE 15–5. Downward Shift in the Saving Function

16. Simon Kuznets, *National Income: A Summary of Findings* (New York: National Bureau of Economic Research, 1946), p. 53.

ity of capital coefficient. A decline in the value of σ means that the impact on capacity of any specific amount of investment is smaller, and, therefore, the extent to which income would have to grow to absorb into use the additions to capacity would also be lessened. A reduction in σ would, in other words, make the problem of attaining a constantly rising volume of investment expenditures less difficult, because with a slower rate of growth of capacity and income, the growth of saving in an absolute sense also will be slower. A decline in σ is the same as a rise in the capital-output ratio, for if a given quantity of investment expenditure has a smaller effect on capacity than heretofore, more capital per unit of output is required. Unfortunately, it is quite unlikely that an advanced economy can easily resolve the problem of maintaining continuous full employment by a downward adjustment in the value σ. For one thing, the productivity of capital coefficient is basically a technological coefficient, and as such not easily adjusted to whatever value might be required for maintenance of a full employment equilibrium. In addition, the long-term trend for the actual capital-output ratio in the United States appears to be downward. If such a trend is characteristic of advanced economies in general, it means higher rather than lower values for the productivity of capital coefficient. Thus, the impact on capacity for any given amount of investment has tended to become greater rather than smaller.

Significance and Limitations of the Domar Analysis of Economic Growth

The analytical system that we have been discussing can be described as dynamic primarily because it goes beyond the assumption of a fixed productive capacity and examines the consequences of an increase in the quantity of a key economic resource, the economy's stock of real capital instruments. Domar's concern with the capacity-creating effect of net investment has a dual significance for ecnomic analysis. First, the analysis follows an old tradition, for nearly all economists who have had something meaningful to say about economic development have accorded the accumulation of capital a priority role in this process.[17] Second, the analysis demonstrates that economic growth is not merely a desirable phenomenon for an advanced capitalistic economy, but an absolute necessity if the economy is to avoid a growing volume of unemployment of both labor and other economic resources. The analysis, moreover, shows that while the economy may grow at a satisfactory rate, there is no reason to expect it to do so automatically.

Our appraisal of Domar's analysis would not be complete if we did not

17. See especially, Benjamin Higgins, *Economic Development: Principles, Problems, and Policies,* 2nd ed. (New York: Norton, 1959), p. 204.

point out some of its important limitations. For one thing, the derivation of required rate obviously depends upon the existence of known and constant values for such crucial factors as the propensity to save and the productivity of capital coefficient. In reality, it is unlikely that either of these are constant all the time. But the difficulty of deriving a required rate does not in any way invalidate the basic theme of the analysis—that there exists some rate of growth that will insure a full employment equilibrium over time.

A second limitation is Domar's use of a productivity of investment coefficient that is an average for the whole economy. The capital-output ratio, both on the average and at the margin, varies widely from industry to industry because of differences in the capital requirements for different kinds of production. This means that it will be very difficult to determine the exact impact of a given volume of investment on capacity unlss we know the composition in an industrial sense of the investment. For example, a given quantity of investment expenditure in an industry characterized by a high capital-output ratio will obviously have a smaller over-all impact on productive capacity than the same amount of investment expenditure in an industry with a lower capital-output ratio.

Finally, Domar's analysis fails to distinguish between a rate of growth of income which will insure full employment of the labor force, and a rate of growth of income which will insure full utilization of the economy's stock of capital. This has been a matter of concern for some economists, who argue that the rate of growth sufficient to absorb additions to the economy's stock of capital will not necessarily provide full employment for a growing labor force.

In spite of these limitations, attention should not be detracted from the important and positive contribution that the Domar type of analysis has made to an understanding of the process of economic development in an advanced economy. Admittedly, Domar's system is overly simplified and, perhaps, overly rigid. But this is a criticism that could be justly leveled at most facets of contemporary economic theory. The real task of economic theory is to direct our attention to a few strategic relationships as a means of understanding somewhat better the vast complexities of the economy in the real world. Not many economists would deny that an enlargement of the economy's productive potential is a factor of key strategic significance in the process of economic growth.

The Harrod Analysis of Economic Growth

Since Harrod's analysis of the growth process in an advanced economy is in many respects similar to Domar's it has become fashionable for economists to speak of the Domar-Harrod theory when they are discussing developments which extend the basic concepts of Keynesian income and employment theory to the general area of economic growth. But there are also enough fundamental differences in their approaches to warrant separate discussion of the ideas of each.

Harrod, like Domar, is concerned with the necessary conditions under which the equality of *ex ante* saving and investment can be maintained over time, but he treats the central element in the growth process, investment expenditure, in a different manner. In Domar's schema we look to the effect that current investment expenditure has on future productive capacity, assuming that this investment expenditure is sufficient to offset the saving of the current income level. In a sense, Domar's analysis is forward looking because such a procedure requires us to determine how much both income and investment will have to grow in the next income period in order to absorb into use at that time the added capacity that is the consequence of investment in the present income period.

Harrod, on the other hand, constructs his analysis in terms of the response of current investment expenditure to a change in the economy's output or real income level. He seeks to determine whether the rate at which income has grown in the immediate past is high enough to induce an amount of investment expenditure sufficient to absorb the saving in the current income period.

The key analytical tool that Harrod employs in his analysis is the *accelerator,* which is defined symbolically as the ratio of a change in the capital stock, ΔK, to a change in the output level, ΔY. Since the change in the capital stock is the same as the net investment, I_n, the ratio $\Delta K/\Delta Y$, or $I_n/\Delta Y$, when defined as the accelerator, represents a behavior coefficient in the sense that it seeks to express as a coefficient the investment response of entrepreneurs to a change in the output level. The acceleration approach makes current net investment a function of the rate of change in output. Fundamental to the notion of the acceleration coefficient, however, is the concept of the capital-output ratio conceived as a technical relationship, for if a relatively fixed relationship did not exist between output and the quantity of capital necessary for the production of that output, there would be no point in asserting that investment expenditure may be induced by changes in output.

Although the treatment of investment expenditure differs in the two analyses, both Domar and Harrod accord identical roles to the saving function. Both analyses are based on the long-run saving function, on an equality between the average and the marginal propensity to save. In both analyses saving *ex ante* and saving *ex post* are presumed to be equal, which means that saving calls the tune. Other variables such as investment, the productivity of capital coefficient and the accelerator must adjust to the rate of saving if full employment over time is to be maintained.

The basic procedure employed by Harrod is to postulate a series of fundamental equations, each of which embodies a carefully defined rate of growth. By means of comparisons between these growth rates, it is possible to determine the conditions under which a steady rate of advance is possible for the economy.

The Warranted Rate of Growth

The most important growth rate developed by Harrod in his analysis is the *warranted rate of growth*, G_w, which he defines precisely as "that overall rate of advance which, if executed, will leave entrepreneurs in a state of mind in which they are prepared to carry on a similar advance."[18] In algebraic terms we have:

$$G_w = \frac{\Delta Y}{Y} \tag{15–7}$$

More explicitly, the warranted rate of growth concept refers to a rate of advance for the economy as a whole that will leave entrepreneurs (in the aggregate or on the average) satisfied with the outcome of economic activity. Within the framework of Keynesian equilibrium analysis, a condition of entrepreneurial satisfaction is a situation in which investment and saving *ex ante* are in equilibrium. This is basically what Harrod means by the warranted rate of growth, except that he is talking of a developing rather than a static situation. The concept of a warranted rate of growth refers to a situation in which a growing absolute volume of *ex ante* investment is in equilibrium with a growing absolute volume of full employment, *ex ante* saving. To express the necessary condition for equilibrium in a steadily advancing economy, Harrod postulates the following equation, which, he says, describes the condition in which producers will be content with what they are doing:[19]

$$G_w \times C_r = s \tag{15–8}$$

Before we examine the significance of this equation, it is necessary to explain the key concepts employed by Harrod in his analysis. We have already discussed G_w. The variable s represents the long-run propensity to save and is the same as α in Domar's analysis. Thus the average and the marginal propensities to save are identical. Harrod assumes that saving intentions are always realized; consequently saving *ex ante* and saving *ex post* are always equal. Algebraically:

$$s = \frac{S}{Y} = \frac{\Delta S}{\Delta Y} \tag{15–9}$$

The variable C_r in Equation (15–8) is somewhat more complex and requires a more detailed explanation. Harrod describes C_r as the symbol

18. Harrod, *Towards a Dynamic Economics*, p. 82.
19. Ibid., p. 81.

for the *capital requirement,* by which is meant "the requirement for new capital divided by the increment of output to sustain which the new capital is required."[20] Harrod conceives the capital-output ratio as a technical relationship, for, as he says, the above definition is "based upon the idea that existing output can be sustained by existing capital that additional capital is only required to sustain additional output."[21] The capital requirement concept must be interpreted with care, for if interpreted too literally it leads to the absurd conclusion that more capital is needed to increase output by the amount that output has just increased. Actually, since capacity is not a precise magnitude, the technical relationship embodied in the capital-output ratio means that at some point near the absolute upper limit of the individual firm's productive capacity, entrepreneurs will feel that more capacity will be required to provide additional output to meet a rising level of demand. Algebraically, we have:

$$C_r = \frac{\Delta K}{\Delta Y} = \frac{I_n}{\Delta Y} \qquad (15\text{–}10)$$

Although C_r as defined above may be said to represent the capital requirement of the economy, the above ratio may also be defined as the accelerator. In this sense, C_r becomes an expression of entrepreneurial behavior, for it represents the coefficient which describes the amount of investment that will be induced by a change in the output level. Investment in the above equation is, in other words, *ex ante* or planned investment, the amount of which depends upon a prior change in output.

Which of these definitions of C_r is appropriate in the context of Equation (15–8), which purports to describe the condition under which equilibrium in a growing economy is possible? Basically, both are appropriate, for although the acceleration concept may be used to explain why investment has attained a particular level in the current income period, it can have no meaning unless an underlying technical relationship between capital and output is assumed.

To clarify this statement, let us make the following algebraic substitutions in Equation (15–8): $\Delta Y/\Delta Y$ for G_w; $I_n/\Delta Y$ for C_r; and S/Y for s. Then we have:

$$\frac{\Delta Y}{Y} \times \frac{I_n}{\Delta Y} = \frac{S}{Y} \qquad (15\text{–}11)$$

Since the ΔY's on the left-hand side of the equation will cancel out, we then have:

$$\frac{I_n}{Y} = \frac{S}{Y} \qquad (15\text{–}12)$$

20. Ibid., p. 82.
21. Ibid.

The basic meaning, therefore, of Harrod's equation that expresses the equilibrium of a steady advance is that the rate of growth must be such that *ex ante* investment is equal to *ex ante* saving. Since, in accord with the accelerator concept, *ex ante* investment depends upon the rise in output, the necessary condition for equilibrium is that output (or income) rise sufficiently to induce enough investment to absorb the saving of the current income period. If this happens, then we can properly speak, as Harrod does, of the growth rate being a *warranted growth rate.*

The Actual Rate of Growth

The second crucial rate of growth in Harrod's analysis is the *actual rate of growth,* which represents the *ex post* percentage change in output between the present and the past income period. Algebraically, the actual rate of growth is:

$$G = \frac{\Delta Y}{Y} \qquad (15\text{–}13)$$

The actual rate of growth, G, to quote Harrod, is "the increment of total production in any unit period expressed as a fraction of total production."[22]

Harrod's fundamental equation pertaining to the actual, or *ex post,* performance of the economy is as follows:

$$G \times C = s \qquad (15\text{–}14)$$

G represents the actual rate of growth as defined above, while s is the actual saving ratio, which is assumed in Harrod's analysis to be the same always as the *ex ante* saving ratio. C may be defined as the actual (or *ex post*) as distinct from the intended (or *ex ante*) capital requirement (or accelerator). In other words, C is simply the ratio of the actual increase in the capital stock, ΔK or I'_n, to the actual change in output, ΔY. If we substitute algebraically in Equation (15–14) in the same way as we did earlier in equation (15–8), we have:

$$\frac{\Delta Y}{Y} \times \frac{I'_n}{\Delta Y} = \frac{S}{Y} \qquad (15\text{–}15)$$

Since once again the ΔY's on the left-hand side of the equation cancel out, we now have:

$$\frac{I'_n}{Y} = \frac{S}{Y} \qquad (15\text{–}16)$$

22. Ibid., p. 77.

This equation simply means that investment *ex post* is equal to saving *ex post*. This is always true, irrespective of the income level. What Harrod has done is simply to place this truism in a growth context.

The Growth Process: The Actual and the Warranted Rates Compared

It should be apparent that, algebraically, the expression $G_w \times C_r$ equals the expression $G \times C$, since both are equal to s, the *ex ante* and *ex post* propensity to save. However, it does not follow that G_w necassarily equals G or C_r equals C. There is no inherent reason, in other words, why the actual rate of growth experienced by the economy should correspond with the warranted rate. Nor need the actual change in the capital stock in an income period coincide with the intended change in capital stock in the same income period. Let us analyze what the results will be if G and G_w do not coincide.

We shall assume, first, that the actual rate of growth is greater than the warranted rate, that is, $G > G_w$. It then follows algebraically that C_r is greater than C. But if this is true it means that *ex ante* (planned) investment is greater than *ex post* (actual) investment in the current income period, because C_r conceived of as the accelerator shows the amount of intended investment induced by a given change income. Thus, if C_r is really greater than C, it has to mean that $C_r \times \Delta Y$ is greater than $C \times \Delta Y$ because ΔY is the same in both instances.

When investment *ex ante* is in excess of investment *ex post*, aggregate demand is greater than aggregate supply, a condition that, in Keynesian terms, will lead to an expansion in income and employment. To put the matter differently, we can say that when G is greater than G_w the economy is in a situation in which output has grown, but aggregate demand has grown even faster. In such circumstances the economy will experience a chronic shortage of capital, as investment *ex post* continously falls short of investment *ex ante*. The outcome will be further pressure on planned, or *ex ante*, investment as entrepreneurs seek to make good the economy's capital shortage, but such a reaction only serves to drive the actual rate of growth further and further from the warranted rate. Thus, it is Harrod's contention that any movement away from the line of steady advance represented by his warranted rate of growth tends to be cumulative in its effect; departures of the actual growth rate from the warranted or equilibrium rate do not, in other words, set in motion forces tending toward a restoration of equilibrium. Equilibrium once disturbed leads to a disequilibrium which becomes progressively worse.

The nature of the process of cumulative expansion envisaged by Harrod when G is in excess of G_w can be demonstrated diagrammatically. For this we can utilize the usual Keynesian type of income determination diagram, as is done in Figure 15–6. Let us assume that the income level, which initially is at Y_1, moves to the level Y_2. The change in income is thus equal to the distance Y_1Y_2, while the actual rate of growth, G, is equal to the ratio Y_1Y_2/Y_1. Since this growth rate is greater than the warranted rate, C_r is greater than C. As a consequence, the amount of investment induced by the change in income from Y_1 to Y_2 is seen to be equal to the distance C_2D_2. But since this amount of investment is greater than the amount prevailing at the prior income level, the aggregate demand schedule has, in effect, shifted from $C + I_1$ to $C + I_2$. Aggregated demand now exceeds aggregate supply at the income level Y_2, and this in turn tends to drive the economy toward the income level Y_3. Again the change in income from Y_2 to Y_3 induces an amount of investment expenditure C_3D_3, that is greater than necessary to achieve equilibrium at the income level Y_3. Investment *ex ante*, in other words, once again exceeds investment *ex post*, and thus the income level will be driven still higher. The departure from the initial equilibrium, the income level Y_1, has not, as shown in the hypothetical model, brought a restoration of equilibrium; rather, forces have been set in motion that drive the economy further and further from the initial equilibrium position. In this situation, saving becomes a virtue, in that a higher rate of saving means, algebraically, an increase in the warranted rate of growth, and thus restoration of equality between the actual rate and the warranted rate. More saving will permit a greater amount of actual investment in each income period, and this will tend to reduce the economy's capital shortage which, in turn, is the main reason why aggregate demand continuously runs ahead of aggregate supply.

The alternative to the situation just described is one in which the warranted rate of growth is greater than the actual rate of growth, that is, $G_w > G$. If this is the case, it must follow that C is greater than C_r; the ratio of actual investment to the change in income is greater than the ratio of intended (planned) investment to the change in income. Investment *ex ante* in the current period falls short of investment *ex post* and consequently, excess capacity will appear, making it impossible for the economy to continue to advance at the same rate as in the past. In other words, a situation in which G_w is greater than G indicates a tendency in the economy toward stagnation and a chronic excess of productive capacity. In such circumstances it will be difficult enough to sustain any growth at all for a significant length of time, let alone at a rate that will justify itself only if net investment is continually increasing in absolute amount.

For a better understanding of what takes place when G_w is greater than G let us refer once again to an income determination diagram. In Figure 15–7 we will begin, as we have done previously, with an assumed full employment equilibrium income level, Y_1. Now if income rises to the

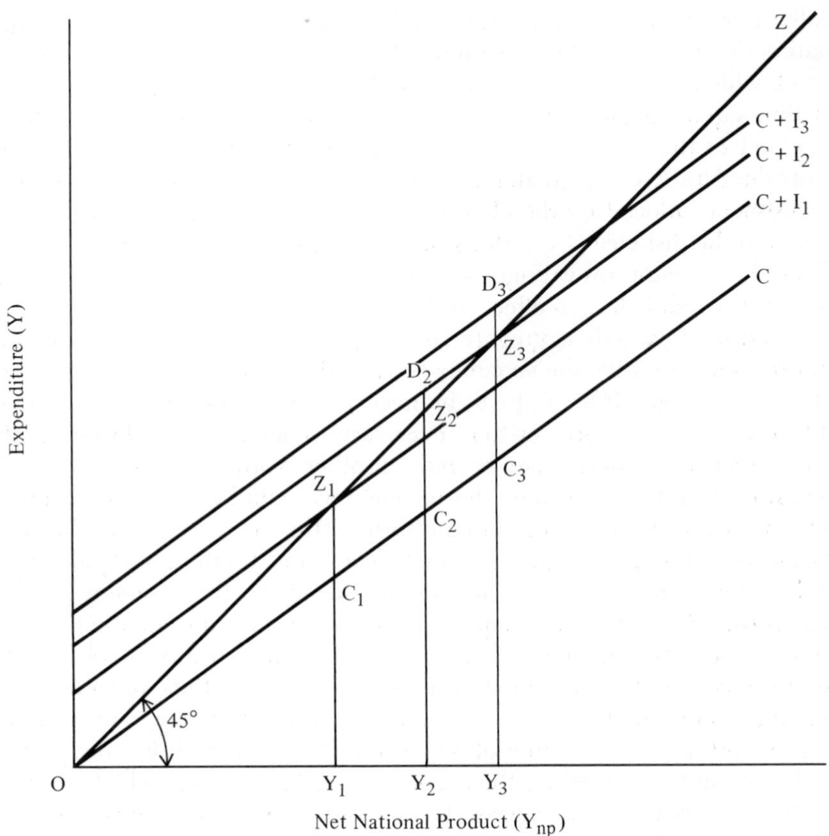

FIGURE 15–6. The Actual Rate of Growth in Excess of the Warranted Rate of Growth

level Y_2, the actual rate of growth, G again is equal to the ratioY_1Y_2/Y_1. Since, however, the accelerator C_r, is smaller than the actual capital coefficient, C, the amount of investment induced by the change in income falls short of the *ex post* investment at the higher income level.

Ex post investment at the income level Y_2 is represented by the distance C_2Z_2, which is also equal to both *ex post* and *ex ante* saving at this income level. The change in income from Y_1 to Y_2, however induces an amount of investment equal to the distance C_2D_2, which falls short of actual investment at the Y_2 income level. Aggregate demand has shifted upward from $C + I_1$ to $C + I_2$ but the shift is not great enough to sustain the actual growth experienced by the economy when income moved from Y_1 to Y_2. At Y_2, aggregate demand now falls short of aggregate supply, so this income level cannot be sustained.

To summarize Harrod's analysis briefly at this point we can say that the necessary condition for an equilibrium rate of growth is that the actual rate be equal to the warranted rate. This means that in each income period investment, which is linked to the rate at which income has grown in the immediate past, will be equal to the planned saving of the income period. Furthermore, Harrod's analysis asserts that if G and G_w are not equal, which is a condition of disequilibrium, the result will not be a restoration of equilibrium or a return to conditions in which G and G_w are equal but rather a greater and greater divergence between G and G_w. The growth process in Harrod's view is an inherently unstable phenomenon, as even the slightest departure from the exceedingly narrow path of an equilibrium rate of growth sets in motion forces making for either secular expansion and inflation or secular stagnation.

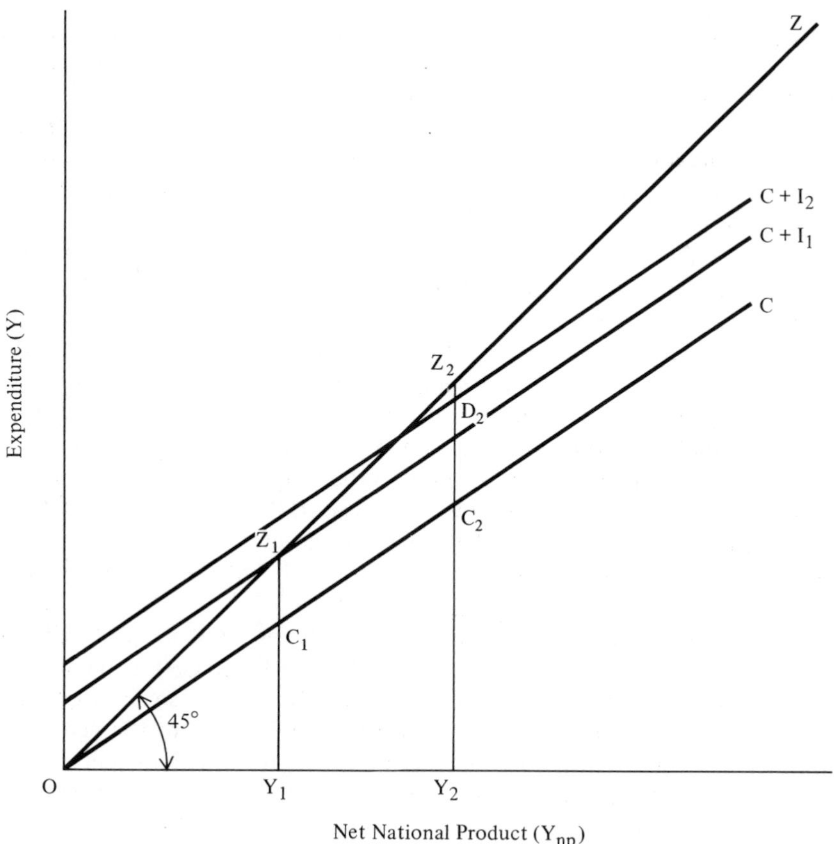

FIGURE 15–7. The Warranted Rate of Growth in Excess of the Actual Rate of Growth

The Natural Rate of Growth

For a complete picture of the growth process as seen by Harrod it is necessary to introduce still another rate of growth. This is the *natural rate of growth,* which Harrod describes as "the rate of advance which the increase of population and technological improvements allow."[23] The use of the term *natural* is somewhat misleading. Harrod is not referring to any growth rate that comes about automatically as a consequence of the free play of market forces. It would be more accurate to describe this particular growth rate as the potential or even *maximum feasible rate of growth,* since Harrod is really talking about the rate of growth required for the full employment of a growing labor force. Such a rate of growth depends upon, first, the average annual rate of increase in the labor force, and, second, the average annual rate of increase in the productivity of labor. If, for example, population and the labor force are growing at an annual average rate of 1 percent while output per worker is increasing, on the average, at the rate of 2 percent per year, the rate of growth necessary to maintain full employment of labor is 3 percent per year.

Introduction of the concept of a natural, or feasible, rate of growth into his analysis better enables Harrod to describe the conditions under which the economy will tend toward a condition of either secular stagnation or secular exhilaration. This is possible because there is no inherent reason, in Harrod's view, for the natural growth rate, G_n, and the warranted growth rate, G_w, to coincide. These two rates may be equal, but the more normal situation, in Harrod's view, is one of divergence between the natural and the warranted rate of growth. For example, Harrod asserts that the economy will tend toward secular stagnation if G_w is greater than G_n. The logic of Harrod's position is that, other than for short intervals of time, G cannot exceed G_n. Because given the rate at which the productivity of labor is increasing, the available labor supply will set a ceiling on the rate at which output can actually grow. If this is true, and if G_w is greater than G_n, it follows that G_w will be greater than G. Most of the time, in other words, the actual rate of growth will be below the warranted rate of growth.

But the above condition is one in which investment *ex post* will run ahead of investment *ex ante*, and, consequently, excess capacity will appear. Because the accelerator is weak, the increase in aggregate demand is not sufficient to absorb into use all additions to the economy's capital stock. Such additions, of course, are determined by net *ex post* investment in the income period. If this is the economy's situation, it means basically that over time the economy will tend toward chronic underemployment of all resources, that is, secular stagnation.

Another way in which we can describe this situation is to say that the rate of growth required for the full utilization of a growing capital stock

23. Ibid., p. 87.

is greater than the rate of growth required for the full employment of a growing labor force. This will foster excess capacity and with it the impossibility of sustaining the existing growth rate, even though this rate is below the warranted rate.

The warranted rate of growth is interpreted as a full capacity (as distinct from a full employment of labor) rate of growth. In what sense is this true? The concept of the warranted rate of growth is concerned with the amount of added capital needed to sustain added output. Therefore, the warranted (or justifiable) rate of growth is one that induces just enough of an upward shift in the schedule of aggregate demand (see Figure 15–6) so that the added capacity represented by net *ex post* investment at each successive higher level of income will be utilized. But the rate of growth that will induce a sufficient shift upward in the aggregate demand schedule to absorb into use a growing productive capacity does not necessarily have to be equal to a rate of growth that will give full employment to a growing labor force. This is basically what Harrod is attempting to demonstrate by asserting that the natural rate of growth does not necessarily have to equal the warranted rate.

The alternative situation suggested by Harrod is one in which the natural rate is greater than the warranted rate. In this instance, Harrod reasons that the actual rate of growth will stay above the warranted rate most of the time. As described earlier, *ex post* investment will continuously fall short of *ex ante* investment, with a consequent chronic shortage of real capital. Aggregate demand will run ahead of aggregate supply, the inducement to invest will remain high, and thus the economy will find itself in a state of secular exhilaration.

Concluding Observations on the Domar-Harrod Analysis of Economic Growth

Both the Domar and Harrod approaches to the broad problem of economic growth in an advanced economy accord investment the central role in the growth process. Furthermore, both Domar and Harrod undertake their analyses of the process of growth within an analytical, Keynesian framework. They agree that the central problem in the growth process in an advanced economy is that of the conditions under which planned investment will be continuously equated with a growing absolute volume of planned saving. Domar and Harrod are also in agreement with respect to the key role of saving, since their analyses are based on the assumption of a constant average and marginal propensity to save, and on the further assumption that actual and planned saving are always equal.

The two analyses differ mainly in the way in which they look at the investment process. Domar's analysis looks ahead in the sense that he stresses the effect of today's net investment on tomorrow's capacity or productive potential, and thus seeks to determine the rate at which the economy must grow if this productive capacity is to be absorbed into use in the future. He is concerned primarily with the essentially technical question of the effect of present investment on future capacity. Harrod's analysis, on the other hand, tends to look backward in the sense that he is seeking to determine if output has actually grown enough between yesterday and today so as to induce an amount of net investment sufficient to absorb today's full employment saving. Although his analysis rests in a fundamental sense on a technological relationship between output and capital, Harrod's key analytical tool is the concept of the accelerator, since this is the coefficient that links current investment to changes in the output level. Harrod's analysis centers primarily on the reaction of entrepreneurs to past changes in the income level, and assumes that if entrepreneurs in the aggregate are satisfied with the past rate of growth, they will act in such a way as to promote future growth in the economy at the same rate.

Both the Domar and the Harrod analyses of the growth process are subject to the same general criticism of being perhaps excessively abstract and too dependent (insofar as their conclusions with respect to the economy's ability to achieve a satisfactory rate of growth are concerned) on some rather rigid assumptions concerning the values and fixity of such critical determinants as the propensity to save and the capital coefficient. Harrod in particular, can be criticized for placing too much stress on the phenomenon of induced investment as the crucial factor in the growth process. As a consequence, there emerges a picture of the economy tied tightly to a very narrow path of growth—with the twin disasters of either secular exhilaration and inflation or secular stagnation threatening in the event of the slightest divergence from the precisely determined path of advance.[24] This has been described as movement along a razor's edge equilibrium path of output.

Despite the shortcomings we have noted, the analyses of Domar and Harrod, by directing our attention to such strategically important ideas as the capacity creating efforts of net investment and the phenomenon of accelerator-induced investment, do succeed in providing important insights into the operation of the real-world economy. More specifically, their theories enable us to understand, first, why the economy must grow

24. Harrod's analysis appears unnecessarily rigid because it is built almost entirely around the concept of induced investment. He does recognize, however, that some investment is autonomous in that it is not directly linked to immediate output requirements. The existence of such investment obviously reduces the amount of current saving that must be absorbed into investment as a consequence of past changes in the income level. The same is also true for net foreign investment, as the excess of exports over imports may also provide an outlet for current saving through foreign lending. The introduction of autonomous investment and the foreign balance makes the economy's growth path somewhat less precarious than originally suggested by Harrod.

if full employment is to be maintained, and, second, why the economy cannot be expected to grow automatically at a rate that will insure full employment.

APPENDIX

Neoclassical Growth Theory

The razor edge character of the Harrod-Domar analysis has been attacked by a number of economists as being excessively rigid and unrealistic.[1] The basic point of contention is the assumption in the Harrod-Domar analysis of a fixed value for the capital-output ratio (K/Y) and its reciprocal, the productivity of capital coefficient—Domar's σ. It is this feature which gives the analysis its razor's edge character, as the economy is tied tightly to a narrow equilibrium path. As Harrod demonstrates, any departure from this equilibrium $(G_w = G)$ leads either to a surging expansion or a plunging collapse.

What the neoclassical critics of the Harrod-Domar analysis seek to show is that the economy in a growth context is stable and that it will, if left to its own devices, seek out a steady-state equilibrium growth path. There is a basic similarity here to the monetarist approach to the economy's behavior, for, like the monetarists, the neoclassical theorists are challenging the Keynesian notion that the economy is inherently unstable.

This approach is called neoclassical for several reasons. It assumes that full employment is normally present as the economy grows; hence savings are continuously absorbed by investment. A competitive economy, diminishing returns, and returns to the factors of production equal to their marginal products are also assumed. But most important for our purposes is the key assumption of the substitutability of capital for labor—and vice versa. In contrast to Harrod-Domar, the capital-output ratio and its converse, the productivity of capital, σ, are variable. It is this feature of the neoclassical theory that permits the system to move toward a steady-state equilibrium path of growth.

The essentials of the neoclassical model can be demonstrated with a simple diagram, as shown in Figure 15–8. The horizontal axis in the diagram shows different values for the output-capital ratio (Domar's σ), and the vertical axis represents the rate of growth of output $(\Delta Y/Y)$ and the capital stock $(\Delta K/K)$. Given a positive value for the propensity to save,

1. See especially Robert M. Solow, "A Contribution to the Theory of Economic Growth," *Quarterly Journal of Economics*, February 1956; and T. W. Swan, "Economic Growth and Capital Accumulation," *Economic Record*, November 1956. The model in this Appendix is a simplified version of the one developed by Professor Swan in the latter article.

the rate of growth of output will be greater, the greater is the value of the output-capital ratio. Domar's analysis should make this clear, for if all saving is invested (an assumption of the neoclassical analysis), then the larger the amount of saving the greater will be the effect on productive capacity as the value of σ increases. Since full employment is assumed, it necessarily follows that the rate of growth of real output will be a positive function of σ. The real output growth line ($\Delta Y/Y$) crosses the vertical axis at a positive growth rate because some growth will take place as a result of a growing labor force and independently of the value of σ.[2]

The rate of growth of the capital stock ($\Delta K/K$) will be proportional to the output-captal ratio (Y/K, or σ), given a fixed value for the propensity to save. This can be shown quite simply. If s is the long-term propensity to save, then S (saving) will be equal to sY. But since the neoclassical model assumes that full employment is the norm and that full employment savings are absorbed by investment, it follows that $sY = I = \Delta K$. If we divide $sY = \Delta K$ by K, we have sY/K or $s\sigma = \Delta K/K$, which shows that, given the propensity to save, s, the rate of growth of the capital stock is proportional to the output-capital rate (Y/K, or σ).

Now let us examine what happens in terms of the model shown in Figure 15–8. Suppose the economy is initially at a point at which the

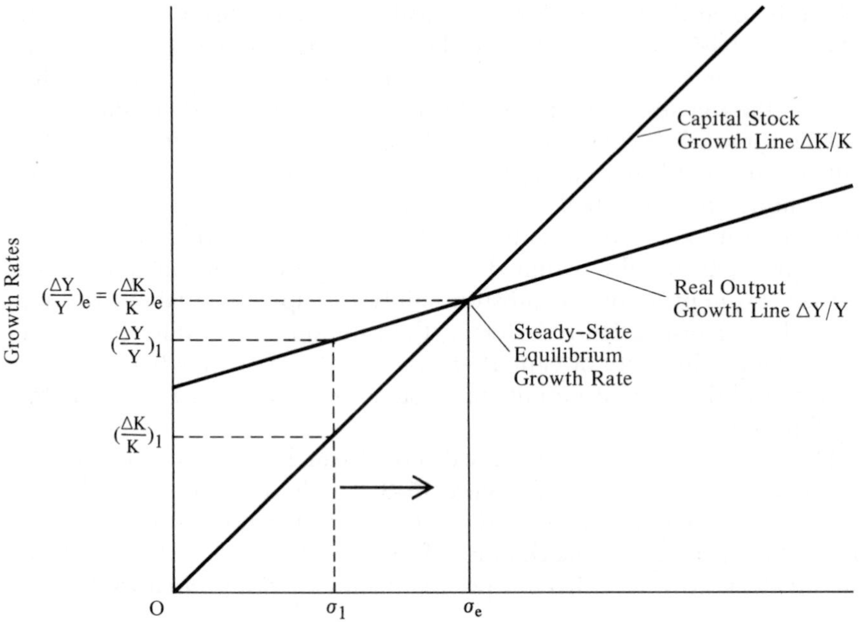

FIGURE 15–8. The Neoclassical Growth Model

2. See the Swan article for elaboration on this point.

value of the productivity of capital coefficient is σ_1. What does this show? If this is the situation it means that output is growing faster than the capital stock, that is, $(\Delta Y/Y)_1 > (\Delta K/K)_1$. In the neoclassical world when this happens, the productivity of capital will rise and capital will be substituted for labor. This will tend to accelerate the rate of growth of both capital and output, but as long as the productivity of capital (σ) is increasing the rate of increase in the capital stock will have to accelerate more than the rate of increase in output. This will continue until the two growth rates become equal—the point of intersection of the capital stock growth line and the real output growth line—and a steady-state equilibrium growth rate will prevail.

Contrast this with the Harrod analysis. If output is growing more rapidly than the capital stock, it means the economy faces a chronic shortage of capital. In Harrod's terminology, G is greater than G_w, which means an explosive upward surge in planned investment and the sytem moves further and further away from the equilibrium growth rate of $G = G_w$. Only the full employment ceiling set by the natural growth rate G_n halts the upsurge.

What happens in the neoclassical model when the output-capital ratio is at a value which has the capital stock growing faster than output? This would be to the right of σ_e in Figure 15–8. In this case, the productivity of capital will decline, labor will be substituted for capital, and this process will continue until the income-capital ratio has fallen sufficiently to bring the rate of growth of the capital stock into line with the rate of growth of output; a steady-state equilibrium will again prevail. In the Harrod analysis, however, this situation is one in which excess capacity develops ($G_w > G$), and a cumulative downward movement gets underway, a collapse that will continue until the system works off its excess capacity. Without public intervention this might take a long while.

Neither the Harrod-Domar nor the neoclassical approach taken in isolation provides a wholly adequate theoretical analysis of the problems an advanced market economy confronts in attempting to attain both growth and full employment over time. Even though its underlying assumptions are more rigid than can be justified, the Harrod-Domar analysis underscores two important aspects of the economy. The first is the capacity-creating effect of net investment, and the second is the inherent instability typical of a market system. Experience tends to confirm this view more than it does the neoclassical (and monetarist) view that the system is inherently stable. On the other hand, the neoclassical analysis helps us understand that the kind of precarious knife edge equilibrium found in Harrod-Domar is probably much too extreme a view of how the system really works. Perfect substitutability of capital for labor does not exist in reality, but neither do absolutely rigid capital-output ratios in most instances. Thus, there must be some blending of the two approaches if we are to obtain a workable and realistic theory.

16

Business Cycles and Forecasting

In a broad sense this chapter extends the theme of the last chapter—economic growth. The difference is that we are concerned now with historical patterns of growth and the tools economists use to predict future changes in the economy. For economic growth does not occur at a steady rate; it proceeds by fluctuations—ups and downs if you will.

Figure 16–1 plots the uneven nature of the economy's performance over nearly two centuries. This chart shows the deviations of an index of general business activity from the long-term trend of the economy. The latter, of course, has been upward; as we saw in the prior chapter the long-term rate of growth of the American economy has been around 3.5 percent per year. But this is a trend, not the reality of any given year. What Figure 16–1 reveals is that progress over time is sporadic, proceeding in a rough cyclical fashion in which a period of expansion is always followed by a period of contraction.

Historically the term "business cycle" has been used to describe the periodic ups and downs which characterize the actual movement through time of the real economy. The reason for using the word *cycle* is because economic activity over the long pull does follow a wavelike pattern with a significant amount of regularity. But there is some danger in using this term because it carries the connotation of more regularity than is the reality. For a period of time after World War II the term "business cycle" fell out of favor among economists, in part because the long post war economic upswing gave rise to a belief—now seen as naive—that the business cycle was a thing of the past. "Fluctuations" came to be the preferred term, particularly because it does not imply a regular wavelike motion as does the word *cycles*. As a result of the experiences of the 1970s—especially the severe downturn in 1974–75—the idea of the business cycle has come back into fashion.[1] In the final analysis, the name used is less important than the reality; our economy has not experienced a smooth growth path in the part nor is it likely to in the foreseeable future.

Our objectives in this chapter are basically three. First, we shall examine the nature of the business cycle—how it is defined, how it is measured, and what happens during the course of a typical cycle. Second, we shall take a broad, historical look at some of the ideas economists have stressed as explanations for the cycle. Finally, we shall examine the general area of economic forecasting, including a review of the nature and effectiveness of the major forecasting techniques. Forecasting exists because the business cycle exists. If the economy always proceeded upward along a smooth trend line, then it would only be necessary to extrapolate the past in order to know what would happen in the future. Unhappily, the world is not that simple. Hence, there is a necessity for economic forecasting.

The Nature of the Business Cycle

We have, in fact, already defined the business cycle. A formal definition would be *a wavelike movement in the general level of economic activity that takes place over time.* Such a definition is broad enough to apply to the business cycle as a general phenomenon encompassing the entire economy, or to the many individual types of economic activity which are a part of a more general picture. A couple of important points need to be stressed. First, the business cycle is wavelike, but it is not regular in an exact periodic sense. Motions of the latter sort are characteristic of many physical phenomena—electrical current, for example—but not of economic activity. Second, the business cycle is an economic phenomenon characteristic of *all* countries organized on market principles, which is to say organized on the basis of private property and the pursuit of private gain. Further, major business cycles occur at the same time in the leading industrial nations. Business cycle research shows, for example that this has been true in both the nineteenth and twentieth centuries for such major industrial powers as Germany, France, Great Britain, and the United States. It is not true for the minor cycles, and it is not true that all major industrial nations have had the same number of business cycles. But in a broad, historical sense it is clear that the business cycle is an international phenomenon deeply rooted in the behavior patterns of market economies.

1. For example, a recent article in *Business Week* magazine discussing the 1974–75 recession was headed "The Business Cycle is Alive and Well." See *Business Week,* April 19, 1976.

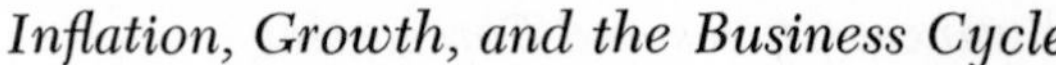

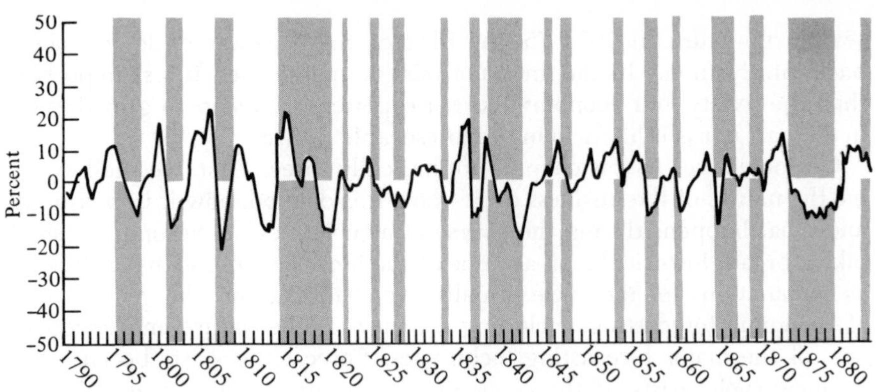

Shaded Areas Represent Recessions and Depressions
Note: Based on data from the Cleveland Trust.

FIGURE 16–1. Business Activity, 1790–1975: Deviation from the Long-Term Trend

In the United States the most important work in defining, measuring, and understanding the business cycle has been done by the National Bureau of Economic Research, a privately funded research organization located in New York City. In Chapter 2, the reader will recall, it was pointed out that the National Bureau pioneered in the development of national income accounting in this country. Wesley Mitchell, a long-time leader in business cycle research, was instrumental in the creation of the National Bureau. Mitchell was the foremost advocate of the view that the cycle involves a continuing, self-generating process which is inherent in a capital-using economy organized around the exchange of money for goods and goods for money in private markets. In his classic study of fluctuations, *What Happens During Business Cycles,* Mitchell defined the cycle as follows (his definition remains as the working concept of the cycle used by the National Bureau of Economic Research):

> Business cycles are a type of fluctuation found in the aggregate economic activity of nations that organize their work mainly in business enterprises: a cycle consists of expansion occurring at about the same time in many economic activities, followed by similarly general recessions, contractions, and revivals which merge into the expansion phase of the next cycle; this sequence of events is recurrent, but not periodic; in duration business cycles vary from more than one year to ten or twelve years; they are not divisible into shorter cycles of similar character with amplitudes approximating their own.[2]

Thus the business cycle as seen by Mitchell pertains primarily to fluctuations in the overall level of economic activity, affecting most industries

2. Wesley C. Mitchell, *What Happens During Business Cycles.* (New York: National Bureau of Economic Research, 1951), p. 6.

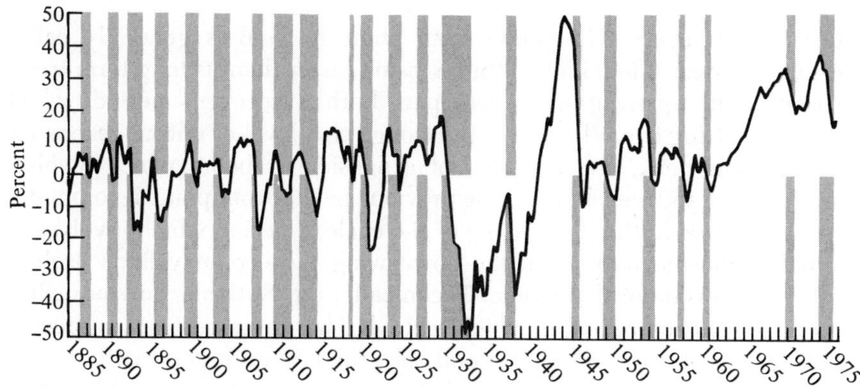

and activities at about the same time. It is a recurrent process, but not regular in either the magnitude of fluctuations or the frequency with which they occur.

Measuring the Business Cycle

There are various possible ways in which the business cycle can be measured but the one most widely used is the method developed by the National Bureau of Economic Research. This method is also used by the U.S. Department of Commerce, which, in its monthly periodical *Business Conditions Digest*, publishes the most comprehensive volume of data from any source on what is happening to the economy in a cyclical sense. For its purposes the National Bureau measures the business cycle from trough to peak to trough, although it is just as possible to measure it from peak to trough to peak.

Figure 16–2 shows a simplified, "idealized" cycle in which real GNP moves from point A (an initial trough or lower turning point) through point B (the peak or upper turning point) and back down to Point C (a second trough), from whence a new cycle will begin. The fluctuations take place around a trend line which incorporates the economy's long-term growth rate. Because the economy is growing, each peak and each trough normally will be a higher level than the prior peak or trough. The word "normally" is used advisedly in this context, as a glance at the long-term behavior of the economy shown in Figure 16–1 shows it does not always happen this way, especially when the economy collapses to the extent it did during the Great Depression of the 1930s.

Figure 16–2 includes additional technical information on the nature of the business cycle. The phase from point A to B is generally called *upswing*, a period in which output is rising faster than its long term trend. Normally an upswing will encompass both a recovery period, which involves getting from the low of the trough to a level of output reached at the previous peak, and a period of expansion or boom which involves output rising to levels beyond the previous peak. From point B to point C the economy is in the *downswing* of the cycle, a period which involves an actual decline of output. In the downswing the economy finds itself in either a recession or depression. Technically, the National Bureau defines a recession as any period in which *real* GNP has dropped for two successive quarters (six months). Beyond this, there is no precise definition of what constitutes a *recession* and what constitutes a *depression*. The difference between the two is a matter of judgment, depending upon the depth of the fall in output (the rise in unemployment) and the length of the downswing or slump in economic activity. Most citizens have no trouble identifying the collapse of the 1930s as a depression because of its length and severity. Since World War II, however, the term recession has generally been used, the reason being the relative mildness of downturns, save for the 1974–75 slump. The extent to which output—or any other economic variable—departs from the long-term trend is described as the *amplitude* of the cycle. It is normally measured as the average deviation (expressed as a percentage) of the series from its trend. Amplitude may be measured with respect to the entire cycle or for specific periods (a month, for example) within the cycle.

How frequent and how lengthy are business cycles in the United

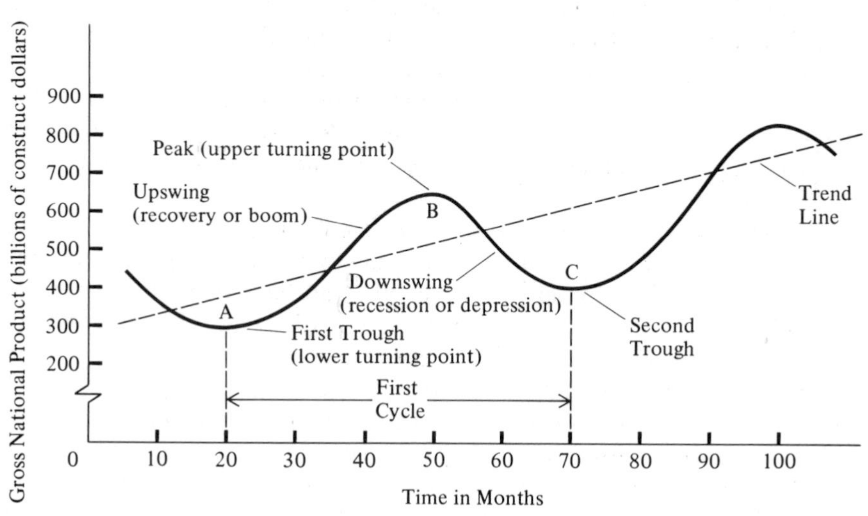

FIGURE 16–2. A Simplified Cycle Pattern

States? Although no precise answer can be given to this question because satisfactory data are lacking for the early years of the nation, reasonably good estimates are available. Figure 16–1 shows 41 periods of recession since 1790. These data, the reader should note, refer only to the downswing in the index of general business activity. Thus, the shaded areas shown in Figure 16–1 do not measure a full cycle as defined by the National Bureau of Economic Research which has developed data on the business cycle using the trough to trough method for the period 1854–1975. These findings are shown in Table 16–1.

In the period covered by the data of Table 16–1 there have been 28 full cycles, averaging 52 months in length (from trough to trough). The expansion phase has been almost twice as long as the contraction phase. On the average, since 1854, periods of expanding economic activity have averaged 33 months—or nearly three years—while the downturns typically have been slightly less than two years, averaging 19 months. The data of Table 16–1 also indicate some significant changes in the cyclical pattern of the economy following World War II. Since 1945 we have had six measurable business cycles, but the significant development has been an increase in the length of the expansion and prosperity phase of the cycle and a reduction in the average length of the downturn. After World War II expansions were 48 percent longer and contractions 42 percent shorter than the long term average for the economy (1845–1975). In part this was the result of the unusually long upswing of the 1960s, but not wholly since upswings for three out of the four cycles recorded between 1945 and 1961 were also longer than the historic average.

It was the mildness of cycles—especially the downswings—in the post-World War II era which gave rise to the belief that the business cycle had been tamed by modern monetary and fiscal policy. This attitude was summed up by the Kansas City Federal Reserve Bank in the following comment:

> Ironically, in the late 1960s, after nearly a decade of almost uninterrupted growth, a widespread notion developed that the old-style business cycle was extinct. It was suggested that the definition of the business cycle be expanded to include periods of retarded growth. The title of a government publication was changed from *Business Cycle Developments* to *Business Conditions Digest.* Unfortunately, the business cycle was not dead.[3]

As mentioned, belief that the business cycle was dead collapsed in the face of the unexpected severity of the 1974–75 slump, the worst economic downturn experienced by the economy since the 1930s. Not only was the falloff in output more severe than any of the other post World War II recessions, but the contraction phase lasted 16 months, a period only

3. Federal Reserve Bank of Kansas City, *Business Conditions,* March 1975, p. 11.

TABLE 16–1. Duration of Business Cycle Expansions and Contractions in the United States, 1854–1975

Business Cycle			*Duration (in months) of—*		
Trough	*Peak*	*Trough*	*Expansion*	*Contraction*	*Full Cycle*
Dec., 1854	June, 1857	Dec., 1858	30	18	48
Dec., 1858	Oct., 1860	June, 1861	22	8	30
June, 1861	Apr., 1865	Dec., 1867	46	32	78
Dec., 1867	June, 1869	Dec., 1870	18	18	36
Dec., 1870	Oct., 1873	Mar., 1879	34	65	99
Mar., 1879	Mar., 1882	May, 1885	36	38	74
May, 1885	Mar., 1887	Apr., 1888	22	13	35
Apr., 1888	July, 1890	May, 1891	27	10	37
May, 1891	Jan., 1893	June, 1894	20	17	37
June, 1894	Dec., 1895	June, 1897	18	18	36
June, 1897	June, 1899	Dec., 1900	24	18	42
Dec., 1900	Sept., 1902	Aug., 1904	21	23	44
Aug., 1904	May, 1907	June, 1908	33	13	46
June, 1908	Jan., 1910	Jan., 1912	19	24	43
Jan., 1912	Jan., 1913	Dec., 1914	12	23	35
Dec., 1914	Aug., 1918	Mar., 1919	44	7	51
Mar., 1919	Jan., 1920	July, 1921	10	18	28
July, 1921	May, 1923	July, 1924	22	14	36
July, 1924	Oct., 1926	Nov., 1927	27	13	40
Nov., 1927	Aug. 1929	Mar., 1933	21	43	64
Mar., 1933	May, 1937	June, 1938	50	13	63
June, 1938	Feb., 1945	Oct., 1945	80	8	88
Oct., 1945	Nov., 1948	Oct., 1949	37	11	48
Oct., 1949	July, 1953	Aug., 1954	45	13	58
Aug., 1954	July, 1957	Apr., 1958	35	9	44
Apr., 1958	May, 1960	Feb., 1961	25	9	34
Feb., 1961	Nov., 1969	Nov., 1970	105	12	117
Nov., 1970	Nov., 1973	Mar., 1975	36	16	58
Average, all cycles:					
28 cycles, 1854–1975			33	19	52
12 cycles, 1919–1975			42	15	56
6 cycles, 1945–1975			49	11	60

SOURCE: *Business Conditions Digest*, April 1973, p. 115; May 1977, p. 11

slightly shorter than the historic average for bad times. Clearly the 1974–75 recession—or "mini-depression," as some choose to call it—was an old fashioned business cycle of the sort that was not supposed to happen. But it did.

Inflation and the Business Cycle

In one important sense, however, the most recent cycles—especially that of 1974–75—differ significantly from the "old-fashioned" business cycle of the pre-World War II years. This difference is inflation and its persistence through *all* phases of the cycle—the downswing as well as the upswing. This change has led the Conference Board to suggest that we are now experiencing a new type of cyclical experience, one characterized by fluctuations of widening intensity not only in output and employment, but also in the inflation rate.[4] In the view of the Conference Board economists, the cycle has changed in a way which makes it increasingly difficult to control by deployment of monetary and fiscal policy in the conventional counter-cyclical fashion. Figure 16–3 uses fluctuations in the industrial production index to illustrate the widening intensity of the cycle.

The root of the problem appears to be the new inflation, an inflation which does not seem to be "fundamentally cyclical; rather, it looks like a new strain, highly resistent to conventional anti-inflationary policy, and flagrantly in violation of theoretical explanations of price behavior. . . ."[5] What happens in the face of a persistent upward thrust in the price level is that attempts to bring inflation under control by putting on the monetary and fiscal brakes push the economy into a recession before they have any significant impact on prices. The recession may slow down the rate of

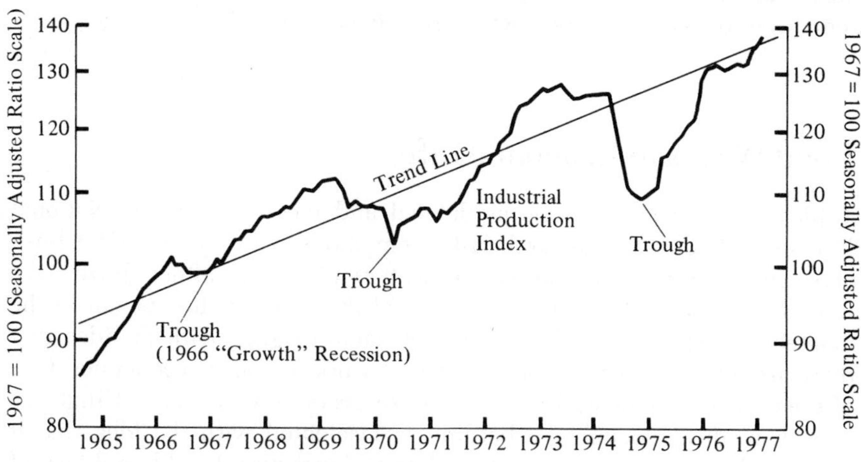

FIGURE 16–3. Cyclical Fluctuations in Industrial Production: 1965–1977

4. Albert T. Sommers with Lucie R. Blau, *The Widening Cycle: An Examination of U.S. Experience with Stabilization Policy in the Last Decade* (New York: The Conference Borad, 1975).

5. Ibid., p. 3.

inflation, but it does not bring about an actual decline in prices. This is the major difference from earlier experiences. But since the public will no longer tolerate a significant rise in the unemployment rate, restrictive policies not only have to be abandoned, but thrown into reverse to pull the economy out of the recession. Thus policy alternates between "stop and go," which, as the Conference Board research suggests, pushes the economy into intensifying recessions as a consequence of our struggle against mounting inflation. It is clear that the 1970s experienced a resurgence and intensification of the economy's cyclical behavior, but it is not certain that this is the pattern of the future. This is yet to be determined, although the Conference Board believes that the renewal of the strength of the business cycle is associated with an inflationary trend that goes deeper than the cycle itself. In its view, the roots of the inflation lie not in any single cause—such as federal deficit spending, for example—but in the mutliple public and private demands placed upon the system from 1965 onwards. These demands mounted rapidly and, in effect, outran the economy's real capacity to satisfy them. Our goals, in other words, have outdistanced our means. Since the society has not developed adequate political mechanisms to adjudicate excessive claims upon a limited national output—fiscal and monetary policy were not adequate for this task—inflation has been the inevitable result. This leads the Conference Board to conclude that stable growth and stable prices will continue to elude us until we undertake a tough-minded, critical review of our national goals and discipline ourselves so that they do not exceed our real resource capabilities.[6] It remains to be seen if our democratic society can meet this challenge.

Long Waves in Economic Life

Typically the business cycle as defined and measured by the National Bureau of Economic Research lasts from three to five years. Most business cycle research has centered on this type of a cycle, although from the time research into the cyclical behavior of the economy first began in the nineteenth century there have been scholars intrigued with the idea that there are much longer economic waves at work in market economies. One of the earliest serious students of the business cycle was Clement Juglar, a French medical doctor who became so fascinated with the idea that it was possible through statistics to isolate and measure the ebb and flow of economic life that he gave up the practice of medicine and became an economist. Juglar was an early advocate of the idea that there were commercial cycles which occurred with considerable regularity. He saw that

6. Ibid., p. 36.

each cycle had a similar pattern, even though there was no uniformity with respect to either frequency or length. He suggested that cycles had three parts—prosperity, crisis, and liquidation—and that they always followed one another in the same order.[7] Juglar did think, however, that the average length of a cycle was 9 to 10 years, which is two to three times longer than the cycles recognized by contemporary theorists.

It was a Russian economist, Nikolai D. Kondratieff, whose name has become almost synonymous with the idea of long waves in economic life.[8] Kondratieff developed his theory of long waves by studying data on wholesale prices, interest rates, wage rates, and physical production for the French, British, and American economies. His studies covered the period from about 1780 to 1920 or almost a century and a half. From these studies he concluded that Western—that is, market or capitalistic—economies are subject to very long waves of a distinct cyclical character. These "Kondratieff cycles" are approximately 50 to 60 years in length with an upswing and downswing of about equal length. Further, they are international in scope and appeared about the same time in the major industrial states of Europe as well as the United States. Kondratieff did not offer any theoretical explanation to account for the existence of long waves, but he did suggest that they are inherent in a capitalistic economy.[9] Kondratieff's published research covered two-and-one-half long waves, extending roughly from the end of the 1780s to the beginning of the 1920s. Table 16–2 shows an "idealized" version of the Kondratieff long waves extrapolated to the present. These data are termed "idealized" because specific dates are shown for the turning points of the cycles, although Kondratieff's research specified a range of four or five years, rather than a specific year for the turning points.

Joseph A. Schumpeter, best known, perhaps, for his theory linking investment to innovation and invention (Chapter 7), developed a "model" of the business cycle which involved an integration of Kondratieffs' long wave theory with the ideas of Juglar and a third economist, Joseph Kitchin, who, writing in the early 1920s developed a theory involving major and minor cycles.[10] His minor cycle averaged 40 months in dura-

7. Wesley C. Mitchell, *Business Cycles: The Problem and the Setting,* (New York: National Bureau of Economic Research, 1927), p. 452.

8. Kondratieff developed his ideas about long waves in the early 1920s. He published a paper on the subject in Russian in 1925 which was subsequently translated into both German and English. The English version of his article may be found in *Readings in Business Cycle Theory* (Philadelphia: Blakiston Co., 1944), pp. 20–42. Kondratieff was a Marxist economist, but he disappeared from the Soviet scene sometime in the late 1920s. It has been reported that he incurred the displeasure of Stalin, was arrested, and banished to a Soviet labor camp. His real fate remains unknown.

9. Wesley C. Mitchell, *Business Cycles*, p. 228.

10. Joseph Kitchin, "Cycles and Trends in Economic Factors," *Review of Economic Statistics*, January 1923, pp. 10–16.

TABLE 16–2. "Idealized" Kondratieff Cycles: 1790–1970s

First Long Wave:	1790–1845	(55 years)
Expansion:	1790–1815	
Contraction:	1815–1845	
Second Long Wave:	1845–1895	(50 years)
Expansion:	1845–1870	
Contraction:	1870–1895	
*Third Long Wave:**	1895–1940	(45 years)
Expansion:	1895–1920	
Contraction:	1920–1935-40	
Fourth Long Wave:	1940–??	(?? years)
Expansion:	1940–70s	
Contraction:	1970s–??	

SOURCE: Nikolai D. Kondratieff, "The Long Waves in Economic Life" in *Reading in Business Cycle Theory* (Philadelphia: Blakiston Company, 1944), pp. 20–42.

*Published research by Kondratieff covered only 2½ cycles, 1790 to 1920.

tion and his major cycle consisted of three minor cycles, which made the Kitchin major about the same length as the cycle Juglar thought he had discovered (9 to 10 years). What Schumpeter did was combine the 40-month Kitchin cycle and the 10-year Juglar cycle with Kondratieff's long wave. In Schumpeter's scheme the Juglar cycle provided the link between the Kondratieff long wave and the much shorter Kitchin cycle. No special significance attaches to this, except in those rare instances when the downswings of all three cycles coincide. As Schumpeter said, "No claims are made for our three cycle scheme except that it is a useful descriptive or illustrative device. Using it, however, we in fact got *ex visu* of 1929, a 'forecast' of a serious depression embodied in the formula: coincidence of the depression phase of all three cycles."[11]

Contemporary students of the business cycle flatly reject the notion of long-waves in economic life, either of the Kondratieff variety or the shorter Juglar-type cycle. There are cycles—of this there is little doubt—but the general consensus among economists is that they average between three and five years in length, as is suggested by the data in Table 16–1. Minor cycles do exist, but most of these appear to be the result of inventory adjustments. Economists do not believe that there is any systematic relationship such as Kitchin described between minor cycles and a longer cycle of perhaps 10 years.

An economic historian, W. W. Rostow of the University of Texas, gives

11. Joseph A. Schumpeter, *Business Cycles* (New York: McGraw-Hill, 1939), Vol. I, p. 174.

credence to the Kondratieff concept of long waves, but interprets the phenomenon different from most business cycles theorists. He sees the long-wave theory primarily in terms of a price cycle whose true significance is found in the movement of the price of basic commodities (raw materials and food) *relative* to other prices. According to Rostow, there have been five times in the past two-hundred years when a rise in the relative price of basic commodities occurred, the most recent being the surge in energy, other raw materials, and food prices which began about 1972. The other four occasions began in the 1790s, the early 1850s, the latter part of the 1890s, and the late 1930s.[12] What happened in each of these earlier periods was food and raw material prices rose sharply and then fluctuated in a relatively high range for approximately a quarter of a century. Figure 16–4 plots an "idealized" Kondratieff cycle against the path of indices for wholesale and retail prices in the United States (1967=100) for the period 1790–1975.[13] As indicated earlier, the path of the Kondratieff cycle from 1920 onwards is an extrapolation, as Kondratieff's original findings covered the two-and-one-half cycles which he had actually measured through the early 1920s. In Rostow's analysis the upsurge of food and raw material prices (the upswing's of the Kondratieff cycle shown in Figure 16–4) were followed by a period of approximately equal length in which food and raw material prices were *relatively* cheap. Down to 1914, Rostow argues, the classic response of the world economy to the Kondratieff upswing was to open new agricultural lands to production (the American west, Canada, Australia, Argentina, and the Ukraine). In the Fourth upswing, which began in the late 1930s, the response took the form of more investment and a diffusion of technology which brought rapid productivity gains to food and other raw materials production. What is the lesson in this? Rostow believes that in the face of a Kondratieff upswing in the *relative* price of basic materials, an industrialized nation must increase or redirect investment in ways which will expand the supply of basic products or economize on their use. "The central operational fact about Kondratieff upswing is that the pattern of investment, the directions of investment, must change."[14] If we are in a Kondratieff upswing, it is fundamentally different from the past because it involves not just changes in the relative price of food and raw materials generally, but quite a new situation with respect not only to the price but also the supply of such absolutely fundamental resources as energy, water, not to mention a livable environment. One consequence, according to Rostow is

12. W. W. Rostow, "Caught by Kondratieff," *The Wall Street Journal,* March 8, 1977. See also "The Bankruptcy of Neo-Keynesian Economics," *Intermountain Economic Review,* Spring 1976, pp. 6–7.

13. These price data are charted by the Conference Board and the "idealized" Kondratieff cycle is imposed upon them.

14. Rostow, "Caught by Kondratieff."'

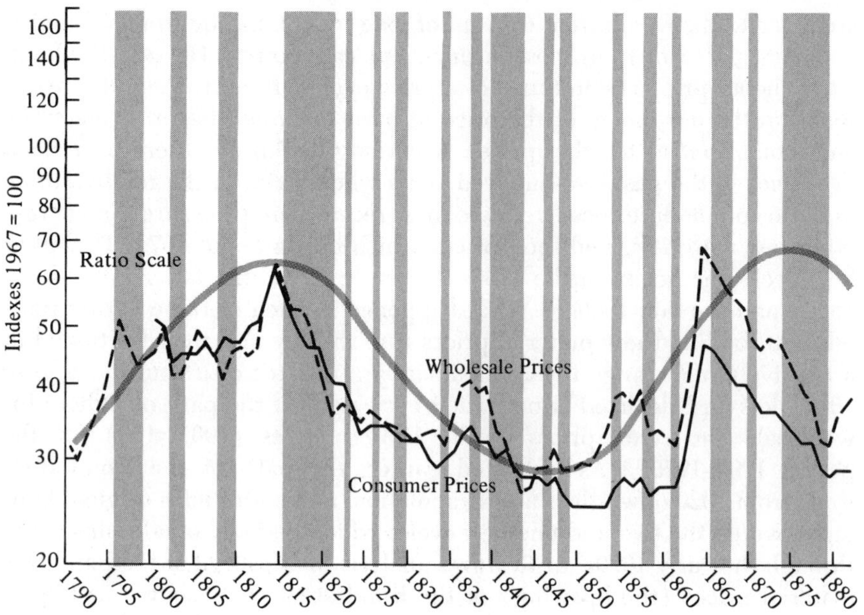

FIGURE 16–4. Long Waves in U.S. Economic Life

that we will have to depend relatively more on government and less on the workings of the market system for the necessary response to price movements during the most recent Kondratieff upswing.[15]

What Happens in a Typical Business Cycle

While it is true that no two business cycles are the same with respect to length, intensity, or other developments, it is also true that there is a basic pattern of events which is similar in all cycles. Thanks largely to the long, painstaking research of Wesley Mitchell, we have a clear picture of

15. Economists use the phrase "terms of trade" to refer to the movement of the prices for one group of commodities *relative* to another. Thus, a rise in food and raw material prices relative to other prices (as happens in a Kondratieff upswing) means a change in the terms of trade in favor of agricultural commodities and other raw material prices. The reason is easily understood. If, for example, the price of a bushel of wheat is going up faster than the price of other goods and services, then each bushel of wheat has more *real* purchasing power in terms of other goods and services. This is what Rostow says happens in the upswing of the Kondratieff cycle—the terms of trade turn in favor of food and other raw materials.

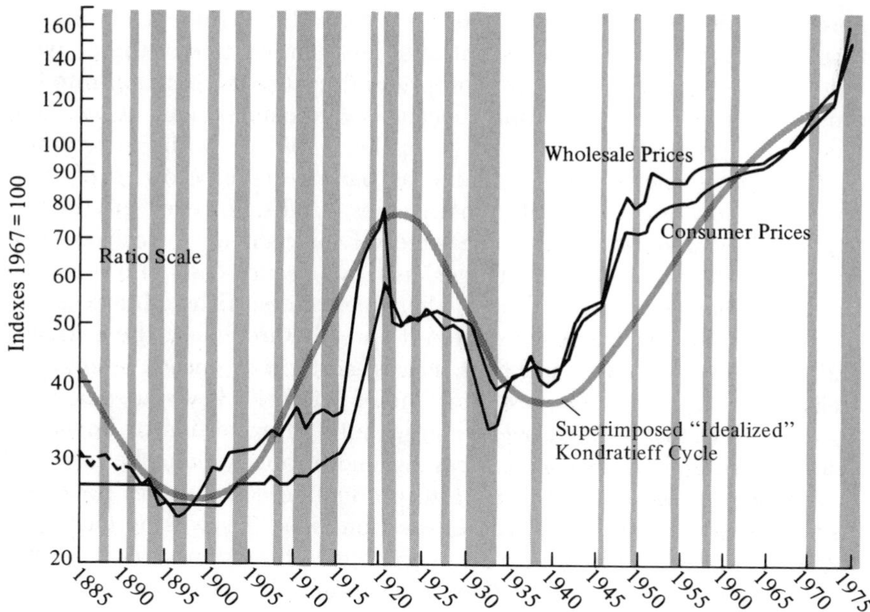

the most important things which happen in a business cycle. To arrive at a composite picture of the cycle, Mitchell examined over the course of his long and productive career the behavior of more than eight hundred time series.[16] He never did develop a precise theory of the business cycle, although when viewed overall his findings provide a reasonable and coherent explanation of the cyclical process.

There are two important points to note and understand with respect to Mitchell's view of the cycle. First, Mitchell—like many other economists—found the cycle to be inherent in money-using, market economies in which the quest for money profits by business enterprises is the dominant fact of economic life. Second, the processes at work in the typical cycle are cumulative and carry within themselves the seeds by which one phase of the cycle is transformed into the next phase.These processes are not only cumulative, but repetitive, from hence comes the fact that *all* cycles have certain common characteristics.

A convenient point of departure is a recession or depression. In the

16. Right up to the time of his death, Mitchell was still trying to find out empirically what actually happened in the cycle. His work over the years is summarized in his last book, published after his death. See Wesley G. Mitchell, *What Happens During Business Cycles: A Progress Report* (New York: National Bureau of Economic Research, Studies in Business Cycles 5, 1951). Our account of the sequence of events in a typical cycle is based largely on Mitchell's findings.

absence of deliberate policy actions by a central government (a tax cut, more spending, lowered interest rates, or any combination of these) what will bring a recovery? In a recession prices drop (or the inflation rate lessens), labor is in ample supply because of unemployment, wages and other costs go down (or at least go up less rapidly), while money and credit become increasingly available as bank reserves grow. Profits, of course, are low or nonexistent in many cases. Profits, however, are the key to a recovery. Somewhere, in some sector of the economy, a recovery will start when the profit picture changes, usually because costs in a recession—or depression—eventually drop farther than prices. Although a recovery tends to be slow at first, once started it spreads throughout the economy and becomes cumulative in effect. Prices start rising once a recovery is well under way. Here we encounter one of Mitchell's key statistical findings, which is that as a recovery merges into an expansion or boom the prices of finished goods and services rise more rapidly than the prices of those things which enter directly into production costs—wages for labor, rents for land and buildings, and interest on loans. There is no guarantee that this pattern will hold in a recovery, but to the extent it does, profits improve and the expansion gathers momentum. An improved profit picture not only stimulates current production which puts people back to work, it also stimulates investment spending as pessimism in the business community gives way to optimism.

Why doesn't prosperity continue indefinitely? What brings an expansion to an end? Basically what happens is that the cumulative process of recovery and expansion (or boom) is subject to two fundamental stresses, both built into market systems organized around profit-seeking business enterprises. One pertains to the production process itself and the other to the financial structure. We must keep in mind that the business cycle is a short-term phenomenon, which means that it takes place within a time period (three to five years) which does not permit large increases in productive capacity. Thus, as an expansion proceeds the costs of doing business will begin to rise, slowly at first but at an accelerating pace as prosperity proceeds. This comes about in part as firms push up against capacity limits set by the existing stock of equipment. The cost of labor will rise, not only because prosperity pushes up standard wage rates as firms scramble for increasingly scarce labor, but also because more overtime will be paid. Further, labor efficiency (worker productivity) declines as less skilled workers are pulled into the job market, older and less efficient equipment is pressed into use, while longer hours and pressure to turn out goods at an even faster pace causes more mistakes, waste, and numerous small inefficiencies, all of which increase the costs of doing business. At some point in an upswing prices of raw materials begin to rise faster than the selling prices for finished products, a development which puts further pressure on cost-price relationships and the profit picture.

In the meanwhile, parallel stresses are developing in the investment and money markets. Essentially what Mitchell found was that the supply of funds available for lending through the usual financial channels (the bond and mortgage markets) fails to keep pace with the demand. Neither does the supply of bank loans, which are necessarily limited by the reserves banks must hold against their expanding liabilities. Firms find that it becomes more and more difficult to negotiate new security issues—bonds especially—except on increasingly onerous terms. High levels of employment and economic activity generally soak up most of the money in circulation, leaving little available for lending or to meet liquidity needs. The demand for bank loans continues to grow, not only because of expanded levels of activity, but also because prices are rising. For a time at least this demand is not responsive to higher interest rates, since profit expectations remain high and firms are optimistic they can turn borrowed money over rapidly enough to come out ahead. The growing tensions in the financial markets are a threat to continued expansion simply because sooner or later higher interest rates will cut into both actual and expected profit margins. When this happens both current production and investment for future production will suffer.

As the foregoing pressures and tensions mount in both the real (goods) and financial (money) spheres of the economy, only one route is open to prevent disaster from overwhelming the economy. This is to continue to push up prices fast enough to keep rising costs from encroaching upon profits. But this proves to be impossible. Some prices, such as those set by law, by long-term contracts, by custom, or even by business policy, simply cannot move up rapidly. Incomes, too, may not keep pace with prices, a factor responsible for the 1974–75 recession. In any event, the accumulated stresses imposed on both the production and financial side of the economy during an expansion end sooner or later in a *crisis*. In Mitchell's view a crisis initially is a situation in which business firms attempt to liquidate some or all of the debts they have incurred during the expansion and prosperity phase of the cycle. The crisis, which marks the upper turning point of the cycle, may be mild or severe, even turning into a full-fledged monetary panic of the sort which led to the temporary closing of the banks in 1933. But once an expansion or boom slides into a crisis, the situation again becomes cumulative, spreading from the banking community to business firms to the entire community. Business firms are forced to concentrate on looking after their outstanding liabilities and husbanding their financial resources, instead of pushing sales and continuing to expand production. Thus, the volume of new orders and with it production and employment begin to fall, a process which is cumulative downward just as a recovery and expansion is cumulative upward. Unless checked by government intervention or some other unforeseen outside event (such as a war), the economy slides into a recession or depression, from whence the cycle will begin all over again.

Are there limits to the amplitude of the cycle? This is a question which

Mitchell never addressed directly, although his notion that each phase of the cycle carries within it the forces which lead the economy into the next phase implies the existence of limits. Professor J. R. Hicks developed a theory of a "constrained" cycle in which the magnitude of fluctuations is limited by both a ceiling and a floor.[17] In Professor Hicks's analysis the cycle results from an interacton between the Keynesian multiplier and the accelerator in a fashion similar to the example developed in Chapter 7 (Table 7–2). Figure 16–5 depicts the Hicksian cycle "model" with the built-in floor and ceiling. The ceiling is set by the rate of growth of the full employment labor force plus the rate of growth in its productivity. Thus, if the fully employed labor force grew at an annual average rate of 1 percent and labor productivity increased annually on the average at 2.5 percent, the ceiling at which output could grow over time would be 3.5 percent. Actual output could not exceed this figure except for a brief interval. Thus, there's an effective upper limit to cyclical fluctuations in the economy.

The floor below which output during its cyclical path cannot fall is determined differently. It results in part from the fact that the working of the accelerator over the course of the cycle is not symmetrical. The accelerator, it will be recalled, leads to more or less investment spending as a consequence of a *change in the rate* at which output is changing. During a downswing the fall in output will, of course, lead to a decline in induced investment, but there will be a limit to the amount by which total investment will fall. The reason is that all investment is not induced. Even in a severe depression some autonomous investment is likely; hence total investment will not normally fall to zero or even become negative (except for very short periods). This means, in effect, that the effective value of the accelerator may be smaller in a downswing than it

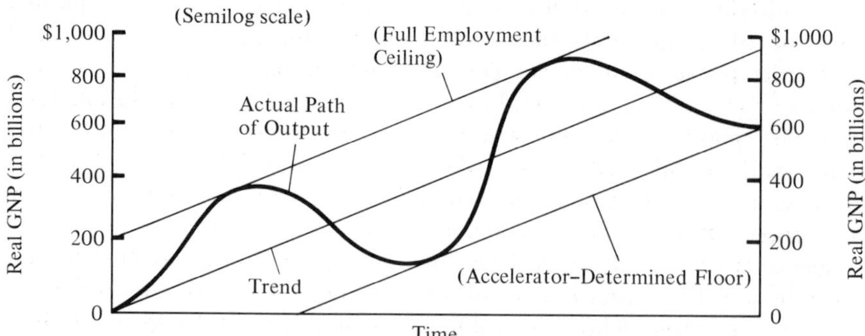

FIGURE 16–5. The "constrained" Business Cycle of J. R. Hicks

17. J. R. Hicks, *A Contribution to the Theory of the Trade Cycle* (London: Oxford University Press, 1950), especially Chapters VII and VIII, pp. 83–107.

is in an upswing, a fact which automatically tends to put a floor under the downswing. Further, we must reckon with the Keynesian fact that as income (that is, real output) falls, consumption does not fall as fast. Even, therefore, if gross investment fell to zero—or became negative for a short period of time—consumption outlays would eventually act to place a limit to the fall in output. This is so simply because at some point they will begin to exceed output. When this happens the floor will have been reached. It almost goes without saying that the economy may experience a level of unemployment which is simply not acceptable politically long before the "floor" is reached, but this does not change the theoretical fact that such a floor may exist. It merely means that positive policy actions will be taken before this point is reached.

Causes of the Business Cycle

Although some economists have tried to understand and explain the business cycle ever since existence of cycles in economic activity was recognized, most of this effort took place outside the mainstream of theoretical economics. The reason, of course, was the dominant position of the classical approach to economic understanding right up until the crash of 1929 (See Chapter 4). Classical economics, dominated by Say's Law and belief that full employment was the normal state of affairs, simply had no place for a view of the world in which serious ups and downs in economic activity were the norm. As a consequence, most theorizing about the business cycle in the nineteenth century did not have much academic respectability, being seen mostly as a part of an "underworld" of economics populated by cranks, crackpots, and assorted charlatans pushing their pet nostrums for the world's economic ills.[18] The situation did not change until the early 1900s, at which time the work of Mitchell, Schumpeter and a few others began to have a recognized impact. Still, business cycle theorizing continued largely outside the mainstream of economic analysis until Keynes's monumental study appeared in the mid-1930s.

Even though there is no agreement even today among economists on *the cause* of the business cycle, one very important thing happened because of Keynes's work: *The General Theory* brought the business cycle into the mainstream of economic analysis. Keynes did not develop

18. Karl Marx is, of course, an exception to this, as he is one of the commanding figures in the history of economic thought and a man of the nineteenth century, as well. Marx believed that the business cycle was so ingrained in the capitalistic system of ownership and production that the only possible cure was a complete change in the nature of the system. The classical economists did not accept Marx's analysis of capitalism.

a definitive theory of the business cycle.[19] But cycles are a phenomenon characteristic of the aggregate economy. Further, they have been viewed historically as an inherent characteristic of profit-oriented, market-based economic systems. Since these viewpoints are in harmony with the content and spirit of *The General Theory*, it follows naturally that analysis of the business cycle can—and should—take place within the unified theoretical framework that Keynes developed.

Explanations for the cycle have fallen into one of two quite broad categories, an approach we shall follow in this discussion. First, there is an approach usually described as *external or exogenous.* This view, which is characteristic of much thinking about the cycle during the nineteenth century, looks upon external shocks—such as a war or a bad harvest—as the fundamental cause of the business cycle. Technically such shocks are said to be stochastic, which means random. It is true, of course, that the way in which the economy reacts to an external shock is important for understanding and explaining the cycle, but the basic cause is held to be external to the system itself. Philosophically, this approach fits in with classical thinking since the classical economists saw the economic system primarily as a self-regulating mechanism which tended (if left alone) toward an equilibrium of full employment. In their view this was its "natural state."

The second stream of thought is much more in tune with modern Keynesian thinking about the nature and behavior of the economic system. It involves the belief that cycles are inherent in the economic system, that their existence is not dependent upon any external forces. This clearly is the spirit of *The General Theory.* Such *internal* or *endogenous* theories of the cycle may be wholly mechanistic, as is the case with the purely formal multiplier-accelerator model developed in Chapter 7, or they may be loose and relatively unstructured, as is a theory which revolves around the key role that Keynes accords to expectations and uncertainty. In any event, all such internal explanations of the cycle have in common a belief that profit-based, market-oriented economic systems are inherently unstable.

External causes

One of the oldest of the external—or *stochastic*—attempts to explain the cycle is the "sunspot theory," an approach developed by the English clas-

19. As we have seen, the purpose of *The General Theory* was to develop a systematic explanation of the forces which determine the level of output and employment in the mature, market (i.e., capitalistic) economy. Keynes did not set out to establish a theory of the business cycle, but he did believe that the theoretical framework which he developed in his classic work could also be used to explain this phenomenon. See Chapter 22, "Notes on the Trade Cycle," in his *The General Theory, Interest and Money* (New York: Harcourt, Brace & World, First Harbinger ed., 1964).

sical economist, W. Stanley Jevons.[20] His investigations into fluctuations led him to suggest a cycle of approximately 10 to 11 years duration. But the main cause of such cycles were periodic upheavals in weather conditions, a development that he thought was traceable to variations in the intensity of sunspots. If there were a strong correlation between sunspots and cycles in the weather, such a theory of the business cycle might make sense for a predominantly agricultural economy, but it would not suffice to explain the business cycle in an economy in which agriculture accounts for only a small part of the output total. Subsequent research doesn't support the close correlation between sunspots and business cycles which Jevons thought existed, although the subject of the impact of sunspots on the earth's climate continues to fascinate scientists and laymen alike. It remains an open scientific question.

Money—especially gold—has sometimes been seen as the source of an exogenous shock capable of initiating a cyclical reaction in the economy. Gold discoveries in California and Alaska are examples of monetary shocks. The difficulty with this view is that such events happen only once in a great while, whereas cycles are a more or less regular occurrence. Under modern conditions a monetary shock theory of the cycle simply will not do, for the money supply is no longer dependent upon such chance happenings as the discovery of a new gold field in the nation or abroad. Although critics of the Federal Reserve maintain that the actions of the men who manage the nation's central bank are often counterproductive, they do not claim that these actions are wholly capricious, unrelated to what is happening in the economy. Thus, there is no real basis for a modern theory of the cycle based upon monetary shocks.

Joseph A. Schumpeter not only studied the business cycle and its length in detail, but he also developed a theory of the cycle which should be classified with other external or exogenous explanations. Briefly, Schumpeter believed that innovation was the major external shock which would start the economy on a cyclical path. Schumpeter is at one with other theorists who see the business cycle as a continuing process, one which moves through successive phases with considerable regularity. But innovation is the key originating cause in such fluctuations. He described the process as follows in an important 1927 article:

> These booms consist in the carrying out of innovations in the industrial and commercial organism. By innovations I understand such changes of the combination of factors of production as cannot be effected by infinitesimal steps or variations on the margin. They consist primarily in changes in methods of production and transportation, or in changes in industrial organization, or in the production of a new article, or in the opening up of new markets of new sources of material. The recurring

20. Jevons is perhaps best known for his role in the development of the law of diminishing marginal utility.

periods of prosperity of the cyclical movement are the form progress takes in capitalistic society.[21]

In this article and in his subsequent voluminous writings Schumpeter made it clear, first, that innovations originate in irregular fashion because a single individual or a relative handful of businessmen see possibilities for gain not seen by the vast majority, and, second, that the cycle of boom followed by collapse is the mechanism through which the benefits of any innovation get spread throughout the economy. The cycle, in other words, is the price of progress. Schumpeter's theory is classified as an external or exogenous approach because the individual entrepreneur (or a small band of entrepreneurs) who gets the process started is in a sense, outside the system. The act of innovation is an extraordinary act, one not normally forthcoming because of the usual, routine operation of the economy. It is in this sense that innovation is an external or exogenous cause of the cycle.

Before we look at the alternative set of explanations for the cycle—those which see it as wholly an internal affair in a market system—let us consider briefly a thoroughly modern version of the external or exogenous approach, a version which puts government in the role of the external cause. This view grows out of the neoclassical and monetarist views of the economy as inherently stable, tending when left alone toward a full employment equilibrium.[22] Some external shock is required to dislodge the economy from its natural, equilibrium state. When this happens, there will be public pressure for government action to restore equilibrium. But because of lags, the government policy reaction will not only come too late, but its response is likely to be too strong in view of the fact that the forces which tend to restore equilibrium start working even before a policy decision is made. What government intervention does is exaggerate the natural corrective response of the economic system to an external shock, thus worsening rather than correcting the effect of the shock. Government is seen as a cause not a corrective to cyclical fluctuations. Milton Friedman is one of the leading proponents of this viewpoint, especially in the realm of monetary policy. The Federal Reserve System, he argues, usually does the wrong thing because it misreads what is happening in the economy, failing to pay enough heed to the economy's self-correcting

21. Joseph A. Schumpeter, "The Explanation of the Business Cycle," *Economica,* December 1927, p. 295.

22. See for example Merton H. Miller and Charles W. Upton, *Macroeconomics: A Neoclassical Introduction,* (Homewood, Ill.: Richard D. Irwin, Inc., 1974). In their Preface, Miller and Upton say "We believe that the course in macroeconomics should emphasize . . . that a market economy left to its own devices will settle into a full employment equilibrium. External shocks, of a variety of kinds, will dislodge it from equilibrium from time to time, but the economy's internal defenses will speedily return it to equilibrium barring new shocks or actively destabilizing policies by the government."

mechanism. For example, the Federal Reserve usually interprets rising interest rates as a sign of insufficient money rather than excess spending. It reacts—wrongly, according to Friedman—by increasing the money supply, which only worsens the situation leading to more spending. Government action is destabilizing rather than stabilizing.

Internal causes

In spite of the ofttime persuasive arguments of Professor Friedman, a majority of economists are not ready to accept the view that the economy is inherently stable. Consequently, cycle theories of an *internal* or *endogenous* character are more in tune with contemporary thinking about the economy's behavior than are external shock theories. Here again, however, there is no single theory, no consensus among economists on how to explain the business cycle. For simplicity in exposition we shall consider, first, some pre-Keynesian views of the internal causes of the cycle and follow that with a brief examination of the cyclical process as seen by Keynes in *The General Theory.*

Pre-Keynesian theorizing about the business cycle may be divided into two broad categories. These are, first, a group of theories usually labeled "underconsumptionist," and, second, another group generally described as "overinvestment" theories. We shall take a brief look at some of the main ideas and economic personalities associated with each of these broad categories.

Although the term "underconsumption" lacks a precise meaning, the "underconsumptionist" approach to the business cycle sees the ultimate collapse in boom conditions as caused by a failure of spending by consumers to keep pace with production, leading eventually to a "glut" of unsold goods. The reasons why consumption fails to keep pace are not always clear, sometimes being the result of hoarding, sometimes of an excess of savings, or sometimes simply because it is believed that the system does not pay out sufficient funds to buy back what is being produced. Why the latter happens is not always clear, although it is a theme which runs through the underconsumptionist literature. The roots of the underconsumptionist viewpoint trace back to Thomas Malthus one of the early classical economists. In one of the many letters he exchanged with David Ricardo, Malthus pointed out that it was possible for demand to be deficient if a society attempts to save at a pace in excess of the willingness to invest (to employ modern terminology), but his arguments made no impression on Ricardo and other classical economists. Say's Law won out over what Keynes called "plain sense."[23]

23. See Keynes's essay on Malthus entitled "Thomas Malthus: The First of the Cambridge Economists," in John Maynard Keynes, *Essays in Biography*, (New York: W. W. Norton & Company, Inc., 1951), p. 117.

Prior to Keynes, the most complete development of the underconsumption approach to business cycles came from John A. Hobson, a British economist writing near the end of the nineteenth century. Hobson took issue with Say's Law, asserting that the business cycle resulted from a combination of oversaving and underconsumption. He did not deny the fundamental premise that production (that is supply) creates the means to make payments or buy back what is produced, but he did argue that many persons produced more (that is, got more income) than they needed to consume, so their production did not translate into an equal amount of effective demand. Consequently, demand could be insufficient in the aggregate. The remedy was in less saving, an end which could be attained by some redistribution of income and wealth. Hobson recognized that redistribution could go too far, thereby impairing saving and ultimately economic progress, but progress was also hurt by the periodic failures of demand to keep pace with the growth in productive power because income was too unequal. Thus society had to thread its way toward a more equal distribution of income, but not one so equal as to threaten all saving and the progress it made possible.

In a way the "overinvestment" theories are a mirror image of the underconsumptionist approach to the cycle. Like the latter, prosperity collapses because of an excess of production—a glut of goods. But in this case the goods in excess supply are capital goods, not consumer goods. Basically what happens is that an upswing in activity is set in motion by a rising tide of spending for new capital goods, a surge whch eventually saturates the economy with more new capital than it can profitably employ. When this happens the investment boom collapses, dragging down the rest of the economy.

What causes the overinvestment boom? No specific answer exists for this question, although the practice in the theoretical literature is to lump the causes of the investment boom into two broad categories—monetary and nonmonetary. Frederick A. Hayek, an Austrian-born economist and recent Nobel laureate, is the best-known exponent of the monetary overinvestment theory of the business cycle. At the root of the problem is the willingness of the banking and financial system to create new bank credit and make this credit available to business enterprises on favorable terms. It is, in other words, an expansion of money and credit which gets the investment boom rolling. For investment to take place, however, there must be "real" savings, which involves a diversion of resources from consumer to investment goods output. In Hayek's scheme the necessary savings are *forced,* not voluntary. This is what eventually causes the investment boom to collapse. Savings are "forced" by the process of rising prices brought about by producers of investment goods bidding for increasingly scarce resources as the boom accelerates. The boom can continue as long as investment spending is fed by expanding bank credit and forced saving. But ultimtely this leads to maladjustments in the structure of production—there are too many new capital goods in relation to the real ability of consumers to buy. Forced savings means that consumers are being priced out of the market by higher prices, a process which must sooner or later lead to a glut of both investment and consumer goods. The inevitable collapse is hastened by growing stringency in the financial markets as the banking system exhausts its excess reserves and interest rates begin to rise. Thus, firms find it more and more difficult to secure on favorable terms the credit needed to keep the investment boom rolling. What the crisis and downturn do, in Hayek's view, is force the economy back into a more normal situation, which is one in which the structure of production—i.e., the relationship between investment and consumption goods output—is adjusted to the level at which voluntary savings are forthcoming. Recession or depression is the price the economy pays for the excesses of an investment boom generated initially by easy money conditions.

Nonmonetary overinvestment theories of the business cycle suggest a similar sequence of events—too much investment, too little consumption demand, and an eventual turning point or collapse when the investment goods produced during the boom begin turning out increased quantities of consumer goods and services. The basic difference is that much less stress is placed upon money and credit as the ultimate causal factors in the investment boom. What is common to all such theories is a belief that the cycle is caused by overproduction which results from overinvestment. Money of necessity plays a role, for no expansion is possible without more money, but the nonmonetary theorists view the money and financial system primarily as a part of the response mechanism rather than a fundamental causative factor. Leading exponents of a nonmentary overinvestment approach to the cycle have been a Russian economist, Michel Tugan-Baranowsky, a German, Arthur Spiethoff, and Gustav Cassel, a Swedish engineer who became an economist. The key studies of these and other overinvestment theorists appeared before publication of Keynes's *The General Theory.*

The General Theory

Keynes did not set out to develop a theory of the business cycle, (in-*The General Theory*) but he did think about the phenomenon and draw upon the theoretical apparatus which he developed in his classic work to suggest why cycles existed in a market economy. Most of the ideas discussed previously in this section can be fitted into the sequence of events which Keynes envisaged. We shall conclude this discussion of the causes of the business cycle with a brief summary of Keynes's views on the phenomenon.

In his "Notes on the Trade Cycle" (Chapter 22 in *The General Theory*) Keynes says that the essential character of the trade cycle—the regularity and the duration of the economy's ups and downs which justify the notion of a cycle—is due mainly to "the way in which the marginal efficiency of capital fluctuates."[24] This, of course, puts investment at the heart of the matter, for the marginal efficiency of capital is the key to what happens to investment spending. Keynes approaches the question of the cycle by asking what happens in the later stages of a typical boom. As with most business cycle theorists, Keynes sees the boom carried forward mainly by investment spending, given the essentially passive role of consumption spending. But investment spending, Keynes reminds us, depends not only on the existing scarcity and cost of capital goods, but on expectations as to the future yield of newly produced capital goods. However, "the basis for such expectations is very precarious. Being based upon shifting and unreliable evidence they are subject to sudden and violent change."[25] The future and its uncertainty—this is a theme to which Keynes returns again and again in *The General Theory*. And here we have the basic reason for the sudden and unpredictable collapse of the marginal efficiency of capital, an event which marks the onset of the "crisis" and the downward plunge of the economy. In the latter stages of any investment boom, expectations of future yields must be optimistic enough to offset the growing abundance of capital, the rising supply price for new capital, and increases in interest rates. At some point, however, all this may collapse, as the longer the boom goes on, the more fragile and uncertain become the basis upon which expectations for future yields rests. Thus, as Keynes says, the "predominant explanation of the crisis is, not primarily a rise in the rate of interest, but a sudden collapse in the marginal efficiency of capital."[26] All else flows from this fundamental fact.

Following the collapse of the marginal efficiency of capital, there will be a sharp increase in liquidity preference, a consequence of the dismay and uncertainty about the future which the crisis precipitates. For a time interest rates will be high, but even after the immediate crisis passes the marginal efficiency of capital remains so low that there is no practical way in which interest rates can be reduced enough to bring investment spending out of a slump. For a period the slump will be intractable. Unless there is outside intervention—government action, for example—some time must elapse before a recovery can begin. But there cannot be a general recovery from the slump until there is a revival in the marginal efficiency

24. Keynes, *The General Theory*, p. 313.
25. Ibid., p. 315.
26. Ibid., p. 315.

of capital. This will not happen, however, until the economy rids itself of surplus inventories of all goods carried over from the crisis and ensuing slump and until normal forces of growth begin to make the stock of fixed capital assets (equipment and buildings) *relatively* less abundant.

Keynes distinguishes his analysis from earlier "overinvestment" theories of the cycle by pointing out that in his opinion the term "overinvestment" should only be used to describe a state of affairs in which every kind of capital good is so abundant that no new investment in any kind of capital could earn more than its replacement cost—a condition in which capital ceased to have any true scarcity value. This, of course, is not the situation he is describing, for a collapse in the marginal efficiency of capital means a collapse in the expected returns based upon uncertain and flimsy knowledge about the future. Such expectations may or may not reflect the scarcity of capital in a more enduring and fundamental sense. It is the relative scarcity of capital in a subjective sense which governs the marginal efficiency and thus determines the pace of investment. This is the true meaning of Keynes's theory which sees wide swings in the marginal efficiency of capital as the key to understanding the business cycle.

The Political Business Cycle

Before we leave the subject of causes of the business cycle, a brief word is in order about a related idea—the political business cycle. In a remarkable prescient article published in 1943, Michal Kalecki foresaw that once governments learned how to control the business (or trade) cycle, they might find themselves confronted with a political cycle.[27] The gist of Kalecki's argument was that attempts to insure full employment by large-scale government spending during a slump would sooner or later encounter strong opposition from the business community. Such opposition would arise in part bceause of straightforward hostility by business to deficit spending as a matter of principle, and in part because of the fear that a prolonged period of full employment would strengthen the economic position of the wage-earner *vis a vis* the property owner and businessman. But the general public will not tolerate a prolonged slump with

27. Originally from Poland, Michal Kalecki visited England in the 1930s, remained there during the war years, and returned to Poland after World War II. He died in 1970. The article in question is entitled "The Political Aspects of Full Employment," *The Political Quarterly*, October-December, 1943, pp. 322–331. It is now generally recognized that Kalecki developed in the early 1930s an analysis of the workings of a market economy which in its broad outline is remarkably similar to Keynes's theory. Because his ideas were first published in Polish they did not become generally known among Western economists until after *The General Theory* appeared in 1936.

high unemployment; consequently, political pressure mounts until the government acts to bring the economy out of the slump by either cutting taxes, increasing public spending, or both. In any event the policy measures taken to counter the slump involve deficit spending, a development which sooner or later arouses the opposition of the business community and forces the government to return to a more orthodox policy of reducing deficits. A new slump follows. Kalecki foresaw a situation in which government policy (fiscal and monetary) was whipsawed continuously between forces demanding action to end slumps and unemployment and forces fearful of the consequences of prolonged deficit spending. In many ways Kalecki's vision of a political business cycle is very much like what both Britain and the United States have experienced in recent years. The basic difference is that it is primarily inflation (not deficit spending) which leads to alternating policies of *stop* (putting on the fiscal and monetary brakes) and *go* (stepping on the fiscal and monetary accelerator) in an effort to cope with the contemporary malaise—stagflation. Modern governments have not been notoriously successful to date in solving the problem of stagflation.

Economic Forecasting

We shall conclude this chapter with a few observations on economic forecasting. An appropriate place to begin is with a question: what is economic forecasting? The answer is simple but important. Forecasting is an attempt to determine what will happen in the economy over the near term, which is to say what will happen in the next quarter or the next year.[28] Most forecasting does not extend further into the future. Forecasting involves, in other words, an attempt to foresee or estimate changes in the major aggregate economic variables—output, employment, and the price level, for example—in the period immediately ahead. Forecasting requires a knowledge and understanding of what has happened in the recent past, what is happening now in the economy, and the *why* of such happenings. The latter implies a need for economic theory, for we cannot understand and interpret the observed performance of the economy without a theoretical frame of reference. Forecasting is both an art and a science, although it is probably more of an art than a science. The reason is the uncertainty which surrounds the economic future. Thus we touch

28. The reader should recall that in Chapter 1 a distinction was made between forecasting and prediction. The latter applies to a specific economic law or generalization and has to do with predicting the value of a dependent variable when there is a change in the independent, causal variable. An example would be the predicted change in consumption given a specific change in income.

once again on a key theme which threads its way through the Keynesian view of the economic universe.

Forecasting is necessary because the economy moves forward in irregular fashion—in the kind of cyclical or wavelike movements which have been the subject of this chapter. If the economy's path through time were regular, then forecasting would not be necessary. We should merely have to extrapolate past trends to know what tomorrow would bring. Unfortunately, the world in general and the economic world in particular does not work this way. Yet man wants to know what is going to happen next week, next month, or next year. Thus, forecasting meets an important human need. Further, accurate forecasting is essential if economic stabilization is to work. We know from the available evidence that the economy is inherently unstable, but we also believe that this instability can be minimized by a judicious use of the policy tools which are the legacy of contemporary macroeconomic theory. But unless we can forecast with a reasonable accuracy forthcoming ups and downs of the economic system, our knowledge of how to apply economic theory to improve the economy's performance will not do us much good.

This brings us to a more specific question: what do we expect from economic forecasting? Basically, forecasting should accomplish two things. First, it should tell us that the economy is approaching a turning point, which is to say that forecasting ought to send out some kind of a signal that a major change in the economic weather is coming. It should in other words, tell us that a downturn or an upturn is in sight. Ideally, forecasts ought to tell us exactly when a turning point can be expected, but this is beyond the current capabilities of the art. Second, a forecast should have something to say about the magnitude of a forthcoming change. For example, if the economic signals say a recession is coming, they also ought to give some indication of the severity or depth of the recession.

There are some knotty problems involved in the foregoing matters which are worth pointing out, although we shall not explore them in depth. For example, if correct policy action is taken in the face of a forecast, the forecast is thereby rendered incorrect. What does this do to the belief in the accuracy of subsequent forecasts? Another and different problem may arise if business firms and private individuals react to a forecast in ways which bring about the conditions being forecast. For example, the forecast of a downturn in economic activity may lead business firms to trim costs in anticipation of hard times by laying off some workers or persuade consumers to save more and spend less. Such actions could make future conditions worse than they might have been in the absence of a forecast. There are no ready answers to these problems, although most economic forecasting is probably not yet accurate enough for these possibilities to affect seriously the economy's performance.

The Methods of Forecasting

There is no one technique widely recognized among economists as *the method* for forecasting. The techniques actually used range from the subjective judgment of a single competent individual to the use of elaborate econometric models involving large numbers of sophisticated equations. We shall review some of the more widely used techniques, although no claim is made that our list is exhaustive.

Extrapolation

The technique which is both the simplest and the most widely used by the nonspecialist is to project into the future what is happening currently or has happened in the recent past. Possibly a simple extrapolation of the present into the future should not be designated as a "technique," but this method is probably used—consciously or unconsciously—more than most people realize. Keynes believed that this was largely the way in which businessmen form their expectations about the future, since he argued there was no scientific bases whatsoever they could employ for the calculation of future values. What they do, he argued, is assume—even though past experience shows this to be risky—that the present is a serviceable guide to the future. In addition, the individual businessman seeks support for his judgment by falling back on the judgments of other businessmen. Unfortunately, they also are doing exactly the same thing—assuming the present is a serviceable guide to the future.[29] What this means, of course, is that such forecasts are based on a flimsy foundation, subject to "sudden and violent change." This technique may work for a while because of the cumulative character of most expansions and contractions, but it cannot—save by chance—forecast turning points in the cycle or provide evidence on the magnitude of the cyclical swing.

The Consensus Approach

Another commonly used forecasting technique is the consensus method. This method is widely employed in the press, especially by business and financial publications. It is labeled consensus because it involves getting opinions from a large number of observers as to what is likely to happen to the economy in the months or year ahead. A consensus outlook is then constructed based on these opinions. This technique is most often employed at the start of a new year. General circulation newspapers tend

29. John Maynard Keynes, "The General Theory of Employment," *The Quarterly Journal of Economics*, February 1937, p. 214.

to develop their forecasts by surveying leaders in business, labor, government, and education, whereas the business and financial press is more likely to direct its probing at professional economists in business and the universities. *Business Week* magazine, for example, normally publishes at the end of the year a major article on the economic outlook for the next twelve months. Their analysis typically pulls together the opinions of a broad sample of academic and business economists and compares their outlook with forecasts turned out by the best-known econometric models. Table 16–3 contains the average of the forecasted percentage changes made by 25 economists and 9 econometric models for 1977 as reported in *Business Week*. The average of the changes predicted by the 25 economists is a good example of consensus type forecasting.

TABLE 16–3. Economic Forecasts for 1977 (in percent)

	Real GNP	*Inflation Rate*	*Unemployment Rate*
Estimates of 25 economists	5.0	5.5	7.1
Estimates of 9 econometric models	4.8	5.6	7.4

SOURCE: *Business Week*, December 27, 1977.

Indicators

One of the most important forecasting tools developed in recent years are the indexes of *leading, coincident,* and *lagging* indicators. These terms refer to statistical series which either lead, coincide, or lag behind the general cycle movement of economic activity. For forecasting purposes the index of leading indicators is most important, because it is designed to tell us that either a downturn or upswing in economic activity is in the offing.

The National Bureau of Economic Research in cooperation with the federal government has been primarily responsible for development of this particular forecasting technique. For more than two decades, Geoffrey H. Moore and Julius Shiskin conducted an intensive study of the behavior of several hundred time series for economic variables, seeking always to discover those series which would enable economists to forecast changes in economic activity. Out of these studies they narrowed the analysis to 88 indicators, of which 36 were placed in the leading category, 25 were put in the coincident group, 11 were classified as lagging, and 16 not classified with respect to timing. The list was further refined and shorted, leading ultimately to the development of a composite index for each of these three categories—leading, coincide, and lagging. These composite indexes are published monthly by the U.S. Department of Commerce in *Business Conditions Digest.* Table 16–4 lists the economic time series included in each of these three composite indexes and Figure 16–6 shows their behavior for the period 1948–77. This chart shows clearly that the downturn in the composite index for leading indicators foreshadowed a recession, although there is a wide variation in the 1948–77 period in the number of months by which the downturn in this index led the overall downturn in economic activity. The average lead time for the last 5 recessions was 10.8 months, although the actual lead time ranged from a maximum of 23 to a minimum of 4 months. If the index of leading indicators turns down for two consecutive months, trouble may lie ahead. This is the current thinking of the Department of Commerce.

TABLE 16–4. Composite Indexes and Their Composition

Index and Series

Composite Leading Index (12 series)

1. Average workweek for manufacturing production workers
2. Layoff rate in manufacturing (per 100 workers)
3. New orders for consumers goods and materials
4. Percent of companies reporting slower deliveries
5. Net business formation
6. Contracts and orders for plant and equipment
7. New building permits for private housing
8. Net changes in inventories
9. Changes in sensitive prices
10. Prices for 500 common stocks
11. Changes in total liquid assets
12. Money supply (M_1)

Composite Coincident Index (4 series)

1. Employees on nonagricultural payrolls
2. Personal income less transfer payments
3. Industrial production
4. Manufacturing and trade sales

Composite Lagging Index (6 series)

1. Average duration of unemployment
2. Manufacturing and trade inventories
3. Labor cost per unit of output in manufacturing
4. Commercial and Industrial loans outstanding as reported by large commercial banks (weekly)
5. Average prime rate charged by banks
6. Ratio of consumer installment debt to personal income

SOURCE: *Business Conditions Digest*

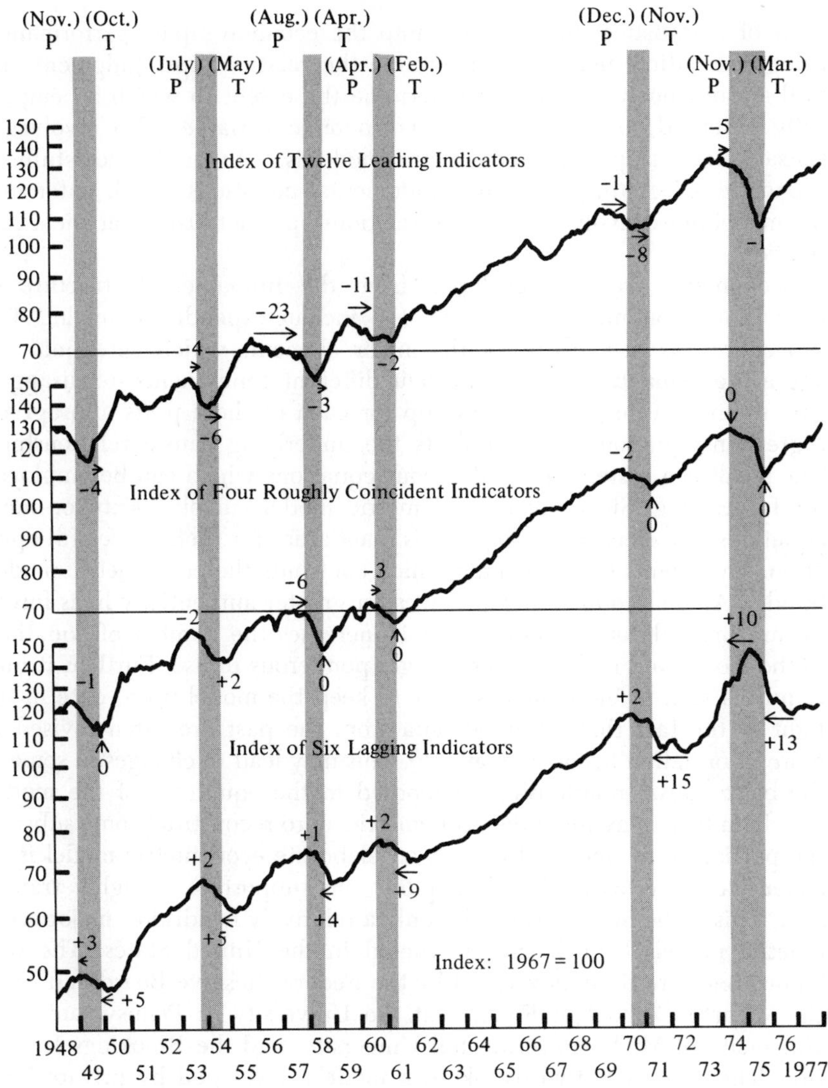

FIGURE 16–6. Major Composite Indexes: 1948–77 (1967 = 100)

Econometric Models

Finally some comments are in order about forecasting with econometric models of the economy. Basically, an econometric model is a mathematical representation of the economy which consists of a series of equations involving dependent (endogenous) and independent (exogenous) variables. The relationships presented in the equations are developed on the basis of a statistical investigation into the economy's past performance, using correlation analysis to determine the relationships. Judgment and skill are obviously required to determine the extent to which an empirically observed correlation between economic variables also involves a causal relationship. If an econometric model is to be used successfully in economic forecasting, then the fundamental equations which enter into the model must involve true casual relationships—not just a statistical correlation.

Econometric models developed from the fundamental structure of Keynesian economics, particularly the income-expenditure model. The procedure has been to break the major elements which enter into the aggregate demand function into their different components—to disaggregate them to a degree—and develop for each of these parts appropriate regression equations which reflects the underlying causal relationships. The result is a system of simultaneous equations which can be employed for forecasting. Since some econometric models involve sixty or more equations, the electronic computer is mandatory for their successful operation. This points up a dilemma which confronts the econometric model-builder. As the econometrician strives for greater authenticity he is forced toward more disaggregation, but this increases the number of equations in the model and makes it increasingly ponderous to use. Further, it may require a staff of individuals simply to keep the model up to date in the light of the fact that observed data from the past are often revised as more information becomes available. This may lead to changes in some of the basic causal relationships embodied in the equations of the model, which, in turn, may force the econometrician to reconstruct some substantial portion of his model. In short, an elaborate econometric model is an expensive undertaking which requires the support of a highly trained staff. This is the basic reason why only a relatively handful of major econometric models have been constructed in the United States. The best known ones are those developed by the Federal Reserve Board and MIT, the Wharton School of Finance at the University of Pennsylvania, the University of Michigan, Princeton University, and the Brookings Institution. There are also two well-known models developed by private business firms, Chase Econometrics (a subsidiary of the Chase Manhattan Bank), and Data Resource Incorporated.

The Effectiveness of Forecasting

Just as there is no single technique for economic forecasting, there is no simple answer to the question of its effectiveness. There has been significant forward progress in this field since World War II, but much remains to be done to improve the accuracy and effectiveness of the art. Numerous studies in recent years have sought to answer this question of the accuracy of economic forecasts.[30] We shall conclude this chapter with some observations on a few of these.

In an analysis of the performance of econometric models in forecasting GNP and changes in GNP over the 1953–64 period, Victor Zarnowitz found that forecast values for GNP were off by only about 2 percent on the average, not an excessively large error. But much larger errors were made by the econometric models in forecasting the actual change in GNP. Here the range was from 28 to 56 percent, with the average error being about 40 percent.

One important body engaged in making forecasts is the Council of Economic Advisers. Since 1962 it has included in the annual *Economic Report* forecasts of current and constant dollar value for the GNP as well as the inflation rate as measured by the GNP deflator. The Council employs a variety of forecasting techniques—including econometric models—to develop its projections. In general, according to Geoffrey Moore's analysis, the track record of the Council in forecasting change in the rate of growth of *real* GNP is pretty good. In ten out of the thirteen forecast years, the Council's forecasts of changes in the rate of growth for real GNP were in the right direction, which is to say they correctly forecast that the rate of growth would either increase or decrease. Their record on forecasting changes in the inflation rate was not satisfactory, for in only four of the thirteen years was the Council able to forecast correctly whether the inflation rate would rise or fall. In four years its forecasts were in the wrong direction, and in the other five years the results were ambiguous because either the forecast rate or the actual rate (but not both) remained constant. With respect to forecasts for actual GNP (real and current dollar amounts), Moore found that the Council's errors were about one-half as large as they would have been if it had been assumed that last year's change was the same as this year (used a single extrapolation, in other words). For inflation, the results were much less satisfactory, since the Council consistently tended to underestimate the inflation rate. Actually, according to Moore, an assumption that the previous year's

30. Readers interested in this question should consult one or more of the following studies. Victor Zarnowitz, *An Appraisal of Short-Term Economic Forecasts* (New York: National Bureau of Economic Research, 1967); Stephen K. McNees, "An Evaluation of Economic Forecasts," *New England Economic Review*, November/December 1975 and an update of the subject by the same author in the September/October 1976 issue of the *New England Economic Review;* Geoffrey H. Moore, "Economic Forecasting—How Good A Track Record?" in *The Morgan Guaranty Survey*, January, 1975; and Maury N. Harris and Deborah Jamroz, "Evaluating the Leading Indicators," Federal Reserve Bank of New York, *Monthly Review*. Other references will be found in these studies.

inflation rate would repeat itself would have produced forecasts as accurate as those found in the *Economic Report*.

Probably the forecasting tool which has proved to be accurate more consistently than any other is the composite index of leading indicators. According to the Harris-Jamroz study cited above this particular index has never failed to signal any of the post-World War II downturns (Figure 16–6), although on occasion when it has dropped no recession followed. As pointed out earlier, the chief weakness of this index is not that it does not give an accurate signal of an impending change, but that there is no consistency to length of the lag between the downturn (or upturn) in the indicator and the subsequent change in the economy's direction.

What these various findings indicate is that no wholly satisfactory technique has evolved for forecasting either the timing or strength of major changes in the aggregate economy. All the various techniques have a role —the National Bureau concluded that there are no major differences between the accuracy of forcecasts based upon informal consensus models, econometric models, or leading indicators. That is, perhaps, to be expected, since all techniques must depend in greater or lesser degree on some extrapolation of present or recent past conditions into the future. But since humans can learn from their experience, the future will never be exactly like the past. Forecasting is a useful art, and efforts should continue to improve it. But given the uncertainties which attach to an unknown future, we can never make it into a "science" in which we push a few buttons on a computer and get an accurate reading of tomorrow's economic weather.

V

Aggregate Income Distribution

17

Theories of Aggregate Income Distribution

In this final chapter we turn to the theory of income distribution, a relatively unexplored aspect of modern income and employment theory. Our approach is from the point of view of the economy as a whole; we are concerned with the distribution of the national income on the basis of ownership of economic resources or factors of production.

The purpose of an analysis of income distribution from the aggregate point of view is not only to determine what role the level of aggregate income plays in the distribution of the national income to the factors of production, but also to study the influence of the distribution of income on the income and employment level. We therefore have two objectives in this chapter: (1) to determine if there is any discernible way in which the pattern of income distribution to the factors of production changes with change in the output level, and (2) to find out if there is a functional relationship between the distribution of income and the level aggregate demand, which, in the short run, is the prime determinant of the income level.

This is an area of economic analysis in which there does not exist any well-established and universally accepted body of economic analysis. David Ricardo, a founder of classical economics, thought that analysis of the principles that determine the distribution of the national output among different classes of claimants ought to be the major objective of economic analysis. However, throughout most of the nineteenth and early twentieth centuries economists were more concerned with the broad problem of resource allocation and the composition of the national output than they were with income distribution. After the appearance of Keynes's analysis in the mid-1930s, interest shifted almost exclusively to the problem of determination of the income and employment level in the short run. Since World War II there has been a renewed interest in the phenomenon of economic growth, inflation, and questions having to do with the distribution of the national income.

The Meaning of Income Distribution

Before we give our attention to various attempts to develop a theory of aggregate income distribution, it will be worthwhile to preface the analysis with a more thorough discussion of the meaning of income distribution. We are interested in *functional* or *factoral* income distribution, the claims on the national output that arise out of the ownership of economic resources. The productive process requires the services of economic resources, and payment must be made to the owners of the resources in order to secure these services. This gives rise to a claim by resource owners to a share of the national output. The broadest possible allocation of the national income is a twofold division with wage and salary income on one side and the various forms of property income on the other. Property income consists of income derived from ownership of economic resources in the form of either capital equipment or natural resources. In national income accounting, property incomes take the form of rents, interest, and profits. Beyond this fundamental division between labor and nonlabor income, the functional distribution concept has to do with the relative share of the income total that accrues to the different types of nonhuman economic resources, that is, the relative share in the income total of different types of property income.

The functional distribution of income is to be distinguished both in theory and empirically from the *personal distribution of income.* Personal distribution involves the distribution of money income among different income classes. Personal income distribution depends upon a prior factoral or functional income distribution, because in modern society the major determinant of the personal money income of each individual is the quantity of economic resources that he owns and the price he obtains for each unit of such resources supplied to the productive process. But this is not the whole story, for the personal income of some individuals may be augmented by transfer payments, while the income claims of others based upon ownership of economic resources may be reduced either by taxation or the fact that all income earned in the productive process is not necessarily paid out to individuals.

If, for the sake of analytical simplicity, we disregard transfer payments and the witholding from personal income of some portion of earned income, the income of an individual during a period of time depends upon the following:

1. The quantity of economic resources owned by the individual. Human labor is an economic resource, and, except in slave societies, such labor cannot be owned by anyone other than the individual who is the basic source of a particular kind and amount of labor power.

2. The extent to which the services of the fundamental kinds of economic resources (that is, labor, capital, and land) are being utilized. With respect to labor it is a matter of the employment level, and with respect to capital and land it is a matter of the degree of utilization of the existing stock of these resources.

3. The price that is paid for each unit of the economic resource utilized in the current productive process.

Thus, if an individual owns only his own labor power as an economic resource, and if his skill is such that his labor power can command a return of $4.00 per hour and, finally, if he is employed on the average a total of two thousand hours per year (forty hours per week for fifty weeks per year), his income will be $8,000 per year.

Because the personal income of an individual depends upon the three elements discussed above, the problem of the distribution of income has usually been regarded as a microeconomic problem that must be treated at the level of the firm and the household. This is so because given the distribution of ownership of nonhuman resources as determined by the society's structure of property rights, the extent to which resources are actually utilized can be seen as an aspect of the theory of the firm, and the problem of the price paid for each unit of a resource utilized is handled simply as a special facet of the theory of individual prices.

Most contemporary textbooks treat income distribution basically as a problem in the pricing of factors of production. These prices are determined presumably by the same basic forces that determine the prices of individual commodities and services, namely the interaction of demand and supply. The demand for an economic resource depends on its physical productivity and on the demand for the good or service whose production requires the use of the resource. The supply of the resource in question depends primarily on the quantity of the resource in existence at any particular time as well as the willingness of the resource owner to allow it to be used in the productive process. The theory of resource pricing is thus not so much a theory of the distribution of the national income as it is a theory that explains both the nature of the business firm's demand for the services of economic resources and the process of relative price determination for economic resources. It does not provide us with an answer to the vital question of how the distribution of the national income into labor income—that is, wages and salaries—and nonlabor (or property) income is determined.[1] This remains an important theoretical problem.

Interest in the general problem of distribution of the national income along functional lines stems in part from the view of many economists that the relative share of labor and nonlabor (or property) income in the national income is remarkably constant. For example, Keynes wrote in 1939:

> the stability of the proportion of the national dividend accruing to labour, irrespective apparently of the level of output as a whole and of the phase of the trade cycle . . . is one of the most surprising, yet best established facts in the whole range of economic statistics, both for Great Britain and for the United States. . . . It is the stability of the ratio for each country which is chiefly remarkable, and this appears to be a long-run, and not merely a short-period, phenomenon.[2]

There have been a number of empirical studies which tend either to support or disprove the thesis that the relative share of labor and nonlabor income in the national income has remained more or less constant over the very long run. For example, a statistical study by Professor D. Gale Johnson of the University of Chicago, dealing with the functional distribution of income in the United States for the period 1850 through 1952 concluded that although there had been some increase in the relative share of labor income in the national income total over this long period, the amount of the increase was relatively moderate and not inconsistent with the basic thesis of long-term stability in labor's share in the income total.[3] Professor Sidney Weintraub argues that the national income data show that the proportion of the gross business product—that is, that part of GNP originating in the business sector—which consists of employee compensation has been, for all practical purposes, a constant.[4]

Among challenges to the thesis of the historical constancy of the share of labor income in the national income is the argument of Professor Irving B. Kravis who, using much the same data as Johnson, has asserted that there has been a decided shift in the distribution of the national income from property to labor income.[5] Skepticism concerning the constant rela-

1. The distribution of nonlabor income between contractual income in the form of interest and rents and residual income in the form of profit is determined basically by the nature and extent of contractual obligations existing in a society.

2. John Maynard Keynes, "Relative Movements of Real Wages and Output," *Economic Journal*, March 1939, p. 48.

3. D. Gale Johnson, "The Functional Distribution of Income in the United States, 1840–1952," *Review of Economics and Statistics*, May 1954, p. 182.

4. Sidney Weintraub, *A General Theory of the Price Level, Output, Income Distribution, and Economic Growth* (Philadelphia: Chilton, 1959), pp. 14, 15.

5. I. B. Kravis, "Relative Income Shares in Fact and Theory," *American Economic Review*, December 1959, p. 917.

tive share of labor in the national income has also been expressed by Professor Robert M. Solow.[6]

These and other studies attest to the continuing interest of economists in the broad problem of the functional distribution of the national income, even though there is neither agreement among them on the extent to which empirical data do or do not support the constancy of relative shares thesis, nor a generally accepted body of theoretical principles which explains the functional distribution of income, irrespective of whether relative shares are in fact constant. This is clearly one of the significant frontier areas of contemporary economic analysis which has yet to be provided with a clearly defined and generally agreed upon body of economic principles.

Classical Theories of Income Distribution

The two most important figures in the classical approach to the distribution of the income of society are David Ricardo and Karl Marx.[7] Both Ricardo and Marx were interested in the long-term evolution of a capitalistic system of production, and as a consequence they developed definite notions on the manner in which this evolution would affect the distribution of income among the major economic classes. We shall first examine Ricardo's effort to develop a theory of relative shares, and then turn our attention to the Marxian theory, which stems directly from the theory developed by Ricardo.

Ricardo's Theory of Income Distribution

David Ricardo thought that discovery of the laws which regulate the distribution of the national output among the chief economic classes of society should be the principal problem in economic analysis. In a famous letter to his contemporary, Thomas Malthus, Ricardo put the matter in these terms:

> Political Economy you think is an enquiry into the natures and causes of wealth—I think it should rather be called an enquiry into the laws which determine the division of the produce of industry amongst the classes who concur in its formation. No law can be laid down respecting

6. Robert M. Solow, "The Constancy of Relative Shares," *American Economic Review*, September 1958, p. 618.

7. Marx is regarded as a classical economist because his analysis is in the classical deductive tradition, and because his fundamental notions are drawn directly from Ricardian theory.

> quantity, but a tolerably correct one can be laid down respecting proportions. Every day I am more satisfied that the former enquiry is vain and delusive and the latter only the true object of the science.[8]

Ricardo's concern with the problem of income distribution arose not only from an interest in the question of relative shares per se, but also because he believed that the theory of income distribution held the key to an understanding of the whole mechanism of the economic system, especially the forces which govern the progress of the economy. Thus Ricardo's theory of relative shares yields a simplified macroeconomic model which shows the inevitable progression of the economy and society toward a stationary state in which all further capital accumulation and technical progress ceases.[9]

In Ricardo's theory the economy is divided into two broad sectors, industry and agriculture, but it is what happens in agriculture that is of crucial importance for the over-all development of the economy. Ricardian analysis rests upon three major assumptions. The first is that agriculture is characterized by diminishing returns if and when additional labor is applied to the production of foodstuffs, because agricultural land is not unlimited in quantity and is not of a uniform quality. Secondly, Ricardo accepts the Malthusian law of population, which asserts that the population tends to increase very rapidly whenever wages rise above the subsistence level, and to decrease when wages fall below this level. Finally, the Ricardian analysis assumes that profit is the essential spur to capital accumulation, which is the key to economic progress.

In Ricardo's theory the output of the economy is allocated among the three major shares of rents, wages, and profits. Rent is the return on land, and it exists by virtue of the principle of diminishing returns. In a technical sense, rent is the difference between the product of labor on marignal land—land that yields just sufficient product to cover production costs—and the product of labor on land that yields more than enough product to cover production costs. Rent is thus a surplus based upon differences in the quality of land. On any given unit of land, rent is the difference between the average and the marginal productivity of successive units of labor.[10]

Wages are defined as the return to labor. In Ricardo's system it is essential to distinguish between the natural price (that is, wage) for labor, and the market price. The natural wage, or price of labor, is the level of wages toward which the actual or market wage will tend in the long run. It is basically a subsistence level of wages, a level of wages just sufficient to maintain the working propulation intact at a minimum of subsistence.

8. *Works and Correspondence of David Ricardo,* Sraffa ed. (Cambridge: Cambridge University Press, 1952), vol. 8, pp. 278–79.

9. Nicholas Kaldor, "Alternative Theories of Distribution," *Review of Economic Studies,* 23 (1955–56): p. 84.

10. Ibid.

In the earliest formulation of classical wage theory, the subsistence level was interpreted to mean a physical or biological level of wages just sufficient to permit the labor force to survive and raise enough children so that, over-all, the size of the labor force would neither increase nor decrease. In Ricardo's analysis, however, the idea of a subsistence level for wages is less a biologically determined minimum and more in the nature of a minimum standard shaped by cultural and social as well as physical forces. Yet Ricardo retains the concept of a natural rate toward which the actual rates tend, and which is such as to just maintain intact the size of the labor force. In contrast to the natural price of labor there is the market wage, by which is meant the level actually prevailing in the market and which is determined by the forces of supply and demand. In Ricardo's analysis the demand for labor is dependent primarily on the rate of capital formation or accumulation, which in turn is a function of the rate of profit. A high level of capital accumulation would cause employers to compete vigorously for labor, thus forcing the market price of labor above the natural price.

The third and final share in the income total is that of profit. In the Ricardian scheme profit is treated as a residual. It is the amount left over after wage payments and rents have been subtracted from the income total. Profits, though, have an extremely important role to play because they determine the rate of net investment or capital accumulation which, in the classical system, is the chief source of economic progress. Moreover, profits are crucial, too, because they are the source of the saving that makes possible capital accumulation.

The Working of the Ricardian System · The basic objective of Ricardo's theory was to demonstrate what happens to the relative distribution of output as it expands. In seeking to explain the behavior of relative shares, Ricardo also provided economics with a very long-run theory on the course of development of a capital economy. (See Chapter 15, pp. 512–15.)

Ricardo's theory of income distribution is based on the operation of two separate principles. Professor Nicholas Kaldor calls these the "marginal principle" and the "surplus principle." The marginal principle is employed to explain the division of national output between rent and the other two shares (wages and profits), and the surplus principle is called upon to explain the division of the national product *less* rent between wages and profit. The operation of these two principles and the resulting impact on the distribution of income into relative shares can be best explained with the use of a simple diagram.[11] This diagram is shown as Figure 17–1 and represents the forces operating in the agricultural sector of the economy.

11. This diagram is derived from Kaldor's discussion of alternative theories of income distribution.

Agricultural output, or the basic means of subsistence, is measured on the vertical axis, and the labor force in the sense of the number of workers employed in agriculture is shown on the horizontal axis. The curve *AP* depicts the average product of labor, and the curve *MP* represents the marginal product of labor. The *AP* and *MP* curves are both separate and downward-sloping because of the operation of the principle of diminishing returns. The one factor that differentiates this presentation from the more customary graphic analysis of the marginal productivity theory of wages[12] is that in Ricardo's analysis the marginal product is assumed to be equal to the sum of wages and profits. This is so because in the long run the level of wages is determined not by the marginal productivity of labor in the modern meaning of the term, but by the natural or subsistence price for labor. In Figure 17–1, therefore, the distance *OW* is equal to the natural, or subsistence, wage. This wage rate represents in real terms—that is, in terms of agricultural output—a level just sufficient to maintain intact the existing labor force at a subsistence (or culturally determined minimum) standard of living. If the marginal product is thus the sum of wages and profits in the Ricardian scheme, then the distance *WP* represents profit per unit of output, on the assumption that the employment level is equal to *ON*. Rent is equal to the distance *PR*, since we have already defined this share as equal to the difference between the average and the marginal product of labor. The actual level of employment—*ON* in Figure 17–1—is determined by the rate of capital accumulation because net investment serves to increase output, which in turn increases the demand for labor.

The fundamental character of Ricardo's theory of relative shares can be seen by analysis of what takes place as output expands in the economy's agricultural sector. In essence, the Ricardian schema postulates a sequence of events as follows: expansion of total production is the consequence of a high rate of capital accumulation (that is, net investment), which in turn results from the lure of high profits. Expansion leads to a high level of demand for labor, which has the effect of raising the market wage above the natural wage. Population will then rise, and there will be an increased demand for agricultural commodities, leading to an expansion of agricultural output. Since the total supply of agricultural land is fixed, the effort to expand the output of agricultural commodities by the employment of more labor (as shown on the horizontal axis of Figure 17–1) will sooner or later encounter diminishing returns, which will ultimately cause a reduction in both the average and the marginal product of labor. The latter effect is illustrated in the figure by the downward slope of both the *AP* and the *MP* curves.

12. Allan M. Cartter, *Theory of Wages and Employment* (Homewood, Ill.: Irwin, 1959), p. 17.

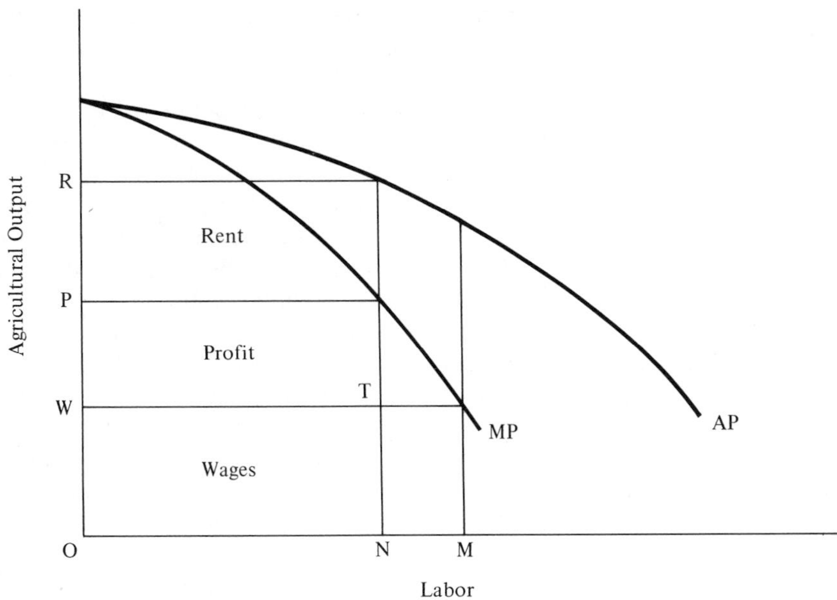

FIGURE 17–1. The Ricardian Theory of Income Distribution

As the attempt is made to expand agricultural output through the employment of more labor, the cost of production and thereby the price of agricultural commodities will rise. This is a consequence of diminishing returns or the decline in the average and marginal product of labor in the agricultural sector. When this happens, rents will necessarily increase, because rent is the difference between the product of labor on marginal land (land that yields just enough product to cover costs of production) and the product of labor on intramarginal or average, land. In Figure 17–1 this development will be reflected in a growing value for rent per unit of output (the distance *PR* with the employment level *ON*) as the volume of employment is expanded. At the same time the rising cost of production of agricultural output means that current money wages will have to rise in order to permit workers to maintain the subsistence standard of living for the labor force. The natural wage in real terms (the distance *OW*) will not change, but the share of the total output that is absorbed by wages will have to increase. This is shown by an increase in the size of the rectangle which represents the wage share of the total output. Initially this was the area *ONTW* at the employment level *ON*. This area will be elongated as employment expands toward the ultimate upper limit represented by the distance *OM*. What happens to profit in the process is readily apparent: As output expands, profit per unit of output (the distance *WP* at the employment level *ON*) continuously shrinks until finally at the employment level *OM* (at which point *MP* has fallen to a level just equal to the natural price of labor) it disappears completely.

The continuous fall in profit per unit of output depicted in Figure 17–1 takes place in the agricultural sector because of diminishing returns on land, but the same tendency toward a declining rate of profit will be at work in the manufacturing sector of the economy, even though the latter may not be subject to diminishing returns. The increase in the price of agricultural commodities with the resultant rise in the money cost of the subsistence standard of living will force manufacturers to pay higher wages. Profits will thus decline in the manufacturing sector. Moreover, as long as mobility of capital is assumed, profit will have to be the same in both agriculture and industry, or else capital will shift from one sector to the other.

We can summarize Ricardo's theory of income distribution by stating that, given the assumption of a constant technology and a constant natural wage in real terms, the relative share of wages in the output total will increase with a rising level of output and employment. The relative share of profit will decline and ultimately fall to zero. This is the point at which the economy reaches the stationary state of classical theory, a situation in which all accumulation, population growth, and technical progress cease. The basic causal force in this schema is the fact of diminishing returns in agriculture, a grim tendency which can only be postponed temporarily by technical progress. Technical progress cannot, in other words, prevent the ultimate disappearance of profit and the onset of the stationary state.

Although Ricardo saw clearly that his system would lead to an increase in the relative share of wages in the total output and that this would come at the expense of profit, he was less certain as to what would happen to the relative share of rent.[13] However, if the economic system reacts to increasing employment as depicted in Figure 17–1, the relative share of rent in the output total will rise along with the rise in the relative share of wages; the rent share depends upon the amount of rent per unit of output, which rises with successive increases in the employment level.

The Marxian Theory of Income Distribution

Karl Marx's theory of income distribution in an advancing capitalistic economy rests basically upon an adaptation of Ricardian ideas, even though his analysis reaches very different conclusions concerning the behavior of relative income shares as the level of income and employment changes. Marx's theory of income distribution is an essential aspect of his

13. Paul Davidson, *Theories of Aggregate Income Distribution* (New Brunswick, N.J.: Rutgers University Press, 1960), p. 7.

general and sweeping theory of capitalistic development because it is his contention that the economic development of capitalism is tied to the distribution of the output among the different economic classes.

The entire Marxian structure rests on the concept of the labor theory of value which, in essence, asserts that the value of a commodity or service is determined by the labor time necessary for its production. Thus labor power is the ultimate source of economic value. The reader should note that we are concerned, first, with the determination of exchange value rather than value in a broader, philosophical sense and, second, that Marx's labor theory of value is basically a cost of production theory because it makes exchange value dependent wholly on factors present on the supply side of the picture, specifically, the amount of labor power necessary to produce a commodity or service. For this reason, Marx's theory is sometimes said to be an objective theory of value in contrast to modern value theory which is in part subjective since it holds that value depends upon the usefulness (or utility) of the good or service to the ultimate purchaser as well as upon the cost conditions under which the commodity or service in question was produced.

What is unique in the Marxian analysis is not so much the labor theory of value—Marx derived this idea from Adam Smith and Ricardo—but the application of the theory to the value of labor power itself, which is to say, the wage of labor. According to Marx, the supply price for labor is determined by the amount of labor power required to produce the commodities and services that make up the minimum level of subsistence necessary to maintain the labor force intact. In the Marxian system, as in the Ricardian analysis, there exists a natural price for labor, a level of real wages which will just permit the labor force to survive and reproduce itself. In Marx's theory the value of the real wage corresponding to this minimum level of subsistence is determined by the amount of labor power necessary to produce the commodities that enter into the subsistence standard of living.

Marx's application of the labor theory of value to the determination of the value of labor itself is crucial because it forms the basis for his theory of surplus value, or theory of the exploitation of labor, which in turn provides the fundamental key to an understanding of the proces of income distribution in a capitalistic society. Surplus value exists, according to Marx, because labor power in a given period of time will produce more economic value than the cost of labor itself as measured by the supply price of labor or the minimum real wage that will maintain intact the labor force. Because labor power is the source of all economic or exchange value, exploitation exists whenever the worker fails to receive the whole of the value of the output. The difference between the value of the total output and the supply price of labor represents surplus value which is expropriated by the capitalists, who, in the Marxian schema, are owners of the nonhuman instruments of production—capital equipment and land. It is through their ownership of the physical means of production that the capitalists exploit the working class and extract surplus value from it. This is the essence of the Marxian theory of exploitation, and its validity is no greater than the validity of its basic cornerstone, the labor theory of value. Non-Marxist economists usually question the correctness of the labor theory as a satisfactory explanation of the phenomenon of exchange value.

Nevertheless, the notion of surplus value is crucial to the Marxian theory of income distribution; surplus value is the source of all profit, and thus the amount of surplus value that can be expropriated by the capitalistic class will determine the relative share of profit in the income total. Marx, it should be noted, was concerned primarily with the distribution of output between wages (or labor income) and profit (or nonwage income). He was not particularly interested in the allocation of the nonwage share among the various forms of property income. Unlike Ricardo, he did not believe in the principle of diminishing returns, and thus he did not distinguish in his analysis between rents and profit.[14]

In Marx's analysis of the productive process the value of a final good or service can be broken down into three component parts. These are: c, which represents raw materials and capital consumption,[15] v, which Marx defined as *variable capital* and which represents the value of the labor power entering into current production (that is, the wage bill in terms of the subsistence wage); and s, which is surplus value or profit. Thus, the value of any single final good or service is equal to $c + v + s$. For the economy as a whole, the value of the gross output may be defined as $C + V + S$, where C is equal to capital consumption alone (since at the level of the whole economy raw materials are intermediate products, and thus their value is included in the value of the final output). V is equal to Σv, and S is equal to Σs. The net output will, therefore, be equal to $V + S$, as it is derived by subtracting C from the gross output. Net output can thus be seen to consist of two basic shares, the wage share, V, and the profit share, S.

The ratio of the profit share to the wage share is of key importance in Marx's analysis, because this ratio, S/V, is more than a measure of the rate of exploitation; a change in S/V means that a change has taken place in the relative share of wage and nonwage (that is, profit) income in the output total. Consequently, if we understand how Marx thought that this ratio would change in response to the basic forces at work in the capital-

14. Kaldor, p. 87.

15. Capital and raw materials present a difficult problem in terms of the labor theory of value, because they contribute to current output, but are clearly not labor. Marx resolved this problem by regarding capital and raw materials currently utilized in the productive process as stored-up labor power from past periods.

istic system, we grasp the essence of the Marxian theory of income distribution. A rise in this ratio represents an increase in the rate of exploitation and, consequently, an increase in the share of profit relative to wages in the income total. A decline in the ratio represents the reverse.

According to Marx, the most important single force at work in the economy centers around the effort of the capitalists to increase the rate of exploitation of labor, that is, to increase the ratio S/V. At the core of Marx's theory of the long-term development of a capitalistic economy is the contention that the basic forces at work in such a system tend to bring about exactly this result. Let us examine the reasons postulated by Marx to explain this tendency. For one thing, Marx believed, as did Ricardo, that the market wage tended to fall toward a real wage equal to the minimum subsistence standard of living. In Marx's analysis this was not caused by population pressure, as was the case in the Ricardian system, but by a continuous excess of labor supply over demand, which Marx saw as the normal condition of a capitalistic economy. The continuous presence of what he termed a vast industrial "reserve army" of unemployed workers prevents the market wage from rising (for other than very short periods of time) above the minimum wage level necessary to maintain the labor force intact.

The excess supply of labor and the industrial reserve army of the unemployed are the inevitable products of certain forces at work in the economic system. One of the most important of these is competition. In Marxian theory competition takes the form of a struggle among the owners of the material instruments of production to increase the rate of exploitation or, and this comes to the same thing, the nonwage share in the income total. This might be done by lengthening the working day, thereby increasing the amount of surplus value expropriated from the labor force. Much the same result could be achieved by an increase in the intensity of labor. There are limits, though, to the extent that the rate of exploitation can be increased by either of these means. Technical progress —or a change in the physical productivity of the labor force—would achieve this result because with a constant length for the working day and no change in the real subsistence wage, the total product will expand with technical progress and thus there is necessarily an increase in surplus value or the rate of exploitation. This is true as long as the market wage does not depart significantly from the subsistence wage. Marx termed the increase in the rate of exploitation from this source an increase in "relative surplus value," and asserted that the latter would vary directly with the productivity of labor.[16]

Technical progress is primarily the result of the accumulation of capital. Consequently the struggle among the capitalists to increase the rate of

16. Davidson, p. 15.

exploitation forces them to accumulate capital—that is, to invest. In the Marxian system capital accumulation or investment is an activity that is not to be explained primarily in terms of the lure of profit, but as a necessary structural feature of the economic system which results from the intensity of competition among capitalists seeking to increase the rate of exploitation.[17] In any event, the combination of capital accumulation and technical progress provides the basis for Marx's fundamental proposition concerning the distribution of income in a capitalistic society: the "law of the increasing misery of the working class." According to this law, capital accumulation and a growing level of real output must lead to a decline in the relative share of wages in the output total and a corresponding increase in the relative share of profit. This is a conclusion on relative shares diametrically the opposite of that reached by Ricardo. The fundamental cause of decline in the relative share of wages is technical progress, the fruits of which go entirely to the owners of the physical instruments of production. The alleged increasing misery of the working class does not come from any decline in the level of real wages, since their misery does not increase in any absolute sense; it is the result instead of the failure of real wages to advance along with gains in productivity. This is the heart of Marx's theory of distribution.

Although the logic of his own theories pertaining to surplus value and the role of competition led Marx to assume that the relative share of wages in the output total would decline as productivity and the income level rose, he also took over from earlier classical theories the view that capital accumulation would be accompanied by a falling rate of profit. Unlike Ricardo and other classical economists, Marx did not attribute this to the operation of the principle of diminishing returns, but to an increase in what he termed the "organic composition of capital," by which he meant, to employ more modern terminology, an increase in the capital-output ratio, or a more capital-intensive productive process. Although there is no compelling reason why a more capital-intensive operation would lead to a decline in profit as long as wage rates remain unchanged at the subsistence level,[18] Marx's law of the falling rate of profits is nevertheless necessary to complete his analysis of the course of development of the capitalistic system. The process of capital accumulation and growth leads inevitably to a severe economic crisis. This crisis is the result of both the falling rate of profit, which must sooner or later adversely affect capital accumulation itself and, second, overproduction because of an insufficiency of aggregate demand. The latter stems from the progressive decline in the relative share of wage income in the output total. Marx thought the capitalistic system would be increasingly wracked by crises of greater and greater severity until finally it would collapse amid an upris-

17. Kaldor, p. 88.
18. Kaldor, p. 86.

ing of the working class that would usher in the era of communism. Marx proved to be a poor prophet concerning not only the behavior of the wage share in the national income, but also the long-term development of capitalism.

Contemporary Theoretical Developments

The development of marginal utility and marginal productivity analysis in the latter part of the nineteenth century had the effect of shifting attention from the macroeconomic or aggregate problem of the distribution of the national income into functional shares to the primarily microeconomic problem of the determination of the prices of the factors of production. Thus, for almost a century, income distribution theory has come to mean the process by which factor prices are determined through the interplay of the firm's demand for the services of economic resources and the conditions under which varying amounts of the resource will be supplied. Analysis of the fundamental forces determining the distribution of income in the sense in which Ricardo saw the problem practically vanished from the literature of the science. Since World War II, though, there has been a revival of interest in the macroeconomic aspects of income distribution. These analyses emerged primarily out of the framework of modern income and employment theory; they should be regarded as probing efforts that seek development of a body of theory in this area rather than as a completed and fully acceptable set of conclusions concerning the forces that determine the functional distribution of income. We cannot touch upon all such theoretical developments pertaining to the distribution of income in an aggregate sense, but we shall deal with the ideas of several individuals whose thinking seems most representative of this trend. Specifically, we shall analyze the theories of Professors Allan M. Cartter, Nicholas Kaldor, and Sidney Weintraub.

A Simplified Keynesian Model

In his *Theory of Wages and Employment,* Professor Cartter has attempted to develop a relatively simple model which links the problem of distribution to the determination of the income level for the economy as a whole.[19] His analysis is considered Keynesian because it ties the distribution of income in a functional sense to the fundamental Keynesian condition of income equilibrium, namely that saving and investment *ex ante* must be equal. The equilibrium income level is Cartter's point of

19. Cartter, p. 155.

departure. His major purpose is to show how an alteration in the functional distribution of income between a wage and a nonwage share may affect the equilibrium income position. His analysis does not, however, come to grips with the problem of the relationship between changes in the income and employment level and changes in the functional pattern of income distribution. For this reason, his model lacks the generality that a true theory of aggregate income distribution ought to possess; it represents, nevertheless, an interesting and worthwhile effort to relate income distribution to some important macroeconomic variables.

Cartter's model rests on four basic propositions that may be summarized as follows.[20]

1. The initial assumption is that equilibrium in the income level depends upon the equality between saving, S, and investment, I, in an *ex ante*, or intended, sense. Thus, our first equation is

$$I = S \qquad (17\text{–}1)$$

2. The rate of *ex ante* investment is assumed to be a linear function of profit, P. This gives us

$$I = \pi(P) \qquad (17\text{–}2)$$

In the above equation, π is a constant defined as the investment-profit coefficient. It is equal to the ratio I/P. It is further assumed that the value of π is normally positive but less than one. The relationship between I and P is shown graphically in Figure 17–2. The value of π is represented by the slope of the curve. An upward, or counterclockwise, movement of the curve depicts a rise in the value of the investment-profit coefficient. The practical meaning of this is that a given amount of profit will generate (or induce) a greater amount of investment than heretofore.

3. Income is assumed to be allocated between two factors, laborers and capitalists, the latter being the owners of all nonhuman economic resources. Thus the two functional shares of the national income are wages and profits. Cartter designates the proportion of the total income, Y, which goes to labor in the form of wages by the symbol λ. The share of the income total going to capitalists in the form of profits is thus $1 - \lambda$. This gives us the following two definitional equations for the total of wages and the total of profits:

$$W = \lambda Y \qquad (17\text{–}3)$$

$$P = (1 - \lambda)Y \qquad (17\text{–}4)$$

From Equation (17–4) and from Equation (17–2) it follows that investment can be further defined as

$$I = \pi(1 - \lambda)Y \qquad (17\text{–}5)$$

20. The model is applicable to a simplified economy with no government and no foreign balance. See Cartter, p. 155.

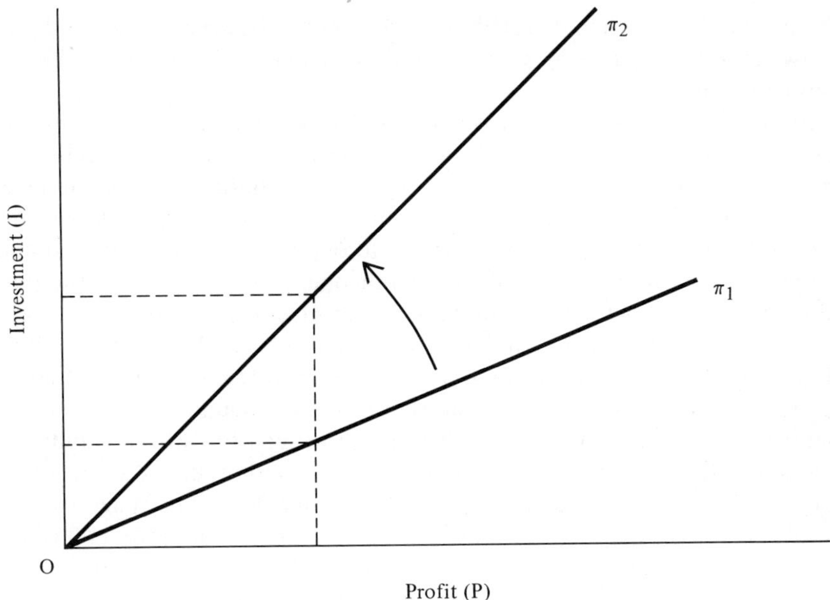

FIGURE 17–2. The Investment-Profit Coefficient

4. The fourth proposition that enters into Cartter's model is that the level of saving in the economy depends upon the marginal (and average) propensities to save of the major groups in the economy; the division of income between these groups; and, finally, the extent to which profits are retained by business firms or distributed to the owners (that is, the shareholders). The foregoing factors are defined symbolically by Cartter as follows:

$a =$ The propensity (marginal and average) to save out of wage income.
$b =$ The propensity to save out of shareholder's income.
$v =$ The share of profit income that is distributed to shareholders or the owners of business firms. This is distributed profit.
$1 - v =$ The share of total profits retained in business firms. This follows from the definition of v.

On the basis of the foregoing, Cartter finds it possible to rewrite the fundamental equation defining the necessary condition for income equilibrium (equality between *ex ante* saving and investment) as follows:[21]

$$\pi(1 - \lambda) = \lambda a + (1 - \lambda)[vb + (1 - v)] \qquad (17\text{–}6)$$

This equation expresses the saving-investment identity in a form which will show the possible impact on the equilibrium income level of a

21. The algebraic derivation of this equation is shown in the Appendix to this chapter.

change in the functional distribution of income between wage and the nonwage (that is, profit) share. Let us examine some of its significant implications.

In the first place, an increase in the relative share of wages in the income total will reduce profits and thereby bring about a decline in investment expenditure.[22] As a consequence the equilibrium income level will decline. The fall in investment might be offset by an equal downward shift in the saving function, but this would depend upon the marginal and average propensities to save of the two income groups as well as the possible effect of a change in the distribution of income on the share of profit income distributed to shareholders (the value of v). It is Cartter's view that an increase in labor's share will reduce investment by more than it reduces saving. This implies that there is not enough of a difference between the saving propensities of the two groups to cause a significant decline in the saving function for the whole economy in the event of an increase in the relative share of wages in the income total. Wage earners would have to have a significantly lower propensity to save (marginal and average) than nonwage groups for such a shift to come about.

A decline in investment brought about by an increase in the relative share of labor income can be offset by an increase in either the investment-profit coefficient, π, or by an increase in v, the proportion of profit income distributed to shareholders. An increase in π implies that a given amount of profit will induce more investment expenditure than heretofore, a condition that will be realized only if expectations of future profits are highly favorable or improving. In the event of a shift in the distribution of income in favor of wage earners and a consequent decline in the relative share of profit, a higher level of investment is likely only if the change in income distribution brings a sufficient increase in consumption expenditure to justify more favorable expectations with respect to future income. This, though, implies that the saving function will fall by more than the investment function in the event of an increase in labor's share.

An increase in the value of v would also tend to offset the decline in investment brought about by the reduction in the relative share of profit in the income total. An increase in v at any income level presumably means a decline in the proportion of income saved, because normally the marginal (and average) propensity to save of profit recipients is less than unity. Thus, an increase in the value of v is tantamount to a downward shift in the saving function. If this shift is large enough, the equilibrium income level will be unaffected.

A second set of possibilities centers around the effect of a decline in the relative share of wages in the income total. Within the strict algebraic framework of Cartter's model, such a decline will automatically increase

22. Cartter, p. 158.

the profit share and thereby cause investment expenditure to rise. If it is assumed that saving increases less than in proportion to the upward shift in investment spending, then the equilibrium income level will rise in the unlikely case that there is no change in any of the other variables that are a part of the analysis. The assumption that the saving function will shift upward, although to a lesser degree than the shift in the investment function, necessarily implies a fall in current consumption. It is difficult to see how such a change can leave the investment-profit coefficient unaffected. The larger level of profit which results from the initial decline in the relative share of wages in the income total will result in a greater investment expenditure only if we totally ignore the unfavorable effects on expectations with respect to future profit possibilities of an absolute decline in the volume of consumer spending. It seems likely, in other words, that a change in the distribution of income in favor of profit and at the expense of wage income will lead, sooner or later, to a decline in the value of the investment-profit coefficient. If this happens, it means that a given amount of profit will induce less investment expenditure than heretofore, and thus the absolute amount of investment may not increase, even though the relative share of profit in the current income total has risen. Less certain is the impact of a decline in labor's share on the value of v. There seems to be no *a priori* reason for the value of v to change one way or another with an initial alteration in the functional distribution of income in favor of the nonwage share. However, if the absolute decline in consumption outlays caused the investment-profit coefficient to fall so drastically that the equilibrium income level fell rather than rose, pressure might be exerted by shareholders to increase the proportion of total profit actually distributed so that the shareholders would be able to maintain customary standards of living. Beyond this, though, no generalization seems possible with respect to changes in the value of v as a result of changes in the distribution of income.[23]

Cartter's analysis represents a thoughtful attempt to bring distributional problems into the framework of modern income and employment theory. His reformulation of the basic investment-saving equilibrium equation, Equation (17–6), is useful because it offers insight into the way in which a shift in the functional distribution of income may affect the income equilibrium itself. The weak link, perhaps, in his analysis is the assumption that investment is a direct function of profit, and the further implicit assumption that the absolute amount of consumer spending will not have any direct impact upon either profit or profit expectations. Beyond this, though, the analysis does not offer an explanation of the behavior of relative shares as the income and employment level changes.

23. As defined by Cartter, v is the share of gross profit that is distributed to shareholders. Replacement investment will limit the extent to which the value of v can be increased.

Kaldor's Theory of Income Distribution

Kaldor's analysis is similar to that of Cartter's in that his point of departure is the fundamental condition for an income equilibirum; saving and investment *ex ante* are equal. But the similarity ends at this point because Kaldor attempts to demonstrate how changes in the ratio of investment to income will cause a change in the relative share of profits and wages in the income total, whereas Cartter's analysis concerns itself with the impact of changes in the distribution of income on the absolute amount of investment. The key characteristics of the Kaldorian theory can be summed up algebraically in a series of equations.[24]

$$Y = W + P \tag{17–7}$$

The above equation is simply an identity which asserts that the national income, Y, consists of the sum of wage payments, W, and profits, P. This is identical with Cartter's proposition that the income of society is allocated between two factors, laborers and capitalists.

$$I = S \tag{17–8}$$

This is the basic condition for income equilibrium. I and S are intended or *ex ante* values.

$$S = S_w + S_p \tag{17–9}$$

This identity asserts that total saving (*ex ante*) for the economy is equal to the sum of saving out of wage income, S_w, and saving out of profit income, S_p. The amount of saving in equilibrium thus depends upon the average propensity to save of each of the two income classes present in the Kaldorian system. If we label the average propensity to save of wage earners as s_w and the average propensity to save of profit recipients as s_p, we then have

$$S_w = s_w \times W \tag{17–10}$$

$$S_p = s_p \times P \tag{17–11}$$

Equation (17–10) gives us the absolute amount of saving out of wage income; Equation (17–11), the absolute amount of saving out of profit income. The sum of the two yield the total of saving.

By the process of substitution and algebraic manipulation, Kaldor derives an equation which describes in symbolic form the essential features of his theory of income distribution.[25]

$$\frac{I}{Y} = (s_p - s_w)\frac{P}{Y} + s_w \tag{17–12}$$

24. Kaldor, p. 95.

25. The algebraic derivation of this equation is shown in the Appendix to this chapter.

Before we discuss the theoretical meaning of the foregoing equation it is essential to make clear the underlying assumptions of the Kaldorian theory. First, he assumes that full-employment conditions prevail in the economy and, second, that the saving propensities for both the wage and the nonwage groups are constant. There are some added assumptions which we shall bring out as we discuss the model.

Given these two assumptions, Kaldor's thesis is that the share of profit in the income total is a function of the ratio of investment to income (or output). This thesis can be expressed in algebraic form by rearrangement of Equation (17–12).

$$\frac{P}{Y} = \frac{1}{(s_p - s_w)} \times \frac{I}{Y} - \frac{s_w}{(s_p - s_w)} \qquad (17\text{–}13)$$

In algebraic terms it can easily be seen that an increase in the investment-output ratio, I/Y, will result in an increase in the share of profit in income, P/Y, as long as it is assumed that both s_w and s_p are constants and, further, that $s_p > s_w$.

Of greater importance to us is the underlying economic rationale for Kaldor's theorem that the share of profit in the income total is a function of the investment-output ratio. Under full employment conditions an increase in investment expenditure must, in real terms, bring about an increase in both the ratio of investment to output, I/Y, and also an increase in the saving-output ratio, S/Y. This is necessary if equilibrium at a higher level of real investment is to be obtained. If the saving-output ratio did not rise, the result would be a continuous upward movement of the general level of prices. The heart of Kaldor's theory lies in his demonstration that a shift in the distribution of income is essential to bring about the higher saving-output ratio which is the necessary condition for a continued full-employment equilibrium with a higher absolute level of investment in real terms.

This brings us to another key assumption in his analysis: propensities to save for the two income classes differ. The propensity to save out of profit income is greater than the propensity to save out of wage income. This assumption, according to Kaldor, is a necessary condition for both stability in the entire system and an increase in the share of profit in income when the investment-output ratio increases.[26] The underlying rationale is that with a fixed level of real income (the full-employment assumption) the only way in which an increase in the saving-output ratio for the whole economy can be brought about is either through a change in the propensity to save itself, which Kaldor rules out by his assumption that both s_w and s_p are constant, or by a shift in the distribution of real income from the income class with the lower propensity to save to the income class with the higher propensity to save.

26. Kaldor, p. 95.

The mechanism which brings about the redistribution of income in favor of the profit share whenever there is a rise in the investment-output ratio is essentially that of the price level. The increase in investment expenditure under full-employment conditions leads initially to a general rise in prices. Since, according to Kaldor, no mechanism exists to insure that money wages rise at the same rate as prices, there presumably will be an increase in profit margins relative to wages. The failure of money wages to keep pace with the rise in the general price level will thus reduce the real income of wage earners, while the increased profit margins increase the real income of nonwage income rcipients. Since the propensity to save of the latter group is, on the average, higher than that of wage earners, the inflation-induced shift in the distribution of real income in favor of profits will raise the over-all level of real saving in the economy. This process will continue until the saving-output ratio is once again in equilibrium with the investment-output ratio. The reader should understand, though, the key importance to the Kaldorian system of the assumption that the propensity to save of profit recipients is greater than that of wage earners. Without this assumption, the real saving-output ratio would not rise, irrespective of any alteration in the distribution of income, and thus the system would be unstable.

Since Kaldor seeks to relate the functional distribution of income directly to variables that are of crucial importance in the determination of the level of income and employment, his analysis is appropriately described as an aggregate or macroeconomic theory of income distribution. But it must be recognized that Kaldor's analysis is severely restricted by its underlying assumptions. The theory does not tell us how the distribution of income in a functional sense will be affected by changes in real income (or output) below the full-employment level, although it does suggest that any attempt to increase capacity once full employment is reached will bring about a relative increase in the nonwage share in the income total. In this sense Kaldor's analysis has a distinct classical flavor, even though his framework is that of modern employment theory.

Weintraub's Theory of Income Distribution

Among the most ambitious efforts to construct an aggregate theory of income distribution is that of Professor Sidney Weintraub. In *An Approach to the Theory of Income Distribution*,[27] he attempts to analyze the functional distribution of income through the device of the aggregate supply function, a concept of key importance in modern income ond employment theory. Weintraub believes that an aggregate supply func-

27. Sidney Weintraub, *An Approach to the Theory of Income Distribution* (Philadelphia: Chilton, 1958).

tion constructed in terms of current rather than constant prices provides the necessary bridge between income and employment theory and a theory of aggregate income distribution. Weintraub employs the aggregate supply schedule to show how the functional distribution of income will change as the level of employment (and output) changes. In addition, he seeks to make his theory complete by relating the level of the aggregate demand function to the functional distribution of income. Thus, Weintraub's analysis has a more ambitious objective than any of the theories we have surveyed to this point.

The Aggregate Supply Function and the Theory of Relative Shares · The point of departure for Weintraub's theory of income distribution is the aggregate supply function. He designates this function with the capital letter Z. In concept, Weintraub's Z is identical with the so-called Keynesian aggregate supply function that we discussed earlier.[28] It is a schedule which relates money proceeds to the employment level. In the Weintraubian system money proceeds are measured in current rather than constant prices. As is true of any aggregate supply function, there will be a unique level of employment associated with each level of money proceeds, and because of the static character of the analysis each level of employment will be uniquely associated with a particular level of output (that is, real income). An aggregate supply schedule of this kind is shown in Figure 17–3.

The money proceeds associated with each and every possible employment level must be allocated in accordance with the following equation:

$$Z = wN + F + R \qquad (17\text{–}14)$$

In the above equation symbols have the following meanings:

w = the money wage rate
N = the employment level
F = fixed or contractual incomes or payments (rents, interest, contractual salaries)
R = the residual or profit

The wage bill in total is thus equal to wN. Weintraub uses the symbol W to designate the total wage bill, as distinct from the level of money wages, w. Therefore, $W = wN$. These three component parts of aggregate supply measured in terms of money proceeds correspond to the three allocative shares of the national income: wages, rentier or fixed incomes, and profits.

The relationship between the three types of incomes which make up the economy's aggregate supply function is depicted in Figure 17–4.[29]

28. Chapter 5, pp. 125–28.
29. Weintraub, *An Approach to the Theory of Income Distribution*, p. 29.

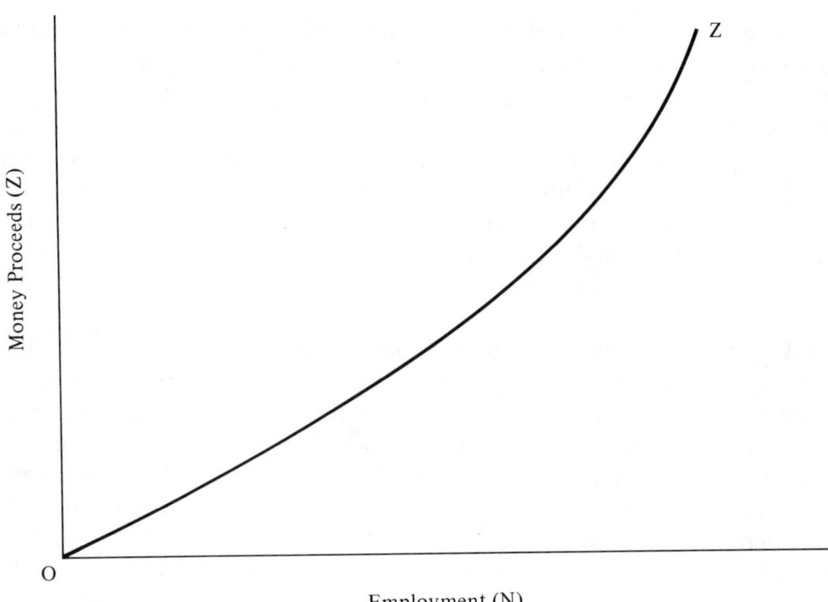

FIGURE 17–3. Weintraub's Aggregate Supply Function

The aggregate supply function is represented by the curve OZ. The line OW represents the total wage bill W on the assumption that money wages are constant. The dotted line FF' represents fixed (or contractual) payments, and it is drawn to exceed W by the absolute amount of these payments. The residual (or profit) is equal to the difference between the schedule OZ and the FF' curve. Thus $R = OZ - FF'$. It may be noted that proceeds fall short of factor costs up to the employment level ON_1, which means that profits are negative until the economy reaches this level of employment. It follows that the economy cannot remain indefinitely at an employment level below ON_1 as this implies that firms, on the average, are experiencing losses.

It is Weintraub's contention that the aggregate supply function, Z, is nonlinear. He employes the concept of the elasticity of aggregate supply as a measure of the shape of the function Z. The elasticity of aggregate supply, which Weintraub designates as E_z, shows the relationship between a change in money proceeds and a change in employment. In equation form we have[30]

$$E_z = \frac{\Delta N}{\Delta Z} \times \frac{Z}{N} \tag{17–15}$$

30. Technically, the elasticity of aggregate supply is the ratio of a percentage change in employment, $\Delta N/N$, to a percentage change in proceeds, $\Delta Z/Z$.

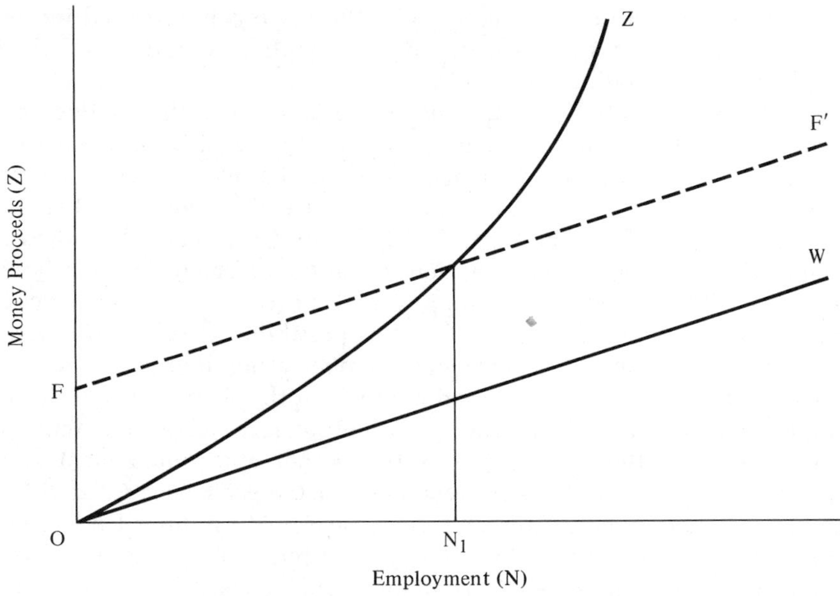

FIGURE 17–4. Construction of Weintraub's Aggregate Supply Function

If the coefficient E_z has a value greater than one, $E_z > 1$, it means that a 1 percent increase in proceeds would lead to a more than 1 percent increase in employment. This would be true under conditions of increasing returns. On the other hand, a value for the elasticity of aggregate supply coefficient of less than one, $E_z < 1$, means that a 1 percent increase in proceeds leads to a less than 1 percent increase in employment. This is the usual situation under conditions of decreasing returns. The static character of Weintraub's analysis means that the normal situation is one of diminishing returns to additional labor and, therefore, the coefficient E_z will have a value of less than unity. If this is correct, and if it is further assumed that the money wage is a constant, it follows that *OZ* will curve upward and to the left in the fashion depicted in Figure 17–4. The combination of diminishing returns to labor and fixed money wages means that labor costs per unit of output will rise as more employment is offered. As a consequence, the general price level will rise with a growing volume of employment, and the aggregate demand function will have to reflect this fact. A straight-line function would be possible only on the assumption of constant prices.

The foregoing discussion sets the stage for consideration of the essentials of Weintraub's theory of relative shares. The key to what happens to the relative importance of the three types of income as changes take place in the income total depends upon what assumptions are made concerning the shape of the *OZ*, the *FF′*, and the *OW* curves. Let us consider each income category in turn, beginning with the share going to fixed income groups. We shall assume we are dealing with a situation in which employment (and output) expands.

If *OZ* has, in reality, the shape shown in Figure 17–4, the relative position of the rentier, or fixed income, group must worsen, because its absolute money income does not change. Therefore its relative position worsens even if prices remain constant. Prices are not constant when the aggregate supply function assumes the shape of the schedule shown in Figure 17–4. The necessary condition for an improvement in the relative income position of the rentier group is a fall in the general price level as output and employment expand, but this possibility is ruled out by the assumption of a constant money wage and decreasing returns.

Figure 17–4 also depicts a situation in which the share of wages in the output total, wN/Z, will decline as the output level advances. Actually, the behavior of the wage share as the output and employment level changes depends upon the value assumed for the coefficient E_z. If $E > 1$ this means increasing returns or a rising marginal product. Under such circumstances the wage share in the income total would rise, because a rising marginal product when combined with a constant money wage implies a falling price level, and the gap between the *OW* curve and the *OZ* curve would narrow. Such would be the graphical representation of an increase in the relative share of wages in the income total. On the other hand, the assumption that $E_z < 1$ implies decreasing returns or a declining marginal product for labor. The consequence would be a decline in the relative share of labor in the income total because the gap between the *OW* and the *OZ* curves becomes larger and larger. This is the kind of situation depicted in Figure 17–4. If we assume diminishing returns to labor, an assumption that is not wholly unrealistic in the short run, the tendency will be for the relative share of wages in the income total to decline with advancing employment and output. This is the basic conclusion reached by Weintraub and rests essentially on the application of the principle of diminishing returns or productivity to the problem of relative shares.

Since profit is a residual, its relative share in the income total is determined primarily by what happens to the other two income categories. The general presumption, though, is that the residual share will increase relatively as employment and output expand. This is true irrespective of the behavior of the wage share because the entrepreneurial groups or profit recipients are the chief beneficiaries of the relative decline in the income position of the rentier class as output expands.[31] If the wage share also declines because of diminishing returns, the gain in the relative importance of the residual share will be all the greater.

31. Weintraub, *An Approach to the Theory of Income Distribution*, p. 47.

In essence, Weintraub's theory of relative shares presumes that, in the short run and under the usual conditions of static analysis, a rise in the income and employment level will bring about a redistribution of income which tends to favor the recipients of income in the form of profits at the definite expense of persons or groups whose incomes are fixed in money terms, and at the probable expense of wage earners—as long as the principle of diminishing returns is assumed operative and money wage rates remain constant. In *An Approach to the Theory of Income Distribution*, Weintraub expands this basic framework to take into account the effect of other influences upon the division of the economy's output into relative income shares. For example, he argues that the general effect of monopoly is to lower the relative share of wages in the income total, while an increase in money wages may or may not favorably affect the wage share. Changes in the physical stock of capital may have a favorable impact on the wage share if such changes increase the marginal productivity of labor, although a definite conclusion to this effect is not always warranted. With respect to labor's productivity, Weintraub demonstrates that a change in the relative share of labor is dependent not upon changes in marginal productivity alone but upon the ratio of the marginal to the average product of labor. Therefore, an increase in the marginal product of labor will not lead to an increase in the relative share of wages if the average product of labor rises in the same proportion.[32] Changes in the capital stock as well as technological improvements may have this effect.

Income Distribution and the Aggregate Demand Function · Weintraub's analysis does not end with this theory of relative shares. He has constructed an aggregate demand function, *D*, which links the spending decisions of the economic system to the distribution of income. In this way he attempts to show not only how the income and employment level affect the functional distribution of income but, further, how the income level itself is related to income distribution through the impact of distribution on the position of the aggregate demand function. As is the case with his aggregate supply function, the aggregate demand schedule worked out by Weintraub is in current rather than constant prices.

For the purposes of simplicity we shall limit our examination of Weintraub's aggregate demand analysis to two categories of expenditure: consumption and investment. We shall assume that investment expenditures are a constant (in real terms), that is, they are autonomous with respect to the income level. Since our analysis is cast in terms of current prices, the current money value of investment outlays will increase as the price level rises.

The crucial consideration, then, in Weintraub's concept of aggregate

32. Ibid., p. 51.

demand is the level of consumption spending. Weintraub postulates an essentially Keynesian consumption function, except that he introduces asset holdings in addition to current disposable income into his analysis as a factor determining current outlays for consumption purposes. In equation form,

$$C = cY_d + \lambda A \tag{17–16}$$

In this equation, c represents the average propensity to consume; λ represents the possible dissavings out of asset holdings, A.

For our purposes the most significant variable in Equation (17–16) is disposable income, Y_d, as this provides the necessary link to the distribution of income. Y_d may be defined in equation form as follows:

$$Y_d = wN + F + kR \tag{17–17}$$

All the variables in this equation have the same meaning as heretofore, except that a new variable, k, is introduced. Weintraub defines this as the fraction of profits, R, that is actually distributed to individuals. (The reader should be careful not to confuse Weintraub's k with the k of the multiplier theory.)

Since the consumption function for the economy as a whole is constructed from the consumption spending patterns characteristic of the three major classes of income recipients (rentiers, wage earners, and profit recipients), we must examine the probable behavior of each of these classes as the level of employment and income rises. In our discussion of the aggregate supply function we saw that the relative income position of the rentier groups would worsen with a rise in the income level. Under such circumstances their current expenditures for consumption purposes would have to increase if such groups attempted to maintain intact their real consumption position. This follows from the assumption built into the aggregate supply function that the general price level will rise as employment and output expand. Thus, the consumption expenditures curve for these groups will slope upward toward an absolute maximum represented by the total of their fixed money receipts. The average propensity to consume will steadily increase, finally reaching 100 percent at that point at which the general price level has risen sufficiently to require the rentier groups to spend the whole of their current money income in order to maintain real consumption unchanged.

The money incomes of wage earners are represented by the *OW* curve in Figure 17–4. This assumes that money wages are a constant. The consumption expenditure pattern of wage earners will move along a curve that is roughly similar to the curve depicting the total wage bill, *OW*, although the slope of the wage earners' expenditure curve is likely to be less than that of the wage-bill curve, if it is assumed that wage earners save greater absolute amounts as their money income grows. The rise in the price level may prevent wage earners from enlarging the proportion of real income saved as the income level rises, but it does not preclude them from increasing money expenditures at a rate sufficient to maintain real consumption. There will be a limit, though, to the extent to which this can be done without ultimately bringing about a decline in the proportion of real income saved if, as was assumed earlier, the relative share of wages in the income total declines with advances in income and employment. In any event, the consumption function of the wage-earner class will most likely slope upward to the right at a rate that is slightly lower than that of the schedule representing the total wage bill.

Consumption expenditures for profit recipients depend, first of all, on the proportion of total profit that is distributed to shareholders in the form of dividends. If this is presumed to be a constant after the economy has reached that level of employment and output at which profits are positive (the employment level ON_1 in Figure 17–4), the consumption pattern of the entrepreneur class is determined largely by what happens to profits with further increases in the income level. In view of our earlier assumptions about constant money wages and fixed money incomes for the rentier class, profit income will rise at a rate in excess of the rise in the price level. If this happens, Weintraub contends that the entrepreneurial class can readily sustain its real consumption position by increasing consumption outlays out of distributed profits at about the same pace at which the general price level is increasing. Thus, he concludes that the consumption expenditure by this group is likely to move upward along a path that is roughly parallel to OZ in Figure 17–4.

When we combine the consumption behavior patterns for the three major groups of income recipients into a single consumption function for the whole economy, the result is a schedule which slopes upward to the right, but at a slower rate than the aggregate supply function. This is explained primarily by the inability of the rentier group to sustain their real consumption position in the face of rising prices and the personal saving of both the entrepreneurial and the wage-earner groups. Even if wage earners succeed in preventing a decline in the proportion of their real income saved as income rises, the rate of increase in consumption outlays will still be less than the rate reflected in the aggregate supply function. Consequently, the over-all slope of the consumption function will be less than that of the aggregate supply schedule.

The construction of the aggregate demand schedule is completed by adding an amount equal to autonomous investment expenditure to the consumption function. That has been done in the D schedule of Figure 17–5. If real investment is assumed to be a constant, then current monetary outlays for investment will rise along with the rise in income and the general price level. The addition of investment expenditure to the consumption function provides us with the aggregate demand which embodies the same price phenomena that are built into Weintraub's aggregate supply function. The equilibrium level of employment and income is determined by the intersection of the *D* and *OZ* schedules. It is at this point and only at this point that there is an employment (and income) volume at which the expected sales proceeds will be exactly equal to expenditures forthcoming from the consuming and investing groups.[33]

A Concluding Note on Distribution Theory

In this chapter we have sought to survey and analyze some of the major contributions that have been made toward the development of an aggregate theory of income distribution. Our discussion has ranged over more than one hundred years of economic thought, for the problem of the functional distribution of the national income is one that has excited the interest and attention of classical as well as modern economic theorists. We conclude as we began by observing that there is no general agreement among economists, classical or modern, on the nature and significance of

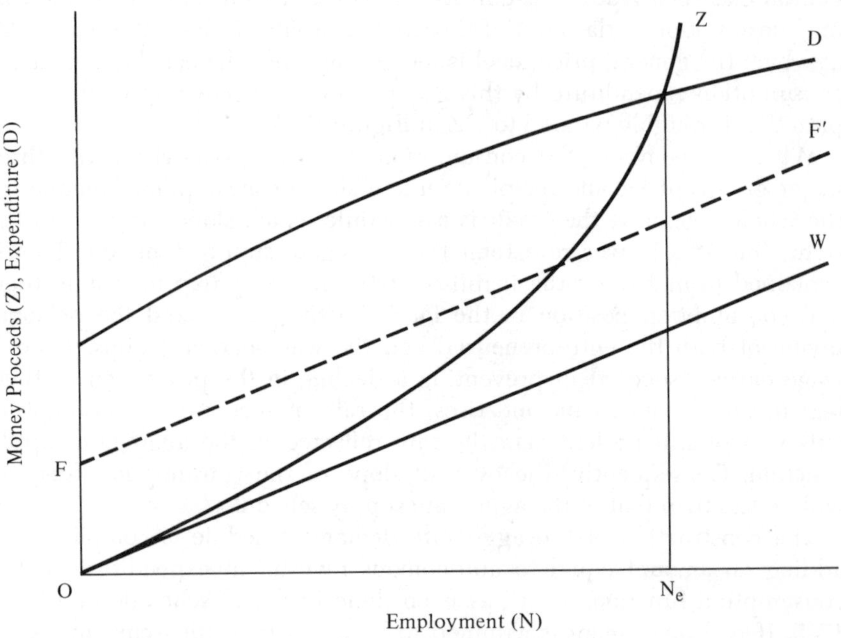

FIGURE 17–5. Weintraub's Aggregate Demand and Aggregate Supply

33. Ibid., p. 44.

the forces that determine the distribution of the national output into relative shares. Ricardo and Marx, both members of the classical school, reached diametrically opposite conclusions about the impact of a change in output on the distribution of income. Modern theorists have not succeeded in developing a wholly accepted body of theory in this area. But there is one element common to all their endeavors. The modern effort to develop an aggregate theory of income distribution takes as its point of departure the now generally accepted theoretical framework that we define as modern income and employment analysis. It is reasonably safe to predict that whenever an adequate theory of the functional distribution of the national income is developed, it will be done within this framework. At the present, though, such a theory is still in an emerging state, and the ideas, concepts, and theoretical schemata that we have surveyed in the chapter must be regarded as pioneering efforts directed toward this still unrealized goal.

APPENDIX

Algebraic Derivation of Equation (17-6)

(1) $I = S =$ the basic equilibrium condition
(2) $I = \pi(P)$ [Equation (17–2).]
(3) $P = (1 - \lambda)\,Y$ [Equation (17–4).]
(4) $I = \pi(1 - \lambda)\,Y$ [Equation (17–5). This is derived from the two preceding definitional equations.]
(5) $a \times \lambda Y =$ saving by wage earners [a is the propensity (marginal and average) to save out of wage income. It is a constant, $O < a < 1$.]
(6) Nonwage saving is derived as follows:
  (a) $bvP + (1 - v)\,P$ [bvP is saving out of distributed profit; and $(1 - v)$ is nondistributed profit. The latter is by definition saving; b is the propensity (marginal and average) to save out of shareholder's income. It is a constant, $0 < b < 1$.]
  (b) $P = (1 - \lambda)\,Y$ [From Equation (3) above.]
  (c) Therefore, nonwage saving equals:
    (1) $bv\,(1 - \lambda)\,Y + (1 - v)\,(1 - \lambda)\,Y$
    (2) $(1 - \lambda)\,Y \times [bv + (1 - v)]$ [This is derived by substitution of $(1 - \lambda)\,Y$ for P in Equation (6a) above.]
(7) Total saving is therefore equal to:
  (a) $S = (a \times \lambda Y) + [Y\,(1 - \lambda)\,(bv + (1 - v)]$
  (b) $S = Y\,[a\lambda + (1 - \lambda)\,(vb + (\mathrm{v} - v)]$

(8) Since $I = S$ (in equilibrium) it follows:

(a) $\pi(1-\lambda)Y = Y[a\lambda + (1-\lambda)(vb + 1 - v)]$

(b) Divide both sides of the above by Y and we have Equation (17–6):

$\pi(1-\lambda) = a\lambda + (1-\lambda)[vb + (1-v)]$

Algebraic Derivation of Equation (17-12)

(1) $I = S$ = the basic equilibrium condition

(2) $Y = W + P$ [Equation (17–7).]

(3) $I = s_pP + s_wW$ [Saving equals the sum of saving out of profit income, s_pP, and saving out of wage income, s_wW.]

(4) $I = s_pP + s_w(Y - P)$ [This is from Equation (2) above. $W = (Y - P)$.]

(5) $I = s_pP + s_wY - s_wP$ [From Equation (4) above.]

(6) $I = P(s_p - s_w) + s_wY$ [From Equation (5) above.]

(7) $\frac{I}{Y} = (s_p - s_w)\frac{P}{Y} + s_w$ [Divide both sides of Equation (6) above by Y. This gives Equation (17–12).]

Index

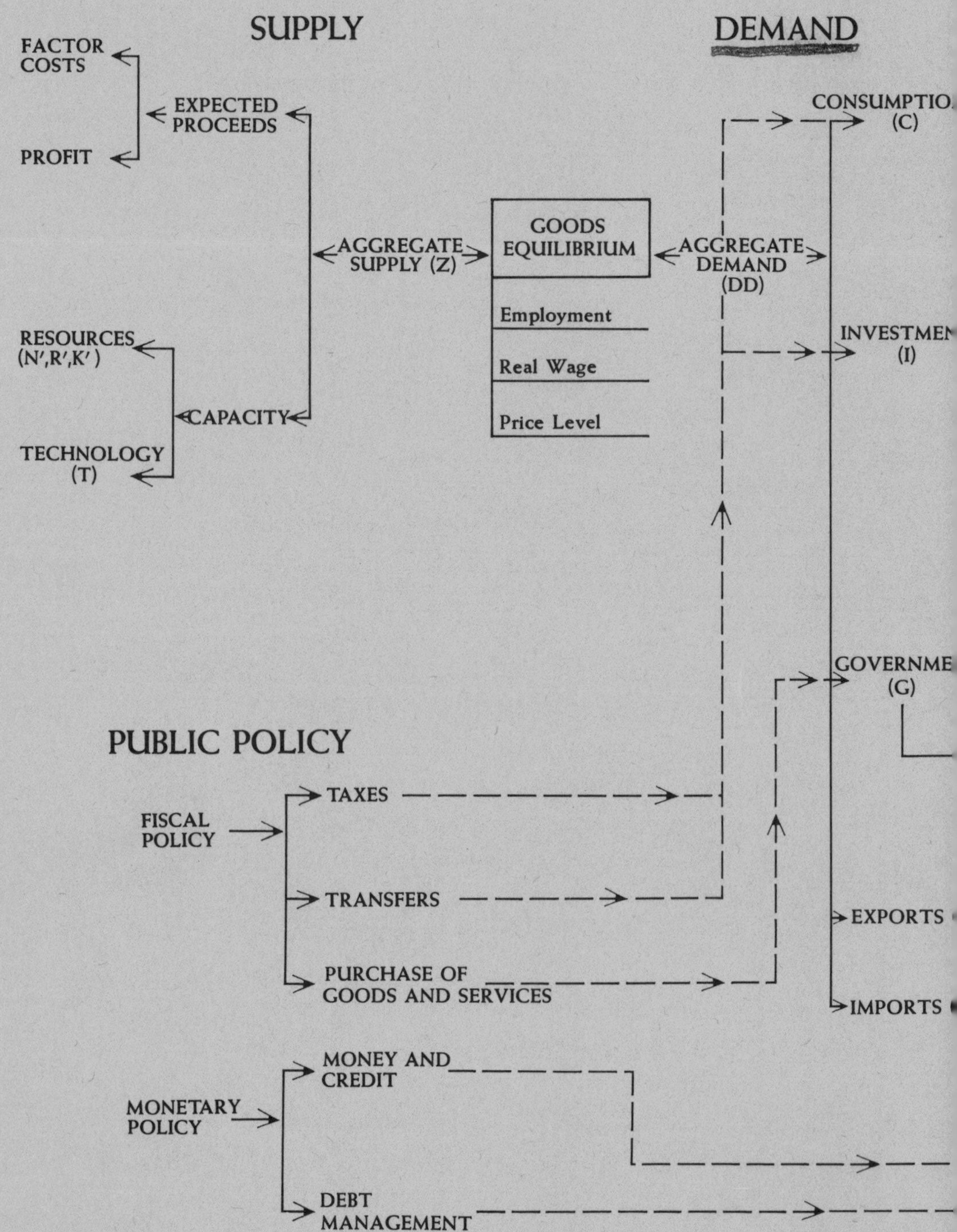
SUPPLY
DEMAND
FACTOR COSTS
EXPECTED PROCEEDS
PROFIT
CONSUMPTIO
(C)
GOODS EQUILIBRIUM
AGGREGATE SUPPLY (Z)
AGGREGATE DEMAND (DD)
Employment
Real Wage
Price Level
RESOURCES (N′,R′,K′)
CAPACITY
TECHNOLOGY (T)
INVESTMEN
(I)
GOVERNME
(G)
PUBLIC POLICY
FISCAL POLICY
TAXES
TRANSFERS
PURCHASE OF GOODS AND SERVICES
EXPORTS
IMPORTS
MONETARY POLICY
MONEY AND CREDIT
DEBT MANAGEMENT